All the MESSIANIC PROPHECIES of the Bible

Books in This Series

All the Apostles of the Bible

All the Divine Names and Titles in the Bible

All the Doctrines of the Bible

All the Men of the Bible

All the Messianic Prophecies of the Bible

All the Miracles of the Bible

All the Parables of the Bible

All the Prayers of the Bible

All the Promises of the Bible

All the Women of the Bible

All the MESSIANIC PROPHECIES of the Bible

Herbert Lockyer

GRAND RAPIDS, MICHIGAN 49530

To
Andrew Gray, M.A., of Scotland,
Managing Director
of
Pickering and Inglis,
the well-known evangelical
publishers, who publish
my works in Britain

ZONDERVAN™

All the Messianic Prophecies of the Bible
Formerly titled *All the Prophecies of Christ in the Bible*

Requests for information should be addressed to:

Zondervan, *Grand Rapids, Michigan 49530*

Appreciation is expressed to the Macmillan Company for their permission to quote verses from *The New Testament in Modern English* Copyright © 1958, 1959, 1960 by J. B. Phillips.

ISBN 0-310-28091-5

Printed in the United States of America

11 12 13 14 • 47 46 45 44 43 42 41

CONTENTS

Page

Introduction 9

PART 1. SPECIFIC MESSIANIC PROPHECIES 23

Chapter 1. *The Twofold Word and the Twofold Witness* 25

Chapter 2. *Prophecies of His Pre-existence* 33

Chapter 3. *Prophecies of His Ancestry* 48
A) His Two Genealogies, *49;* B) His Descent From Shem, *53;* C) His Descent From Abraham, *53;* D) His Descent From Judah, *54;* E) His Descent From David, *54;* F) His Descent From Joseph, *56*

Chapter 4. *Prophecies of His Birth* 58
A) As to the Seed Resulting in Birth, *59;* B) As to the Virgin Birth, *60;* C) As to the Time of Birth, *62;* D) As to the Place of Birth, *64;* E) As to the Forerunner of His Birth, *65;* F) As to Names Given at Birth, *65;* G) As to the Reception of Birth, *75;* H) As to the Purpose of Birth, *85*

Chapter 5. *Prophecies of His Character* 86
A) His Holiness, *85;* B) His Righteousness, *85;* C) His Goodness, *88;* D) His Faithfulness, *88;* E) His Troth, *89;* F) His Justice, *89;* G) His Guilelessness, *90;* H) His Spotlessness, *91;* I) His Innocency, *91;* J) His Obedience, *92;* K) His Zeal, *92;* L) His Meekness, *93;* M) His Mercy, *94;* N) His Forgiveness, *95;* O) His Patience, *96;* P) His Benevolence, *97;* Q) His Self-denial, *97;* R) His Love, *99*

Chapter 6. *Prophecies of His Ministry* 101
A) To Begin in Galilee, *101;* B) To Continue in Jerusalem, *101;* C) To Function in the Temple, *101;* D) To Proclaim a Jubilee, *101;* E) To Jews and Gentiles, *102;* F) To Be Anointed With the Spirit, *102;* G) To Be a Teaching One, *103;* H) To Be As a Miracle Worker, *106*

Chapter 7. *Prophecies of His Dual Nature* 108
A) The Son of God – Deity, *109;* B) The Son of Man – Humanity, *111*

Chapter 8. *Prophecies of His Death* 146
He Was To
A) Be Betrayed by a Friend, *147;* B) Be Sold for Thirty Pieces of Silver, *148;* C) Be Forsaken by His Disciples, *148;* D) Be Accused by False Witnesses, *148;* E) Be Mocked and Beaten, *149;* F) Be Pierced in Hands and Feet, *150;* G) Be Crucified With Thieves, *150;* H) Pray for His Persecutors, *151;* I) Be the Object of Ridicule, *151;* J) Have His Garments Gambled For, *152;* K) Be Deserted by God, *152;* L) Agonize With Thirst, *153;* M) Commit Himself to God, *153;* N) Have His Friends Stand Afar Off, *154;* O) Be Spared Having His Bones Broken, *154;* P) Be Pierced, *155;* Q) Be Hid by Darkness, *156;* R) Be Buried With the Rich, *157;* S) Die a Voluntary, Substitutionary Death, *157*

Chapter 9. *Prophecies of His Resurrection* 159
A) Forecasts and Fulfillments of Power Over Death, *160;* B) Features of Power Over Death, *160;* C) Fervent Witnesses of Power Over Death, *162*

Chapter 10. *Prophecies of His Ascension and Exaltation* 167
A) The Memorable Forty Days, *167;* B) The Marvelous Power of the Risen Body, *168;* C) The Messages of Post-Resurrection, *169;* D) The Manner of His Ascension, *169;* E) The Manifold Benefits of His Exaltation, *181*

Chapter 11. *Prophecies of His Second Advent* 184
A) Two Events of the Second Advent, *185;* B) The Events of the Advent, *188;* C) A Triad of Great and Related Promises, *189;* D) The Dramatic Prophetic Program, *194;* E) The Inauguration of the Millennium, *200;* F) The Great White Throne, *206;* G) The Surrendered Kingdom, *209;* H) The New Creation, *209*

PART 2. SYMBOLIC MESSIANIC PROPHECIES 211

Chapter 1. *Prophetic Gleams From Conspicuous Persons*......213
Christ and...
A) Adam, *213;* B) Abel, *214;* C) Melchizedek, *215;* D) Abraham, *217;* E) Isaac, *218;* F) Joseph, *221;*

G) Moses, *223;* H) Aaron, *224;* I) Joshua, *226;* J) Judges, *229;* K) Boaz, *230;* L) Samuel, *232;* M) Job, *233;* N) David, *238;* O) Solomon, *243;* P) Jeremiah, *249;* Q) Elijah and Elisha, *253;* R) Daniel, *255;* S) Jonah, *258;* T) Hosea, *260;* U) Zerubbabel, *262*

Chapter 2. *Prophetic Gleams From Prescribed Offices*.........265
A) The Prophet, *266;* B) The Priest, *268;* C) The King, *270;* D) The Daysman, *272;* E) The Surety, *273*

Chapter 3. *Prophetic Gleams From Historical Events*.........276
A) The Ark, *276;* B) The Ladder, *280;* C) The Blood-Sprinkled Door, *283;* D) The Miraculous Bush, *286;* E) The Two Pillars, *289;* F) The Red Sea, *291;* G) The Healing Tree, *295;* H) The Manna, *299;* I) The Smitten Rock, *308;* J) The Two Stone Tablets, *314;* K) The Nazarite Vow, *317;* L) The Magnificent Benediction, *318;* M) Aaron's Rod, *320;* N) The Brazen Serpent, *321;* O) Six Cities of Refuge, *326;* P) Mount Pisgah, *333;* Q) The Twelve Stones, *337*

Chapter 4. *Prophetic Gleams From Religious Rituals*..........343
A) The Constructed Tabernacle, *345;* B) The Ceremonies of the Tabernacle, *372*

Chapter 5. *Prophetic Foregleams From Levitical Offerings* 477

Chapter 6. *Prophetic Foregleams From Feasts and Festivals*...512
A) The Seven Feasts of Jehovah – Commanded, *513;* B) Minor Feasts – Uncommanded, *518*

Chapter 7. *Prophetic Foregleams From Christ's Own Teaching* 519
A) The Double Function of the Prophet, *519;* B) His Predictions Fulfilled, *520;* C) His Predictions in Process of Fulfillment, *520;* D) His Predictions Yet to Be Fulfilled, *522;* E) Apostolic Use of His Prophecies, *522*

Appendices:

A. Prophetic Foregleams From Metaphors 525

B. Christ's Quotations From the Prophets 525

C. Old Testament Prophecies Quoted in the New Testament 525

ABOUT THE AUTHOR

Dr. Herbert Lockyer was born in London in 1886 and held pastorates in Scotland and England for twenty-five years before coming to the United States in 1935.

In 1937 he received the honorary Doctor of Divinity degree from Northwestern Evangelical Seminary.

In 1955 he returned to England where he lived for many years. He then returned to the United States where he continued to devote time to the writing ministry until his death in November of 1984.

We praise Thee for the radiance
    That from the hallowed page,
A lantern to our footsteps,
    Shines on from age to age.

It is the golden casket
    Where gems of truth are stored;
It is *the heaven-drawn picture*
    Of Christ, the living Word.

INTRODUCTION

Originally, it was my intention to classify and comment upon all the subjects of divine prophecy in the Bible. But as I set out to enumerate all the prophecies about and from God, Christ, the Holy Spirit, the angels, the devil, the saints, the Jews, the Gentile nations and the church, I knew that such a colossal task would require volumes to cover and years of close study to complete – years I may not have, seeing I am well beyond fourscore. Thus I decided to concentrate upon all the prophecies about Christ, seeing that the divine perfections of foreknowledge and fulfillment can be observed better in the realm of prophecies concerning our blessed Lord than in any other sphere of prophecy.

We begin our meditation of Christ in prophecy with the premise that because of His omniscience, God alone can foreknow and foretell the future, and that He chose to confine His foretelling to the pages of His prophetic Word. Justin Martyr, overwhelmed by this fact said, "To declare a thing shall come to pass long before it is in being, and to bring it to pass, this or nothing is the work of God." We have the explicit statement that God alone, in the Bible alone, gave the world true prophecies:

> I am God, and there is none else; I am God, and there is none like me; Declaring the end from the beginning, and from ancient times things that are not yet done; saying, My counsel shall stand, and I will do all my pleasure (Isa. 46:9, 10).

The prerogative of God alone to forecast and fulfill prophecy is recorded by other writers. In no uncertain terms Moses outlines the test of a prophet's validity (Deut. 18:20-22). Isaiah likewise calls on those who declare things to come, to produce their credentials (Isa. 41:21-23; cf. Jer. 28: 7-17). Jesus had the mark of a true prophet (John 13:19). All Scripture, including its prophetic element, is given by inspiration of God (II Tim. 3: 16. See also II Peter 1:19-21). But more of this aspect later.

Setting out on this further literary pilgrimage of mine, I took as my rod and staff four precious portions of the Word. I classified them thus:

My Double Revealer

Earnestly desiring to see light in His light, I turned to our Lord's message on "The Holy Spirit," and claimed anew His inspiration and direction, seeing that as "The Spirit of Truth" He came to testify of Christ, and to take of those things pertaining to Christ and reveal them to us (John 14:16, 17; 15:26; 16:14, 15). Having inspired the prophets of old to record all that they did of the coming Christ, the Spirit is the best Revealer of those prophetic truths they wrote.

The other Revealer is Christ Himself, who unfolded to His disciples after His fulfillment of many Old Testament prophecies the inner significance of *all* that the prophets had written concerning Him (Luke 24: 25-27, 44). My prayer was that as I followed Christ's footprints through Old Testament Scriptures, I, too, might experience the burning heart (Luke 24:32).

My Double Reward

Confident that as the foregoing Scriptures were appropriated they would prove sufficient for my spiritual enlightenment and enthusiasm, I was likewise assured that the following promises would act as a spur to personal encouragement in the quest for truth. That one's own meditation upon Christ is both pleasurable and profitable is implied. "My meditation of him shall be sweet" (Ps. 104:34). Is this not the equivalent of delighting ourselves in the Lord and in the Word revealing Him (Pss. 1:2; 19:14; 37:4, 23)? Such a delight is mutual, for if we delight ourselves in the Lord, He will delight Himself in our ways. The word "sweet" as used by the psalmist, means "acceptable," "pleasing," and is associated with an acceptable sacrifice (Jer. 6: 20; Hos. 9:4). Any phase of meditation upon the Saviour is pleasant to the taste and rewarding.

Another passage I endeavored to keep before me as I followed Christ through the Scriptures was the one contained in God's warning to Eli: "Them that honour me I will honour" (I Sam. 2:30). Here we have a *double honor,* with one aspect depending upon the other. A person has the assurance that if, by the Spirit, the effort is made to magnify the inestimable value of Christ as Scripture presents Him, He in turn will reward such glorification of Him by making our presentation of Him an avenue of blessing to the saints. May He be pleased to honor the writer in this way!

As a preparation for our study of all the prophecies of Christ, as given by the prophets, by Himself, and by the apostles, let us seek to understand some of the principles governing the ministry of the prophets themselves, and also of prophecy in general as found in the Bible as a whole. When we realize that about one-fourth of the Bible is related to predictive prophecy, or predictions which, at the time of their utterance, were still future, we see that negligence of such an element of Scripture is inexcusable. As a knowledge of Bible prophecies is essential to an understanding of the nature and completeness of the revelation of God's will and purpose, it is essential to examine every aspect of prophecy.

A. *The Channels of Prophecy*

Holy men of God, moved or carried along by the Holy Spirit, were the media and messengers of God's prophetic purpose. Who were these prophets who gave witness to the divine will in general, and to Christ in particular? Although the whole of the Old Testament is of immense value, the presence and preaching of the prophets constitute its greatest glory, as well as the glory of the Jewish people. Their revelation of religion and philosophy was both progressive and unique. As William E. Gladstone, Prime Minister under Queen Victoria, looked back in his later years upon his long career, he said, "My only hope for the world is in bringing the human mind into contact with Divine revelation." What this statesman said of the Bible can be said of the mission of the prophets. They revealed God to man, and sought to bring men to God. It may help us to know more of their place in the divine order if we understand the way they are classified.

Another occurrence of the term "prophet" is in connection with Saul: "Is Saul also among the prophets?" (I Sam. 10:9–13). Such an expression appears to have been proverbial. Although Samuel is thought of as a prophet (I Sam. 3:20), actually he is not referred to as such but as a "seer" (I Sam. 9:9, 18, 19). Samuel also served as a "priest" (I Sam. 7:9), and as a "judge" (I Sam. 7:15–17). He was the first prophet and founder of the monarchy and its last judge, and the sole ruler of Israel between Eli and Saul. The etymology of the word "prophet" helps to determine the nature of prophecy.

1. *Its Hebrew significance.* Although there is some uncertainty as to the original meaning of the Hebrew word for prophet, a common theory is that it meant to "bubble" or "gush," the reference being to the excited or frenzied manner of speech of the early prophets. The Hebrew word *hittiph* sometimes translated "prophecy," primarily meant "to let drop," referring to the saliva dropping from the mouths of prophets as they prophesied. But the term *nabi* means "to call" or "name" or "announce." So the *nabu* or prophet was an "announcer," or "herald," of the divine will and word – the essential characteristic of the prophet as he is known to us in history. *Nabi* is from a verb meaning "to boil forth" as a fountain, and represents one who speaks out freely from a full heart impelled by an inspiration from God.

2. *Its Greek significance.* The literal meaning of the Greek word for prophet is "to speak forth" or "a forth-teller," that is, one who speaks forth the message which has been communicated to him through divine inspiration, whether of practical duties or future events. It would seem that the emphasis of the prophet's work lay on the former. A prophet, therefore, was a *forth-teller* and a *fore-teller,* whose message was for the people of his own age, and also for ages beyond his own. In fact, he was:

a. A *preacher,* or spokesman for God, a messenger with God's message. It was thus that Nathan the prophet functioned when he said to David after his seduction of Bathsheba, "Thou art the man!" (see II Sam. 12:7). Similarly, John the Baptist, greatest among the prophets, apart from Christ, proclaimed, "Repent ye: for the kingdom of heaven is at hand" (Matt. 3:2).

b. A *predictor,* or one who declares by divine inspiration something that will take place in the future, near or distant. Thus Isaiah the preacher became a predictor when he spoke predictively of a virgin who would conceive and bear a son whose name was to be "Immanuel." Predictive prophecy is that form of Bible prophecy foretelling what God is going to do.

Dr. A. T. Pierson, who reminds us that the words prophet and prophecy occur over four hundred times in Scripture, commenting on the two senses conveyed by the term prophet, summarizes:

> When a prophet predicts, or foretells, he sees and represents the future in the light of the present; when he rebukes, reproves, counsels, or admonishes as Jehovah's representative messenger — *forth*-telling rather than *fore*-telling — he portrays the present in the light of the future. . . . *Predictive* prophecy is the foremost proof to which the Word of God appeals on its own behalf. It was the standing miracle by which God challenged faith in His inspired Word, defying all the worshipers of other gods and their sages and seers to produce any such proofs that their gods were worthy of worship or their prophets true representatives of a Divine religion (see Isa. 41:21-23).

Among other terms used to designate an Old Testament prophet, we have:

c. *Seer,* or See-er (I Sam. 9:9, 10). From a verb meaning "to see," this name implies supernatural insight or foresight, or second sight, or all three. A seer was one who saw divine visions, divine truths, and spoke of what he had seen from God. Such a supernatural gift of insight into things divine was not possessed by the common run of men. Seers of old entered into the "counsel" of God, the "secret" of God, the "plan" of God, the "ways" of God, and the "thoughts" of God. A great variety of expressions are used to denote the content of the revelation made to them, but hidden from men in general.

The prophet was also known as:

A man of God (I Sam. 2:27; 9:6; I Kings 17:18).

A servant of God, or Jehovah (I Kings 18:36; I Chron. 6:49; Isa. 20:3).

A messenger of Jehovah (Isa. 42:19; Hag. 1:13).

A watchman (Jer. 6:17; Ezek. 3:17).

All the terms used imply a close relationship of the Prophet to God, each term expressing some aspect of such a relationship, or of the prophet's mission, or of the way he achieved his religious insight. The central idea contained in them all, however, was that the prophet was a mediator by speech between man and God. With minds and mouths controlled by the Holy Spirit, they spoke as He gave them utterance. Of all the prophecies made under the control and inspiration of the Spirit, we can apply the words of the angel to John, "These are the true sayings of God" (Rev. 19:9). It is ridiculous to affirm that God inspired the thoughts of the prophets, but left them to express these thoughts in the way most natural to them. You cannot have an unclothed thought in your mind. Language surrounds the thought from the moment of its birth. As the Bible is the only authoritative revelation of God's mind and will, it was essential that it be expressed in words of His choosing. If there be divine inspiration at all, verbal inspiration is a necessity. As Dean Burgon put it:

> What music would be without notes, mathematical sum without figures, so would an inspired book be without words controlled by the inspiring Spirit.

When our Lord spoke about "every jot and tittle," He had in mind the significance of every atom of Scripture — choice of exact words and precise phrases, terms, and grammatical forms. This is why it is of great importance to examine the very language God instructed the prophets to employ to make known His will. "Every word of God is pure" (Proverbs 30:5). (See also Pss. 12:6; 18:30; 19:8; 119:140.)

d. A further characteristic feature of Old Testament prophets is that they were not only preachers, predictors, and seers, but also *patriots.* Not only did they possess the combination of vision and understanding of man and God, but also a passion for patriotism. Theirs was a patriotic fervor for the sake of the nation which they wanted to be in right relationship to God. They could foresee the inevitable consequences of rebellion against God's will for the nation of which they were part, and loyally warned their native land. To them, religion and nationalism were inseparable. Robert Browning wrote of the land under whose blue skies his happiest years were spent:

> Open my heart and you will see
> Graved inside it — *Italy.*

If we could have opened the hearts of those noble prophets of Israel, we would have found graven in them — *Canaan.* All their thinking was colored by the conviction that Israel was especially chosen by God for a great destiny, with the land of Canaan as their divinely chosen habitation. This was the star leading the prophets even through the darkest night of their national history. It was thus that they became mighty preachers of righteousness and judgment, using wind and sea, thunderstorms and earthquakes, as well as the gentler scenes of the land of Israel, as symbols most fit for their themes (Isa. 5:1; Jer. 8:7; 17:11; Hos. 14:5; Mic. 5:7). If we would fully appreciate their prophecies, we must in some measure see the romance and riches of Canaan through their eyes.

e. "Holy men of Old." This further designation of the prophets that Peter uses is indicative of their character. There are two ways of judging any life, namely by (1) the dignity of the character possessed, and (2) the range of the influence exerted. At their best, the Old Testament prophets were men of the highest moral character, obedient to the inspiration of the Holy Spirit, and therefore regarded with veneration amounting to fear. The people looked on them as men not only with superhuman knowledge, but also with superhuman power. Many of these godly men in the rank and order of the prophetic order were ready to seal with their blood their loyalty to God-imparted truths (II Kings 9:7; 21:10-16; Jer. 26:20-23). No wonder the utterances of those preacher-patriots are as powerful today as when they were first delivered! Our present civilization could be saved from its impending doom if only it would pause and listen to the warnings of those ancient messengers of Jehovah.

Godly and influential though the prophets were, they were but men, and being human, subject to failure. As Pierson reminds us, "Even prophets and apostles, *apart from their character and capacity as such,* being only fallible men, were liable to mistakes" (I Kings 19:4; Gal. 2:11-14). There were times when they were not altogether correct and things did not turn out as they had foretold. Sometimes their messages were changed (II Kings 20:1-5). There were times when they deliberately concealed the truth (Jer. 38:14-28). On one occasion Jeremiah did not receive a message from God concerning a course of action on which his advice had been sought until ten days later (Jer. 42:7). Gradually the prophetic order deteriorated, losing the spiritual and moral power it once possessed; hence, the emergence of false prophets.

In spite of any blemishes true prophets may have had, they occupy a unique place in religious history, exhibiting as they did that prophecy was the supreme gift of Israel to the world. There is nothing comparable to this in the religious history of mankind. As Dr. Albert C. Knudson expressed it in 1914 in his volume on *The Beacon Lights of Prophecy:*

> Other peoples have had their great religious teachers: the Hindus their Buddha, the Persians their Zoroaster, the Arabians their Mohammed. But nowhere do we find a succession of men extending over several centuries of time, who entertained such lofty conceptions of religion, devoted themselves with such passion and power to the realization of these conceptions, and contributed so much to the permanent moralization and spiritualization of religion, as did the prophets of Israel.

The prophecies of these heralds, who were not simply preachers of repentance, clearly prove that they regarded Jehovah not only as the God of history but also as the God of destiny. They never spoke as mere social reformers, for to the very core of their beings they were teachers of divine truths, interpreters of the mind of God for the spiritual benefit of the minds of men. Their task was to announce the coming of Jehovah and no element in their teaching was more common to all of them than this and none more fundamental. It binds all their utterances together into unity, and connects them also with the fuller revelation of a later day.

Luke the historian reminds us that, "To [Christ] gave all the prophets witness" (Acts 10:43), and we herewith tabulate alphabetically all the persons who are named as prophets.

Aaron Exodus 7:1
Abraham Genesis 20:7
Agabus Acts 21:10
Ahijah I Kings 11:29
Amos Amos 7:14, 15
Asaph Matthew 3:35 (Ps. 78:2)
Balaam Numbers 24: 2
Daniel Daniel 10; Matthew 24:15

David Acts 2:25
Eldad Numbers 11:26
Elijah I Kings 18:36
Elisha II Kings 6:12
Ezekiel Ezekiel 1:2, 3
Gad I Samuel 22:5
Habakkuk Habakkuk 1:1
Haggai Ezra 5:1; 6:15; Haggai 1:1
Hananiah Jeremiah 28:17
Hosea Hosea 1:1; Romans 9:25
Iddo II Chronicles 13:22
Isaiah Isaiah 1:1; I Kings 20:11; Matthew 3:3
Jehu Kings 16:7
Jeremiah II Chronicles 36:12; Jeremiah 1:2
Joel Joel 1:1; Acts 2:16
John the Baptist Luke 7:28
Joshua I Kings 16:34
Jonah II Kings 14:25; Jonah 1:1; Matthew 12:39
Malachi Malachi 1:1
Medad Numbers 11:26
Micah Jeremiah 26:18; Micah 1:1
Moses Deuteronomy 34:10
Nahum Nahum 1:1
Nathan I Kings 1:32
Obadiah Obadiah 1
Oded II Chronicles 15:8
Paul Acts 13:9-11; 27:10
Samuel I Samuel 3:20
Shemaiah II Chronicles 12:5
Zacharias Luke 1
Zechariah Zechariah 1:1
Zephaniah Zephaniah 1:1

Prophetesses were also included in the prophetic order. These holy women of God likewise knew what it was to be borne along by the Spirit in their predictions and proclamations. Among those specially named are:

Anna Luke 2:36
Deborah Judges 4:4
Huldah II Kings 22:14
Miriam Exodus 15:20
Noadiah Nehemiah 6:14

"Prophetess was the courtesy title of a prophet's wife, as well as the term describing those who prophesied according to the prophecy "your daughters shall prophesy" (Joel 2:28; cf. Ps. 68:11, R.S.V.). The New Testament gift of prophecy was bestowed on women as well as on men (Acts 21:9; I Cor. 11:5). Jezebel was a false prophetess and the temptress of the Christians at Thyatira to whom was given the name of Israel's wicked queen.

Christ was also predicted and proclaimed as a prophet (Deut. 18:15-19; John 6:14). The people knew Him as a prophet (Matt. 21:11; Luke 7:16), His disciples also called Him a prophet, and He referred to Himself as such (Matt. 13:57; Luke 24:19). It was as a prophet that He was mocked (Luke 22:64). According to the teaching of the New Testament, the exalted Christ still continues to exercise His prophetic function, guiding His disciples into all the truth by His Spirit whom He has sent (John 16:7-13), and "building up the body" by bestowing upon it apostles, prophets, and teachers (Eph. 4:8-12).

The authentic marks of true prophets and of their prophecy are clearly stated:

Prophets are sent by God (Isa. 58:1; Jer. 1:4; 23:28; 25:4; Ezek. 2:3; Amos 8:14, 15).
Prophets were to be received with faith and reverence (Luke 24:25; I Thess. 5:20; II Pet. 1:19).
Prophecy has God as its Author (Isa. 44:7; 45:21; Luke 1:70; II Pet. 1:19, 21; Rev. 1:1).
Prophecy is a gift of Christ (Eph. 4:11; Rev. 11:3).
Prophecy is from the Spirit (John 16:13; I Cor. 12:4, 10).
Prophecy can be tested (Deut. 13:1-5; 18:20-22; Jer. 14:15; 23:16).

That the Lord Jesus Christ was the *supreme and final Prophet of God* (Hebrews 1:1, 2) and superior in every way to the other prophets who were both called and qualified of God is clearly evident, as Pierson points out in his section on *The Written and Living Word.* The prophets were finite and fallible, human and necessarily imperfect, and inferior to Him who was without sin.

In numbers the prophets were many –
Christ was one, alone, solitary.
The prophets were limited in the scope of power –
Christ had all power in heaven and on earth.
The prophets were sinful and imperfect –
Christ was sinless and flawless in character.
The prophets were inspired at given times only –
Christ was also the mouthpiece of God.
The prophets were not always understanding –
Christ was omniscient and original.
The prophets had only partial foreknowledge –
Christ was the Framer and Controller of the ages.
The prophets witnessed to the Light –
Christ was Himself the Light of of the world.
The prophets were partial in the revelation of truth –
Christ was the perfect Truth of God.
The prophets had to give place to others –
Christ is without rival or successor.

References must be made to the false prophets the Bible mentions and strongly denounces. Like all similar institutions, the prophetic order was exposed to the danger of corruption which grew partly out of the fact that, as a whole, the prophets were dependent for their support upon the gifts of the people. Thus they were consequently in danger of delivering such messages as would serve their own selfish ends, as Micah points out (3:5; cf. II Kings 5: 20). There was likewise the danger of formalism and professionalism. We have an illustration of prophetic deterioration in the case of Micaiah and the four hundred prophets who gathered about Ahab (I Kings 22:5-28). Zedekiah, Shemaiah, and Bar-josus are among the false prophets so named (I Kings 22:11; Jer. 29:31; Acts 13:6). As to divine denunciations pronounced upon false prophets and their false prophecies, the reader is referred to the following passages: Deuteronomy 13; 18:20; Isaiah 9:15; Jeremiah 6:13; 14:13; 23:9, 34; 28:15; 29:21, 31; Ezekiel 13:3; 14:9; Matthew 7:15; 24:11; II Peter 2:1; I John 4:1.

B. *The Constraint of Prophecy*

There are those who seek to dismiss the study of prophecy as being visionary and impractical, and who affirm that such a study is not only a waste of time but often results in paralysis for real, present constructive work. There are some preachers who look upon prophecy as a "hot potato" and best left alone. But, surely, if one-third of the Bible is taken up with prophecy, it is a positive sin to neglect such an integral part of Scripture. Further, as prophecy is history written in advance, we are up-to-date in the trend of international events today if we have a knowledge of the unfolding plan of God which prophecy provides. The Christians who live at their best and give of their best, meeting thereby, the challenge to accomplish great things for God, are those who live near to "the more sure word of prophecy."

The study of prophecy is obligatory for several important reasons that we are apt to forget when we say that it is a subject best left alone.

1. *The study of prophecy is imperative if we would know the mind of God.* If those holy men of old spoke as they were carried along by the Holy Spirit, which means that He inspired them in what they were

to say, is it not our unbounded duty to find out what they declared from and for God? If He has spoken, then what He has said makes all the difference in the world. If He has given any indication of His purposes in creation, redemption, and history, it is of great importance for us to find out what He has said about the life and destiny of men and nations.

2. *The study of prophecy is essential if we are to have a right perspective of history.* Whether we admit it or not, these are days heavy with prophetic significance and we cannot have an understanding of our times and an inner grasp of the crises through which we are passing unless we study God's prophetic plan. There cannot be the right perspective of history unless there is a true appreciation of the significance and the meaning of the truth of Christ's coming. Scientific scholars may argue that students of prophecy present truth in a narrow, arbitrary fashion, but what else can they do, seeing the truth is of God? If a train does not keep to the parallel narrow rails, there will be disaster. If modern scholars had lived in the days of Isaiah, they would have rebuked him for daring to announce that the coming Messiah would be born of a virgin and then die for the sins of the world.

3. *The study of prophecy imparts the note of authority into preaching, making it living and vital.* Prophecy, any phase of it, is a part of the divine revelation, and witness for Christ is impoverished if the prophetic aspect of truth is neglected. We become prophets to our day as the desire to know the exact mind of God becomes a deep conviction. Although we may not be prophets in the sense that Isaiah and Jeremiah were, we can speak as from God, and for God, as they did. As they were sent into the world with a divine message, so Christ sends us out to proclaim His Gospel. Ours is the privilege to witness for Him, with power from Him.

The true students of prophecy are those who stand strong and firm even as nations crumble and as the shadows deepen and mens' hearts fail them because of fear. What is the secret of their calm confidence? Is it not the assurance that God is in all crises moving toward the great consummation in which Jesus shall come, fulfilling the dream of prophets and realizing the inner hope of all inspired prophecy? Is this not why the most ardent preachers, fruitful evangelists, sacrificial missionaries, and soul-saving Christians are among those who believe and blazen forth "the words of the prophecy of this Book"?

C. *The Credentials of Prophecy*

Prophecy is the *diapason* of the Bible – its great, dominant note from Genesis to Revelation. Then it must not be forgotten that the precious promises of God shine through the Scriptures as prophecies, as well as all the other predictive passages, and that no promise of His can possibly fail. Scriptural prophecy shares in the Bible's infallibility. "Prophecy came not in old time by the will of man: but holy men of God spake as they were moved by the Holy Ghost" (II Pet. 1:21). Peter uses the word "sure," or as the A.S.V. has it, "word of prophecy *made* more sure" (II Pet. 1:19), which carries the idea of being firm, steadfast, solid, or incapable of being removed or destroyed. Peter is not giving us a comparison between the prophecies of the Old Testament and those of the New Testament, but he is proving that the former have been confirmed in the latter in the person and work of Christ, and are therefore to be relied on.

In the most outstanding prophetic book of the Bible, in which John gives us the unveiling of Jesus Christ, his estimation of the revealed prophecies is, "These are the *true* sayings of God." "These words are *true*" (Rev.

19:9; 22:6), just as the One revealed is "Faithful and True" (19:11). As the prophecies concerning Christ's first coming were correct and infallible, being fulfilled to the most minute detail, so all prophecies associated with His second advent must be literally fulfilled. Acceptance of the credibility and infallibility of the one set of prophecies involves the same admission of the second set. Human oracles are fallible, but the inspired Word, containing divine oracles is different. Instead of ambiguous and untrustworthy utterances, we find teachings distinct and definite, inspired and infallible, authoritative and authentic. Under the figure of a scroll, sealed with seven seals, John gives us a pictorial exhibit of the authority and majesty of Holy Scripture. A "seal" stands in the Bible for silence, mystery, completeness, but especially for the sacredness connected with authority, authenticity, and inviolability. Divine authority is stamped upon Holy Scripture, which is rightly called the "Word of God." Of the many facets of Scripture truth, prophecy ever carries with it the credential of divine inspiration. Dealing with *The Prophetic Element* in Scripture, A. T. Pierson observes that

> This is one of the seven elements which together constitute the whole body of the Word of God, namely, History, Biography, Prophecy, Ethics, Devotion, Messianic Revelation, and Spiritual Guidance. This prophetic element pervades all the rest. It is the *eye* of Scripture, with supernatural vision — backsight, insight, and foresight, or power to see into the past, present, and future. It is, therefore, the miracle of utterance, as other miracles are wonders of power, and evinces omniscience, as they do omnipotence, thus reflecting the image of God.

The literal fulfillment of a prophecy is the seal of its divine origin. Prophecies of centuries concerning the final sufferings of Christ were fulfilled during the twenty-four hours leading up to His crucifixion. According to the law of compound probabilities, the chance that they all happened together by accident is 1 in 537,000,000.

In Pierson's *God's Living Oracles*, this renowned Bible scholar says that there are

> Over 300 predictions about the Messiah to be found in the Old Testament. According to the law of compound probability, the chance of their coming true is represented by a fraction whose numerator is one, and the denominator eighty-four followed by nearly one hundred ciphers. One might almost as well expect by accident to dip up any one particular drop out of the ocean as to expect so many prophetic rays to converge by chance upon one man, in one place, at one time. God has put especially upon these prophecies as to His Son the *stamp of absolute* verity and indisputable certainty, so that we may know whom we have believed. Mistakes in so solemn a matter are fatal and God meant that none should be possible.

D. *The Contradictions of Prophecy*

To some minds it may appear as if the Old Testament presents a mysterious prophetic puzzle of strange combinations of prophecies concerning the first coming of Christ that appear at times so conflicting that they seem impossible of fulfillment. Such prophecies that are seemingly contradictory and apparently irreconcilable are known as "Prophetic Paradoxes." A "prophetic paradox" is, by definition, a prophecy containing a *seeming* contradiction, with no real absurdity involved, and presenting an enigma which, without the clue or fulfillment, seems impossible of solution. Prophetic paradoxes concerning Christ abound in the Old Testament and would remain as mysteries if they had not been solved by the appearance of Christ in the flesh. The astonishing feature about these prophetic paradoxes is the perfectly normal, artless way in which they were providentially, even miraculously fulfilled in the life of Christ. There is no need to strain or force either the facts or the predictions to make them match. They fit each other as a key and lock.

Let us consider one or two of these apparent contradictions or impossible contrasts, as they have been called. How could God come to earth, be born as a child yet remain God? "Great is the mystery of godliness . . . God manifest in flesh." Listing further paradoxes, we have:

Jesus, Father of Eternity, yet a Son in time
Chosen of God and elect, yet despised by men
Born King of the Jews, yet rejected by them
Born of a woman, a virgin, yet had no father
Came from Bethlehem, Egypt, Nazareth.

Where really was the place of His earthly origin? Prophecy says:
"Out of [Bethlehem] shall he come forth" (Mic. 5:2).
"I have called my son out of Egypt" (Hos. 11:1; Matt. 2:15).
"He shall be called a Nazarene" (Isa. 11:1; Matt. 2:23).

Are these passages contradictory? There are no contradictions in Scripture, or should we say, Scripture never contradicts itself. The solution of the paradox came when Jesus appeared. He was *born* in Bethlehem, and later was *taken* to Egypt, and, later still, *settled* in Nazareth and grew up there.

Further, Jesus was:

David's Son, yet David's Lord
the Chief Cornerstone, yet a Rock of Offense
a Priest, yet a King upon His throne
pleasing to God, yet abhorred by His own nation,
priceless, yet sold for thirty pieces of silver
not only rejected by men, but forsaken by God
wounded and pierced, yet not a bone was broken
cut off, yet His days are prolonged

These most thrilling prophetic paradoxes of Scripture would be hard to unravel if Jesus had not come to make the obscure most real. In Him, these seeming opposites are harmoniously blended.

E. *The Condition of Prophecy*

The prophet Hosea has the phrase, "Then shall we know (the significance of any Scripture), if we follow on to know the Lord" (6:3). The latter phrase of verse 2 and the whole of verse 3 can be rendered:

> So that we shall live in His presence, and shall know and strive after the knowledge of Jehovah, whose coming forth is sure, like the dawn, so that He may come as the plentiful rain for us, as the latter rain which watereth the earth.

We take out two phrases – "Live in His presence" and "strive after knowledge" – to emphasize necessary conditions for an understanding of messianic prophecies. If we seek to live in the presence of the One prophesied, and prayerfully strive after the inner knowledge of Him, revelation will be granted. What must not be forgotten is that truth is revelation, and that such a spiritual unfolding is dependent upon obedience to the divine will. "Happy are ye if ye know these things, *and do them.*" Is it not an obvious and important truth that we cannot grow into a living apprehension of the simple and advanced truths associated with prophecy until we have fully apprehended the antecedent underlying basic truths of holiness, obedience, and reliance upon the divine Revealer Himself? The more we seek to live in harmony with the *indwelling Christ,* the more we shall understand the marvel of the *prophetic Christ*.

Revelation is never separable from obedience, which is ever the organ of spiritual revelation. A true biblical understanding of prophecy is not so much *mental* as it is *experimental*. Dr. Norman McLeod once quaintly put it like this:

> There are professed teachers and preachers who no more grasp the truth they nominally hold than does the sparrow grasp the message that passes through the telegraph wire on which it perches.

The clean conscience, the obedient will, and the candid mind are all necessary to the open eye. Only the pure in heart can see God as He is reflected in His Word. A maxim of Gregory the Great was, "We are to learn the mind of God from the words of God," but it is essential, first of all, to have His mind. Whatever aspect of Scripture we desire to study, we must remind our hearts that we stand on holy ground, and that it should be trodden with reverent feet. In our quest for truth our attitude must be that of Job:

> That which I see not teach thou me: if I have done iniquity, I will do no more (34:32).

It has been suggested that distinction must be drawn between revelation, interpretation, illumination, and inspiration.

Revelation is the divine impartation and communication of truth to the mind of man, independent of his mental ability and acquirements. Truth, hid from the wise and prudent, is revealed to babes (Matt. 11:25; Rom. 1:17; Eph. 3:3-5; Amos 3:7).

Interpretation is the science of discovering and disclosing the true meaning, not only of prophecy, but also of other aspects of divine truth. It is the Holy Spirit alone who is able to help a prophet or preacher to unfold the authoritative meaning of a divine utterance (Dan. 2:19-28; 4:24-28; 5:17-28).

Illumination is associated more to the province of the Spirit in so enlightening the mind of the believer as to enable him to discern, and in a measure beyond his natural, unaided powers to apprehend and comprehend the beauty and glory of a divine revelation (Eph. 1:17, 18; 3:16-19).

Inspiration is the method of revelation, rendering its subject capable of receiving and transmitting it to others without error, either by tongue or pen. Obviously, the value of a written revelation must depend upon its divine inspiration. Essential in inspiration, Pierson goes on to enforce, is *the action of the mind of God upon the mind of man*, in such a way and measure as to quicken and qualify the human medium for the true conveyance of the divine message. Revelation expresses the *informing* process, inspiration the *implanting*.

The Bible gives us the assurance and a guarantee that the willingness to discover, know, and obey the truth will be rewarded: "If any man will do his will, he shall know of the doctrine, whether it be of God, or whether I speak of myself" (John 7:17).

Dr. George F. Pentecost, who was one of the outstanding preachers during the early part of this century, used to relate an argument he had with an atheist who did not believe the Bible because he did not know the Author. Pentecost's question was, "Well, my friend, is the multiplication table a work of authority with mathematicians?"

"Most certainly," was the atheist's reply.

"Do you happen to know who the author of that table is?"

When the atheist frankly confessed his ignorance of the author, the preacher rammed home the point: "Then I suppose, as a matter of fact, being a scientific man and a conscientious sceptic, you never use the multiplication table?"

"Oh, yes," the atheist replied. "It proves itself to be true by its work."

"Then, my friend," said the preacher, "leaving on one side all those hair-splitting questions of academic science and criticism, shall we not be allowed to say that we know the Bible is a work of absolute authority in religion and morals – whether we know its human authors or not – because it works well in its own sphere, just as the multiplication table works in its sphere?"

We do know who the divine Author of the Bible was, and who the human writers were whom He chose to set forth the revelation of Himself in promise, parable, and prophecy. And did the Author not say, "My Word will not return unto me void"?

F. *The Center of Prophecy*

Christ is the subject and goal of prophecy, and it was the Holy Spirit, as "the Spirit of prophecy," who inspired the prophets of old to testify beforehand concerning the sufferings of Christ and the glory that should follow (I Pet. 1:10-12; Rev. 19:10; cf. Eph. 1:9, 10). "It is of *Jesus* that thy brethren, *the prophets*, testify by the Spirit in them." Prophecy is concerned chiefly with Jesus, and bears testimony to Him in His redemptive life and work, and His coming glory. We see the exact fulfillment of the many prophecies converging on one Man – the Man Christ Jesus. Later on, as we shall see, the testimony of Jesus in the Book of Revelation is of a definitely prophetic nature, being taken up with Christ's return to assume governmental control of all things to be displayed in the kingdom (Rev. 1:2).

The distinction must be observed between fulfilled prophecies and unfulfilled prophecies of the Bible.

Fulfilled prophecies are those found in the Old Testament and which were fulfilled in the birth, ministry, death, and resurrection of Christ. These prophecies testify to the omniscience and omnipotence of God, who said of Himself, "I have spoken, I will also bring it to pass; I have purposed, I will also do it" (Isa. 46:11).

Unfulfilled prophecies are what theologians name "eschatology," or the science or doctrine of last things. This aspect of predictive prophecy is found in the New Testament and is related to the return of Christ for His Church, the tribulation era, the millennium, the final judgments, and eternity. Eschatology brings us to the revelation of God's eternal purpose and to our fascinating future as believers.

Old Testament prophecies, particularly those prophetic paradoxes we have already mentioned, have an element of obscurity, presenting as it were a lock for which only the New Testament has the key – and that key is the One to whom all the prophets gave witness.

A story is told of H. Houdini, one of the greatest magicians the world has known, concerning a demonstration he gave in Paris of his ability to unlock locks. A local magician claimed he could do all that Houdini did, and publicly offered to extricate himself the next day from a cage locked by Houdini's special lock. The wily French contender had an accomplice, unknown to Houdini, who wormed the combination of the lock from the American magician. But somehow Houdini suspected a trick, and that night he changed the combination. The next day the cocky French magician had himself locked in the cage, but to his chagrin he could not unlock the combination lock. He tried in vain to discover the new combination, amid the jeers of the crowd. Finally, he had to beg Houdini to release him, which the magician did after a little showmanship. Then Houdini showed him and the audience what the new five-letter combination was: F-R-A-U-D.

The one who worked out the combination was the one who could unlock it. In like manner, the One who gave those Old Testament prophecies, as a lock, knew the combination who would unlock the mysteries. It was another five-letter combination: J-E-S-U-S. Everywhere in Old Testament Scriptures there is the air of expectancy – Someone is coming! Thus, over this portion of the Bible with its thirty-nine books, we can write EXPECTATION. The New Testament opens with the appearance of that expected One, and so over its twenty-seven books we can place the word MANIFESTATION. As. Dr. W. Graham Scroggie puts it: "Christ is the focal Fact of history. All history before Him was a preparation for His first Advent, and all history since He came has been a preparation for His Second Advent."

Schaff, the renowned church historian, says of Christ:

> He is the centre and turning point not only of chronology, but of all history, and the key to all its mysteries. Around Him, as the Sun of the moral universe, revolve at their several distances all nations and all important events in the religious life of the world; and all must, directly or indirectly, consciously or unconsciously, contribute to glorify His name and advance His cause. The history of mankind before His birth must be viewed as a preparation for His coming, and the history after His birth as a gradual diffusion of His spirit and progress of His Kingdom.

As we are to find, all messianic prophecies concerning Christ's life and work were accurately verified in history. Forecasts and fulfillments answer as perfectly to one another as the fingers of one hand do to the fingers of the other hand. Prophecy and performance are set over against one another in such a way as to leave all but the willfully blind, convinced and worshipful. That renowned Bible teacher and preacher, the late Dr. A. J. Gordon of Boston once gave his children a jigsaw puzzle and told them to take it into the nursery and that he would come in later to see how they were getting on. After a while Dr. Gordon went into the playroom and found them excited as they stood round the completed picture. "Why, children, how did you manage to put it together so quickly?" asked the father. "Because we found a man on the back," they joyfully replied. The secret of the sublime unity of Scripture is the Man on the back. The Bible, then, is a mirror of Jesus, revealing and magnifying Him for whom it was originally written. Augustine's great phrase was, "Be prepared to find the Lord Jesus *latent* in the Old Testament as He is *patent* in the New."

Dr. A. T. Pierson, who affirmed that there are over 300 prophecies relating to Christ, reminds us that there are three canons by which all true prophecy can be tested.

1. It must be such an unveiling of the future that no mere human foresight or wisdom could have guessed it.

2. The prediction must deal in sufficient details to exclude shrewd guesswork.

3. There must be such lapse of time between the prophecy and the fulfillment as precludes the agency of the prophet himself in effecting or affecting the result.

Judged by these principles, all the messianic prophecies are shown to be genuine, and their value as evidence is beyond serious challenge. "There failed not aught of any good thing which the Lord had spoken . . . ; all came to pass" (Josh. 21:35). Further, such a prayerful, diligent study of prophecy ought to lead us into a fuller comprehension of the divine mind and will, and a richer devotion to Him whose glory is the culmination of all prophecy – the Lord Jesus Christ.

Part One

SPECIFIC MESSIANIC PROPHECIES

Chapter One

THE TWOFOLD WORD AND THE TWOFOLD WITNESS

The absorbing meditation we are now undertaking enables us to appreciate the sentiment of the psalmist when he wrote, "I have rejoiced in the way of thy testimonies, as much as in all riches" (Ps. 119:14; cf. vv. 72, 127). To follow the unfolding of the testimony Scripture gives of our Savior is a most enriching as well as an enlightening and edifying experience, especially as we remember that the divine Expositor Himself is near to guide us to those Scriptures concerning Himself. Before actually discovering that the Bible is "the Heaven-drawn picture of Christ, the Living Word," there are preliminary considerations which, when grasped, enable us to appreciate more fully the inseparable connection between the Holy Oracles and the Holy One.

A. *The Twofold Word (Living and Written)*

Both Christ and Scripture bear the designation, "The Word," the former being the living Word and the latter, the written Word. In the declaration of the psalmist, "Thou hast magnified thy word above all thy name" (138:2), the whole body of Holy Scripture is included. A translation commonly accepted reads, "Above all Thy Name, Thou hast made glorious Thy Word." John Calvin has it, "Thou hast magnified Thy name above all things, by Thy Word." As for Martin Luther, he translates it, "Thou hast made Thy Name glorious above all, through Thy Word." The evident meaning of the verse is that beyond all works of creation and providence, or other ways God has made Himself known, He has exalted His written Word.

Why has God exalted the Scripture thus? Is it not because it unveils and magnifies His Son who came as the revelation of God's inner Self? In His Incarnation, Jesus became the Word incarnate: "The Word was made flesh and dwelt among men," and it is only in the written Word that His whole character and commission have been revealed. Thus, in prophetic vein, He could say, "In the volume of the book it is written of me" (Ps. 40:8; Heb. 10:7, 8). Our Lord is found in the Word, that is, in the letter; the Word is found in Him, in the life. Because of the identity of the written Word with the living Word, faith in the infallibility of the former is essential to the revelation and authority of the latter.

As Pierson expresses it,

> The Holy Scripture and the Person of the Lord Jesus Christ are so inseparably bound together, that whatever impairs the integrity and authority of the one correspondingly affects the other. The Written Word is the Living Word enfolded: the Living Word is the Written Word unfolded. Christ is the Cornerstone of all faith, but that Cornerstone is laid in Scripture as a bed-rock, and to disturb the Scripture authority unsettles the foundation of the believer's faith and of the Church itself.... The Bible is Christ portrayed; Christ is the Bible fulfilled. One is the picture, the other is the Person, but the features are the same and proclaim their identity.

A devout Hebrew scholar has pointed out that the Old Testament is a book of consonants without vowels, as Hebrew students know. But Christ came as the Alpha and the Omega, the initial and final vowels of the New Testament language, to all the vowel points to the old revelation; to be the interpreter of difficulties and the filler of gaps. And so, as Luther exhorts, "In the Word thou shouldest hear nothing else than thy God speaking to thee."

The Greek term *Logos,* then, is used of the Lord Jesus Christ and of the Scriptures of truth. *Logos* means the spoken or written word because it makes manifest and reveals to us invisible thoughts. Christ is the *living Word* because He reveals the invisible God (John 1:1, 18). Essentially, the Bible is not something we have to interpret, but that which God has given in order to interpret Himself and His will to us, in and through the life and mission of His Son. The Bible is called the *Word of God,* or the written Word, because it interprets and testifies of Christ. The Holy Spirit is the interpreter of both Words, for He receives and shows us "the things of Christ" through the printed Word (John 16:14; I Cor. 2: 9-14; 12:7, 8). How solemn is the charge, "Preach the word" (II Tim. 4:2)!

The Word that is written makes known Christ the living Word.

The Word that is preached makes known both the living and the written Word.

The spiritually-minded hymnist Joseph Hart brings the two Words together in the verse

> The Scriptures and the Word
> Bear one tremendous name,
> The Living and the Written Word
> In all things are the same.

Here are a few illustrations of how precisely the same things are proclaimed of both the one and the other. Both produce the same effects in our lives. When Paul went to Thessalonica he reasoned with the people there "out of the *Scriptures,*" and then we are told immediately that his preaching consisted of "opening and setting forth that *Christ*... is the Messiah" (Acts 17:1-8). The reader may be able to add a few more evidences to the following list of similarities, all of which can come under the category of prophecies. To save time and space we have used "W." for "written Word" and "L." for "living Word."

W. – "They pressed upon him to hear the *Word of God*" (Luke 5:1). L. – "His name shall be called the *Word of God*" (Rev. 19:13).

W. – "The *gospel* of *peace*" (Rom. 10:15). L. – "The *Prince of Peace*" (Isa. 9:6).

W. – "Make me go in the path of thy commandments" (Ps. 119:35). L. – "No man cometh unto the Father, but *by me*" (John 14:6).

W. – "Teach me, O Lord, *the way* of thy statues" (Ps. 119:33). L. – "Jesus saith ... I am *the way*" (John 14:6).

W. – "Thy Word is *truth*" (John 17: 17; cf. Pss. 119:151; 19:9). L. – "Jesus saith ... I am ... *the truth*" John 14: 6; cf. 1:14; Rev. 3:7).

W. – "Begotten ... through the *gospel*" (I Cor. 4:15). L. – "Begotten ... by ... *Jesus Christ*" (I Pet. 1:3).

W. – "Thy precepts ... with them thou hast *quickened me*" (Ps. 119: 93; cf. v. 50). L. – "You hath he *quickened* who were dead" (Eph. 2:1).

W. – "Desire the sincere milk of *the word* that ye may *grow*" (I Pet. 2:2). L. – "He that *eateth* me, even he shall *live by me*" (John 6:57).

W. – "The *truth* shall make you *free*" (John 8:32). L. – "*Christ* hath made us *free*" (Gal. 5:1).

W. – "Ye are *clean* through the *word* which I have spoken" (John 15:3). L. – "The *blood* of Jesus Christ ... *cleanseth* us from all sin" (I John 1:7).

W. – "The engrafted word, which is able to save your souls" (James 1:21). L. – "*He* is able to save them to the uttermost" (Heb. 7: 25).

W. – "*Sanctify* them through *thy*

truth" (John 17:17; cf. I Tim. 4:5). L. — "*Sanctified* through the offering *of the body of Jesus Christ* once for all" (Heb. 10:10; cf. I Cor. 1:2).

W. — "*The holy scriptures* . . . able to make thee wise unto salvation" (II Tim. 3:15). L. — "*Christ Jesus,* who of God is made unto us *wisdom*" (I Cor. 1:30).

W. — "He sent *his word,* and *healed them*" (Ps. 107:20). L. — "*Jesus* . . . *healed* them" (Matt. 4:23, 24).

W. — "*The word of God,* which effectually *worketh* also in you that believe" (I Thess. 2:13). L. — "Serving according to *his working* which *worketh* in me mightily" (Col. 1:29).

W. — "*The word* that I have spoken . . . shall *judge* him" (John 12:48). L. — "*The Lord Jesus Christ* . . . shall *judge* the quick and the dead" (II Tim. 4:1).

W. — "Born . . . by *the word of God*" (I Pet. 1:23). L. — We are "*born* of God" (I John 5:18).

W. — "*Thy Word* was unto me the *joy* and rejoicing of my heart" (Jer. 15:16). L. — "I will go . . . unto *God,* my exceeding joy" (Ps. 43:4).

W. — "Holding forth *the word* of life" (Phil. 2:16). L. — "*Jesus Christ* . . . eternal life" (I John 5:20).

W. — "The scripture cannot be *broken*" (John 10:35). L. — "A bone of him shall not be *broken*" (John 19:36).

W. — "Man shall not *live* by bread alone, but by every *word of God*" (Luke 4:4). L. — "I am the *living bread* . . . if any man eat of *this bread* he shall *live* for ever" (John 6:51).

W. — "The *law* . . . is a *fountain of life*" (Prov. 13:14). L. — "With *thee* is the *fountain of life*" (Ps. 36:9).

W. — "*Thy Word* is . . . a *light* unto my path" (Ps. 119:105; cf. Prov. 6:23). L. — "*I am* the *light* of the world" (John 8:12; cf. 1:4).

W. — "*Thy word* is a *lamp* unto my feet" (Ps. 119:105). L. — "*Thou* art my *lamp,* O Lord" (II Sam. 22:29).

W. — "Is not *my word* like as a *fire, saith the Lord* . . . ?" (Jer. 23:29; cf. 5:14). L. — "*I, saith the Lord,* will be unto her a *wall of fire*" (Zech. 2:5; cf. Isa. 10:17).

W. — "Exceeding great and *precious* promises" (II Pet. 1:4). L. — "To you . . . which believe, He is *precious*" (I Pet. 2:7).

W. — "*The law* of thy mouth is better unto me than *thousands* of gold and silver" (Ps. 119:72). L. — "*My beloved* is . . . chiefest among *ten thousand*" (Song of Sol. 5:10).

W. — "How *sweet* are *thy words* unto my taste!" (Ps. 119:103). L. — "*His mouth* is most *sweet*" (Song of Sol. 5:16).

W. — "*Thy* testimonies are *wonderful*" (Ps. 119:129). L. — "*His name* shall be called *Wonderful*" (Isa. 9:6).

W. — "The *gospel* is the *power* of God" (Rom. 1:16). L. — "*Christ,* the *power* of God" (I Cor. 1:24).

W. — "Thy judgments are *good*" (Ps. 119:39). L. — "*Thou* art *good,* and doest *good*" (Ps. 119:68).

W. — "Thy *word* is true from *the beginning*" (Ps. 119:160). L. — "Ye have known *him* that is from *the beginning*" (I John 2:13).

W. — "The righteousness of *thy testimonies* is *everlasting*" (Ps. 119: 144). L. — From everlasting to *everlasting, thou art God*" (Ps. 90: 2).

W. — "*Thy testimonies* . . . thou hast founded them *for ever*" (Ps. 119: 152). L. — "*Thy throne,* O God, is *for ever and ever*" (Heb. 1:8).

W. — "The *word* of the Lord *endureth for ever*" (I Pet. 1:23, 25). L. — "*The Lord* shall *endure for ever*" (Ps. 9:7; cf. John 12:34).

W. — "*The Word* of God . . . *liveth* . . . *for ever*" (I Pet. 1:23). L. — "Worship *him* that *liveth for ever*" (Rev. 4:10).

W. — "*The word* of our God shall

stand for ever" (Isa. 40:8). L.—"[His] kingdom... shall *stand for ever*" (Dan. 2:44).

W.—"Is not *my word*... like a hammer that *breaketh* the rock in pieces?" (Jer. 23:29). L.—"*That stone*... will *grind* him to powder" (Luke 20:18).

W.—"[They] *stumble* at the *word*" (I Pet. 2:8). L.—"[*Christ*] a *stumblingstone*" (Rom. 9:33).

W.—"Thy *commandments* . . . are *ever with me*" (Ps. 119:98). L.—"Lo, *I* am with you *alway*, even unto the end" (Matt. 28:20).

W.—"Let the *word* of Christ *dwell* in you richly" (Col. 3:16). L.—"*Christ* may *dwell* in your hearts by faith" (Eph. 3:17).

W.—"The *word of God abideth* in you" (I John 2:14; cf. John 15:7). L.—"Hereby we know that *he abideth* in us" (I John 3:24; cf. John 15:4).

W.—"Thy *testimonies* . . . are very *faithful*" (Ps. 119:138). L.—"*He*... was called *Faithful* and True" (Rev 19:11).

W.—"*The Word of God* is... *sharper* than any two-edged *sword*" (Heb. 4:12). L.—"Out of *his mouth* goeth a sharp sword" (Rev. 19:15). (Can it be that *two-edged* implies both the *living* Word and the *written* Word?)

W.—"The *word* of the Lord is *tried*" (Ps. 18:30). L.—"[*He* is] a *tried* stone" (Isa. 28:16).

We cannot meditate on these pairs, and others we could cite, without recognizing how Christ and the Scriptures are one. It is to be doubted whether Jesus had any books beyond the *Bible*—which was only the Old Testament at that time—and *Himself*. But He read in these two great Books of God till they became one Book in His hand, and He, Himself, the living embodiment of Scripture. He could say, "My Father and I are one." It is likewise true that the living Word and the written Word are one. As the eternal Word, Christ compared the inviolability of Scripture revealing Him to the permanence of the very heavens and earth (Matt. 5:18; John 5:46, 47).

B. *The Twofold Witness*

Of the Scriptures, Jesus could say, "These are they which testify of me" (John 5:39). In turn, as "the true witness," He testified to divine inspiration of the Scriptures (John 17:8, 14, 17). It is a most absorbing study to trace how the Word testifies of Jesus, and how He witnessed to its authority.

1. *The witness of Scripture to Christ*. The master key to a spiritual understanding of any or of all books of the Bible is our Lord's explicit declaration concerning them: "These are they that testify of *me*." It is only with this key that we are able to unlock the precious treasures of the Word and arrive at the hidden meaning of words and hints. There are apparently casual expressions, circumstances, and events, which in themselves, and apart from Christ, are meaningless, but if we use this key prayerfully and carefully, then we come to share the wonder and joy of those who found, "*him* of whom Moses in the law, and the prophets, did write" (John 1:45).

From earth's earliest ages saints looked forward, not only to events in the future, but also to the coming of One to fulfill all divine promises and prophecies. With the choice and development of Israel as a nation, there emerged one central figure as the hope of the people—the seed of the woman (Gen. 3:15). Their redemption and that of lost sinners was to be accomplished by one Man, the promised Messiah who would be descended from Abraham and from the tribe of Judah (Gen. 22:18; 49:10). This was the promised Deliverer from Satan's dominion, and from Moses on, the writers of the Old Testament fill in the picture, each adding a fresh, vivid touch.

By the aid of the Holy Spirit they were able to *testify beforehand* to the sufferings of Christ, but their vision stretched beyond the cross and the Resurrection. The vision of the Saviour's final triumph was theirs also. Zechariah, for example, saw the Lord as King over all the earth with His saints assisting Him in the governmental control of all things (14:4-9). What the Old Testament saints had no knowledge of, and therefore were not able to prophesy about, was the mystery hid from the past ages, namely, the Church of the living God. Paul speaks of the Church composed of saved Jews and saved Gentiles as "the mystery of Christ," and of himself as a revealer of such a mystery (Eph. 3:1-12). Those saints of old saw the cross and the millennial glory of Christ, but had no vision of the valley – the Age of the Church – between those two great mountain-peaks of prophecy.

The whole of Scripture revolves around Jesus and can be divided in a threefold way:

Jesus is coming – Genesis to Malachi
Jesus has come – the four gospels
Jesus is coming again – the Acts to Revelation.

From the first prophecy of the Bible – which was given to Satan – all hope was centered on the Man who would be born of a woman to accomplish God's redemptive purpose, and all through the thirty-nine books of the Old Testament one breathes the air of expectancy – Someone is coming – the One to whom *all* the prophets gave witness.

Then at Bethlehem, the Christ of prophecy became the Christ of history, and through His brief career He was forever laying hold on Old Testament prophecies and relating them to Himself. Openly, He declared that His life and work were but the fulfillment of all that had been written in the first part of the volume of the Book. At an early age He was cut off, or slain. Death, however, could not keep its prey. Although Jesus often spoke of His return to earth after His Ascension, it is with the angelic announcement after He was received up into heaven that all associated with the coming again of this same Jesus is unfolded by the apostles, Paul being the outstanding exponent of Christ's Second Advent who had no doubt about His coming "the second time" (Heb. 9:28).

Our obligation is to believe *all* that *all* the prophets have written of Christ, and search out how their prophecies of Him were fulfilled. His own method of expounding in *all* the Scriptures concerning Himself was to begin at Moses, meaning, the books written by Moses, namely, the first five books of the Bible, then journey through all the poetical books, and conclude with all the prophetical books. The Scriptures which the Master expounds were all the books from Genesis to Malachi (Luke 24:25, 27, 44, 45). The one great all-pervading Subject of these thirty-nine books is Christ; all else stands in relation to Him. He is their "Beginning and the Ending," as He is of the entire Bible.

In a most profitable way, A. M. Hodgkin, in his valuable work *Christ in All the Scriptures,* takes us from Genesis to Revelation and points out the prophetic portraits of Christ in each book of the Bible. For readers desiring to pursue this method, the following outline could be used around which to group the successive prophecies of Christ in the Bible.

a. *The Old Testament*
Prophecies of Christ in historical books – Genesis to Esther
Prophecies of Christ in poetical books – Job to Song of Solomon
Prophecies of Christ in prophetical books – Isaiah to Malachi

b. *The New Testament*

Prophecies of Christ in the four gospels
Prophecies of Christ in the Acts
Prophecies of Christ in the epistles – Romans to Jude
Prophecies of Christ in the Book of Revelation

2. *The Witness of Christ to Scripture.* Old Testament Scriptures point forward to Christ, and when He came as the Goal of prophecy, He referred His friends and enemies to what had been written of Him. If anything can convincingly show the respect and reverence due the Old Testament, it surely is the extent to which the Lord Jesus Christ endorsed its authority. Think of statements like these:

"Abraham rejoiced to see my day: and he saw it, and was glad" (John 8:56).
"Moses wrote of me" (John 5:46).
"David called me Lord" (Matt. 22:43, 44).
"The words . . . which were written . . . concerning me" (Luke 24:27, 44).

When He was tempted by the devil in the wilderness, Jesus fell back upon written words which have strengthened the saints of succeeding ages and selected as "pebbles from the clear brook" three conclusive answers to the tempter from the fifth book Moses wrote: Deuteronomy 6: 13, 16; 8:3. In His Sermon on the Mount, Jesus declared that He had come to fulfill all the law and the prophets had prophesied of Him (Matt. 5:17-19).

Few of us realize how many our Lord's quotations of the Old Testament are. Careful study reveals that He referred to twenty Old Testament characters and quoted from nineteen different books (see appendices). As regards the Psalms and the prophetical books, if possible the divine authority of our Lord is yet more deeply stamped on them than on all the rest of the Old Testament. The ground of His constant appeal was *"It is written!"* He called some of His disciples "fools" and "slow of heart" because they did not believe all that the Old Testament prophets had written of Him. For Him, the holy oracles were His meditation day and night.

The eye-catching biographical statement that young Timothy had known the Scriptures from childhood is an indication that scribe-written scrolls of the Old Testament were universally treasured among the Jews as the family Bible was a century ago in Christian homes. Robert Burns, in "The Cotter's Saturday Night," depicts the head of the humble home reading from the large Bible:

> The sire turn o'er, wi' patriarchal grace,
> The big ha'-Bible, ance his father's pride.

As the home of Joseph and Mary was a thoroughly Jewish one, it is certain that a copy of the much-prized ancient Scriptures was revered and daily read as the God of Israel enjoined His covenant people so to do:

> These words of mine shall be in thine heart:
> And thou shalt teach them diligently unto thy children, and thou shalt talk of them when thou sittest in thine house, and when thou walkest by the way, and when thou liest down, and when thou risest up.
> And thou shalt bind them for a sign upon thine hand, and they shall be as frontlets between thine eyes.
> And thou shalt write them upon the posts of thy house, and on thy gates (Deut. 6:6–9).

In all Jewish homes, whether the occupants were rich or poor, learned or simple, the commandment concerning family worship with the reading of Scripture was strictly observed. It was into such a home that Jesus was born and brought up, and if Mary read the daily portion to her first-born, we can imagine with what emphasis she would utter the verse:

> Thou shalt shew thy son in that

> day, saying. This is done because of that which the LORD did unto me when I came forth out of Egypt . . . that the LORD'S law may be in Thy mouth" (Exod. 13:9).

Then as soon as the Holy Child Jesus was able to hold the scroll in His own hand, how earnestly He would search the Scripture, something which, later on, He rebuked His disciples for *not* doing. The question arises as to how old Jesus was when He discovered from His own prayerful and constant reading of the Scriptures that they testified of Him. Coleridge confessed that he loved the Bible because it *found* him. It must have been so with Jesus, for He both found Himself in the Holy Scriptures and was found by them. Through almost thirty years of Bible meditation, He discovered Himself, and then for some three years He went about saying, "It is written of me."

Alexander Whyte says,

> Never did Moses, nor David, nor Isaiah, nor any other psalmist or prophet in all the House of Israel, search into and meditate on Holy Scripture as did Jesus of Nazareth; and never were its precepts kept to such an illumination, to such a revelation, and to such a glorious reward. With what an unfathomable depth of awe and wonder did Jesus search into the Scriptures concerning Himself! And with what boundless adoration and praise did He more and more discover and find Himself in them! He would exclaim, "O how I love Thy law! It is my meditation all the day.

As Jesus came to the full knowledge of Himself as He increased in wisdom by hearkening to the witness of Holy Writ, searching and receiving the testimony with an inner consciousness and confidence that He was the One predicted, He came to affirm of the Scriptures, "These are they which testify of me." If He was not the One all the prophets gave witness to, then He was a colossal fraud and liar to take such a witness and relate it to Himself as He did, declaring publicly that He was the Messiah for whose coming men longed.

There was that memorable day in the Temple when He took the ancient scroll on which Isaiah had written his prophecy, and "He found the place" – so familiar was Jesus with the book He had no need to fumble to find the place as we often have to when the Bible portion is announced from the pulpit – quickly turning to the prophet's description of the mission of the coming Messiah. Authoritatively, Jesus affirmed that the portion He read related to Himself. He said: "This day is *this* Scripture fulfilled in your ears" (Luke 4:16-21; cf. Isa. 61:1). We have a fuller, clearer, and much richer Book than Jesus had. He did not have the wonderful New Testament. He came that this might be written after His return to the Father. Ours is the completed Book of God, for us there is the privilege to search the Old Testament and the New.

With the whole Bible in our hands, is ours the mind of Christ to meditate on the glorious revelation it contains? Do we daily appropriate the unsearchable riches such a treasure house of truth contains? C. H. Spurgeon once said that it did not matter what text he chose to preach on, as soon as he opened the gate, he scampered over the fields to find Jesus as quickly as possible. Do we have the same quest to find our Beloved as He feeds among the lilies?

Our estimation of the infallibility and worth of Scripture is affected by our relationship to the Person the Bible predicts and presents. Unless there is personal intimacy with Jesus Christ our Lord, there cannot be that spiritual discernment so necessary to an understanding of the Scripture. If we would know the Book of God, we must be fully acquainted with the God of the Book. If we are His and

He is ours, then the Scriptures are instinct with the deity and authority of the Lord they portray, and provide us with a world of spiritual and intellectual treasure. By the illumination of His presence in their pages, by the seal of His authority upon all its principles, precepts, and promises, by His own invariable assumption of the Scriptures' infallibility, there is wrought into our deeper spiritual consciousness the unwavering conviction that the Bible, in its entirety, is the Word of God that liveth and abideth for ever.

> Should all the forms that men devise
> Assault my faith with treacherous art,
> I'd call them vanity and lies,
> And bind the Bible to my heart.

Although, as we have already indicated, one most profitable way of tracing the relationship between Christ and prophecy is to take the Bible and, commencing with Genesis, go through it book by book, marking down all prophecies to our Lord in specific pronouncement, in type and symbol, in events and experiences, in persons and names. With pastors and teachers in mind, I have chosen to set forth the prophecies of Christ as related to the various phases of His life and mission, so that this work can be used as sermonic material for pulpit and classroom.

Chapter Two

PROPHECIES OF HIS PREEXISTENCE

Old Testament Theophanies | His Personal Affirmations

A. *Old Testament Theophanies (Foregleams)*

As we seek to trace and place Old Testament prophecies to Christ, it may be reasoned by some shortsighted people that such a form of Bible meditation is somewhat impractical and perhaps visionary. Why not concentrate upon the Christ of history, upon the One whose personality dominates the New Testament, rather than upon the shadowy forms of Him in Old Testament Scriptures? But is not this false reasoning? If the actual Christ, as He lived on earth, said, "In the volume of the book it is written of me," is it not incumbent upon us to find out what was written about Him before He came among men?

What were all those things holy men of old recorded about Christ's purpose in history? How can we have a right perspective of Christ's presence in the world unless there is a true appreciation of these questions: Where did He come from? Who is He? Why is He the focal point of all history? Why was it necessary to make prophecies some 1,000 to 500 years before the predicted events concerning Him occurred? Why were facts of His life foretold in Old Testament prophecy and prefigured in many types and symbols? How is it that when we open the gospels we find "him of whom Moses in the law, and the prophets, did write" – Jesus?

Surely the first advent of Christ was vastly important when God made such unusual preparation for the appearance of His Son among men! As He predicted that a new and final revelation of Himself would be seen in Christ, is it not imperative to study these predictions? The fact is that we cannot account for, nor explain, the Christ of history apart from the Christ of prophecy. As He Himself prophesied that the consummation of our present age will be precipitated by His Second Advent and that we must study "the more sure word of prophecy," in like manner we must be able to read those prophetic signs associated with His first Advent.

A careful and intelligent study of Old Testament prophecies regarding Christ under the guidance of the Holy Spirit is most vital in order to discover how they moved toward the great consummation of the Incarnation when the dream and hope of all the prophets was realized. Predictive prophecy is related to Israel, the Gentile nations, and the Messiah; and it is with the direct and literal predictions of the Messiah that we are presently concerned – a study as fascinating as it is fruitful.

When Jesus deliberately fitted Himself into the prophetic utterance of Zechariah, "Thy King cometh, sitting upon the foal of an ass," we read that "all the city was moved saying, Who is this?" All ages since He rode into the city of Jerusalem have asked the same question concerning the same Person. Touch history at any point, and you will find men making this inquiry about Christ – *Who is this?* Almost 2,000 years have come and gone since this Galilean Peasant lived among men, and today the question is more pertinent than ever — *Who is this?*

Well, strange though it may sound, this Man *lived before He was born.* In contrast, we were born in order to live. From the past eternity He was the Son of God before, in time, He became the Son of Mary. Through the dateless past, heaven was His home before, for our sakes, He came to a humble home in Nazareth. In His former mode of existence, He had been so rich, but, for man's salvation, He became poor — so poor that at times He had nowhere to lay His head that had been adorned with glory. Let us examine, therefore, the fact and the forecast of our Lord's pre-existence.

The Old Testament abounds in references to our Lord's pre-existence. The first is to be found in the majestic opening verse of the Bible. "In the beginning *God created*" (Gen. 1:1). English has only singular and plural, but Hebrew has singular, dual, and plural. Here the word for *God* is "Elohim," cast in the plural, used some 2,500 times throughout the Bible, including at least three times in the story of creation. The term corresponds with "let *us*" (1:26), and clearly asserts the Trinity — God the Father, God the Son, God the Spirit.

Thus, Christ was a Co-Creator, as Paul confirms when he says that "by him all things were created . . . all things were created by him, and for him: and he is *before all things,* and by him all things consist" (Col. 1:16, 17; cf. John 1:3). Further, were we not chosen in Him *before* the foundation of the world? Christ then existed before the creation of the world and man which He shared in (Heb. 1:8, 10; Rev. 4:11). The statement opening John's gospel, *"In the beginning* was the Word, and the Word was *with* God, and the Word was God" (1:1), precedes the *beginning* of Genesis which is limited to the creation of the universe and of man. *In the beginning* — the past eternity which had no beginning, Christ, as *the Word of God* was *with,* or dwelt with, God.

Again, one of the names of deity given to Jesus before He was born was that of *Everlasting Father,* or *Father of Eternity.* Names, as used in Hebrew, express that which a person *is;* being called anything means *being* that thing. As the eternal Son, Jesus came as the embodiment and revelation of the eternal God, just as He will act in judgment as the predicted *Ancient of days* whose august appearance that Daniel describes corresponds to that which John gives us of the glorified Jesus he saw (Rev. 1; Daniel 7:9, 13, 22).

We have no doubt whatever that the One so described was called by the prophet "the Ancient of days" because He was *from everlasting to everlasting.* Some commentators, however, suggest that a very aged man with a majestic appearance is meant, as Ezekiel describes (1:26-28), and is not intended to indicate the existence of the Judge from eternity. Keil writes, "What Daniel sees is not the eternal God Himself, but an aged man, in whose dignified and impressive form God reveals Himself." But in his delineation of "the fourth beast" — a prediction of what John fully develops in the beast rising up out of the sea (Rev. 13:18) — the horn prevails against the saints "until the Ancient of days *come.*" If this one has not yet arrived, then he could not have been some venerable-looking judge of Daniel's time. When Christ, as "the Ancient of days" returns to earth, His saints will share in His Kingdom age (Rev. 20:4).

Among other forecasts of our Lord's pre-existence we have the psalmist's declaration, "His name shall continue as long as the sun" (72:17), the original Hebrew of which reads, "Before the sun was, His name was *YINON*"

– the only occurrence in Scripture of this word, which ancient Jewish commentators agree is a name of the Messiah.

Solomon had an insight into the eternalness of the prophesied Messiah when he wrote, "The *Lord* possessed *me* in the beginning of his way, before his works of old. I was set up from everlasting to everlasting, from the beginning or ever the earth was" (Prov. 8:22, 23). That Solomon's description of *Wisdom* personified is a portrayal of the eternal Messiah is beyond doubt. Solomon goes on to give us a further delightful evidence of Christ's pre-existence in the words, "Then was I by him, as *one brought up with him;* and I was daily his delight, rejoicing always before him" (Prov. 8:30).

Eternity alone gives expanse for Christ, who was "in the beginning" whenever such a *beginning* was, "whose goings forth have been of old, from everlasting" (Mic. 5:2), of whom Jehovah declares, "Thy throne, O God, is for ever and ever" (Heb. 1:8). It is of this One that it is asserted, "From everlasting to everlasting thou art God" (Ps. 90:2). See John 1:3, where the phrase "not anything made that was made" forces the conclusion that either He created Himself or He was the uncreated Creator of all things. As none will claim that He could or did create Himself, there is only one conclusion, namely, that Christ was the Author of all in the universe of God? (Rev. 4:11).

The word "eternity" occurs only once in the Bible. Isaiah speaks of God as being "the high and lofty one that inhabits eternity" (57:15), and who, just as surely inhabits the hearts of the lowly and humble in whom He ever delights. The ASV of Ecclesiastes 3:11 reads, "He hath set eternity in their heart." *Eternity* along with its cognate *eternal* implies "the endless past, the unending future, or God's present experience for all time." It is in this sense that the term is used of:

God – "The *eternal* God is thy refuge, and underneath are the everlasting arms" (Deut. 33:27).

Christ – "The king eternal" (I Tim. 1:17).

The Holy Spirit – "The eternal Spirit" (Heb. 9:14).

The saints – Through grace all the children of God have the assurance of life forevermore. "God hath given to us *eternal* life, and *this* life is *in* his Son" (I John 5:11).

Eternal life, then, is not something but *Someone,* even the eternal Son Himself.

B. *Christ's Personal Affirmations (Fulfillments)*

Having considered a few of the foregleams of Christ's pre-existence as indicated in Old Testament Scriptures, as we take up the gospels, can it be proved that after His birth He was conscious of having existed previously to His human life on earth? If He was, when did such a consciousness become His? At what period in His life did such an awareness overtake Him? As already suggested, Jesus was familiar with the Old Testament from childhood days, and as He came to those statements regarding His pre-existence, did His heart glow as He thought upon the dateless past spent with His everlasting Father? Although we have no record of anything Jesus said during the first thirty years of His life, apart from the single occasion when He was twelve years of age and said, "Wist ye not that I must be about my Father's business?" through all those years as "*God* manifest in flesh," He must have had the inner consciousness that He had come down from heaven.

We cannot agree with those who affirm that it was not until His baptism when He entered His public ministry that Jesus was given the divine revelation that He was indeed the long-promised Messiah sent by God. Even though, through the silent years at Nazareth, He may not have given utterances and evidences of His pre-existence and deity, nevertheless, because He was the eternal Word made flesh, ever within His mind must have been the consciousness of who He was, and from whence He had come.

The Apostle John, for whom Jesus had a deep affection, is spoken of as "leaning on Jesus' bosom." Such physical closeness was symbolic of his nearness to the heart of his Lord. This is why the gospel bearing his name is distinct from the other three gospels. It is John who records more than any other writer the proofs of the Master's pre-existence and deity. Was it not John who wrote that the whole world could not contain the books that could be written about the words, wisdom, and works of the One he magnified as the Lord from heaven? Here are John's references to Him who existed before the world began:

"In the beginning... the Word was ... with God" (1:1).

Before John goes on to speak of the creative works of the Lord in time, he asserts the pre-existence of the Creator. The words "with God" express not only *pre*-existence, but *co*-existence. Distinct from God the Father, yet as God the Son, Christ, being "in the bosom of the Father" (1:18), was ever "throned face to face with God," or had "his gaze ever directed towards God." Completing his graduated sentence, John declares that Jesus *was God,* a phrase maintaining the distinction of person, yet at the same time asserting the oneness of essence characteristic of the Godhead.

"The world was made by him.... he came unto his own" (1:10, 11).

To John, the Creator was the true Light who came into the world, and the identification of Him with the historic event of creation was a proof that He had an existence before He was made flesh.

"We beheld his glory, the glory as of the only begotten of the Father" (1:14).

The words "only begotten," meaning "having glory as is the attribute of an only begotten Son" are used of Him only by John (1:14, 18; 3:16, 18; I John 4:9). "Only begotten," implying as of an only begotten child, or "the only child" is used four times by others (Luke 7:12; 8:42; 9:38; Heb. 11:17). As employed by John, the words carry the sense of the eternal generation of the Word—"the only begotten Son of God, begotten of his Father before the worlds." The outflashings of glory were an evidence of uncreated deity.

"He that cometh after me... was before me" (1:30).

John the Baptist is speaking of Christ his cousin according to the flesh. John was six months older than Christ as a babe, yet he here distinctly testified, "He was *before* me." Christ came *after* John, as far as public ministry was concerned, but He was *before* the Baptist in that as the eternal One He came from "the bosom of the Father." Some of the oldest manuscripts read, "Only begotten God, which is in the bosom of the Father." Oneness of eternal essence and eternal existence are here implied.

"We have found the Messias, which is, being interpreted, the Christ" (1:41; cf. 4:25).

This declaration of Andrew indicates the fulfillment of the Old Testament forecast. Prophecies of old had led men to expect Christ, and hearing John the Baptist proclaim Him as the foreordained Lamb of God, his hearers felt instinctively that this must be He of whom the prophets had spoken. An attribute of deity is omniscience which Christ manifested when He told Nathanael that He knew all about him. "He knew what was in man" (2:24, 25; cf. 4:17).

"He that came down from heaven" (3:13).

In His midnight conversation with Nicodemus, Jesus told the seeking Jewish ruler that He spoke only of those things He knew, and testified only to what He had seen. He was speaking to Nicodemus of heavenly things. He could do so with authority, for He had been in heaven, and therefore was qualified to speak of eternal truths. "... even the Son of man which is in heaven." There is no contradiction here. Away from heaven in a physical body, He ever maintained contact with heaven, for His was an unbroken communion with His Father, of whom Jesus said, "Thou hearest me always" (11:42).

"God sent ... his Son into the world" (3:17, 34; 4:29, 34; 5:23).

"Sent" is an oft-repeated word on the lips of Jesus and, as used here of and by Himself, implies a previous presence in the company of the Sender. Webster defines the word as meaning "to cause to be conveyed by an agent to a destination." In this case the agent was God the Son, sent by His Father, and the destination was this world of sinners, lost and ruined by the Fall. When did the actual sending take place? Well, the Agent first appeared in a manger, but His choice as the Agent was made in a past eternity because Jesus came as the Lamb slain *before* the foundation of the world.

"He that cometh from above is above all" (3:31).

John makes it clear that the message Jesus declared was from the Father, brought down to earth by the Son Himself. The message the Baptist declared was but that of a servant who did not fully know its meaning. But with Jesus it was different, for He was divine in origin, divine in nature, divine in teaching and works.

"He whom God hath sent speaketh the words of God" (3:34).

He could do no other for He Himself was "the Word of God."

"The bread of God is he which cometh down from heaven" (6:33).

Preaching in the great synagogue at Capernaum, Jesus repeated and expanded the symbol of Himself as heaven-given Bread, and affirmed that His pre-existence was the warrant of His life-giving power. The religious leaders, not understanding the claims He advanced as the pre-existent One, stoutly protested these claims and accused Jesus of blasphemy. But He reaffirmed His life before birth and proclaimed that since He was the heaven-descended Bread of Life, His flesh was meat indeed, and His blood was drink indeed, and that unless He was appropriated, they could not have life. Life eternal, resurrection at the last day, and His own presence even now within the soul, follow upon the partaking of Christ, as food from heaven.

Such a mysterious presentation of Himself caused His disciples to murmur. To them, His reference to a preexistent state was a "hard saying." But Jesus relieved their questioning hearts by predicting that His coming ascension into heaven as an event would justify His allusions to His pre-existence, no less than to His lifegiving virtue as the God-Man. Could anything be more explicit and authoritative than the following statements?

"What and if ye shall see the Son of man ascend up *where he was before?*"

"I know *whence I come,* and whither I go; but ye cannot tell *whence I come* and whither I go."

"*I am from above* ... I am not of the world."

"I proceeded forth and *came from God.*"

"*I came forth from the Father,* and am come into the world; again I leave the world, and go to the Father."

". . . the glory which I had with thee *before the world was.*"

Does not the reality of our Lord's pre-existence lighten up such mysterious sayings as these, as well as similar ones? How many millennia the world has been in existence is not easy to compute, yet here was One who had been born as a babe in Bethlehem, standing in the midst of men and claiming in His powerful intercessory prayer on the eve of offering Himself to the eternal Father as the incarnate Saviour, that He was coequal with God *before the world was* (John 17:5). If He was nothing more than an enthusiastic, revolutionary peasant of Galilee who, knowing of the prophetic messianic traits, related them to Himself and acted them out, then He was nothing but a deceitful charlatan – a rank impostor, as the Pharisees said He was when they accused Him of blasphemy.

What impresses us most in our Lord's remarkable discourse on "the Bread of Life" is His acquisition of the awesome, mystic name of Jehovah – *I am* that *I am!*

"*I am* the bread of life" (6:35).

"*I am* the living bread which came down from heaven" (6:51).

Isaiah records the divine message, "Ye are my witnesses, saith the LORD, and my servant whom I have chosen: that ye may know and believe me, and understand that *I am he*" (43: 10). Jesus made the same claim to be the great *I am* because the Father and He are one. The Samaritan woman was the first to hear Jesus use this expression of His Person. When Jesus spoke to this woman at the well concerning the water of life and spiritual worship, she, with a knowledge of Old Testament prophecies, said, "I know that Messias cometh, which is called Christ; when he is come, he will tell us all things" (John 4:25). What was the reply of Jesus? Study it closely: "*I* that speak unto thee *am he*" (v. 26). No wonder the woman testified, He "told me all things that ever I did," and the Samaritans, after hearing Jesus for themselves, confessed, "This is indeed the Christ, the Saviour of the world." His omniscience and Saviourhood were evidences of His pre-existence as the august *I am* – a description He often used of His person and work, as John records:

"*I am* he" (4:26) – as the divine-human One, He meets our need of a perfect Saviour from sin.

"*I am* the bread of life" (6:35) – as such He meets and satisfies our soul hunger.

"*I am* the light of the world" (8:12) – seeing there is no darkness in Him at all, He can banish our spiritual darkness.

"*I am* the door of the sheep" (10:7) – as He is the only way into fellowship with God, we are homeless without Him.

"*I am* the good shepherd" (10:11) – because He is *good*, His Shepherd-care cannot fail.

"*I am* the resurrection and the life" (11:25) – no other can remove the sting of death.

"*I am* your Master and Lord" (13:13) – if this divine One is not our Lord, He is not Lord at all.

"*I am* the way, the truth, and the life" (14:6) – as such He meets our threefold need: we are lost and need the way, in error and need the truth, in a state of spiritual death and need life.

"*I am* the true vine" (15:1) – being the vine, He meets our need of union with Himself.

"*I am* Jesus of Nazareth" (18:8) – becoming man, He understands our human needs; as God, He can meet them.

The most striking aspect of His assertion of being the great *I am* is that He thus identified Himself with the covenant name of Jehovah in the Old Testament. The Pharisees recognized that Jesus claimed deity when He applied this title most emphatically to Himself, for when He said, "Before Abraham was, *I am*," they took up stones to kill Him, considering it blasphemy, which by the law was punishable by death. Abraham lived 2,247 years before Christ was born, yet here He is affirming that He was in existence *before* Abraham.

Moses asked God the question about His identity. "When I come unto the children of Israel, and shall say unto them, The God of your fathers hath sent me unto you; and they shall say to me, What is his name? what shall I say unto them?" God answered Moses:

> "I AM THAT I AM. . . . Say unto the children of Israel, I AM hath sent me unto you" (Exod. 3:13, 14).

Although Egypt had numerous gods, each had a distinct name, and while the Israelites had known God as *Elohim* ("The Lofty One") and *Shaddai* ("The Powerful"), yet somehow they had not passed into proper names, and Moses, sensing that the Israelites, Egyptian-like, would want a distinct and proper name, asked God by what name he should call Him. Yet the reply, "I am that which I am," was a deep and mysterious statement of His nature, and not actually a proper name.

It was as if God were saying to Moses, "I cannot be declared in words, cannot be conceived of by human thought. I exist in such sort that My inscrutable nature is implied in My existence. I exist, as nothing else does — necessarily, eternally, really. If I am to give Myself a name expressive of My nature, so far as language can be, let Me be called *I AM*."

Assumed as a name, then, I AM implies, as Ellicott suggests:

1. An existence different from all other existence; "*I AM* . . . and there is none else" (Isa. 45.6).
2. An existence out of time, with which time has nothing to do; "Before Abraham was, I AM" (John 8:58).
3. An existence that is real, all other being shadowy.
4. An independent and unconditioned existence, from which all other is derived, and on which it is dependent.

Continuing His conversation with Moses about His name, God said, "Thou shalt say unto the children of Israel, '*Jehovah*, God of your fathers' " (which is the Hebrew of "The Lord God of your fathers"). He added: "This is *my name* for ever, and this is my memorial unto all generations" (Ex. 3:15). Thus the "I AM that I AM" is modified and becomes *Jehovah*. Although there is a substitution of the third person for the first, the meaning remains the same. Thereafter, Jehovah became the predominant name of God throughout the rest of the Old Testament. In the New Testament, Lord — the name Jesus used of Himself — takes its place. An equivalent of the name occurs in the Revelation where the Lord appears as "He which is, and which was, and which is to come" (1:4, 8; 4:8; 11:17; 16:5). "Necessary, self-sustained, independent, eternal existence, must always be of His essence."

We may deem God's "*I AM THAT I AM*" to be enigmatic, and somewhat of a dignified refusal on God's part to reveal Himself. Yet as used both by God and the Lord Jesus, it suggests essential and unconditional existence — absolute, self-determined, self-sustaining, and eternal. Here is everlasting Being, unvarying faithfulness, and measureless vitality. The Israelites, God's people, brought into redeeming connection with Him, were to count upon and appeal to Him as thus described. H. E. Govan, to whose *Studies in the Sacred Name,* we are greatly indebted says,

> Perhaps the vast possibilities implied can be more fully grasped if we give the verb — as is now done by most scholars — a future sense: *I WILL BE THAT I WILL BE.* Here is the promise of increasing self-manifestation. He is to be to us "a God of ever-developing potency", always going on to express Himself to us under fresh aspects according to our need.
>
> Does it seem to us somewhat vague and undignified? Do we seek a more precise description of God? But how *could* we define the Perfect, the Absolute, the Infinite? The Moslems, we are told, have a thousand names for God; but could even a thousand be adequate?

There is a sense in which the divine *I am* is a divine blank check for all our unknown future, no matter what emergencies may present themselves. He who said to the woman at the well, *I am He,* has a limitless supply. In our pre-existent, pre-eminent Lord, we have the promise of strength, counsel, protection, provision, guidance, and a thousand other possessions.

God said that His name, *Jehovah,* would be ever remembered, and so it was. "His name is great in Israel" (Ps. 76:1). "Our help is in the name of *Jehovah*" (Ps. 124:8). "In the name of *Jehovah* will I destroy them" (Ps. 118:10). Those who went up to the Holy City to worship God were spoken of as "going up in the name of *Jehovah.*" Associated with all these acts of worship, performed in spirit and in truth, was the assurance that the great *I will be that I will be,* who had so amply justified His covenant name in the redemption of His people, was pledged to undertake for them in all things as long as they trusted Him.

Thus the name Jehovah, in all its glorious significance, became God's memorial, as He said it would — God's "forget-Me-not." This is why the sacred name occurs almost 8,000 times in the Old Testament, 50 of which is in the briefer form JAH. It also was frequently used as a component part of personal names, in the form of Jeho as a prefix, or as a suffix in the form of Jah. The name came to be regarded among the Jews with superstitious reverence, with the pronunciation of it being forbidden. He who dared to speak it, said one rabbi, forfeited his place in the world to come. *Adonai* or *Elohim* were substituted in the reading of the sacred text. But, wherever our version prints the word GOD or LORD in small capitals, it represents the personal name Jehovah in the original. The American Revised Version uses this name wherever it occurs in the Hebrew. Some modern translations print the form YAHWEH, but the richly resonant, full-sounding, impressive Jehovah will hardly be superseded.

What a comfort it is to know that all the characteristics and features of Jehovah of the Old Testament are exhibited for our edification and encouragement in Jesus of the New Testament. All the prophecies, titles and types of Jehovah are exemplified and carried to perfection in Him whose name was called JESUS. Faith throws us back upon *I will be that I will be* in all its glorious indefiniteness of possibility. We do not know what awaits, but we are assured of the inexhaustible sufficiency of our Jehovah-Jesus. Pressing emergencies may arise, but He will be present in all His adequacy to meet the need.

Proud, conceited man, puffed up with the thought of self-sufficiency as the humanist, may say in his heart, "I AM, and [there is] none else beside me" (Isa. 47:8; cf. Zeph. 2:15), and in his self-existence act in a Jehovah-like way, but apart from *the* Jehovah, he *is* nothing, *has* nothing, and *can do* nothing. Paul could say, "By the grace of God, I am what I am," because he had experienced the emancipating power of the divine *I am that I am* – even the Saviour who is alive forevermore. How enlightening it is to compare the wonderful Jehovah Psalm with Christ's declaration of the nature of His mission among men (Ps. 146, with Matt. 11:2-6; Luke 4:18).

PRAISE YE JEHOVAH!

Praise ye Jehovah!
Praise Jehovah, O my soul!
While I live will I praise Jehovah:
I will sing praises unto my God while I have any breath.
I will sing praises unto my God while I have any being.
Put not your trust in princes,
Nor in the son of man, in whom there is no help.
His breath goeth forth, he returneth to his earth,
In that very day his thoughts perish.
Happy is he that hath the God of Israel for his help,
Whose hope is in Jehovah, his God,
Who made heaven and earth, the the sea, and all that in them is;
Who keepeth truth for ever;
Who executeth judgment for the oppressed;
Who giveth food to the hungry.
Jehovah looseth the prisoners;
Jehovah openeth the eyes of the blind;
Jehovah raiseth up them that are bowed down;
Jehovah loveth the righteous;
Jehovah preserveth the sojourners;
He upholdeth the fatherless and the widow,
But the way of the wicked He turneth upside down.
Jehovah shall reign for ever,
Thy God, O Zion, unto all generations.
Praise ye Jehovah!

In John's Gospel there are further affirmations of our Lord's pre-existence we could dwell upon, such as:

"*I am* from him [God], and he hath sent me" (7:29).

"I go unto him that sent me" (7:33).

"I know whence I came, and whither I go" (8:14).

"Jesus knowing . . . he was come from God, and went to God" (13:3).

"I came forth from the Father" (16:28).

"Thou lovedst me before the foundation of the world" (17:24).

One of the most striking evidences of Christ's pre-existence which John records is where Jesus, in citing the vision of divine glory that Isaiah the prophet had received, distinctly declared that "the Lord high and lifted up on a throne" was none other than He Himself. "He saw his glory and spake of him" (Isa. 6 with John 12:38-41). This glory was of the pre-incarnate Word, who was in the beginning with God, and was God. When Jesus turned aside from the ivory palaces to come to a world of woe, He did not leave His glory behind, but brought it with Him. Although such glory was veiled by His humanity, there were outflashings of His inherent glory as at His Transfiguration, making even His garment white and glistening. Such a manifestation of glory blinded the three disciples for the time being (Matt. 17:1-8).

Then are not the truths of His deity and His pre-existence implied in several Pauline passages? Think of this majestic, conclusive, and final ascription as given in Colossians 1:15-20, according to Phillips' *New Testament in Modern English*:

> Now Christ is the visible expression of the invisible God. He existed before creation began, for it was through him that everything was made, whether spiritual or material, seen or unseen. Through him, and for him, also, were created power and dominion, ownership and authority. In fact, every single thing was created through, and for, him. He is both the first principle and the upholding principle of the whole scheme of creation. And now he is the head of the body which is the Church. Life from nothing began through him, and life from the dead began through him, and he is, there-

> fore, justly called the LORD of all. It was in him that the full nature of God chose to live, and through him God planned to reconcile in his own person, as it were, everything on earth and everything in Heaven by virtue of the sacrifice of the cross.

Then we have Paul's praise for "the generosity of Jesus Christ, the Lord of us all. He was rich beyond our telling, yet he became poor for your sakes so that his poverty might make you rich" (II Cor. 8:9 Phillips). The phrase "He was rich" cannot apply to the outward aspect of our Lord's life on earth. Born of a poor woman, He had poverty as a companion until He died. He had nothing to leave. His only bequest was a legacy of peace to His disciples. "For our sakes he became poor"; the Greek word for "poor" means almost a beggar. Riches, then, refers to the eternal wealth He surrendered when He became Man. "He was rich in the ineffable glory of divine attributes, and these He renounced for a time to the mystery of the Incarnation, and took our nature with all its poverty."

Further, there is the wonderful passage that has caused many a theologian a headache, and has aroused much controversy through the centuries, becoming known as the "*kenosis* theory." The phrase "he humbled himself" (Phil. 2:8) means, "He emptied Himself." Although in "the form of God" and "equal with God," Christ yet stripped Himself. The question is, of what? Did He not pray for the return of the glory He had had with the Father before the world was, which was akin to the *Shechinah* of the divine presence (John 17:5)? Our Lord did not empty Himself of His divine nature, nor of all His precious attributes, but only of the outward and visible manifestation of the Godhead. Bishop Lightfoot puts it, "He emptied, stripped Himself of the insignia of Majesty."

We know from the miracles of our Lord that when occasion demanded, He exercised His divine attributes. As for the glory of the Godhead, "He resumed it for a moment in the Transfiguration; He was crowned with it anew at the Ascension." Here we quote Philippians 2:6-8 – again from Phillips' translation:

> He, who had always been God by nature, did not cling to his prerogatives as God's equal, but stripped himself of all privilege by consenting to be a slave by nature and being born as mortal man. And, having become man, he humbled himself by living a life of utter obedience, even to the extent of dying, *and the death he died was the death of a common criminal.*

While there are other direct and indirect evidences of Christ's pre-existence we could adduce, we conclude with the magnificent statement found in Hebrews 1:2-12. Let these startling phrases speak for themselves:

> His Son . . . by whom also he made the worlds;
> Who being the brightness of his glory . . .
> The express image of his person . . .
> Upholding all things by the word of his power . . .
> He bringeth in the first begotten into the world . . .
> Unto the Son, he [God] saith, Thy throne, O God, is for ever . . .
> Thou, Lord, in the beginning hast laid the foundation of the earth; and the heavens are the works of thine hands . . .
> Thou art the same, and thy years shall not fail.

Language has no meaning if this remarkable affirmation does not teach the deity, the essential Lordship, the pre-existence, and eternity of God's eternal Son. Here we have a divine portrait of the supreme dignity of the Saviour who came as God's Representative on earth, and as the Redeemer of mankind. As a reward for all He surrendered for our sakes, God has invested Him with unlimited dominion. Presently, He rests after the accomplishment of His work on earth, but when He takes to Himself to reign, then will the subjection of His enemies be complete and final (Dan. 7:14; Eph. 1:20-23).

F. H. Faber has taught us to sing —

> Backward our thoughts through ages stretch, onward through endless bliss —
> For there are two eternities, and both alike are HIS!

As we conclude our study of Christ's pre-existence, a word or two is necessary as to the significance of the *theophanies,* as the visible appearances of God in the Old Testament are called. Did Jesus come occasionally to earth before He came to live on it for thirty-three years? In the early days of the human race before men had any portion of the Written Word, and before the full revelation of the Holy Spirit as the Inspirer and Revealer of truth, God appeared, generally in human form, and talked with men. Before Adam and Eve sinned, they walked and talked with God, but after sin entered to disturb such close fellowship, they hid themselves and only heard His voice (Gen. 3:8) as Cain did (4:6).

Both Enoch and Noah are spoken of as having "walked with God" (Gen. 5:24; 6:9), with Noah being in close contact with God to receive instructions concerning the ark built according to divine specifications. Several times the Lord is spoken of as having revealed His will and purpose in dreams and visions to those He was to use. But we have a series of remarkable appearances of God, forming a prominent feature of the early history of the Old Testament. One of the most attractive and instructive of these theophanies, so closely akin to Christ's pre-existence, is that of the experience the patriarch Abraham had by the oak of Mamre (Gen. 18).

Divine appearances usually occurred when men were asleep as in the vision Jacob had at Bethel (Gen. 28:10-17), but with Abraham it was different. When he lifted up his eyes to see the One spoken of as "Jehovah appeared" (Gen. 18:1), "lo, three men stood by him." Abraham bowed himself to the ground and offered his visitors hospitality, and under the oak tree, they ate. One of the three, who acted as spokesman, bore the sacred name of Jehovah, and was the same Person who said to Abraham, "*I am* the Almighty God" (Gen. 17:1; 18:1). So we read, "Jehovah said, Shall I hide from Abraham that thing which I do?" (18:17).

This distinguished spokesman is not to be confused with either of "the two angels" sent to Sodom. With Jehovah Abraham intercedes for Sodom; and by Him judgment is afterward executed upon the godless, guilty city. When it is said that "Jehovah rained upon Sodom and upon Gomorrah brimstone and fire from Jehovah out of heaven," it will be noticed that a sharp distinction is established between a visible and an invisible Person, each bearing the most holy name. The temporarily visible Jehovah was, we believe, the Lord Jesus, the pre-incarnate Christ, to whom the invisible God committed all judgment (John 5:22). It was the visible Jehovah who promised Abraham that Sarah would have a son, and that "all the nations of earth shall be blessed in him [Abraham]."

Then we come to the appearances and utterances of that very exalted and mysterious Being, spoken of as "the Angel of the Lord," whom Canon Liddon, in his masterly work on *The Divinity of Our Lord,* said "is certainly distinguished from Jehovah; yet the names by which this Angel is called, the powers which he assumes to wield, the honour which is paid to him shew that in Him there was at least a special presence of God." For our part, we have no difficulty in believing that the appearances of this

Angel were manifestations of the pre-incarnate Son of God, with whose appearance as God manifest in the flesh all theophanies ceased.

This supreme Angel spoke sometimes in His own name, and sometimes as if He were not a created personality, but only a veil or organ of the higher nature that spoke and acted through Him. Take, for instance, His appearance to the distressed Hagar, when He spoke in the character of an ambassador from heaven, that the Lord had heard her affliction (Gen. 16:11). Yet He had just before promised Hagar, "*I* will multiply thy seed exceedingly." How did the slave-wife of Abraham reply? "She called the name of the LORD (Jehovah) that spake unto her, Thou God seest me." To Nathanael, Jesus said, "When thou wast under the fig tree, *I saw thee*" (John 1:48).

Later on, this same august Angel prevented Abraham from fulfilling God's command to offer his son Isaac as a sacrifice. Yet in the same narrative the Angel associates Himself with Him from whom "Abraham had not withheld his son, his only son." The Angel accepted for Himself Abraham's obedience as rendered to God. If we have here another manifestation of the pre-incarnate Christ, then how conscious He must have been of the time when He would be offered up – and slain – as God's only-begotten Son! In His second appearance to Abraham, the Angel gave the promise, "In thy seed shall all the nations of the earth be blessed; because thou hast obeyed my voice" (Gen. 22:18). Christ Himself came to exhibit what it was to be obedient, even to the death of the cross.

Another theophany was the one Jacob experienced when in a dream he heard a voice announcing, "I am the God of Bethel, where thou anointedst the pillar, and where thou vowedst a vow unto *me*" (Gen. 31:11, 13). The speaker was "the Lord" (Jehovah) who in the vision at Bethel stood above the ladder saying, "I am the LORD God of Abraham thy father, and the God of Isaac." Then it would seem as this One was the chief of that angel-host Jacob met at Mahanaim (Gen. 32:1); and with whom Jacob wrestled for a blessing at Peniel; and of whom the patriarch could say, "I have seen God face to face, and my life is preserved" (32:30). If the One Jacob saw and heard at the ladder was Jesus in a pre-appearance form, how vivid would the occasion be as He came to speak of angels ascending and descending upon Him (John 1:51). It is somewhat interesting to observe that when it came to the blessing of the sons of Joseph that Jacob, the dying patriarch, invoked the benediction of "the God which fed me all my life long unto this day" (Gen. 48:15) but also of "the Angel which redeemed me from all evil" (48:16) – a ministry no ordinary angel could exercise.

Moses was another who received a visit from this conspicuous Angel of the Lord to whom we read that He addressed Moses "face to face" (Ex. 33:11). While in Midian, Moses had the awesome experience of hearing a voice speaking to him "in a flame of fire out of the midst of a bush" (Ex. 3:1-6). In spite of the fire, the bush remained miraculously unconsumed, a token to Moses that the people he was to lead would be indestructible. We have here a combination of titles. "The angel of the Lord appeared unto him," "Jehovah" observed that Moses turned aside to see, and "Elohim" called to Moses out of the burning bush. Moses felt the very ground he stood on was holy and hid his face, "for he was afraid to look upon *God*." The speaker out of the bush – the Angel of the Lord – announces Himself as "the God of Abraham, the God of Isaac, and the God of Jacob." The divine attributes of mercy, wisdom, providence, power, and authority manifested by "the Angel of the Lord" found expression in and through the One who became the "Stranger of Galilee."

Amid all their trials and tribulations from Egypt to Canaan, the Israelites had the presence and protection of "the Angel of the Lord." As they made their escape from Egypt, it was He who placed Himself between their camp and the host of Pharaoh (Ex. 14:19, 20). He also granted them His protecting care as they journeyed from Egypt (Num. 20:16). God promised that His Angel – the Angel of His presence – would keep Israel in the way until Canaan was reached; and that His presence would be a guarantee that the Amorites and other idolatrous races would be cut off. But Israel was urged to obey this Angel, and never provoke Him, seeing that the holy "name is in him."

How assuring the promises must have been: "Mine Angel shall go before thee," "My presence shall go with thee, and I will give thee rest" (Ex. 32:34; 33:14, 15). Is it not easy to distinguish the One God spoke of as "Mine Angel" as the Lord who assured His own that He would be with them alway, even unto the end? Even after the tragedy of the golden calf, the promised guardianship of the Angel was not withdrawn. Although fully representing God, the Angel is clearly shown as distinct from Jehovah Himself.

Balaam was another who had an encounter with the Angel of the Lord. How authoritatively this Angel withstood Balaam on his faithless errand, bidding him go with the messengers of Balak, adding, "Only the word that I shall speak unto thee, that thou shalt speak" (Num. 22:35; cf. 23:16; 24:12). Surely it is clearly evident that no mere created being, speaking and acting in his own right, could have spoken to men, or have allowed men to act toward himself in worship, reverence and honor, as did the Angel of the Lord who, to our way of thinking, was the Son of God, God's messenger whom He ever delighted in (Mal. 3:1-6).

We now come to the contact Joshua had with the "captain of the host of the LORD," whom he, the successor of Moses as leader of Israel, first saw as a man "with his sword drawn in his hand" (Josh. 5:13-15). No angel from the legion heaven possesses would dare ask for a token of reverence and worship. Did not an angel reprove John for falling down at his feet to worship him because of the revelation he had brought to the apostle (Rev. 22:8, 9)? But Joshua fell on his face and worshipped "the captain of the host of the LORD," and called him LORD. Because of the presence of this Defender, the place both He and Joshua stood on was holy ground. Is not Jesus the brave and victorious captain of our salvation, and worthy of all worship and adoration for all He is in Himself, and for all He has accomplished (Heb. 2:10)?

Among other references to the Angel of the Lord we have the following, which Canon Liddon groups together for us. Each appearance is worthy of more space than we can allot.

In the Song of Deborah the curse against Merog is pronounced by the Angel. The Book of Judges contains three appearances of His, in each of which we are scarcely sensible of a created personality, so completely is the language and bearing that of a higher nature present in the Angel.

At Bochim He expostulates with the assembled people for their breach of the covenant in failing to exterminate the Canaanites. God speaks by the Angel in His own name, and refers to the covenant which He had made with Israel, and to His deliverance of the people out of Egypt. He declares that on account of their disobedience He will not drive the heathen nations out of the land (Judges 2:1-5).

In the record of the Angel's appearance to Gideon, he is called "the Angel of the Lord," "Lord," "Jehovah." This august One urged Gideon to attack the Midianite oppressors of Israel, adding the promise, "I will be with thee." Did not Someone from heaven give the Church a similar promise: "I will never leave thee, nor forsake thee" (Heb. 13:5)?

When Gideon placed an offering before the Angel with the request that He would manifest His heavenly character by some sign, the Angel touched the offering with a stick, and fire rose up out of the rock and consumed the offering. Gideon was afraid that he would die because he had seen the "Angel of the LORD face to face" (Judges 6:22).

The nameless wife of Manoah was also honored with an appearance of this angel. At first she said that "a man of God" came to her. Then she described Him as having a "countenance like the countenance of an angel of God, very terrible." When the angel appeared to Manoah, he failed to recognize the Visitor. When Manoah asked, "What is thy name?" the reply was, "it is secret"—secret, meaning "wonderful," seeing "he did wondrously" (Judges 13:17, 18). When the angel mounted up visibly to heaven in the flame of the sacrifice, Manoah and his wife, like Gideon, feared they would die because, as they said, "We have seen God" (13:6-22).

Wisdom in Jewish Scriptures, as Liddon points out, is far more than a human endowment, or even an attribute of God. Job asked the question, "Where shall wisdom be found?" and then went on to state that it is personified in God. In the Book of Proverbs the wisdom is co-eternal with Jehovah—assisting Him in the work of creation. Wisdom reigns, as one specially honored, in the palace of the King of heaven, and is the adequate object of the eternal joy of God. God not only possesses wisdom, He *is* wisdom, and all true wisdom delights in Him (Prov. 8).

Faith believes that wisdom is personal, co-eternal with God, who made His beloved Son to be "unto us—wisdom" (I Cor. 1:30). In Christ alone "are hid all the treasures of wisdom" (Col. 2:3), and, as "wisdom ... from above," He answers to the matchless wisdom James so fully describes (3:15-18). In our quest for divine wisdom, "the spirit of wisdom and revelation," is ever within us to unfold its manifold facets. Francis Bacon (1568-1626) has the quotation "*De Sapientia Veterum*" (The Wisdom of the Ancients). With our Ancient of days there can be found the eternal and internal depths of all wisdom. The Word being the personification of perfect wisdom, we can understand how the early fathers with general unanimity saw in all of these theophanies, the *Word,* the vocal expression of wisdom. To them, "the Angel of the LORD" was the Son of God Himself. For our final word concerning the fact and forecasts of our Lord's pre-existence, whether direct or indirect, literal or symbolic, we turn to Canon Liddon whose great volume, *The Divinity of Our Lord,* which first appeared well over 100 years ago, we have leaned so heavily upon in this aspect of our study:

> Whether in the Theophanies the Word, or the Son, appeared actually, or whether God made a created angel the absolutely perfect exponent of His thought and will, do they not point in either case to a purpose in the Divine mind which would only be realized when men had been admitted to a nearer and more palpable contact with God than was possible under the patriarchal or Jewish dispensations? Do they not suggest, as their natural climax and explanation, some personal self-un-

veiling of God before the eyes of His creatures?

Would not God appear to have been training His people, by this long and mysterious series of communications, at length to recognise and to worship Him when hidden under, and indissolubly one with a created nature? Apart from the specific circumstance which may seem to have explained each Theophany at the time of its taking place, and considering them as a series of phenomena, is there any other account of them so much in harmony with the general scope of Holy Scripture, as that they were successive lessons to the eye and to the ear of ancient piety, in anticipation of a coming Incarnation of God?

Chapter Three

PROPHECIES OF HIS ANCESTRY

His Two Genealogies
His Descent from Shem
His Descent from Abraham
His Descent from Judah
His Descent from David
His Descent from Joseph

When Paul warned Timothy against wasting time over "endless genealogies," he was not referring to "genealogies" in their proper sense, as found in the Scriptures, but to the wild and improbable legends some early Jewish schools attached to them. Inquiries into matters of controversy could have no bearing on practical life. There were more certain questions for Timothy to search out to godly edification (I Tim. 1:4). Although lists of names may appear to be dry and uninteresting and may not be considered the parts of Scripture to meditate on, yet they must not be neglected by students of the Word. In our time, genealogical societies have sprung up to help those who are interested in their ancestry to help them learn something about their forefathers.

The genealogies of Scripture are important, for they form the generation-to-generation tie-up of all preceding biblical history and are both the skeletal framework of the Old Testament and the cords binding the whole Bible together, giving it its characteristic unity. They also separate real history from mere legend. The Jews, as we know, were meticulous about keeping a record of succeeding generations. Public registers of all members of families had to be scrupulously preserved. Think of the long, official genealogies given in I Chronicles 1-9 and Ezra 2! There are also the lists Nehemiah introduces with testimony to divine sanction for them (Neh. 7:5-67):

> And my God put into mine heart to gather together the nobles, and the rulers, and the people, that they might be reckoned by geneaology (v. 5).

Priests who could not trace their ancestry were put out of their office (Neh. 7:64). Any Jew ought to have been able to trace his genealogy, for "all Israel were reckoned by genealogies" (I Chron. 9:1). Kept in the cities, these lists were public property.

Further, each Israelite's genealogical record constituted his title to his farm or home; so he also had a pecuniary interest in preserving the genealogical records of his family. These national records were carefully kept until the destruction of Jerusalem, the Temple, and the Jewish nation in A.D. 70. Therefore, during the life of Jesus, no one could dispute that He was of the house and lineage of David as He claimed to be, because there were the public records to prove it. Israel's genealogical records — except those in the Bible — were destroyed or confused as the result of the plunder of Jerusalem by Titus. After A.D. 70 no pretending Messiah could prove" that he was the prophesied son of David.

Edmund Burke (1729-1797), in his *Reflections on the Revolution in France,* says that "people will not look forward to posterity who never look backward to their ancestors." The Jews of old were inspired to look forward to their posterity as they mused on all that their God had been to their ancestors since the time of Abraham, Isaac, and Jacob. In another essay Burke writes of possessing "the wisdom of our ancestors."

Richard B. Sheridan (1751-1816), in *The Rivals*, pertinently remarked, "Our ancestors are very good kind of folk; but they are the last people I should choose to have as visiting acquaintances." As we go over the genealogies of Jesus, we may share the same sentiment about some who are mentioned as ancestors. For instance, consider the first four women who are mentioned:

Tamar, the daughter-in-law of Judah
Rahab the harlot,
Ruth the Moabitess,
Bathsheba, the object of David's adulterous love.

As it was without precedent in Jewish genealogies to include women, why were *these* women included in the genealogies of Jesus? Should not the genealogist have observed discreet silence regarding these women, two of whom were stained by sin, and one of whom was a foreigner? But all became monuments of God's grace and serve to show how He can give vile and dishonored vessels a place of honor. Did not the prophesied Jesus come to save sinners of every type and race? The Gospel suggested by the genealogies is the revelation of Jesus who came as the Friend of sinners to "save that which was lost."

A. *His Two Genealogies*

We thus come to the genealogies of Jesus as given in the New Testament in order to trace His lineage according to the flesh. As we know, there are two genealogies – one by Matthew, and the other by Luke (Matt. 1:1-17; Luke 3:23-38). From earliest days these two lists have formed the subject of endless discussion, with skeptics asserting that there are contradictions in them that cannot be reconciled. Dr. T. M. Lindsay suggests that "if we start with the fact that Matthew, in order to get his generations into sets of *fourteen*, omitted several names – a common practice among the Jewish genealogists – the reconciliation of the two descents is very simple, and the supposed difficulties are easily explained by well-known Jewish practices." Dr. H. B. Swete reckons that "most of the difficulties are removed at one stroke, and the known facts harmonized, by the simple supposition that Luke has given us the meeting point of the lineage, both of Joseph and Mary who are akin." In this connection, Dr. W. Graham Scroggie comments that if Matthan, thirty-eight in Matthew's genealogy, and Matthat, seventy-first in Luke's, were the same person, we see that Jacob and Heli were brothers.

> Luke tells us that Joseph was the son of Heli, and it is conjectured with much probability that Mary was the daughter of Jacob. If it is assumed that Jacob, having no son, adopted Joseph, his nephew and heir, we see that Mary married a relation, and that she, as well as Joseph, was descended from David, Joseph in the line of Solomon, and Mary, his wife, in the line of Nathan.

With these two genealogies before us, there are one or two conspicuous features we might consider in passing. First of all, there are *two* lists. Why? Would not one have been sufficient and saved scholars the trouble of trying to reconcile their apparent differences? Three views have been expressed as to the necessity of the two lists:

1. Both genealogies give the descent of Joseph – Matthew's the *real*, and Luke's the *legal* descent.

2. Matthew gives Joseph's legal descent as successor to the throne of

David, and Luke gives his real parentage.

3. Matthew gives the real descent of Joseph; and Luke, the real descent of Mary.

But there is a further explanation of the two lists. *Two,* in Scripture, carries with it the thought of confirmation or verification: "At the mouth of *two* witnesses . . . shall the matter be established (Deut. 19:15). "For God speaketh once, yea *twice*" (Job 33:14). "God hath spoken once; twice have I heard this" (Ps. 62:11).

Then there is the reason of showing Christ's descent through David from Abraham and Adam set forth in an unbroken line in both genealogies. Both were needed to prove that redemption was no afterthought on God's part, but designed from the beginning. In Matthew's list, Abraham and David are singled out to prove the fulfillment of the promises and prophecies to Abraham 2,000 years before, and to David 1,000 years before. Luke takes us back to Adam, the father of the human race, and brings the *first* Adam and the *last* Adam together — the two federal heads — Adam, of the human race; Christ, the Head of a redeemed people, His Church. In Adam we die, in Christ we are made alive.

The Old Testament begins with Genesis, which means "generation," and the New Testament opens with the "genesis" or "generation of Jesus Christ." The Old Testament ends with the word "curse," which summarizes the sin of succeeding generations from Adam down. Because of the sin of Adam and Eve, the serpent was cursed, the earth was cursed, and man likewise came under the curse (Gen. 3:14, 17; cf. 4:11; Deut. 21:23). *Thorns* appeared as the emblem of the curse. But the first subject of the New Testament is Jesus, and this is as it should be, for according to prophecy He came to redeem us from "the curse of the law." Thorns were woven into a crown which was placed upon His lovely brow. "Cursed is every one that hangeth on a tree" (Gal. 3:13). There shall be no more curse" (Rev. 22:3).

> Death and the curse were in our cup,
> O Christ, 'twas full for Thee!
> But Thou hast drain'd the last dark drop —
> 'Tis empty now for me.
> That bitter cup — love drank it up;
> Now blessings' draught for me.

Sir Wm. S. Gilbert (1836-1911), in *The Mikado,* has this biographical paragraph:

> I can trace my ancestry back to a protoplasmal primordial atomic globule. Consequently, my family pride is something inconceivable. I can't help it. I was born sneering.

Our human ancestry is traceable not to a fishlike substance cast up by the sea, but to Adam who was created by God and bore His image. But the first Adam sinned, causing all who followed him to be born in sin; thus we were "born sinning." But man can be born again, and the necessity of the genealogies is to provide us with the ancestry of Him who was manifested to destroy the works of the devil. The "old man" is the man of old, or one in whom the old Adamic nature prevails. Jesus came that there might be the "new man." Descended from Adam, the son of God, the Last Adam through grace makes the sinning sons of men to become anew the sons of God.

Another impressive feature of the first genealogy is Matthew's use of the mystic number fourteen (see Num. 29:13; I Kings 8:65). It is the double of seven, the number of completeness. Matthew also uses the sacred three so that there are the three "fourteen generations" (1:17). Surely, there is nothing casual about such divisions. Fausset observes that the period from Abraham to David is that of the patriarchs; from David to the Babylonian captivity, that of kings;

from the captivity to Christ, that of private individuals. The first and second periods have illustrious beginnings, but the third does not. It is the period of captivity because of sin and rebellion; yet, it ends with the Messiah who came to set prisoners free. His coming gives this period preeminence over the first two periods of fourteen generations each.

The first period is that of *promise,* beginning with Abraham and ending with David, the receivers of the promise. During this period the people were a theocracy, governed by judges.

The second period foreshows Christ's eternal *Kingdom* through the temporary kingdom of David's line. Throughout these generations the people were a monarchy, ruled by kings.

The third period breathes the air of *expectation,* with the cry, "How long, O Lord? How long?" During this period the people were a hierarchy, with priests as mediators. Israel's career is reflected by these three periods: growth, decline, ruin; her utter failure pointing emphatically to the need of redemption through Him who heads each genealogy.

A word is necessary in connection with the disparity in the length of these two genealogies: Matthew gives forty-one names, whereas Luke lists seventy-four – the full number, as following the natural line. Much controversy has raged around the omissions in Matthew's shorter list. Had the enemies of Christ seen anything false or mutually contradictory between these lists, they would have erased them from the public documents. But evidently they saw nothing irreconcilable in them. It will be seen that from Abraham to David both lists agree, but thereafter the names differ, with Luke giving us forty-two from David on, and Matthew only twenty-seven. The reason for the lesser number in Matthew is intelligible, if he is tracing only heirs to the throne, for "the heir of my heir is my heir." So intermediate heirs are omitted, at the risk of misconception, for spiritual reasons; for example, Simeon is omitted in Moses' blessing on account of his cruelty (Deut. 33) and Dan is excluded because of his idolatry (Rev. 7:4-8).

A comparison of the two genealogies reveals the different standpoints of the genealogists. For instance,

Matthew appropriately, as writing for Jews, gives Christ's legal descent, and sets Him forth as Israel's King.

Luke, probably of Gentile extraction, writes for Gentiles, and gives the natural descent.

Matthew records the names downward, from Abraham the natural father of the Jews, but the spiritual father of the Gentiles (Gen. 17:5; Rom. 4:16, 17).

Luke writes his list of names upward from Christ to Adam, "who was the son of God" and the father of Gentiles and Jews, all sinners alike (Rom. 5:19). Luke writes of Christ as the Son of man.

Among other comparisons and contrasts between the genealogies that can be noted are the following:

Matthew presents Jesus as the legal and royal heir to the promises and prophecies given to Abraham and David. Luke gives us the line of Mary, showing Jesus' blood or physical descent, "seed of David according to the flesh" (Rom. 1:3).

Whereas Matthew is concerned with the kingship of Jesus, and Luke His humanity, both writers are entirely one in their witness to the Virgin Birth and to the deity of our Lord. Both agreed that although He was the Son of Mary, He was yet "the Son of the highest."

Mark and John do not give space to these genealogies for different reasons. Mark does not mention Christ's Virgin Birth. Why does Mark pass over the first thirty years of the earthly life of Jesus, and introduce Him suddenly to us when the Holy Spirit came upon Him at the commencement of His service (1:9, 10)? It was because Mark was given the task of presenting Jesus as the true Servant of Jehovah. Servant means "slave," and who cares about the ancestry of a slave! All that is required is character and fitness for prompt and willing service. This is why Mark repeats the words "straightway," "immediately," "anon" – all implying immediate action.

John omits any reference to the human descent of Jesus for another reason. The first phrase of his gospel indicates that his mission as a writer was to emphasize the deity of his Lord, and no earthly genealogy has any place in such a presentation of Christ. "In the beginning was the Word, and the Word was with God, and the Word was God" (1:1). The divine, eternal origin of Christ goes back before there were any earthly genealogies of men to record.

The four Gospels as a whole display the glories and beauties of God's well-beloved Son who came fulfilling all past predictions of His life and work. These four divinely given gospels are faithful portraits of the same Person who came as King, Servant, Man, and God. Each gospel is the complement of the other, and when the four gospels are studied in this light, they take on a new significance.

As we come to pinpoint some of the persons mentioned in these genealogies with whom our Lord was associated prophetically, we cannot but admire the retention of these family lines through which a promise or prophecy of a Person was transmitted, a fact unexampled in history. From the creation of the first man, Adam, the coming of Christ was anticipated, and in the early days of human history God was pleased to choose one family line, namely, that of Abraham, through whom His Son (around whom prophecy gathers) should enter to the world to fulfill all that the prophets had declared of Him. We heartily concur with the excellent introduction which Dr. A. T. Pierson wrote for the guidance of those setting out to study Christ and prophecy.

> The most ordinary reader may examine the old curious predictions of the Messiah's person and work found in the Old Testament, follow the graded progress of these revelations from Genesis to Malachi, and trace the prophecies as they descend into details more and more specific and minute, until at last the full figure of the Coming One stands out. Then, with this image clearly fixed in his mind's eye, he may turn to the New Testament, and beginning with Matthew, see how the *historic* personage, Jesus of Nazareth, corresponds and coincides in every particular with the *prophetic* personage depicted by the prophets. . . . There is not a difference or a divergence, yet there could have been no collusion or contact with the prophets of the Old Testament and the narrators of the New Testament. Observe, the reader has not gone out of the Bible itself. He has simply compared two portraits; one in the Old Testament of a mysterious Coming One, another is in the New of One who has actually come: and his irresistible conclusion is that these two blend in absolute unity.

It is not the Bible that gives values to Christ, but Christ who gives value to the prophetic Scriptures. The Bible may dwell upon numerous subjects of great importance, but at the center and circumference of all the truth presented is the One who could declare, "In the volume of the book, it is written of *me*" (Heb. 10:7). He is the Secret of the structural, historical, prophetical, doctrinal, and spiritual unity of the Bible.

Christ is the end, for Christ was the beginning; Christ is the beginning, for the end is Christ.

B. *His Descent From Shem*

Jesus was born a Jew. What an illustrious Jewish ancestry was His who came, not only as "the glory of his people Israel," but also as "a light to lighten the Gentiles" (Luke 2:32). Going back over His lineage, we know from both forecast and fulfillment that He came from the line of Shem.

Forecast: "Blessed be the LORD God of Shem . . ." (Gen. 9:26, 27).
Fulfillment: ". . . which was the son of Shem" (Luke 3:36).

"The generations of Shem" (Gen. 11:10-26) stretch from Shem to Abraham, covering ten generations – 427 years. Shem himself may have recorded this entire genealogy, for his life spanned the period covered by it. Shem lived from 98 years before the Flood until 502 after the Flood, which means that he lived until 75 years after Abraham entered Canaan. Noah had three sons – Shem, Ham, and Japheth (Gen. 6:10) – who became the fountainheads of the new nations after the Flood. Eliminating two-thirds of the nations, God indicated that the Messiah must come from Shem – not Ham or Japheth. It was from Shem that the Jews sprang, through Abraham, as we shall see.

"Blessed be Jehovah, the God of Shem" (Gen. 9:26, R.V.). In the following verse there is no word answering to the word *"he"* found in the A.V., and so the verse correctly reads: "God will enlarge Japheth, and will dwell in the tents of Shem."

The Chaldee of Onkelos paraphrases the verse like this: ". . . will make His glory to dwell in the tabernacles of Shem." The final fulfillment of this prediction came when Jesus, the eternal Word, was made flesh, having been born of a Jewish woman, and men "beheld his glory, the glory as of the only begotten of the Father" (John 1:14).

The name *Shem* means in Hebrew "name" – a designation subsequently given him as one of *note* or great among Noah's sons, as one of the two sons who dutifully covered their father's shame. The prophecy that *Jehovah* would be specially the God of Shem was fulfilled in the choice of Abraham and of Israel, his descendants as God's peculiar people. Shem is called "the father of all the children of Eber"; the term *Hebrews* is derived from Eber (Gen. 10:21; cf. Num. 24:24). The Greek for "Shem" is *Sem* from which we have the word "Semites." Anti-*Semitism* means "hatred of the Jews."

C. *His Descent From Abraham*

Matthew begins his genealogy with this introduction: "The book of the generation of Jesus Christ, the son of David, *the son of Abraham*" (1:1).

All nations were excluded except one, namely the one with Shem as its progenitor and which had its beginning with the call of Abraham. By such a choice, the God of history divided the many nations of the earth into two groups. The majority of the peoples became "the Gentile nations," while a very small family became known as God's "chosen people," the Jewish nation. To this privileged people God gave a land, and a prophecy that He would make the people "a great nation" and through them bless the earth (Gen. 12:1-7; 17:1-8, 15-19).

Forecast: "In thee shall all families of the earth be blessed" (Gen. 12:3).
Fulfillment: "Jesus Christ . . . the son of Abraham" (Matt. 1:1).

"Now to Abraham and his seed . . . which is Christ" (Gal. 3:16).

Matthew's gospel deals principally with the Messiah's relation to Israel, and Abraham was the head of the Israelitish race. Coming from the Ur of the Chaldees, he was originally a Gentile, but he became the first man to be a Hebrew (Gen. 14:13), a designation which means "one who has passed over or beyond the river." How immeasurably has the world been blessed through Abraham's Seed, which is the Saviour! Both Jews and Gentiles alike have experienced the riches of His grace.

"And the scripture, foreseeing that God would justify the heathen through faith, preached *before* the gospel unto Abraham, saying, In thee shall *all* nations be blessed" (Gal. 3:8).

Abraham had many sons, including his firstborn, Ishmael, and Isaac. Here, again, we have a divine choice, for God decreed that the Messiah was to come through *Isaac* ("In Isaac shall thy seed be called") and not through Ishmael, progenitor of the modern Arabs.

Forecast: "And the Lord appeared unto [Isaac], and said, . . . In thy seed shall all the nations of the earth be blessed" (Gen. 26:2, 4).

Fulfillment: "Who are Israelites . . . , whose are the fathers, and *of whom as concerning the flesh Christ came,* who is over all, God, blessed for ever" (Rom. 9:4, 5, 7; cf. Heb. 11:18).

D. *His Descent From Judah*

Jesus came as "the Star out of Jacob" and "out of Jacob shall come he that shall have dominion" (Num. 24:17, 19). Jacob had twelve sons, and another choice had to be made by God. *Judah* is selected, and it was from the tribe bearing that name that Jesus came.

Forecast: "He . . . chose the tribe of Judah" (Ps. 78:67, 68).

"The sceptre shall not depart from Judah . . . until Shiloh come" (Gen. 49:10; cf. Luke 3:33).

Fulfillment: "For it is evident that our Lord sprang out of Judah" (Heb. 7:14).

"The Lion of the tribe of Juda" (Rev. 5:5).

The tracing of Christ's descent through Judah's *royal* line harmonizes with the kingly aspect of Jesus Christ in Matthew's gospel. Jacob gives us the meaning of the name of his fourth son by Leah: "Thou art he whom thy brethren shall *praise*" (Gen. 49:8; cf. 29:35). *Judah* means "praise," and his wonderful Descendant, *Jesus,* is worthy of all praise and honor and glory. By the *sceptre* we are to understand, not so much a king's staff, but a *tribal* staff. Each tribe had its own rod or staff as an ensign of authority upon which was inscribed the name of the tribe. The tribal *identity* of Judah was not to pass away until Shiloh came.

Shiloh has ever been taken to be a name of the Messiah. It means "peace" or "one sent." As the Messiah, or Sent One, Jesus came *before* Judah lost its tribal identity. Since He came, our Shiloh has had the obedience of countless myriads as the prophetic Word said He would (Gen. 49:10).

E. *His Descent From David*

Among Old Testament prophecies of Christ quoted in the New Testament, those relating to David and Christ hold the place of preeminence. We can gather only a few references from the abundant quotations regarding David and his niche in prophecy. From the thousands of families comprising the tribe of Judah, the choice of *one* family line had to be made. God chose the family of *Jesse.*

Forecast: "And there shall come forth a rod out of the stem of Jesse, and a Branch shall grow out of his roots; And the spirit of the Lord shall rest upon him" (Isa. 11:1, 2).

Fulfillment: "Jesus . . . which was the son of Jesse" (Luke 3:23, 32).

"There shall come out of Sion the Deliverer" (Rom. 11:26).

"The Spirit of the Lord is upon *me*" (Luke 4:18).

"*He* shall rule them with a rod of iron" (Rev. 2:17; cf. 12:5).

The word "rod" occurs in one other Old Testament passage ("a rod of pride," Prov. 14:3) and there it carries the idea of "a twig, a shoot such as starts up from the roots of a cut-down tree." Isaiah gives us a clear prophecy of God taking a man with no standing – a mere "stump" of a tree cut down – and engrafting new life into it. Jesse was an unknown person; he was not even the head of a royal family, but God made him the father of a king, thereby placing him in the royal, messianic line. The prophecy of the women when Obed, the father of Jesse and grandfather of David, was born has been abundantly fulfilled in Jesus, descended from Jesse: "Blessed be the Lord, which hath not left thee this day without a kinsman, that his name may be famous in Israel" (Ruth 4:14).

Divine choice is again manifest in the selection of *David* to be the ancestor of Jesus, David's greater Son. Of Jesse's eight sons, David, the youngest, seemed the most unlikely to be selected. But God's choice is always *choice*, and in David he had a man after His own heart. When we come to Matthew's genealogy of Christ, the name *David* occurs five times. In fact, his name dominates the New Testament, appearing fifty-eight times in all. Our Lord's frequent mention of Israel's illustrious king reveals the profound regard He had for him and for the *Psalms* he wrote.

The story of the Old Testament is a prophetic one, unfolding God's dealings with a chosen nation through which He would ultimately bless all the nations on the earth. As this fascinating story unfolds, one humble family is taken, and from it one member was selected to bless the world. From him One would come who would be the most glorious King of kings, One who would live forever and establish a Kingdom of endless duration. Of the numerous Davidic promises and prophecies we can cite only a few.

Forecast: "Thy throne shall be established for ever" (II Sam. 7:16).

"The Lord hath sworn in truth unto David; he will not turn from it; Of the fruit of thy body will I set upon thy throne" (Ps. 132:11).

"In that day will I raise up the tabernacle of David" (Amos 9:11).

"Of the increase of his government and peace there shall be no end, upon the throne of David" (Isa. 9:7).

"Thou Bethlehem [city of David] ... out of thee shall he come forth unto Me that is to be ruler in Israel. ... For now shall he be great unto the ends of the earth" (Micah 5:2, 4).

"I will raise unto David ... a King" (Jer. 23:5).

"In that day ... the house of David shall be as God" (Zech. 12:8; cf. 13:1).

Over a period of 500 years, the prophecy of an eternal King, to arise from David is repeated over and over – by David himself, especially in his *Psalms;* by his son Solomon; and by several of the prophets. With the aid of your Bible concordance, trace out all references to *David* in the Old Testament and then match them with the almost sixty complementary passages in the New.

Fulfillment: "Jesus Christ, the son of David" (Matt. 1:1).

"The Lord God shall give unto him the throne of his father David" (Luke 1:32).

"What think ye of Christ? whose son is he? *They* say unto him, The Son of David" (Matt. 22:42).

"Jesus Christ our Lord, which was made of the seed of David according to the flesh" (Rom. 1:3).

"Christ cometh of the seed of David, and out of the town of Bethlehem, where David was" (John 7:42).

"For unto you is born this day in the city of David a Saviour, which is Christ the Lord" (Luke 2:11).

"I am the root and the offspring of David" (Rev. 22:16).

"Whose kingdom is an everlasting kingdom" (Dan. 7:27).

"Of his kingdom there shall be no end" (Luke 1:33).

During our Lord's sojourn on earth, no one came forward to dispute the well-known fact that He was of the house and lineage of David, because His ancestry was in the public records that all had access to. When Jesus asked the Pharisees, "What think ye of Christ? whose son is he?" they replied, "The son of David" (Matt. 22:42). We might ask David himself, "What do you think of the Messiah?" for he had so much to say about Him. Did not Jesus expound from *the Psalms* the things concerning Himself? All students of the Word recognize the fact that Jesus is presented in all His messianic character in the Psalms of David, as we shall be indicating as we proceed with our meditation.

Who, from all of David's many sons, was the one through whom the Messiah should come? Solomon was God's choice – and David's, too! Messiah's right to the throne of David was to come through Solomon's regal line. So we read, "And of all my sons, (for the Lord hath given me many sons,) *he* hath chosen *Solomon my son* to sit upon the throne of the kingdom of the LORD over Israel" (I Chron. 28:5; cf. 29:24). Turning to the New Testament, we see that this prediction was fulfilled, for Jesus came of Solomon in the royal line of David (Matt. 1:6). Our Lord's references to Solomon should be noticed.

From early days, Solomon had a consuming passion for many branches of knowledge and became the literary prodigy of his time. His intellectual attainments were remarkable, making him the wonder of the age. As a scientist, he knew a great deal about botany and zoology. As a ruler, a business man with vast enterprises, a poet, a preacher, and moralist, Solomon compelled kings from the ends of the earth to see and hear him (I Kings 3:9-12; 4:9). Among those who came to see the glory of his palace and hear his wisdom was the Queen of Sheba. But Jesus, in all humility, yet with all authority, could say of Himself, "Behold, a greater than Solomon is here" (Mat. 12:42).

In spite of all the splendor and magnificence of Solomon's reign, Jesus, plucking a few lilies from the field, dared to say that "even Solomon in all his glory was not arrayed like one of these" (Matt. 7:29). The beauty of lilies is God-fashioned, pleasing to behold, and perennially renewed; whereas that of Solomon's glory was self-conceived, artificial, and transient.

F. *His Descent From Joseph*

When Christ came to earth, He had two Josephs to care for Him – one when He was born, the other when He died. The first Joseph was poor, the second rich. As Joseph, "a just man," has the last place among the males in the genealogical list of Matthew, consideration is necessary regarding his inclusion: "And Jacob begat Joseph the husband of Mary, of whom was born Jesus" (Matt. 1:16).

The change of expression in the list is important. All through it, the Old Testament characters are linked together by the word *begat* – a term implying natural generation. But *begat* no longer applies, for Jesus was not *begotten* of natural generation, as the rest were. He was born of Mary, not of Joseph and Mary. Jesus had a human mother, but not a human father, as our next section will more fully show.

Luke, in his genealogy, has the phrase "Jesus . . . being *(as was supposed)* the son of Joseph" (3:23). Matthew speaks of Joseph as "the son of Jacob," but Luke describes him as "the son of Heli." Of course, it was impossible for him to be the natural son of both. Luke, writing of Jesus as *the Son of man,* gives His genealogy on His mother's side through Heli who was Mary's father. Luke does not say that Heli *begat* Joseph who was the actual son of Jacob, but became *son* (in-law) to Heli on his marriage with Mary. Fausset has an enlightening comment on the seeming contradiction here:

> Mary must have been of the same tribe and family as Joseph, according to the law (Num. 36:8). Isaiah implied that Messiah was the seed of David by *natural* as well as legal descent (11:1). Probably Matthan of *Matthew* is the Matthat of *Luke,* and Jacob and Heli were brothers; and Jacob's son Joseph, and Heli's daughter Mary, first cousins. Joseph as *male* heir of his uncle Heli, who had only one child, Mary, would marry her according to the law. Thus the genealogy of the *inheritance* in Matthew's list and that of *natural descent* in Luke's list would be primarily Joseph's, then Mary's also.

Further, the word "supposed" indicates that Christ's sonship to Joseph was only a *reputed,* not a real one. Yet Jesus was God's extraordinary gift to Joseph through his proper wife Mary, and *the fruit of his marriage to her,* not as natural offspring of his body but *as supernatural fruit.*" Hence attention is drawn to Joseph as a "son of David" and "of the house and lineage of David" (Matt. 1:20; Luke 2:4; cf. Luke 1:32). Later on, Joseph and Mary are spoken of as the *parents* of Jesus.

Here, again, we see a fulfillment of the prophetic Scriptures. Portraying Christ, some 700 years before He was born, Isaiah could say, "Unto us a child is born, unto us a son is given" (9:6). At Bethlehem was born the holy Child Jesus, Mary's firstborn, but as a Son He was given by God, whom Jesus claimed as His Father. He was born of a woman, but not of a woman and a man as in natural generation. As the *Child* born, we have a revelation of His humanity; as the *Son* given, His deity.

Chapter Four

PROPHECIES OF HIS BIRTH

As to the Seed Resulting in Birth	As to the Forerunner of Birth	As to the Reception of Birth
As to the Virgin Birth	As to Names Given at Birth	As to the Purpose of Birth
As to the Time of Birth		
As to the Place of Birth		

As the Power of the Highest overshadowed Mary, since the "Holy Thing" to be born of her was to be Son of God, we dare not enter the meditation before us without seeking the same divine overshadowing in order to understand the unique work of the Spirit within her. Without the aid of the Holy Spirit, who is the Power of the Highest, and who as such made the womb of Mary His workshop, we cannot understand the truth of the incarnation of Christ, of which Paul wrote, "Great is the mystery of godliness – God manifest in flesh."

> Seek not the cause, for 'tis not in thy reach,
> Of all the truths prophetic volumes teach,
> Those *secret things* imparted from on high,
> Which speak at once, and veil the Deity.
> Pass on, nor rush to explore the depths that lie
> Divinely hid in sacred mystery.

A striking wonder in connection with the prophecies concerning Christ is their minuteness of description and their precision of performance. They reveal that God is never before His time – nor after! "Ye shall not see me, *until the time come . . .*" (Luke 13:35). An outstanding fact isolating Christ from all others is that He is the one Man in the history of the world of whom explicit details of His birth, life, death, and resurrection were given centuries beforehand. The challenge of this pure miracle is that it has happened to one Man only in the entire history of the world. He is the only Person whose life and ministry were prewritten in the most remarkable manner before He came into the world. As Canon Dyson Hague puts it:

> Who could draw a picture of a man not yet born? Surely God, and God alone. Nobody knew over 500 years ago that Shakespeare was going to be born; or over 250 years ago that Napoleon was to be born. Yet here in the Bible we have the most striking and unmistakable likeness of a Man portrayed, not by one, but by twenty or twenty-five artists, none of whom had ever seen the Man they were painting.

The astounding miracle of these predictions of Christ proves that "the inspiration of that portrait came from the Heavenly Gallery, and not from the studio of an earthly artist. Nothing but Divine prescience could have foreseen it, and nothing but Divine power could accomplish it." Peter confirms such a sentiment, for he wrote, "For the prophecy came not in old time by the will of man: but holy men of God spake as they were moved by the Holy Ghost" (II Pet. 1:21).

It is our endeavor to show that "the Christ of the New Testament is the fruit of the Tree of Prophecy, and Christianity is the realization of a plan, the first outlines of which were sketched more than 1500 years before," as David Baron expresses it in *Rays of Messiah's Glory*.

It is the fulfillment of specific, detailed prophecies that provides the Bible with its divine seal – a seal that can never be counterfeited, since it is affixed to the truth which it attests, namely, that God's foreknowledge of the actions of free and intelligent agents is one of the most "incomprehensible attributes of Deity and is exclusively a Divine perfection." We readily concede that the prophets themselves may not have understood the full import of the predictions they gave when they pictured beforehand the expected Messiah, yet the language they used could not refer to anyone else in history. It was thus that Paul was able to persuade the Jews that Jesus was the predicted One "out of the prophets" (Acts 28:23).

The drama of fulfilled prophecy is most evident in connection with the birth of Jesus, the details of which were exactly accomplished when He was born of Mary. Men must be blind if they cannot see that the identification between the One predicted and the One presented is most positive and complete. "Then said the Lord unto me, ... I watch over my word to perform it" (Jer. 1:12, R.V.). Thus, having spoken, and guarding all, He inspired the prophets to set forth the truth carefully and accurately, for nothing short of *absolute accuracy* will suffice in the fulfillment of all He spoke concerning the Son He promised to send into the world.

A. *As to the Seed Resulting in Birth*

The only key to all messianic prophecy is found hanging at the front door of the Bible, and, strange though it may be, this key was given by God to that "old serpent, the devil." He was the first to learn of a Deliverer who would come to destroy his devilish works. To him was given the initial promise and prophecy of redemption from the sin he had brought into God's fair universe.

> And the Lord God said unto the serpent, ... I will put enmity between thee and the woman, and between thy seed and her seed; it shall bruise thy head, and thou shalt bruise his heel (Gen. 3:15).

From this point on, the chain of promises and prophecies concerning "the seed of the woman" lengthens until it ends in the birth of Jesus, who was not only "the seed of the woman," but "the seed of Abraham," and "the seed of David."

Forecast: "The woman ... and her seed" (Gen. 3:15).

Fulfillment: "Mary was found with child of the Holy Ghost" (Matt. 1:18).

"... to thy seed, which is Christ" (Gal. 3:16).

"Till the seed should come to whom the promise was made" (Gal. 3:19).

Forecast: "And the Lord appeared unto Abram, and said, Unto thy seed will I give this land" (Gen. 12:7).

Fulfillment: "Now to Abraham and his seed were the promises made" (Gal. 3:16).

Forecast: "Now therefore so shalt thou say unto my servant David, ... I will set up thy seed after thee, which shall proceed out of thy bowels" (II Sam. 7:8, 12).

Fulfillment: "The gospel of God ... concerning his Son Jesus Christ our Lord, which was made of the seed of David according to the flesh" (Rom. 1:1, 3).

With the first direct messianic prophecy in the Bible there commenced "the highway of the Seed." What God said about "the Seed of woman" constitutes "the Bible in embryo, the sum of all history and prophecy in a germ," for here is intimated, not only the Virgin Birth of Christ, but also His vicarious sufferings – "Thou shalt bruise His heel"; and His complete and eventual dominion over Satan and his works – "It (Christ) shall bruise thy head" (see Heb. 2:9-15).

Attention must be drawn, however, to the fact that divine prophecy began when God said to Adam and Eve in the garden: "In the day that thou eatest thereof thou shalt surely die" (Gen. 2:17; cf. 3:3, 4). It was then that the prophecy test began. Adam, made in the image of God, and in his original sinlessness and communion with God in the perfect environment of Eden enjoying to the uttermost every blessing and liberty, was also given the divine prophecy of warning not to eat of a certain tree. But Adam and Eve failed to meet the prophecy test and partook of the forbidden fruit, bringing ruin and death to all mankind through their rejection of the prophetic warning. Then came the precious prophecy of redemption through the seed of the woman who had sinned first. The first prophecy was a warning of *death,* but the second prophecy was a promise of *life.*

Thus there started the gulf stream of Bible prophecy, continuing ever wider, fuller, and deeper throughout the thirty-nine sacred books of the Old Testament, until Jesus came, "born of a woman." But a fascinating line of study, sometimes forgotten, is the ever-increasing determination of Satan to destroy the prophesied Seed. Although we can touch only briefly on such antagonism, the reader will find this subject fully dealt with in the author's small work on *Satanic Conflict of the Ages,* in which he outlines the many devices and arts which Satan employed to destroy the Royal Seed, Christ, who was Satan's great Antagonist and glorious Conqueror.

There were times when Satan almost succeeded in destroying the "Seed," through the exceeding sinfulness of men, causing God to send, for instance, the Flood; in the intended massacre of the entire Jewish nation at the instigation of Haman, the Jews' enemy; and at the massacre of the innocent babies when Herod thought the child Jesus would be among them. If the devil, through his diabolical deeds, had caused the Old Testament to close with the word "curse," nevertheless, he had nothing to crow about. "He who laughs last, laughs longest," and God always has the last laugh, for He kept the messianic line unbroken until the Messiah came to bear the curse and overcome the devil by His Cross.

It is in this light that we can understand the purpose of the genealogies of Jesus who came as "the Seed of the woman." Do they not remind us of the failure of Satan to destroy the direct messianic line stretching from Adam to Christ? These seemingly dry records of names are a testimony to the fact that all the evil methods of the enemy to annihilate the House of Judah had miserably failed. What a ring of triumph there is about the announcement: ". . . Mary, of whom was born Jesus, who is called Christ!"

B. *As to the Virgin Birth*

The phrase we have just considered, "her seed," is not found elsewhere in the Bible. Well over one hundred times we read of "the seed" and "seeds," but in all cases *the seed of the man* is meant. But *the seed of the woman* is a unique concept and can be interpreted only as a foreshadowing of the virgin birth of our Lord. If He was not to be born of a virgin, then Adam would have been referred to: "his seed," not "her seed." When the Prince of Glory came, the prince of this world could find nothing in the One who sprang from "her seed." The reason? "Mary . . . was discovered to be pregnant – by the Holy Spirit" (Matt. 1:18, *Phillips*).

It is with hesitation that one approaches the solemn, holy mystery of our Lord's entrance into our world as a human Babe. The theme is so vast and delicate, so profound and incomprehensible, that one trembles lest a single word should be expressed that misinterprets to the least degree any aspect of such a wonderful revelation. Bishop Handley Moule asserts that "in Scripture a mystery may be a fact which, when revealed, we cannot understand in detail, though we can know it, and act upon it. . . . It is a thing to be known only when revealed." With reference to the Virgin Birth, it is certainly true that "we cannot understand it in detail, though we can know it, and act upon it."

In the presence of such a holy miracle, "there can be no fitting attitude of the human intellect save that of acceptance of the truth, without any attempt to explain the absolute mystery." With this "mystery of godliness" in mind, we should give heed to this dictum:

I will seek to believe rather than to reason;

to adore rather than to explain;

to give thanks rather than to penetrate;

to love rather than to know;

to humble myself rather than to speak.

Forecast: "Behold, a virgin shall conceive, and bear a son, and shall call his name *Immanuel*" (Isa. 7:14).

"For unto us a child is born, unto us a son is given" (Isa. 9:6).

Fulfillment: "And behold, thou shalt conceive in thy womb, and bring forth a son. . . . Then said Mary unto the angel, How shall this be, seeing I know not a man? And the angel answered and said unto her, The Holy Ghost shall come upon thee" (Luke 1:31, 34, 35).

"When as his mother Mary was espoused to Joseph, before they came together, she was found with child of the Holy Ghost" (Matt. 1:18).

"Behold, a virgin shall be with child, and shall bring forth a son, and they shall call his name Emmanuel" (Matt. 1:23).

To fulfill the amazing prophecies of the birth of Christ, God performed a biological miracle, for the manner of His begetting was somthing unknown in human history and experience. Huxley declared that as a scientific man he could not reject Christianity on the ground of the virgin birth of Christ, as there were millions of such births in the lower forms of life. Reason may declare that among humans what happened to Mary is impossible; however, Mary also had to learn that, "with God nothing shall be impossible." Responding by faith to the divine revelation, the virgin said, "Be it unto me, according to Thy word."

Is it not somewhat remarkable that whenever the birth of the Messiah is spoken of in prophecy, reference is made to His mother, or to the womb, never to a human father, which, of course, Jesus did not have.

"The Lord hath called me from the womb" (Isa. 49:1).

"The Lord . . . formed me from the womb to be his servant" (Isa. 49:5).

"The Lord hath created a new thing in the earth, A woman shall compass a man" (Jer. 31:22).

"Thou art he that took me out of the womb" (Ps. 22:9).

". . . until the time that she who travaileth hath brought forth" (Micah 5:3).

Although we speak about the supernatural or miraculous birth of Christ, we must understand that there was nothing unique or exceptional about the process of His birth, which came about in a completely natural way. The miraculous element was not in the formation of our Lord's body or in its appearance in the manger, but in the manner of its begetting or conception. His birth was supernatural in that He was virgin-born, that is, He was conceived apart from natural generation by the method of intercourse. This is what Mary herself meant when she said, "I *know not* a man." She bore the prophesied One as the result of a divine creative act, and was *virgo intacto*. Thereafter, Mary lived in the usual relations of wedlock with her husband, Joseph, bearing children in a natural way (see Matt. 13:55, 56).

What exactly is a *virgin* – a term having a two-fold application when used of a woman? The Hebrew word *almah* denotes any young unmarried woman, whether she has kept her virginity or not. In these days of loose morality, permissiveness, premarital sexual experiences, and even school girls being taught contraceptive methods, fewer young women are virgins. But when the Septuagint translators came to the Hebrew word that Isaiah used, they gave us the word *parthenos* for *almah* because it conveyed the significance implied, which is the word the angel used in his instruction to Joseph. Concerning *parthenos,* Cruden says that it represents "a young unmarried woman who had preserved the purity of her body." Mary was a *virgin* in this sense.

Approach, Thou gentle Little One,
  Of stainless Mother born to earth,
Free from all wedded union
  The Mediator's two-fold birth.
What joys to the vast universe
  In that chaste Maiden's womb are
    borne;
Ages set free from sorrow's curse
  Spring forth, and everlasting morn.

All who are born after the ordinary course of nature have the root of sin within them. Had our Lord been born according to the laws of natural procreation, having a human father as well as a human mother, then He would have had to cry, "Behold, I was shapen in iniquity, and in sin did my mother conceive me" (Ps. 51:5), but He was born "holy, harmless, undefiled, separate from sinners" (Heb. 7:26). Because He was conceived of the Holy Spirit, His substance was pure and immaculate, and without original sin. To save sinners, it was imperative for Him to be sinless; hence, the necessity of a *virgin* birth. So He came, "Offspring of a virgin's womb." The miracle of His birth is seen in that in spite of the sinful pedigree His genealogies prove, He yet entered the world a perfectly sinless Person. "That holy thing which shall be born . . . shall be called the Son of God (Luke 1:35). Professor James Orr affirms:

> Doctrinally it must be repeated that the belief in the Virgin Birth of Christ is of the highest value for the right apprehension of Christ's unique and sinless personality. Here is One, as Paul brings out in Romans 5:12-17 who, free from sin Himself, and not involved in the Adamic liabilities of the race, reverses the curse of sin and death brought in by the first Adam, and establishes the reign of righteousness and life. Had Christ been naturally born, not one of these things could be affirmed of Him. As one of Adam's race, not an entrant from a higher sphere, He would have shared in Adam's corruption and doom — would Himself have required to be redeemed. Through God's infinite mercy, He came from above, inherited no guilt, needed no regeneration or sanctification, but became Himself the Redeemer, Regenerator, Sanctifier, for all who receive Him.

C. *As to the Time of Birth*

All the prophecies relating to Christ were accurate, and their performance exact. Forecast and fulfillment are in perfect agreement. All specifications as to His ancestry and the manner and time of His birth came to pass as predicted. What Jesus said as He entered His public ministry, can be equally applied to the hour of His birth. "The *time* is fulfilled and the kingdom of God is at hand" (Mark 1:15). Paul reminds us that "when the fulness of the *time* was come, God sent forth his Son, made of a woman" (Gal. 4:4) – not a day before the *time,* not a day after, but precisely in the hour striking on God's prophetic clock.

Forecast: "The sceptre shall not depart from Judah ... *until* Shiloh come" (Gen. 49:10).

"I shall see him, but not *now*" (Num. 24:17).

"Know therefore and understand, that from the going forth of the commandment to restore and to build Jerusalem *unto* the Messiah the Prince shall be seven weeks, and threescore and two weeks.... *After threescore and two weeks* shall Messiah be cut off, but not for himself" (Dan. 9:25, 26).

"The Lord ... shall suddenly come to his temple" (Mal. 3:1).

Fulfillment: "And it came to pass in *those days* ... she brought forth her firstborn son" (Luke 2:1, 7).

"For unto you is born *this day* in the city of David a Saviour, which is Christ the Lord" (Luke 2:11).

"When the fulness of the time *was come*" (Gal. 4:4).

How unwilling man is to see the Mind of the Infinite planning the details of Christ's birth, and His hand as the Almighty executing all prophesied specifications. As the time of His birth drew near, Mary was actually living at the wrong place if her Son, the Messiah, was to be born in Bethlehem of Judea. But see how the intricacies of God's overruling Providence fulfills His prophetic Word. Sir William Ramsay – the noted British chemist and archaeologist, as well as Bible scholar – in 1923 discovered at Ankara, Turkey, a Roman temple inscription which stated that in the reign of Caesar Augustus there were three great tax collections. The second was ordered *four years* before the birth of Christ; the third, several years after His birth.

The second special tax was the one the proud Jews resented; so they sent a commission to Rome to protest about it. Quirinius, the local governor of Syria, did not have the authority to settle the problem. Further, those were days of slow communications and slower travel, and as the commission finally failed, the Jews had to submit to the enrollment and taxing. By the time the official tax collectors had worked their way eastward, town by town, and after the time-consuming delays caused by the Jewish protests, exactly enough delay was caused, and all in the natural course of events, so that when the enrollment was put in force in Judea the exact time had come for Mary to give birth to her Child (Luke 2:1-3).

Dr. F. J. Meldau put it this way in his booklet on *Messiah in Both Testaments,* to which I am greatly indebted:

> Neither Mary nor Caesar nor the Roman tax collectors did the *timing,* nor were they in charge of affairs; but the God who rules the world behind the scenes had His hand on the wheel, and He literally "moved the peoples of the world" and timed everything to the very day, so that Mary and Joseph got to Bethlehem in *the nick of time,* that Jesus, the chosen Messiah, might be born in the right place, the place designated by the infallible finger of prophecy.

Further, as to the time of His coming, Christ had to appear while the Temple was yet standing, as Malachi prophesied: "The Lord shall suddenly *come to His Temple*" – which Temple was destroyed in A.D. 70, when Titus ransacked the city of Jerusalem.

Forecast: "The desire of all nations shall come: and I will *fill this house* with glory, saith the Lord of hosts" (Haggai 2:7).

"And I took the thirty pieces of silver, and cast them to the potter in *the house of the Lord*" (Zech. 11:13).

"We have blessed you out of *the house of the Lord*" (Ps. 118:26).

Fulfillment: "And the blind and the lame came to him in the temple; and he healed them" (Matt. 21:14).

"... and the children crying in the temple, ... Hosanna" (Matt. 21:16).

"And Jesus went into the temple of God" (Matt. 21:12).

"They found [Jesus] in the temple, sitting in the midst of the doctors" (Luke 2:46, 47).

The Messiah had to come 483 years after a specific date given in Daniel's time – a prophecy given by the prophet almost 500 years before Jesus came to the Temple. Thus the public entry into the Temple in Jerusalem was pre-arranged and predicted by God, and perfectly fulfilled when Jesus of Nazareth went into the Temple, the destruction of which He Himself predicted (Matt. 24:1-3). Step by step, His movements matched the blueprint of prophecy. Daniel, in his timetable of the Messiah, prophesied that He would be *cut off*, or killed, before the destruction of the Temple. Christ was crucified some thirty-five years before it was demolished.

D. *As to the Place of Birth*

Another instance of the perfect planning of God is seen in the way the place of our Lord's Birth, as well as its time, are pinpointed in prophecy. How precise He is in His arrangements! He never leaves anything to chance. We appear to have an involved series of predictions as to the place of Christ's appearance at Birth – Bethlehem, Egypt, Nazareth.

Forecast: "Nevertheless the dimness shall not be such as was in her vexation, when ... [he] afterward did more grievously afflict her by the way of the sea, beyond Jordan, in Galilee of the nations. The people that walked in darkness have seen a great light: they that dwell in the land of the shadow of death, upon them hath the light shined" (Isa. 9:1, 2).

"And there shall come forth a rod out of the stem of Jesse, and a Branch shall grow out of his roots" (Isa. 11:1).

"I ... called my son out of Egypt" (Hos. 11:1).

"But thou Bethlehem ... out of thee shall he come forth" (Mic. 5:2).

Fulfillment: "He shall be called a Nazarene" (Matt. 2:23). When Isaiah spoke of Jesus as *the Branch*, he used the word *neh-tzer*, meaning "the separated One," or "the Nazarene."

"When [Joseph] arose, he took the young child and his mother by night, and departed into Egypt.... Out of Egypt have I called my son" (Matt. 2:14, 15).

"Jesus was born in Bethlehem" (Matt. 2:1; cf. 2:5, 6; John 7:42).

"And he came and dwelt in a city called Nazareth: that it might be fulfilled which was spoken by the prophets, He shall be called a Nazarene" (Matt. 2:23).

"He turned aside into the parts of Galilee" (Matt. 2:2).

We must not be confused by all these places and deem them contradictory, for all were touched by Him in the course of His divinely planned life. As Micah prophesied, Jesus was born in Bethlehem, but soon after was taken into Egypt by Joseph and Mary, to escape the foul plot of Herod to destroy Him. After the wicked king's death, Joseph and Mary along with the holy Child, returned to Palestine, where Jesus was reared and spent the best part of His life. This is why He was known as "Jesus of Nazareth" and was called a *Nazarene*. His ministry was exercised in and around Galilee. Although He never went beyond these small provinces of Palestine, yet His name is spread abroad throughout the whole earth.

E. *As to the Forerunner of His Birth*

Jesus said of John the Baptist, that he was more than a prophet – that among those born of women no one greater than John had arisen (Matt. 11:9, 11). Shunning the habitation of men, he lived in the solitude of the desert, knowing from his childhood that the Event of the Ages was about to take place and that he had been prophesied and born to herald its arrival. He knew he was to be the Elijah of prophecy; in habits and dress he was Elijahlike; and, Elijahlike, he heralded the coming of the predicted Messiah, the latchet of whose shoes he was not worthy to unloose.

Forecast: "The voice of him that crieth in the wilderness; Prepare ye the way of the Lord" (Isa. 40:3).

"I will send my messenger, and he shall prepare the way before me" (Mal. 3:1).

"Behold, I will send you Elijah the prophet" (Mal. 4:5).

Fulfillment: "In those days came John the Baptist, preaching in the wilderness of Judaea . . . this is he that was spoken of by the prophet Esaias, saying, The voice of one crying in the wilderness, Prepare ye the way of the Lord . . ." (Matt. 3:1, 3; cf. Luke 3:3-6).

"I am the voice of one crying in the wilderness" (John 1:23).

"This is he, of whom it is written, Behold, I send my messenger before thy face" (Luke 7:27; cf. Mark 1:2-4).

This predicted forerunner of Jesus was six months older than his illustrious cousin, and earned the title of being "the prophet of the Highest," because of his special honor of being the subject of prophecy ages before the birth of Christ. God's interposition in the wonder of his birth caused all the people to muse in their hearts whether he were the promised Messiah (Luke 3:15). John's life and ministry greatly impressed Herod, but his faithfulness in rebuking the king for his sin cost the baptist his life. Elijah, after whom John was fashioned, escaped death, being translated to heaven in a chariot of fire; but John was murdered. Thus the forerunner was like his Lord at the end.

F. *As to Names Given at Birth*

Prospective and expectant parents have to wait for their baby to arrive and its sex to be known before they can actually name it. In view of the blissful event of a birth, a list of both male and female names is made, and from it a choice is subsequently made. But Jesus was given several names *before* birth. A frequent authoritative declaration used of Him is "He shall be called." A name is often a synonym for the nature of any object, or of any being. Names, and their meaning, is a most profitable study. This is why the prophesied names of the Saviour demand our attention. But, although we may be able to explain the significance of the Names given to Mary's Holy Child in the two birth-narratives, it is impossible for the human mind to unfold the overwhelming mystery of the Incarnation itself. Truly, His names are like the ointment the priests of old used – compounded of several spices! His names are like such ointment poured forth.

1. *Called Jesus.* This was the personal name of Him who was born of a virgin, and is the one used of Him more often than any other in the New Testament. It is mentioned in both the first and the last verses of this section of the Bible (Matt. 1:1; Rev. 22:21). The last verse contains a triad of His outstanding designations. *Jesus* is the Greek form of Joshua, Jeshua, or Jehoshua – all of which mean "Salvation of Jehovah."

Forecast: "Which also our fathers that came after brought in with Jesus" (margin: Joshua) (Acts 7:45).

"For if Jesus (margin: Joshua) had given them rest" (Heb. 4:8).
Fulfillment: "Thou shalt call his name *JESUS*" (Matt. 1:21).

"[Joseph] called his name *JESUS*" (Matt. 1:25).
Jesus means, "Jehovah Salvation." Salvation is not some*thing*, but Some*one*. "He *Himself (autos,* not merely like Joshua, He is God's *instrument* to save) *saves* His people from their sins. He was born a *Saviour* (Luke 2: 11). In his profitable study *YESHUA IN THE TENACH* (the name *Jesus* in the Old Testament), Arthur E. Glass draws attention to the fact that the name Jesus is actually hidden in the Old Testament, being found about one hundred times from Genesis to Habakkuk. The author affirms that

> Every time the Old Testament uses the word SALVATION (especially with the Hebrew suffix meaning "my," "thy," or "his," with very few exceptions (when the word is used in an impersonal sense) it is identically the same word as YESHUA (Jesus). This is actually what the angel said to Joseph — Thou shalt call His name YESHUA (salvation).

Author Glass then goes on to show how this works out in some of the Old Testament passages. What David actually said was, "I will rejoice in thy YESHUA" (Jesus) (Ps. 9:14). That *Jesus* was the fulfillment, embodiment, and personification of the oft-repeated term "*salvation*" is borne out in the great passage from the prophet Isaiah: "Behold, God is my YESHUA [a reference to Jesus in His preincarnate, eternal existence (John 1:1)]; I will trust, and not be afraid; for JAH-JEHOVAH is my strength and my song; he also is become my YESHUA [Jesus, the Word made flesh (John 1:14)]. Therefore with joy shall ye draw water out of the wells of YESHUA" [Jesus crucified, waters of salvation flowing from Calvary (John 7:37-39)] (Isa. 12:2, 3).

No other name has endeared the Saviour to our hearts, or has been enshrined in so many Christ-honoring hymns as JESUS. It will ever remain "sweet . . . in a believer's ear. It soothes his sorrows . . . and drives away his fears."

> Many names are dear, but His is dearer;
> How it grows more as life goes on!
> Many friends are near, but He is nearer,
> Always what we want, and all our own.

2. *Called Christ.* The name Christ is the Greek equivalent of *Messiah,* meaning "anointed." Prophets, priests, and kings of old were anointed, being prophetic types of Him who, as the *Christ,* combines all three offices in Himself. It was the Messiah (or Christ) who was eagerly anticipated by all godly Jews. "He that should come" (Matt. 11:3). *Christ* was the official title of the Saviour. Throughout the New Testament there is the undesigned confirmation that "Jesus is *the* Christ" (the article being almost always used in the Greek); Matt. 16:16; John 6:69. See John's solemn pronouncements in I John 4:3 and 5:1.
Forecast: "Thy God hath anointed thee with the oil of gladness above Thy fellows" (Ps. 45:7).

"... against his anointed" (Ps. 2:2).
Fulfillment: "Unto you is born this day . . . Christ (Messiah, the Anointed) the Lord" (Luke 2:11).

"The Spirit of God descending . . . upon Him" (Matt. 3:16).

He put the seal to the claim of Messiahship when He said, "Ought not *Christ* to have suffered these things?" Peter recognized in Him the manifestation of the prophesied Anointed One, "Messiah the Prince" (Dan. 9:25), when he confessed, "Thou art *the* Christ, the Son of the living God" (Matt. 16:16) — the One who came as the divinely appointed Fulfiller of prophecy. When His Messiahship became generally accepted,

"Christ" was used as His personal designation and as the evidence of His consecration and qualification for His mission among men. He was "the Christ of God" (Luke 9:20), that is, the Anointed of the Father to do His will. Further, it is the name associated with the believer who is a "Christian" – an anointed follower of the Anointed One. Then the term "in Christ," which Paul uses over seventy times in his epistles, expresses our living union with Christ – a union He emphasized under the figure of the vine and the branches (John 15:1-10). How apt are the lines of F. W. H. Myers (1843-1901) in his *Saint Paul:*

> Yea, thro' life, death, thro' sorrow and thro' sinning,
> He shall suffice me, for He hath sufficed:
> Christ is the end, for Christ is the beginning,
> Christ is the beginning for the end is Christ.

3. *Called Lord.* This title, denoting authority, dominion, deity, is equivalent to Jehovah of the Old Testament as already indicated. Next to Jesus, occurring more than 542 times, the title next most frequently used of Him is Lord, appearing 174 times. It is employed by Himself five times in John's Gospel, and by others of Him forty-three times. Although there is a variety of Hebrew and Greek terms under this name, which is one applied to both God and men and expresses varied degrees of honor, dignity, and majesty, the prevailing Greek term *kurios,* usually rendered "Lord," "master" or "owner," one who possesses power or authority over property or persons; it is a term of respect. *The Lord's* is a possessive and means "belonging to Christ," whether identified with His people, His day, His supper, His money.

Forecast: ". . . the Lord hath said unto me, thou art My Son . . ." (Ps. 2:7).

"The Lord said unto my Lord . . ." (Ps. 110:1).

Fulfillment: "For unto you is born this day . . . Christ the Lord" (Luke 2:11).

"Ye call me Master and Lord . . . so I am" (John 13:13).

". . . your Lord and Master . . . do as I have done to you" (John 13:14, 15).

"Sanctify the Lord God in your hearts" (I Pet. 3:15).

It is sadly possible to know Jesus as a Saviour, yet not honor and obey Him as the *Lord* of all we are and have. As Hudson Taylor used to put it, "If He is not Lord of all, He is not Lord at all." How blessed we are when we fully recognize Him as our "*Lord* Jesus Christ." God hath made Jesus "both Lord and Christ" (Acts 2:36). Have we acknowledged Him as Lord? Is He the "Lord of our life" as well as "God of our salvation"?

> Lord of all being, throned afar,
> Thy glory flames from sun and star.
> Center and soul of every sphere:
> Yet to each loving heart how near.
>
> Lord of all life, below, above,
> Whose light is truth, whose warmth is love.
> Before Thy ever-blazing throne
> We ask no luster of our own.

4. *Called Emmanuel* (Immanuel). When Isaiah used the exclamation *Behold* in connection with this divine name, he wanted to arrest attention to an extraordinary prophecy. *Emmanuel* was not a mere appellation like the common name "Jesus." It was not a name men were to use in an ordinary way of the prophesied One, but a name revealing His character and His contact with man.

Forecast: "Behold a virgin shall conceive, and bear a son, and shall call his name Immanuel" (Isa. 7:14).

"The stretching out of his wings shall fill the breadth of thy land, O Immanuel" (Isa. 8:8).

Fulfillment: "Now all this was done that it might be fulfilled which was spoken of the Lord, by the prophet, saying, Behold a virgin shall be with child, and shall bring forth a son, and they shall call his name Emmanuel, which being interpreted is, God with us" (Matt. 1:22, 23).

Two truths are suggested by this remarkable name: Christ's Deity and His fellowship with men. He became "*God* manifest in *flesh.*" In His last commission to His own, He said, "Lo, I am *with you* alway, even unto the end of the world" (Matt. 28:20). His full manifestation as *God with us* will be experienced in the coming glory when "the tabernacle of God is with men, and He will dwell with them, ... and *God Himself shall be with them,* and be their God" (Rev. 21:3). In the Old Testament, God had a Tabernacle for His people. Now He has a people as His Tabernacle, for the redeemed are "an habitation of God through the Spirit" (Eph. 2:22; cf. 2:21).

Scripture can be summarized in this threefold way:

> In the Old Testament it is — God *For* Us
> In the Four Gospels — God *With* Us
> In the Acts and Epistles — God *In* Us

"Christ *in* you, the hope of glory." Of course, He is *for* us, and *with* us, but now, by His Spirit, He is ever *in* us. He is our eternal Inhabitant – the Indweller Who will never leave us – the Comforter, abiding with us for ever (John 14:16).

Is this not a revelation of His character that we can cling to in the dark and difficult hours of life? Think of the marvel of it – The Mighty God with *us,* poor mortals of the dust! Why should we ever doubt or despair, or charge our souls with unnecessary care when we have such "a never failing treasury, filled with boundless stores of grace" at hand for instant possession? From an ancient Latin hymn we have the lines –

> O come, O come, Emmanuel,
> And ransom captive Israel.

5. *Called King.* When we reach the section dealing with *Prophetic Titles,* the subject of Christ's Kingship will be dealt with more specifically. At this point we only want to examine the arrestive phrase used by Matthew that Christ was *born King* of the Jews. Born King! Queen Elizabeth II of Great Britain was *born* a Princess, but only became Queen on the death of her father, King George. Her son Charles was *born* a Prince, and as heir to the throne, will not be King unless his royal mother dies or abdicates.

History records a very rare exception to this monarchical role of one in a royal family being *born* a King. When Alfonso XII, King of Spain died in 1885, he left behind a pregnant wife, Maria Christina, who, six months after her husband's death, gave birth to a posthumous son, Alfonso XIII, who was immediately proclaimed King under the Regency of his mother. But although born a King he had no pre-existence as "another King, one Jesus." Having lived before He was born, as the Sovereign Lord, He was *born King* because He came as "the King Eternal."

The prophets, in general, and the psalms in particular, have much to say about the coming Messiah as God's anointed King to establish a Kingdom in righteousness.

Forecast: "Yet have I set my king upon my holy hill of Zion" (Ps. 2:6).

"I will raise unto David ... a King (who) shall reign and prosper" (Jer. 23:5).

"(The Lord) shall give strength unto his king, and exalt the horn of his anointed" (I Sam. 2:10).

Fulfillment: "Where is He that is born King of the Jews?" (Matt. 2:2).

"Saying that he himself is Christ a King" (Luke 23:2).

"Behold, thy King cometh" (John 12:15).

That Christ was a truer king than Herod who sought the young Child's life is evident from the expressions used in the Birth narrative. When Herod is mentioned, it is with a small 'k' (king), but for Christ it is a capital 'K' (King), which is only proper, as He is *King* of kings. Born king! Yet a strange insignia of royalty awaited Him, for His palace was a stable, His throne a mother's knee, His courtiers the lowly shepherds, His robe the swaddling clothes. Truly He was a king in disguise. May we be found among the number who recognize and revere Him as the king of saints who yield unto Him the undivided sway of our lives He demands and deserves!

The valiant Knights of King Arthur said of their Sovereign, "We never saw his like, there lives no greater leader." But the glory of King Arthur pales into insignificance alongside the richer glory of Christ our King. It is thus we sing, "Hail Jesus, King of my days and nights!" One of the marvels of Grace is that He has made us to be kings. The question is, Do we reign in life by the power of the King of Love? We shall have more to say in another connection about His prophesied millennial reign as prince of the kings of earth.

> My Christ, He is the Lord of lords,
> He is the King of kings;
> He is the Sun of Righteousness,
> With healing in His wings.

6. *Called Governor.* While all the names we are considering are more or less associated with the Jews of which Christ is King, they yet carry with them a larger application. For instance, as *Governor,* Jesus has power to rule His people Israel, but of the increase of His government over Jew and Gentile there is to be no end. A large variety of Hebrew and Greek words are used to express the significance of the English term *Governor.* Generally, it represents one holding a most responsible official, governmental position. Thus Joseph is called "Governor" over Egypt. Several of the Roman procurators are referred to as "Governors." It is also employed, prophetically and actually, of Christ.

Forecast: "He is governor among the nations" (Ps. 22:28).

"Their governor shall proceed from the midst of them" (Jer. 30:21).

"He shall be as a governor in Judah" (Zech. 9:7).

"The government shall be upon his shoulder" (Isa. 9:6; cf. 22:21).

Fulfillment: "Out of thee shall come a Governor" (Matt. 2:6).

"All dominions shall serve and obey him" (Dan. 7:27 with Col. 1:16).

The word for *governor* can mean "one who goes first, leads the way, chief in war." Has not He Who came as *Governor* the right to lead the way, seeing He triumphed gloriously in His war against sin and Satan? Some governors who rise from the ranks often become officious and unsympathetic. But our Heavenly Governor is no hard despot. He rules by love, and sways our souls, not by a sword, but by His scars. His sufferings brought Him sovereignty. Triumph is His because of the Tree. Have we learnt that if we too would govern in life we must go to a *Tree;* that the death of self leads to a diadem, that we rise as we "lay in dust life's glory dead"?

Isaiah would have us remember that of the increase of His Government in the World there is to be no end. Universal dominion is to be His when He reigns from shore to shore. "The government shall be upon His shoulder." Can we say that His Government is increasing personally and spiritually? Does He have more of us today than He had yesterday? Is path as a shining light, shining m[illegible] and more unto the perfect day? Is His love breaking down all barriers and crossing all frontiers in the narrow realm of our life? We can be sure of this fact, that Satan will contest every inch of ground we yield to Jesus who was born to govern.

Direct, control, suggest this day,
All I design, or do, or say;
That all my powers, with all their
might,
In Thy sole glory may unite.

7. *Called Son.* This most frequent designation of the Second Person of the Blessed Trinity, speaking of a specific relationship, covers several aspects of His Sonship. Matthew, in his Genealogy of Jesus uses the term *Son* to express different affiliations. When we come to deal, particularly, with our Lord's dual nature, full attention will be given to the titles *Son of God* and *Son of Man.* At this point, we simply outline the various ways *Son* is dealt with by Matthew and Luke.

a. *Son of Abraham*

"In thee shall all families of the earth be blessed" (Gen. 12:3; 22:18).

"The son of Abraham" (Matt. 1:1).

"The blessing of Abraham might come on the Gentiles through Jesus Christ" (Gal. 3:14).

In His wondrous Birth, Jesus laid hold of the seed of Abraham, and as his Son, covenant relationship with Israel is implied.

b. *Son of David*

"I have made a covenant with . . . David. . . . Thy seed will I establish for ever" (Ps. 89:3).

"Jesus Christ, the son of David" (Matt. 1:1).

"Concerning his Son Jesus Christ our Lord, which was made of the seed of David according to the flesh" (Rom. 1:3).

Kingship and royalty are prominent here. Jesus was of the Davidic line and was born in the City of David. Coming of the lineage of David, He was successor of David and heir of all the promises granted to him (Luke 1:32; 2:4).

c. *Her firstborn son*

"Unto us a child is born" (Isa. 9:6).

"She brought forth her firstborn Son" (Matt. 1:25).

Nine times over Jesus is referred to as "The young child." As Mary's child, He possessed true humanity, and He never forgot such a relationship. When He came to die, He said to His mother, "Behold *thy* Son!" and then committed her to John's care with the request that he treat her as *his* mother. Keble reminds us that Jesus was

A Son that never did amiss,
That never sham'd His mother's kiss,
Nor cross'd her fondest prayer.

d. *Out of Egypt have I called my son*

"The Lord hath said unto me, Thou art my Son" (Ps. 2:7).

"Unto us a son is given" (Isa. 9:6, 7).

"Out of Egypt have I called my son" (Matt. 2:15).

My Son! When God gave up His only-begotten Son, He emptied heaven of the very best for the worst of earth. Here we have emphasized the divine, filial relationship, embracing, as it does, implicit obedience to the Father's will. Jesus is also called "The Son of the Highest" (Luke 1:32). The Holy Spirit responsible for the miracle of His birth is named "The power of the Highest" (Luke 1:35), while the Baptist who heralded Christ's coming as the Messiah is referred to as "The prophet of the Highest" (Luke 1:76).

A further miracle of Grace is that God has condescended to call those redeemed by the blood of Jesus His "sons." "Ye are sons" – "Now are we the sons of God" (Gal. 4:6; I John 3:1, 2). But has He brought us right out of Egypt, or are we prone to yearn after its fleshpots? As with the Divine Son, so with ourselves, sonship implies unquestioning obedience to the Father's will, and separation from the world.

8. *Called a Nazarene.* The appellation *Nazarene* is akin to *Nazarite,* al-

though there is a distinction between the two words. The Nazarite vow involved complete dedication to God, and forecasted Jesus, who fulfilled the *spirit* of such a vow, although He shunned the outward rules of such. (See Matt. 11:18.) Matthew tells us that Jesus "came and dwelt in a city called Nazareth: that it might be fulfilled which was spoken by the prophets, He shall be called a Nazarene" (Matt. 2:23). Nathaniel, quoting a popular opinion, asked the question, "Can there any good thing come out of Nazareth?" (John 1:46).

Who were the prophets who predicted that Jesus would be a *Nazarene?* "Called" is a word expressing what He should be in His earthly manifestation, but none of the prophets gave Him the literal name "Nazarene," though His contemporaries did. "Nazarene" is derived from *Natzri,* meaning "pain." What the prophets foretold was that One would come Who would be a "pain sufferer." Thus, the general description of the Messiah is that of One abject and despised (Isa. 53:2, 3), so the nickname *Nazarene* agreed with His foretold character, namely, One Who was glorious in Himself but despised in man's eyes.

Further, the people of Nazareth at the time of Christ's birth had established a very poor reputation in morals and religion, hence, the proverb "Can any good thing come out of Nazareth?" When Jesus was crucified His crucifiers wrote above His Cross – Jesus of *Nazareth* – a man out of a place like that! As a true Nazarene, as well as a Nazarite, He stooped to the lowest depths of ignominy on our behalf. Willingly, He endured shame, hatred, contempt, and all that was despicable that He might seal our pardon with His blood. Nazareth might have been a place with a character, but Jesus lived an undefiled life in it, and was the world's "Good Thing" that came out of it.

Nazareth, O Nazareth!
Tho' a name of evil holding
There was brought "The Undefiled,"
Like a dove, a serpent folding
There grew up "The Holy Child."
Nazareth! Cross-like we see
Thy stained name from all stains free.

Surely we have here a type of grace, for is not Jesus the new cruse of salt sweetening every bitter spring in life. Many in Nazareth must have lost their stain of sin because of Christ's sojourn there. His virtues were dowries sufficient to enrich His environment, and His character was glory set in grace. Outside the camp, bearing His reproach, may we prove to be a blessing in the Nazareth we may find ourselves in.

Our God has sanctified all ages; He
Not for twelve years but those long
thirty-three
Dwelt in our world, the ever-
undefiled;
Loving, obedient, gentle, stainless,
mild,
Exemplar He alike to sire and boy.

9. *Called Wonderful, Counsellor, the Mighty God, the Everlasting Father, the Prince of Peace.* Although Isaiah gives us such a galaxy of names the Divine Child was to receive at His birth, he yet uses the singular – "His *name* shall be called" – as if the five he gives were but varied facets of the one name. Ellicott comments that we have four elements of the compound name:

Wonderful – Counsellor
God-the-Mighty-One
Father of Eternity
Prince of Peace

Taking the five titles as they appear in the King James' version, let us try to trace their combination of prediction and performance in the Word.

a. *Wonderful*

This first of the five gathered for us in one garland expresses a marvelous burst of eloquence on the part of Isaiah as, some 700 years before Christ was born, he was able with such accuracy of delineation to picture all that He would be in Himself, and likewise accomplish. The full description tallies to the last letter with the description of the Son of God while here among men. *Prophecy,* it has been said, is God's finger mark on the leaves of the book, preparing us for miracles – God's footprints on the life of the world. Because of all Christ taught and accomplished – and is accomplishing – He is worthy of the name *Wonderful.*

Forecast: "Who is He that . . . things too wonderful for me" (Job 42:3).

"Thy testimonies are wonderful" (Ps. 119:129).

"Such knowledge is too wonderful for me" (Ps. 139:6).

"Thou hast done wonderful things" (Isa. 25:1).

"The LORD of hosts, which is wonderful in counsel" (Isa. 28:29).

"His name shall be called Wonderful" (Isa. 9:6).

The Hebrew word for "wonderful" is *secret.* Manoah asked "The Angel of the Lord" His name and He replied, "Why askest thou thus after my name, seeing it is *secret?*" (Judg. 13:18). The same word *secret* is given as "wondrously" in the next verse. Did wondrously! This is what we know of Jesus. His wonderful words, works, and witness proved Him to be "the Son given." It would have been more wonderful if Jesus, being all He evidently was, had performed no mighty works.

Fulfillment: "The chief priests and scribes saw the wonderful things that he did" (Matt. 21:15).

"All bare him witness, and wondered at the gracious words" (Luke 4:22).

"Jesus of Nazareth, a man approved of God . . . by wonders" (Acts 2:22).

"Wonders . . . done by the name of thy holy child Jesus" (Acts 4:30).

How worthy He was of His name *Wonderful!* Because He was, in Himself, all this name implied, He was wonderful in His *teaching,* which has never been surpassed by the world's greatest scholars. He was wonderful in His *character,* the marvel being that while others became repentant and were converted under His influence, He, Himself, never had anything to repent of. He was wonderful in His *life,* because of its purity and plan – a saving plan He brought about through His death and Resurrection.

> O Wonderful! round whose birth-home
> Prophetic song, miraculous power
> Cluster and turn like star and flower.

b. *Counsellor*

Often these first two names are linked together and made to read "Wonderful-Counsellor," or "Wonder of a Counsellor." The Bible has the combination "Wonderful in Counsel." The Hebrew for "The Spirit of Counsel" is rendered in the LXX Version as "The Angel of great counsel." If we seek divine counsel we shall never walk in darkness. How grateful we should be for a Guiding Mind to think for all, Guiding Heart to feel for all, Guiding Hand to act for all.

Forecast: "His name shall be called . . . Counsellor" (Isa. 9:6).

"Who . . . being his counsellor hath taught him?" (Isa. 40:13).

"I beheld . . . and there was no counsellor" (Isa. 41:28).

"Thy testimonies also are . . . my counsellors" (Ps. 119:24).

Fulfillment: "Who worketh all things after the counsel of his own will" (Ephes. 1:11).

"The immutability of his counsel" (Heb. 6:17).

"Whence hath this Man this wisdom?" (Matt. 13:54).

"Christ . . . the wisdom of God" (I Cor. 1:24).

The term Isaiah employed embodied the idea of the perfect wisdom the future Messiah would manifest. Having come as the personification of divine wisdom, how foolish we are if we ask not "counsel at the mouth of the LORD"? (Josh. 9:14). Problems and perplexities arise that seem to be insoluble, but we have a Counsellor who can explain all the enigmas of life. With His every other grace, guidance can be ours. He offers to lead us into all truth by His Spirit. We are thrice happy if we can say, "Blessed be the Lord, Who hath given me counsel."

J. B. Figgis, in his heart-warming volume on *Emmanuel,* tells us that

> We must steer clear between two opposite dangers: the one, not to ask or to expect counsel; the other, to except it so clearly as to overturn the balanced judgment of older and more experienced Christians. A compass is an excellent thing, and compass and a sail two excellent things; but a ship wants something more than a compass and sail — a ship wants ballast, and this is what some good people utterly and entirely lack. The Word, common sense, and the wishes of others, are, to such people, mere cobwebs, to be brushed aside that the handwriting on the wall may be seen; whereas, it is this notion often that are the cobwebs — the handwriting may be hardly there at all.

> O Counsellor! Your thousand years
> One question, tremendous with tears,
> One awful question vexed our peers
> . . .
>
> But Thou hast come, and now we
> know
> Each wave hath an eternal flow,
> Each leaf a life-time after snow.

c. *The Mighty God*

This remarkable feature of this third name is that the word Isaiah uses for *God* was not "Elohim," which is used not only of God Himself, but of human agents whom He uses. "The Lord said unto Moses, See, I have made thee a god (elohim) to Pharaoh" (Exod. 7:1), but *El,* which was never used by any Old Testament writer in any lower sense than that of Absolute Deity. It is the term applied directly to *Jehovah,* "The mighty God" (Isa. 10:21, etc.). He is the Mightiest among the mighty.

Forecast: "A great God, a mighty" (Deut. 10:17; Neh. 9:32).

"His name shall be called . . . The mighty God" (Isa. 9:6).

"Great in counsel, and mighty in work" (Jer. 32:19).

"Thy name is great in might" (Jer. 10:6).

Fulfillment: "He that cometh after me is mightier than I" (Matt. 3:11).

"His mighty works were done" (Matt. 11:20; Luke 19:37).

"All power is given unto me" (Matt. 28:18).

"He that is mighty" (Luke 1:49).

"In him should all fulness dwell;" . . . "The fulness of the Godhead bodily" (Col. 1:19; 2:9).

The natural meaning of this third name is *Mighty God,* and nothing less is the Lord who came mighty with the might of God. His was an uncreated might. *Immanuel,* the name already considered, is the very same name in compound with *with us.* The Promised, Predicted One, then, was nothing less than God. All the apostles gave witness to Christ that He was "very God of very God." Thomas echoed their faith when he exclaimed, "My Lord and my God." Peter spoke of Him as "Our God and Saviour, Jesus Christ," while Jude added, "Our only Lord God, even our Lord Jesus Christ." Did Jesus Himself not claim "I and My Father are one" — one in the manifestation of the might of deity? We cannot account for His peerless life, His matchless teaching, His efficacious death and Resurrection, His abiding influence on nations and men apart from the fact that He was the mighty God manifest in flesh. If He was only a man, why were there not more men like Him? He was, as John Milton puts it, "The Son of God, with Godlike force endured."

d. *The Everlasting Father*

Richard Crashaw, that quaint poet

of the sixteenth century who coined that phrase in connection with our Lord's miracle of turning water into wine, "The conscious water saw its God, and blushed," wrote a "Hymn of The Nativity" in which he describes the birth of "the mighty Babe" and concludes with the couplet:

> Welcome, all wonders in one sight!
> Eternity shut in a span.

When God became man, eternity was indeed shut up in His earthly span of thirty-three years. While it may seem as if we are confounding the Persons of the Trinity when we use the names of the Father and the Son interchangeably, the term *Father* is often used in a broad sense as the source or originator of a quality or an object (See Job 29:16; Isa. 22:21). In ancient Rome, when a citizen had accomplished some brave and noble deed of infinite value and of willing self-denial, soldiers would raise him on their shields, maidens would throw garlands at his feet, and the populace would hail him in their songs as *Pater Patrioe,* Father of his country. Such an honorable title illustrates the inner significance of the name before us, "The Everlasting Father," of "The Father of Eternity – the King, Immortal and Invisible."

Forecasts: "The name of the LORD, the everlasting God" (Gen. 21:33).

"From everlasting to everlasting, thou art God" (Ps. 90:2).

"I am the LORD, I change not" (Mal. 3:6).

"His name shall be called . . . The everlasting Father" (Isa. 9:6).

Fulfillments: "Out of thee (Bethlehem) shall he come forth . . . whose goings forth have been from of old, from everlasting" (Mic. 5:2).

"Before Abraham was, I am" (John 8:58).

"Christ abideth for ever" (John 12:34).

"Jesus Christ the same yesterday, and to day, and for ever" (Heb. 13:8).

It is because of His everlastingness that He can make all who believe the recipients of everlasting life (John 6:47). With Christ, they are to become the sharers of the eternity of Jehovah. The LXX version translates *The Everlasting Father,* as "The Father of the age to come." "The age to come" was how ancient Jews spoke of the future messianic dispensation. As the Father of the Ages, Christ has accomplished far more for succeeding ages than any other noble person.

> O everlasting Father, God!
> Sun after sun went down, and trod
> Race after race the green earth's sod,
> Till generations seemed to be
> But dead waves of an endless sea,
> But dead leaves from a deathless tree.

The Father of Eternity, however, became the Babe of Bethlehem, and brought liberty from bondage and life from the dead. Because He lives and has ever lived, we also can live. Through His grace, by faith, we are the recipients of eternal bliss.

e. *The Prince of Peace*

All foregleams of the coming Messiah in Old Testament Scriptures are taken up with the idea that peace, not war, is characteristic of His ideal kingdom. This is why "peace" dominates so many messianic prophecies. Such a hope was embodied in the name David gave to his son Absalom, which means "Father of Peace." The name "Solomon" likewise implies "peaceful." Old John Trapp uses the phrase *Pacis Omnimodoe,* suggesting all kinds of peace – outward, inward, of country or of conscience, temporal or eternal; and Jesus, as prince of all the aspects of peace, has full power to bestow them upon mankind.

Forecasts: "His name shall be called . . . The Prince of Peace" (Isa. 9:6).

"The mountains shall bring peace to the people" (Ps. 72:3).

"This man shall be the peace" (Mic. 5:5).

"He shall speak peace unto the heathen" (Zech. 9:10).

Fulfillment: "Born . . . a Saviour . . . on earth Peace" (Luke 2:11-14).

"In me ye might have peace" (John 16:33).

"Jesus . . . saith unto them, Peace be unto you" (John 20:19, 21, 26).

"He is our peace" . . . He "preached peace" (Ephes. 2:14, 17).

Christ became our peace, that He might reconcile sinners unto God, and in His teaching He re-echoes the voice of prophecy. "Let him take hold of my strength, that he may make peace with me; and he shall make peace with me" (Isa. 27:5). Sometimes sinners are urged to "make their peace with God," but such is as impossible as it is unnecessary. Peace has been made by the blood of the Cross. The Saviour *is* our peace, and in accepting Him we possess the peace He procured and is! It is only as the hymn puts it, "the blood of Jesus whispers peace within." This is the peace the world cannot give nor take away. Peace *with* God – Peace *from* God – Peace *in* God.

> O prince of Peace! crowned, yet discrowned,
> They say no war nor battle's sound
> Was heard the tired world around;
> They say the hour that Thou didst come,
> The trumpet's voice was stricken dumb,
> And no one beat the battle drum . . .
> And when, not yet in God's sunshine,
> The smoke drifts from the embattled line
> Of warring hearts that would be Thine,
> We bid our doubts and passions cease,
> Our restless hearts be stilled with these,
> Counsellor, Father, Prince of Peace.

G. *As to the Reception of the Birth*

In our modern family life, the coming of a baby is the occasion of much joy. After long expectation and preparation, the very little bundle of humanity arrives and the parents are grateful to God for such a gift, and others in the home circle rejoice. How was the birth of earth's most illustrious child received – a birth which the Bible predicted more than 4,000 years before Jesus was actually born in a manger? Did all share the sentiment expressed by Richard Crashaw in his unusual *"Hymn of Nativity"*?

> Gloomy night embrac'd the place
> Where the noble Infant lay.
> The Babe look'd up and shew'd His face;
> In spite of darkness, it was day.
> It was Thy Day, sweet! and did rise
> Not from the East, but from Thine eyes . . .
> We saw Thee; and we blest the sight
> We saw Thee by Thine own sweet light.

Through the centuries the British have observed an unvarying custom as a royal babe is about to be born. When the Court physicians are assured that within an hour or so a new prince or princess will see the light of day in the royal household, government leaders are advised, and the Home Secretary must hasten to the palace, to remain there until the child is born. The moment he receives official notification from the attendant physicians, he is the first to intimate it to the nation.

Once in the more degenerate days, so far as royalty is concerned, the Home Secretary (or his equivalent) had to be actually present at the birth, to assure the nation that a royal heir had really been born. Some royal couples in the distant past were childless and anxious to keep the throne attached to their own royal line. They were not above trying to impose a child that was not theirs upon the nation as a natural heir to the throne. To avoid any such fraud, the representative of government and people was present at the birth to bear witness that a child had actually been born to the reigning queen. In those days, when the Church of Rome lusted for power and had a rival successor to the throne ready, there was great disappointment in Rome if a babe was born to a Protestant queen, and great care had to be taken lest the babe be stolen or destroyed. That danger is past, for no Catholic can now ascend the English throne, by law. Thus the attendance of the Home Secretary at a royal birth is a mere formality, though doubtless he sees the babe before leaving the palace, and gives his best wishes to the reigning king and queen.

As every Christmas Day comes round we think of another princely birth, Who came of the royal house and lineage of David. Not only did Jesus come from a royal line, He was *born* a king, something that never happens in any royal household, as already indicated. As we gather anew around the Babe, let us think of the spectators of that wondrous event and advent. Who were the witnesses of Christ's birth? They were holy and human, devout and diabolical, enquiring and exalting.

1. *The Holy Trinity.* First of all, the Three Persons comprising the Trinity were at Bethlehem. The Father was present, for it was His love that drew salvation's plan. He it was who predicted and promised the Coming One. Long ago, God declared that Christ would appear as the seed of the woman to destroy Satan's authority (Gen. 3:15). Through the thousands of years represented by the Old Testament, God prepared the mind of man and the world for the advent of His blessed Son. What holy joy, then, must have been His when ultimately Christ emerged from the womb of Mary as God manifest in flesh!

Christ, also, was a spectator of His own birth. We deem it unnecessary to discuss the question as to when He became conscious He was the promised Messiah. We have no doubt whatever that when the human body was fully prepared for Christ to indwell, He entered it as God, the Son. While His glory was not manifested until He commenced His ministry, yet within Him as the Babe, there was the full consciousness of who and what He was.

It goes without saying that the Holy Spirit was likewise present at the manger, as He was responsible, as the Begetter of Life, for the conception within Mary's womb. He it was who implanted the seed necessary for the production of a body, and who graciously overshadowed Mary during the months she was with child. Yes, and it was the Spirit who possessed our Lord from the beginning of His earthly career until, by the same Spirit, Christ offered Himself up to God.

2. *The Devil.* Another onlooker, and a frustrated one at that, was the Devil. The one event he sought to prevent was the coming of Christ into the world. Ever before him was the announcement he had received in Eden, and from that hour he had set out to destroy the royal seed from which Jesus was to spring. There were times when he almost succeeded, but God saw to it that the tribe of Judah was kept intact. Thus Christ came to earth as the Promised One in spite of the powers of hell. Witnessing the coming of the seed, Satan was just as determined to destroy Mary's child and thereby prevent the Cross. All satanic efforts, however, were foiled, and Christ finished His God-given task.

Bethlehem's crib is the test of character. Man's true worth is revealed as he stands at the feet of the Babe, wrapped in swaddling clothes. Further, what man does with Christ's wondrous birth determines his destiny. Dealing with it as an ordinary birth and treating Christ as a child with a human father, shuts a man out from all the Man-Child made possible. No one can be a Christian after the New Testament order if he discredits the virgin birth. Rejection of this initial miracle of Christianity means the rejection of all the miraculous content of the Bible, even to the rejection of the miraculous work of the Spirit.

Somehow the cradle and the cross are bound together. The overthrow of one means the elimination of the other. This is why the modernist, who will not accept the truth of the Incarnation, has little room in his theology for the atoning death of Christ. Certainly there is mystery associated with our Lord's Incarnation, but this is no reason why it should be discredited. If we try to explain the virgin birth, we lose our reason – if we deny it, we lose our soul. Therefore let us seek out those who are mentioned in the birth narratives, and who were present that day when Christ was born, and note their personal reactions as they gazed upon the Babe, who came for the redemption of sinners.

3. *Priestly Zacharias.* In his song concerning Jesus, Zacharias blessed God for His Advent as a fulfillment of prophecy and as a source of spiritual blessing. As the father of John the Baptist, forerunner or advance-courier of Christ, Zacharias' testimony cannot be neglected, At their advanced time of life, both Zacharias and Elisabeth had ceased to mention the subject of offspring. Their past prayers for a child, however, had not been forgotten by God. "Thy prayer is heard and thy wife Elisabeth shall bear thee a son."

To the ancient Jews to be childless was a weighty affliction, one of the bitterest of sorrows (I Sam. 1:11). Thus, when Gabriel appeared with the message that Elisabeth would conceive, Zacharias doubted such a miraculous interposition and was smitten with dumbness until John was born. Old Bengel says, "Loss of speech was a kind of medicine to Zacharias lest he should become swollen with pride because of the predicted greatness of his son."

Godly though he was, Zacharias felt the message of Gabriel incredible. But familiar as he was with Old Testament Scriptures, such an announcement should not have cast doubt into his mind. The wonderful births of Isaac, Samuel, and Samson should have reminded priestly Zacharias that what God had accomplished in the past, He was able to repeat. Forgetting God's ability to fulfill His word, however, Zacharias resorted to arguments of human sense and reason. Yet it was not for him to reason why when God uttered His voice.

After nine long months, the illustrious son appeared, and so we come to the witness of Zacharias to Christ as the dayspring from on high who visited us (Job 38:12; Luke 1:78). All doubt and dumbness disappeared and Zacharias, vocal with praise, blessed God for the honor his son was to have in going before the face of the Lord to prepare His ways.

4. *Godly Elisabeth.* Elisabeth, the aunt of Mary's child, also adds her quota to the fact of the Incarnation. Her name, meaning "God her oath," testifies to her pious upbringing. Although she had been barren through the years of expectancy, yet her barrenness was not the result of sin as the Jews so often taught. When she realized a child was to be hers, she hid herself, for "modesty is ever the fruit of piety."

As soon as Mary conceived, she visited the home of Elisabeth, and there is delicacy yet profundity in the conversation of these two miraculously pregnant women. What happiness they shared! As soon as they met, Elisabeth's babe leaped within her womb – mysterious effect of sympathy. With clarity of spiritual insight, Elisabeth called Mary "the mother of my Lord," witnessing thereby to the truth that the child Mary was to bear the long-promised Messiah. Thus Elisabeth recognized the truth of Christ's Incarnation, for how could an unborn Child be called Lord if He was not coming as such? Why, the leaping of her own babe was a pre-recognition by the unborn John of the unborn Saviour-Lord!

Commending Mary for her precious faith, Elisabeth said, "Blessed is she that believed." Here was a faith laughing at the impossible. When it came to Mary's time to be delivered, Elisabeth thanked God for all His mercy in bringing her through a time of severe trial.

5. *John the Forerunner.* The testimony of John the Baptist as to the authenticity of the virgin birth must be reckoned with, seeing that his was the high privilege of preparing the way for Christ to appear. Having a conception as miraculous as the one about to be born, John had no doubt as to the Incarnation. Spirit-filled from his birth, he was certain of his mission, and at all times declared that he was not that Light the prophets spoke of, but only a witness to that Light. His office was to herald the approach of the king, and to prepare the people for His coming. Think not of me but of the one about to appear, John seemed to say. And when Jesus came, John, with true magnanimity, was ready to vanish from the scene. "He must increase, I must decrease."

After Christ came and His ministry was established, John, although in prison, maintained his witness to his Lord. His last act, as a prisoner in chains awaiting a cruel death, was to send men to Jesus. He, himself, had no doubt as to Christ's authority. His question, "Art Thou He that should come or look we for another?" cast no reflection upon John's faith in Christ. He wanted his two disciples to receive from Christ's lips an answer leaving an indelible impression on their minds which, of course, was what happened. The words and works of Jesus revealed to John's disciples that the faith of their master in Christ had been fully justified.

Just as John prepared the way for Christ's first coming when he preached sin, repentance, and judgment, so there is a need, in these last days, for an army of John the Baptists to proclaim an identical message and prepare, thereby, the way for the second coming of Christ.

6. *The Virgin Mary.* No other proof of the Incarnation is so conclusive as that which came from her who was chosen to be the mother of our Lord. She, more than any other, was intimately associated with Him who came from her womb.

It is interesting to compare the questions of Zacharias and Mary. When Gabriel appeared to the former with the announcement of John's birth, he replied, "Whereby shall I know this?" When the same angel came to Mary, telling her of the favor to be hers, she said, "How shall this be, seeing I know not a man?" The reply of Zacharias suggested doubt of all Gabriel had declared. Mary's question, however, entertained no doubt as to her becoming the mother of such a child as Gabriel described. She did not understand the manner of its accomplishment until Gabriel further explained the share of the Spirit in conception.

Reverently and readily Mary acquiesced in the purpose of God. She knew there was nothing too hard for the Lord. She also knew that her reputation would be at stake, but no questions were asked and no objections were raised. Accepting the honor laid upon her, she humbly replied: "Behold the handmaiden of the Lord; be it unto me according to thy word."

Saluting Mary, Gabriel did not pray to her as a goddess. He recognized her saintly character and gave due recognition to her fitness for the honor bestowed upon her. The Roman Catholic Church falsely holds

Mary as an object of worship and someone to be prayed to. Catholics also affirm that Mary was "conceived without sin." Yet she herself recognized the need of the Saviour she was about to bear, for in her "Magnificat" she sang, "My spirit hath rejoiced in God *my* Saviour."

The marvel and mystery of the Incarnation was emphasized by Gabriel in the remarkable words, "The Holy Spirit shall come upon thee, and the power of the Highest shall overshadow thee: therefore also that holy thing which shall be born of thee shall be called the Son of God" (Luke 1:36). Although chosen to be the Messiah's mother, she never used the terms "sinless" and "immaculate" of herself. She was only too conscious of her low estate. Thus it came about that within Mary, the Spirit laid hold of deity and humanity and fused them together, making possible the Lord Jesus, who came as the unique combination, the God-Man.

In the overruling providence of God, when Augustus decreed the taxing, Mary must needs be at Bethlehem, which the prophets had declared would be the birthplace of the promised Messiah. This poor virgin, of an obscure town, was reminded by Gabriel of the greatness of her firstborn son, in that He was coming as the Son of the Highest, and as the Messiah, with a kingdom spiritual, universal, and eternal in nature.

Full of wonder that it was no more strange for her, a virgin, than for aged Elisabeth to become a mother, her faith in and surrender to God enabled her to accept the situation and face the suspicion of Joseph and the world. Visiting Elisabeth and receiving her salutation, it must be noted that Elisabeth did not say to Mary, "Blessed be thou *above* women," only "*among* women." The unusual honor thrust upon Mary by the Catholics is foreign to New Testament teaching.

In the fulness of time, Jesus was born of a woman, thus Bethlehem atoned for Eden. "If woman was guilty of the world's first sin, on her breast the Redeemer was nourished." What a glorious song of praise was Mary's! Honor, gratitude, and joy were all hers, as she declared that her babe would put down the mighty from their seats. Before long thrones of power, boasting of security, were to tremble before Him, as He scattered the proud in the imagination of their hearts.

How many things about the Holy One to be born of her, uttered by angels and men, Mary kept in her heart and pondered over! Her musings continued not only through the months of pregnancy, but as long as Jesus tarried among men. Perhaps she did not fully understand at all times the import of Simeon's prophecy that the birth of her Son would be a sword piercing her soul. As she gazed upon Christ dying at Calvary and heard Him say, "Woman, behold thy Son!" then she experienced a sword-pierced heart. How poignant her grief must have been! But courageously Mary stood by the cross and did not waver in her allegiance to Him who was her Saviour-Son.

7. *Just Joseph.* Joseph was present at the manger. He had every right to be there, even though he was not the father of the One about to be born. His presence there witnessed to a severe test that had emerged triumphant. Mary was the pure young woman he had fallen in love with and was about to make his wife, yet the child she was about to bear would not be his. Seeing her "great with child," without fanfare Joseph was minded to put her away. He never acted rashly with his espoused wife, although he was baffled by her condition. How this serves for all time as an example of godly wisdom and tender consideration for others!

Bitterly disappointed that Mary had apparently betrayed him, yet believing, he made no haste (Isa. 28:16). As a praying man he waited upon God, and his love for and patience with Mary were rewarded. God understood his mental difficulties and rewarded godly Joseph's conscientious attitude toward Mary by revealing His redemptive plan. God never fails those who carry their anxieties to Him. Joseph received a direct and distinct revelation from God, and at once his fears were banished and his line of duty made clear.

Tenderly he cared for his dear one as if the child she was bearing were his own. Overawed by the mystery of it all, that his beloved Mary had been chosen as the mother of the Lord he as a devout Jew had eagerly anticipated, we can imagine how he superintended every detail of the nativity.

What holy thoughts must have filled the mind of Mary's guardian? Where suspicion regarding Mary's purity once lurked, strong faith now reigned as he looked into the lovely face of Mary's child. At last God's promises had been fulfilled and before him was the Babe through whom God's covenants would be established!

When it became necessary because of Herod's hatred to flee into Egypt, Joseph cared for Mary and her child with reverent devotion until tidings came that Herod was dead and that they could safely return to their own land. While a shroud of secrecy covers the thirty years that Christ spent at home, we can be sure of this, that between Jesus and Joseph there was an affection strong and deep, as long as Joseph lived.

8. *The Angelic Host.* What a striking contrast the birth of Christ affords! Around Him impoverished circumstances – above, the glorious and glad angelic host. While the multitude of the heavenly host, welcoming and witnessing Christ's birth, knew they could never share in all that His Incarnation was to make possible, they yet proclaimed to a needy world the first Christmas carol.

Paul reminds us that Christ as "God manifest in flesh" was "seen of angels" (I Tim. 3:16). Peter also tells us that the angels stooped down to look into the amazing depths of grace revealed in the sufferings of Christ. But as angels they could only look and wonder. They could only *see* but never *share* in the redemptive plan of God.

In dealing with the angels as witnesses of Christ's birth, we must discuss, first of all, the part Gabriel, the archangel, played in such a momentous event, as that of the Ancient of Days becoming a babe. The same angel also appeared to Daniel (Dan. 8:16) and now comes to Zacharias and Mary on the same business. Gabriel did not act on his own initiative. He was sent by God on such a high commission. "The account which Gabriel gives of his own office should raise in our minds great searchings of heart," says Bishop Ryle. "This mighty spirit, far greater in power and intelligence than we are, counts it his highest honor to stand in God's presence and do His will. Let all our aims and desires be in the same direction."

The message Gabriel bore to Zacharias should have produced boundless joy. Instead, Zacharias was guilty of unbelief and his questionings resulted in heavy chastisement. Mary treated Gabriel somewhat differently. What a glorious account he gave of the One to be within her womb! Mary was overawed by the announcement. As a virgin, she rightly wondered how she could bear the Christ-Child, but Gabriel quickly silenced all questionings as to the Incarnation by telling Mary that "with God nothing shall be impossible." So, although "a wicked angel came to Eve, in order that through her man might be separated from God, a good angel came to Mary, that through her God might be united to men."

The first to herald the tidings that Christ was coming to save men, and who could praise God for such a provision, were the angels who had never sinned, and who needed no Saviour. The first hymn, then, honoring Christ came from a multitude of the heavenly host. Thus the homage of angels confirmed the faith of a godly remnant, who looked for redemption in Israel. Angels, as we know, were to occupy prominence in the life and teaching of Him whom they knew before He was born.

9. *The Lowly Shepherds.* How fitting it was that the Good Shepherd who was coming to give His life for the sheep first announced His birth to good shepherds watching over their flocks! As a heavenly revelation never comes to unprepared minds, but always to noble hearts, just as the loftiest peaks are always the first to hail the dawn, the shepherds were spiritually prepared for the news. They were in the habit of meditating upon the prophetic Scriptures, so when the heavenly ambassadors came to them, they were ready to receive the message.

Thus it was that the good tidings of the advent of "the Shepherd and Bishop of our souls" came to shepherds and, through the office they typified, to all men. The venerable Bede expressed it, "The angels of Heaven bring the glad tidings – not to the Scribes and Pharisees at Jerusalem – but to shepherds keeping their flocks by night," who immediately obeyed the heavenly commandment and told others of what had come to pass.

To those of us who are undershepherds, there is much to learn from the conduct of these godly shepherds. Bishop Hooper's counsel to those pastors he refers to as "those godly and faithful prisoners which were taken together at prayer in a house in Bow Churchyard," should be hid in the heart.

> Read the second chapter of Luke, and there we shall see how the shepherds that watched their sheep all night, as soon as they heard that Christ was born at Bethlehem, by and by must go to see him. They did not reason nor debate with themselves who should keep the wolf from the sheep in the meantime, but did as they were commanded, and committed their sheep to Him Whose pleasure they obeyed. Let us so do, now we be called; let us commit all other things unto Him that called us. He will take heed that all things shall be well. He will help the husband; he will comfort the wife. He will guide the servants; he will keep the house. He will preserve the goods: yea, rather than it should be undone, He will wash the dishes and rock the cradle. Cast, therefore, all your care upon God.

10. *The Lowing Cattle.* Pusy, the renowned commentator, wrote: "His attendants were the rude cattle, less rude only than we, the ox and ass, emblems of our untamed, rebellious nature, yet owning, more than we, their Master's crib." Although forced from their stall to make room for Mary and her child, these oxen were not as dumb as they looked. The One about to be born was their creator, and instinctively they would recognize Him.

Mrs. Browning's exquisite lines, as to the intelligent recognition of the Babe by the cattle, come to mind

> The dumb kine from their fodder
> turning
> Softened their horned faces
> To almost human gazes
> Toward the Newly-Born.

Why was He being born? Was not one reason the ultimate good of all within a dumb creation? Does not the whole creation, including beast as well as man, groan and travail in pain as it awaits complete deliverance from the curse? When Christ appears the second time on earth, is He not going to transform the present cruel, rapacious character of the beasts of the field? Listen to the description

Isaiah gives of the benefits accruing to dreaded animals during Christ's millennial reign:

> The wolf also shall dwell with the lamb, and the leopard shall lie down with the kid; and the calf and the young lion and the fatling together, and a little child shall lead them. And the cow and the bear shall feed; their young ones shall lie down together: and the lion shall eat straw like the ox. And the sucking child shall play on the hole of the asp, and the weaned child shall put his hand on the cockatrice's den. They shall not hurt nor destroy in all my holy mountain: for the earth shall be full of the knowledge of the LORD, as the waters cover the sea (Isa. 11:6–9).

What a day that will be, when "beasts and all cattle" as well as "the kings of the earth" shall shout "Praise ye the Lord" (Ps. 138:4; 148:11). The presence of cattle, then, at His birth, is a prophecy of His universal dominion.

11. *The Ignorant Innkeeper.* Reading that "there was no room in the inn" for the expectant mother, we can imagine that the innkeeper had been approached for suitable accommodation, but none could be found. Owing to the edict for all to register, travelers crowded the highways, and space in the small inn was at a premium. It was thus that the innkeeper had a cattle stall prepared for Mary, in which she might bear her child. Yet had the innkeeper known the royalty of the One to be born, he would have made room for Him, although it might have meant surrendering his own room. But Christ came as a king in disguise. He came as a king and must have a palace, which was the manger. He came as a king and must have courtiers, which were beasts.

If the inn, a place of public resort, represents social life, then there is little room for Christ in such today. Social circles have a way of treating Christ with cold indifference. They have no room for Jesus, King of Glory. The outside place is good enough for Him. They have plenty of room for business, pleasure, and activities of all kinds, but little room for Christ. Let us take heed lest we exclude Him from any part of our life.

Why was the stable chosen as the birthplace of our Lord? Was it not that He might reprove the glory of the world and condemn the vanities of life? That babe in the stall, outside the inn, speaks eloquently of the truth of His willing condescension on our behalf. Though he was rich, for our sakes He became poor. Although His surroundings were so mean, angels above shouted their hallelujahs, and a star brought the wise and great to His side! Although He never had a magnificent retinue of servants attending His birth, yet He came as the king who would cause the kings of earth to tremble.

12. *The Wise Men.* Conspicuous among the visitors to the young child were the learned men from the East. They were those predicted by Isaiah who would render homage to the king (Isa. 42:6; 60:3, 6). How deeply they were moved by the birth of one who was to change the course of events! These students of Scripture and the stars were guided by a miraculous star to the very place where Christ was to be found. That they were more desirous of finding Him than the Scribes, whose advice they sought, is evident from the fact that the Magi came to Christ, while the Scribes did not.

As it was a practice in the East for all approaching a king to make him the recipient of gifts, so the Wise Men presented to Christ, born King of the Jews, their gifts, enabling Joseph and Mary to find their way back to Egypt. These men of faith and purpose had no doubt about the fulfillment of prophecy, neither regarding the kingship of Christ. They traveled weary miles over the hot desert sands and never halted until they saw Him of whom the prophets spoke.

Although at the end of their arduous journey they only saw a babe, they yet believed in Him and worshipped Him as a king. Truly, as Bishop Ryle remarks,

> Theirs is a striking example of faith. They believed in Christ when they had never seen Him — but that was not all. They believed in Him when the Scribes and Pharisees were unbelieving — but that again was not all. They believed in Him when they saw the little Infant on Mary's knee and worshipped Him as a King. This was the crowning point of their faith — they saw no miracles to convince them. They heard no teaching to persuade them. They saw nothing but a new-born infant, helpless and weak and needing a mother's care, like any one of ourselves. When they saw the infant, they believed they saw the divine Saviour of the world. "They fell down and worshipped Him." We read of no greater faith in the whole volume of the Bible.

13. *Saintly Simeon.* Another spectator of the most significant birth of all history was old Simeon, who without doubt was endued with a prophetic spirit. This "just and devout man" kept the light of prophecy burning when religion was at a low ebb in Israel. Simeon means "one who hears or obeys." Well, he certainly knew the voice speaking in the prophets of old, and obeyed the light received. Coming into the Temple, Simeon took the Babe up in his arms and blessed God, and every word of his blessed benediction is worthy of prayerful study.

At last faith had been justified, and Simeon could die without fear. "Lord, now lettest thou thy servant depart in peace, for mine eyes have seen thy salvation." In this swan song, Simeon was not ashamed to declare that this One, born in the city of David, was the Saviour of the world, the light to lighten the Gentiles, and the glory of His people Israel. This was more than the letter-learned Scribes of his time had discerned. These were the men who looked upon Christ as a sign to be spoken against and to whom He would become a stone of stumbling and a rock of offense. With Simeon it was so different. No wonder his prophecy caused Joseph and Mary to marvel over all that was being said regarding Jesus. Every additional witness added to their knowledge of Him for whom they were to care through the years. Shepherds, angels, now a spirit-taught prophet, all alike contributed to the adoration the parents of our Lord felt.

Ere long, ours will be the thrill of having our eyes see our salvation, for Christ is our salvation. What joy will be ours to gaze upon Him, whom our souls have loved so long!

14. *Adoring Anna.* How imperative it is to count the aged Anna among the witnesses of Christ's birth! Mentioned nowhere else in the New Testament, a distinction Anna shares with saintly Simeon, we can detect divine wisdom in that a woman and a man should testify to the fact of the Incarnation. "Simeon and Anna, standing near the infant Jesus, are types of the Old Covenant decaying in the presence of the New, which shall never grow old." In the mouth of two witnesses it shall be established.

This woman, whose brief yet precious biography speaks of an unsullied character, of self-denial, of unceasing prayer, had no doubt regarding the identity of the Babe born in Bethlehem. To all who looked for redemption, this prophetess had the rich reward for all her godliness of seeing the long-promised Redeemer, and with joy assured the saints of the fulfillment of God's promises as to the Messiah.

There is much about Anna worthy of our imitation. She was not carried away by the wickedness surrounding her. She kept herself unspotted from the world and, living in the promises, patiently awaited the coming Saviour. At this distant time, can we say that the same life of faith is ours? Are we looking for our complete redemption from sin, sorrow, and Satan? By character and conduct are we declaring our eager anticipation for the second advent of Christ?

15. *The Cynical Scribes.* The reaction of the religious leaders to the birth of Christ is also worthy of consideration. Troubled Herod sought the advice of the Scribes and Pharisees as to the place where Jesus should be born. Quoting the Scriptures that answered the anxious monarch, they said, "in Bethlehem of Judea." This very knowledge condemned them, for they did not go to Christ, although they aided the Wise Men in finding Him. These Scribes were like milestones pointing out the way to travelers, but themselves remaining motionless. "If the actual birthplace of Christ did not agree with their Scriptural reply, there would be strong evidence, to start with, against the claims of Jesus. On the other hand, if it did, the motive to examine His subsequent claims would be strong, had they been sincere."

The attitude of these Scribes and Pharisees teaches us that it is not always those who are blessed with most religious privileges who give most honor to Christ. With their knowledge of the prophetic Word, they should have been the first to hasten to Bethlehem and look upon the babe, whose day Abraham longed to see. But Christ came unto His own, those of His own religious persuasion, and they received Him not.

> These men of grave and moral word,
> With consciences defiled,
> Said, "Let the old truth still be heard,
> We want no Child."

Familiarity, we say, can breed contempt, and this was certainly true with these religious leaders who had the Scriptures in the head, but no grace in the heart. They told Herod where Christ should be born, but never went to the manger to welcome the Saviour.

When the Wise Men saw the child, they believed and surrendered of their best, but the Scribes and Pharisees remained aloof and unbelieving. They never recognized the royalty and deity of the One born of Mary, and right on until He died in agony and shame, they were conspicuous Christ-haters. Alas, their ilk are not dead, for in the ministry today we have those who, with all their Bible knowledge and religious privileges and position, reject His virgin birth and His claims as the Son of God!

16. *Hateful Herod.* The opposite effects of the birth of Christ on those around Him is borne out by the troubled state of mind experienced by Herod the King. No wonder he was agitated. "Jesus in His cradle is mightier than Herod on his throne." All earthly potentates pale into insignificance alongside the glory and splendor of "the King Eternal."

But what was it that gave Herod the jitters when he heard of what had happened at Bethlehem? Well, he had reason to be afraid seeing the Pharisees had warned him of the end of the Herodian dynasty. Therefore, if the One the Wise Men had spoken of was truly a king, he must seek to destroy Him, which he tried to do in the slaughter of the innocents (Jer. 19:4), once he found the Wise Men had failed to return from their visit to the Child, with the desired information (Matt. 2:18).

Says Joseph Parker, commenting upon this incident, "No man has troubled the human heart so much as Christ. His whole course is a rebuke to evil. A Babe 'troubling' a king! The good have ever 'troubled' the bad. The nefarious bookkeeper is troubled by the eye of his honest companion."

One concluding question. How has

the fact of Christ affected us? Is ours the attitude of the adoring shepherds or that of Herod, mad with jealousy, trembling because of the possible loss of his throne? When the Lordship of Christ is fully recognized, many Herods are troubled. Dagon must fall to pieces when the ark is carried into the temple.

H. *As to the Purpose of the Birth*

When we come to *Prophecies of His Ministry,* we shall deal more fully with all that was involved in our Lord's condescension in taking upon Himself the likeness of His flesh. It was not a question of having to come because His birth was predicted. Christ was virtually slain *before* the foundation, which means that in the dateless past before man was created, "Love drew salvation's plan," He preceded all prophecy. While He came fulfilling all predictions made of Him, He came, primarily, because of the decision made by the Cabinet of the Trinity before time commenced (Rom. 8:29, 30; Ephes. 1:5, 11).

The angelic announcer of Mary's unborn Son said that when He did appear that His name must be Jesus, because, true to His name, He was to save sinners. This was the supreme purpose of His humiliation in being made lower than the angels. It was because of that that His Incarnation and Crucifixion were born together. We were born to live – Jesus was born to die! The sole design of the crib was the cross, as we shall discover when we come to examine the *Prophecies of His Death.*

As His birth was a *manifestation,* there are various aspects of it emphasized in the New Testament:

He manifested God in human flesh (I Tim. 3:16).

He manifested forth His inherent, pre-existent glory (John 2:11).

He manifested the righteousness of God (Rom. 3:21).

He manifested His word (Titus 1:3).

He manifested life in all its fulness (I John 1:2).

He manifested God's purpose to take away sin (I John 3:5).

He manifested complete triumph over Satan (I John 3:8; Gen. 3:5).

He manifested the sacrificial love of God (I John 4:9).

There was no other good enough
To pay the price of sin,
He only could unlock the gate
Of Heaven, and let us in.

The account was settled in a past eternity and the price paid when Jesus took a human body, and after living in it for thirty-three years, died in it, bearing in His body the terrible load of human sin (I Pet. 2:24; Isa. 53:5).

Chapter Five

PROPHECIES OF HIS CHARACTER

His Holiness	His Guilelessness	His Mercy
His Righteousness	His Spotlessness	His Forgiveness
His Goodness	His Innocency	His Patience
His Faithfulness	His Obedience	His Benevolence
His Troth	His Zeal	His Self-Denial
His Justice	His Meekness	His Love

Thomas Dekker, who lived around 400 years ago and who was no mean poet, left us one of the finest portraits of the earthly life of Jesus ever etched. It reads:

> The best of men
> That e'er wore earth about Him, was a sufferer,
> A soft, meek, patient, humble, tranquil spirit,
> The first true Gentleman that ever breath'd.

But did Jesus exhibit all these gentlemanly virtues in the days of His flesh? Was He, as W. E. Gladstone, the renowned British statesman, proclaimed Him, "The greatest the ages have ever shown us," or as John Stuart Mill eulogized Him, "The one perfect life lived in Nazareth"? Is it true, as Canon Liddon would have us believe, that Jesus is exalted among men as being "indefinitely above us all as the true representative, the ideal, the perfect Man"? Canon Liddon continues, "His is the Human Life which does justice to the idea of Humanity. He is the Archetypal Man." Was the commendation of Pilate somewhat far-fetched when he said concerning the actions of Jesus, "I find in Him no fault at all"? Are we justified in believing that He was "fairer than the children of men"?

Turning to the New Testament, we find it replete with the fulfillment of predicted aspects of His character. The portrait of all He was in Himself is complete. Character, it has been said, is what a man is in the dark, and the life of Jesus, privately as well as publicly, was without blemish. He was a stranger to any kind of sin or human failing. There is, of course, a difference between character and reputation. Character is what we *are;* reputation represents what people think and say about us, which may be altogether contrary to what we actually are.

Our Lord paid the strictest attention to His character, and without fear of contradiction could say, "I do *always* the things pleasing to My Father." Facing His enemies, who tried hard to ruin His character, He could challenge them, "Which of you convicted me of sin?" But when it came to His reputation, He threw it to the winds. In fact, Paul tells us that Jesus "made Himself of *no* reputation." What men thought and said about Him never troubled Him, for at all times, and in all things, He lived as unto God and thus became His well-beloved Son in whom He was well pleased. If there are those who, spitefully or jealously, falsely portray us, we must so live as to give the lie to all they wrongly accuse us of.

The traits of character Jesus manifested fit in with the prophetic description of the Messiah, who filled and overflowed all past conceptions of Him. He never came short of any of the good things the prophets wrote concerning His life among men. He lived as God's perfect man, and as man's perfect God. As it is most impressive to read in parallel statements the prediction in comparison with the performance, let us see if we classify several of these parallels in the living Word who came and tabernacled among us.

A. *His Holiness*

As a member of the Godhead, and coming from God's holy habitation, Jesus brought with Him the attribute of pre-existent holiness and was thus born holy. Describing to Mary the nature of the child she was to bear, the angel said, "that *holy thing* which shall be born of thee" (Luke 1:35). Because Jesus was born without sin or the possession of inbred sin, the Devil had no foothold in the child when He appeared. All others born into the world since earth's first child were born with the old Adamic nature. But Jesus, born holy, had no original sin. There was nothing in Him the Devil could appeal to. He had none of those things within, defiling a man.

Forecast: "Who is like unto thee, O LORD . . . glorious in holiness" (Exod. 15:11).

"Yet have I set my king upon my holy hill of Zion" (Ps. 2:6).

Fulfillment: "Thy holy child Jesus" (Acts 4:27).

"These things saith He that is holy" (Rev. 3:7).

"Which of you convinceth me of sin?" (John 8:46).

"He . . . knew no sin" (II Cor. 5:21).

Although, as Paul reminds us, Jesus was made sin for us, the Devil never made Him a sinner. Had His life been stained by one sin, He would have forfeited the right to bear away the sins of the world. But born holy, He was likewise born a Saviour. Because He could claim when the prince of this world came that he had nothing in Him, He triumphed gloriously over the satanic foe (John 14:30).

B. *His Righteousness*

The root meaning and essential idea of the term "righteousness" is that of *right*ness, or being right or just in all things. The act of making right in God-ward relationship is known as *justification.* In Biblical usage, "righteousness" is conceived as judged by the standard of God's holy law, which is derived from His holy character, and summarily comprehended in the Decalogue (Exod. 20:1-17). Unrighteous man is totally incapable of making himself righteous enough to be accepted by Him who is our righteousness.

Forecast: "By his knowledge shall my righteous servant justify [make right] many" (Isa. 53:11).

"Their righteousness is of me, saith the Lord" (Isa. 54:17).

Fulfillment: "Unto the Son, he (God) saith . . . a sceptre of righteousnss is the sceptre of thy kingdom" (Heb. 1:8).

"Thou hast loved righteousness" (Heb. 1:9).

"To declare his righteousness . . . that he might be just (right), and the justifier (one who puts right) of him which believeth in Jesus" (Rom. 3:25, 26).

"He is righteous" (I John 2:29; 3:7).

> Jesus, Thy blood and righteousness
> My beauty are, my glorious dress;
> Midst flaming worlds, in these
> arrayed
> With joy shall I lift up my head.

Here, again, it was because Jesus was just and right in all His ways and witness, ever obedient to His righteous Father, never crooked in His dealings with others, that He was qualified to become our righteousness. His life was never out the least fraction against the plumbline of truth and morality.

C. *His Goodness*

How can we define "Goodness"? If *good* is a contraction of *God*, then the virtue of goodness is God-likeness. In *Paradise Lost*, John Milton writes:

> Abashed the Devil stood,
> And felt how awful goodness is, and saw
> Virtue in her shape how lovely.

This must have been the quality of goodness Jesus manifested as He went about doing good. In his essay on *Goodness*, Bacon would have us know that "the inclination to goodness is imprinted deeply in the nature of man: insomuch, that if it issue not towards men, it will take unto other living creatures." The goodness of Jesus compassed saint and sinner alike, not only because it was imprinted deeply in His nature, but because He came as the personification of divine goodness.

Forecast: "Good and upright is the LORD: therefore will he teach sinners in the way" (Ps. 25:8).

"For thou, Lord, art good, and ready to forgive" (Ps. 86:5).

"The Lord is good to all" (Ps. 145:9; 100:5; Nah. 1:7).

Fulfillment: "One came and said unto him, Good Master . . . Why callest thou me good?" (Matt. 19:16, 17).

"Jesus of Nazareth . . . who went about doing good" (Acts 10:38).

The reply of Jesus to the question of the young seeker seems to suggest that He disclaimed the possession of goodness – "Why callest thou me good? There is none good but one, that is, God." Ellicott suggests that one old manuscript gives a different form to our Lord's answer, which reads, "Why askest thou me concerning that which is good? There is One that is the Good." Then the comment follows:

> The questioner had lightly applied the word *good* to One whom he as yet regarded only as a human teacher, to an act which, it seemed to him, was in his own power to perform. What he needed, therefore, was to be taught to deepen and widen his thoughts of goodness until they rose to Him in whom alone it was absolute and infinite, through fellowship with whom only could any teacher rightly be called good, and from whom alone could come the power to do any good thing.

The psalmist prayed, "Do good, O LORD, unto those that be good, and to them that are upright in their hearts" (Ps. 125:4). Divine goodness, however, is no respecter of persons, and showers its benefits upon the just and the unjust alike. If the goodness of the Lord is spurned and rejected, then His severity must be endured (Rom. 11:22).

> The King of Love my Shepherd is,
> Whose goodness faileth never.
> I nothing lack if I am His,
> And He is mine for ever.

D. *His Faithfulness*

Because of the attractiveness and value of His attributes, God desires His people to experience and exhibit many of them. This is why such a quality as faithfulness is applied in the Bible to God and man. How impressive is the estimation of Paul that "God is faithful" (I Cor. 1:9). Moses described Him as "the faithful God, which keepeth covenant" (Deut. 7:9). Again and again we are reminded that He is faithful in keeping all His promises and, therefore, is worthy of our trust. As God, absolute reliability, firm constancy, and complete freedom from arbitrariness and fickleness are His. He is ever steadfast and loyal towards His own; and being unchangeable in His ethical nature, expects them to be faithful to Him and to His Word and Cause. Hence the several exhortations to faithfulness.

Forecast: "Faithfulness [shall be] the girdle of his reins" (Isa. 11:5).

"His seed . . . as a faithful witness in heaven" (Ps. 89:36, 37).

"Great is thy faithfulness" (Lam. 3:23).

Fulfillment: "Faithful is he that calleth you" (I Thess. 5:24).

"Yet he abideth faithful" (II Tim. 2:13).

"Christ, who is the faithful witness" (Rev. 1:5; 3:14).

"He that sat upon him was called Faithful and True" (Rev. 19:11).

Loving the faithful Saviour, martyrs of old imbibed His spirit and were faithful unto death. Faithfulness and not our fame is to be the basis of reward in eternity (Rev. 2:10). Although we may not be clever, brilliant, conspicuous, or famous, by the grace of our faithful creator we can be loyal, true, and faithful both to Him and to those around us. The least among the saints can aspire to the reputation John Milton gives the seraph Abdiel in *Paradise Lost*:

> . . . Faithful found
> Among the faithless, faithful only he:
> Among the innumerable false, unmoved,
> Unshaken, unseduced, unterrified
> His loyalty he kept, his love, his zeal.

E. *His Troth*

Allied to the virtue just considered is that of trueness, representing fidelity, conformity to fact, accuracy. The phrase "true blue" came from some especially fast blue dye or color and denotes uncompromising loyalty or orthodoxy. This is why the blue color was adopted by the Covenanters and Scottish Presbyterians. We have the proverb, "It pays to be true." But the true God expects us to be true, not because of any advantage that may accrue. Trueness is a part of the divine nature and should be a virtue loved for itself by all who profess Him who, ever true, cannot deny Himself or act contrary to His own nature. "Let God be true" (Rom. 3:4).

In "Macbeth," Shakespeare asks the question, "What! can the Devil speak true?" The answer is, No! because, as He who was all that is true said, "he is a *Liar,* and has been one from the beginning."

Forecast: "The stem of Jesse . . . shall reprove with equity for the meek of the earth" (Isa. 11:1, 4).

"The LORD be a true and faithful witness" (Jer. 42:5).

"The LORD is the true God" (Jer. 10:10).

Fulfillment: "Master, we know that thou art true" (Matt. 22:16).

"The same is true, and no unrighteousness is in him" (John 7:18).

"That we may know him that is true" (I John 5:20).

"He . . . was called Faithful and True" (Rev. 19:11).

Him that is true! What a coveted character to possess! What an example to follow! When amid all the deceptions and fluctuations of the world around he penned the words "the whole world lieth in wickedness," John felt, with the most absolute and penetrating and thankful conviction of his own true heart, that the followers of the true One were safe and secure if rooted and grounded in Him and in His perfect, unshakable, unassailable truth.

> Truehearted, whole-hearted, faithful and loyal,
> King of our lives, by Thy grace we will be!
> Under the standard exalted and royal,
> Strong in Thy strength we will battle for Thee.

F. *His Justice*

Robert Browning in "The Guardian Angel" wrote of

> Infinite mercy . . .
> As infinite a justice too.

God would not be infinite if He were not just. But everywhere the Bible extols His justice, which is never unjust or capricious (Job 8:3). To quote John Milton again,

> Just as the ways of God,
> And justifiable to men;

Unless there be who think not God
at all.

How full of meaning is the quotation from a speech of Benjamin Disraeli in Parliament, "Justice is Truth in action"! Divine justice is always the demonstration of divine truth. Edmund Burke wrote that "there is but one law for all, namely, that law which governs all law, the *law of our Creator,* the law of humanity, justice, and equity — the law of nature, and of nations." Written large over Holy Writ is the Creator's law of justice.

Forecast: "Keep the way of the LORD, to do justice" (Gen. 18:19).

"He executed the justice of the LORD" (Deut. 33:21).

"Of the increase of his government and peace . . . upon the throne of David . . . to establish it . . . with justice" (Isa. 9:7).

Fulfillment: "Behold, thy King cometh . . . he is just" (Zech. 9:9).

"I judge: and my judgment is just" (John 5:30).

"Ye denied the Holy One and the Just" (Acts 3:14; 7:52; 22:14).

"He might be just, and the justifier" (Rom. 3:26).

"Christ . . . the just for the unjust" (I Pet. 3:18).

The beneficence of Him who is "excellent . . . in plenty of justice" (Job 37:23), is seen in that "He sendeth rain on the just and on the unjust" (Matt. 5:45), a truth the Pharisees had to learn from Jesus (Matt. 9:13). When divine justice is scorned and sinned against, the present delay of punishment affords no presumption of final exemption. God may not pay every payday, but at last He pays. Under grace, justice is mingled with mercy.

There's a wideness in God's mercy,
Like the wideness of the sea:
There's a kindness in His justice,
Which is more than liberty.

Our sins deserved the utmost punishment justice demanded, but the just God gave His Son to bear our load, and by the cross He was thus just, yet the justifier of all who accept the One who died in our room and stead. What a different end Pilate would have had had he liberated the "Just Man" who had troubled his wife's dreams.

G. *His Guilelessness*

Beilby Porteus, 1731-1808, in his poem on Death, gives us a sketch of a godly soul within his ken:

In sober state,
Through the sequester'd vale of rural
life,
The venerable Patriarch guileless
held
The tenor of his way.

Such honesty and simple-mindedness in character constitute an enviable virtue. Guile, when it represents duplicity or trickery, is to be deplored. This is the aspect John Milton expresses in *Paradise Lost* when he describes Satan as

The infernal serpent; he it was,
whose guile
Stirr'd up with envy and revenge,
deceived
The mother of mankind.

That the Bible has some practical and pointed things to say about guile and guilelessness is evident from the following verses:

Forecast: "Blessed is the man . . . in whose spirit there is no guile" (Ps. 32:2).

"Keep . . . thy lips from speaking guile" (Ps. 34:13).

Fulfillment: "Laying aside all . . . guile . . . Neither was guile found in His mouth" (I Pet. 2:1, 22).

Jesus could say of Nathaniel that he was an Israelite in whom there was no guile, but the Master Himself, as a truer Israelite, was the most guileless man who ever breathed. Guileless, or harmless, means freedom from evil, or the admixture of evil, or transparency of character — a lamblike disposition. Thus, the redeemed from among men, first-fruits unto the

Lamb are spoken of as having no guile in their mouths (Rev. 14:4, 5).

When Paul told the carnal Corinthians that he caught them with guile (II Cor. 12:16), he was apparently quoting the language of his critics. We should not misunderstand the apostle's assertion, "Being crafty, I caught you with guile." This was not a phase of Satanic subtlety he previously warned the Corinthians against (11:3). The word *guile* itself means "a bait for fish or a snare for fowls," and represents any cunning contrivance for deceiving or catching. In a right way, without any evil trickery, Paul, in a wise way, laid a trap to make the ungenerous Corinthians give more liberally to the support of the apostles. To coin a phrase, it was a kind of *guileless* guile he adopted, a virtue all of us must emulate if we would be as wise as serpents, yet harmless as doves.

H. *His Spotlessness*

P. B. Shelley, the poet, could write of Sir Philip Sidney that he was "Sublimely mild, a Spirit without spot," a sentiment true of Him who was "holy, harmless and undefiled." In Bible usage, to be "without spot" implies a person without any bodily defect or stains or marks, and goes back to the Levitical law under which the lambs offered in sacrifice to God had to be without any bodily blemish (Exod. 12:5).

Forecast: "Bring thee a red heifer without spot" (Num. 19:2).

"Lift up thy face without spot" (Job 11:15).

"There is no spot in thee" (Song of Sol. 4:7).

Fulfillment: "Offered himself without spot" (Heb. 9:14).

"As of a lamb without blemish and without spot" (I Pet. 1:19).

"Found of him, in peace without spot" (II Pet. 3:14).

Jesus is the perfect Saviour, well able to remove our evil stains, because of His own spotlessness. He left the world, in spite of all He had to endure, without a stain on His character. When His church is complete and glorified it will be without "spot, or wrinkle, or any such thing . . . without blemish" (Ephes. 5:27). Presently, we are spotted and blemished (II Pet. 2:13), but it is assuring to know that His blood can wash away all stains. In "Macbeth," Shakespeare makes one of the characters say, "Out, damned spot! out, I say," but there was no one and nothing to "raze out the written troubles of the brain." Bless God, there is radical cure for the life or garment spotted by the world, flesh, and the Devil! It is found at Calvary, where the spotless Son of God died.

I. *His Innocency*

Harmless, guileless, spotless, innocent are simply rays of the unflecked holiness Jesus manifested while on the earth. He never offended in one point. Although severely tempted of the Devil, He remained innocent of any transgression. In every phase of life, He was impeccable, faultless. Applied to Him, *innocent* implies "not deserving punishment," because He was guiltless. To condemn and kill a known innocent man is a dastardly crime. The religious leaders made haste to shed innocent blood, once Pilate declared that he was innocent of shedding "the blood of such a just person as Jesus."

Forecast: "I will wash mine hands in innocency" (Ps. 26:6; 73:13).

"Strive not with a man without cause, if he have done thee no harm" (Prov. 3:30; I Sam. 19:5).

"Innocency was found in me" (Dan. 6:22).

Fulfillment: "I have betrayed the innocent blood" (Matt. 27:4).

"Jesus . . . harmless, undefiled" (Heb. 7:22, 26).

"Harmless, the sons of God" [and as the Son of God] (Phil. 2:15).

Robert Browning wrote the phrase, "Ignorance is not innocence but sin." Adam was created innocent, but not with ignorance. Coming from the hand of the Creator, he was complete in every way and therefore had a mind comprehending all around him. Alas! he was not long losing his innocency. But Jesus was born innocent, and His innocency was never lost. John Milton says, "Assuredly we bring not innocence into the World, we bring impurity much rather." Condemnation becomes ours when we allow original sin, with which we are born, to develop into practiced sin. We speak about being as "innocent as a child," but as soon as a child knows the difference between right and wrong, and follows the wrong, the fragrance of innocence vanishes.

J. *His Obedience*

To quote Milton the blind poet, yet again, he would have us remember:

> Wouldst thou approve thy constancy, approve
> First thy obedience.

Born into a human family, obedience was the first lesson Jesus learned, and because He learned to love and exhibit this admirable quality, He was ever constant and true. "Keep ye the Law – be swift in all obedience," wrote Rudyard Kipling, and Jesus never deviated from the Law, but was swift in obedience to its enactments regarding God and also earthly relations and obligations. In one of her expressive children's hymns, C. F. Alexander has the couplet:

> Christian children all must be
> Mild, *obedient*, good as He.

Forecast: "If ye will obey my voice indeed . . . ye shall be a peculiar treasure unto me" (Exod. 19:5; Jer. 11:7).

"I have obeyed the voice of the LORD" (I Sam. 15:20).

"Obey the voice of the LORD your God" (Jer. 26:13).

"Jacob obeyed his father and his mother" (Gen. 28:7).

Fulfillment: "By the obedience of one" (Rom. 5:19).

"The obedience of Christ" (II Cor. 10:5).

"Learned he obedience by the things which he suffered" (Heb. 5:8).

"He . . . became obedient unto death" (Phil 2:8).

"He . . . was subject (obedient) unto them (His parents)" (Luke 2:51). Our Lord did not obey His heavenly Father because He *had* to. He never found obedience a hard yoke, or an irksome task. He delighted to do His Father's will. He could confess:

> Now have I found obedience that is joy,
> Not pain, not conflict of the heart and mind,
> But harmony of human souls with God.

Faber has taught us to sing that obedience to

> God's will on earth is always joy,
> Always tranquility.

We are truly "obedient children" (I Pet. 1:14) if we follow Christ as the supreme example of obedience to God. Saintly George Herbert left us a prayer to offer in sincerity:

> Oh let Thy sacred Will
> All Thy delight in me fulfill!
> Let me not think an action mine own way,
> But as Thy love shall sway,
> Resigning up the rudder to Thy skill!

K. *His Zeal*

One of the twelve apostles Jesus selected was "Simon called Zelotes" (Luke 6:15). *Zelotes* being the Greek for "a zealous one." In those far off days the "Zealots" were members of a patriotic party of the Jews inspired by Judas the Galilean against the Romans when Cyrenius was Governor. Later the term degenerated when the "Zealots" became a band of assassins. After meeting Jesus, the zeal of Simon was directed into the channel of His service. The word *zeal* is from a root meaning "to boil, seethe," and in a wrong sense covers any vehement passion, especially jealousy. In a right sense it implies enthusiasm, fervor, warmth in endeavor.

Forecast: "The zeal of the LORD of hosts shall do this" (II Kings 19:31).

"The zeal of thine house hath eaten me up" (Ps. 69:9).

"He . . . was clad with zeal as a cloak" (Isa. 59:17).

"He was zealous for his God" (Num. 25:13).

Fulfillment: "The zeal of thine house hath eaten me up" (John 2:17).

"I must work the works of him that sent me" (John 9:4).

"And the child grew, and waxed strong in spirit" (Luke 2:40).

"I must be about my Father's business" (Luke 2:49).

The fire of enthusiasm to accomplish all He had been sent to do ever burned upon the altar of His heart. Like the fire in the Tabernacle millenniums before His birth, it never went out. How apt are the lines of Browning at this point:

> Belief's fire, once in us
> Makes all else mere stuff to show it itself!
> We penetrate our life with such a glow
> As fire lends wood and iron,
> Enthusiasm's the best thing, I repeat!

That zeal can be misdirected is indicated by Paul in his description of those who had "a zeal of God, but not according to knowledge" (Rom. 10:2; See Phil. 3:6). The apostle, however, commended the Corinthians for the right brand of zeal — "What vehement desire, yea, what zeal!" (II Cor. 7:11; 9:2). The "great zeal" of Epaphras likewise earned the praise of Paul (Col. 4:13). Having suffered from the wrong kind of zeal, the apostle set high value upon true zeal inspired by the Spirit (Acts 22:3; Gal. 1:14), and exhorted the saints ever to be "zealous of spiritual gifts" (I Cor. 14:12).

Many years ago a pastor friend of mine spoke of a sermon he preached on "Sinners, Saints, and Cinders." I could imagine what he had to say about the first two categories, but the last puzzled me. "What were the cinders?" I asked. "Burnt out saints!" he replied. He meant those who had lost their early fire. Ashes instead of a flame were on the altar. They still went the round of religious activities, but the old-time enthusiasm had evaporated, and they had need to be zealous again, and repent (Rev. 3:19).

> O not for Thee my fading fires
> The ashes of my heart.

Do you remember the sigh of Longfellow:

> O bring us back once more
> The vanished days of yore,
> When the world with Faith was filled!
> Bring back the fervid zeal,
> The hearts of fire and steel,
> The hands that believe and build.

L. *His Meekness*

The virtue of meekness, lowliness of heart, or the absence of fleshly ostentation should be the possession of all those who follow Him who, living under the dominion of proud Rome, was meek and lowly in heart. Born in humble circumstances, Jesus remained clothed in humility.

> With taunts and scoffs they mock what seems Thy meekness,
> With blows and outrage adding pain to pain:
> Thou art unmoved and steadfast in Thy meekness;
> When I am wrong'd, how quickly I complain.

What a spirit of meekness and modesty was His! What grandeur of humility He manifested! He did not shun the lowest seat. He walked through the valley of nothingness, as the prophets said He would. His was the stainless peace of blest humility.

His life when here, as well as birth,
Was but a check to pomp and mirth;
And all men's greatness you may see
Condemn'd by His humility.

Forecast: "He is brought as a lamb to the slaughter" (Isa. 53:7).

"He is . . . lowly, and riding upon an ass" (Zech. 9:9).

"The meek shall inherit the earth" (Ps. 37:11).

"Thou hast made him a little lower than the angels" (Ps. 8:5).

"Who remembered us in our low estate" (Ps. 136:23).

Fulfillment: "That it might be fulfilled which was spoken by the prophet . . . thy King cometh unto thee, meek" (Matt. 21:4, 5).

"I am meek and lowly in heart" (Matt. 11:29).

"I Paul . . . beseech you by the meekness and gentleness of Christ" (II Cor. 10:1).

Such meekness must not be interpreted as a weak or supine attitude. Jesus was no "Simple Simon," as His firm, defiant, and courageous handling of the Pharisees when He drove them from the Temple proves. Meek and humble, He was yet capable of righteous indignation against all forms of hypocrisy. The quality of meekness so often commended in the Bible is a mark of true discipleship (Ephes. 4:2; Phil. 2:5-8; Titus 3:2; I Pet. 3:15, etc.). This commended and commanded meekness implies the ability to endure all things with an even temper, and to shun all haughty self-sufficiency. It is gentleness in action, the exhibition of tenderness in bearing with others.

Jesus! Who deemdst it not unmeet
To wash Thine our disciples' feet,
Though THOU were Lord of All:
Teach me thereby this wisdom meek,
That they who self-abasement seek
Alone shall fear no fall.

M. *His Mercy*

An outstanding feature of the divine dealing of a world of sinners lost and ruined by the Fall is that of mercifulness (Ps. 78:38).

With mercy and with judgment,
My web of time He wove.

The mercy of the Lord is akin to the tender, compassionate spirit He exhibited toward saint and sinner alike. He was in no way self-opinionated when He said, "I will have mercy on whom I will have mercy," for mercy, tenderness. and compassion represent the divine character. In English literature there is nothing comparable to Shakespeare's tribute in "The Merchant of Venice" to the transcendant attribute of divine mercy:

The quality of mercy is not strained.
It droppeth as the gentle rain from heaven
Upon the place beneath. It is twice blest:
It blesseth him that gives and him that takes.
'Tis mightiest in the mightiest; it becomes
The throned monarch better than his crown.
His sceptre shows the force of temporal power,
The attribute to awe and majesty,
Wherein doth sit the dread and fear of kings;
But mercy is above the sceptred sway;
It is enthroned in the hearts of kings;
It is an attribute to God himself,
And earthly power doth then show likest God's
When mercy seasons justice. Therefore, Jew,
Though justice be thy plea, consider this,
That, in the course of justice, none of us
Should see salvation. We do pray for mercy,
And that same prayer doth teach us all to render
The deers of mercy (act IV, Sc. I).

Forecast: "The LORD is . . . of great mercy" (Num. 14:18).

"I will trust in the mercy of God" (Pss. 52:8; 59:10, etc.).

"Thy mercy, O LORD, held me up" (Ps. 94:18).

"To the LORD our God belong mercies" (Dan. 9:9).

"I will...have compassion on them" (Jer. 12:15; Lam. 3:22).

Fulfillment: "Jesus had compassion on them" (Matt. 20:34).

"He was moved with compassion" (Matt. 9:36; Luke 15:20).

"To perform the mercy promised" (Luke 1:72).

"Jesus, Master, have mercy on us" (Luke 17:13).

"The merciful... shall obtain mercy" (Matt. 5:7).

What a proof of divine inspiration it is to see how performance completely matches prediction when it comes to the delineation of our Lord's character! How He revealed Himself as our merciful high priest, personifying the divine mercy so prominent in Old Testament Scriptures! Such mercy is divine compassion in action, the effort to relieve the ills of others, which is more than mere pity. A cry for mercy implies a sense of guilt and is a cry the merciful Saviour quickly responds to. Ebenezer Elliott (1781-1849) wrote "the People's Anthem," a verse of which reads

> When wilt Thou save the people?
> Oh, God of Mercy! when?
> The people, Lord, the people!
> Not thrones and crowns, but men!

But is not this question unwarranted since we know that God waits to be merciful to the repentant? Jesus was deeply moved with compassion as He saw the multitudes as sheep without a shepherd, but they would not turn to Him that they might have life. As soon as the cry, "God, be merciful to me a sinner" reaches His compassionate ear, response is immediate. Once we are made the recipients of His mercy, it is incumbent upon us to exhibit the same virtue. Shakespeare asks, "How shalt thou hope for mercy, rendering none?" Does not James remind us that "he shall have judgment without mercy, that hath shewed no mercy; and mercy rejoiceth against judgment" (2:13)?

N. *His Forgiveness*

Divine forgiveness is the outworking of divine mercy because it means the acquittal of the guilty seeking mercy. The heart moved with compassion is the heart ready to forgive. In Biblical usage, "to forgive," means to graciously remit a person's debt or sin, or to set him at liberty from his guilt. Prophecy and history are combined in the forgiveness offered the sinner under grace. As the *Zondervan Pictorial Bible Dictionary* has it, "Those forgiven by God *before* the Incarnation were forgiven because of Christ, whose death was foreordained from Eternity. Christ's atonement was *retroactive* in its effect" (Heb. 11:40). The only ground of the forgiveness of our sin is Christ's death and Resurrection coupled with our sincere repentance for committed sin. In this respect, all sin remains unpardonable, if offered pardon is rejected.

Forecast: "Forgive thy people that have sinned" (I Kings 8:50).

"Thou, LORD, art good and ready to forgive" (Ps. 86:5).

"To the LORD our God belong... forgivenesses" (Dan. 9:9).

Fulfillment: "The Son of man hath power on earth to forgive sins" (Matt. 9:6).

"For Christ's sake hath forgiven you" (Ephes. 4:32).

"Father, forgive them; for they know not what they do" (Luke 23:34).

"He is faithful and just to forgive us our sins" (I John 1:9).

If, as Alexander Pope reminds us, "To err is human, to forgive, divine," how grateful we should be that as erring humans we can receive forgiveness from Him who is to be feared. Too often we forget that if divinely forgiven it is our obligation to manifest such a grace in our dealings with others. Forgiven by God for Christ's sake, we are to be "kind one to another, tenderhearted, forgiving one another." Faber would have us know that

> 'Tis not enough to weep my sins —
> 'Tis but one step to Heaven:
> When I am kind to others, then
> I know myself Forgiven.

Ever being in need of the forgiveness Jesus secured by His cross, the least that we can do is to forgive. There may be times when it seems impossible to forgive those who have caused us much harm, but He who forgave the men who murdered Him can enable us to forgive. Is this not the sentiment Tennyson expressed in the following lines?

> O Man, forgive thy mortal foe,
> Nor ever strike him blow for blow;
> For all the souls on earth that live
> To be forgiven must forgive —
> Forgive him seventy times and seven!
> For all the blessed souls in Heaven
> Are both Forgivers and Forgiven.

O. *His Patience*

The divine teacher, who, in instructing His disciples in the art of patience, said, "In your patience possess ye your souls," came as the personification of prophesied patience. In every particular His life illustrated His teaching, as can be seen in the way He bore reproach and silently endured the insults heaped upon Him. What a perfect model of longsuffering Jesus is! He far outstripped Job, who is held out to us as an outstanding example of patience under trial. Divine patience is never exhausted. Dear old George Herbert said, "God takes a text, and preacheth patience." The revelation of the Gospels is that God took His Son and by Him preached patience. F. Von Logan (1605-1655) wrote that

> Though the mills of God grind
> slowly, yet they grind exceeding small;
> Though with Patience He stands
> waiting, with exactness grinds
> He all.

Forecast: "The patient waiting for Christ" (II Thess. 3:5).

"I waited patiently for the LORD" (Ps. 40:1).

"He was oppressed, and he was afflicted, yet he opened not his mouth" (Isa. 53:7).

"He shall not fail nor be discouraged" (Isa. 52:4).

"The LORD, The LORD God . . . longsuffering" (Exod. 34:6).

"The longsuffering of God waited in the days of Noah" (I Pet. 3:20).

Fulfillment: "LORD, have patience with me" (Matt. 18:26; Rom. 15:4, 5).

"A companion . . . in the patience of Jesus" (Rev. 1:9; 13:10).

"(Herod) questioned with Him . . . but he answered him nothing" (Luke 23:9).

"Let us not be weary in well doing . . . faint not" (Gal. 6:9).

"Jesus Christ might shew forth all longsuffering" (I Tim. 1:16).

"The longsuffering of our LORD is salvation" (II Pet. 3:15).

Christ's brief sojourn on earth was one long sermon on patience and long-suffering, or long on suffering. Think of those thirty silent years He spent in Nazareth waiting patiently for the hour of His anointing for service! But He was not discouraged as He lingered in the shadows. He knew His hour would come. Yet when it came, how patient He was with His erring, backward disciples and with His jealous foes. How truly He exemplified the Pauline cameo of love suffereth long and is kind! Jesus never at any time revealed the least trace of impatience or of undue haste. Calmly He waited — and still waits — for the fulfillment of the divine purpose.

> Thy work this hour is Patience! —
> If the Past
> Hath set its image there where
> naught decays,
> Deny not its own work to this thy
> last,

Strong yearnings ever mark'd thy vanished days,
And outstretch'd longings after absent ways;
That all is past; and now thy heart incline
To Heaven's all-gracious Will thyself resign! —
The Heavenly kingdom this; and this is Life Divine.

P. *His Benevolence*

Benevolence, or bountifulness in a person, means that he or she has a personal graciousness in doing good, has a kind disposition bent on dispensing favors. Such was the virtue of Him who is described as going about doing good, which goodness was divinely inspired, for God was with Jesus in the bestowal of benefits. At Calvary, ungrateful beneficiaries crucified goodness (Acts 10: 38, 39). They tried to destroy the fountain of heavenly bounty. But, as Shakespeare reminds us in "Measure For Measure," "Virtue is bold, and goodness never fearful." As the predicted and personified goodness of God, Jesus was never fearful, even when His kindness of heart was rejected. Robert Burns, the Scottish bard, could write of

The heart benevolent and kind
The most resembles God.

Forecast: "He hath dealt bountifully with me" (Ps. 13:6).

"Who daily loadeth us with benefits" (Pss. 68:19; 116:12).

"Thou shalt deal bountifully with me" (Ps. 142:7).

"They that exercise authority... are called benefactors" (Luke 22:25).

Fulfillment: "Jesus went about... teaching ... preaching ... healing" (Matt. 4:23, 24).

"The Son of man came ... to minister" (Matt. 20:28; Mark 10:45).

"Jesus ... went about doing good" (Acts 10:38).

"The words of the Lord Jesus ... It is more blessed to give than to receive" (Acts 20:35).

The word "benefit," we are told, denotes kindness or favor on the part of the benefactor, and gratitude and respect on the part of the beneficiary. Alas, the angels coming down loaded with benefits material, physical, and spiritual return to heaven with hands empty of thanks and praise from earth! The psalmist asked, "What shall I render unto the LORD for all his benefits toward me?" (116:12). One response was to pay his vows, or give God His full due. One of the beautiful traits of the earthly life of Jesus was His kindness toward some who treated Him most unkindly. Those who spat on His serene face saw in His eyes the look of forgiving grace. "Reviled, He reviled not again." How true is the couplet Robert Browning gives us in *The Ring and the Book:*

'Twas a thief said the last kind word to Christ:
Christ took the kindness and forgave the theft.

Shakespeare in "The Two Gentlemen Of Verona" asks the question about "Sylvia"

Is she kind as she is fair?
For beauty lives with kindness ...

Jesus our wonderful benefactor is as fair as He is kind, but in Him beauty and benevolence are happily blended. Seraphic Samuel Rutherford loved to speak of Him "as my ever-running over Lord Jesus." Shall we not praise Him from whom all our blessings flow?

Q. *His Self-Denial*

While we appreciate the fine sentiment of Francis Bacon, "Be so true to thyself as thou be not false to others," yet the fact remains that we can only be true to others as we die to the unworthy traits of self. We are truest to ourselves when, like Jesus, we are willing to save ourselves.

The life of self is death.
The death of self is life.

William Cowper would have us remember at all times that

> Self-love no grace in sorrow sees,
> Consults her own peculiar ease;
> 'Tis all the bliss she knows:
> But nobler aims true Love employs;
> In self-denial her joy,
> In suffering her repose!

As we are to see, this is the way the Master went when He emptied Himself of all self-pity, self-comfort, self-love, and self-preservation. His life and death were a powerful illustration of the truth He taught about losing our life. But we are so slow to learn that

> If we live for self we live in vain.
> If we live for Christ we live again.

A striking example of the Master's self-denial is seen in the fact that He wrought no miracle till He was thirty years of age, and then no miracles afterwards to promote His own ease and comfort. The intention of those He wrought for the preservation of His own life was that He might reserve Himself for that to which He often distinctly alluded, namely, the sacrifice of Himself in the agony of the cross. Had He wished He could have summoned legions of angels awaiting His command (Matt. 16:21; 26:53).

Forecast: "Keep that thou hast unto thyself" (Gen. 33:9).

"I will freely sacrifice unto thee" (Ps. 54:6).

"He hath poured out his soul unto death" (Isa. 53:12).

"Though thou be little . . . out of thee shall he come" (Mic. 5:2).

Fulfillment: "Whosoever shall seek to save his life shall lose it" (Luke 17:33).

"To give his life a ransom for many" (Mark 10:45).

"He saved others; himself he cannot save" (Matt. 27:42).

'He humbled himself . . . Wherefore God also hath highly exalted him" (Phil. 2:8, 9).

How true was the jibe of the chief priests they hurled at Jesus as He died in agony and shame! "He saved others." No greater compliment could be paid Him. But those mockers were wrong when they said, "himself he cannot save." He could have saved Himself – His self. He could have made that blood-stained tree a throne, and commanded fire from heaven to destroy those gloating over His brutal death; but He died, not only for our sin, but to self. Had He saved Himself, there would have been no salvation for a lost, guilty world. He laid "in dust life's glory dead," and now "from the ground there blossoms red life that shall endless be" (II Cor. 8:9).

Paul reminds us that it is our reasonable service to present our bodies as a living sacrifice to Him who gave His all for us (Rom. 12:1). As Jesus did not please the self-life, so like Him we are not to please or pamper ourselves (Rom. 15:1-3). Henry Drummond has reminded us that "No man is called to a life of self-denial for its own sake. It is in order to be a *Compensation* which is always real and always proportionate."

Another aspect of the Master's death to self was His manifest unworldliness. The psalmist prayed that he might be kept "from men of the world" (17:14), and David's Greater Son lived out the truth about being crucified unto the world, and having the world crucified unto Him. Born to die, Jesus died all along to the inducements of the world and the flesh. In every way, He overcame the world (John 16:33). All its kingdoms had no attraction for Him (Matt. 4:8). And He exhorted men not to try and gain the world and in doing so lose their soul. Did He not pray concerning His own, "They are not of the world, even as I am not of the world" (John 17:16; See I John 2:15, 16; 3:1; 4:5)? That quaint writer Quarles would have us know

Thus in our gain become we gainful losers,
And what's enclosed, encloses and enclosers;
Now, reader, close thy book! — and then advise;
Be wisely-worldly, be not worldly-wise:
Let not thy nobler thoughts be always raking
The world's base dunghill!

R. *His Love*

Jesus could confess, "I and the Father are one," and they were indeed one in the possession of transcendant attributes, the most conspicuous of which is Love. John reminds us that "God *is* Love" (I John 3:1; 4:7, 8). Note the word "is"! Love is not only one of the divine virtues; it is an integral part of the divine being. Jesus was not only loving in all His ways, but was Himself the perfect personification of love. As prophesied, He came as the culmination of the revelation of God as a loving heavenly Father. Thus, without fear of contradiction Jesus could say, "He that hath seen me hath seen the Father."

My God, Thou art all Love!
Not one poor minute 'scapes Thy breast
But brings a favor from above —
And in this Love — I rest.

Forecast: "The Lord . . . set his love upon you" (Deut. 7:7; Ps. 91:14).

"In his love and in his pity he redeemed them" (Isa. 63:9).

"He will rest in his love" (Zeph. 3:17).

"Many waters cannot quench love" (Song of Sol. 8:7).

"I have loved thee with an everlasting love" (Jer. 31:3).

"I drew them with . . . bands of love" (Hos. 11:4).

Fulfillment: "Having loved his own . . . he loved them unto the end" (John 13:1).

"Greater love hath no man than this . . . lay down his life" (John 15:13).

"The love wherewith thou hast loved me may be in them" (John 17:26).

"God so loved . . . he gave his only begotten Son" (John 3:16).

"The love of Christ constraineth us" (II Cor. 5:14).

"Unto Him that loved us, and washed us from our sins" (Rev. 1:5). In his "Hymn of Love," Paul extols Love as the greatest of all divine and Christian virtues, as it is the very nature of God and also lies at the very heart of Christianity. Love found its supreme expression in the self-sacrifice of God's loved and loving Son at Calvary.

Inscribed upon the Cross we see,
In shining letters, *God is Love!*

Had God not been the very essence of love, He could never have been compassionate towards a world of wickedness and corruption and surrendered His well-beloved Son to die for its redemption. The liberal-minded say that it does not matter what man believes so long as he believes something. But it is of great importance *what* he believes, for that belief shapes behavior. Thus a faith that does not manifest itself in love both towards the Lord and man is dead and worthless (Gal. 5:6, 13; James 2:17-26). Tennyson wrote the lines

God give us Love. Something to love
He lends us; but, when love is grown
To ripeness, that on which it throve
Falls off, and Love is left alone.

Jean Ingelow asked the question in her "Hymn," "And didst Thou love the race that loved not Thee?" Is this not the miracle of Grace? Of old, those whom God set His love on, failed to love Him in return, yet He went on blessing them. Then when Jesus came, the world He loved nailed Him to a cross. How we should rejoice that His banner over us is LOVE, a love that will not let us go! As Whittier reminds us,

I know not where His islands lift
Their fronded palms in air;
I only know I cannot drift
Beyond His love and Care.

Does not this meditation on the prophetic profile of the character of Jesus constrain us to assert with Tennyson that "What the Sun is to the flower, Christ is to my soul." In His life among men, He was all — and more — that the prophets of old said He would be; and the fact that features of His life were described in detail and then fulfilled in like manner is overwhelming evidence of the existence and working of a mind transcending the human mind to a degree that forces us to stand in awe. Our solemn responsibility is to expressive and progressive conformity to His character — forecast and then fulfilled. Did He not come from the eternal past and die that we might be conformed to His image (Rom 8:29)? Are we being changed into the same image by the Spirit whose holy task it is to reproduce Jesus in our lives (II Cor. 3:18)?

Chapter Six

PROPHECIES OF HIS MINISTRY

To Begin in Galilee To Continue in Jerusalem To Function in the Temple	To Proclaim a Jubilee To Jews and Gentiles To Be Exercised in the Spirit	To Be a Teaching One To Be a Miraculous One

The sacred, sublime task of the Christ of prophecy when He became the Christ of history was to become the Christ of redemption. Thus He came as the pre-existent Lamb slain from before the foundation of the world. But as He moved among men after His heavenly authentication as the Sent One from the Father, how were they to know that He was the promised and prophesied Messiah? Did He have credentials corresponding to those predicted by the prophets? Was He the authoritative representative of God, or were they to look for another? Well, how did Jesus prove that He was the Son of God who came into the world to bear the iniquity of all? The evidences He gave were the life He lived, the truth He taught, and the works He wrought. As we have just considered the kind of life He lived for more than three years (the curtain is drawn over His first thirty years), we now concentrate upon His teaching and His miracles as proofs of His authenticity.

A. *His Ministry Was to Begin in Galilee*

Forecast: "Beyond Jordan, in Galilee . . . the light shined" (Isa. 9:1, 2).

Fulfillment: "Jesus . . . departed into Galilee" (Matt. 4:12-17).

B. *His Ministry Was to Continue in Jerusalem*

Forecast: "Rejoice greatly . . . shout, O daughter of Jerusalem: behold, thy King cometh" (Zech. 9:9).

Fulfillment: "They drew nigh unto Jerusalem . . . Behold, thy King cometh unto thee" (Matt. 21:1-11).

Matthew tells us that all the people of Jerusalem were moved when they saw Jesus, and asked, "Who is this?" But those who followed Him knew that He was the One of whom the prophets had spoken, and replied, "This is Jesus the prophet of Nazareth of Galilee."

C. *His Ministry Would Function in the Temple.*

Forecast: "I will fill this house with glory" (Hag. 2:7).

"The Lord . . . shall suddenly come to his temple" (Mal. 3:1).

Fulfillment: "They found him in the temple" (Luke 2:46).

"Jesus went into the temple of God" (Matt. 21:12).

D. *His Ministry Was to Proclaim a Jubilee to the World*

Forecast: "Loose the bands . . . undo the heavy burdens . . . let the oppressed go free" (Isa. 58:6).

"The spirit of the Lord God is upon me . . . to preach . . . to bind up . . . to proclaim (Isa. 61:1, 2).

Fulfillment: "He hath put down the mighty . . . as we spake to our fathers" (Luke 1:52, 55).

"He (Jesus) found the place where it was written, The Spirit of the

Lord is upon me . . . to preach . . . to heal" (Luke 4:17-18).

Our Lord's whole dignified manner in the synagogue on the Sabbath Day, His familiarity with the Old Testament, and the application of prophecy to Himself as He said; "This day is this scripture fulfilled in your ears" amazed the worshipers whose eyes were fastened upon Him, yet they only saw Him as "Joseph's son," not as the Son of God with all power and authority. His ministry maddened them, for they "were filled with wrath."

E. *His Ministry Was to Jews and Gentiles*

John reminds us that "the Father sent the Son to be the Saviour of the world" – the world Jesus said "God so loved" (John 3:16; I John 4:14). *All* have sinned, and all, whether Jews or Gentiles need to be saved, and at His birth it was declared that He would be "a light to lighten the Gentiles, and the glory of thy people Israel" (Luke 2:32).

1. *Salvation for Jews.*

Forecast: "My people hath been lost sheep" (Jer. 50:6).

"They say, . . . our hope is lost" (Ezek. 37:11).

Fulfillment: "Go rather to the lost sheep of the house of Israel" (Matt. 10:6).

"I am not sent but unto the lost sheep of the house of Israel" (Matt. 15:24).

2. *Salvation for Gentiles.*

Forecast: "Rejoice, O ye nations, with his people [Jews]" (Deut. 32:43; Ps. 18:49).

"He shall bring forth judgment to the Gentiles" (Isa. 42:1-4).

Fulfillment: "In his name shall the Gentiles trust" (Matt. 12:21).

"Will he go unto the dispersed among the Gentiles, and teach the Gentiles?" (John 7:35).

"God also to the Gentiles granted repentance unto life" (Acts 11:18).

Announcing His mission, Jesus said that He had come to seek and save the lost, not only lost Jews, but lost Gentiles. True, He was born a Jew, yet He died not only as the King of the Jews but as the Saviour of all men. He came into the world to save sinners, irrespective of their creed, caste, color, or condition. John Milton tells us that

> To the Cross He nails thine enemies,
> The Law that is against thee, and the sins
> *Of all mankind,* with HIM there crucified —
> Never to hurt them more, who rightly trust
> In this His satisfaction.

F. *His Ministry Required the Anointing with the Spirit*

Although born of the Holy Spirit and filled with Him from birth, Jesus received at His baptism before He entered upon His brief ministry not only the acclaim of the Father but the anointing with the Spirit. How amazing it is that it took God thirty years to prepare His Son for a very short ministry of some three years! God is never in a hurry when it comes to the molding of those He desires to use mightily in His service.

Forecast: "Thy God, hath anointed thee with the oil of gladness above thy fellows" (Ps. 45:7).

"The spirit of the LORD shall rest upon him, the spirit of wisdom and understanding, the spirit of counsel and might, the spirit of knowledge and of the fear of the LORD; and shall make him of quick understanding" (Isa. 11:2-3).

"The spirit of the Lord GOD is upon me" (Isa. 61:1).

Fulfillment: "The Spirit of God descending like a dove, and lighting upon him" (Matt. 3:16).

"The Spirit of the LORD is upon me" (Luke 4:18).

"God giveth not the Spirit by measure unto him" (John 3:34).

"Rivers of living water . . . this spake he of the Spirit" (John 7:39).

"Jesus returned in the power of the Spirit" (Luke 4:14).

That Jesus was anointed with the Holy Spirit "above His fellows," meaning in a manner and degree far beyond any man or men, is evident from all He accomplished among and for men. When He left heaven, Jesus died to self-reliance in that He was ever subordinate to the will of God and unceasingly dependent upon the Holy Spirit. "I, by the Spirit of God," was the secret of His wonderful words and mighty miracles. Spirit-possessed, Spirit-led, Spirit-blessed, He fulfilled the prophetic word as to the anointing He would receive. "The healthful Spirit of thy grace" was ever His portion, and in turn, became His Ascension gift to His church, whose birth took place, historically, at Pentecost.

> Dwell in us as in the Son,
> With His Father ever One
> In adoring union;
> Comforter Divine.

G. *His Ministry Was a Teaching One*

How true it is that it is the quality of a life that tells, and not its length! Methuselah lived for 969 years, but all he did, as far as the record shows, was to "begat sons and daughters," all of whom perished in the Flood, if not before it. The earthly ministry of Jesus extended to only 3½ years, but what He accomplished in that short span changed the course of history (see the author's two volumes on *The Man Who Changed The World*). His public witness, commencing when He was thirty years of age, divided itself broadly in a three-fold way:

Preaching, or proclaiming the Gospel, when, speaking generally, His appeal was to the multitude.

Teaching, or the exposition of the Gospel, which was confined to His disciples.

Healing, or the illustration of the Gospel, with the miracles as parables of grace.

All three phases are given by Matthew, who reminds us that Jesus went about all Galilee "teaching . . . preaching . . . and healing" (Matt. 4:23). In this section we are to concentrate on His unique influence as a preacher and teacher, in which realm there has never been His like. When we think of His methods, style, and themes, what those who heard Him said was a true estimate, "Never man spake like this man." As Jesus wrote nothing, all His utterances were oral, and delivered wherever people gathered by the sea, on mountain slopes, on dusty roads, and beneath a friendly roof.

Prophetic forecasts prepared the world for the coming of its greatest teacher, as the messenger of God.

1. *As a prophet.*

Forecast: "The LORD thy God will raise up unto thee a Prophet from the midst of thee, of thy brethren . . . I . . . will put my words in his mouth" (Deut. 18:15, 18).

"He that is now called a Prophet was beforetime called a Seer" (I Sam. 9:9).

Fulfillment: "A prophet is not without honour" (Matt. 13:57).

"This is Jesus the Prophet of Nazareth" (Matt. 21:11; Acts 3:20, 22).

"A great prophet is risen up among us" (Luke 7:16).

The prophet of old was the *seer* and the *announcer* of the message of Jehovah, the method of reception and delivery of divine truth being indicated by these two words, descriptive of his holy office. First, he saw (see-er) the truth, through a dream, oral word, or theophany, then proclaimed not his own personal opinions but a "Thus saith Jehovah." What he perceived, he proclaimed. Jesus was a true seer and announcer, for He could say, "We speak that we do know, and testify that we have seen." These are the two guiding terms in the divine revelation: "seen," "speak." A false prophet was one who spoke without seeing. A disobedient prophet was one who saw but failed to speak.

2. *As a preacher.*

Forecast: "It is written of me . . . I have preached . . . I have not refrained my lips, O LORD" (Ps. 40:7, 9).

"The preacher sought to find out acceptable words" (Eccles. 12:10).

"How beautiful upon the mountains are the feet of him . . . that publisheth peace . . . salvation" (Isa. 52:7).

"The LORD hath anointed me to preach" (Isa. 61:1).

Fulfillment: "From that time Jesus began to preach" (Matt. 4:17).

"The poor have the gospel preached to them" (Matt. 11:5).

"He preached the word unto them" (Mark 2:2).

"He went throughout every city and village, preaching" (Luke 8:1).

"All . . . wondered at the gracious words which proceeded out of his mouth" (Luke 4:22).

In the realm of homiletics, one of the most remarkable books on preaching is that by Dr. Albert Richmond Bond, under the title *The Master Preacher,* a book which offers preachers and students for the ministry a study on "The Homiletics of Jesus." In his unique treatise, Dr. Bond says:

> Jesus of Nazareth was the world's Master Preacher. His ministry was brief but epochal. Through His own custom and His directness for the later ministry of the Apostles Jesus created the Christian pulpit. His preaching was cast in the Oriental, Hebrew forms and was delivered to audiences that varied in size from the single listener to the vast multitude. His personality, message, and method drew attention from all classes of people. His success as a Preacher should be measured both by his personal mastery of His audiences and by His creation of the ideals that have controlled the homiletical methods of all ages. . . . The preaching of Jesus in methods and purpose is described by two Greek words which mean "the proclamation of a herald" and the publication of good tidings.

How privileged the people of His time were to listen to such a pulpiteer who preached peace to "those afar off, and to them that were nigh" (Ephes. 2:17)! Jesus will ever remain the divine ancestor of Christian preaching. To quote Bond again, "The history of oratory discovers the literary contribution to the Preaching of Jesus. The pulpit is the distinctive product of Christianity."

3. *As a teacher.*

Forecast: "Behold . . . who teacheth like him" (Job 36:22)?

"For a long season . . . without a teaching priest" (II Chron. 15:3).

"I am the LORD thy God which teacheth thee to profit" (Isa. 48:17).

Fulfillment: "Thou art a teacher come from God" (John 3:2; 8:2, 28).

"I sat daily with you teaching in the temple" (Matt. 26:55).

"He began to teach them many things" (Mark 6:34).

"Thou hast taught in our streets" (Luke 13:26; John 18:20).

While preaching and teaching contain common traits, in our Lord's oral ministry *exposition* is more prominent than *exhortation.* The characteristics of His teaching were simplicity, clarity, brevity, and picturesqueness. Great moral truths were enforced by impressive homely illustrations which, in many cases, were parables. About seventy of these are to be found in the Gospels. Narrative parables are not quite so numerous. Christ's chief method was to preach and teach by parables.

Forecast: "I will open my mouth in a parable" (Ps. 78:2).

"I will incline mine ear to a parable" (Ps. 49:4).

"Speak a parable unto the house of Israel" (Ezek. 17:2; Mic. 2:4).

Fulfillment: "He spake many things unto them in parables" (Matt. 13:3).

"Know ye not this parable . . . all parables" (Mark 4:13)?

"Unto you it is given to know . . . in parables" (Luke 8:10; 5:36).

Because of His genius in parabolic preaching, Jesus was largely responsible for the contributions of the parable to religious literature. As the word "parable" occurs forty-eight times in the first three Gospels, one can see how this method of presentation was constantly used by Jesus. In the main, His illustrations and parables reflect His observations and experiences during His thirty silent years. He lived in a home where domestic duties were unsoured by poverty and where all the simplicities of home life were carefully preserved by those whose hearts were simple. This is why He drew heavily on such for illustrative material in His preaching and teaching, giving it a heavenly application. John Oxenham wrote:

> The good intent of God became the Christ
> And lived on earth — the Living Love of God,
> That men might draw to closer touch with Heaven,
> Since Christ in all the way of man hath trod.

The memories of His home and social life in Nazareth stayed with Him and appeared in His picturesque teaching as He moved among men. Often He had watched Joseph toil and Mary spin and knew that but for them He would have had neither food or raiment. On the hillside among the lilies, He spoke of them never toiling or spinning. Boy-like, He would watch His mother's bread-pan with its heaving, fermenting mass rising to fall and falling to rise again, and saw in the gradually forming dough an illustration of the changing fortunes and ultimate triumph of the divine purpose in the world, and also a picture of Himself as being set for "the falling and rising again of many."

Guests coming late at night to the cottage, and the necessity of securing a batch of bread to feed them, and a call on a drowsy neighbor to help out, enabled Jesus to teach His disciples to knock at God's door and find Him ready and willing to help.

Every night He watched His mother light the domestic oil lamp, and its soft light shining on all in the room, and such a memory is captured in Himself as the Light of the world, and as the Light that must not be hid. Using her lamp to find a coin she had dropped and which rolled out of her sight, and then Mary's delight in finding it and calling in her friends to rejoice with her, gave Jesus a picture of heaven when lost souls are found.

Outside His humble home Jesus often saw the clucking hens calling their chicks under their wings, with some wilfully staying outside. This simple, common sight found an echo in His sob of the unwanted, when the people rejected His covering wings.

As a boy, He would join in the innocent play of children around, engaging in mock weddings and funerals, and rebuking those who would not play. When He became a teacher, remembering such a game, He could say, "We have piped unto you, and ye have not danced; we have mourned unto you, and ye have not wept."

Then there were those times when He passed a few workmen waiting for hire, clad in only one coat, or, as we would say, in their shirt-sleeves, after the custom of the time, in token they were ready for service, but no man hired them. The boy with watching eyes took it all in and in after years when He sent out His disciples, He commanded them to be clad in only one coat, a mark of earnest diligence in service.

Could He have seen one of His sisters absent-mindedly wash "the outside of the cups and plates" only and then receive Mary's rebuke for neglecting to wash the inside? Was it this backward glance that enabled Jesus to condemn the Pharisees of hypocrisy in being clean without but full of rottenness within?

We can imagine that as a lad He often helped to wash the feet of visitors and cook a meal for them in His little home. Years later He washed the feet of His disciples as He talked to them about "humility." Then there came a day when He cooked a breakfast on the lake shore for them. The reader will find it profitable to expand this connection between our Lord's home life and the use of early experiences as preaching material. Jesus came to experience what Wordsworth called "The sad, slow music of humanity." Such sources of imagery in His teaching can be conveniently summarized in this way:

Illustrations From Natural Phenomena

Sun — Light — Darkness — Lightning — Earthquakes — Fire — Clouds — Rain — Storm.

Illustrations From Animate Nature

Creatures

Camels, Oxen, Sheep, Goats, Horses, Lions, Eagles, Wolves, Serpents, Asses, Foxes, Swine, Dogs.

Plants

Olive, Sycamore, Vine, Fig, Mustard, Tree, Lilies, Reed, Thorns, Thistles, Anise, Mint, Cummin, Trees, Branches, Roots.

Illustrations From Human Life

The Physical Realm

Flesh, Blood, Eye, Ear, Hands, Feet, Hunger, Thirst, Sleep, Sickness, Laughing, Weeping, Death.

The Domestic Realm

Houses, Lamp, Seats, Food, Oven, Cooking, Bread, Salt, Birth, Husband, Mother, Sister, Brother, Children, Marriage, Service.

The Commercial Realm

Fisherman, Tailor, Potter, Builder, Merchant, Business, Money, Talents, Treasure, Debts.

The Agricultural Realm

Shepherds, Sheep Husbandmen, Soil, Tillage, Sowing, Growth, Harvest, Vineyards, Laborers.

The Civil Realm

Robbery, Violence, Judgment, Punishment, Taxes, Slavery.

The Social Realm

Marriage, Hospitality, Feasts, Salutations, Journeyings.

The Religious Realm

Alms, Tithes, Fastings, Prayer, Sabbath, Temple.

The Historical Realm

References to John the Baptist, Slaughter of the Galileans, Tower of Siloam, Herod Antipas, Herod the Tetrarch, Herod Archelaus, Good Samaritan.

The Unseen Realm

Angels, Demons, Satan, Heaven, Hell.

For a fuller treatment of our Lord's use of illustrations and parables, reference can be made to the author's volume on *All the Parables of the Bible*.

H. *His Ministry Was as a Miracle-Worker*

Having dealt with His *words*, we now come to His *works*, or the miracles He performed, which were, as He said, "the works of Him that sent me," and as such they established Christ's claims of pre-existence and deity. The miracles, manifestation of power which could not have taken place from natural causes or without superhuman aid, attested to the truth and authority of Christ's spoken word. Repeatedly, He appealed to His miracles, which no other man ever did, as an evidence of His heaven-given mission. Just as His miracles testified to His place in the Godhead, so the bestowal of miraculous gifts upon the apostles at Pentecost established the church that Christ bought with His blood as a divine institution. As with Christ, so with His church, though not thus primarily designed, the display of superhuman power accented the note of authority and compelled those who witnessed it to confess the presence of the extraordinary in the miracle-worker.

Forecast: "Shew a miracle for you" (Exod. 7:9).

"My glory, and my miracles" (Num. 14:22).

"Thine eyes have seen... those great miracles" (Deut. 11:3; 29:3).

"Where be all his miracles?" (Judg. 6:13).

"Then the eyes of the blind shall be opened" (Isa. 35:5; 42:7).

"The spirit... of might... shall rest upon him" (Isa. 11:2).

Fulfillment: "This beginning of miracles did Jesus" (John 2:11, 23).

"No man can do these miracles... except God be with him" (John 3:2).

"Will He do more miracles" (John 7:31)?

"This man doeth many miracles" (John 11:47; 12:37).

"The blind receive their sight" (Matt. 11:4, 5; Acts 2:22).

A striking difference between the miracles of Jesus and those performed by the prophets and apostles is that the latter came as answers to prayer, as, for example, when Elias prayed about rain (James 5:7, 18), but with Jesus, miracles manifestly flowed forth from the majestic life resident within Him. Further, as Canon Liddon puts it, "Christ's miracles are physical and symbolic representations of His redemptive action as the divine Saviour of mankind. Their form is carefully adapted to suit this action. By healing the palsied, the blind, the lame, Christ clothed with a visible form His plenary power to cure spiritual diseases." His miracles also manifested forth His mediatorial glory.

From the Gospels we learn that Jesus entered the world by a miracle, His Virgin Birth; and left it by another miracle, the miracle of miracles, His Resurrection and Ascension. These miracles alone prove Him to be an altogether superhuman Being. How utterly blind Matthew Arnold must have been when he said, "Miracles do not happen... The Time-Spirit is sapping the proof from miracles... The human mind, as its experience widens, is turning away from them." As Arnold has been dead for more than eighty years, he has had ample time to learn the error of his thinking. If a miracle is an alteration of the established course of nature, then surely the One who created nature can interrupt its recognized course if He deems fit. A comprehensive coverage of the miraculous in Scripture can be found in the author's volume *All the Miracles of the Bible.* How appealing are the lines of Jean Ingelow:

> What is thy thought? — *There is no miracle?*
> There is a great one, which thou hast not read,
> And never shalt escape — *Thyself,* O man! —
> *Thou* art the Miracle...
> Thou art thy Father's copy of HIMSELF! —
> Thou art thy Father's Miracle!
> MAN is the Miracle in nature. God
> Is the One Miracle to man! Behold!
> "There is a God," thou sayest. Thou sayest well;
> In that thou sayest all. TO BE is more
> Of wonderful, than, being, to have wrought,
> Or reigned, or rested!

Chapter Seven

PROPHECIES OF HIS DUAL NATURE

The Son of God – Deity	The Master's Tears	The Master's Joy
The Son of Man – Humanity	The Master's Hunger	The Master's Sorrows
His Human Body	The Master's Thirst	The Master's Love
His Human Soul	The Master's Sleep	The Master's Anger
His Human Limitations	The Master's Weariness	The Master's Compassion
His Human Emotions and Experiences	The Master's Toil	The Master's Humility
	The Master's Poverty	The Master's Prayers
	The Master's Temptations	The Master's Amazement

We have now reached a phase of our study as mysterious as it is marvelous, incomprehensible as it is inspiring, namely, that of our Lord's dual nature, or two persons in a single indivisible personality. Dr. Handley Moule remarks that "God did not send His Son to join a man born of a woman; which would have been an alliance of two persons, not a harmony of two natures related to one person." That man should be made in God's image was a wonder, but that God should be made in man's image is a greater wonder. A recognition of this wonderful truth is basic in the meditation of any aspect of His messianic activities. It was at His birth that the mingling of His two natures took place, for in the womb of Mary the Holy Spirit fused deity and humanity together, becoming the Creator of the love-knot between God and man. Thus, Jesus appeared not as God exclusively or as man exclusively, but as the unique combination of the God-Man, very God and perfect man in one body. God became manifest in the flesh. "Veiled in flesh the Godhead see." Zechariah has the impressive prediction, "Awake, O sword, against my shepherd, and against the man that is my fellow, saith the LORD of hosts" (13:7). Here the prophet speaks of the Messiah, not only as the coming shepherd, but as the One co-equal with God, "my fellow," one who is one with me yet who is also the man, "the man Christ Jesus," "equal with God."

Then another remarkable feature of this divinely-conceived union of two natures is that it altered the composition. From the past eternity the three members of the Godhead had been one in essence – the same in that they had no visible form.

The First Person of the Trinity was referred to in this manner by Jesus: God is Spirit.

The Third Person of the Trinity is spoken of some 100 times in the Bible as the Holy Spirit.

The Second Person of the Trinity until His birth must have shared the same entity, but His Incarnation brought about a dramatic change. He was no longer *Spirit*, so we have the invitation of Jesus: "Behold my hands and my feet, that it is I myself; handle me, and see; for a spirit hath not flesh and bones, as ye see me have" (Luke 24:39).

God the Son is no longer a *Spirit*-form, but has hands and feet, and can be handled. Now, the amazing wonder in heaven is a visible Person of the Trinity clothed in humanity's dust, glorified. The human body the Holy Spirit prepared for Jesus, and in which He lived and died, was raised from the grave, and taken up to heaven when He ascended on high. An aspect of "the blessed hope" is that we are to see Him "as He is," that is, in His glorified body, and seeing Him we are to be like Him, meaning, possessing a "glorious body," or as Paul expresses it, "fashioned like unto his glorious body" (Phil. 3:21; I John 3:1-3).

The miracle of the Incarnation, then, was the transformation of Christ, who had been "in the form of God," into "the form of a servant, and made in the likeness of men." God sent His own Son, who had shared His *likeness* from the dateless past, to earth made in the likeness of sinful flesh, but with sin excluded (Rom. 8:3; Phil. 2:7). When we read "The spirit of the LORD came upon Gideon," the phrase "came upon" literally means "clothed Himself with Gideon" – deity covered humanity. This is the same word used by Jesus before His Ascension: "I send the promise of my Father upon you (to clothe you)" (Judg. 6:34; Luke 24: 49). Paul employs the same term, "put on Christ," clothe yourself with Christ (Gal. 3:27). When Peter urges us to be "clothed with humility," he uses this word indicating a covering (I Pet. 5:5).

Thus our Lord's dual nature meant that God clothed Himself with man, and man was clothed with God. God the Son, becoming man, humanized deity, and deified humanity. Throughout His mission, these two natures were never separated but acted in unison, as His miracles prove. As the human One, Jesus enjoyed the marriage at Cana, but as God He turned the water into wine. As the man, He knew what it was to require sleep, but as the God He calmed the angry deep when the boat in which He slept was rocked by the storm. As the man, He could weep with those who wept at Bethany, but as God He was able to raise from the dead the friend He loved. Is this not a source of comfort for our hearts? As the man Christ Jesus, He knows all about our human need, but as God our Saviour, He is able to meet any and every need that may arise. Having considered His two natures conjointly let us now deal with them separately.

A. *The Son of God – Deity*

Already we have seen how our Lord's theophanic, or pre-Incarnation, appearances testify to His preexistence and deity and to His position in the Godhead. Three simple words form the most vital question that can be asked of Jesus of Nazareth, *was He God?* This is not a question we can equivocate about. Each of us must answer a *Yes* or *No*. If we have wrong views about His deity, we cannot have right views about other aspects of the Christian faith. The question Was He God? forms the cleavage line between orthodoxy and heterodoxy. If we can join with John in affirming, "We know that the Son of God is come . . . and we are in him that is true, even in his Son Jesus Christ. This is the true God, and eternal life" (I John 5:20), then we are safe and secure for time and eternity.

While the terms *deity* and *divinity* convey the same truth of Christ being God, we prefer the former term, as the latter has been given wider connotations. Modernists speak of the "divine" in man, a God-spark that only needs fanning. We refer to a sunset or a painting as being "divine." Madame Bernhardt, the renowned singer, is billed as "The *divine* Sarah." But deity, from *deus*, means "God," and cannot be used of a man. Predictions and performances of Christ's deity abound.

Forecast: "The LORD hath said unto

me, Thou art my Son" (Ps. 2:7, 12).

"He is thy Lord; and worship thou him" (Ps. 45:11).

"I will make him my firstborn, higher than the kings of the earth" (Ps. 89:27).

"The LORD said unto my Lord" (Ps. 110:1).

"The mighty God" (Isa. 9:6).

"He will save us: this is the LORD" (Isa. 25:9).

"The Lord GOD will come with strong hand" (Isa. 40:10).

"He shall be called, THE LORD OUR RIGHTEOUSNESS" (Jer. 23:6).

"Ruler in Israel; whose goings forth have been from of old, from everlasting" (Mic. 5:2).

Fulfillment: "This is my beloved Son, in whom I am well pleased" (Matt. 3:17).

"Where is he that is born king... we... are come to worship him" (Matt. 2:2).

"The firstborn among many brethren" (Rom. 8:29; Col. 1:15).

"My Lord and my God" (John 20:28).

"Whence hath this man... these mighty works" (Matt. 13:54; Luke 24:19).

"God our Saviour... the great God and our Saviour" (Titus 2:10, 13).

"Strong is the Lord God who judgeth" (Rev. 18:8; Luke 11:22).

"Christ Jesus, who of God is made unto us... righteousness" (I Cor. 1:30).

"Thou lovedst me before the foundation of the world" (John 17:24).

In addition to these instances of expectation and manifestation, we have the evidence of Christ's miracles as to His deity, which declared Him to be the Son of God with power. For a full treatment of all the miracles He performed, proving Him to be "the mighty God," reference is made to the author's volume *All the Miracles of the Bible.* All we can cite at this point is a general classification of same.

Christ had power over diseases in all their ramifications in the human race. He had power over all the elements of Nature, power over sin and death, power over demons, power over hades and the spirit world.

Further, Christ's inclusion in the Trinity is a further proof of His deity. As God the Son, He is associated with God the Father and God the Spirit in at least seven vital aspects of our Faith:

In *election* (I Pet. 1:2). All three are in unison in creation and redemption.

In *redemption* (Heb. 9:12, 14). All three were involved at Calvary.

In *sonship* (Rom. 8:16, 17). All three are linked on to heirship.

In *baptism* (Matt. 28:19). All three are the guarantee of acceptance.

In *judgment* (Heb. 2:3, 4). All three witness to our negligence.

In *benediction* (II Cor. 13:14). All three bless us in their own way.

In *revelation* (Rev. 1:4, 5; 22:17-21). Seal of deity is the last verse.

Then the oft-repeated term "The Son of God" is eloquent with the truth of His deity. It indicates the verity of His statement as "the faithful and true witness" that He is "the beginning of the creation of God" (Rev. 3:14). The title "The Son of God" is never used of His supernatural birth, because it was not by birth that this relationship was brought about, but by the election of God in a past eternity. He was God's eternal Son before He became the Son of Mary. Thus, when He is referred to as "The Son of the Father," there is emphasized the complete and solemn setting forth of the union of Jesus with the Father in the essence of the Godhead, a union existing before the world began. A kindred title, "The Son of the Highest," has a theocratic significance, and points to Him as God's anointed king as predicted (II Sam. 7:14; Ps. 2:7).

The one Old Testament reference to "The Son of God" (Dan. 3:25) is given in the R.V. as "a son of the gods" and was evidently a phrase spoken by a heathen. In the New Testament, it is the exclusive title of Jesus, except once when it is used of Adam (Luke 3:38). The title is more common in the R.V. than in the A.V., occurring forty-four times in reference to Jesus, and always represents a special relationship. As the same nature of God, Jesus is of the Father, sent by the Father as the instrument of the Father's will. There are scores of passages in which Jesus called God "Father," and other passages in which He is called "The Son," and "The Beloved Son."

Angels are spoken of as "sons of God" (Job 1:6; 38:7), and so are Christians (Rom. 8:14, 19). All men may be the creatures of God but are not His sons. The ungodly are not God's children. *Son* implies a relationship by birth, and sinners can only become sons of God by the regenerating power of the Spirit (John 1:11-13; 3:7). It is most important to observe that Christ *alone* is "The Son of God," and distinguishes Himself as such from the sons of God when He says, "My Father, and your Father" (John 20:17). The deity of Jesus Christ could not be more fitly or forcibly expressed than in the opening sentence of Mark's Gospel: "The beginning of the Gospel of Jesus Christ, the Son of God." Mark then goes on to declare His deity in every chapter.

Christ, then, is not one among many sons, but the Only, the well-beloved Son of the Father—a relationship unshared by any other, and absolutely unique—a revelation of which was given to Peter by the Father leading him to exclaim, "Thou art the Christ, the Son of the Living God." Aspects of this wonderful Sonship are:

It was the claim made for Jesus by John the Baptist (Matt. 3:16, 17; Mark 1:10, 11).

It was substantiated at the Transfiguration (Matt. 17:5; Mark 9:7; Luke 9:35).

It was Christ's insistence upon this relationship which incensed the Sanhedrin, causing it to denounce the claim as blasphemy (Matt. 26:63-66).

It was accepted by Paul and the apostles without question, and given the central place in their preaching (Rom. 1:4).

A companion title to "The Son of God" is "The Son of the Highest," as already indicated. The Holy Spirit as "The Power of the Highest" overshadowed Mary in the preparation of a human body for Christ, who, when He came would be "The Son of the Highest." God is described as The Highest: "The Highest himself" (Pss. 18:13; 87:5), and as the Highest receives the praises of men and angels (Luke 2:14; 6:35). Christ came as the day-star from on high, bringing a new day to those who sat in the darkness and death shadows of the world. Christopher Smart (1722-1771) composed a somewhat remarkable hymn under the title "The Son of David," the last verse of which magnifies Him as the Son, obedient unto death.

> Glorious — more glorious is the
> crown
> Of Him that brought salvation down
> By meekness, call'd *Thy Son;*
> Thou that stupendous truth believed,
> And now the matchless deed's
> achiev'd,
> Determined, dared, and done.

B. *The Son of Man—Humanity*

If the title "Son of God" forcefully expresses His God-consciousness, the companion title "Son of Man" most strongly emphasizes His messianic consciousness. The main distinction between these two most prominent titles is clearly evident. As "Son of God," Jesus is related to His heavenly Father; as "Son of Man," He is related to His dominion in the earth. Benjamin Warfield, in his monumental work *The Lord of Glory,* says of the designation before us:

> It intimates on every occasion of its employment our Lord's consciousness of being a super-mundane Being, Who has entered into a sphere of earthly life on a high mission, on the accomplishment of which He is to return to His heavenly sphere, whence He shall in due season come back to earth, how, however, in His proper majesty to gather up the fruits of His work and consummate all things. It is a designation, therefore, which implies at once *a heavenly pre-existence, a present humiliation,* and a future glory; and He proclaims Himself in this future glory no less than the universal King seated on the throne of Judgment for quick and dead (Matt. 25:31; Mark 8:38).

Forecast: "God is not a man, that he should lie; neither the son of man, that he should repent" (Num. 23:19).

"The son of man, which is a worm" (Job 25:6).

"Son of man, stand upon thy feet, and I will speak to thee" (Ezek. 2:1).

"Understand, O son of man" (Dan. 8:17).

To Daniel the prophet the ultimate triumph was to be "one like the Son of man" over the beasts which envisaged victory over humanity itself (Dan. 7:13, 14, 17).

Fulfillment: "The Devil . . . is a liar . . . I tell you the truth" (John 8:44, 45).

"I am a worm . . . a reproach of men . . . despised" (Ps. 22:6; Isa. 53:3; Matt. 27:30, 31).

"I have given unto them the words which thou gavest me" (John 17:8).

"All that heard him were astonished at his understanding" (Luke 2:47).

Because of the many times "Son of Man" appears in the Gospels we cannot enumerate all references to the title, which signifies humanity itself, not merely what it resembles, but what essentially belongs to man. The title is never used of the Lord by anyone but Himself in the Gospels, where it occurs some eighty-five times. He almost always calls Himself the Son of Man. Paley observes that "The title *Son of Man* is in all the Gospels found under the peculiar circumstances of its being applied by Christ to Himself, but of never being used of Him, or towards Him, by any other person. It occurs 17 times in Matthew's Gospel, 12 times in Mark, 21 times in Luke, and 11 times in John, and always with this restriction." Outside the Gospels it appears four times: Acts 7:56; Hebrews 2:6; Revelation 1:3 and 14:14. The first and last references afford a striking contrast:

"The Son of Man *has nowhere to lay his head*" (Matt. 8:20 R.V.).

"The Son of man, *having on His head a golden crown*" (Rev. 14:14).

By such a title Jesus declared His role in the story of redemption and in eschatological history. Bullinger says of this designation "Son of Man" that by it:

> He is raised above the general sons of men, and as given by Jesus Himself it becomes a Messianic name, adopted by Him on account of the relation in which He stands as the promised "seed of the woman" to His brethren. *Son of God* indicates the Divine side, referring to His personal and Divine glory. *Son of Man* is the human side of Son of God, and denotes not merely His need and rejection, but in this connection, as yet securing blessing and righteousness rule over the earth "as second man," "the last Adam."

The Chief Priests did not charge Jesus with blasphemy when He called Himself "The Son of Man" – the triumphant human of Daniel. Their animosity knew no bounds when He claimed Messiahship and used the title "Son of God" of Himself. That He identified the two designations as belonging to Himself is brought out in His appearance before the High Priest, who asked Him if He claimed to be the Son of God. Jesus referred to Himself as the Son of Man but claimed that the Son of Man would be seen in the position in which they would expect the Son of Man to be (Matt. 26:63, 64). "The Jews felt, as our Lord intended, that the Son of Man in Daniel's prophecy could not but be Divine; they knew what He meant by appropriating such words as applicable to Himself" (Dan. 7:13; Matt. 24:30).

When John saw that no man was worthy enough to open the seven-sealed book, he wept much. But from heaven he was told to dry his tears for "The Lion" was able to loose the seven seals and turning to see the strong Lion, instead he beheld a slain "Lamb." And Christ was both – as the *Lion* He was the strong Son of God, but as the *Lamb* He became man's innocent yet suffering Son of Man, to be tried in all points as men were, yet without sin.

> O Saviour Christ, Thou too art Man;
> Thou has been troubled, tempted, tried;
> Thy kind but searching glance can scan
> The very wounds that shame would hide.

Forecast: "Thou art my bone and my flesh" (Gen. 29:14; II Sam. 5:1).

"I have laid help upon one that is mighty; I have exalted one chosen out of the people" (Ps. 89:19).

"A man shall be as an hiding place from the wind" (Isa. 32:2).

"A man of sorrows, and acquainted with grief" (Isa. 53:3, 4).

"Behold the man whose name is The BRANCH" (Zech. 6:12; Isa. 4:2).

"There is a friend that sticketh closer than a brother" (Prov. 18:24; 17:17).

Fulfillment: "Flesh and bones, as ye see me have" (Luke 24:39).

"The Lord is my helper" (Heb. 13:6).

"How often would I have gathered thy children together... under [my] wings" (Matt. 23:37).

"I am the true vine" (John 15:1).

"The Son of man... a friend of... sinners" (Matt. 11:19).

As we are to see, Jesus named Himself the Son of Man because it was part of the divine plan that He should enter into a full human nature, bearing the burdens of sorrow and disappointment, experiencing the onslaught of temptation, enduring certain limitations of the flesh, and under the dual disposition of Son of God and Son of Man present God with a human face. Behind all His participation in the full life common to man were divine forces enabling Him to triumph over adversities and prove Himself to be the Sinless One. Yet His manhood was not unreal because it was sinless.

Christ's possession of deity in no degree interfered with or overshadowed the complemental truth of His perfect manhood. Although the Eternal Word, He took upon Himself human nature in its reality and completeness (John 1:1, 14; 8:40; I Tim. 2:5), and as the ancient Creed has it, He became "Perfect Man, of a reasonable soul and human flesh subsisting." But Jesus did not merely assert His real incorporation with our humanity, He exalted Himself indefinitely above all men as the Representative, the Ideal, the Pattern Man. He alone was the genuine offspring of the human race. He was *The* Son of Man, "the Fairest among the children of men": the very prime and flower of human kind.

Awhile ago we mentioned how Jesus humanized deity, which is seen, for instance, in His capacity of judge. All authority was given to Him to execute judgment because He is the

Son of Man, and having a genuine humanity, He is touched with a feeling of the infirmities of the human race He is to Judge. He knew what it was to be judged unjustly by men, who caused Him such humiliation that in His humanity He was humbled below the level of natural dignity. Behind His execution of judgment there will be the justice of a perfect human heart. Such a truth is of the utmost comfort to those who are His, for having come in the flesh and sharing our life, He touches the very heart of the inner life of the believer. He is our mediator, who bridged the chasm which parted earth and heaven, and that "touch of Nature," making Him, most holy as He is, in very deed kin with us. Because He became one of us we know assuredly that now "There is no place where earth's sorrows are more felt, Than up in Heaven."

In the four Gospels Christ's humanity is everywhere assumed and announced. His was not a transitory theophanic appearance as in the Old Testament, but a permanent abode in human form. His body was like any other man's, and so we have references to His body, head and hair, fingers and hands, legs and feet, eyes and face, side and death. As the first Adam was a perfect man in every way, because he was fashioned by God, so the last Adam came forth with a perfect body through having been conceived by the Holy Spirit. Jesus must have been the most attractive man of His time, "the Fairest of all the earth besides." A classification of His human traits may enable us to praise Him more than ever as, "The wonderful man of Galilee."

1. *His human body.* Are we not informed that when Jesus came into the world, He said, "A body hast Thou prepared Me" (Heb. 10:5)? Born of a human mother and dependent upon her in childhood, His body grew in stature, and His mind expanded in knowledge and wisdom. Later on, He came to speak of His body as a "temple" (John 2:21). As a babe, He wore infant clothes and was held in the arms of aged Simeon, as well as in His mother's, whose firstborn Son He was. That He was born is an historical fact millions upon millions testify to as they date their letters today. Nothing could be more explicit than the genealogical item, "Mary, of whom was born Jesus," or the declaration of Paul that Jesus became a partaker of flesh and blood (Heb. 2:14; John 1:14). He appealed to the senses of His disciples to prove His humanity. "Behold my hands and my feet, that it is I myself" (Luke 24:39). "Behold my hands . . . my side" (John 20:27). Then there is John's great confession:

> "That which was from the beginning, which we have *heard,* which we have *seen* with our eyes, which we have *looked* upon, and our hands have *handled,* of the Word of life" (I John 1:1).

As He ever illustrated by life the truth He taught, "out of His body there flowed rivers of living water," which have never ceased to refresh thirsty hearts in the dry, arid wilderness of this world.

2. *His human soul.* Jesus referred to His *soul,* as well as to His body, the cabinet of the soul. "My soul is exceeding sorrowful, even unto death" (Matt. 26:38). "He was troubled in spirit" (John 13:21). Isaiah prophesied that He would see the travail of His soul (53:11). David, with prophetic insight knew that Christ's soul would not be left in hell (Acts 2:31). Knowing how priceless a possession the soul is, Jesus warned Peter that if a man gained the whole world and lost his soul, he lost his greatest treasure (Matt. 16:26). But what actually did Jesus mean when He said His soul was troubled? What is the nature of this invisible inhabitant of

the human body, which is separated from the body at death?

> Death is parting,
> 'Tis the last said adieu 'twixt soul and body.

When God breathed into the nostrils of Adam the breath of life, he became "a living soul" (Gen. 2:7). Evidently this immaterial substance gave life to the body, and in the R.V. of our Lord's question, "life" is given for "soul." "What shall a man give in exchange for his life?" While it may be true that the Bible does not contain a scientific psychology acceptable to present-day non-Christian psychologists, yet it clearly teaches that man is a tripartite being, having spirit, soul, body (I Cor. 15:44; I Thess. 5:23; Heb. 4:12). At times "soul" and "spirit" are used interchangeably, with the former indicating the individual organism possessed of life in the creature and the latter standing for the universal principle imparting life from the Creator (Isa. 26:9; Luke 1:46, 47). The "one mind" Paul speaks of is given as "one soul" in the R.V. of Phil. 1:27. A distinction between "soul" and "spirit" can be stated thus: "Soul expresses man as apart from God, a separate individual; "spirit" expresses man as drawing his life from God (John 10:11; 19:30).

"Spirits" and "souls" are likewise interchangeable terms. "Spirit is the self when thought of apart from earthy connections. When the blessed dead in heaven are spoken of as having been put to a martyr's death, they are called souls (Rev. 6:9). When there is no reference to their former bodily experience, they are called *spirits* (Heb. 12:23)." At death, the body, the tabernacle housing soul and spirit, returns to dust, awaiting the resurrection, or redemption of the body. But the non-material self, the *I*, if regenerated goes to heaven; if not born anew before death comes, then the person within the body goes to the abode of lost souls.

The *Zondervan Pictorial Bible Dictionary* defines the word "soul" as being used in the Bible "to designate the non-material ego of man in its ordinary relationship with earthly and physical things. It is one of a number of psychological nouns, all designating the same non-material self, but each is a different functional relationship." With the soul-part of man there is a trinity in unity, namely, mind, heart, and will. With the mind we *think,* it being the self in its rational functions, or self as deeply contemplating. With the heart we *love,* it being the self as manifesting a complex of attitudes. With the will we *act,* it being the self as choosing and deciding. The mind sees an object, thinks about it; the heart comes along and loves it; the will surrenders to it. Often all three possessions do not act in harmony. For instance, many are persuaded in their minds that they are sinners, needing Christ as Saviour, yet are not prepared to love Him and surrender to His claims. When the psalmist prayed, "Unite my heart to fear thy name" or sang, "With my whole heart will I praise Him," he was emphasizing the necessity of having *all* his inner powers in unison for prayer and praise.

What relevance has this preamble about the soul to Christ who will yet see of His soul-travail and be satisfied? When He said, "Now is my soul troubled," He was describing how *all* of His inner self was afflicted by His anguish. We will never know how He suffered in mind, heart, and will – then in body on our behalf. As E. C. Clephane puts it,

> But none of the ransomed ever knew
> How deep were the waters crossed,
> Nor how dark the night which the Lord passed thro'
> Ere He found His sheep that was lost.

3. *His human limitation.* It may

seem to appear contradictory to speak of Him who came as "The Mighty God" as having limitations, but while the Infinite has no limitations, the Finite has. Thus, when the Son of God became the Son of Man, with the acquisition of a human body, He became subject to some of its restrictions. "Being found in fashion as a man, He humbled – or emptied – Himself." In his Commentary on *Philippians,* Lightfoot translates, "He emptied, stripped Himself of the insignia of Majesty." Yet "when occasion demanded He exercised His Divine attributes," as Professor Moorehead puts it. But one of those attributes He did not exercise was that of *omnipresence.* His miracles testify to His *omniscience* and *omnipotence.* If, however, He was in one place yet wanted in another, He could not be in two places at the same time, as He was in the body. Still, healing *where* He was, He could heal in another by remote control.

The last promise to His own when, by His Resurrection, He was emancipated from all physical limitations, was, "Lo, I am *with you* alway," whether His saints are in Canada or China. This was why it was *expedient* for Jesus with a human body to go away, in order that His own, no matter where they may be, can rejoice in His spiritual presence. "Christ *in* you." Although thousands of miles apart, when His redeemed meet for worship, each gathering can sing in his own language.

> What if Thy form we cannot see?
> We know and feel that Thou art here.

Is this not the full fulfillment of the forecast of David?

"If I take the wings of the morning, and dwell in the uttermost parts of the sea;
Even there shall thy hand lead me, and thy right hand shall hold me" (Ps. 139:9-10).

Further, there is a passage that appears to suggest a limitation of our Lord's *knowledge* while here in the flesh. It is to be found in His Parable of the Fig Tree, where He says, "But of that day and that hour knoweth no man, no, not the angels which are in heaven, *neither the Son,* but the Father" (Mark 13:32). Do these words mean that Jesus did not know the hour of His parousia? If with His omniscience, He knew what was in man, surely as "The Everlasting Father" He would know what was in the counsels of God. As His first advent was planned in a past Eternity, and He was fully cognizant of it, would not the entire plan of God, even the second advent with all related to it, be known to Jesus?

When God had in mind the choice of Abraham as father of the Jewish race, a great and mighty nation, what did He say? "Shall I hide from Abraham that thing which I do" (Gen. 18:17)? He did not hide His counsel, but revealed His purpose to Abraham. We cannot, therefore, imagine God withholding from His only begotten Son anything concerning His mission. Not only so, if Jesus came with full consciousness of His Messiahship, all related to His second advent and messianic reign must have been known to Him. What, then, is the answer to the somewhat problematic passage before us? Sidney Collett in his most helpful work *The Scripture of Truth* has a most satisfactory answer.

> It ought to be more widely known that the Greek, translated "but," consists of two words, the simple English of which is "if not" — thus *ei* meaning "if," and *me,* meaning "not." The late Archbishop Trench, one of the greatest authorities on words, when lecturing at a London college, called attention to this about 100 years ago; and it can be seen by any one on reference to a good Greek lexicon. So that the clause should read — "Neither if the Son *if not the Father.*" In other words, "If I were not God as well as man, even I should not know." We have

exactly the same thought in John 9:33, where these two Greek words are rightly translated, "if not," namely, "IF ("ei") this Man were *not* ("me") of God, He could do nothing."

Jesus could declare, "I and the Father are one," and as He loved and was ever obedient to His Father, the secret of God's full purpose must have been known to His Son. Thus this much misunderstood passage, instead of being a confession that Christ's knowledge was limited, is in reality a declaration of His omniscience – since He claims in this very passage to be one with the Father, and as such to know *all* things.

4. *His human emotions and experiences.* In his description of Jesus, as the Great High Priest, the author of *Hebrews* says that, "We have no superhuman High Priest to whom our weaknesses are unintelligible – he himself has shared fully in all our experience of temptation, except that he never sinned" (Heb. 4:14, 15 *Phillips*). The word "temptation" can mean "trial" or "testing," and it brings Jesus very near to our hearts when we realize that He was tested or tried in all points as we are, but never once failed. Prophecy depicted the coming Messiah as One who would be closely identified with the lives of those among whom He was to dwell.
Forecast: "In all their affliction he was afflicted" (Isa. 63:9).

"He hath borne our griefs, and carried our sorrows" (Isa. 53:4).

"I sat where they sat" (Ezek. 3: 15).

Fulfillment: "Fill up that which is behind of the afflictions of Christ" (Col. 1:24).

"Jesus . . . healed all that were sick: That it might be fulfilled which was spoken by Isaiah the prophet, saying, Himself took our infirmities, and bare our sicknesses" (Matt. 8:14-18).

"He journeyed, came where he was" (Luke 10:33).

In very truth, Jesus journeyed down to where we are and touched our human life at all points. He sat where we sit, and thus became a scholar in the school of trial. Although now the Captain of our salvation, in *all* things it behooved Him to be made like unto us. He became perfected by the experience of our human lot. Says John Keats, "Nothing ever becomes real till it is experienced – even a proverb is no proverb to you till your life has illustrated it." Experiencing our human emotions, Jesus came to know how real they were, and His perfect human life illustrated all that prophecy had portrayed of Him as the Messiah who was to become man.

a. *The Master's Tears*

Christ would not have been human had He not cried as a baby and wept many a time through the years of His boyhood and youth. The only authentic record we have of his tears, however, is when He reached manhood. Three times we are told of His sacred tears:

He cried over a doomed city –
"He beheld the city [Jerusalem], and wept over it" (Luke 19:41).

He cried over the death of a much loved friend –
"When Jesus therefore saw her [Mary] weeping . . . Jesus wept" (John 11:33, 35).

He cried as He offered up prayers –
"He had offered up prayers and supplications with strong crying and tears" (Heb. 5:7).

As Jesus prayed without ceasing, His eyes must have been often red with crying. With His royal ancestor David, He, too, could say, "My tears have been my meat day and night." Weeping is a human emotion that Jesus shared to the full. "His dropping of warm tears revealed not only His sensitive feelings, but heart-sorrow over the sins and sorrows of those around Him. His was that ". . . Heart, the fountain of sweet tears, And love, and thought, and joy" that Wordsworth could write about. Thomas Hardy uses the phrase, "That long drip of human tears," and Jesus certainly experienced such a "long drip." Earth fed Him with the bread of tears. Swinburne declares that with the making of man there came

> Time with a gift of tears
> Grief with a glass that ran.

In the making of the man Christ Jesus, there was added the human ability to weep and grieve. Describing *The Nameless One,* J. Clarence Mangan (1803-1849), says,

> He, too, had tears for all souls in trouble
> Here, and in Hell.

Living among men, the Master knew what it was to weep with those who wept. He had tears for all souls, whether saints or sinners. Can we not hear His sob of unwanted love, in His lament, "O Jerusalem, Jerusalem"? Solomon would have us know that there is "a time to weep." Such a time was ever present with Jesus, who throughout His brief ministry experienced what it was to "sow in tears." He was given "tears to drink in great measure." When He asked His disciples, "Whom do men say that I the Son of Man am?" they replied, "Some say . . . Jeremiah" (Matt. 16: 14).

Why was it that some of the people thought Jesus to be Jeremiah? Was it because, like the "Weeping Prophet," He was intensely emotional? Tears and weeping are common to Jeremiah's prophecy. He could exclaim, "Oh that my head were waters, and mine eyes a fountain of tears, that I might weep day and night for the slain of the daughter of my people!" (9:1, 15). Again, he cried, "Let our . . . eyes run down with tears, and our eyelids gush out water," and his compassionate tears ran down and saturated his book. If tears are liquid pain, or agony in solution, then Jesus, like Jeremiah, who was one of the prophets who gave witness to Him, knew a great deal about such watery anguish. The tears of Jesus sanctify our crying eyes, and beget in us a like sympathy. Paul was one who witnessed with tear-stained eyes (Phil. 3:18), and who served, warned, and wrote with tears (Acts 20:19, 31; II Cor. 2:4). A cold, unfeeling, dry-eyed religion has no influence over the souls of men. Tears win victories. The age is coming when with His handkerchief, God is to wipe away all tears from our eyes.

b. *The Master's Hunger*

How contradictory it seems to be that in our affluent society, countless thousands yet perish with hunger! The terrible tragedy of children, as well as adults, suffering the pangs of hunger has evoked the practical sympathy of prosperous nations for their relief. Jesus knew what it was to be hungry and thirsty, yet His soul never fainted in Him. George Bernard Shaw in "Major Barbara" says, "I can't talk religion to a man with bodily hunger in his eyes." This was how Jesus felt as He looked upon the hungry faces of the multitude and fed them before He preached to them about food to satisfy the hunger of the soul.

Forecast: "Thou has withholden bread from the hungry" (Job 22:7).

"He . . . suffered thee to hunger" (Deut. 8:3).

"If I were hungry, I would not tell thee" (Ps. 50:12).

"Draw out thy soul to the hungry" (Isa. 58:7, 10).

Fulfillment: "When they were come from Bethany, he [Jesus] was hungry" (Mark 11:12).

"As He returned into the city, he hungered" (Matt. 21:18).

"I was an hungered, and ye gave me no meat" (Matt. 25:42).

"He had fasted forty days and forty nights, he was afterward an hungered" (Matt. 4:2).

Human-like, Jesus appreciated "eating and drinking." To those of His day, He seemed to be much more dependent on the physical supports of life than John the Baptist, that great ascetic who had prepared a way for Him. Yet He came to know by experience the pangs of physical hunger. When we read of Him taking no food during the forty days of temptation, the language implies the contrast presented by His ordinary habit of eating normally. His presence at the marriage feast in Cana, the lavish entertainment in the house of Levi and at the table of Levi, the supper which He shared at Bethany with His friend He had raised from the dead, the Paschal festival which He desired so earnestly to eat before He suffered, the bread and fish breakfast He prepared and of which He partook before His disciples, even after His Resurrection, testify to regular habits of eating to sustain His physical frame. How grateful we should be if we have good food to eat and a healthy appetite to enjoy it! And at all times we serve our bodies best when we eat to live – not live to eat.

That He could not bear to see people hungry is evidenced by His concern for the foodless crowd that had followed Him, and in the miracle He performed to ease their hunger. Yet such was His complete identification with our human experiences that although He miraculously fed the hungry, He never performed a miracle to banish His own hunger, but endured it. That He often fasted, not as a stated, ostentatious ceremonial as the Pharisees did, but as the natural expression of the spiritual state, finds record in the Gospels. He missed many a meal in order to be alone with God, or to bring blessing to needy hearts. If physically hungry, the will of His Father was His meat and drink.

To those smitten with spiritual hunger, He offered Himself as "the Bread of Life." He likewise invited His own to eat His flesh and to drink His blood. Then His promise is that they shall hunger no more for, as the Lamb, He is to feed them for ever (Rev. 7:16, 17).

Thou bruised and broken Bread
My lifelong wants supply;
As living souls are fed,
O feed me, or I die.

c. *The Master's Thirst*

Jonathan Swift, in a description of a voyage, wrote that he and other travelers "ate when we were not hungry, and drank without the provocation of thirst." But many face the provocation of thirst without water to combat such a sensation. There are some parts of the world where a rainfall at the right time can make the difference between life and death. Constantly thirsty, thousands of cattle die, and human life is tragically impoverished. In the life and times of Jesus, people and cattle depended upon wells for their necessary water. The Bible has much to say about wells, water, thirst, and drinking.

Forecast: "[Thou] broughtest forth water for them . . . for their thirst" (Neh. 9:15).

"My tongue cleaveth to my jaws" (Ps. 22:15).

"In my thirst they gave me vinegar to drink" (Ps. 69:21).

"Give me . . . a little water to drink; for I am thirsty" (Judg. 4:19).

Fulfillment: "Whosoever drinketh of this water shall thirst again" (John 4:13).

"Jesus saith unto her, Give me to drink" (John 4:7).

"I was thirsty, and ye gave me no drink" (Matt. 25:42).

"Jesus knowing . . . that the scripture might be fulfilled, saith, I thirst" (John 19:28).

Canon Liddon says that "The profound spiritual sense of His redemptive cry, 'I thirst,' uttered while He was hanging on the Cross, is not obscured when its primary literal meaning, that while dying He actually endured that wellnigh sharpest form of bodily suffering, is explicitly recognised." Exercising His prerogative as "The Mighty God," He could have slaked His thirst, but dying as the man Christ Jesus for sinful men, He willingly endured the depth of human anguish.

Two drinks were offered Jesus by His crucifiers. First, they gave Him vinegar to drink mingled with gall, or "wine mingled with myrrh," as Mark states it. This concoction was both narcotic and nauseating, and was given to those being crucified to dull the fearful pain of execution. Jesus tasted it but, discovering that it was a narcotic, refused it because it was His resolute purpose to drink the cup the Father had given Him to the last drop in the full possession of His senses. He did not want to die doped, or have the clearness of His communion with His Father blurred as the result of the slumberous potion. How magnificently our Mighty Monarch died!

The second drink was the one a Roman soldier gave Him in response to His cry "I thirst!" A vinegar-filled sponge on the end of a stick was pressed against the lips of the parched sufferer, which He did not refuse, but must have been grateful for (John 19:29). Prompted by a rough pity, the offerer was responsible for the last kind act for Jesus before He died. That sour wine, or wine and water, cooled His fevered lips, and enabled Him to cry with a *loud* voice as He yielded up the ghost (Matt. 27:50). Thus prophecy was fulfilled, for His tongue was relieved of its dryness as it cleaved to His jaws. Such agony was borne on our behalf that we might have Him as the Well of Living Water springing up forevermore, and being to our hearts the promise, "They shall neither thirst any more" (Rev. 7:16).

I heard the voice of Jesus say,
"Behold, I freely give
The living water: thirsty one,
Stoop down, and drink, and live."
I came to Jesus, and I drank
Of that life-giving stream;
My thirst was quenched, my soul revived,
And now I live in Him.

d. *The Master's Sleep*

What an indispensable, refreshing boon natural sleep is! Because of our complex physical make-up, sleep is necessary for both mind and body. John Fletcher of the fifteenth century could write of

Care-charming Sleep, thou easer of all woes,
Brother to Death.

William Ernest Henley (1849-1903) wrote the couplet

Night with her train of stars
And her gift of sleep.

Beneficial sleep is indeed a gift, as the Old Book tells us: "He giveth His beloved sleep." God's beloved Son, taking upon Himself a human body, needed such a gift, and slept as peacefully as other men, and woke refreshed after a night's "magic sleep" with the gratitude of David on His lips:

"I laid me down and slept; I awaked; for the LORD sustained me" (Ps. 3:5).

"I will both lay me down in peace, and sleep: for thou, LORD, only makest me dwell in safety" (Ps. 4:8).

Yet there were nights upon nights when He denied Himself sleep, and retired to the solitude of a mountain, where, with the darkness of the night as a blanket to cover Him, He spent the lonely hours in communion with His Father. Other men might go to their homes to sleep, but this man, who had nowhere to lay His head, slept when and where He could. After an all-night session of prayer, Jesus came to His disciples and found them "heavy with sleep." They were too drowsy to watch with Him for only one hour, so He sent them back to sleep (Mark 14:41). He was ever the considerate, understanding Master.

Forecast: "I will not give sleep to mine eyes ... Until ..." (Ps. 132:4, 5).

"Thou shalt lie down, and thy sleep shall be sweet" (Prov. 3:24).

"They shall dwell safely in the wilderness, and sleep in the woods" (Ezek. 34:25).

Fulfillment: "He ... continued all night in prayer" (Luke 6:12).

"But He was asleep ..." (Matt. 8: 24).

"The Son of man hath not where to lay His head" (Luke 9:58).

Christ's deep sleep in that small boat was not disturbed by the storm that threatened momentarily to engulf it, but by His frightened disciples who, waking Him up, rebuked Him by saying, "Carest Thou not that we perish?" It was beyond them to know how He could sleep in such peril. Those distressed and frightened disciples failed to remember that

> No waters can swallow the ship where lies
> The Master of ocean, and earth, and sky.
> They all shall sweetly obey My will.

So aroused out of a peaceful sleep, He calmed the angry waves, saying, "Peace, be still!" While this is the only explicit reference to Christ sleeping, as He often lodged at Bethany with Mary, Martha, and Lazarus, He must have spent many a restful night beneath their hospitable roof, without the aid of pills or drugs to induce sleep.

In His teaching, Jesus often used sleep as an illustration to enforce a point. The sleepy sower must not be surprised if weeds appear. Death was likened unto a sleep. Much loss will be experienced by those who, instead of watching, will be asleep when He returns. While the virgins slept, the Bridegroom came, and when they awoke the door of the marriage chamber was closed against them. How pertinent was the question put to Jonah, "What meanest thou, O sleeper?" Of heaven John says, "There shall be no night there," implying that in our glorified bodies, there will be no provision for sleep. Over there, we are to unceasingly serve Him who never slumbers nor sleeps. Ours will be the joyful privilege of fulfilling His purposes without interruption.

d. *The Master's Weariness*

Such a physical feeling is related to sleep in that it often induces and ends in refreshing slumber. Shakespeare in one of his sonnets has the phrase, "Weary with toil, I haste me to my bed." Weariness besets the most robust and is often nature's alarm clock warning us to have a slower pace. Sir Walter Scott in *Rokeby* wrote that

> A weary lot is thine, fair maid,
> A weary lot is thine.

But is it not the lot of us all? Perhaps we are not all like the one Yeats describes in his "Ballad of Father Gilligan," who

> Had pity on the least of things
> Asleep upon a chair.

Of this character the poet says

> The old priest Peter Gilligan
> Was weary night and day;
> For half his flock were in their beds,
> Or under green sods lay.

Laziness as well as labor can result in weariness of the flesh. It was the mariner's excessive struggle against the storm that Coleridge depicts in the lines

> There passed a weary time. Each throat
> Was parched, and glazed each eye.
> A weary time! A weary time!
> How glazed each weary eye.

As a mirror of human life, the Bible has a good deal to say about the physical infirmity of weariness. In fact, it is profitable to go over references, and list the various causes.

Family strife can produce it (Gen. 27:46).

Disappointment with life can bring it on (Job 10:1; Ps. 69:3).

Overmuch study leads to it (Eccles. 12:12).

God speaks of being wearied by man's iniquity (Isa. 43:24).

Sin impoverishes one's physical vigor (Jer. 9:5; Gen. 19:11; Eccles. 10:15).

Weariness is no respecter of age (Isa. 40:30).

Weariness is associated with divine Persons. In one passage we are told that "The LORD, the Creator of the ends of the earth, fainteth not, neither is weary" (Isa. 40:28). Yet we find Malachi saying "Ye have wearied the LORD with your words." But the accused replies, "Wherein have we wearied him?" (Mal. 2:17). Because of His unceasing service of teaching, preaching, and healing, with all the travel and lack of rest Christ's ministry involved, He must have been often weary. We have only one reference, however, to His tiredness of body — Jesus therefore, being weary with his journey, sat thus on the well" (John 4:6). How glad He was for the rest, and for the water He found there to refresh Him!

Isaiah prophesied that even "the youths . . . shall be weary," and Jesus was not much beyond thirty years of age, when He took advantage of a rest on His journey of mercy. Is this not a striking evidence of His full participation in our humanity? The long walk from Judaea, and the exhaustion it caused, proves that He was subject at times to extreme physical fatigue. Before the Incarnation, God appears remote, inaccessible, far removed from the experiences of human life, but the references to all Jesus suffered in His physical frame brings God so near to us. His true association with the material side of our common nature assures us of His sympathy, and also of His aid in time of need.

The word John uses for *weary* is a forceful one meaning "having become beaten out," "to work one's self weary," or as we would say, absolutely "all in." It was this same word Jesus employed for "*labor*" in His invitation, "Come unto me, all ye that labour" (Matt. 11:28). There is a further suggestion in the action of Jesus when He reached the well. "Jesus, tired with His journey sat down beside the spring, *just as He was*," as Phillips states it. "Just as He was" conjures up the picture of a man thoroughly exhausted, throwing Himself down, too tired to journey another inch. In prophecy, He is offered as the shadow of a great rock in a weary land, and here He is, Himself, so grateful for the rest and refreshment at "Jacob's Spring." Isaiah portrays the Messiah as being able to "speak a word in season to him that is weary" (Isa. 50:4), and here is the Messiah so weary, receiving a word in season from the woman at the well. Ellicott's comment is

> John saw Jesus, wearied by the noontide journey, sitting thus by the well, while the disciples went on to the city to procure food. The reality of this fatigue, as one of the instances witnessing to the reality of His human nature, is important.

Although so weary, He did not faint. It was not the kind of weariness Keats had in mind when he wrote

> The weariness, the fever, and the fret,
> Here, where men sit and hear each other groan.

What must be borne in mind is the fact that although Jesus was weary *in* His service, He was never weary *of* it. Paul would have us know that we are not to fever and fret, if we become weary *in* well-doing, for in due season we shall reap, if we faint not.

The hands of Moses became heavy or weary when held up so long (Exod. 17:12), as Cowper reminds us in his *Olney Hymns*

> While Moses stood with arms spread wide,
> Success was found on Israel's side;
> But when thro' weariness they fail'd,
> That moment Amalek prevail'd.

Paul served the Lord in weariness and painfulness (II Cor. 11:27), yet he never seemed to give way to feelings. When so weary that he felt he would faint in his mind, he would say to his tired heart, "Up, trudge another mile!"

The world is so full of weary hearts, of many who can say with Job, "Weary nights are appointed unto me." Jeremiah could write, "My soul is wearied because of murderers," and the excessive crime and violence of our time has a wearying effect upon one. Running with the footmen, keeping pace with things today, is likewise exhausting (Jer. 4:31; 12:5). Anne Bronte, in "Appeal" sighs

> Oh, I am very weary,
> Though tears no longer flow;
> My eyes are tired of weeping,
> My heart is sick of woe.

If we would also know how to speak words of encouragement to the weary hearts we meet on life's dusty highway, let us turn them to the age-long promise the prophet gave us over 2,500 years ago:

> "They that wait upon the LORD shall renew their strength; they shall mount up with wings as eagles; they shall run, and not be *weary;* and they shall walk, and not faint" (Isa. 40:31).

f. *The Master's Toil*

We are taken up in this section not so much with the arduous labors of Jesus during His public ministry but with His earlier years when He earned His own bread by the strength of His hands and the sweat of His brow. As a carpenter, He must have had nights when He was so weary and tired, and glad of the sleep bed would provide. John Keble, in "The Christian Year," would have us remember that

> The trivial round, the common task,
> Would furnish all we ought to ask;
> Room to deny ourselves; a road
> To bring us, daily, nearer God.

For well-nigh thirty years in Nazareth, Jesus knew all about this "trivial round, the common task," and yet never forgot to be about His heavenly Father's business. Dr. John Horton says that, "The message of the Gospel was essentially a message from business men to business men." This is true as we think of the four fish-merchants, custom-house officer, doctor, tent maker who knew all about the strain of toil. As for Jesus, the master-builder of the church, was He not also the first master-carpenter in it? Christ would have endorsed the saying of Marcus Aurelius: "The craft that thou hast learned, love."

It was from Joseph, His foster-father, that Jesus learned all about wood and nails, which cruel men provided for His death. Isaiah speaks of the carpenter stretching out his rule, and the young Carpenter was deft in the use of His tools. When the villagers pointed to Him, and said, "Is not this the carpenter?" (Mark 6:3), they knew they could rely upon His workmanship for He never made anything shoddy nor countenanced anything shady in business transactions. The Devil was to tempt Him – "Make bread for yourself" – but for years Jesus labors hard for His bread, and proved Himself to be a human workman, as well as the divine Lord. (See the author's volume *All the Trades and Occupations of the Bible*).

Like every other Jewish boy of His time, He would attend the synagogue school until He was about fourteen or fifteen years of age, and then according to Jewish custom would follow the trade of the home, which in His case was carpentry. When Christ the carpenter came, He not only built the way, but laid Himself across the yawning chasm of division between humanity and God and became the living bridge, so that He could say "I am the Way to Zion." Day in and out, for some fifteen years, He labored at the bench making yokes for the oxen, the furniture for the people of His town, and His carpentering skill would be seen in the quality of work leaving the shop in which the toil of divinity revealed the divinity of toil.

Those hard years of honest labor, mending broken chairs, tables, doors, and yokes, prepared Jesus for the mending of a broken world, and the repair of damaged lives. Not only so, but His craft gave Him sympathy with those who had trials and difficulties in business. When the carpenter became the preacher, He knew how to speak about strained relations between employer and employed, and the problem of wages (Matt. 20:1-14; 21:28). Not only was He well-versed in the affairs of heaven, He could discourse on the perils of business, of bankrupt debtors, of burdens of the market, of enormous profits and the responsibility of sharing the same with those in need. Having led a very frugal life as a carpenter, He warned the rich of their peril. Dr. Harrington C. Lees sounds the warning:

> In the day of the great cleavage, when from field or mill or couch one is taken and another left, may it be granted to every Christian man of business — as the Master looks into His ledger, and declares the profits of the talents which He entrusted to His servant — to hear the glad "Well done," and to receive the great promotion from the office to the Palace, from the desk to the Throne.

We cannot do better than end our brief homily on the blessed carpenter Christ with the appropriate verses by that most prolific writer *Anon*, to be found in Dr. W. B. Hinson's Christ-honoring volume *Jesus the Carpenter:*

> That evening, when the Carpenter swept out
> The fragrant shavings from the work-shop floor,
> And placed the tools in order and shut to
> And barred for the last time the humble door,
> And going on His way to save the world,
> Turned from the labourer's lot forevermore;
> I wonder — was He glad?
>
> That morning, when the Carpenter walked forth
> From Joseph's doorway in the glimmering light,
> And bade His loving mother long farewell,
> And through the rose-shot sky with dawning bright,
> Saw glooming the dark shadow of a cross,
> Yet seeing, turned His face toward Calvary's height,
> I wonder — was He sad?
>
> No, when the Carpenter went on His way,
> He thought not of Himself for good or ill;
> One was His path through shop, or thronging men
> Craving His help, e'en to the thorn-crowned hill;
> In toiling, healing, teaching, suffering, all
> His joy; His life, to do the good God's will;
> And heaven and earth are glad.

g. *The Master's Poverty*

Among the Words of Agur, we have the request "Give me neither poverty nor riches; feed me with food convenient for me" (Prov. 30:8). Jesus had both riches and poverty and, at times, not enough food to sustain Him. Rich in glory, for our sakes He became poor, so poor, on earth. In his tribute to Wordsworth, Shelley says of the poet, "In honoured poverty thy voice did weave," and the poverty Jesus was closely acquainted with was of the honored sort. His association with poverty and with the poor contradicts the sentiment of Samuel Johnson in his *Life of Boswell,* in which he said

> Resolve not to be poor: whatever you have, spend less. Poverty is a great enemy to happiness; it certainly destroys liberty, and it makes some virtues impracticable and others extremely difficult.

But in His humble home at Nazareth, poverty was not an enemy to happiness therein; and when Jesus became a poor, itinerant preacher, poverty did not cripple His liberty or make the manifestation of all His commendable virtues impracticable or difficult. Sydney Smith, in his *Wit and Wisdom,* remarks that "Poverty is no disgrace to a man, but it is confoundedly inconvenient." But Jesus never found that it was inconvenient to be poor. Such a state enabled Him more effectively to judge the poor with righteousness (Isa. 11:4). His foes mocked Him as He came out from the poor home in the peasant village of Nazareth. If only they had had the warning of old Ben Johnson they might have acted differently: "When I mock poorness, then Heaven make me poor."

The Bible depicts Jesus as "an honest exceeding poor man," to appropriate Shakespeare's phrase; and not one of "the murmuring poor, who will not fast in peace" George Crabbe wrote about. How right was dear, saintly George Herbert, when in "The Temple" he wrote that

> Man is God's image; but a poor man is
> Christ's stamp to boot.

Describing *Soul of Man Under Socialism,* Oscar Wilde says that "As for the virtuous poor, one can pity them, of course, but one cannot possibly admire them." Jesus, however, was a virtuous poor man who begged for no one's pity who was certainly admired by friend and foe, and who has inspired an uncounted host of saintly souls to take upon themselves the vow of poverty for His dear sake.

Forecast: "If he be poor . . . [offer] two young pigeons" (Lev. 14:21, 22).

"The poor committeth himself unto Thee" (Ps. 10:14).

"Yet setteth he the poor on high" (Ps. 107:41).

"Zion . . . the poor of his people shall trust in it" (Isa. 14:32).

Fulfillment: "They brought him [Jesus] . . . to . . . present him to the Lord . . . [with] two young pigeons" (Luke 2:22, 24).

"Jesus . . . lifted up his eyes to heaven" (John 17:1).

"He humbleth himself . . . God also hath highly exalted him" (Phil. 2:8, 9).

"He trusted in God; let him deliver him" (Matt. 27:43).

That the human experience of poverty Jesus knew all about colored His teaching is evident from His warning to the rich and from His encouragement to the poor. "Blessed be ye poor: for yours is the kingdom of God. Blessed are ye that hunger now: for ye shall be filled" (Luke 6:20, 21). Do you think there was an indirect reference to Himself when He said "The poor ye have always with you"? Alas! Judas had no care for the poor – not even for his poor Master (John 12:6). Among the poor God chose, but who were rich in faith and are now the heirs of God, is His own beloved Son, who had nowhere to lay His head. To the church at Smyrna, Jesus could write, "I know . . . thy poverty" (Rev. 2:9). Yes, He had had an intimate acquaintance with poverty Himself.

Evidences of His poor estate are found in the way He lived on borrowed things. He was born in a borrowed stable; He dined at another's table; when He slept in a bed, it was a borrowed one at Bethany; He sailed in another man's boat; He rode on another man's ass; for His need, He lived upon the money and food ministered unto Him by women who were His true followers; He was ultimately buried in a borrowed grave. Poor, He had nothing to leave, not even His clothes, which were gambled for by the soldiers who crucified Him. But although He had no tangible possessions to leave His relatives and friends, He left them a treasure money cannot buy. To His own He gave a legacy of peace, and to John, the disciple He loved, Jesus bequeathed the care of His precious mother. Rich before He became poor, He is vastly richer now, for through all He endured as man, He is peopling heaven with a glorious host of redeemed souls. Charles Kingsley answers a pressing question in the lines

> How was He,
> The Blessed One, made perfect?
> Why, by grief —
> The fellowship of voluntary grief —
> He read the tear-stained book of
> poor men's souls,
> As I must learn to read it.

h. *The Master's Temptation*

James reminds us that "God cannot be tempted," but when God the Son became man, He likewise became the target of the assaults of hell. Paul affirms that temptation is "common to man," as the man Christ Jesus came to experience. While God permitted His Son to be tempted of the Devil, He did not provide the temptation. At the outset, let it be made clear that temptation is not sin. It is not a sin to be assailed by the enemy of our souls. The sin comes when we give in to the tempter.

> Yield not to temptation,
> For *yielding is sin.*

Jesus always resisted the Devil, and the Devil fled from Him; and each victory over him helps us some other to win. In His initial temptations by Satan, Jesus repelled him by quoting Scripture. Rejecting Satan's suggestion about taking a shortcut to the throne, Jesus found solace in prayer. He preferred the long, hard way of shame and sorrow to a cross. From the real struggle of His soul in the wilderness temptation, Jesus secured a better contact with those who were tempted by the Devil. As the result of His own battles, He could appeal to those oppressed by the Devil for the right to succor them. As A. R. Bond expresses it,

> His brave heart, mindful of the force of suggestive evil and conscious of the power to conquer for others as for self, overflowed with love for the tempted soul. The gentleness of compassion and the compassion of gentleness moved him to give himself for men in a ceaseless endeavor to empower them to gain the victory over self and sin.

Forecast: "Ye shall not tempt the LORD your God" (Deut. 6:16; Exod. 17:2).

"The great temptations which thine eyes saw" (Deut. 7:19).

"They tempted God in their heart" (Ps. 78:18).

"The serpent was more subtil than any beast of the field" (Gen. 3:1).

Fulfillment: "Thou shalt not tempt the Lord" (Matt. 4:7).

"Why tempt ye me?" (Matt. 22:18).

"Ye . . . have continued with me in my temptations" (Luke 22:28).

"When the devil had ended all the temptations" (Luke 4:13).

"Blessed is the man that endureth temptation" (James 1:12).

When the tempter tempts us, the victorious Saviour is at hand to lead us in the train of His triumph. He who suffered being tempted, and who was tempted in all points like as we are yet who never succumbed to temptation will see to it that we are not tempted above what we are able to endure, and is ready with a way of escape from the satanic net (I Cor. 10:13).

> O Saviour Christ, Thou too art Man;

Thou hast been troubled, tempted, tried;
Thy kind but searching glance can scan
The very wounds that shame would hide.

The question may arise in some hearts, holy by birth, nature, and practice, was there any possibility of Jesus yielding to the Devil in his fierce temptations, and sinning thereby? Dr. W. Graham Scroggie answers such a question by saying that, "The fact of importance is not was He 'able not to sin' — *posse non peccare* — nor was He 'not able to sin' — *non posse peccare* — but that He did not sin. And let us not suppose that, on that account, His humanity was not real, for real humanity is not what we are, but what God intended us to be."

As Jesus was born without sin, the Tempter without was seconded by no pulse of sympathy within. Canon Liddon reminds us that

> The human will of Christ was incapable of willing evil. . . . As God and Man our Lord had two wills; but the Divine will originates and rules His action; the human will is but the docile servant of that will of God which has its seat in Christ's Divine and Eternal Person. Here we touch upon the line at which revealed truth shades off into inscrutable mystery. We may not seek to penetrate the secrets of that marvellous working of One Who is both Divine and Human: but at least we know that each nature of Christ is perfect, and that the Person which unites them is one and indissoluble.

It was because He remained sinless that He destroyed the works of the Devil. Victorious, He could ask of His foes, "Which of you convinceth me of sin?" (John 8:46). Made like us, and tempted like us, He yet remained sinless (Heb. 4:15), and thus when tempted we can approach Him and find help in time of need. "In him is no sin," says John. Had there been, He would never have had the power to take away our sins (I John 3:5). How assuring are the lines of Frances Ridley Havergal on the theme before us!

To whom, Saviour, shall we go?
The Tempter's power is great:
E'en in our hearts is Evil bound
And lurking stealthily around,
Still for our souls doth wait.
Thou tempted One, Whose suffering heart
In all our sorrow bore a part,
Whose life-blood only could atone;
Too weak are we to stand alone,
And nothing but Thy shield of light
Can guard us in the dreaded fight.

i. *The Master's Joy*

Our Lord was not only subject to and partaker of our infirmities (Heb. 4:15; 5:7), He also shared our human emotions, especially those of joy, sorrow, love, anger, and compassion. First of all, let us think of His joy, about which He had much to say. Contradictory though it may seem, He was the gladdest as well as the saddest man of His time. Terms like gladness, joy, rejoicing, happiness, appearing in the Gospels, are very much akin. *Joy* is sometimes translated "gladness" (Mark 4:16 RV), and as "rejoicing" (Rom. 12:12). As for *happiness,* or *"happy,"* the same is sometimes rendered "blessed" (Acts 26:2 RV). The word *happen* means "to go or come together" (Mark 10:32). We have the phrase "things *that happened* in the way" (Luke 24:35).

While we prone to think of happiness and joy as being equivalent, yet there is a distinction between the two emotions. Happiness often depends upon what *happens.* If all goes well and nothing disturbs our pleasure then we are happy. But if our circumstances are adverse, then we are gloomy and not happy. Happiness and unhappiness cannot exist together, as joy and sorrow can do. Shipley in *Dictionary Of Word Origins* says that "*Happy* first meant lucky; and if you were lucky you'd be *happy* too."

'Twixt gleams of joy and clouds of Doubt
Our feelings come and go,
Our best estate is toss'd about
In ceaseless ebb and flow.

Deep-seated joy, however, is independent of all circumstances or change. Wordsworth reminds us of "Peace – The central feeling of all happiness." But if trials and tribulations ruin such peace, happiness goes. When Jesus spoke of "*my* joy," He had in mind a deep feeling within that nothing could disturb or change. It was a joy enabling Him to endure even the cross (Heb. 12:2). Faber would have us know that

God's will on earth is always joy,
Always tranquillity.

Even Gethsemane could not disturb Christ's tranquillity of heart, for He could ascribe to the sentiment expressed by an unknown poet:

Now have I found obedience that is Joy,
Not pain, not conflict of the heart and mind,
But harmony of human souls with God.

His was an unchangeable and inextinguishable joy, demons, or men, or sorrow, could not rob Him of – the nature of Joy, E. Young so expressively depicts

A soul in commerce with her God, is Heaven,
Feels not the tumults of the shocks of life;
The whirls of passions, and the strokes of heart:
A *Deity* believ'd is a joy *begun;*
A *Deity* ador'd is joy *advanced;*
A *Deity* belov'd is joy *matured.*

Forecast: "Thou hast put gladness in my heart" (Ps. 4:7; 30:11).

"Serve the Lord with gladness" (Ps. 100:2).

Gladness

Fulfillment: "To shew thee these glad tidings" (Luke 1:19).

"Thy God hath anointed thee with the oil of gladness" (Ps. 45:7).

Forecast: "I have rejoiced in the way of thy testimonies" (Ps. 119:14).

"My heart rejoiced in all my labour" (Eccles. 2:10).

"As the bridegroom rejoiceth over the bride" (Isa. 62:5).

Rejoicing

Fulfillment: "In that hour Jesus rejoiced in spirit" (Luke 10:21).

"Rejoiceth greatly because of the bridegroom's voice" (John 3:29; Rev. 19:7).

Forecast: "The joy of the Lord is your strength" (Neh. 8:10).

"In thy presence is fulness of joy" (Ps. 16:11).

"To give . . . the oil of joy for mourning" (Isa. 61:3).

Joy

Fulfillment: "Rejoice in that day, and leap for joy" (Luke 6:23; 15:7).

"My joy . . . your joy might be full" (John 15:11; 16:24).

"That they might have my joy fulfilled in themselves" (John 17:13).

The joy of Jesus was not superficial or effervescent but a "joy unspeakable and full of glory" and in the steadfast joy He makes His own the recipients of (I Pet. 1:8). Twice over He declared that His joy was fulfilled in His disciples. While we have no explicit record of Jesus laughing, He must have done so, otherwise He would not have been human. We cannot imagine Him carrying a dour, forbidding countenance. His must have been a smiling and gracious face revealing an inner joy, hence the way all classes flocked to Him, and the children as well as the needy felt He was their friend. The common people heard Him gladly, without fear in their hearts.

It would seem as if He found His greatest joy in seeing men and women emancipated from sin's thralldom. In the lost being found there was great rejoicing in heaven, He taught (Luke 15). When the seventy came back with the report of mighty things accomplished in His name, we read that He rejoiced in the Holy Spirit, and said, "I thank Thee, O Father." Weymouth translates the passage, "Jesus was filled with rapturous joy by the Spirit" (Luke 10:21). Gratitude to God was an element of His joy because He was ever conscious that He was fulfilling the divine plan. Here we have a glimpse into His inner life, a heart-throb.

Ever quiet in His joy, He knew how to share the joys of others. He freely accepted invitations to social functions where gladness was intended. Because He experienced the whole range of human emotions, He was able to arouse similar emotions in a masterly way, by His attitude, words, and works. Amazement, wonder, anger, joy, sorrow, jealousy, hope, and hatred show the range and depth of emotions He stirred up. Wonder or marvel was a common emotion of His audiences. He understood as no other the spiritual value of emotions, and never aroused them to gratify Himself. A sensational emotionalism found no favor with Jesus, whose purpose was to direct the emotions towards right-thinking and right-living. As A. R. Bond says, "Jesus came that men might know the truth, which is an *intellectual* process: that they might love God and men, which is an *emotional* process; and that they might live righteously, which is a *volitional* process."

It is His express desire that His joy might possess us so that our joy might be full. Such joy or gladness is —

The Fruit of the Holy Spirit (Gal. 5:22).

The Companion of True Life (I Thess. 3:8, 9).

The Outcome of Faith and Hope (Rom. 5:2; 15:4).

The Nature of God Himself, who is its ground (Ps. 35:9; Phil. 3:1; 4:4).

Persecution for Christ's sake enhances joy (Matt. 5:11, 12; Acts 5:41), and seeking the joy of others is distinctive of Christian sympathy (I Thess. 3:9). If we would truly joy in God, then we must follow the implication of the word as an Acrostic:

J esus First
O thers Second
Y ou Last

John Masefield tells us that

He who gives a child a treat
Makes joy-bells ring in Heaven's street.

By living and laboring for the ingathering of young and old, even though we may sow in tears, we shall add to the music of heaven's joy-bells, by our own rejoicing as we bring our sheaths with us. If we would live noble and triumphant lives, then, as Shelley puts it, we must be "Good, great and joyous, beautiful and free."

j. *The Master's Sorrow*

The Prophet Isaiah condenses into three words all the anguish and grief Jesus experienced in the days of His flesh, "man of sorrows," an illustration, surely, of the maximum of truth in the minimum of words. The Gospels fully record His close acquaintance with grief. Was there ever any sorrow like unto His sorrow (Lam. 1:12)? Sorrow is one of the most common of human emotions or feelings, man being born to it as the sparks fly upwards — the man Christ Jesus being no exception. Because He became the suffering Son of man, He is ever precious to suffering hearts, as H. Hamilton King poetically states:

Men as men
Can reach no higher than the Son of God,
The Perfect Head and Pattern of Mankind.
The time is short and this sufficeth us
To live and die by: and in Him again
We see the same first starry attribute.
"*Perfect through* suffering," our salvation's seal,
Set in the front of His Humanity . . .
While we suffer, let us set our souls
To suffer perfectly: since this alone —
The Suffering—which is this world's special grace
May here be perfected and left behind.

Prophecy and history make it clear that there were many causes for the Master's sorrow, grief, suffering, anguish, and pain. Burdens came from different sources to bow His head and break His heart. In a marvelous way He illustrated the truth

That the mark of rank in nature
Is capacity for pain,
That the anguish of the singer
Makes the sweetness of the strain.

It may be fitting at this point to consider the full implication of the prophetic portrayal of the Messiah as One who would bear our griefs, carry our sorrows, and heal us with His stripes (Isa. 53:4, 5). The fulfillment of this forecast as given by Matthew reads, "[Jesus] healed all that were sick: that it might be fulfilled which was spoken by Esaias the prophet, saying, Himself took our infirmities, and bare our sicknesses" (Matt. 8: 17). Many so called faith healers take this as their basic text for their assertion that sin and sickness are associated in Christ's redemptive work and that, regarding healing as an integral part of His ministry, as the Great Physician made possible our physical as well as our spiritual and moral healing by His cross.

Those who teach that there is divine healing in the Atonement and that bodily health can be claimed as a redemption right summarize their arguments thus:

(1) Sickness is the result of sin.
(2) Christ came to save from sin and its conquences.
(3) He bore our sicknesses as He bore our sins. As the sickless Christ He bore our sickness; as the sinless Christ He bore our sins.
(4) He is enthroned in heaven to make good the purpose of His redemptive work in both body and soul.
(5) The Holy Spirit was given to carry out this purpose.
(6) Christ is the sufficient Saviour of the body as well as the soul.
(7) He ordained the ministry of healing by the anointing with oil and the prayer of faith.
(8) Healing is among His abiding gifts to His church.
(9) Healing is not the exceptional privilege of the few, but the heritage of the children of faith and of holy obedience. This redemptive right can be humbly and boldly claimed by any believer as he walks humbly and obediently with the Lord.

The present writer disassociates himself from this Magna Charta atonement healing. There are extremists who assert that we are living below our blood-bought privilege if we are sick or diseased in body, seek the service of doctors or resort to means of healing. Their dictum is, "If you can't trust the Lord, then call the doctor. If you can't take God's best, take His second best." A preacher was heard to say that "doctors were God's gracious gifts to unbelieving sinners," implying that saved sinners had no need of physicians. But many a teacher of this doctrine of healing as a birth-right of grace in a time of sore affliction has had to seek the relief medical science offers.

Our position is that physical healing is not an integral of the gospel of salvation. Paul never included it in his proclamation of the evangel. Nowhere does he associate the healing of the body with the cross. Atonement, to him, was for sin and sin only. When his companion Timothy was afflicted with stomach trouble and his oft infirmities, Paul did not tell him to claim healing from Christ as his redemptive right but to take some medicinal wine to relieve his discomfort. As already indicated, the authority of healers that Christ bore the sickness of mankind vicariously as He bore our sins is Matthew's application of Isaiah's prophecy.

"Jesus healed all that were sick ... Himself bare our sicknesses."

But Christ *at that moment* was not making atonement. To identify His healing of the sick *at this juncture* with His work at the cross "is to shift the great transaction of Calvary to an early point in His ministry. Such teaching vitiates the whole doctrine of Atonement by making Christ live an atoning life. But Christ was not here making Atonement, nor did He until some three years later. Nowhere in the Gospels do we find Him declaring that sickness needed His death. Old Testament healings were not associated with any redemptive act." Sin *alone,* demands expiation by blood. Jesus never affirmed that there were any vicarious elements in His healings. He did, however, forecast the vicariousness of His death.

If physical sickness requires atonement, then sickness implies a clouded conscience and broken fellowship with such as sin produces. But what a cruel, as well as false doctrine this is, especially when we remember that some of the saintliest men who ever lived experienced in the direst sicknesses most precious and sweet fellowship with God. Paul knew how the most exalted spiritual revelations and thorns in the flesh often went together. What, then, is the explanation of Christ bearing our sicknesses? It simply means that He entered sympathetically into the sobs, sorrows, and sufferings of those He encountered as He went about doing good. We have not an High Priest that cannot be touched with the feelings of our infirmities. Jesus bore sickness inasmuch as He bore the mortal suffering life, in which alone He could bring them to an end and finally swallow up death, and all that led death to victory.

In His willingness to stoop and lift the burden of human weakness and at great cost in physical and mental virtue bear it away, He was but illustrating the divine tenderness, in which God is represented by Old Testament writers as being "the nerve-center of His people's pain." "In all their affliction he was afflicted" (Isa. 63:9). This is the Law of Christ Paul would have us emulate as we encounter the burdens of others (Gal. 6:2). That there is healing in the Atonement is only true in that *all* gifts and blessings come to us from the cross. Having delivered up His Son for our salvation, "how shall he not with him [Christ] also freely give us all things?" (Rom. 8:32). There are many blessings in the Cross, the fulness of time for the enjoyment of which has not yet arrived.

> Deliverance from death is ours through the Atonement, yet death, as a grim reality, is still here.
>
> Atonement covers the millennial age as well as the age in which we presently live.
>
> Calvary removed the curse of sin, but this curse is still with the whole creation groaning to be delivered from its thralldom.

Therefore, as we cannot claim *in this age* all that is included in the cross, we cannot claim universal exemption from sickness until He comes with healing for the nations. What must be made clear, then, is the fact that where sickness is directly due to sin, the first thing is to deal with the cause and find its remedy in the cleansing blood. Where sickness is produced by natural causes, God, who is the author of natural law, can give wisdom and understanding to rightly remedy the cause by natural means. If such means fail, God can be supplicated to restore in a supernatural way, and if healing is for His highest glory and the sufferer's greatest benefit, His miraculous power will be displayed. Ultimately *only* God can heal.

Our summary of the question, then, is as follows:

Atonement was wrought out at Calvary, and there alone.

The apostles are emphatic that all Christ bore on the cross was our sin.

The healings and resurrections by Christ were before and apart from the cross and therefore contained no vicarious element.

The Risen Lord, while the life-giving or vitalizing One, accomplishes by His Resurrection our justification, not our physical health.

Being the unchanging and unchangeable Christ, He can apply His power to the degree of our need and the measure of His ever blessed will concerning us, just as He did to sufferers before His death and Resurrection.

We return, for a moment, to consider what faith-healers affirm as to Jesus being "the sick-less Christ." While there is no stated record of His ever suffering from sickness or physical ailments, apart from the extreme exhaustion manifest when, worn out, He sat by the well, and also in Gethsemane when He sweated, as it were, drops of blood, yet He would not have been human during childhood and boyhood days if He had not been subject to the common ills of growing children. Further, when He became a man, He suffered a good deal of pain, particularly when the furious mob plucked the hair from His face, and rained hard blows upon it, and subjected Him to all the terrible cruelties that death by crucifixion involved.

> We may not know, we cannot tell
> What pains He had to bear.

The most dreaded aspect of any sickness or disease is pain, a physical infirmity Jesus experienced to the limit when He loosed us from the pains of death (Acts 2:24). Keats wrote the phrase "Yearning like a God in pain." Do not the Gospels present us with God manifest in flesh – and in pain? In any pang rending the human heart, the Man of Sorrows has a part, and it is in this way that He bore, and still bears, our infirmities. He *knows,* He *loves,* He *cares.*

Let us now examine more specifically the cause and nature of the sufferings and sorrows of Jesus. There is a saying to the effect that "To have suffered much is like knowing many languages. You have learnt to understand all, and to make yourself intelligible to all." Having suffered much, the Saviour understands a suffering humanity, and waits to make Himself intelligible to all who are willing to listen to His voice. To many of old, the idea of a suffering Messiah seemed a contradiction of terms. Had not the prophets depicted Him as One "Kings will see and arise, princes also will worship" in deep religious awe, "kings shall shut their mouths at him" (Isa. 52:15)? But in harsh and utter contrast, when Jesus the Messiah came born in a stable, and allowed Himself to be buffeted and beaten, and was seen as a sobbing, suffering man, even saints like John the Baptist asked, "Is this He that should come, or look we for another?" Then we have the despairing lament of the disciples on the Emmaus Road, "We thought it had been He who would have redeemed Israel," as they visualized Him still dead in Joseph's tomb.

Forecast: "A man of sorrows . . . oppressed . . . afflicted" (Isa. 53:3, 7).

"If there be any sorrow like unto my sorrow" (Lam. 1:12).

"For thy sake I have suffered rebuke" (Jer. 15:15).

"Consider my trouble which I suffer of them that hate me" (Ps. 9:13).

Fulfillment: "He . . . began to be sorrowful . . . My soul is exceeding sorrowful" (Matt. 26:37, 38).

"He must . . . suffer many things" (Matt. 16:21).

"It behooved Christ to suffer" (Luke 24:46).

"Jesus . . . suffered without the gate" (Heb. 13:12).

While there are many more passages we could weave proving the connection between prediction and performance, sufficient have been cited that when Jesus entered His ministry it was to be honored by the few but hated by religious leaders. His lines did not always fall unto Him in pleasant places. Yet suffering as He did, He ever retained serenity of soul. He is the perfect model of a man who never murmured or who was discontented with His lot. Jesus could sing in His suffering, for when He went out with His disciples to Calvary, He joined in the singing of a hymn. What were some of the ingredients of His suffering?

Sufferings came from His temptations

Do we not read, "In that he himself hath suffered being tempted" (Heb. 2:18)? As the thrice Holy One, sin was never any temptation to Him, for He was not of this world, of which Satan is prince. When he assailed Jesus in the wilderness, he found nothing in Him he could appeal to (Matt. 4:1-11; Heb. 4:15). Holy, He recoiled from and could not but resist him. But how He suffered! Forty days without food, during the battle with the powers of hell, left Him physically and mentally exhausted, but angels came and ministered unto Him.

Sufferings came from his environment

The world around Jesus was sinful, and one in which saints would find tribulation, if they lived a life of separation from its evil ways. But His surroundings could not and did not contaminate Him. The wicked deeds of His sinful contemporaries could not injure Him morally. Gracefully He endured the contradiction of sinners against Himself. He ever remained "separate from sinners." A sunbeam loses none of its glory although it shines on a dunghill. But coarse jests, ribald laughter, lies, caused Him suffering. Some said that He was devil-possessed, and others affirmed He was mad and took up stones to kill Him. Although now saved, we were once sinful, but Christ, who had never sinned, lived above His environment.

Sufferings came from His sympathy

When the diseased woman touched Jesus, He felt that virtue had left Him. In all of His healings He gave part of His own being. Perfect compassion for the sick, the sorrowing, and the sinful made inroads upon His physical make-up. He made the sorrows of others His own, or as Isaiah puts it, "He carried their sorrows." Cries of need always secured His never-failing aid. No wonder He was weary on His journey of mercy. He was constantly touched with feeling for the infirmities of others (Heb. 4:15). Ours is the privilege of being a partaker of Christ's sufferings (I Pet. 4:13).

Sufferings came from His disappointments

It was true that He was never discouraged as Isaiah prophesied (Isa.

42:4), yet the Gospels reveal that human-like, Jesus was often disappointed. "Purposes are disappointed" (Prov. 15:22). A keen disappointment can cause mental suffering as intense as any form of physical suffering. Alexander Pope wrote that "Blessed is the man who expects nothing, for he shall never be disappointed," as being the "ninth beatitude." Jesus expected a fitting response to His teaching, and when not forthcoming He was disappointed.

Can you not detect the feeling of disappointment when many of His disciples went back to their old way and walked no more with Him, and with pathos in His voice said to The Twelve, "Will. ye also go away?" (John 6:66, 67). Then something of His failure can be sensed in His wail over a lost city. "O Jerusalem, Jerusalem! how often would I have gathered thee . . . but ye would not!" Nicholas Rowe (1674-1718) has the appealing phrase "I feel the pangs of disappointed love." These were the pangs Jesus felt as He wept over the so-called Holy City. Then what about His heart-sorrow when His friend came and betrayed Him with a kiss? Because He lived in the will of God, Jesus knew how to spell *dis*-appointment as *His* – appointment.

Sufferings came from Gethsemane

None of the ransomed will ever fully understand all the sorrow and soul-anguish of the garden, in which Jesus sweated clots of blood as He sought to prayerfully prepare for all He knew awaited Him at Calvary where He was to bear the sin He loathed. We read that when He entered the garden, "He . . . began to be sore amazed and to be very heavy" (Mark 14:33), and that while He remained in it He was "exceeding sorrowful" and prayed "in an agony" (Luke 22:44). "The intensity of this emotional experience could hardly have found more truthful record, though one may not perceive the full extent of the experience."

There are at least two flowers we can gather from this garden of shadows: the one, the flower of *sympathy* – Christ became one with us in our sorrow; the other, the flower of *substitution* – Christ made Himself as though one with us in regard to our sin. A preacher of over a century ago bids us say with him, "O dark Gethsemane, thou art, as thy name signifies, a very vile press, or wine-press, of the wrath of God. But out of thy darkness what lights have risen! From those tremors of the Son of God, what strength has come to the sons of men. From thy rocky soil have sprung flowers that now bloom freshly over all the earth." It was Keble who gave us one of the most moving poems about Gethsemane:

There is a spot within this sacred dale
That felt Thee kneeling — touch'd Thy prostrate brow:
One angel knows it, O might prayer avail
To win that knowledge! sure each holy vow
Less quickly from th'unstable soul would fade,
Offer'd where Christ in agony was laid.

Might tear of ours once mingle with the blood,
That from His aching brow by moonlight fell,
Over the mournful joy our thoughts would brood,
Till they had fram'd within a guardian spell
To chase repining fancies, as they rise,
Like birds of evil wing, to mar our sacrifice.

So dreams the heart self-flattering, fondly dreams;
Else, wherefore, when the bitter waves o'erflow,
Miss we the light, Gethsemane, that streams
From Thy dear name, where in this page of woe
It shines, a pale kind star in winter's sky?

Who vainly reads it *there*, in vain
had seen Him die.

Suffering came at the hands of men

It was because Jesus put His own heart of compassion beside the world's heart-sorrow and sadness that He left Gethsemane for Calvary. As He left the garden, the traitor met him, then His disciples left Him, Peter denied Him with an oath. He looked for comforters, but He found none (Ps. 69:20). His foes basely and cruelly maltreated Him; He was buffeted, smote, beaten, spat on, hair plucked from His cheeks. He was sent from one tribunal to another; mock trial followed mock trial. Herod set Him at nought and mocked Him. Pilate had Him scourged with the Roman scourge; the soldiers crowned Him with thorns and robed Him in mock insignia of royalty.

But, mystery of mysteries, reviled, He reviled not. He never tried to escape. Although having all power in heaven and on earth, He did not perform a miracle and slay His foes. He was passive in their hands; He opened not His mouth. He was willing to be led as a lamb to the slaughter. The Creator submitted to His cruel creatures, and allowed them to carry out their wicked will on Him. No wonder Pilate marveled at His silence in suffering, His self-restraint and calm dignity.

Bearing shame and mocking rude
In our place condemned He stood.

Suffering came at the cross

No other than Oscar Wilde wrote in his "Ballad of Reading Gaol"

How else but through a broken heart
May the Lord Christ enter in?

It is because of His own broken heart that Jesus is the healer of hearts crushed by sin and sorrow. On the cross He revealed not only His thoughtfulness for others, but also His own terrible sufferings. Not only were there the sobs of men and women as they gazed upon His blood-spattered form, but His own sobs, as He cried in the daytime (Ps. 22:1-12). Hating sin, He yet bore it. Although He made Himself responsible for it, He was never defiled by it. He was not able to save Himself from the sufferings of the cross. He could not because He would not.

What did the cross mean for Him, the sinless sinbearer? The depth of desolation came when God forsook Him. He had no sympathy from man, no aid from angels, but the crown of His anguish was the seeming lack of support from the sin-hating, sin-punishing Jehovah. It was man's hour, and men did their worst. All restraint was removed, as they derided Him, made Him the butt of their ridicule and object of their scorn. It was the hour of darkness, with hell let loose to rejoice over the waves and billows of divine wrath going over His soul. His dreadful sufferings were nothing to those who passed by (Lam. 1:12, 13). But He endured the cross for two reasons:

(1). Because God is holy, sin must be put away, and only the Sinless One could do that.

There was no other good enough
To pay the price of sin;
He only, could unlock the Gate
Of Heaven, and let us in.

(2). Because salvation for sinners could be provided in no other way. Pitying the lost and yearning to save them, He went to Calvary and died that they might be forgiven. Was He not born to die for a world of sinners lost and ruined by the Fall? (Luke 19:10; I Tim. 1:15; 2:6).

In "A Prayer For Holy Week," as given in her volume of great thoughts from many minds, Mrs. Lyttelton Gell, fitingly summarizes what we have endeavored to say of the sufferings of the Saviour:

By all the sufferings of Thine early years, Thy fasting and temptation, Thy nameless wanderings, Thy lonely vigils on the Mount; by the weariness and painfulness of Thy ministry among men — Good Lord, deliver us!

By Thine unknown sorrows, by the mysterious burthen of the Spiritual Cross, by Thine agony and bloody sweat — Good Lord, deliver us!

O Jesus Christ, Who wast lifted up from the earth that Thou mightest draw all men unto Thee, draw us also unto Thyself!

k. *The Master's Love*

Love was not only one of Christ's transcendant attributes, but an integral part of His being. He *is* love, and came as the personification of the love of God. "He that hath seen Me, hath seen the Father." Our finite minds cannot grasp or diagnose all that is related to such eternal love. Tersteegen has taught us to sing

> Thou hidden love of God, whose
> height,
> Whose depth unfathomed, no man
> knows.

The three aspects of the divine nature of *Life, Love,* and *Light* are applied to Jesus by John on numerous occasions. To the apostle, his Lord was "The Word," or "The Logos":

(1). *The Logos Is Light.*

Not only Light, but *The* Light, the only *true* Light (John 1:9). All that has ever illuminated any soul of man radiated from Jesus Who proclaimed Himself to be "The Light of the World."

(2). *The Logos Is Love.*

Not only does He impart Life, He is *"The Life"* — the essence of God (John 11:25; I John 5:20). He is called "The Word of Life" (I John 1:1), because He has life in Himself (John 5:26).

(3). *The Logos Is Love.*

With Jesus, love was not only a human emotion, but the essence of His being. From a past eternity, His Father had been the recipient of His divine love (John 14:31). Then it was the Father's love for His Son that sent Him into the world, and out of love, Jesus obeyed (John 3:16). Thomas A Kempis, a devout lover of the Lord would have us remember that "Love is born of God, and cannot rest but in God, above all created things. He that loveth . . . giveth all for all, and hath all in all . . . O Fountain of Love unceasing, how can I forget Thee? Is it any great thing that I should serve Thee, Whom the whole creation is bound to serve."

Forecast: "His banner over me was love . . . strong as death" (Song of Sol. 2:4; 8:6).

"I have loved thee with an everlasting love" (Jer. 31:3).

"I will love them freely" (Hos. 14:4).

"A friend loveth at all times" (Prov. 17:17).

Fulfillment: "We love him, because he first loved us" (I John 4:19).

"Having loved his own . . . he loved them unto the end" (John 13:1).

"God so loved the world, that he gave his only begotten Son" (John 3:16; 15:13).

"Him whom thou lovest is sick" (John 11:3).

God demonstrated His love for a lost world in the act of the Incarnation, and Jesus came as the Son of His love to complete the divine approval of the self-giving of love. From the outset of His public ministry, Jesus revealed Himself as the ideal and pattern lover of men. His tears at the grave of the one He loved at Bethany called forth the testimony of the other mourners, "Behold how He loved him!" The promise for every faithful disciple of trust and companionship is, "I will love him and will manifest Myself unto him." The fulness of love can only be measured by divine capacity, yet Jesus could say to His own, "Even as the Father hath loved Me, I also have loved you." Cardinal Newman left us an appealing prayer to pray:

O Lord, how wonderful in depth and
height,
But most in man, how wonderful
THOU art!
With what a love, what soft
persuasive might
Victorious o'er the stubborn
fleshly heart;
Thy tale complete, of saints THOU
dost provide
To fill the throne which angels lost
through pride.

The question can be asked, What is Love? The dictionary answers, "A feeling of strong personal attachment induced by sympathetic understanding, or by ties of kinship." We have already thought of the inner life of Jesus under the three-fold analysis of intellect, emotion, and will, which existed not as separate and distinct compartments of His Person, but features of His soul's functioning. Where there is no heart, there cannot be love, for love is an emotion of the heart, and the love Jesus manifested towards men was induced by a sympathetic understanding of their need. As the Son of Man, He had ties of kinship with humanity, and His love for mankind, like all His other emotions, was regal and victorious. No emotion of His ever reached a low level. Here are some features of His shining like the different facets of a diamond:

(1). *His Love Is Divine*

Although it was the warm love of a human heart experienced as they came into contact with Jesus, the nature of His love was divine. As the Father and He were one, their love was one in essence. He could say, "Therefore doth my Father love me" (John 10:17), and it was heavenly love that Jesus exhibited. Mere human love can wane and cease, but divine love knows no diminution (John 14:21). "As the Father hath loved me, so have I loved you (John 15:9).

(2). *His Love Is Immeasurable*

Paul uses a blessed contradiction when speaking of the Love of Christ. "Know, the Unknowable," he says. "To know the love of Christ which *passeth* knowledge." Then dealing with the measurements of such love, the apostle implies that it is like trying to comprehend the incomprehensible to apply a yardstick to its breath, length, depth, and height (Ephes. 3:18, 19). Charles Wesley, writing of Christ's love as being stronger than death and hell, says that we

Desire in vain its depths to see;
They cannot read the mystery
The length, and breadth and height.

Faber also emphasized the immeasurability of divine love when he wrote

For the Love of God is broader
Than the measure of man's mind.
And the Heart of the Eternal
Is most wonderfully kind.
But we make His love too narrow
By false limits of our own;
And we magnify His strictness
With a zeal HE will not own.

(3) *His Love Is Personal*

Separating himself from the multitudes around, Paul could say, "The Son of God, who loved me, and gave himself for me" (Gal. 2:20). John describes himself as the disciple whom Jesus loved, and is the writer who tells us that Jesus loved Martha, Mary, and Lazarus. Beholding the rich young ruler, Jesus loved him. Thus He was able to discriminate and focus His love upon an individual pouring out the wealth of His love for one. My finite mind cannot grasp how He can isolate me from the 3,000 millions in the world and say, "I love *you*," yet, with Paul, I know He loves *me*. He loves, then, with a discriminating affection.

(4). *His Love Is Filial*

Because the Saviour loves *each* believer, He loves all believers who form His church. "Having loved His own." While Paul was assured of Christ's love and sacrifice for *him*, he went from the personal to the collective aspect of divine love when he wrote "Christ also loved the church, and gave himself for it" (Ephes. 5:25). We have the plural instead of the personal in "Christ also hath loved us" (Ephes. 5:2).

> From Heaven He came and sought her
> To be His holy bride;
> With His own blood He bought her,
> And for her life He died.

(5). *His Love Is Universal*

Jesus shared God's love for a sinful world. In His intercessory, priestly prayer, He prayed that "the world may know that thou hast sent me, and hast loved them, as thou hast loved me" (John 17:23). Had He not loved those who rejected Him, He would not have wept over them. He not only taught that the greatest love is seen in a man dying for his friend, but that His own love and self-sacrifice included in its benefits His enemies. He told His disciples to love their enemies, and He lived what He preached, for while we were yet enemies He died for us.

(6). *His Love Is Unchangeable*

Loving His own, He will love them to the end. Divine love knows no fluctuation or termination. Nobody and nothing can possibly separate us from the love of the Father and of the Son (Rom. 8:35-39). As a true friend, He loves at all times, and under all circumstances.

> Mine is an unchanging love,
> Higher than the heights above,
> Deeper than the depths beneath:
> Free and Faithful, strong as death.

Owen Meredith (Lord Lytton) reminds us that

> Life's sorrows still fluctuate; God's love does not,
> And His love is unchanged, when it changes our lot.

We can readily understand how this deep, immeasurable, and constant love became the motive-force in Paul's dynamic ministry, "The love of Christ constraineth us" (II Cor. 5:14), or as Phillips has it, "The very spring of our actions is the love of Christ." Can we say that we are impelled and compelled by the same wonderful love? Do we love the lover of our soul with all our mind, heart, and will? Is ours the sentiment of Madam Guyon as she writes the following lines?

> Why have I not a thousand thousand hearts,
> Lord of my Soul — that they might all be Thine?
> If THOU approve — the zeal Thy smile imparts,
> How should it ever fail? Can such a fire decline?
> Love, pure and holy, is a deathless fire, —
> Its object heavenly; — it must ever blaze!
> Eternal Love a God must needs inspire,
> When once He wins the heart, and fits it for His praise!

1. *The Master's Anger*

In "The Task," William Cowper wrote of "Anger insignificantly fierce." But there was nothing insignificant about the fierce anger of Jesus. Horace (65 B.C.) gave us the epigram that "Anger is a short madness." The anger the Master displayed was not rage, but righteous indignation. Often human anger is simply revenge. Divine anger, however, is never revengeful or spiteful. When Moses struck the rock, his anger was loss of temper, and he began to experience "the long, long echo of some angry tone." Entrance into the Promised Land was denied him because "he spake unadvisedly with his lips." Angered at the waters of strife, it went ill with Moses (Ps. 106:32).

The serious effects of immoderate passion or of inordinate temper are only too well known. Uncontrolled bursts of anger or "brain-storms" as they are called can be disastrous. But Jesus was never guilty of that excessive vehemence of feeling, taking years to heal. Paul gave sanction to the kind of anger having a legitimate place in human character and life – "Be angry and sin not." But he went on to speak of an anger that is sin, namely, the wrath we manifest if we give place to the Devil (Ephes. 4:26, 27). Such wrath and anger must be put away (Ephes. 4:31). Jesus never gave place to the Devil. All His emotions were divinely controlled. He never uttered a wrong word, never had an occasion to apologize for any action of His. Therefore, His anger was not the reflection of an imperfect human nature, but a mirror of the perfection of the eternally righteous God He manifested to men.

Forecast: "The LORD was angry" (Gen 18:30, 32; Deut. 1:37; II Kings 17:18).

"Kiss the Son, lest he be angry" (Ps. 2:12).

"God is angry with the wicked" (Ps. 7:11).

"Who may stand in thy sight when once thou art angry?" (Ps. 76:7).

"The day of the LORD cometh... with wrath" (Isa. 13:9).

Fulfillment: Anger, indignation and wrath are associated with Jesus several times in the New Testament as an integral faculty of His nature, and as a weapon He used against injury, injustice, and unbelief.

"He had looked round about on them with anger" (Mark 3:5).

What a withering look He must have had as He focused His eyes of fire upon the Pharisees who refused to answer His question about healing the sick and infirm on the Sabbath.

"He was moved with indignation" (Mark 10:14).

John Milton could write of Satan being "incensed with indignation." Because the disciples hindered the little children coming to Jesus for a benediction and a touch of His gentle hand, He, too, was "incensed with indignation."

"Jesus straitly charged them, saying, See that no man know it" (Matt. 9:30).

The phrase "straitly charge" means, strictly or sternly charge. He had healed a leper and two blind men, and gave His command for silence about the miracle so sharply as to border on anger. Yet this severe command did not prevent their disobedience.

"He groaned in spirit" – "groaning in Himself." The margin has it "moved with indignation" (John 11:33, 38). Perhaps Jesus was indignant within because of the failure of those He loved to appreciate the divine purpose in the death of Lazarus (John 11:37).

Then was He not moved by just anger when He cleansed the Temple, and rebuked Satan through Peter (Matt. 16:23; 21: 12-17; John 2:13-22)? Such divine-human anger was free from bitterness and spite; it was always judicial and just. John writes of "The Wrath of God" and this was exhibited in His Son.

A lamb is the symbol of gentleness, docility, meekness, and does not protest even when led to slaughter. Yet, if on a rare occasion it should become angry, we are told that it becomes most ferocious. Is this not the thought Shakespeare had in mind when in "Julius Caesar" he wrote the following lines?

> O Cassius! you are yoked with a lamb
> That carries anger as the flint bears fire;
> Who, much enforced, shows a hasty spark,
> And straight is cold again.

The wrath of Jesus as the Lamb will indeed be terrible as it is matched against the "great wrath" of Satan and his deluded hordes. In His just and righteous indignation, provoked by the wickedness and apostacy of the Great Tribulation Era, His intense abhorrence against all that is alien to His holy mind and purpose will result in just judgment. Coupled with "the wrath of the Lamb" is "the indignation of the wrath of Almighty God." What terrible anger awaits all haters of God and His Christ, and the murderers of their people!

While it may seem incongruous to us that both love and anger, gentleness and indignation featured in Christ's ministry, yet a glowing wrath existing side by side with heavenliest grace characterized not only our Lord but Paul and John. As for Christ, He was a perfect psychologist, and maintained an unusual equipoise, knowing how to balance His human emotions so that one did not master another. His emotional life so free from the baseness marring the emotional life of other men reveals that "He was not so far removed from the common human life as to forbid the tie of the same emotions that stir the heart of the man in the streets, though His own life on earth was without fault or flaw. Jesus impressed His contemporaries with His normal emotional life, even though the purity of His life was such as to create constant wonder."

m. *The Master's Compassion*

Written large over the Gospels is the gentleness of compassion and the compassion of gentleness. The exhibition of divine and human gentleness and sympathy made Jesus great. It was foretold of Him that He would not break a bruised reed or quench the smoking flax, and His interest in and consideration for others was a master passion with Him who gave His life as a ransom for many. His compassionate interest in the needy was not a make-believe. Often we read, "He was moved with compassion," which means that His heart sympathized with human suffering. Walking the common road with men, He earned the title of "The Man of Sorrows." How assuring are those lines of Robert Browning for our hearts:

> That one Face, far from vanish, rather grows,
> Or decomposes but to recompose,
> Become my universe that feels and knows.

Forecast: "That the LORD may . . . have compassion upon thee" (Deut. 13:17).

"He, being full of compassion, forgave" (Ps. 78:38).

"Thou, O Lord, art a God full of compassion" (Ps. 86:15).

"Because his compassions fail not" (Lam. 3:22).

"I will show mercy on whom I will have compassion" (Rom. 9:15; Exod. 33:19).

Fulfillment: "He was moved with compassion" (Matt. 9:36).

"I have compassion on the multitude" (Matt. 15:32).

"The Lord . . . hath had compassion on thee" (Mark 5:19).

"A certain Samaritan . . . He had compassion on him" (Luke 10:33).

Following His steps, we are to have compassion one of another, and never to shut up the bowels of our compassion (I Pet. 3:8; I John 3:17). Is it not with shame that we confess how far short we come of emulating the Master's mercy, sympathy, and compassion? Bishop Westcott, the renowned theologian once wrote, "Touched by the love of Christ . . . Compassion will gain for us again its true meaning. We shall minister to the weak and the erring, not in condescending pity, but as enabled to share evils which are indeed our own."

> We hold a Creed
> Of deeper Pity, who know what chains of ill
> Bind round our petty lives.

Jesus gained sympathy through His temptations. The real struggles of His own soul gave Him a better contact with those being tempted of the

Devil. Having emerged victorious from battle with the Devil, He gained the right to speak to others in life's conflicts. Having overcome the world and its god, Jesus could lead the way to victory over Satan, sin, and self.

In His miraculous ministry as the loving physician, He maintained a gentle patience and lovable disposition, making Him the ideal friend of the needy. He was ever ready to respond to the cry of distress, and with tender words consoled the sick and the sorrowing. A divine graciousness characterizes His miracles, which, with one exception, were miracles of mercy (See the Author's volume *All the Miracles of the Bible.*)

Then as the friend of the friendless and Saviour of sinners, Jesus revealed the gentleness of attitude that made the cold, heartless formalism of the Pharisees so conspicuous. The outcast, the condemned, the lost, were His deepest concern. To the tired, sinful, struggling hearts around Him, He could bare His heart, saying, "Come unto Me, and I will give you rest." He was indeed "The Knight of the Lowly," as A. R. Bond describes Jesus. In the spirit of chivalry, He championed the causes of the despised and down-trodden. "His knighthood flowered in fragrant acts of mercy." His compassions never failed. As John Milton expressed it:

> The Son of God was seen
> Most glorious; in HIM all His Father shone
> Substantially express'd, and in His Face
> Divine Compassion visibly appear'd.

n. *The Master's Humility*

The manifest humility of Christ is the key to His whole life. Had He not been the eternal Son Who humbled Himself in becoming man, He would have been guilty of the most flagrant and fake egotism when He said to His disciples, "Learn of me; for I am meek and lowly of heart." His humility was in sharp contrast to the glaring pride of ancient philosophers. True lowliness is the measuring line of the actions, sufferings, words, movements of Jesus. Deny His deity, and you have no answer to His perfect sincerity, unselfishness, and humility. The charge made against Him, "Thou being a man, makest thyself God," was literally true. Not only did He act in a Godlike way, *He was God*, and in the flesh displayed human emotions to perfection.

> His life while here, as well as birth,
> Was but a check to pomp and mirth;
> And all man's greatness you may see
> Condemn'd by His humility.

We have met those with a pretense of humility, who were proud of it. But as Marcus Aurelius would have us know, "Nothing is more scandalous than a man that is proud of his humility." Archbishop R. C. Trench, who wrote the greatest books on *The Miracles* and *The Parables*, also left us the couplet

> If humble, next of thy Humility beware!
> And, lest thou should'st grow proud of such a grace,
> Have care!

But there was no sham about the humility of Jesus. His was indeed "The stainless peace of blest humility." Peter would have us to be clothed with humility, but with Jesus this virtue was not a garment He put on – He was the perfectness and personification of divine humility (Isa. 57:15).

Forecast: "Thou hast made him a little lower than the angels" (Ps. 8:5).

"Lowly, and riding upon an ass" (Zech. 9:9).

"Better it is to be of an humble spirit with the lowly" (Prov. 16:19).

"I dwell... with him also that is of a contrite and humble spirit" (Isa. 57:15).

Fulfillment: "We see Jesus, who was made a little lower than the angels" (Heb. 2:9).

"Behold thy King cometh unto

thee meek and sitting upon an ass" (Matt. 21:5).

"I am . . . as he that serveth" (Luke 22:27; John 13:5).

"Learn of me; for I am meek and lowly in heart" (Matt. 11:29).

The utter humility of Jesus is a marked feature of His earthly life. Lowliness, not only as to His birthplace and the humble home in which He lived for thirty years, but as to the manner of His living, was evident to all around. He not only preached meekness and humility, He refused the honors of men (John 5:41; 6:15). He practiced every virtue He proclaimed. He *was* the Truth He taught. Jesus served God and man with all humility, and He would have us follow His example. As no other, He humbled Himself under the mighty hand of God, ever placing humility before honor. He believed that it was better to be of a humble spirit with the lowly, than to divide the spoil with the proud (Prov. 15:18, 19).

Jesus appeared to human eyes as One who was humble, as

> One naturally contented with obscurity, lacking the restless desire for eminence and distinction which is so common in great men; hating to put forth personal claims; disliking competition and disputes who should be greatest; . . . fond of what is simple and homely, of children, and poor people. It might have seemed as if His preternatural powers were a source of distress and embarrassment to Him, so eager was He to economise their exercise and to veil them from the eyes of men. He was particularly careful that His miracles should not add to His reputation. Again and again He very earnestly enjoined silence on those who were the subjects of His miraculous cures.

Such is the comment of Canon Liddon on the humility of Christ.

> Jesus! Who deemdst it not unmeet
> To wash Thine own disciples' feet,
> Though Thou wert Lord of All;
> Teach me thereby this wisdom meek,
> That they who self-abasement seek
> Alone shall fear no fall.

Pride, it would seem, is the sin above all others God hates. It was pride that brought about the fall of Lucifer and turned him into the Devil. Archbishop Trench reminds us that

> God many a spiritual house has reared, but never one
> Where Lowliness was not laid first the corner-stone.

We should be ever humble before the Lord, for we have nothing whereof to boast. "What hast thou, thou didst not receive?" Does not Tennyson embody this thought in the lines

> In me there dwells
> No greatness, save it be some far-off touch
> Of greatness to know well I am not great.

Humble love, not proud reason, keeps the door of heaven. May we, therefore, condescend to things of low estate, experiencing the power of the lowly one Himself in overcoming our pride with His humility!

o. *The Master's Prayers*

One of the mysteries of our Lord's Incarnation was His dependence upon the Father, and upon the Holy Spirit. He could do nothing without the Father; and His phrase, "I, by the Spirit of God" indicates His reliance upon the power of the Spirit. If Jesus in His humanity had need of constant prayer, then how deep must our need be. The Gospels present Him praying not only for others but for Himself. Pre-eminently, Jesus was a man of prayer, and his intercourse with heaven was never broken. He not only taught His disciples the principles of effective prayer, but made prayer His "vital breath" and His "native air."

In my volume on *All the Prayers of the Bible*, readers will find a section devoted to our Lord's teaching about prayer, and a summary of the prayers He prayed. His life illustrated

His own precept that "men ought always to pray, and not to faint." He knew from experience that invigorating power of prayer Trench wrote of in this poem:

Lord, what a change within us one short hour,
Spent in Thy Presence will prevail to make;
What heavy burdens from our bosoms take,
What parchéd grounds afresh, as with a shower;
We kneel! and all around us seems to lower;
We rise! and all, — the distant and the near —
Stands forth in sunny outline, brave and clear!

Forecast: "He is a prophet, and he shall pray for thee, and thou shalt live" (Gen. 20:7).

"Evening, and morning, and at noon, will I pray" (Ps. 55:17).

"I give myself unto prayer" (Ps. 109:4).

"He . . . made intercession for the transgressors" (Isa. 53:12).

"He . . . wondered that there was no intercessor" (Isa. 59:16).

Fulfillment: "These words spake Jesus, and lifted up his eyes to heaven" (John 17:1).

"Men ought always to pray, and not to faint" (Luke 18:1).

"[Jesus] continued all night in prayer" (Luke 6:12; Heb. 5:7).

"He ever liveth to make intercession for them" (Heb. 7:25).

While it is true that the public ministry of Jesus commenced in prayer, and continued in its atmosphere, those silent years in Nazareth were not prayerless ones. Learning as a child to pray, at the age of twelve He was about His Father's business — which surely involved contact with the Father for all necessary strength and guidance. His thirty-three years on earth were one long prayer. He prayed at all times, under all circumstances, and about all things. How He loved those seasons of withdrawal from the world, when without interruption He could commune with His Father! Such occasions were not regulated by the clock. Often they continued through the entire night. He became the man to fill the gap as a mighty intercessor.

The marvel of His intercessory ministry is that it did not finish with His death when He prayed for His murderers. "He *ever liveth* to make intercession." He entered heaven as our advocate to plead our cause.

I have a Saviour,
Who's pleading in Glory.

His hands are always lifted up in prevailing intercession, and will never tire as those of Moses did as he sat on the mount.

There is a way for man to rise
To that sublime abode;
An Offering and a Sacrifice,
A Holy Spirit's energies,
And *Advocate with God.*

For an enumeration of all the prayers Jesus offered in the days of His flesh, same will be found in the volume mentioned above. Suffice it to say that sixteen times the Gospels say that Jesus prayed, eight times of which the substance of the prayer is briefly given. Six of His prayers were offered during His last week, including His high-priestly prayer of John 17. The Gethsemane prayer is the only one given by the first three Gospels. Various details of the common narratives are given by the writers, namely, eight are peculiar to Luke, three to John, one to Mark. In six instances reference is made to Christ's retirement for prayer.

Prophesied as the One who would come to intercede for transgressors and to pray for all men, in His prayer-ministry He has left us an example to follow. But are we taking advantage of the privilege of bringing everything to God in prayer? Have we not need to re-echo the request of the disciples who, watching the Master's prayer-habits, asked, "Lord, teach us to pray!" Said Thomas A Kempis, "This is that which most of all hindered heavenly consolation, that thou art too slow in turning thyself to Prayer." As we come to pray may we ever remember the words of John Newton:

Thou are coming to a *King!*
Large petitions with thee bring!
For His grace and power are such
None can ever ask too much.

p. *The Master's Amazement*

Although there are a few other aspects of Christ's emotional life we might mention, we conclude this section dealing with His natural sense of wonder. In "Hamlet," Shakespeare describes the actor who can not only "drown the stage with tears" but...

... Amaze, indeed,
The very faculties of eyes and ears.

There were some things that amazed our Lord's "faculties of eyes and ears." *Marvel* and its cognates appear more than twenty times in the Gospels and carry the idea of looking on with wonder and amazement. An equivalent term, *wonder,* is found more than twelve times, and suggests a kindred thought of astonishment and surprise at a strange or unusual deed or occurrence. People are often referred to as being awe-struck at the miracles of Jesus. Our present interest is in His own amazement, or human emotion of wonder. Amazement was not only a common emotion of His audiences; it was a part of His own physical make-up.

Forecast: "They shall be amazed one at another" (Isa. 13:8).

"I will make many people amazed at thee" (Ezek. 32:10).

"Wonder marvellously: for I will work a work in your days" (Hab. 1:5).

Fulfillment: "Great things Jesus had done... all men did marvel" (Mark 5:20).

"He began to be sore amazed" (Mark 14:33).

"They were all amazed at the mighty power of God" (Luke 9:43). Three times over, reference is made of the amazement of Jesus. The faith of the heathen centurion and the second rejection at Nazareth caused the human Jesus to marvel (Matt. 8:10; Mark 6:6). Then as Jesus faced Gethsemane, we read that "He... began to be greatly amazed, and sore troubled" (Mark 14:33). What caused Him to marvel as He entered the agony of the garden we will never know. Perhaps He stood in wonder at the deeper and more crushing acceptance of the burden of the world's redemption through His coming death, shadows of which were already closing in upon His heart and across His path. On our part, "Love so amazing, so Divine" demands our all.

Can I Gethsemane forget?
Or there Thy conflict see,
Thine agony and bloody sweat,
And not remember Thee?

Remember Thee, and all Thy pains,
And all Thy love to me;
Yea, while a breath, a pulse remains,
Will I remember Thee.

It is to be hoped that our coverage of the Deity and Humanity of Jesus has widened our personal horizon of all He is in Himself as Son of God and Son of Man. Because He fits the hundreds of Old Testament prophecies as nobody else can, filling every mold and every crevice, we know that He is the child who was born and the Son who was given for our redemption. As we ask Him again, "What sayest Thou of Thyself?" we hear Him answer "Bone of your bone, flesh of your flesh, and likewise the Son of the Living God."

It was R. W. Gilder who taught us to sing

If Jesus Christ be a Man,
And only man, I say,

That of all mankind I will follow
Him,
And to Him will cleave alway.

If Jesus Christ be a God,
And the only God, I swear,
I will follow Him through Heaven,
or Hell,
The earth, the sea, the air.

Chapter Eight

PROPHECIES OF HIS DEATH

He Was to Be Betrayed by a Friend	He Was to Pray for His Crucifiers	He Was to Have His Friends Stand Afar Off
He Was to Be Sold for Thirty Pieces of Silver	He Was to Be the Object of Ridicule	He Was to Be Spared Broken Bones
He Was to Be Accused by False Brethren	He Was to Have His Garments Gambled For	He Was to Be Hid by Darkness
He Was to Be Mocked and Beaten	He Was to Be Deserted by God	He Was to Be Buried with the Rich
He Was to Be Pierced in Hands and Feet	He Was to Agonize with Thirst	He Was to Die a Voluntary Death
He Was to Be Crucified with Thieves	He Was to Commit Himself to God	

The heart of Christianity is the Bible, God's infallible Word; the heart of the Bible is the cross of the Redeemer; the heart of the cross is the very heart of God, making provision for the salvation of a lost world. As Christ came as the Lamb slain before the foundation of the world, the Bible is fittingly eloquent with the message of God's sacrificial gift. It would seem as if we have more foreshadings, more types prefiguring the cross of Christ than of any other fundamental theme. As Dr. A. T. Pierson expressed it, "From the hour of Abel's altar-fire down to the last Passover of the Passion Week, pointed as with flaming finger to Calvary's Cross, we see the emergence of a thousand lines of prophecy and indirect forecasts . . . as in one burning focal point of dazzling glory."

Sir J. Bowring, in his famous hymn in which he wrote of the cross as "towering o'er the wrecks of time," reminds us that

> All the light of sacred story
> Gathers round its head sublime.

Concerning all the events leading up to the Crucifixion and the cross itself, Matthew says, "All this was done, that the scriptures of the prophets might be fulfilled" (Matt. 26:56). What are these Scriptures of the prophets but the books of the Old Testament in which prophecies of the sufferings of Christ were set forth some 1,000 to 500 years before these events occurred. All that concerns us in this particular section are the many specific prophecies associated with the death of God's Lamb. Indirect or symbolic forecasts of the cross will be dealt with when we reach the second general division of our study.

When ultimately the predicted Messiah appeared on earth, it was as both prophet and preacher, in which dual capacity He excelled. In His utterances, the predictive element was conspicuous, for He not only laid hold of past prophecies and related them to Himself, but more than once forecast His approaching sufferings, death, and resurrection. With His predictive power, He warned His followers of the harsh treatment He would receive. Prophecies about Him, and from Him, were all literally fulfilled when He was lifted up from the earth upon a rugged cross. "Such a recognition of the Divine source removes predictive prophecy from the realms of human ignorance and errors."

Of all the Old Testament prophets who gave witness to the redemptive ministry of the coming Messiah, David and Isaiah are most conspicuous, as the following references show. Apart from the Gospels, with their actual description of the cross, there is nothing in Calvary literature comparable to the climax of anguish David gave almost a thousand years before the cross; and then the portrait of an archetypal sorrow minutely sketched by the hand of Isaiah some 700 years before Christ was born to die. Both psalmist and prophet, by the Holy Spirit, dealt with the deepest humiliations and woes as the prelude to an assured and glorious victory.

David passes from a detailed description of the Crucifixion to the announcement that by the unexampled sufferings of the Messiah the heathen will be converted, and all the hundreds of Gentiles brought to adore the living and true God (Ps. 22).

Isaiah presents the Servant of God as the One despised and rejected of men, but who, through His vicarious death, will bear the "iniquity of us all." His designed death, however, will be the designed instrument whereby He will achieve His mediatorial reign in glory. His death is to be the condition of His victory (Isa. 53).

It is Isaiah who gives us the central messianic prediction. In fact, in his book are to be found more predictions about the coming Christ, whose portrait he gives, than in any one or all of the other prophets. This being so, we can readily discern the master device of Satan to impugn and impair the prophetic value of the book bearing Isaiah's name. David Baron says that Isaiah 53 reads more like "an historical summary of the Gospel narrative of the sufferings of Christ and the glory that should follow, instead of a prophecy." Augustine said of the chapter: "Methinks Isaiah writes not a prophecy but a Gospel." Without doubt it reads as if it had been written beneath the cross of Golgotha. "It is the deepest and the loftiest thing that Old Testament prophecy, outstripping itself, has ever achieved."

As at least one-half of all the Old Testament forecasts converge upon the Lord Jesus Christ, such predictive prophecy is not only an impregnable rock fortress for rational faith, defying all attempted assaults, but a double defense, proving the divine origin, inspiration, and authority of Scripture – and a vindication of His deity and messiahship. Entering our meditation of all that our Lord endured as He came to the final hours of anguish, may our personal prayer be

> O help me understand it, Lord,
> Help me to take it in.
> What it meant for Thee, the Holy
> One,
> To take away my sin.

A. *He Was to Be Betrayed by a Friend*

Wordsworth would have us know

> . . . That Nature never betrays
> The Heart that loved her.

Although chosen as an apostle, Judas could never have had a deep love in his heart for Jesus; otherwise he would never have heartlessly betrayed Him as he did. No wonder that, after he realized the enormity of his foul deed, he committed suicide.

Forecast: "Yea, mine own familiar friend, in whom I trusted, which did eat of my bread, hath lifted up his heel against me" (Ps. 41:9).

"It was not an enemy that reproached me: then I could have borne it . . . It was thou . . . mine acquaintance" (Ps. 55:12-14).

Fulfillment: "Judas . . . came to Jesus,

and said, Hail, master; and kissed him. And Jesus said unto him, Friend, wherefore art thou come?" (Matt. 26:47-56).

"He that eateth bread with me hath lifted up his heel against me... that the scripture might be fulfilled" (John 13:18).

"One of you shall betray me" (John 13:21).

B. *He Was to Be Sold for Thirty Pieces of Silver*

What an illustration of false values we have in this bargain Judas struck with those who wanted to murder his Master! What a measly sum to pay for Him Who declared that all the silver and the gold belonged to Him, and whose price is above rubies!

Forecast: "They weighed for my price thirty pieces of silver" (Zech. 11:12).
Fulfillment: "They covenanted with him for thirty pieces of silver" (Matt. 26:15-16).

Such ill-gotten money burnt the fingers of Judas. It was blood-money and brought no sense of pleasure to the avaricious heart of Judas, so the prophet's prediction covers the potter, silver, amount thrown down in the house of the Lord.

Forecast: "Cast it unto the potter... I took the thirty pieces of silver, and cast them to the potter in the house of the LORD (Zech. 11:13).
Fulfillment: "Judas... brought again the thirty pieces of silver... and he cast down the pieces of silver in the temple" (Matt. 27:3-10).

C. *He Was to Be Forsaken by His Disciples*

What hopelessness and pain are often associated with the term *forsaken!* Yet it can represent a noble decision. For instance, it is used twice in connection with the disciples of Jesus' choice. As He entered His public ministry and commenced to preach and teach the Gospel, hearing Him, the disciples responded to His call and, as we read, "They *forsook all* and followed Him." Their own ambitions, vocations, homes, were surrendered to His claims. What a sacrificial and courageous forsaking that was! Through almost three years they continued following the lowly Nazarene, but when they saw the swords and staves raised against Him, and saw that close discipleship might mean death, "They forsook Him and fled." What a heartless desertion that was! When He needed their companionship most, they ran away and left Him to face His agony alone.

The disappointment the disciples were guilty of was enough to break any leader's heart. At the end of the training of the twelve, how miserably they failed Him. We know our own hearts only too well to harshly condemn them for their desertion of such a friend. Jesus had to appear alone and undefended before the corrupt Jewish hierarchy and the representatives of the greatest Gentile power on the earth at that time. In the hour of His greatest need, not one person stood by Him. Alone, He had to face His trial and the early hours of His Crucifixion

> Alone, alone!
> He bore it all alone.

Forecast: "Smite the shepherd, and the sheep shall be scattered" (Zech. 13:7).
Fulfillment: "Then all the disciples forsook him, and fled" (Matt. 26:56).

"Jesus saith... I will smite the shepherd, and the sheep shall be scattered" (Mark 14:27).

D. *He Was to Be Accused by False Witnesses*

If, as Edmund Burke states, "Falsehood has a perennial spring," then the source of all false accusation or lying is Satan, who falsely or rightly accuses the brethren unceasingly (Rev. 12:10). The foes of Jesus were ever on the alert for the least flaw in His actions so that they might accuse Him. But He never made a mistake.

He remained without fault (John 8:6). When falsely accused, He did not try to defend Himself, but endured the contradictions of sinners. He never tried to silence false tongues. When Jesus was arrested, it was not by proper officials but by a mob inspired by the priests and elders. He rebuked the inconsistency of approach when He asked: "Are ye come out as against a thief . . . to take me?" (Matt. 26:55, 56).

False witnesses were suborned to witness against Him, to put Him to death, and He was tried at night, which was an illegal action. Words of reason and justice on the part of Pilate had no influence. In the Roman Court, Pilate gave verdict that he could find no fault in Jesus, but the lying mob prevailed and the innocent prisoner was put to death. That trial was the most despicable miscarriage of justice in the annals of all history.
Forecast: "False witness did rise up; they laid to my charge things that I knew not" (Ps. 35:11).

"They have spoken against me with a lying tongue" (Ps. 109:2).
Fulfillment: "The chief priests . . . sought false witness against Jesus" (Matt. 26:59).

"Many false witnesses came . . . two false witnesses" (Matt. 26:60).

Before His accusers, Jesus remained silent. He never opened His mouth to expose their lies. *He held His peace.* As one has expressed it, "In sublime and magnanimous silence Messiah will endure to the uttermost because Jehovah wills it . . . Here we look down into the unfathomed mystery of infinite love." Jesus had no incriminations against His accusers and executioners. One cannot but be startled by both the strange prophecy of this unjust procedure and its remarkable fulfillment.
Forecast: "I was as a dumb man" (Pss. 38:13; 39:2).

"He openeth not his mouth" (Isa. 53:7).

Fulfillment: "Accused . . . he answered nothing" (Matt. 27:12).

"He answered him to never a word" (Matt. 27:14).
Peter elaborates on Christ's majestic silence by telling us that "When he was reviled, reviled not again; when he suffered, he threatened not; but committed himself to him that judgeth righteously" (I Pet. 2:23).

E. *He Was to Be Mocked and Beaten*

The prophets were inspired by the Holy Spirit to testify beforehand minute details of the indignities the coming One was to endure. How else can we explain the most accurate descriptions of the humiliation of Christ, who did not appear until some 700 years after these were prophesied? Note how prediction and performance exactly agree.

Jesus was smitten with a rod upon His cheek.

Forecast: "They shall smite the judge of Israel with a rod upon the cheek" (Mic. 5:1).
Fulfillment: "They . . . smote him with the palms of their hands" (Matt. 26:67).

Jesus was to be spat upon, as well as smitten.

Forecast: "I gave my back to the smiters, and my cheeks to them that plucked off the hair. I hid not my face from shame and spitting" (Isa. 50:6).
Fulfillment: "Then did they spit in his face, and buffeted him . . . Prophesy unto us, thou Christ, Who is he that smote thee?" (Matt. 26:67, 68).

"They spit upon him . . . and smote him on the head" (Matt. 27:30).
Is it not most impressive to read in these parallel statements the prediction in comparison with the fulfillment? No wonder Isaiah said as, in prophetic vision, he saw God's Suffering Servant battered and bleeding, with a holy face covered with man's

spittal, "When we shall see Him, there is no beauty that we should desire Him." What else can the saints do but hide their faces from One so stricken, smitten of God, and afflicted? Robert Browning could write "O, word, as God has made it! all is Beauty." But in His shame and ignominy, the bruised and bleeding form of Jesus was surely the most unbeautiful object in the beautiful world He created. How great was His beauty! But ugly men tried to destroy it, for Isaiah saw His face marred more than any man's. The shocking and brutal abuse Jesus suffered can be gathered from the following prophecy:

> "As many as were astonished at thee; his visage was so marred more than any man, and his form more than the sons of men" (Isa. 52:14).

The renowned German Delitzsch translates this passage thus:

> "Just as many as were astonished at Him, for so disfigured was He that His appearance was not human, and His form was not like that of the children of men."

His bruised and swollen face the smiting with the reed produced must have looked more terrible when, after the crown of thorns had been pressed onto His forehead, the oozing blood made Him a pitiable sight to behold, blindfolded as He was (Luke 22:64). The grim fact is that He was not guilty of any crime deserving of such suffering. "He was wounded for our transgressions, he was bruised for our iniquities" (Isa. 53:5).

> O Sacred Head once wounded,
> With grief and pain weighed down
> How scornfully surrounded
> With thorns, Thine only crown!
> How art Thou pale with anguish,
> With sore abuse and scorn!
> How does that visage languish
> Which once was bright as morn!

F. *He Was to Be Pierced in Hands and Feet*

One of the most remarkable features of the Psalm of the cross is its prophecy of death by Crucifixion, which was unknown among Jews until their captivity, 600 B.C. The Jews executed their criminals by stoning. Crucifixion was a Roman and a Grecian custom, but the Grecian and Roman empires were not in existence in David's time. Yet here is a prophecy written 1,000 years before Christ was born by a man who had never seen or heard of such a method of capital punishment as crucifixion. No other form of death could possibly correspond to the details David gives of the piercing of hands and feet, and the stripping of the tortured one to tell all the bones (see further on — *He Was To Be Pierced.*)

Forecast: "They pierced my hands and my feet" (Ps. 22:16).

Fulfillment: "Except I shall see in his hands the print of the nails . . . and thrust my hand into his side, I will not believe . . . Then saith he . . . behold my hands . . . thrust [thy hand] into my side" (John 20:25-29).

Comparing this Calvary Psalm, or "The Psalm of Sobs," as it has been called, with the crucifixion narratives in the Gospels, we can see that not a jot or a tittle miscarried. Such an "ancient document is a photograph of the fact, fulfilled in flawless detail."

G. *He Was to Be Crucified With Thieves*

The word Isaiah used for *transgressors* among whom Christ was numbered does not refer to the usual run of sinners, but to *criminals,* or those who were open transgressors of the law of God and man. Voluntarily, He permitted Himself to be reckoned with malefactors, and to all appearances as far as the mob was concerned, Jesus was a felon like His companions in death — perhaps considered a shade worse than the other two, as He was given the middle place.

Forecast: "He made his grave with the wicked ... he was numbered with the transgressors" (Isa. 53:9, 12).

Fulfillment: "With him they crucify two thieves ... he was numbered with the transgressors" (Mark 15:27, 28; Luke 22:37; 23:39-43).

Here, again, prediction and performance present "one of those remarkable coincidences which were brought about by Providence between the Prophecies and the Savior's Passion, that Christ should have been crucified between two robbers."

H. *He Was to Pray for His Persecutors*

For the pains Jesus received, He responded with prayers for those who ill-treated Him; He met indignities with intercession, suffering with supplication. He had taught His disciples to pray for those who would despitefully treat them; and at the Cross, He practiced what He had preached. What incomparable magnanimity! He certainly exhibited what George Meredith calls "the magnanimity of love." He never paid people back in their own coin. He overcame evil with good. It takes much grace to kiss the hand that wounds. Retaliation was not in our Lord's vocabulary.

Forecast: "For my love they are my adversaries: but I give myself unto prayer" (Ps. 109:4).

"He ... made intercession for the transgressors" (Isa. 53:12).

Fulfillment: "Then said Jesus, Father, forgive them; for they know not what they do" (Luke 23:34).

Inspired by our Lord's noble example, Stephen, too, prayed for his murderers:

> "They stoned Stephen ... he kneeled down, and cried ... Lord, lay not this sin to their charge" (Acts 7:59).

The recent crucifixion of his Master and his intercession for those who crucified him enabled Stephen to die bravely as the first martyr of the Christian church.

I. *He Was to Be the Object of Ridicule*

The varied attitudes of those around the cross reveal the kind of impression the dying One made upon their minds. In the main, Jesus was surrounded by enemies. Not only so, but crowds gathered when any crucifixion took place, just as they did in the days of public execution in Britain. First of all, we are told of those who shook their heads as they watched the Saviour die.

Forecast: "When they looked upon me they shaked their heads" (Ps. 109:25).

"They shoot out the lip, they shake the head" (Ps. 22:7).

Fulfillment: "They that passed by reviled him, wagging their heads" (Matt. 27:39).

The word Matthew uses for *wagging*, means "the moving, nodding, or tilting of their heads as a contemptuous gesture," as if to sneeringly suggest that this was the end of a supposed Messiah. Job, in his answer to Eliphaz, said, "I could heap up words against you, and shake mine head at you" (Job 16:4). This was the attitude of those who shook their heads at Jesus as they tauntingly defied Him to prove His claims to messiahship by coming down from the cross. Their heads should have been bowed in shame at such a ghastly scene.

Ridicule is implied in the prophetic description in the reaction of those who abused Jesus:

> "He trusted on the LORD that he would deliver him: let him deliver him, seeing he delighted in him" (Ps. 22:8).

Re-echoing these words some 1,000 years later, the mockers used, "He said, I am the Son of God" instead of "He delighted in him." What those who chided Him were ignorant of was the wonderful truth that because He was the Son the Father delighted in He stayed upon the cross till the bitter end in order to complete God's redemptive plan. Jesus could not save Himself and us at the same time. Salvation became ours through His sacrifice.

Further, when it is said that "the people stood beholding," theirs was not the attitude of wonder, or worship, but of stolid indifference. "The rulers *also* with them derided Him." This qualifying phrase suggests that both people and rulers were unmoved by such a gory sight.

Forecast: "All they that see me laugh me to scorn" (Ps. 22:7).

"Behold . . . as many as were astonished at thee" (Isa. 52:13, 14).

Fulfillment: "The people stood beholding. And the rulers also . . . derided Him" (Luke 23:35).

David used a very expressive word in his prophetic portrayal of the crucified One: "They *gaped* upon me with their mouths" (Ps. 22:13), which prophecy finds fulfillment in the phrase "sitting down [the people] watched him there" (Matt. 27:36). What exposure to public scorn, ridicule, and contempt Jesus endured!

J. *His Garments Were to Be Gambled for*

The clothes Jesus wore were His only possession in the world, yet even these were taken from Him. Those coarse, heartless soldiers might have had the decency to leave His seamless robe to hide His emaciated body. Confirmed gamblers are often destitute of tender, human feelings.

Forecast: "They part my garments among them, and cast lots upon my vesture" (Ps. 22:18).

Fulfillment: "The soldiers . . . took His garments . . . cast lots . . . that the scripture might be fulfilled, which saith, They parted my raiment among them, and for my vesture they did cast lots" (John 19:23, 24).

In David's prophecy of Messiah's tragic and horrible sufferings, for exquisite detail dramatically fulfilled, this item as to His clothing is surely the gem of the psalmist's prediction. Divinely inspired, he was able to look down through ten centuries of time and see and record an incident so trivial. Is this not a proof that the Omniscience wrote the prophecy and Omnipotence fulfilled it when "the soldiers parted His raiment, and cast lots"?

K. *He Was to Be Deserted by God*

It was heart-rending enough for Jesus to have His disciples forsake Him and flee; but to be forsaken by His own Father was surely the crown of His anguish. The psalmist declared that he had never seen the righteous forsaken, yet here is Jesus the most righteous One who ever breathed, forsaken not only by earth but by heaven. Martin Luther said of the fourth cry of the cross that it was "God forsaken by God."

As we know, all the utterances from the cross had their roots in the Bible of the Jews, the Old Testament. What else can we do but be impressed that in those hours of agony Jesus, breaking His silence, expressed His deepest thoughts and feelings in words written long centuries before. By connecting prediction and performance, He set His seal about the divine inspiration of Old Testament Scripture. Readers are struck with the large space given in the New Testament to the details of the death of Christ. Very little is said about the death of others, with the exception of Stephen. The reason for this is obvious. So much was given in prophecy to His life, sufferings, and death, and space was necessary to prove that in every detail prophecy was fulfilled. A case in point is the cry of desertion we are now considering.

Forecast: "My God, my God, why hast thou forsaken me?" (Ps. 22:1).

Fulfillment: "Jesus cried with a loud voice . . . My God, my God, why hast thou forsaken me?" (Matt. 27:46).

The face of God was turned, not so much from His Son in whom He always delighted, but from what His Son was bearing, namely, the sin of a lost world, for He was of purer eyes than to look upon iniquity. "God made Him to be sin for us, Who knew no sin." Thus, it was more from Christ as the sin-bearer than from His actual Son that the Father hid His face. The strange enigma of God-forsakenness can only be understood in the light of Christ's mediatorial office. What is evident is the way the Lord Himself laid hold of the first verse of the Calvary Psalm and used it verbatim as expressive of His desolation.

A. T. Pierson in *Living Oracles* reminds us that

> The Hebrew shows not one completed sentence in the opening verses of Psalm 22, but a series of brief ejaculations, like the gasps of a dying man whose breath and strength are failing, and who can only utter a word or two at a time: "My God — My God — why forsaken Me — far from helping Me — words of my roaring" — presenting a picture overwhelmingly pathetic, the Suffering Saviour, forsaken by God, gasping for life, unable to articulate one continuous sentence. . . . The writer thus forecasts the mystery of the Cross which remained unsolved for a thousand years. It was like a dark cavern at the time, but when the Gospel narrative portrays Jesus as the Crucified One, it is like putting a lighted torch in a cavern.

How amazing is divine grace! Jesus was forsaken of God in that dark hour as He bore – and bore away – the sin of the world, that He might be able to promise every blood-washed child of His, "I will never leave thee; I will never forsake thee" (Heb. 13:5). Have you ever noticed that this is about the only verse you can read backwards, and it means the same? "Thee forsake never will I: Thee leave never will I." The feeling of divine desertion need never be ours.

L. *He Was to Agonize With Thirst*

Dealing with the human emotions of Jesus, we drew attention to the significance of the twofold reference to the relief offered to moisten the parched lips and tongue of Jesus. Here, we simply note the prediction and fulfillment of same.

Forecast: "My tongue cleaveth to my jaws" (Ps. 22:15).

"In my thirst they gave me vinegar to drink" (Ps. 69:21).

"My throat is dried" (Ps. 69:3).

Fulfillment: "Jesus knowing . . . that the scripture might be fulfilled, saith, I thirst" (John 19:28).

"They gave him vinegar to drink mingled with gall: and when He had tasted thereof, he would not drink" (Matt. 27:34).

"One of them filled [a sponge] with vinegar . . . and gave him to drink" (Matt. 27:48).

Coupled with His extreme physical exhaustion His cruel sufferings had produced were the perspiration and terrible thirst and the pitiless beating of the oriental sun upon His uncovered head until "He was poured out like water . . . Strength dried up like a potsherd." Do we, from our smitten hearts, with tears, these two wonders confess?

> The wonders of His glorious love,
> And my own worthlessness.

M. *He Was to Commit Himself to God*

As Jesus lingered in the shadows, God was still *His* God. So we have the repetition of the pronoun of personal possession *My* God, *My* God. But leaving the shadows, His work being accomplished, He used the endearing term which was always upon His lips, *Father!*

Forecast: "Deliver . . . my darling from the power of the dog" (Ps. 22:20).

"Into thine hand I commit my spirit" (Ps. 31:5).

Fulfillment: "Let him deliver him now, if he will have him" (Matt. 27:43).

"Jesus had cried with a loud voice

. . . Father, into thy hands I commend my spirit: and having said thus, he gave up the ghost" (Luke 23:46).

This final saying of the cross has enabled many a saint to die triumphantly. Beginning with the first martyr of the faith, Stephen, who, as he was being stoned to death, "called upon God, saying, Lord Jesus, receive my spirit," martyrs and saints down through the ages have made Christ's last words their own. The phrase added by the historian, "He gave up the ghost," literally means, "He dismissed His spirit," a Greek phrase suggesting an act of the will. While He was crucified by Jews and Gentiles alike, actually He died by His own volition. Had He not said, "I have power to lay down My life – I have power to take it again"? Further, He declared, "No man taketh my life from Me, but I lay it down of myself." Thus, His life was not taken, but *given*. In life and death, we are ever safe in the hand of God.

N. *He Was to Have His Friends Stand Afar Off*

On His way to the judgment hall, Jesus had the disappointment of seeing Peter, who had vowed to follow Him to prison and death, "following afar," and to have His disciples as a whole desert Him. Now, as He was dying, so few of His "friends," as He called His own, were near to give Him some consolation by their presence. He Himself had proved to be a friend, sticking closer than a brother, but He was left to die alone. What John Dryden wrote of in "Alexander's Feast" was truer of Jesus

> Deserted at his utmost need
> By those his former bounty fed;
> On the bare earth expos'd he lies,
> With not a friend to close his eyes.

Forecast: "My lovers and my friends stand aloof from my sore; and my kinsmen stand afar off" (Ps. 38:11).

"Thou hast put away mine acquaintance far from me" (Ps. 88:8).

Fulfillment: "All his acquaintance, and the women that followed him from Galilee, stood afar off" (Luke 23:49).

"I have trodden the winepress alone" (Isa. 63:3).

The one ray of comfort for Jesus in His agony was the sight of His broken-hearted mother, Mary, as she "stood by the cross." Others might desert, but courageously she was at His side to see Him die, even as she had nursed Him that day in the manger when He became her firstborn son. The grief of it all might have seen her prostrate on the ground in sobs and deep distress. But no! She *stood*, sustained in that dark hour by divine grace. John also must have been standing with her, supporting her in her sorrow, for the last words of Jesus to those on earth were addressed to the mother He ever reverenced, and to John, the disciple He dearly loved.

O. *He Was to Be Spared Having His Bones Broken*

Ellicott in his *Bible Commentary* informs us that the breaking of the legs of those crucified by means of clubs was a Roman punishment, known by the name of *crurifragium*, which sometimes accompanied crucifixion, and appears also to have been used as a separate punishment. Its purpose and effect was to cause death. The soldiers broke the legs of the two thieves crucified with Jesus to ensure their death, but when the soldiers came to Jesus, they saw that He was dead and "broke not His legs." He had by His own will committed His spirit to His Father. Yet again, prophecy was literally fulfilled.

Forecast: "Neither shall ye break a bone thereof" (Exod. 12:46).

"Nor break any bone of it" (Num. 9:12).

Fulfillment: "The scripture should be fulfilled, A bone of him shall not be broken" (John 19:36).

"He keepeth all his bones: not one of them is broken" (Ps. 34:20).

While it is true that onlookers saw His bones protruding from His naked and emaciated body – "I may tell all my bones; they look and stare upon me" – yet in a miraculous way not a bone of the suffering Messiah was broken, even although some were out of joint. God kept His word, no bone of His Son was broken. But His bones waxed old through His roaring all the day long. It was a miracle of divine providence that Jesus was already dead when the soldiers came to club Him and thus hasten His death and the sooner remove His body from the cross. The application of broken bones the psalmist mentions refers to his restored, spiritual privileges, "That the bones which thou hast broken may rejoice" (Ps. 51:8). His whole being had felt the crushing weight of his sin; to its very fibers, David's frame had suffered, but he was divinely forgiven and renewed.

P. *He Was to Be Pierced*

The longer we meditate upon that "wondrous Cross, on which the young Prince of Glory died," the more humiliated we are by the realization that it was for us the Saviour bled and gave up His life. What else can we do or should we do but out of repentant, grateful hearts pray

> For Thy wounding, for Thy dying, for Thy dire separation from all sensible consolations, how can I praise Thee? For standing out there alone, alone amid the ashes of Golgotha, amid the darkness and the sense of desertion — and all for me, for me a sinner — corrupt, and covered with iniquity? Thou, Who knewest no sin, made sin for me, that I might be made the righteousness of God in Thee. Thy love for me, Thy blood for me: it is too good; it is too great; it is too blessėd. But at least let me love and trust and serve Thee for it, world without end.

Perhaps no features of the cross have so moved and won the hearts of multitudes all down the ages as the pierced hands and feet, and the riven side of Jesus.

> See from His head, His hands, His feet,
> Sorrow and love flow mingled down:
> Did e'er such love and sorrow meet,
> Or thorns compose so rich a crown.

As the nails were driven into those bountiful hands and holy feet, and the sword thrust into His holy side, His once beautiful form became blood-bespattered.

> His dying crimson, like a robe,
> Spreads o'er His body on the tree.

Forecast: "They pierced my hands and my feet" (Ps. 22:16).

"They shall look upon me whom they have pierced" (Zech. 12:10).

"What are these wounds in thine hands?" (Zech. 13:6).

"Awake, O sword, against my shepherds" (Zech. 13:7; Mark 14:27).

Fulfillment: "Except I shall see in his hands the print of the nails . . . saith he [Jesus] to Thomas . . . reach hither thy hand, and thrust it into my side" (John 20:25-27).

"One of the soldiers . . . pierced His side" (John 19:34).

"Every eye shall see him, and they also which pierced him" (Rev. 1:7).

Jesus, as the carpenter, was accustomed to wood and nails, and He had them as He died. Those nails holding Him to His cross likewise nailed our sins to it (Col. 2:14), and made Him, for the redeemed, a nail fastened in a sure place (Isa. 22:23). Although there is no mention of the actual piercing in the Crucifixion narratives, it is implied in the phrase "They crucified Him," for in such a terrible mode of death, Roman nails held the victim to the cross.

> Was it the nails, O Saviour
> That bound Thee to the tree?
> Nay, 'twas Thine everlasting love,
> Thy love for me, for me.

Aged Simeon, who was thrilled at the privilege of taking the child Jesus up in his arms, and blessed God for His gift, warned Mary, "Yes, a sword shall pierce through thy own soul also," and what inner anguish must have been hers as she watched her son dying such a death. What a thrust she must have felt as an actual sword was driven into the side of the child of her womb! In prophecy Jesus cried, "My heart is like wax; it is melted in the midst of my bowels" (Ps. 22:14), which phrase we link on to "a spear pierced his side, and forthwith came there out blood and water" (John 19:34). This related phrase proves that Jesus literally died of a broken heart. Not only was it punctured by the soldier's sword thrust, but the extreme mental and spiritual torture was so great that His heart was ruptured before the point of the sword pierced it. Appearance of blood and water indicated that the lymphatic fluid apparently had separated from the red blood, producing "blood and water." The word "lymph" comes from the Latin *lympha,* meaning "water."

"This is he that came by water and blood, even Jesus Christ" (I John 5:6). Toplady has given us the spiritual significance of this physical feature:

> Let the water and the blood,
> From Thy riven side which flowed,
> Be of sin *the double cure,*
> Cleanse me from its guilt and power.

The blood is the symbol of Calvary, by which we are cleansed from the guilt of sin; the water is the symbol of Pentecost, when the Spirit came as "rivers of living waters" to deliver us from the power of sin. Too many of us are living with only half the cure Jesus provided by His death. Through our acceptance of Christ as Saviour, past guilt has been cancelled; but we are not fully emancipated from the government of sin. Yet through the unhindered, indwelling Holy Spirit we can experience the claim Paul emphasizes:

"Sin shall not have dominion over you."

Q. *He Was to Be Hid From a Gaping Crowd by Darkness*

Here we have one of the minor miracles enacted at the cross, namely, the sudden turning of mid-day into midnight. As Isaac Watts has taught the church to sing,

> Well might the sun in darkness hide,
> And shut His glories in,
> When Christ, the mighty Maker, died,
> For man the creature's sin.

The alternate periods of light and darkness when Jesus died are recorded in the cry, "O my God, I cry in the daytime, but thou hearest not; and in the night season, and am not silent" (Ps. 22:2).

Forecast: "It shall come to pass in that day, saith the Lord GOD, that I will cause the sun to go down at noon, and I will darken the earth in the clear day" (Amos 8:9).

Fulfillment: "Now from the sixth hour [noon] there was darkness over all the land unto the ninth hour [3 p.m.]" (Matt. 27:45).

Those who had rough-handled Jesus took His clothes from Him and then nailed His almost naked body to the tree. But the sun refused to shine on its naked Creator writhing in agony. Thus, the miraculous darkness was Nature's sympathy with her suffering Lord, as well as another prediction performed. Halley, in his remarkable *Bible Handbook*, offers the suggestion that possibly

> Inanimate nature hid her face in shame at the unspeakable wickedness of man, and was, perhaps, trying to express her sympathy with the Son of God in His final grapple with the dark powers of Hell. God may have meant the darkness to be Creation's symbolic mourning for Jesus while He was suffering the expiatory pains of the lost.

The contrast between His birth and death is marked. At His birth the darkness of night was turned into the brightest glory. Now, at His death the brightest hour of the day is supernaturally turned to night by a pall of darkness, the degree and nature of which is not defined. A more intense darkening of the sun will trouble the earth in "the great and terrible day of the LORD" (Joel 2:31, 32; Matt. 24:29, 30).

R. *He Was to Be Buried With the Rich*

An important feature to be noted is that Jesus was *buried*, according to prophecy (I Cor. 15:3-4). The Roman custom in disposing of the corpses of those crucified was to throw them to the wild, roaming dogs. Hence, David's phrases in the Calvary Psalm, "Dogs have compassed me . . . Deliver . . . my darling from the power of the dog" (Ps. 22:16, 20). But Jesus did not share the fate of His companions, the two thieves, whose mangled bodies were fed to the hungry dogs. Joseph of Arimathaea, a secret disciple of Jesus, begged Pilate for the body of Jesus, and receiving permission, Joseph, along with Nicodemus, took His body, washed, anointed, and clothed it, and buried it in the grave Joseph had prepared for himself.

Forecast: "He made his grave . . . with the rich in his death" (Isa. 53:9).

Fulfillment: "There came a rich man of Arimathaea, named Joseph . . . and laid it [the body] in his own new tomb" (Matt. 27:57-61).

The Jewish rulers who thought Jesus was dead and done with would have given the same dishonorable treatment to His body as that meted out to the two thieves. But He had an honorable burial because "He had done no violence, neither was any deceit found in His mouth." Once again we see an agreement with prophecy and history – a further proof that only God could make fulfillment fit forecast. It was impossible for any human design to make the latter fit the former.

S. *He Was to Die a Voluntary, Substitutionary Death*

Dealing with the events fulfilled in the last twenty-four hours in the experience of Jesus of Nazareth, we have already seen that His life was not *taken* but *given*, as Scripture makes clear.

Forecast: "He hath poured out his soul unto death" (Isa. 53:12).

"I gave my back to the smiters" (Isa. 50:6).

Fulfillment: "The Good Shepherd giveth His life for the sheep" (John 10:11).

"No man taketh it [my life] from me, but I lay it down of myself" (John 10:18).

Of His own volition He entered the fierce battle and emerged with the cry of victory, "It is finished." As He died, He could rejoice because "no blot had marred His stainless past; no word that needed to be forgiven could be recalled; no deed left undone now vexed His spirit."

What Jesus fully realized was that in and by His death He was fulfilling Scripture as to the provision of a Saviour for the lost. Did He not say to the disciples on that Emmaus Road that He should suffer, rise again from the dead in order "that repentance and remission of sins should be preached in his name among all nations" (Luke 24:44-47 R.V.)? Says Paul, "Christ died for our sins, according to the scriptures" (I Cor. 15:3); and "gave himself for me" (Gal. 2:20). Thus, dying for sinners, His death was substitutionary.

Forecast: "With his stripes we are healed . . . the LORD hath laid on him the iniquity of us all . . . he shall bear their iniquities" (Isa. 53:5, 6, 11).

"Shall Messiah be cut off, but not for himself" (Dan. 9:26).

Fulfillment: "The Son of man came ... to give his life a ransom for many" (Matt. 20:28).

"When he had by himself purged our sins" (Heb. 1:3; I Pet. 2:24).

What else can we do but join in John's Calvary Doxology: "Unto Him that loved us, and washed us from our sins in His own blood" (Rev. 1:5)? Countless numbers of volumes have been written expounding the wonders of messianic prophecy and fulfillment and the glorious truth that Jesus died an atoning death. C. H. Spurgeon could say that all his theology could be condensed into four words: *"He died for me."* The only passport to heaven is the inner assurance that we have been saved by His matchless grace.

> Yea, Thou wilt answer for me, righteous Lord;
> Thine all the merits, mine the great reward;
> Thine the sharp thorns, and mine the golden crown;
> Mine the life won, and Thine the life laid down.

One of the most impressive and heart-moving descriptions of the cross is to be found in Bishop Fulton Sheen's volume *Life Is Worth Living* (Fourth Series). In his Chapter on "Why Do The Innocent Suffer?" the Roman Catholic Bishop reminds us that "the Cross is evil at its worst and Goodness at its best ... When we look, not to a broken law, but at the broken Person of Christ on the Cross, we begin to see the full gravity of our sin. We see there our own biography." Then comes this remarkable paragraph:

> The Cross is the desk upon which it is written —
> His blood the ink —
> His nails the pen.
> His flesh the parchment.
> We see our evil thoughts in the Crown of Thorns —
> Our avarice in the Hands that are pierced with nails —
> Our wanderings away from the path of goodness in the Feet pinned with nails
> And all our false loves are the open and rent side.

Concluding, the Bishop says, "On the Cross He poured forth His blood, not because bloodship pleased the Father, but because the sinner deserved to die and He, willing to be one with sinners, chose to bear the punishment our sins deserved." No Protestant Evangelical writer could surpass such an impressive Calvary Manifesto.

Chapter Nine

PROPHECIES OF HIS RESURRECTION

Forecasts and Fulfillments of Power Over Death	Features of Power Over Death	Fervent Witnesses of Power Over Death

Believing, as we do, that Jesus actually rose from death and is, as He Himself declared, "alive for evermore," it is not a simple thing to indicate the exact order of events that transpired on that glorious Resurrection morning. First of all, the disciples had not expected their Master to rise again, hence the embalming of His body for permanent burial. Although He had repeatedly told them that He would rise on the third day, they were slow to believe what He – and the prophets – had declared about His resurrection. Mary Magdalene had only one thought when she saw the empty grave, namely that someone had stolen His body. When told by the women that the risen Jesus had appeared, the report was treated as an "idle tale." John alone, of all the disciples, believed at the sight of the empty tomb (John 20:8).

With their lack of expectation, then, the missing body of Jesus, the angelic announcement of His resurrection, the hurrying back and forth in alternate joy, fear, anxiety, wonder, and bewilderment, resulted in a somewhat mild excitement. Thus we have fragments of what happened – one giving us this detail, and another disciple an added event. But no one witness gives a complete account. Yet the main fact was evident. "He could not be holden of death" – a fact, all of the disciples came to realize in transformed lives, and in dynamic service as they witnessed in "the power of His resurrection." It has been said that "all that Christ asked of mankind wherewith to save them was a cross whereon to die" – and die He did! and then rose again for their justification before a righteous God.

Strange, is it not, after almost two millenniums during which millions upon millions have believed that Jesus rose from the dead, that there are those today, even among religious leaders who, like the Sadducees of old, deny the Resurrection. They chant the mournful creed,

> Now He is dead! Far hence He lies
> In the lorn Syrian town;
> And on His grave, with shining eyes,
> The Syrian stars look down.

But, for those who have been raised with Him and made to sit in heavenly places, they have a different song to sing – one vibrant with confidence and joy.

> He lives! He lives!
> Christ Jesus lives today.

Paul asked the question of King Agrippa, "Why should it be thought a thing incredible with you, that God should raise the dead?" (Acts 26:8). Destitute of such power, He would not be God. But events are recorded with the utmost clarity and confidence, and with a most conclusive authenticity and historical value, namely,

That Jesus died on the Cross at Calvary
That Jesus was buried in Joseph's new tomb
That Jesus rose again three days later (I Cor. 15:1-4).

When Paul affirmed that Jesus rose again "according to the Scriptures," he was referring to the prophetic utterances of the Old Testament, and possibly to the forecasts Jesus Himself gave of His death and resurrection. We cannot but be impressed by the fact that Jesus never made a claim to supernatural power or prerogative but what He performed a miracle of like kind to substantiate it. For instance, He said —

"I am the Bread of Life" — and proved it by performing a miracle of feeding 5,000 from a lad's lunch of fish sandwiches.

"I am the Light of the World" — and He opened the eyes of the man born blind to manifest His claim.

"I am the Resurrection and the Life" — and He raised at least three others — and Himself — to verify His declaration.

A. *Forecasts and Fulfillments of Power Over Death*

Christ was identified as the promised Messiah in that His resurrection was an accomplishment of Old Testament type and prophecy. Such a revelation beforehand of that which was to come to pass was a merciful provision to aid the faith of those "who looked for redemption in Jerusalem," and to lead their minds to Him. Thus Simeon could die in peace when he had seen the Lord's Christ, who came as the consolation of Israel. J. M. Neale, the renowned hymnist would have us remember that

> 'Tis the Spring of souls to-day;
> Christ hath burst His prison,
> And from three days' sleep in death
> As a sun hath risen!

Forecast: The miracle Elisha performed for the dead child was a forecast of Christ's similar miracle (II Kings 4:34).

The miracle at the tomb of Elisha foreshadows the Resurrection (II Kings 13:20, 21).

The confidence of Job as to his resurrection after death is explicit (Job 19:25-27).

"Thou wilt not leave my soul in Sheol [abode of the departed spirits]; neither wilt thou suffer thine Holy One to see corruption" (Ps. 16:10).

"I shall be satisfied, when I awake, with thy likeness" (Ps. 17:15).

"O Lord, thou hast brought up my soul from the grave" (Ps. 30:3).

"Thy dead men shall live together . . . shall they arise" (Isa. 26:19; Ezek. 37:7-10).

"Them that sleep in the dust of the earth shall awake" (Dan. 12:2).

"In the third day he will raise us up, and we shall live in his sight" (Hos. 6:2).

"I will ransom them from the power of the grave" (Hos. 13:14).

Fulfillment: "God is not the God of the dead, but of the living" (Matt. 22:32).

"He is not here, but is risen" (Luke 24:6).

"All that are in the graves shall hear his voice" (John 5:28).

"I will raise him up at the last day" (John 6:40, 54).

"Thy brother shall rise again . . . I am the resurrection" (John 11:23, 25).

"He that was dead came forth" (John 11:43, 44).

"He shewed himself alive after his passion" (Acts 1:3).

"This Jesus hath God raised up" (Acts 2:32).

"They laid him in a sepulchre. But God raised him from the dead" (Acts 13:29, 30).

B. *Features of Power Over Death*

Of the miracle of a dead man being restored to life by only touching the bones of the Prophet Elisha in his grave, Hales, a gifted expositor of a past century, wrote: "This miracle was the immediate work of God, and concurred with the translation of Elijah to keep alive and confirm, in a degenerate and infidel age, the grand truth of a *bodily resurrection,* which the translation of Enoch was calculated to produce in the antedeluvian world, and which the resurrection of Christ, in a glorified body, fully illustrated." There are now these three bodily inhabitants in heaven:

Enoch – the first before the Law,
Elijah – the second under the Law,
Christ – the third under the Gospel.

There was this difference in the form of their translation:

Christ raised Himself to and above the heavens by His own immediate power: He ascended as the Son, Enoch and Elijah as servants.

Elijah ascended by the visible ministry of angels,

Enoch was caught up insensibly at God's invitation.

As for the earthquake accompanying both the death and resurrection of Jesus (Matt. 27:51; 28:2), the earthquake was one of God's ways of drawing attention to a momentous event. For instance, the giving of the Law at Mount Sinai was accompanied by an earthquake (Exod. 19:16-18). Does not the Resurrection stand out as one of the most momentous events in the history of mankind? The holy vocation of Jesus took Him to the cross, and His Resurrection was God's receipt for Calvary, the seal that the debt had been paid. Such a triumph over Satan, and over his power of death, earned for Jesus immortal honor and worship. His own predictions of final victory make impressive reading.

Using Jonah as a sign, He said that as the runaway prophet was "three days and three nights in the whale's belly; so shall the Son of man be three days and three nights in the heart of the earth" (Jon. 1:17; Matt. 12:40). After three days, Jesus rose again from the grave in which His body had rested from Friday afternoon till Sunday morning, and to Him, Jonah was a sign or symbol of His death and Resurrection. The implication seems to be that Jonah actually died in the great fish, but lived again once he was vomited out by the fish. A man *miraculously kept alive* in spite of death surrounding him could not be a fitting symbol of another man dead and buried, yet miraculously raised from the dead.

That Jesus claimed to be Lord of the realm of death is evident from His many utterances, a few of which we cite and which, when linked on to Old Testament predictions, indicate why He had to rise again:

"Destroy this temple, and in three days I will raise it up . . . He spake of the temple of his body" (John 2:19, 21).

"I lay down my life, that I might take it again . . . I have power to take it again" (John 10:17, 18).

"I am the resurrection, and the life" (John 11:25).

"Now is Christ risen from the dead, and become the firstfruits of them that slept" (I Cor. 15:20).

The initial event of the first Resurrection was the raising of the Lord Jesus. Paul declares that "as in Adam all die, even so in Christ shall all be made alive. But every man in his own order, Christ the Firstfruits; afterwards they that are Christ's at his coming" (I Cor. 15:22, 23; Rev. 20:6).

"Jesus began to shew unto his disciples . . . that he must . . . be killed, and be raised again the third day" (Matt. 16:21; Mark 9:31).

"Tell the vision to no man, until the Son of man be risen again from the dead" (Matt. 17:9, 23).

"The Gentiles . . . crucify him: and the third day he shall rise again" (Matt. 20:19; Luke 18:33).

"After I am risen again, I will go before you into Galilee" (Matt. 26:32; 27:63).

"Remember how he spake unto you when he was yet in Galilee, saying, The Son of man must be delivered into the hands of sinful men, and be crucified, and the third day rise again" (Luke 24:6, 7).

"Two men . . . spake of His decease which he should accomplish at Jerusalem" (Luke 9:30, 31).

The *exodus* He spoke of was more than a "decease"; it was a *way out*, and only by His Resurrection could there have been such a way. "His rising from the dead was the complement of His Incarnation, Ministration, and Crucifixion." Because of all He was as the God-Man necessitated an empty tomb. How could the Lord of Life be holden of death? As Dr. Graham Scroggie puts it, "In the light of His origin and character it is impossible to believe that He did not rise from the dead. With His Resurrection everything else that has been revealed of Him assumes proportion, order and harmony; without it all is a mystery; a lock without a key; a labyrinth without a clue; a beginning without a corresponding end."

C. *Fervent Witnesses of Power Over Death*

As He emerged from a virgin womb by a miracle, so now by a further miracle He comes forth from a virgin tomb. Although His timid and short-sighted disciples failed to grasp the place His death and Resurrection should occupy in His Saviourhood and consequently did not share His confidence of victory and future glory, He Himself knew the glory that would follow the cross. Now, power is His to wake the sleeping dead (John 5:28, 29), and at His girdle can be found the keys of death and hell (Rev. 1:18). Nothing is more historically certain than that Jesus rose from the dead and appeared to His disciples. The Resurrection is the best established fact in history, as the following evidences prove. Such a cornerstone of Christianity does not rest upon the testimony of any one person. The hallelujah of the Resurrection is not a *monologue* but a *chorale*, with the voices of rejoicing saints joining in the strain. Who were those who had the privilege of seeing and hearing the risen redeemer? The ten appearances of our Lord after His Resurrection, proving and elaborating the certainty of it, were made under a great variety of circumstances: to men and women, to individuals and groups, in the house and on the street, to disciples glad and sad. The testimony of all who saw Jesus is unmistakable and irrefutable.

Evidence for the Resurrection has been presented in the interesting form of a supposed trial in a court of justice, in which witnesses are examined, counsel heard, the judge sums up, the jury give their verdict. The first we call to testify is Mary Magdalene.

Three women are identified with the ruin and restoration of our race. Eve, earth's first woman, was first in transgression; Mary, the mother of our Lord, was, in God's mercy, first in the promised salvation for sin; Mary Magdalene, the first witness of the Redeemer, who by His death and Resurrection, made possible such a salvation. We would have thought that the Mary who bore Jesus would have been the one most likely to proclaim the victory of her son over the grave. But no! It was vouchsafed to another Mary, her of Magdala, the privilege to proclaim the fact of the empty tomb. Hastening back to the disciples, she said, "They have taken away my Lord," and when they came and saw that the grave was empty, they believed what Mary had said.

This Mary of Magdala was the last to leave the sacred spot. "She wept *without* before the sepulchre," and what else can we do, so long as we stand before any grave? But when we look into it fixedly, look death steadily in the face, the terror vanishes. To the longing of love and to the patience of hope, "angels are within, messengers of peace." Mary wept because she could not find the body of Jesus. Had she seen the dead body where it had been lain, she would have still wept. But at that very moment there stood beside her the very Jesus whom she loved and for whom she wept. "Her tears wove a veil that shut out His face." It was farthest from her thoughts that He would rise from the dead. "She was prejudiced not *for* the resurrection, but *against* it."

Then the living Lord spoke, and the first recorded words to leave His lips, no longer parched with thirst or pale with death, were words of comfort. His last word on the cross affirmed His trust in God; His first word at the sepulchre was that of consolation for man. "Why weepest thou? Whom seekest thou?" Observe, *Whom*, not "*what* seekest thou?" Jesus knew that *He* alone, and no thing, could fill the void in the human heart. For all our questions, He is the answer. To every question of the heart, He has the answer, for He is love; of the mind, for He is the truth; of conscience and the life, for He is our sacrifice and our Sanctification.

Mary came seeking Jesus, and He was at hand, and as the Good Shepherd who calleth His own sheep by name, seeing a wounded lamb bleating out its passionate grief, said unto her, "Mary!" At the sound of her name uttered by the musical voice of Jesus, the portals of her soul opened, and the dull pulses of her joy awoke and beat in rapture. One word escaped her joyful lips – *Rabboni,* which is to say, "Master." Then came His first declaration: "Go to My brethren," and hastily Mary went and declared to the disciples that she had seen the Lord, and that He had spoken unto her (John 20:11-18). The psalmist has the message, "The Lord gave the word: great was the company of those that published," which literally means, "The Lord gives a word. Of *the women* who bring the news, the host is great" (Ps. 68:11). Mary Magdalene was the first herald to publish the news of the Risen Lord, and the first of a great army of women to witness for Him.

Here, again, prediction became performance. In forecast, the One who was to die and rise again said, "I will declare thy name unto my brethren" (Ps. 22:22). In fulfillment, He said to Mary, "Go to my brethren" (John 20:17), and declared to His brethren the name *Father.* "I will declare Thy name" – "I have declared unto them thy name, and will declare it" (John 20:17; 17:26). The prophetic words of David are cited as coming from the lips of the risen Saviour Himself by the writer of *Hebrews* 2:11, 12.

Mary was quick to carry the glad tidings to the disciples, and meanwhile Jesus greeted the other women also, and entrusted them with like messages. It is somewhat impressive how when He, by His angel, sent them on a similar errand, He singled out one disciple with special emphasis: "Go your way; and tell His disciples and *Peter.*" Paul tells us that sometime on that Resurrection Day, "He was seen of Cephas" (I Cor. 15:5). When the two disciples returned from Emmaus that evening, they were greeted with the tidings, "The Lord is risen indeed, and hath appeared to Simon" (Luke 24:34). Peter was among "His disciples" yet it was as if He had said "Tell Peter first, Peter especially, be sure not to leave out Peter." Of the interview between the Saviour and Simon, we know nothing. How eloquent are the silences of the Bible! What a meeting it must have been! As the result of it, Peter was restored to himself and to his office. "The wounds of conscience though generally received in public, must always be healed in private." The meeting with Jesus in secret and alone resulted in Peter's full committal to the Master, and from that interview he went forth to become the mighty leader of the early church.

Paul tells us that the fact of the Resurrection was attested to by the weighty evidence of Jesus being seen by more than 500 brethren at once (I Cor. 15:6). The record of the dramatic and dynamic witness of the apostles in *The Acts* cannot be explained apart from the phenomenon of the Resurrection. Countless thousands were converted and added to the church, as the apostles preached Jesus and the Resurrection. While we cannot identify all who saw the risen Saviour, let us try to set forth the order of His appearances to His own ere He ascended on high.

In the early morning of the day Christ rose from the dead, He appeared first of all to Mary Magdalene (Mark 16:9-10), also to the other women (Matt. 28:1-16).

In the afternoon, He appeared to the two on their way to Emmaus (Mark 16:12-13; Luke 24:13-32), also to Peter (Luke 24:34).

In the evening, He appeared to the Ten (John 20:19-25), and sometime a week later, He appeared to the Eleven, Thomas being present (John 20:26-31).

Sometime later, He appeared to the Seven at the Sea of Galilee, and perhaps also to the 500 brethren Paul mentions. It may be that the commission to go into all the world was given then (Matt. 28:16-20; John 21).

Time and place of appearance to James are unknown (I Cor. 15:7).

Final appearance to all His disciples at His Ascension (Mark 16:14; Acts 1:3, 11).

Paul's list of appearances reads: [Christ] was seen of Cephas [Peter], then of the twelve: After that, of about five hundred brethren at once ... After that he was seen of James, then of all the apostles. And last of all he was seen of me also (I Cor. 15:5-8).

One of the most striking proofs of the credence of the Resurrection was the transformation in the state of mind and conduct of the apostles, the most outstanding of which was Paul, whose remarkable, sudden conversion on that Damascus Road ever remains as a mighty testimony to the reality of the Resurrection. When Paul affirmed, "He was seen of me also," he meant an actual, visible appearance just as the other apostles had had. Nothing but a real objective appearance of Christ will satisfy the case in the record of his conversion (Acts 9:1-19). Thereafter, for more than twenty-five years he served and suffered for Jesus as few have done; and the driving consciousness behind all his marvelous labors was the assurance that his Lord was alive, and that he had seen Him in His glorified body.

The Resurrection, then, is one of the best attested facts in history. Paul had no need to test and sift evidences of such a fact. His eyes had seen Him and not another and he came to give to the church "The Magna Carta of The Resurrection," as I Cor. 15 has been called. George Bowen, in his most profitable "Daily Meditations," says

> Given the Resurrection, and Paul's Epistles are explained; deny the Resurrection, and you cannot account for them.
> Given the Resurrection, and Paul's own character is the natural consequence of it, Paul's conversion its natural product;
> Deny the Resurrection, and he is the greatest of all inconsistencies, and his conversion, *with its effects,* the most inexplicable of all enigmas.

Paul insists, in the strongest language his brilliant mind was capable of, that except for the hope of Christianity there is no excuse for the existence of Christianity. "Our faith is in vain" (I Cor. 15:13-19). What we cannot understand is why a gifted translator and expositor like Professor William Barclay, Dean of Divinity at Glasgow, who, although "he smokes forty to fifty cigarettes a day, and drinks whisky," as one interviewer records, has done so much helpful Bible exposition, "is not even sure Jesus rose from the dead, not on the strength of the Biblical evidence." Dr. Barclay dismisses the miracles of Jesus by saying, "There were many miracle-workers in Jesus's time." But, Dr. Barclay, was Paul a liar when he deliberately asserted that he saw the risen Lord? As a Scottish Presbyterian, Dr. Barclay keeps the Sabbath, or the Lord's Day, and must surely know that Sunday was named the Lord's Day by the apostles to commemorate the miracle that happened that Easter morn.

Paul would have us remember that we can only be saved, or fashioned, into Christians, if we believe that Jesus died *and rose again* (Rom. 10: 9-10). No man, in spite of any religious profession and position he may have, is a Christian after the apostolic order if he denies the Resurrection of Jesus. If He did not rise, all of us are still in our sin. What is it, however, that makes His shed blood and triumph so efficacious? If Jesus was only a man, withal a holy man, who died as a martyr for truths He believed, then His blood would have no more virtue than the blood of any martyr. But Paul uses a pregnant phrase in describing how the church of *God* came into being: "which He [God] hath purchased with his own blood" (Acts 20:28). *The Blood of God!* As Christ died as the God-man, "God manifest in flesh," in some mysterious yet marvelous way deity and humanity mingled in that "precious blood," as Peter calls it, and this is why the crimson tide can wash away the stain of sin (I John 1:7; Rev. 1:5). It was Christ, "the Mighty Maker," who died. Isaac Watts has taught us to sing that the Saviour who bled and died was our *Sovereign*. Charles Wesley expresses it another way:

> 'Tis mystery all! The *Immortal* dies!
> Who can explore His strange design?
> In vain the first-born seraph tries
> To sound the depths of love divine!

Another impressive fact of Scripture is that our Lord's risen body bore the evidence of the form of His death. When he appeared to Thomas, He showed him the woundprints in His hands; and those "rich wounds are still visible above." Zechariah describes the time to come when one shall ask him, "What are these wounds in thine hands?" (Zech. 13:6). Those wounds in His hands, feet, and side are His credentials. Thomas Aquinas has the comment on Jesus showing His friends His wounds:

> With what rapture gaze we on those glorious scars — the scars that remained in Christ's body belong neither to corruption nor defeat, but to the greater increase of glory, inasmuch as they are the trophies of His power; and a special comeliness will appear in the places scarred by the wounds.

The scars of sacrificial service which Paul bore in his body, and which he spoke of as "the marks of the Lord Jesus," displaying them as proudly as a soldier does his medals, disappeared with the corruption of his body and will not adorn his glorified body. But the Calvary scars of Jesus remain and are the object of eternal worship in heaven, where He has the characteristic glory of a crucified, glorified body.

> When my life's work is ended, and I
> cross the swelling tide,
> When the bright and glorious
> morning I shall see;
> I shall know my Redeemer when I
> reach the other side . . .
> By the print of the nails in His
> hand.

Experimentally identified with Jesus in His death, burial, and Resurrection, we are richly blest (Rom. 6:1-10). What else can we do but praise and honor Him who died and rose again on our behalf? How right Charles Lamb was when, in addressing a company of literary men, he said: "If Shakespeare came in we should all rise; but if Jesus Christ we should all kneel." Said an old hero, "I will bend one knee before you my liege king — I bend two knees alone to God." What else can we do — and should we do — but bend both knees in His presence, magnifying Him for His finished work on our behalf? There is the story of the man who came to Talleyrand, the renowned French statesman, telling him that he had thought out a new religion. He said to Talleyrand, "I have come to you that you may tell me how to launch it, and to so conduct this religion that men may generally give to it their assent." The wise statesman replied, "Well, you might be crucified and rise again after three days, and so start it."

For almost two millenniums Christianity has been triumphant over human sin and misery because it is not just one of the comparative religions of the world, but a divine force in the lives of men. Christianity is Christ — Christ crucified, risen, exalted, and returning to the earth bearing the stain of His blood, as its rightful Lord and King. Canon Little enlarges on this thought in his chapter on *The Witness of His Work:*

> Intellectually and morally, Christ is Christianity. Detach Christianity from Christ and it vanishes before your eyes into intellectual vapour. For it is of the essence of Christianity that, day by day, hour by hour, the Christian should live in conscious, felt, sustained relationship to the ever-living Author of his creed and life. Christianity is non-existent apart from Christ; it centres in Christ; it radiates, now as at the first, from Christ. He is indissolubly associated with every movement of the Christian's deepest life. "I live," exclaims the Apostle, "yet not I, 'but Christ liveth in me'." When we do see our Bridegroom's face,
>
> We will not gaze at glory,
> But on our King of Grace:
> Not at the crown He giveth,
> But on His pierced hand;
> The Lamb is all the glory
> Of Immanuel's land.

Chapter Ten

PROPHECIES OF HIS ASCENSION AND EXALTATION

The Memorable Forty Days	His Priestly Benediction	Reward of an Accomplished Task
The Marvelous Power of His Risen Body	His Miraculous Ascent	Privilege of a Universal Presence
The Messages of Post-Resurrection	His Awestruck Disciples	Fulfillment of a Parting Promise
The Manner of His Resurrection	His Predicted Return	Exercise of a Predicted Priesthood
	His Ascension Gifts	
	The Manifold Benefits of His Exaltation	

An infallible proof of the Resurrection was that of Christ "showing Himself alive" after the terrible death He died. The word "shew" has the implication of presenting, or placing Himself before His disciples.

> This exhibition or manifestation provided conclusive evidence of His actual Person. After sending Mary Magdalene as the apostle of the Resurrection to the Apostles, the Risen One followed up the good tidings with personal appearances to confirm their faith, and also that they, in turn, might become eyewitnesses of His being alive. Forty days elapsed between the day of His victory over the grave, and the day He was taken up to Heaven; and during those forty days, the disciples had many opportunities of walking, talking, and eating with their Risen Lord. Such days were necessary in order to equip the disciples to function as heralds of His Resurrection, Ascension and Exaltation. They were days of memorable spiritual instruction when they learned of the work they had to do, and of the doctrines they were to teach.

A. *The Memorable Forty Days*

Then, do you never wonder how the risen Lord Himself spent those forty days, apart from the few appearances to His own? For over three years before His death, His days were so crowded with preaching, teaching, and healing. Intense and exhausting activity was His. Now, there was no public ministry, and what spiritual instruction there was was confined to His disciples. He was about to leave. Not yet ascended to the Father, and in His glorified body which required no sleep, did He use the time for intercession, thereby creating the spiritual atmosphere among His little flock for the coming of His Spirit?

The exact time Jesus spent with His own is some significant – *forty* days. "Forty" is the prominent probation number in Scripture. This specific period is conspicuous in the experience of several Old Testament saints:

Forty days Noah witnessed the flood destroying the godless of earth (Gen. 7:14, 17).

Forty days Moses was in the Mount after the sin of the people in their worship of the Golden Calf (Deut. 9:18, 25).

Forty days of the spies, issued in the penal sentence of the Forty Years (Num. 13:25; 14:34).

Forty days Elijah spent in Horeb (I Kings 19:8).

Forty days of Jonah and Nineveh (Jon. 3:4).

Forty days Ezekiel lay on his right side to symbolize the forty years of Judah's transgression (Ezek. 4:6).

Then twice over in our Lord's sojourn on earth we have the same period:

Forty days of His temptation of the Devil in the wilderness (Matt. 4:2).

Forty days when, alive for evermore, He was seen of His disciples (Acts 1:3).

B. *The Marvelous Power of the Risen Body*

The visible marks of the nails in His hands and feet, and the wound in His side; His references to His "flesh and bones"; and His participation in a breakfast of "broiled fish," convinced the apostles of their Master's identity. They knew He was their Lord (John 21:7, 12). What wonderful days those must have been for the disciples as Jesus suddenly appeared in their midst, and just as suddenly vanished back into the nowhere! Such was His power that in His risen body, He could appear in a room even though its doors were fast closed, for fear of hostile Jews. With our finite minds we cannot understand how a body so tangible, bearing nailprints, and capable of assimilating food could become invisible at will.

Although the body of the risen Lord was the same body of His human life, but glorified, it was no longer subject to the ordinary conditions of human life. "The power that had upheld His body as He walked upon the Sea of Galilee, made it during those forty days independent of laws of gravitation and of material resistance." The locked door of Peter's prison was miraculously opened (Acts 12:10), but the shut doors behind which the disciples sat (John 20:19, 26) were not miraculously opened. They were still shut when Jesus suddenly appeared out of nowhere and stood in the midst of His followers. His appearance was thus preternatural, just as His disappearance was when He withdrew or ceased to be seen by the eyes of those around Him.

Even before His cross, Jesus had a similar power somewhat strange to us. For instance, He could pass through the midst of His enemies, and go on His way – convey Himself away – hide Himself – leave the temple as if He had vanished into thin air (Luke 4:30; John 5:13; 8:59). Do these instances not prove that even in "the days of His flesh" the sinless human will of Jesus possessed a power over His body which is wholly beyond our experience and comprehension? He became visible or invisible only by a distinct act of His will. This we do know, He has the key of David and can therefore open doors no man can shut; and shut doors no strong man can open (Rev. 3:7). At the rapture, the saints are to have a glorious body like unto His and, caught up to meet Him, will share His supernatural power to pass through material substances.

Lenski, in his most helpful exposition on *John*, puts the present mystery in this way:

> In His risen and glorified state, time, space, the rock of the tomb, the walls and doors of buildings no longer hamper the body of Jesus. He appears where He desires to appear, and His visible presence disappears when He desires to have it so. This is wholly supernatural, wholly incomprehensible to our minds . . . When our bodies shall eventually enter the heavenly abode of existence, we may know something of these supreme mysteries, but no doubt if even then we shall really comprehend the profundities of the Divine omnipresence of which the human nature of Jesus partakes and which He exercised since His vivification in the tomb as in these wondrous appearances. "He came and stood in their midst" is all that human thought and language can say. He did not walk through anything. The disciples did not see Him take so many steps from the door

> or the wall to their midst. He was there, and that was all.

Jesus, then, came to His own, though *the doors were shut.* What a comfort it is to know that when a gathering of the saints are reduced to privacy and secrecy for fear of hostile powers, as in countries where Communism prevails, no closed doors can shut out Christ's presence from them. He is ever in the midst speaking peace to troubled hearts.

C. *The Messages of Post-Resurrection*

What were some of the truths the risen One emphasized when He appeared to His disciples? Knowing that they would become the pillars of His church, which the coming of the Holy Spirit would bring into being on the day of Pentecost, He wanted them to be thoroughly convinced that He was indeed the Messiah of prophecy and the fulfillment of all Old Testament types concerning His whole ministry.

Among His post-resurrection utterances we have His assurance that the power and authority of the Holy Spirit would equip those He was leaving behind to witness in His name to take His Gospel to the ends of the earth. Then there was His promise that He Himself would be with them – and us – even unto the end of the age. Luke informs us that during those forty unforgettable days Jesus spoke of

The things pertaining to the kingdom of God (Acts 1:3).

The promises of the Father that they should wait for (Acts 1:4, 5).

The times and seasons of His Second Advent (Acts 1:6, 7).

The dynamic witness among all peoples (Acts 1:8).

D. *The Manner of His Ascension*

As soon as Jesus had finished His precise instructions, He ascended on high. The Greek implies that His discourse was ended, and not interrupted, when He was suddenly taken, or lifted up, from earth to heaven. Those forty days gave Him the necessary time to fully explain those Spirit-inspired commandments which were to become the body of doctrinal truth the apostles were to teach. *The Acts, The Epistles,* and *The Revelation* contain the expansion of those truths received from the lips of the divine teacher. Now let us think of the Ascension itself.

Forecast: Altogether, three ascensions to heaven, in three successive stages of the plan of Redemption, appear in Scripture:

Enoch went up to Heaven, without dying, by the direct act of God (Gen. 5:24).

Elijah, likewise, did not taste death, but ascended to heaven in a whirlwind (II Kings 2:11).

Emmanuel died, rose again, and was received up to heaven (Acts 1:9).

Each ascension provides an evidence of immortality, and the last one is the foundation of our title to it. "Because I live, ye shall live also."

"Lift up your heads, O ye gates; and be ye lift up, ye everlasting doors; and the King of glory shall come in" (Ps. 24:7-10).

"Thou hast ascended on high" (Ps. 68:18).

"If I ascend up into heaven, thou art there" (Ps. 139:8).

Fulfillment: As with other great evangelical truths, the Ascension of Christ is a subject dealt with by the writers of the New Testament, as well as by those of the Old Testament. Christ Himself joined with the ancient prophets to declare His Ascension. He asked the question of His disciples, "What and if ye shall behold the Son of man ascend up where he was before?" (John 6:62). What He had said about His pre-existence proved to be a "hard saying" to those who heard Him, but He assured them that His exaltation would justify all His utterances about proceeding forth from the Father and of returning to Him. The following references bear record of Christ's own predictions as well as the assertions of others concerning His disappearance from Earth:

"When the time was come that he *should be received up*" (Luke 9:51).

"And no man hath *ascended up to heaven,* but he that came down from heaven" (John 3:13).

"What and if ye should behold the Son of man *ascend* up where he was before?" (John 6:62).

"I go unto him that sent me" (John 7:33; 16:5).

"And I, if I be *lifted up from the earth*" (John 12:32).

"He was come from God, and *went to God*" (John 13:3; 14:12).

"I go to prepare a place for you" (John 14:2-4).

"Now I go my way to him that sent me" (John 16:5; 16:7, 10).

"A little while, and *ye shall not see me*" (John 16:16-19; 17:11).

"I am *not yet ascended* unto my Father" (John 20:17).

"The Lord . . . was *received up into* heaven" (Mark 16:19).

"Ought not Christ . . . *to enter into his glory?* (Luke 24:26).

"He was parted from them, and *carried up into heaven*" (Luke 24:51).

"A *cloud received him* out of their sight . . . Jesus, which is taken up from you *into heaven*" (Acts 1:9-11).

D. *The Manner of His Ascension*

An examination of the foregoing passages and others bearing on the same theme reveal that no fewer than thirteen words are used to describe the manner of our Lord's departure from this world into heaven. Different shades of meaning are reflected as to such a stupendous event by these terms. Ascending on high, Jesus was taken, was received, was borne, was lifted up, was taken up, was raised, was separated, was raised up. All of these descriptions declare that He went bodily to heaven, and emphasize the *fact* rather than the *mode* of His disappearance, and of a transition from one condition of existence to another more than that of one location to another. He who came to this world as a babe went from it the glorified man, and never since has been physically in it. A fact we must bear in mind is the one Dr. Graham Scroggie reminds us of, namely,

> Christ's disciples did not see Him rise from the dead, but they did see Him ascend into Heaven. For the confirmation of the certainty and reality of the Resurrection it was not necessary that they should see Him rise, but only that they should see Him risen. But it *was* necessary that they should see Him ascend in order to be sure that He had ascended. In the one case they saw the effect, but not the act; and in the other case they saw the act, but not the effect.

There is one Ascension passage somewhat perplexing to the ordinary reader of the Word, namely, the one Jesus uttered to Mary Magdalene once she discovered that her precious Master was no longer dead, but alive for ever more: "Touch me not; for I am not yet ascended to my Father" (John 20:17). Later on the same day, He told Thomas to thrust his hand into His side. Then He invited the ten disciples when He appeared to them to *handle* Him, to discover if He was actually the man they had known, the One John affirmed their hands had handled (I John 1:1). Why, then, did Jesus prohibit the first witness of His Resurrection even to *touch* Him? The somewhat abrupt request is softened and clarified for us in Weymouth's translation, "Do not cling to Me for I have not yet ascended to the Father."

Our Lord's one word in tones fondly remembered, "Mary," revealed Him to her heart, and her deep joy could find vent in no other utterance than one word, "Master!" This had been His former relation to her. As yet, she had not risen to His higher relationship as her Lord and her God. Seeing Jesus alive, a touch of her clasping hand accompanied her exclamation, to assure her that He was the very one whose grateful and loving disciple she had been. But Jesus checked her eager touch – "Be not touching me," He said, implying that a mere earthly love expressed in the embrace between friends in the flesh was unsuited to the new relations between His own and Himself in His resurrection body. Henceforth, they were not to know Him after the flesh (II Cor. 5:16).

When Jesus went on to explain, "For I am not yet ascended to My Father," He assured Mary for her comfort that the close fellowship, now not yet seasonable, would be restored, and that His people would touch Him, but with the hand of faith, more really than ever, though no longer visibly, when, after His ascension the Holy Spirit would come to make each saint conscious and confident of Him as the indwelling One. He would return to live *in* them, and not merely among them (Gal. 2:20). When Jesus invited Thomas to touch and handle Him it was for the purpose of convincing this cautious disciple that He was indeed the very same Jesus who had died upon the tree. But Thomas did not grasp the opportunity of thrusting his fingers into the woundprints, but immediately identified Him and became the only disciple to call his Lord "God."

Lenski, in his *Interpretation of John's Gospel,* reminds me that the word Jesus used does not mean "to touch lightly," but has the thought of "clinging to," "grasping tightly." Recognizing Jesus, the impulse of Mary's heart was to seize hold of Him whom she had lost and feared not to find again, and clasp Him as her own, never to lose Him again. Such an act had already begun, hence the imperative, "*Stop* clinging." C. H. Scofield, dealing with this passage and pointing out the seeming contradiction between it and the one saying "they came and held him by the feet" (Matt. 28:9), says that there are three explanations given for Christ's prohibition as Mary clasped Him.

1. That Jesus speaks to Mary as the high priest fulfilling the Day of Atonement (Lev. 16). Having accomplished the sacrifice, He was on His way to present the sacred blood in heaven, and that, between the meeting with Mary in the garden and the meeting of Matthew 28:9, He had so ascended and returned: a view in harmony with types.

2. That Mary Magdalene, knowing as yet only Christ after the flesh (II Cor. 5:15-17), and having found her beloved, sought only to hold Him so; while He, about to assume a new relation to His disciples in ascension, gently teaches Mary that now she must not seek to hold Him to the earth, but rather become His messenger of the new joy.

3. That He merely meant, "Do not detain me now; for I am not yet ascended; you will see me again; run rather to my brethren." In his remarkable hymn on *The Lord's Supper,* Horatius Bonar writes the verse

> Here, O my Lord, I see Thee
> face to face;
> Here faith can touch and handle
> things unseen;
> Here would I grasp with firmer
> hand Thy grace,
> And all my weariness upon Thee
> lean.

Allied to the Ascension of Jesus is His Exaltation, the former being necessary for the latter. While on the earth, He was subject to humiliation, of which the cross was the climax. Man lifted Him up on a tree – God now lifts Him up on to a throne.

Forecast: "The Lord . . . I will exalt him" (Exod. 15:2).

"Thou art exalted far above all gods" (Ps. 97:9).

"The Lord said unto my Lord, Sit thou at my right hand" (Ps. 110:1).

"Thou hast ascended on high... that the LORD God might dwell among them" (Ps. 68:18).

"Who shall ascend into the hill of the LORD?" (Ps. 24:3).

Fulfillment: "This same Jesus, which is taken up from you into heaven" (Acts 1:11).

"[Stephen] saw... Jesus standing on the right hand of God" (Acts 7:55, 56).

"Raised... and set him at his own right hand in the heavenly places" (Eph. 1:20).

"Wherefore God hath highly exalted him" (Phil. 2:9).

"Christ... who is even at the right hand of God" (Rom. 8:34).

"His Son... sat down on the right hand of the Majesty on high" (Heb. 1:2, 3).

"Who is gone into heaven, and is on the right hand of God" (I Pet. 3:22).

Wordsworth, describing how "we live by admiration, hope and love," goes on to say something truer of Jesus than of any other. "In dignity of being we ascend." With what dignity of being, majesty, honor, glory, and praise, He ascended to heaven, the highty victor who was once a victim. Heber, in his hymn extolling the martyrs who died for His dear sake, says of them,

> They climbed the steep ascent to
> Heaven,
> Through peril, toil and pain.

Our Lord's ascent to heaven was a very steep one indeed, for He endured the cross, despised its shame, and now sits down at the right hand of the throne of God (Heb. 12:2). Before we come to examine the necessity of His Ascension and Exaltation, let us take a look at one or two features of the Ascension itself, which took place at Bethany, the town of hallowed and happy memories for Jesus. What precious seasons of fellowship He had had there with the much-loved Mary, Martha, and Lazarus whom He raised from the dead! How His mind must have gone back to Olivet near to Bethany, for it was in that area that He had experienced some of His greatest joys and His deepest sorrows.

The place of His final departure was so very representative of His earthly life He was about to leave behind. Was it not in this district that He had known His best friends and basest foes? That sacred Mount of Olives witnessed His hours of solitude as every man went to his own home, but Jesus found His way for an all-night prayer session on its slope. It was on this self-same mount He had sat to preach the greatest sermon the world has ever heard. Further, when He returns as the prince of the kings of earth, His feet will first touch the Mount of Olives. Here, He ascends to heaven from this mount (Acts 1:12), thus making it the place of His solitude, sovereignty, and separation.

1. *His priestly benediction.* Reaching the pre-determined spot from which He was to ascend, "He lifted up his hands, and blessed them" (Luke 24:50). Up He went to heaven, with upraised hands, symbolic of a phase of the ministry He was to exercise therein, for "He ever liveth to make intercession for us." Just over forty days before, those same hands were forcibly lifted up and nailed to the cross, now voluntarily He lifted them up to bless His own. We wonder what particular benediction it was that Jesus pronounced? Could it have been the Mosaic blessing He could recite by heart?

> The LORD bless thee, and keep thee:
> The LORD make his face to shine
> upon thee, and be gracious unto
> thee:
> The LORD lift up his countenance
> upon thee, and give thee peace.
> (Num. 6:24-26).

Whatever the wording of the parting

blessing was, those who heard it must have stored it in their memories. Luke, to whom we are indebted for the features of the Ascension, both in his Gospel and also in *The Acts,* tells us that it was *while* Jesus was engaged in this priestly act that He was parted from His disciples. What better way could there be of going to heaven than that of blessing others! As His feet left the grass, and He rose heavenwards, He was still praying over His own.

A question that comes to mind is whether with His *open,* uplifted hands, the palms were turned toward the gaze of those He was leaving? If so, did they catch their last sight of those scars they must have seen several times during the forty day interval between the Resurrection and the Ascension? We say "scars" because there is a good deal of difference between a wound and a scar. Very few of the disciples saw those ghastly nail-torn hands of Jesus. Mary, His mother, and Mary Magdalene, and probably John saw those ugly, bleeding open wounds, covered with tormenting flies. But when He rose again, those wounds were healed and doubtless all of the disciples saw the scars. Luke, as a physician, would know about the scars wounds leave behind. Shakespeare, describing the valiant soldier prepared to fight and die on the day called "The Feast of Crispian," has the couplet:

> Then will he strip his sleeve and
> show his scars,
> And say, "These wounds I had on
> Crispin's Day."

In heaven, the scarred hands and feet of Jesus will eternally remain as the evidence of the terrible cost of our redemption.

2. *His miraculous ascent.* Luke says that Jesus was *carried up* into heaven. By whom, or how, was He carried or borne up? Then, as a meticulous historian, Luke goes on to say that He was *"taken up* into Heaven." Who took Him up? Further, the writer says that "a cloud received him out of their sight" (Acts 1:9, 11; Luke 24:51). Did Jesus ascend by His own volition, or was He borne on high by others? Some scholars affirm that the words "carried up into Heaven" are wanting in some of the best manuscripts, but we are grateful for their insertion in the A.V. because they remind us of the unfailing assistance Jesus received from the angels of heaven. The old Negro spiritual speaks of "the angels comin' to carry us home." While no chariot of fire nor horses of fire were needed, because Jesus knew the way back home, yet a legion of angels may have formed His triumphal chariot.

In full view of the disciples, Jesus was "taken up," a phrase implying that He was lifted above the surface of the ground, and the "cloud" is said to have produced this action. The Greek means "to take under"; and Weymouth says the cloud "closing beneath Him, hid Him from sight." *Receive* actually means "to raise a thing by getting under it, and then to catch up or raise suddenly, as a wind or a storm does." The way Luke expresses it, that was no ordinary fleecy cloud that enveloped Jesus, but a cloud of beings swooping down, surrounding Him, and bearing Him up until He was lost sight of by those who saw Him rise in triumph to His throne. Artists who have tried to portray the Ascension usually show Jesus wrapped around with angels. Angelic clouds are likely those accompanying Jesus when He returns (Rev. 1:7). Such an unusual cloud must have recalled to the minds of the spectators the marvelous and familiar symbol of Jehovah's presence in Old Testament times, the covering cloud, "The Shekinah Glory" (Exod. 40:34-38). J. A. Alexander, in his "Commentary On The Acts," speaks of the difference between the fiery translation of Elijah and that of our Lord's Ascension as prefiguring that between the spirit of the old and new economy, or of the Law and Gospel (Luke 9:52-56).

Alexander further comments that the phrase "As he went up" does not suggest that Jesus did not vanish or miraculously disappear, but simply passed beyond the boundary of vision, as He previously had done when the eyes of those disciples on the way to Emmaus were opened and they knew Him; "and *he vanished out of their sight*" (Luke 24:31). Man, by his own inventions, can now rise from the earth and ascend 250,000 miles to the moon and journey back, but apart from such mechanical aids, it is impossible for a man to rise a foot above the ground. It would be a miracle, and cause you to stare, if, while walking along, a man in front of you suddenly ascended into the air, unaided in any possible way.

Enoch and Elijah were only men, withal holy men, yet they went straight up into heaven, but not by any power of their own. God took them. Because of all He was in Himself, the man Christ Jesus could have ascended without any aid. As the Lord of Nature, all its laws, even the Law of Gravity, were under His control, and obeyed the will of their Creator. The supernatural elements of His miracles prove this. Jesus did not only exhibit the power of moral and mental superiority over common men, but His authority and power to go beyond the rules and bounds of an ordered universe. A word from His lips stilled a storm. By His almighty hands a few loaves and fishes were multiplied into an abundant feast to appease the hunger of thousands. At His command life returned to inanimate corpses; and a fig-tree withered up. He declared that He had power to raise Himself from the dead, which He did. Thus, having *all* power in heaven and on earth, He could have ascended by the exercise of His own will.

3. *His awestruck disciples.* What a marvelous experience it was for those who witnessed Jesus slowly leave their presence and rise and rise until He was beyond sight! Not one of His disciples had seen Him rise from the dead, but all of them beheld the glorious Ascension and from the day of such had no doubt whatever that the Master whose call to service they followed was indeed their risen, ascended, and exalted Lord. Luke reminds us it was the very moment Jesus had finished His discourse that, with His disciples still gazing upon Him, He was taken up from them (Acts 1:9).

Their reaction to His disappearance is also indicated. "They looked steadfastly toward heaven, as he went up." Heaven, then, is *up.* Looking "steadfastly" is the same as "gazing" (Acts 1:10, 11), which terms imply a tension or straining of the eyes. "Toward heaven" is more correctly rendered "*into* Heaven," as if the disciples were straining to penetrate its secrets and discern their now invisible Redeemer. We can imagine them standing at Olivet with upturned faces, glowing with wonder, and with their minds exercised as to what it was like in the heaven to which their Lord had gone. Luke says that before they left that sacred spot "they worshipped him" before they returned to Jerusalem with great joy in their hearts (Luke 24:52). After His death and burial they sorrowfully returned home from the tomb with a feeling that they would have to live on the memories of a dead Christ. But all is now changed. From Olivet they went out to live and labor in fellowship with a living, risen, and exalted Lord.

Back at Jerusalem, the disciples were often found in the Temple, praising and blessing for all they had witnessed. Jesus had taught them that the temple was "the house of prayer," in which as true worshippers they could find access to God (Luke 19: 46; John 2:16). As they tarried, waiting for the promised Holy Spirit, "all the memories of the precious days that had preceded the Passion would be with them in their fullest intensity." Congregating in an upper room in the city, the disciples continued with one accord in prayer and supplication, preparing themselves, thereby, for Pentecost. Historically, the church Jesus said He would build was born in a prayer-meeting, and its life can only be maintained in the same atmosphere. Dean A. B. Stanley has the verse

> He is gone—and we remain
> In this world of sin and pain:
> In the void which He has left,
> On this earth of Him bereft.
> We have still His works to do;
> We can still His path pursue;
> Seek Him both in friend and foe,
> In ourselves His image show.

We are not *bereft* of Him, as the poet puts it. Does not Mark tell us that even after Jesus was received up into heaven and had sat down on the right hand of God, as the disciples went forth after the Ascension preaching everywhere, the exalted Lord worked with them and confirmed the word with signs following? (Mark 16:20).

4. *His predicted return.* Right on the heels of Christ's departure came the promise and prophecy of His return. As soon as He was received in heaven, the disciples heard the message about their reception by Christ when He appeared the second time. The words of the saintly Bishop Hall are most pertinent as we come to consider the presence and proclamation of the two men who came from heaven, as soon as Jesus re-entered heaven.

> Our blessed Savior raised Himself to and above the heavens by His own immediate power . . . O God, Thou hast done this, but to give us a taste of what we shall be; to let us see that Heaven was never shut to the faithful; to give us an assurance of the future glorification of this mortal and corruptible part? Even thus, O Saviour, when Thou shalt descend from Heaven with a shout, with the voice of the archangel, and with the trump of God, we that are alive and remain shall be caught up together with the raised bodies of Thy saints, into the clouds to meet Thee in the air, to dwell with Thee in glory.

As the disciples were still standing, gazing up at the sky through which Jesus had passed, two men in white apparel from heaven appeared to them, and they saw them and heard them speak. The question of these heavenly messengers, "Why stand ye gazing up?" conveys the idea that they had been standing at Olivet for a long time. Jesus was already in heaven, for in His glorified body space was no criterion. One moment, He was on earth, the next in heaven. Such an immediate transition is also suggested by Paul when he speaks about being "absent from the body – present with the Lord." Then there is the way the two men from heaven addressed the overwhelmed disciples. "Ye men of Galilee," or "Men," "Galileans," that is, 'Men (who are also) Galileans." Why such a designation, seeing it came to be derisively applied to Christians? It was a respectful recognition of the disciples as the countrymen and tried friends of the One who had just ascended, the Man of Galilee.

Was the question of the two advent heralds not a mild rebuke of the disciples who continued standing, still wondering at their Master's disappearance and feeling that He should have stayed on earth? In their astonishment did they despair of ever seeing Him again, even though they had heard Him promise that He would return and receive them unto Himself (John 14:3; 17:24)? Well, quickly the messengers from heaven assured the disciples who were idly gazing after

One who was no longer visible that He, the same Jesus they saw vanish, would return *in like manner* as He went into heaven. "In like manner" is a phrase that does not imply a vague resemblance but exact identity of mode or manner. The descension of Christ will correspond to His ascension.

How did Jesus go? He went up to heaven, visibly, bodily, personally, suddenly, and will return in the very same way. Did He not say "Behold, I come quickly"? When He does appear, it will be in a moment, in the twinkling of an eye. Those "men of Galilee" were His chosen disciples, His church in representation. As the result of Pentecost, they became with the Lord the foundation of the church, and His promised return is related to the church, and is the confirmation of His own prediction, "I will come again, and receive *you* [His church] unto myself" (John 14:1-3 with Acts 1:11 with I Thess. 4:15-18). This is the aspect of His return Paul calls "that blessed hope" (Titus 2: 13), and which John speaks of as a hope that "purifieth" (I John 3:1-3).

In passing, it is necessary to point out that the two who came from heaven, announcing Christ's entrance into heaven and then His return at some future time, were not *angels* but *men!* Regularly, they are referred to as "the two angels," but Luke says that they were two men in white apparel. The saints, we are told, walk with Him in white. The young priests of the temple were clothed in white, and Jesus appeared in a similar garment in His glorified priesthood (Rev. 1:13). While we are not told the identity of these two men thus privileged to come from heaven with a message for earth, we believe that in all likelihood they were the same two men who came to Jesus while He was in the flesh, to talk with Him about the decease He should accomplish at Jerusalem, namely, Moses and Elijah. Now, the same pair appear again to tell the church of His coming the second time without sin unto salvation.

If these two Old Testament warriors were the men who appeared to the men of Galilee, then it was a fitting choice on God's part to send such messengers. Moses died but rose again and was seen by Peter, James, and John on the Mount of Transfiguration. Elijah never died, but was changed into his glorified body instantaneously and ascended to heaven, but likewise appeared with Moses on the Mount (Matt. 17:3-4). Although both were in their glorified bodies, their identity was unchanged because Peter recognized them as soon as they appeared. If Moses and Elijah were the two men who came proclaiming the second advent, then they can typify those who are to share in the rapture of the saints. Moses can represent the dead in Christ who are to rise first, and Elijah, those who are alive when Jesus comes and, escaping death, are changed in a moment of time (I Cor. 15:51-53). T. W. H. Myers bids us live and labor in the light of His predicted Parousia:

> Lo! as some venturer, from his stars receiving
> Promise and presage of sublime emprize,
> Wears evermore the seal of his believing
> Deep in the dark of solitary eyes,
> So, even I, and with a heart more burning
> So, even I, and with a hope more sweet,
> Groan for the hour, O Christ, of Thy returning,
> Faint for the flaming of Thine Advent feet.

5. *His Ascension gifts.* Among the sayings of Jesus, so hard for the disciples to understand, was the one about it being "expedient" for Him to leave them (John 16:7). All their hopes had come to be centered in Him; therefore, to them it was incom-

prehensible that going away would be an advantage. How was it possible for them to be better off without such a friend? The word *expedient* itself has a double significance. It can mean "a contrivance," "an unworthy scheme," "a shifty action." It was said of Edmund Burke that he was "Too fond of the *right* to pursue the *expedient*." But the word also means "advantageous," "profitable," "advisable," and is always used in this sense in the New Testament. Just how were the disciples to "profit withal" by Christ's withdrawal from them?

What else could they be but sorrowful when the disciples heard their Master say, "A little while and ye shall see Me no more"? But John Keble has left us this poetic description of all the saints were to acquire by the absence of their Lord, and of the way they have proved all down the ages that His going was indeed their gain.

> My Saviour, can it ever be
> That I should gain by losing Thee?
> . . .
> " *'Tis good for you that I should go,*
> *You lingering yet awhile below!*"
>
> 'Tis Thine own gracious promise, Lord!
> Thy saints have proved Thy faithful Word.
> When Heaven's bright boundless avenue
> Far open'd on their eager view,
> And homeward to Thy Father's throne,
> Still lessening, brightening on their sight,
> Thy shadowy car went soaring on,
> They track'd Thee up th' abyss of Light.

The Ascension was most necessary as the culmination of our Lord's redemptive work. It was the climax of all that was involved in His Incarnation, and was likewise the evidence of His Resurrection and demanded by it. As for the Resurrection and the Ascension, they stand or fall together. If Jesus was not able to rise again from the dead, He was not able to rise bodily to heaven. But the whole manifestation of God in Christ was supernatural – not contrary to nature but above it, and so He ascended on high having completed in history the work He came to do.

Forecast: "Thou hast ascended on high, thou hast led captivity captive: thou hast received gifts for men; yea, for the rebellious also, that the LORD God might dwell among them" (Ps. 68:18).

"He shall divide the spoil with the strong" (Isa. 53:12).

Fulfillment: "He . . . hath put all things under his feet" (Eph. 1:20-23).

"Wherefore he saith, When he ascended up on high, he led captivity captive, and gave gifts unto men" (Eph. 4:7-16).

Scofield's footnote on the passage about Jesus lifting up His hands in blessing, as He left them is apt – "The attitude of our Lord here characterizes this age. It is one of Grace: an ascended Lord is blessing a believing people with spiritual blessings. The Jewish age was marked by temporal blessings as the reward of an obedient people (Deut. 28:1-15). In the kingdom-age spiritual and temporal blessings unite."

The phrase capturing our attention in connection with His Ascension, in that of the victor triumphantly entering heaven leading His captives captive. Arthur Way translates Paul's description of the divine conqueror and His gains and gifts thus:

> "This is the significance of the words, *He went up to Heaven's height; He led captive a train of vanquished foes; He bestowed gifts on men*" (Ps. 68:18; Eph. 4:8).

The victor of the newly-conquered heights of Zion is addressed as He ascends with His train of captives to receive gifts among men, offered either by His defeated foes or by others seeking His favor. Deborah in her triumphal song calls upon Barak to lead his captivity captive, that is, lead in triumph his long train of captives (Judg. 5:12). John reminds us that "he that leadeth into captivity shall go into captivity" (Rev. 13:10). The psalmist wrote of those leading captives into captivity and of receiving "gifts for men" (the margin puts it "gifts *of* men"), the gifts being the captives or hostages themselves, *the rebellious,* who become subject to Jehovah, and whose land He makes His dwelling place.

Paul, citing this verse, applies it to the variety of gifts and functions the exalted One bestows upon His church, and uses the phrase about a multitude of captives as referring to His victory over the principalities and powers. He made an open show of triumphing over them when He died and rose again (Col. 2:15). The powers of evil, hitherto victorious over men, were conquered, and became subject to the victor, who makes them captive by His redemptive work. The Gospel of the Ascension is that Jesus triumphed over the world, over sin, over death, over Satan. Everything that went to make up our cruel captivity He had led captive. And now, seeing He is for us, none can be against us (Rom. 8:31).

But because Paul provides the contrast between Jesus, descending into "the lower parts or regions of the earth" before He ascended up "far above all heavens" (Eph. 4:9, 10), there may be another application of the phrase about leading captivity captive as He ascended on high, as the *Scofield Reference Bible* suggests (page 1098). From our Lord's encounter with the Pharisees when He recited the incident of the rich man and Lazarus, it would seem as if He taught that before His Ascension, those who died did not go direct to their final abode in heaven or hell, but to an intermediate state of disembodied spirits in a sphere having two divisions or compartments, with a gulf between, namely, *Abraham's Bosom,* to which Lazarus went, not because he was poor but because in spite of his poverty his heart was in a Godward direction. The rich man went to hell, not because he was rich but because he forgot the source of his wealth and his negligence to use same for the relief of the poor.

a. *Before the Ascension*

Up until the time of Christ's death, there was the section of the unseen abode of the departed known as *paradise* or Abraham's Bosom. As Jesus hung on the cross, He comforted the repentant dying thief with the words, "Today shalt thou be with me in *paradise*" – not heaven. This beautiful term of Persian origin means "a garden" and is used to describe man's first habitation – The Garden of Eden. Then it came to signify the temporary, invisible residence of the blessed who died in the Lord. John Wesley, in one of his *Sermons,* affirmed that "it's plain that Paradise is not Heaven. It is, indeed, if we may be allowed the expression, 'the ante-chamber of Heaven'."

The other section Christ called *hell,* where the ungodly are in torment, is also referred to as *The Pit* and *Tartarus* (Luke 16:23; II Pet. 2:4, R.V.; Rev. 9:1, 2, 11). *Hades,* or its corresponding word *Sheol,* represents the abode and state of the dead in general. Hell is not the final depository of the wicked, but the lake of fire (Rev. 20:15). From our Lord's teaching it is clear that death does not terminate our existence, but the dead, whether good or bad, are alive, conscious, in the full exercise of their faculties such as pain and the ability to feel pain and concern for others. Further, using the phrase "the great gulf *fixed,*" He also teaches the impossibility of contact between the saved and the lost, as well as that of the latter being able by purgatorial fires to transfer to the company of the former. There is no second chance after salvation. Once death claims a person, destiny is fixed.

b. *After the Ascension*

The intriguing question is, Where was Jesus Himself during the time His body was in the tomb? Well, His own answer to such a question was that He was in paradise. Thus, to His companion in suffering He promised, "Today shalt thou be *with me* in paradise." He did not go unto the Father, as He said He would, until He ascended on high. How the saints in paradise must have welcomed the crucified One! They were prisoners of hope, captives, so to speak, awaiting their translation to heaven. Did He preach unto these spirits in their paradise-prison of the joy awaiting them in the Father's home? When Paul says "When Jesus ascended up on high He led a multitude of captives," were they those in paradise He had spent three days with, assuring them that as He was being taken up to heaven He would gather them as His companions and lead them as His love-captives into heaven?

This is evident, that since His Ascension all saints dying go not into the ante-chamber of heaven, but straight into heaven itself. When Stephen was dying he saw Jesus in heaven, and at death went right into His presence. Now, paradise is emptied of its captives. They are with the Lord, which is far better. Then possibly added to those paradise saints ascending with Jesus may have been those saints who were raised from the dead when He was. Matthew records how an earthquake opened graves and that bodies of buried saints came alive "after his resurrection" (Matt. 27:51-53). If these resurrected saints from paradise joined the rest who did not share the privilege of rising from the dead when Jesus did, what a glorious, adoring multitude of captives they must have been, as with their victor they ascended into heaven.

The other section of sheol associated with the torments of the wicked remained and is still the abode of those who die without God. "The wicked shall be turned into hell," *which*, with all its remorse, anguish, and despair, will one day be cast into the Lake of Fire, the final abode of all those whose names are not "written in the Lamb's Book of Life." At the Judgment of the Great White Throne, the wicked dead are raised for the ratification of their condemnation. "Death and Hell delivered up the dead which were in them." The ultimate and eternal depository of the lost, of Satan, of the Beast, of the False Prophet, of death and hell is the blackness of darkness for ever.

We now come to consider the nature of the predicted Ascension gifts Christ bestows upon saved men and women; for "*every one* of us is given grace according to the measure of the gift of Christ" (Eph. 4:7). There is no believer without a regeneration gift made possible by the exaltation of Christ (Rom. 12:3-8). What may we not expect from Him who has led captive such a captivity? Holding the key of all the treasures of heaven, He is able to pour down the golden showers of grace on His people here below. What were and are our Lord's Ascension gifts? They are of a spiritual nature and represent a spirit-filled ministry, with a view to the development of a spirit-filled church, united in the spirit to the Lord Himself.

Paul makes it clear that those possessing in any degree the Ascension gifts must use them for—

The perfecting of the people of God,

the work of the ministry,

the edifying of the whole body of Christ.

The whole purpose of these ministry gifts is for the continuation of the work He inaugurated while among men, and must be continually exercised until the glorious head of the church shall have for the vehicle of His action a mystical body complete and perfected, faultless and immortally mature (Ephes. 4:12-16). The three *for's* in verse 12 should be noted. Together they stand for the equipment, adjustment, adaptation, and the furnishing of saints for service in the Lord's name and for the Lord's glory.

To the list of gifts given in Ephesians, namely, apostles, prophets, evangelists, teachers, we can add those he mentions in Corinthians: miracles and healings, helps, government, tongues (I Cor. 12:4-13; Rom. 12:3-8). Dead men need evangelists; living men need pastors and teachers. Apostles, prophets, evangelists are devoted to the *extension* of the church; teachers to its *edification.* Evangelists are the Christ-given quarrymen who dig out the stones. Pastors are the stone-squarers who take off their rough edges. Teachers are the masons who put the stones in place. From all these specified gifts, responsibility passes to "every one of us" to receive them and respond to their ministry that the entire body shall be built up into the head.

A rule of divine procedure in respect to gifts is the one thrice intimated by the divine Giver Himself and that with much emphasis, namely, that gifts habitually exercised are increased, but those habitually neglected are withdrawn (Matt. 13:12; 25:29; Luke 19:26). It was to such a spiritual church at Ephesus that Jesus said that unless it repented of its fallen condition and returned to its first love that He would remove such a "candlestick out of his place" (Rev. 2:5). Thus, with any gift the Lord bestows it is a matter of *use it* or *lose it.*

Without doubt the first and greatest gift of the ascended Lord was the predicted, promised Holy Spirit, who came that unction might be provided for all endowed with gifts to be used for the building up and perfection of the body of Christ.

Forecast: "I will pour out my spirit unto you" (Prov. 1:23).

"I will pour my spirit upon thy seed" (Isa. 44:3).

"I will pour out my spirit upon all flesh" (Joel 2:28).

Fulfillment: "I will put my spirit upon him" (Matt. 12:18).

"When he, the Spirit of truth, is come" (John 16:13).

"They were all filled with the Holy Spirit" (Acts 2:4).

"In the last days, . . . I will pour out of my Spirit" (Acts 2:17, 18).

"Therefore being at the right hand of God exalted, and having received of the Father the promise of the Holy Spirit, he hath shed forth this" (Acts 2:33).

"All power" (Matt. 28:18-20).

The story of The Acts is eloquent with the outcome of such a gift, for on almost every page of the book we have evidences of the presidency and presence and power of the paraclete. Thus a more fitting title of this fifth Book of the New Testament should be *The Acts of the Holy Spirit Through the Apostles.*

Just before Christ left His disciples He astounded them by saying, "Greater works than these shall he do; because I go unto my Father" (John 14:12 R.V.). But it was a prediction to be fully realized as the result of His Ascension. The spiritual conquests for well over 1900 years have been "greater works" than the miracles Jesus performed, for they were temporal, but these "works" are spiritual.

Although we have briefly considered the gifts our exalted victor made possible for His church, we must not lose sight of what His Ascension meant for Himself. If it was profitable for His own that He should go away, what gains were His as He returned to the eternal abode He had left to become a man on earth? What was the pleasure prospering in His hand, and the portion the Father divided with His Son (Isa. 53:10, 11)?

a. *The Reward of His Accomplished Task*

We read that "when He had by Himself purged our sins," "*He . . . sat down* on the right hand of the Majesty on high," as the margin puts it (Heb. 1:3). Here, again, prediction was performed, for centuries before the Ascension David wrote "The LORD said unto my Lord, Sit thou at my right hand, until I make thine enemies thy footstool" (Ps. 110:1). During His sojourn on earth, Jesus, who went about doing good, did little sitting down. Once we are told that He was so weary with His travel and tasks that He sat down by a well, but it was not for long. During His last days there was hardly any time to rest, but with the work He came to do finished, He now sits down. While Jesus is usually represented as sitting at the right hand of God, the post of honor and co-equal power (Matt. 26:64; Eph. 1:20; Col. 3:1; Heb. 10:12, etc.), twice we read of Him *standing*. Stephen, facing a terrible death, looking up to heaven, saw not only the glory of God, but "Jesus standing" (Acts 7:55). Such a changed posture seems to imply that He had risen from His throne to greet His servant who had perished as the first martyr of His church He had bought with His own blood.

Then John, in his vision of Jesus, saw Him as a Lamb standing as it had been slain (Rev. 5:6, 7). Presently He sits with His Father in His throne (Rev. 3:21), but the session of patience is at an end. *Standing* between the throne and the elders implies the first step to the assumption of His blood-bought inheritance. Christ, bearing in His person the scars of the cross, is about to take to Himself His great power and reign. So the "throne" and "right hand" are vacated, and He stands, poised ready to act. *Sitting* suggests a state of quiescence; *standing* intimates readiness for action.

b. *The Privilege of His Universal Presence*

There seems to be an apparent contradiction between these two sayings of our Lord while here below: "I leave the world, and go to the Father" (John 16:28) and "Lo, I am with you alway" – "I will never leave thee" (Matt. 28:20; Heb. 13:5). Predicting His coming Death, Resurrection, and Second Advent, we also find the somewhat opposite statements, "Ye shall not see Me" – "I will see you again" (John 16:7, 16-22). How could He be taken up from His own, yet be with them through all the days? Well, it was expedient for Him to go away that His *localized* presence might become a *universal* presence. While here on earth, because of His possession of a human body, Jesus could not be in two places at a given moment. If He was in Jerusalem, He could not be in Capernaum at the same time. Like the rest of humans around Him, He had to move from one point to another. Men knew where to find Him as the local and visible friend in need.

But one of His Ascension gains is His universality – a blessing His universal church is grateful for. As the result of His exaltation, He ceased to be the seen, local Christ and became the universal Christ by the Holy Spirit's advent. So His going was, spiritually and mystically, His coming again to His own. There is, of course, the promise of His personal return for His church. "Surely *I* come quickly." But how advantaged and comforted we are to know that whether His saints are in America or Africa, Japan or Jamaica, Britain or Borneo, all of them, no matter where they are, can all claim the promise at the same time – "I will never leave thee, nor forsake thee." You in your small corner of the globe, and I in mine, can both realize at the same moment the invisible and inspired and constant presence of Him who is always at hand and never far away from any child of His.

> In the palace of my soul
> He dwells, my Lord and I.

c. *The Fulfillment of His Parting Promise*

Having announced that He was to leave His disciples, Peter asked, "Lord, whither goest Thou?" – a question leading Jesus to utter sublime words myriads of saints all down the ages have rested their hearts upon, "Let not your heart be troubled... In my Father's house are many mansions... I go to prepare a place for you" (John 14:1-3). This, then, is part of His present joy as the result of His return to His original home, to prepare a place for His redeemed children within it. What kind of place it is to be, we do not know. This is evident, that it is a prepared place for a prepared people, and that if we desire the assurance of being heaven-bound we must be heaven-born. "Except a man be born again, he *cannot* see the kingdom of God" (John 3:3).

As the good man prepared a large upper room furnished for the Passover Feast (Mark 14:15; Luke 9:52), so the master Himself is preparing a larger upper room for the many guests He wishes to have with Him. "That where I am, there ye may be also." From His high-priestly prayer we gather that it is His express wish to have those who are married unto Him continually in His presence. "Father, I will that they also, whom thou hast given me, be with me where I am; that they may behold my glory, which thou hast given me" (John 17:24). Paul knew that at death he would depart to be with Christ, which was a companionship far better than any earth could offer.

> There is a Home, where all the soul's deep yearnings
> And silent prayers shall be at last fulfilled.
> Where strife and sorrow, murmurings and heart-burnings
> At last are stilled, at last are stilled.

d. *The Exercise of His Predicted Priesthood*

When we come to the section dealing with "Prophetic Offices" we shall deal more fully with Jesus as priest. At this point all we want to indicate is that on His return to heaven, He entered upon His unique ministry as intercessor, a ministry He will exercise all through the church age or from His Ascension to His Advent, or return for His church. Dealing with the unchanging, unfailing priesthood of Jesus, Paul tells us that He entered within the veil as our forerunner (Heb. 6:19, 20). The term "forerunner" is a most interesting one, suggesting a person who goes in advance, acting as a scout, especially in military matters. It can also represent one sent before a king to see that the way was prepared. It was thus that John the Baptist functioned as the forerunner of Jesus (Isa. 40:3; Matt. 11:10).

Used of Christ, it means that He went on in advance of His followers to take up an office on their behalf. But the writer expresses an entirely new idea, lying completely outside of the Levitical system. In *Hebrews* much is said of Jesus as the High Priest, but the High Priest of old did not enter the tabernacle or temple as a "forerunner" but only as the people's representative. None could follow him into the inner sanctuary. By divine command, he *only* could enter "the holy of holies." He went in the people's stead to plead on their behalf – not as their pioneer! The article *the* is not in the original. The phrase should read "Whither as a forerunner Jesus entered."

This, then, is the peculiarity of the ministry of priesthood that Jesus entered upon, namely, that as the High Priest, He goes nowhere where His people cannot follow Him. He, it is, Who introduces us into full fellowship with God. We have "boldness to enter into the holiest by the blood of Jesus" (Heb. 10:19). One phase of priesthood ministry is that of intercession.

Forecast: "He . . . made intercession for the transgressors" (Isa. 53:12; Gen. 18:23-33).

"He . . . wondered that there was no intercessor" (Isa. 59:16).

"Let them now make intercession to the LORD of hosts" (Jer. 27:18).

"I will pray unto the LORD your God . . . the LORD shall answer you" (Jer. 42:4).

Fulfillment: "When he had offered up prayers and supplications" (Heb. 5:7).

"He ever liveth to make intercession for them" (Heb. 7:25).

"The Spirit itself maketh intercession for us" (Rom. 8:26).

"We have an advocate with the Father, Jesus Christ the righteous" (I John 2:1).

The Bible presents us with many who prevailed in intercession, but Jesus excels them all. In Gethsemane, the prayers He presented as a sacrificial offering were drenched with His tears. His sobs gave weight to His supplications (Heb. 5:7). But in heaven, where there are no tears, His scars enforce His pleas.

Five bleeding wounds He bears,
 Received on Calvary;
They pour effectual prayers,
 They strongly plead for me.

Unceasingly, He exercises His priestly function on our behalf and is ever heard of the Father because of His godly fear. It has been suggested that the idea expressed by Paul is not merely *intercession* or prayer, but *intervention*, which includes every form of Christ's identifying Himself with all our human interests here below. It is in this sense that He functions as our *advocate* with the Father, the term meaning "a pleader who comes forward in favor of and as a representative of another" (I John 2:1). "Advocacy is that work of Jesus Christ for sinning saints which He carries on with the Father whereby, because of the eternal efficacy of His own sacrifice, He restores them to fellowship" (see Ps. 23:3).

In the goodness of God we have two almighty intercessors, the Lord Jesus and the Holy Spirit. The Holy Spirit is within us that we might not sin, and Jesus pleads His precious blood on our behalf if we do sin (Rom. 8:26, 34; I John 2:1, 2). Can we not adapt the phrase of Shakespeare and apply it to the divine intercessors – "Our prayers for ever and forever shall be yours." How apt are the lines of that saintly poetess, Frances Ridley Havergal:

The holy hands, uplifted
 In suffering's longest hour.
Are truly Spirit-gifted
 With intercessive power . . .
For evermore the Angel
 Of Intercession stands,
In His Divine High-Priesthood
 With fragrance-filled hands—
To wave the golden censer
 Before His Father's throne,
With Spirit-fire intenser,
 And incense all His own.

As we linger amid the shadows in a world so broken by sin and sorrow, our advocate on high would have us emulate His ministry in the realm of intercession for those in need. Paul exhorted young Timothy to place *first* in his service for others "Supplications, prayers, intercessions . . . for all men" (I Tim. 2:1, 2). Bishop Westcott would have us remember that "The lonely sufferer is still a fellow-worker with Him: . . . a sleepless voice of Intercession, unheard by man, but borne to God by a 'surrendered soul,' may bring strength to combatants wearied with a doubtful conflict."

Nor Prayer is made on earth, alone;
 The Holy Spirit pleads,
And Jesus, on the eternal Throne,
 For mourners intercedes.

Chapter Eleven

PROPHECIES OF HIS SECOND ADVENT

Two Events of the Second Advent
The Events of the Advent
A Triad of Great and Related Promises
The Dramatic Prophetic Program
The Inauguration of the Millennium
The Great White Throne
The Surrendered Kingdom
The New Creation

A matter of grave concern is the fact that although the vast majority of professing Christians are one with the writer in all that he has endeavored to set forth in relation with the First Coming of Christ, there are far too many among them who seem to be ignorant of what the Scriptures clearly teach us as to His Second Coming. A large class of Christian people neglect the revelation of God's program, as foretold by Christ, prophets, and apostles, with clarity in His Word; and without a definite and comprehensive view of events connected with the Second Coming they cannot rightly divide the Word of Truth. Ministers of the Word who fail to present "the more sure word of prophecy" to their people keep back from them an important aspect of a divine revelation. Vague ideas are held, and so pew, like pulpit, is robbed of truth most absorbing and inspiring.

The threadbare excuse some preachers vent is that there are so many varying, and oft-times opposing, interpretations of prophecy; and that there seems to be such an inherent difficulty in the attainment of certainty as to some features of Christ's return and future events that the whole subject is best left alone. Before the First Coming of Christ, there were pious souls who failed to distinguish between the First and Second Comings, foretold in the Old Testament. To them many of the prophecies passed almost insensibly from things accomplished at Christ's First Advent to those awaiting accomplishment at His Second Advent. Thus it was thought that there were discrepancies, which were explained away by the theory of two Messiahs: One who would suffer; One who would reign in glory. But with the fulfillment of Christ's predicted birth, life, and labors, the true solution became apparent that He was the one and only Messiah who came, first to suffer and afterwards to return to reign.

What must be borne in mind by those who fail to understand what God's program for the future really involves is that as the events for the First Coming were marvelously and minutely fulfilled – some twenty-four distinct predictions being accomplished during the twenty-four hours on the day Jesus died – so all that is clearly recorded in connection with His Second Coming will receive a like fulfillment. "There hath not failed *one* word of all His good promise, which He promised" – a fact applicable to all the promises and predictions of the return of the Redeemer. Apathy, indifference, carelessness, then, regarding interest in an intelligent understanding of events associated with Second Advent truth is to be deplored. The history of the church proves what a dynamic force the revelation of Christ's return can be in her life and service. Love is quickened and faith strengthened by the knowledge that Jesus is returning for His people, and will ultimately set up His everlasting and glorious kingdom. Further, nothing can more effectually stimulate evangelistic efforts at home and abroad than the quiet, calm assurance that all the future God has planned for His beloved Son is about to unfold.

As we have sought to follow God's plan for the First Advent of Christ, let us now seek His aid in a study of the many features of His Second Advent – prophecies of which were given by Old Testament prophets, and the apostles of the New Testament, to which are added the prophecies of Christ Himself as to His return and future events. We start by affirming that there is as much proof of His coming back to earth as there is for His first appearance on it in Old Testament Scriptures. The two focal points of the bulk of prophecy are the First and Second Advents of our blessed Lord. Peter reminds us that the Holy Spirit inspired the prophets to *testify beforehand*, "the sufferings of Christ, *and* the glory that should follow" (I Pet. 1:11). The cross and the crown belonged to one person, namely, He that has come – and is to come!

A. *Two Events of the Second Advent*

In previous sections of our study we dealt with those messianic prophecies which were fulfilled when Christ became man, lived out His life, died and rose again. What was written in the volume of the book concerning His First Advent found manifestation in all that He accomplished. We now come to examine unfulfilled prophecy, referred to as *eschatology*, or the doctrine of last things. This realm of predictive prophecy, found in both Old and New Testaments, covers themes like Christ's return for His church, the Great Tribulation, the end of the Gentile Age, the judgments, the millennium, and eternity. Such a revelation of God's eternal purposes is of vital interest, and most fascinating to follow.

The aspect of truth we are now about to take up ought to lead us into a fuller comprehension of the divine mind and will, and to a richer devotion to Him whose glory is the culmination of prophecy – God's beloved Son and our Saviour, Jesus Christ. Further, ours is the confidence that the numerous prophecies concerning Him already fulfilled are the guarantee that all the predictions as to His future appearance and activities will receive a like fulfillment. "I have spoken it, I will also bring it to pass; I have purposed it, I will also do it" (Isa. 46:11). May our personal comprehension of all the coming days hold both for Christ and ourselves result in a life that is holy and filled with an eager expectancy!

While the term "Second Advent," as well as that of "First Advent," is not to be found in Scripture, all that such terms imply flood its sacred pages. The word "Trinity" is not in the Bible but the fact is everywhere proclaimed. We are distinctly told that Christ is coming *the second time* (Heb. 9:28), and what else can this phrase mean but His Second Advent, or coming – *Advent* meaning, "Coming." In fact, in the narrative, the three distinct appearings of Jesus are brought together as a three-fold cord that cannot be broken –

"Now once . . . *hath he appeared* to put away sin by the sacrifice of himself" (Heb. 9:26) – PAST

"Christ . . . entered . . . into heaven itself, *now to appear* in the presence of God for us" (Heb. 9:24) – PRESENT

Christ . . . *shall appear* the second time" (Heb. 9:28) – PROSPECTIVE

The *backward* look – the *upward* look – the *forward* look offer a complete revelation of Him around whom the Bible gathers, but what a great loss is ours if we neglect the *forward* look, striving, thereby, to live without hope. Dr. J. G. Simpson in his great work *Christus Crucifixus* says that

> There are abundant indications that the Confidence with which the author of The Epistle to the Hebrews looked forward to the return of the Great High Priest, Who had passed into the sanctuary of the heavens, was shared by multitudes of believing men for many generations, inspiring the hope of confessors, sustaining the faith of martyrs, establishing the patience of saints . . . In times of stress, when the winds and waves have roared and hearts have failed for fear, God's saints have been upheld by the vision of the Son of Man sitting at the right hand of power and coming in the clouds. The joy of the thought of His return turned the lonely Aegean rocks and the dark Roman catacomb into the ante-chamber of Heaven itself.

May we experience that such a "blessed hope" is no mere idle theory or a vain though beautiful vision that can have no possible practical result, but an aspect of divine truth kindling our energies into flame, banishing all lifeless inactivity! The whole of life will be ennobled if we live in the light of the constant expectation of Christ's return. It is said that on one occasion during the sitting of the American Senate a sudden and very dense darkness fell upon the city. So awful, so intense did this become that the probability of the end of the world was freely discussed, and one of the Senators moved the immediate adjournment of the House. But another well-known member rose to his feet and in reply to the proposal said, "President, I propose that lights be brought in, and that we proceed with our business. If the Judge comes, He had better find us at our duty." Surely this is the sentiment that should animate all who believe that He who said He would come again will return and not tarry. "Blessed is that servant, whom his lord when he cometh shall find so doing" (Matt 24:46).

The term "the Second Advent" is a general one covering many events that are associated with our Lord from the time of His return for His church right on until the end of the millennium when He surrenders the kingdom to God. But there are two specific events or stages of His coming that must be distinguished. When the hour arrives for Jesus to leave heaven to fulfil His own prediction or promise, "I will come again," He will not descend to earth without a break. On the way down He is to pause in the air for a most stupendous event, and then after awhile continue His coming and journey to the world He left at His Ascension. There are two phrases suggesting intervening events occurring between the two stages of His one coming, and confusion will be ours if we fail to observe these two stopping places, namely,

> "to meet the Lord *in the air*" (I Thess. 4:17)
>
> "his feet shall stand . . . upon *the mount of Olives*" (Zech. 14:41).

The first event on His way down is related to His true church, and takes place in the heavenlies, or somewhere between earth and heaven. The second event is connected with His millennial reign on earth, when He is manifested as the prince of the kings of the earth. As Paul reminds us that the saints are to reign with Him, it seems likely that after coming for His saints and gathering them around Him as He tarries in the air, they will accompany Him to earth when the time comes to assist Him in the governmental control of all things here below.

A prophetic student of the last century drew an analogy between Christ's return and the return of Charles II from his exile. In this historical event there were two distinct stages. The first was concerned with the king's loyal and devoted adherents who had been true to him all through the time of the Commonwealth under Cromwell. They went across to France to meet him, and in their midst he who had long been absent from them reappeared. At first he appeared only to those true and faithful loyal subjects and spent an interval of time with them, discussing with them his plan of campaign and his order of proceedings. All concerning his return to reign was settled at this stage. The second stage came when Charles, with his company of loyal adherents, crossed the sea, landed in England, and was revealed to the nation as the returning king.

Then there followed his enthronement as the sovereign, the trial and judgment of the leading rebels, and, subsequently, the undisputed reign of Charles over the whole land. Apart altogether from the character of Charles II, the two aspects of his return closely resemble the gathering of saints to the returning heavenly king, and afterwards His manifestation of such to the whole world. Later on, we shall consider the separate series of incidents connected with these two main events: namely, *heavenly* scenes, then *earthly* happenings. Among the several words used to set forth the coming again of Christ, we have these three conspicuous ones, all of which imply that the One spoken of is personally present with those who participate in the event.

Parousia, indicating presence, arrival — "the being or becoming present." In Matthew we read, "So shall the *coming* (parousia) of the Son of man be" (Matt. 24:27, 39). He who was not formerly seen, is now here.

Apokalupsis, meaning "revelation," "unveiling," "exposure to view" (Luke 17:30; I Pet. 4:13). This word is from *apokalupto,* "to take off the cover," and gives us *Apocalypse,* the term used of "The Book of Revelation."

Epiphaneia implies "appearing" or "bringing forth into light," "causing to shine," and assures us that Christ will naturally appear and be manifested in a visible way (I Tim. 6:14; II Tim. 4:8). We are to see Him as He is, and such a disclosure is to be accompanied with the outshining of glory. Our Lord will shine *(epiphaneia)* upon those brought into His presence *(parousia).*

A tabular comparison of the passages in which these three terms occur, or those closely related to them, may help, as John Bloore suggests —

COMING (Parousia)

For the saints

(Heavenly)

John 14:3; I Cor. 4:5; 11:26; 15:23; I Thess. 1:10; 2:19; 4:15; 5:23; II Thess. 2:1; James 5:7-8 (or both); Jude 14; Heb. 10:36 (or both); Rev. 2:25, 28; 22:7, 12, 20.

With the saints

(Earthly)

Matt. 16:27; 24:3, 27, 30, 37, 39; 25:31; Mark 8:38; 13:26; Luke 9:26; 18:8; 21:27; I Thess. 3:13; II Thess. 2:8; II Pet. 1:16; 3:4; Rev. 1:7.

Mark 13:32-37 and Luke 12:31-48 may be considered as applicable to both.

REVELATION (Apokalupsis)

For the saints

(Heavenly)

I Pet. 1:7; I Cor. 1:7 (A.V. "coming").

With the saints

(Earthly)

Luke 17:30; II Thess. 1:7, 10; Rom. 8:18-19 (A.V. "manifestation").

APPEARING (Epiphaneia)

For the saints

(Heavenly)

I Tim. 6:14.

With the saints

(Earthly)

II Thess. 2:8 (A.V. "brightness").

APPEAR

Matthew 24:30; Colossians 3:4 refer to the coming with the saints. I Peter 5:4; I John 2:28; 3:2; Hebrews 9:28 clearly refer to the result for the saints consequent upon Christ having come for them.

A study of these passages establishes the two distinct parts of our Lord's coming, shows the difference of relation as to heavenly and earthly scenes, and necessitates an interval of time between them.

The following, fuller classification should help the reader to discern the things that differ in connection with the return of the Redeemer who will soon be leaving His chamber, "perfumed with myrrh and frankincense, with all the powders of the merchant."

B. *The Events of the Advent*

FIRST EVENT

Private – as a king privately visiting new relations of royal blood.
N.T. – *Revelation*, see John 14:1-3; Philippians 3:20; I Thessalonians 4:13-18.
Comes to the *Air* (I Thess. 4:17).
Comes to His *Church*.
Comes for His *Church*.
Comes to a *Marriage*.
Comes as a *Bridegroom*.
Comes to *present* to Himself a holy and acceptable church.
Symbolized by:
Morning Star.
Thief, coming without warning.
Church *caught away, secretly* as Enoch before the Flood.
Parousia – bodily presence.
Our *Gathering* unto Him.
The Day of *Christ*.
The *Hope* of the *Church*.
Church listens for *Sounds*.

SECOND EVENT

Public – as a king riding in state, and acclaimed everywhere as king.
O.T. – *Prophecy*, see Zechariah 14:1-9; Colossians 3:4; Jude 14.
Comes to *the Mount of Olives* (Zech. 14:4).
Comes to *Israel*.
Comes with *His Church*.
Comes to a *Judgment*.
Comes as a *King*.
Comes to *establish* His kingdom, and with His church reign over the earth in righteousness.
Symbolized by:
Rising Sun.
Lightning and thunder.
Church *openly and publicly manifested* with Christ, to assist in His rule.
Epiphaneia – unveiling of bodily presence.
Our *Appearing* with Him in Glory.
The Day of the *Lord*.
The *Hope* of *Israel*.
Israel looks for *Signs*.

There are several points to observe in connection with these two events. First of all, there will be an interval of time between them of at least the seven prophetic years, predicted by Daniel's seventieth week (Dan. 9:27). This inter-period forms the burden of the books of *Daniel* and *Revelation*.

Secondly, between the present Church or Grace Age and the return of our Lord to fulfil what is called "our gathering unto Him," there is no single predicted event to be fulfilled. But in the second or public part of His coming, there are many predicted events to be fulfilled, as we hope to show.

In the third place, present-day believers awaiting the Master's promised coming have a twofold responsibility, namely to live and function as members of His Body, so that when we see Him we shall not be ashamed before Him. Then, in view of the fact that the unsaved will not be caught up when Jesus comes, we must labor as soul-winners, striving to bring them to Him who alone can emancipate them from sin's thralldom and thereby preserve them from the fearful tribulation to overtake a godless world.

The Second Advent of Christ was

the burden of John Milton, the wonderful blind poet in this sublime supplication:

> Come forth out of Thy royal chambers, O Prince of all the kings of the earth; put on Thy visible robes of Thy imperial majesty; take up that unlimited sceptre which Thy Almighty Father hath bequeathed Thee. For now the voice of Thy bride calls Thee, and all creatures sigh to be renewed.

It is said that a friend of Rufus Jones, the renowned Quaker leader, once remarked: "To meet him was to feel set up for the rest of the day because he always made one confident that the best was yet to come." Is this the way to live? Upheld by the glorious hope the future holds for us in the Saviour's return, do we bear such a joyous expectation in our look, making others confident that the best is yet to be?

C. *A Triad of Great and Belated Promises*

Among the thousands of promises the Bible contains (a full treatment of which will be found in the author's volume *All the Promises of the Bible*), those that come from the lips of the Lord Jesus are among the most precious. Many of His very clear and definite promises were actually *predictions,* many of which have already been realized in the history of His church. Such fulfillment leads us to believe that other prophecies yet unfulfilled will receive a like literal performance. Before His final rejection and crucifixion, Jesus gave His disciples three outstanding promises or predictions which form a trinity in unity.

1. *He promised the gift of the Holy Spirit.* Troubled over His predicted departure from them, the disciples were assured that they would not be left in the world as orphans but that He would send them *another* Advocate, another, like Himself, to take His place among them. "I will pray the Father, and he shall give you another Comforter, that he may abide with you for ever; Even the Spirit of truth" (John 14:16, 17). As the Spirit of Truth, He was to take of the truths concerning Christ and reveal their inner significance to their minds. Further, as the One who inspired the prophets to depict coming events, He would be with the disciples to show them things to come.

Such a promise was redeemed on the day of Pentecost, when the Holy Spirit came as the gift of the ascended Lord for His people. On that historic day the Spirit was manifestly and abundantly bestowed upon the assembled believers in the upper chamber, and He still abides in the true church – "the habitation of God through the Spirit." He it is who indwells each follower of the Saviour, combating ignorance and infirmity and making intercession for the saints (Rom. 8:26).

> Our blest Redeemer ere He breathed
> His tender last farewell,
> A Guide, a Comforter bequeath'd
> With us to dwell.

2. *He promised to build His church.* As the previous promise was abundantly fulfilled, the one before us is *being* fulfilled day by day, for every newly born child of God is another living stone added to the mystic fabric the Scriptures call "The Church of the Living God." The building of this marvelous, spiritual structure will not be completed until, in the counsels of God, the last stone has been quarried out of the world to consummate the divine plan. Further, the first promise and this second one are closely related, for as the Holy Spirit was vitally and intimately associated with the Birth of Christ, so was He directly connected with the birthday of the church, which took place as the result of Pentecost (Acts 2).

Continual additions to the church, the Lord's body, are the result of the convicting and regenerating ministry of the Holy Spirit (John 3:3-8). He also maintains the spiritual power of the church and, as the Vicar of Christ on earth, ever seeks to further His cause among men. For over 1900 years now, the Spirit has remained here below, and will continue His manifold ministry until the church is complete. The first explicit disclosure of such a body as the church came from Christ Himself in response to Peter's astounding statement concerning the messiahship and deity of His master (Matt. 16:13-19): "Upon this rock I will build my church; and the gates of hell shall not prevail against it." The future tense, *I will*, must be noted, implying as it does that the church, as we know it from The Acts and The Epistles, was not in existence when the prediction was made. Dr. A. T. Pierson speaks of the necessity of observing "The Law of First Mention." In this first declaration of our Lord's purpose, it is important to observe the personal pronoun He used: "my church." Now we have numerous designations such as *Anglican* Church, *Baptist* Church, *Methodist*, etc., etc. But as its head, Christ spoke of it as *my* church. The Greek word for *church* means "The Lord's," and accurately describes its ownership. *Ecclesia* was a familiar term at the time. Stephen in his defense referred to "the church in the wilderness" (Acts 7:38).

The Hebrew use of the word marked the Jews as a separate people, distinct from all other nations in the fact that before they became a monarchy, governed by a visible, titular head, they constituted a *theocracy*, or God-governed people. Thus when Jesus laid emphasis upon the personal pronoun *my*, He was intimating His plan to create a people who would become a spiritual theocracy – a God-governed, Christ-honoring, Spirit-indwelt people.

Further, with divine authority He said "*I* will build," and since Pentecost this is what He has been doing through the Spirit. As for the word *build*, it signifies more than the mere act of building. It implies to "build a house," and carries the suggestion of the formation of a spiritual dynasty – my *ecclesia!* Then Jesus went on to declare that the spiritual house He was to build could be impregnable and invincible. "The gates of Hell shall not prevail against it." The visible, organized church may be hopelessly divided in itself, "by schisms rent asunder, by heresies distrest," and impotent as it faces a world of sin, crime, violence, and bloodshed; but *His* church, of which He is "the chief cornerstone, in whom all the building fitly framed together [and] groweth unto an holy temple in the Lord," is ever potent in spiritual influence, invincible and indestructible.

Another striking feature is that Jesus only used the word *church* twice, that is, according to the records. First, when He spoke to Peter as the representative of the rest, all of whom, Judas excepted, became the foundation of the church (Eph. 2:20). The second time He employed the term was when He addressed the group when gathered together – the nucleus of the church He was to build (Matt. 18:17). But the remarkable fact is, as Dr. Campbell Morgan points out in his volume on *Peter and the Church*, that "neither in the words of Peter recorded in The Acts, nor in his two Letters, is the word *Church* ever used." True, as Luke reminds us in The Acts, Peter acted for the church and was prayed for by the church. But while the apostle is not recorded as uttering the word, he certainly gave the world the most wonderful and complete description of the nature of the church of God to be found anywhere else in the New Testament –

> "But ye are a chosen generation, a royal priesthood, an holy nation, a peculiar people: That ye should

shew forth the praises of him who hath called you out of darkness into his marvellous Light" (I Pet. 2:9).

Elvet Lewis, the famed Welsh poet-preacher, once said that Jude had intended to write a treatise on salvation but was prevented – "While I was giving all diligence to write unto you of the coming salvation" – from doing it and had to write something else because Paul was already the writer of the great document on salvation. Dr. Morgan suggests that "Peter, the one to whom came the first word about the Church, under the guidance of the Holy Spirit, knew that the mystery of the Church, and its interpretation, were not committed to him, but to Paul." Without doubt, Paul was raised up to be the most remarkable interpreter of the constitution, nature, and ministry of the church Jesus purchased with His blood.

It is this fact of Pauline instruction that leads us to say that the church is not the subject or object of revelation in the Old Testament. This is why all references to the future ministry of the Messiah are related to what will happen on the earth, once the church has been caught up. As the result of Calvary, the building of the church commenced at Pentecost and will be consummated when He, whose church it is, receives her as a bride unto Himself as the bridegroom. Paul emphatically declares that the composition of the church was the mystery hid from the ages, that is from Old Testament saints. Boldly, the apostle announces that Christ Himself had made him the recipient of the inner significance of this mystery he calls "the mystery of Christ" (Eph. 3:1-12).

What was the content of this mystery "which in other ages was not made known unto the sons of men," but which is no longer a "mystery"? Well, Paul tells us. It was God's eternal purpose to bring regenerated Jews and regenerated Gentiles together and make them fellow-heirs of the unsearchable riches of Christ, and members of His body – His church. Thus, while salvation came from the Jews, it is no longer confined to Jews, but is for all who believe, whether Jew or Gentile. This mystery, once hid in God, constitutes the Gospel of His redeeming grace.

The Prophetic Gap or Leap

Although the conception and composition of the church of God was unknown to Old Testament prophets, theirs was a sense of wonderment regarding what lay between the First and the Second Advents of the Messiah. Daniel, more than any other prophet, had a clear insight as to the coming of the Messiah who would be "cut off," or killed, but who would reign after "the week" – a week of years – or the seven years of desolations and abominations were ended (Dan. 9:20-27). But there was something in between the cutting off and the setting up of the Messiah as king that Daniel could not fathom – a gap he was not able to bridge. In common with other prophets, he testified years before Christ came of "His sufferings, and of the glory that should follow." But between His redemptive work at Calvary and His entrance upon His predicted government of the earth, there seemed to be a parenthesis that Daniel and his co-prophets could not explain.

Perhaps this was why Daniel's "cogitations" or meditations troubled or baffled his mind (Dan. 7:28), and why, with others, he takes a prophetic leap from one event to another far distant, without a knowledge of what goes between. The Holy Spirit operative even in Old Testament days as the One who would show the saints "things to come" did not disclose to them the valley between the mountain peaks of "the sufferings of

Christ, and the glory that should follow" (I Pet. 1:11). The comma between "the sufferings" and "the glory" represents the undisclosed period of church history and the prescribed periods of the Great Tribulation and then the Millennial Reign of Christ. It is in the once hidden valley that the church exists and exercises her ministry as the agent and avenue of salvation to a lost world.

"The glory that should follow" literally means "the glories after them" – the plural corresponding to the plural "sufferings" – the one as multiform as the others. What are the "glories" following the gory cross – the glory of His Resurrection, the glory of His Ascension, the resumed divine glory (John 17:5), the glory which is His in the triumphs of the church He purchased with His blood –but most conspicuous in prophetic Scripture, the world-wide glory of His millennial reign – a glory covering the earth, as the waters cover the sea?

3. *He promised to return for His church.* We now consider, more specifically, Christ's third promise He gave His own. All three promises are backed by His authoritative will and power of fulfillment. Three "I will's" –

"I will send my Spirit."
"I will build my church."
"I will come again."

The place where this third promise was given, and its exact phraseology, must be noted. Jesus was gathered with His eleven apostles in the Passover chamber. Judas was missing from the company, having gone out to complete the arrangements of the betrayal of his master. A deep gloom rested upon the small assembly because Jesus had told them that He was about to leave them. "Whither I go, thou canst not follow me now" (John 13:36). Then He gave utterance to some of the most sublime words ever to leave His holy lips. Jesus spoke to His distressed friends about the secret of an untroubled heart, namely,

Faith in Himself – "Believe also in me"
Faith in Heaven – "In my Father's house are many mansions"
Faith in His Return – "I will come again" (John 14:1-3).

Later on Jesus, linking His Death, Resurrection, and Second Advent together gave His disciples the comforting hope, "I will see you again, and your heart shall rejoice" (John 16:22). What must be borne in mind is the fact that He was speaking to His *own*, as He called the disciples – "having loved his own" (John 13:1). As such they formed His church in representation, for when He said "I will . . . receive *you* unto myself," He did not imply the eleven men around Him only, but the multitudes all down the ages who would believe in Him, and of whom the disciples were forerunners. The assurance of His coming is repeated, "Ye have heard how I said unto you, I go away, and come again unto you" (John 14:28).

This, then, is a particular promise for a particular people, namely, for those who have proved that no man cometh unto the Father save through the mediation of His Son (John 14:6). There are those who descry any thought of a personal return of Christ, but language has no meaning if He is not coming as He said He would. "*I* will come again." Because of all He is in Himself, He must return. If He does not, then He is a liar and not *The Truth,* as He here declares Himself to be (John 14:6). "Hath he spoken, and shall he not make it good?" (Num. 23:19). Looking for the man who left us a promise to return, we know that we shall not be disappointed.

If this were the only place in the New Testament where this first event of the Second Advent is mentioned, it would be sufficient for faith to lean upon, seeing it is a divine promise.

But there follow many ratifications of the promise. For instance, as soon as Jesus entered heaven, two glorified men left heaven to confirm His declaration –

> "This same Jesus, which is taken up from you into heaven, shall so come in like manner as ye have seen him go into heaven" (Acts 1:11).

He went away in the presence of His own, and will return in like manner. In unmistakable language, Paul enlarges upon the promise of His coming, declaring that the church is to gather around the Lord in the air (I Thess. 4:13-18). Peter tells us that the Lord will not be slack concerning the fulfillment of His promise (II Pet. 3:9). From *Hebrews* we gather that Christ is to appear "the second time" and that, "he that shall come *will* come, and will not tarry" (Heb. 9:28; 10:37). The last recorded words of Jesus reiterated His promise given in the upper chamber, "Behold, I come quickly" (Rev. 22:7, 12, 20). No wonder John gave as the last prayer of the Bible a yearning for His return, "Even so, come, Lord Jesus."

The *fact* of His coming, then, is *certain,* but the *time* of His coming is as *uncertain* as the fact is certain, and ours is the literal acceptance of the certainty of such a blessed event, the supporting evidence of which is clear, cumulative, and conclusive. That the truth of the Second Advent dominates the New Testament, being mentioned more often than any other fundamental doctrine, is seen in its appearance some 318 times. It is computed that one verse in about every twenty-five throughout the New Testament refers to it. Out of the twenty-seven books forming this sacred part of Holy Scripture, twenty-three mention the coming of Christ in some way or another – the exceptions being *Philemon* and *III John. Galatians* is also cited as an epistle carrying no reference to Christ's return, but this is not true for Paul distinctly says "For we through the Spirit *wait* for the hope of righteousness" (Gal. 5:5). We are not waiting for *righteousness* itself. This has been imputed unto us through faith in Him who has made us (Rom. 3:22), but we do *wait* for the *hope* of righteousness. What is this specific hope? Is it not *the crown of righteousness,* which the righteous One Himself will grant those at His return if they believed in and loved the truth of His appearing (II Tim. 4:8)? Crowns represent not gifts but *rewards,* and as such must be earned. May negligence of or indifference to "the blessed hope," called "The Pole-Star of the Church," not rob us of this particular crown!

Both before and after His death, Jesus made it perfectly clear that He would come again. More than twenty times in prediction, promise, and parable, He spoke of events that would end in a climax, glorious for some, gloomy for others. In fact, His Second Advent is found in the warp and woof of His teaching, taught, for instance in parables, many of which gather around His *departure,* His *absence,* and His *return.* If there be no Second Advent, then these particular parables are absolutely pointless.

Parable of the Lord and His Servant (Matt. 24:45-51). The phrase "My lord delayeth his coming" indicates that he went away, was absent, but means to return.

Parable of the Bridegroom and the Virgins (Matt. 25:1-13). The bridegroom depicted as "tarrying" likewise suggests that he intended to come – as he did!

Parable of the Lord and the Talents (Matt. 25:14-30). Here, the actions are most emphatic –

The lord went away – "a man traveling into a far country."

The lord was absent – "after a long time."

The lord eventually returned –

"the lord of those servants cometh."

Parable of the Master of the House (Mark 13:34-37). Specifically, Christ refers to Himself when He says, "the Son of Man is as a man taking a far journey," and such a journey implies a going away, absence, and return. "Ye know not when the master of the house cometh."

Parable of the Good Samaritan (Luke 10:30-35). Once this sympathetic man had helped the robbed and wounded traveler, "on the morrow . . . he *departed*," and as he did so, he assured the innkeeper, "when *I come again*, I will repay thee."

Parable of the Nobleman and the Pounds (Luke 19:12-27). Again our Lord dwells on the triple fact that He was here, went away, is now absent, and pledged to return. There is the *going away* — "went into a far country"; the *absence* — "to receive for himself a kingdom"; the *return* — "when he was returned."

One of the great objects, not only of the prophetic parables, but of all our Lord's references to His return, as well as the teaching of the apostles on the same theme, is that the saints should hold the truth as a glorious hope, and in the light of it live lives of holiness, faithfulness, and watchfulness.

With such a blessed hope in view,
We should more holy be.
More like our gracious, glorious Lord,
Whose face we soon shall see.

D. *The Dramatic Prophetic Program*

As God is the God of order and not of confusion, we expect all that concerns the future of the church, of the nations, and of the earth to be clearly set forth in His infallible Word. The Holy Spirit, whose office-work is "to show us *things to come*," inspired the writers of Holy Writ to indicate succeeding events in respect to the coming ages. How imperative it is "to rightly divide the word of truth" as we enter the realm of prophecy, in which there is no room for haphazard guesses!

1. *The rapture of the church.* As already indicated, "The Church of God" is not the subject of any Old Testament prediction, but is a specific New Testament revelation, and the next event in the divine program is the gathering unto Christ of His redeemed people gathered out of the world. Being a signless, dateless event, it may occur at any moment. By "the Word of the Lord," a phrase signifying divine inspiration and authority, Paul revealed that when Jesus comes again according to His own prediction, those who died in Him will be raised, and the saints alive as He returns are changed and receive, along with the raised dead, a glorious body like unto His own (Phil. 3:20, 21).

Then follows the dramatic ascension, for we are to be "caught up to meet the Lord in the air." It is from this swift action that we have what is known as "the Rapture," because the words "caught up" in the Latin are *rapera, rapt*, meaning to "carry off" or "to snatch away." Latterly it came to mean, "carried away by joy," which will be our experience when Jesus appears, and we, seeing Him as He is, become like Him. Many key passages of this immediate translation and transformation were cited in the preceding section on Christ's promise to return. Passages like I Corinthians 15:51-58; I Thessalonians 4:13-18; I John 3:1-3, should have the prayerful and careful attention of every believer. As to the time of this most blissful event, the majority of prophetic students place it before the period of "The Great Tribulation" which is to try the whole earth (Rev. 3:10). While the saints are with the Lord, two episodes directly affecting them will take place.

2. *The judgment seat of Christ.* This particular judgment must not be con-

fused with the final assize, The Great White Throne, at which sinners only appear (Rev. 20:11-15). Saints only are to assemble at the judgment seat of Christ, as Paul so clearly teaches in passages like Romans 14:9-11; I Corinthians 3:12-15; II Corinthians 5:10. This is when their lives and labors are reviewed and rewarded – or condemned – as the case may be. Constantly living in the light of this judgment exercises a revolutionary influence over one's life. The rewards are spoken of as "crowns." The tragedy is that many of us will stand before the Judge with a saved soul, but a *lost life* – "saved; yet so as by fire." May we be found living to the limit for the Lord, not merely to receive a reward, but because Calvary has a claim upon the best we can give Him in time, talents, and treasure!

3. *The marriage of the Lamb*. God said of His ancient people Israel, "I will betroth thee unto me for ever" (Hos. 2:19, 20). Paul, describing our deliverance from sin, and from God's broken law, speaks of us as "married ... to him who is raised from the dead" (Rom. 7:4). But before Christ continues His return and journeys to the earth with His church, there will take place this blessed event which will prove to be a season of culminating joy for both the bride and the bridegroom. Apart from what John gives us of "the marriage of the Lamb" (Rev. 19:7-9), we do not have fuller details in Scripture. The Passover supper Jesus Himself instituted is a foretaste of this most marvelous occasion, when "the Bride will not eye her garment, but her dear Bridegroom's face."

4. *The Great Tribulation*. It is most necessary to distinguish between *tribulation* and what John calls *The Great Tribulation*, or, as the original puts it, "The Tribulation – The Great." The saints have always had to endure tribulation for Christ's sake. He Himself told us to expect it – "In the world ye shall have tribulation." But the period of universal trial, coming between the Rapture and the Millennium, is to be a time of unparalleled woe for the inhabiters of earth. Israel and all other nations are to be caught up in unprecedented judgments and devastating anguish. While the Old Testament has no prophetic declaration of the church, it abounds in prophecies of this dread time which covers Daniel's seventieth week, that is, a week of years (Dan. 9:24-27; cf. Ezek. 4:6).

Forecast: "Enoch ... prophesied ... saying, Behold, the Lord cometh with ten thousands of his saints, To execute judgment upon all, and to convince all that are ungodly among them of all their ungodly deeds ... and of all their hard speeches which ungodly sinners have spoken against him" (Jude 14, 15).

Many of the Psalms are heavy with prophecy related to a time of world tribulation and the millennial reign of the Messiah. Here is one striking instance:

> "Our God shall come, and shall not kept silence; a fire shall devour before him, and it shall be very tempestuous round about him. He shall call to the heavens from above, and to the earth, that he may judge His people."

Then follows a verse which has a double application:

> "Gather my saints together unto me; those that have made a covenant with me by sacrifice" (Ps. 50:3-5).

This is what will happen when Jesus returns for those who are His saints in virtue of His sacrifice. But during the days of fierce tribulation, the Lord will overshadow not only those who refuse the mark of the Beast, but also His ancient people, the Jews:

> "The Lord will come with fire, and with his chariots like a whirlwind, to render his anger with fury, and his rebuke with flames of fire" (Isa. 66: 15; cf. 2:10-22).

"I beheld even till the beast was slain... the rest of the beasts,... had their dominion taken away" (Dan. 7:11, 12).

"Behold, I will make Jerusalem a cup of trembling unto all the people round about... all that burden themselves with it shall be cut in pieces" (Zech. 12:2, 3).

"Behold, the day of the Lord cometh" (Zech. 14:1).

"For it is the day of the Lord's vengeance" (Isa. 34:8).

"Hold thy peace at the presence of the Lord God: for the day of the Lord is at hand" (Zeph. 1:7; cf. Joel 2:1, 2).

"The great day of the Lord is near ... a day of wrath, a day of trouble and distress, a day of wasteness and desolation, a day of darkness and gloominess, a day of clouds and thick darkness" (Zeph. 1:14, 15; cf. 2:2, 3; Jer. 30:7).

Many of these Old Testament prophecies have both a partial and a final fulfillment. For instance, in Zephaniah, the approaching invasion of Nebuchadnezzar is treated as a forecast of the true day of the Lord in which all earth-judgments will culminate in the judgment of the living nations and the rebellious of earth at the release of Satan from the bottomless pit.

Fulfillment: "Then shall be great tribulation, such as was not since the beginning of the world" (Matt. 24:21).

"There shall be... upon the earth distress of nations, with perplexity" (Luke 21:25).

"Antichrist shall come...;whereby we know that it is the last time" (I John 2:18).

"For the great day of his wrath is come; and who shall be able to stand"? (Rev. 6:17; cf. 11:18).

"These are they which come out of great tribulation" (Rev. 7:14).

"Woe to the inhabiters of the earth ... for the devil is come down unto you, having great wrath" (Rev. 12:12).

"And he [the beast] opened his mouth in blasphemy against God.... And the beast was taken and... cast into a lake of fire" (Rev. 13:6; 19:20).

"As many as would not worship the image of the beast should be killed" (Rev. 13:15).

Paul divides the human race in a threefold way. The Jews, the Gentiles, the church of God, which is composed of regenerated Jews and Gentiles. As the church is to be caught up to meet and to be with the Lord, she is not present on earth during the Great Tribulation. Such a period of gathering anguish and desolation surrounds Israel and the Gentiles, with the last three and a half years of this season of trial being spoken of as "the time of Jacob's trouble." In the center of the stage of world affairs at this "end time," the prophetic spotlight is focused upon conspicuous groups.

a. *The Western Alliance*

Some semblance of the ancient Roman Empire is to emerge, of which N.A.T.O. (North Atlantic Treaty Organization), the Common Market, and the suggested "United States of Europe," governed by the Rome treaty, are foregleams.

Forecast: "And the fourth kingdom shall be strong as iron... the kingdom shall be partly strong, and partly broken" (Dan. 2:40, 42).

Fulfillment: "The seven heads are seven mountains, on which the woman sitteth" (Rev. 17:9; cf. 13:1).

Rome is notable as "the city of seven hills," and in John's vision we have the last form of Gentile world-power — "a confederation ten-kingdom empire covering the sphere of authority of ancient Rome. Much as we would like to tarry over other features of this section and others of absorbing interest in the book of Revelation, the reader is referred to the author's exposition of same on *Studies in the*

Book of Revelation by the Zondervan Publishing House.

b. *The Northern Confederacy*

One of the most striking prophecies of the Old Testament is that which Ezekiel gives us of Russia and her allies in chapters 38, 39. As Communism pushes onward most relentlessly, and under demonic inspiration, to its goal of world domination, it is important to bear in mind Russia's part in the prophetic program. The R.V. gives us "Prince of Rosh," and it is from *Rosh* that the name "Russia" comes. *Meshech* is the present "Moscow," former European capital, and *Tubal*, now "Tobolsk," the Asiatic capital. The dramatic yet dreadful prophecy against Gog that the prophet Ezekiel gives us should be read along with passages like Matthew 24:14-35 and Revelation 14:14-20; 19:17-21. What terrible judgment awaits this atheistic, cruel, and inhuman Northern European nation – the subtle instigator of much of the bloody revolution around the world today!

c. *The Nations of the Far East*

While they are not cognizant of it, the kings and rulers of the East are rising to power against the great and terrible day of Armageddon. Would that the blinded eyes of "the kings of the sunrise" might be opened to the fearful judgment awaiting them!

"Loose the four angels which are bound in the great river Euphrates" (Rev. 9:14).

"The water thereof was dried up, that the way of the kings of the east might be prepared" (Rev. 16:12; cf. Isa. 41:25; 44:27).

The growing might of eastern nations, such as the Chinese giant, does not augur well for the peace of the world. Now that she is developing her own nuclear bombs, what other nation is there with manpower sufficient to stand up against China's 700,000,000 population? The fact is that the world today is wilting under the unrelenting strain of conflicting ideologies, and the gap between East and West widens.

With the prophecies of prophets and apostles before us it would seem as if three great leaders come into strong focus in the prophetic picture they give us, with others fitting into it who are less conspicuous.

There is the leader of the Northern Confederacy, described as "the chief prince" (Ezek. 38:1-4; 29:1).

There is the political and military leader of the West, the notable beast rising out of the sea – sea being a symbol for agitated nations (Dan. 7:3; Rev. 13:1-8).

There is the religious leader of the West, the false king of the Jews portrayed for us in passages like Daniel 11:36-39; II Thessalonians 2:3-10; I John 2:22; Revelation 13:11-18. This second beast – ape of the Lamb – will, like his companion beast, be satanically inspired. The term *antichrist* (I John 2:18-22) is a religious one, and describes not only a particular person but all the great figures of the last days who will be anti-God and anti-Christ in spirit and action.

d. *The Universal Church*

In his Divine view of "Babylon," symbolic of an apostate Christendom, John portrays *ecclesiastical* "Babylon" as distinct from *political* "Babylon," in terms so arrestive and suggestive of the Romish church in all her wealth, splendor, and also in her cruelty towards those who dare to flout her authority and power (Rev. 17:1-6). When all true believers are removed from the earth at the coming of Christ, and His church is with Him, churches, as buildings, and organizations, with their religious but unregenerated leaders and members, will be left behind. Quickly all religious denominations will be unified under the sway of "the woman arrayed in purple and scarlet colour, and decked with gold and precious stones and pearls." Strong will be the

Lord judging and destroying her (Rev. 18:8).

Already we are witnessing the slow development of the amalgamation of religious forces. It would seem as if the only Gospel some preachers have to preach is church union, the basis of which is the present World Council of Churches. Efforts are being made to unite Methodists and Anglicans, and Anglicans with the Roman Catholic Church. As far back as 1919, Lloyd George, Prime Minister of Britain (1916-1922), who was a Welsh Baptist and a man of great foresight, in an address given to the National Free Church Council, advocated a central conference of all churches of Christendom in the interest of world peace. "It would have to be summoned by the leaders of all the Churches, and *perhaps the Pope would have to preside over it. Let it be Rome if you like.*" Dr. A. Ramsey, present Archbishop of Canterbury, or titular head of the Church of England, is most friendly toward the Romish church, and openly advocates union with it, with the Pope as head of such a united church.

The history of the Church of Rome is not a pleasant one to read, especially during those periods when she seems to reign over the kings of the earth, an influence that John depicts will be here again in the Tribulation (Rev. 17:18). Today, Rome is succeeding in most subtle ways to increase her hold over strategic governments and councils, so much so that when the religious, false beast emerges out of the earth he will not have much trouble in securing the alliance of all the religions of the world. When this takes place, there will reappear, in accentuated form, the autocracy, the religious-political power, the enormous wealth, and the cruel attitude toward those who dare to defy the bidding which Rome presently tries to hide. As the shadows gather around a guilty world, the saints should be wary at the effort to unite religious forces. The true children of God have always been *"One* in Christ Jesus." We do believe in the unity of believers.

e. *The Agony of Israel*

Satan, like Haman of Esther's time, has always been the arch-enemy of the Jews. Since the revelation of God which He gave to Abraham to make of him a great nation, and in turn to bless all the families of the earth (Gen. 12:1-3), Satan has relentlessly sought the destruction of the Jewish people, knowing full well that from them Jesus would come as the Promised Seed to end satanic dominion. All down the ages, the Jews have suffered for their rejection of God's commands, and of their predicted Messiah. Scattered among the nations of the earth they endured captivities. Jesus prophesied their terrible slaughter after His death, and in 70 A.D. the Romans, led by Titus, entered Jerusalem and killed 1,300,000 defenseless Jews and took many others into bondage. The city itself was plowed up as a field, as Micah had predicted it would be (Mic. 3:8-12).

From then on, the Jews have had a fierce struggle to survive. In 1492 Spain forced 800,000 Jews into the sea, the majority of whom perished. Russia has been responsible for the blood of countless thousands, and now under Communism, the Jews find life very hard indeed. Under Adolph Hitler, almost 6,000,000 Jews suffered horrible deaths. Before the six-day war, when Israel was so victorious over the Arabs, Nasser boasted that he would drive all the Jews into the sea. The continuing conflict in the Middle East is resulting in severe persecution for Jews living in Arab countries. Through the centuries, God's ancient people have experienced, at bitter cost, the prediction given through Moses:

> And among these nations shalt thou

find no ease, neither shall the sole of thy foot have rest: but the Lord shall give thee there a trembling heart, and failing of eyes, and sorrow of mind. And thy life shall hang in doubt before thee; and thou shalt fear day and night, and shalt have none assurance of thy life: In the morning thou shalt say, Would God it were even! and at even thou shalt say, Would God it were morning! for fear of thine heart wherewith thou shalt fear, and for the sight of thine eyes which thou shalt see" (Deut. 28:65-67).

But all the agonies the Jews have faced are but the forecast of the threat of annihilation awaiting them in the Tribulation era when Satan himself, knowing his time is short, will make one last bid to destroy the hitherto indestructible Jews, as John describes in the remarkable twelfth chapter of Revelation (cf. Matt. 24: 15). Israel is symbolized as the woman who brought forth a man child to rule the nations with a rod of iron. Here again we have one of those prophetic leaps we have drawn attention to. "She brought forth a man child" – Christ in His Incarnation – who was to rule all nations with a rod of iron," as predicted by the psalmist, and which will be fulfilled when He comes to reign on earth. Satan, cast down from his position as prince of the power of the air, seeks to persecute the woman, or Israel, but God and nature intervene to preserve the people, who by this time "keep the commandments of God, and have *the testimony of Jesus Christ*" (Rev. 12:17). The latter phrase suggests that they had seen Him whom they pierced and mourned because of their share in His death.

Toward the close of the Tribulation, there will be a coalition of hostile powers against the Jews, as the psalmist describes:

"They have said, Come, and let us cut them off from being a nation; that the name of Israel may be no more in remembrance" (Ps. 83:4).

The chief actors in this confederacy would seem to be the Assyrian Isaiah often mentions (Isa. 10:24; 14:25, etc.) and who is "the king of the north" or "the little horn" Daniel describes. This dread figure is the first beast, or head of some form of the ancient Roman Empire (Rev. 13:19). Behind antagonistic leaders is Satan inspiring them in their purpose to destroy Israel (Rev. 19:19). As to the outcome, there is no doubt (II Thess. 2:8).

Jerusalem is again, and finally, delivered, as Zechariah prophesied (Zech. 14:1-4), with the Messiah making it His seat of government, with Israel as His glory. "I will place salvation in Zion for Israel my glory" (Isa. 46:13). A great body of Old Testament prophecy is related to the regathering and permanent establishment of Israel in the land which has ever been theirs by divine right and gift (Deut. 30:3; Jer. 12:15). Israel is to be exalted above the Gentile nations from whom it had received so much desolation and death (Isa. 14:1, 2; 61:6, 7) and become a continual witness to the Gentiles (Zech. 8:23). For the overthrow of Israel's foes, compare Daniel 2:44 with Revelation 19: 11-21.

At present we are to recognize in the Jew God's prophetic clock, for by his temporary presence in the land of promise, *as a nation*, we know that time is running out. Jerusalem, again surrounded by armies, reminds that the end of the Gospel age is near, and that the coming of the Lord draweth nigh. The Jews is always God's index finger as far as prophecy is concerned, and will always remain as an amazing evidence of the sovereignty and mercy of God. Performance of the prediction will soon be a reality, "And ye shall be unto me a kingdom of priests, and an holy nation" (Exod. 19:6). Our present obligation is to "pray for the peace of Jerusalem."

E. *The inauguration of the Millennium*

Because of the magnitude of the study we have undertaken in this volume, we can only give a broad outline of all that is involved in our Lord's return to earth. Many details need to be added to give a complete picture. Still, we hope that we have set forth sufficient evidence to stimulate a deeper interest in these future events deserving a more exhaustive study than we are providing. What a golden age the Millennium will be, when, during the thousand years of righteousness and peace, every promise and covenant with Abraham and David, as well as the glowing predictions of the prophets, will be literally fulfilled to the uttermost! During this period, mankind in general will have its final test under the most favorable and glorious conditions to prove whether or not men can justify themselves in the sight of a holy God.

In contrast to Christ's coming to the air for His saints, this second stage of His return will be a public display of His judicial authority, and His power and glory; the crushing of His foes, and the setting up of His predicted kingdom. In these days of stress and strife, of war and wickedness, and of apostacy, it is as well to envisage the glories of a universal reign of righteousness and peace. Presently we are suffering from the contentions and jealousies of rival nations and the tyranny of ambitious and atheistic dictators, but, as predicted, the earth will yet have an almighty king who will reign in undisputed royalty. Isaiah's prediction of a glorious era will be abundantly fulfilled –

"And he shall judge among the nations, and shall rebuke many people: And they shall beat their swords into plowshares, and their spears into pruninghooks: Nation shall not lift up sword against nation, Neither shall they learn war any more" (Isa. 2:4).

Christ's appearance with His saints will set off a chain of succeeding and culminatory events which we are now to distinguish. Scripture speaks in no uncertain way of the inauguration of the millennial kingdom of the once-despised Galilean.

Forecast: "And in the days of these kings shall the God of heaven set up a kingdom, which shall never be destroyed: . . . It shall break in pieces and consume all these kingdoms, and it shall stand for ever" (Dan. 2:44).

"And there was given him dominion, and glory, and a kingdom, . . . which shall not be destroyed" (Dan. 7:14).

Fulfillment: "Pray ye: . . . Thy kingdom come. Thy will be done in earth, as it is in heaven" (Matt. 6:9, 10).

"To receive for himself a kingdom, and to return" (Luke 19:12).

"Jesus Christ . . . the prince of the kings of earth" (Rev. 1:5).

"They lived and reigned with Christ a thousand years" (Rev. 20:4).

1. *The end of Gentile dominion.* When, in His Olivet prophetic discourse, Jesus spoke of the end of the age, and "then shall the end come," He had in mind the end of Gentile dominion, characterized by nations and kingdoms in constant conflict with other nations and kingdoms (Matt. 24). We are living in what is known as "the times of the Gentiles" which "times" will cease when Jesus returns as the King of Nations (Luke 21:24). All the nations of the earth today are Gentile in nature, with the exception of the Jewish nation and the partly-Jewish Arab peoples. The rest of the nations, Gentile in origin, dominate international affairs.

This Gentile supremacy had its rise when God, through the prophet Daniel, said to Nebuchadnezzar – "Thou, O king, art a king of kings: for the

God of heaven hath given thee a kingdom, power, strength, and glory. And wheresoever the children of men dwell . . . [God] hath made thee ruler over them all" (Dan. 2:37, 38). All down the ages Gentile dominion has continued, and will do so until Christ returns to take over the control of the nations of the earth. Commencing with Nebuchadnezzar, such supremacy will become Christ's, and thus the same language is used of Him as of the original head of Gentile world-sway –

> "KING OF KINGS, AND LORD OF LORDS" (Rev. 19:16). "The kingdoms [Gentile] of this world are become the kingdoms of our Lord . . . ; and he shall reign for ever and ever" (Rev. 10:15).

It is in this connection that Jesus is likewise named "*Prince* of the kings of earth," *Prince* meaning "*Ruler*," and He will rule even over His greatest and most powerful enemies. There will appear the proud monarch of the West, the haughty despot of the East, but Christ will be "higher than the kings of earth." All the kingdoms of this world are His by right and title, but His sovereign rights are now in abeyance. The time is hastening on, however, when He will become king of all who reign, and Lord of all who exercise authority. Public universal government will pass into His hands (Isa. 9:6, 7), and then He will shiver every imperial scepter and break the crowns of all opposing authority, and reign supreme without a rival.

It is profitable to observe that Jesus is also called "The *Prince* of Peace" and "The *Prince* of Life." He is the Prince of Peace, seeing He alone is the purchaser and procurer of peace between God and man (Isa. 53:5), and also of peace between Jews and Gentiles (Eph. 2:11-15). Then the legacy He left His disciples was one of peace (John 14:27).

He is also named "*Prince* of life" (Acts 3:15). As co-creator, He is the author of our temporal life, the realm in which we live and move, and in whose hand is our breath; as our mediator, He is the guide and way to eternal life (John 14:6). Therefore, as such a mighty prince, He will be more than able to subjugate the Devil, the "prince of the power of the air" (Eph. 2:2).

2. *The judgment of the living nations.* As Jesus appears to manifest His kingship, and enters upon His inheritance of wider glories when "all dominions shall serve and obey him" (Dan. 7:27), it would seem that consequent upon His appearing, He will act after the pattern of David, and judge everything He finds according to righteousness.

> "Give the king thy judgments, O God, and thy righteousness unto the king's son.
>
> He shall judge thy people with righteousness, and thy poor with judgment" (Ps. 72:1, 2).

It will be imperative for Him to "gather out of his kingdom all things that offend, and them which do iniquity" (Matt. 13:41) and so begins the remarkable scene He Himself predicted of all the nations gathered before Him for judgment (Matt. 25:31-46). This is the only time in the Gospels that Jesus applies the title of *King* to Himself – "Then shall the *King* say unto them" (Matt. 25:34). This particular judgment, then, marks the introduction and inauguration of His millennial sway.

Examining the features of this session of judgment, we discover how wrong it is to confuse it with the Great White Throne (Rev. 20:11-15), when the wicked *dead* are made to stand before the Judge. The judgment at the beginning of His reign is one of "*living* nations," with three classes present: the *Sheep* nations, the *Goat* nations, *My* brethren. Treatment of the king's *brethren* is to be the ground of classification, whether the nations are among the *sheep* or *goats.* This is the key to the whole scene. The question is, Who are we to understand are meant by *His brethren* (Matt. 25:40)? Without doubt, they are the Jews, His kinsmen according to the flesh. During the days of fierce tribulation, many of them had gone forth as the ambassadors of the coming king, as He Himself predicted that the Gospel of the kingdom should be preached among all nations before the end of Gentile dominion (Matt. 24:14).

And so, the basis of judgment is to be the way the Gentile nations had received such Jewish evangelism. "He that receiveth you receiveth Me," He had said. Hence the king will say to those nations kindly disposed toward the Jews, "inherit the kingdom prepared for you from the foundation of the world"; but to those who had despised the Jew, the punishment is everlasting woe (Matt. 25:34-46). From the display of His power in righteous judgment, the king goes forth to exercise universal dominion with all kings bowing before Him, and all nations serving Him (Ps. 72: 10, 11). In this we can rest that as the judge of all the earth He will do that which is right as He breaks in pieces the nations and destroys kingdoms (Jer. 51:20; cf. Ps. 2:9).

> Oh quickly come, dread Judge of all;
> For, awful though Thine advent be,
> All shadows from the truth will fall,
> And falsehood die, in sight of Thee.
> Oh quickly come: for doubt and fear
> Like clouds dissolve when Thou art near.

It is not easy to determine the location of this awesome, decisive judgment. Joel has the prediction about all nations being gathered for judgment in "the valley of Jehoshaphat," and as Jehoshaphat means "Jehovah Judges," perhaps the new valley to be created by the cleaving of the Mount of Olives as the king's feet stand upon it (Zech. 14:4), this may be the place of such a momentous assize. Regarding the symbolism of dividing the nations, on His right hand and on the left, Scripture often employs *Sheep* to denote those who trust in God, and *Goats,* naturally, to represent the worst side of a man or nation. Of this we may be certain, that the eternal outcome of this judgment will be more solemn than we are able to derive from the simplest or the most sublime figures of speech. (See Ezekiel 34:22: "I will judge between cattle and cattle.")

How apt are the lines of Wordsworth on the symbolism of the last Book of the Bible!

> Characters of the great Apocalypse,
> Of types and symbols of Eternity,
> Of first, and last, and midst, and without end.

3. *The battle of Armageddon.* Again we witness the judicial authority of Him who is coming to judge. When here in the flesh, Jesus predicted that He would return to earth as judge of all mankind, and that He would sit upon a throne attended by legions of angels, and with all nations gathered before Him, adjudicate accordingly. The Messiah is pictured in prophecy exercising His jurisdiction as the universal judge, and coming to judge the earth, Jesus claims such an official position as being His right. Had not the Father given Him authority to execute judgment because He became the Son of man? Messiahship implies His real humanity and, as Canon Liddon reminds us, "His human nature invests Him with special fitness for judgment as for the rest of His mediatorial work . . . He is more than human; but He is to judge, because He is also Man."

Forecast: "He cometh to judge the earth: with righteousness shall he judge the world, and the people with equity" (Ps. 98:9).

"Say among the heathen that the Lord reigneth: . . . he shall judge the people righteously. . . . he shall judge the world with righteousness, and the people with his truth" (Ps. 96:10, 13).

Fulfillment: "The Father . . . hath committed *all* judgment unto the Son. . . . And hath given him authority to execute judgment also, because he is the Son of man" (John 5:22, 27).

"It is he which was ordained of God to be the Judge of quick and dead" (Acts 10:42).

The marvel and miracle of grace is that the saints are to assist the judge in His judicial activities, for Paul asks, "Do ye not know that the saints shall judge the world? . . . Know ye not that we shall judge angels?" (I Cor. 6:2, 3). Did not Jesus assure the apostles, who had forsaken all and followed Him, that with the coming of His kingdom when He shall sit upon the throne of His glory, theirs would be the privilege to "sit upon twelve thrones, judging the twelve tribes of Israel" (Matt. 19:28; cf. Isa. 1:26)?

What exactly is the Battle of Armageddon, when judgment will be swift and severe? It is to be Messiah's personal dread battle. "And *he* gathered them together into a place called in the Hebrew tongue *Armageddon.*" The preceding *Vials* in this chapter are filled with "the wrath of God," but this "battle of the great day of God Almighty" will present "the cup of the wine of the fierceness of his wrath," and will be accompanied by a great earthquake, not only natural, but symbolic of an anarchic revolt provoked by the intolerable despotism of the Beast, and also by the desperate sufferings resulting from the fearful Vial judgments (Rev. 16).

Forecast: "Then shall the Lord go forth, and fight against those nations, as when he fought in the day of battle" (Zech. 14:3).

"I will tread them in mine anger, and trample them in my fury" (Isa. 63:3).

"I will also gather all nations, and will bring them down into the valley of Jehoshaphat" (Joel 3:2).

Fulfillment: "I saw . . . the kings of the earth, and their armies gathered together to make war against him" (Rev. 19:19).

"The kings of the earth and of the whole world" (Rev. 16:14).

"The cup of the wine of the fierceness of his wrath" (Rev. 16:19).

"Gathered . . . together into a place called . . . Armageddon" (Rev. 16:16).

The period of desperate trial and persecution under the rule of Antichrist (Rev. 13), particularly for Israel, will culminate in the titanic struggle at Armageddon, and will be a war that will immeasurably exceed in horror anything hitherto experienced in the history of the human race. A prediction of this tremendous conflict can be found in Ezekiel 38 and 39. The last and greatest war is to take place at *Megiddo,* meaning the "Mount of Slaughter." As many of Israel's past wars were fought in the plain of Jezreel, it is fitting that this historic site is chosen for such a grim conflict, as it will witness the final deliverance of the people of Messiah and usher in a time of inconceivable blessedness and prosperity for the Jews, who through centuries endured such terrible persecutions.

What drama of indescribable magnificence will be enacted when Christ, in person, and followed by the armies of heaven, appears to make war with the kings of the earth and their armies, and with the Beast who had controlled them (Rev. 19:11-21)! Paul's prediction, given in striking and vigorous language, will then be literally fulfilled. "And then shall be revealed the lawless one, whom the Lord Jesus shall slay with the breath of his mouth, and bring to nought [literally, *paralyze him*] by the manifestation of his coming, [or presence]" (II Thess. 2:8, R.V.). Armageddon will thus become the scene of Christ's coronation as victor, and the victory secured will mean a glorious era for the world, now that godless, hostile nations have been eliminated.

Summarizing the manifold results of the Battle of Armageddon, Dr. J. Dwight Pentecost, in his most illuminative volume *Things To Come*, cites the following:

1. The armies of the South are destroyed.
2. The armies of the Northern Confederacy are smitten by the Lord.
3. The armies of the Beast and the East are slain by the Lord.
4. The Beast and the False Prophet are cast into the lake of fire.
5. The unbelievers have been purged out of Israel (Zech. 13:8).
6 The believers have been purged as the result of these invasions (Zech. 13:9).
7. The Enemy, Satan, is bound (Rev. 20:2).

Thus the Lord destroys every hostile force that would challenge His right to rule as Messiah over the earth. As the smiting stone, He has crushed the Image. Figurative uses of stone are numerous in Scripture, but none is so impressive as that of its application to the Lord and the messianic kingdom. Jesus is depicted as the stone which the builders rejected, yet He will be the stone destroying them (Ps. 118:22, 23; Matt. 21:42). He is also the chief cornerstone of the habitation of God (Eph. 2:20, 22; cf. Isa. 28:16), and the saints are living stones fitted into such a temple (I Pet. 2:5, 6).

Forecast: "The Shepherd, the stone of Israel" (Gen. 49:24).

"A stone was cut out without hands" (Dan. 2:34).

"He shall bring forth the headstone thereof" (Zech. 4:7).

Fulfillment: "And whosoever shall fall on this stone shall be broken: but on whomsoever it shall fall, it will grind him to powder" (Matt. 21:44).

"He should smite the nations" (Rev. 19:15).

The times of the Gentiles, beginning with Nebuchadnezzar, arc brought to an end by Christ, the stone "cut out without hands," a phrase implying His deity, in His destruction of Gentile world power symbolized by Daniel's image of succeeding empires. What emancipation from tyranny and godlessness the earth will experience when the messianic kingdom crushes the kingdoms of men! It is the last form of world-dominion, "the feet of iron and clay" part of the Image, that the smiting stone strikes at with disastrous effect.

As Satan has ever been the subtle and invisible instigator of the world hostility towards Christ, and as the god of this world, the force behind the hatred of His Word and ways, it is but fitting that after dealing with Satan's dupes the victorious Messiah sets about the silencing of the enemy of nations and of men. The presence and liberty of such a foe during the millennium would defeat the purpose and program of the Messiah, and so in dramatic language John describes the angel binding Satan, the old serpent, with a great chain, and shutting him up in the bottomless pit for 1000 years, in order that during the millennium the nations will not have him to deceive them (Rev. 20:1-3). With the source of sin removed and outward temptation removed, in the age of divine righteousness man will be given the opportunity of complete obedience to the will of his deliverer and king.

4. *The glorious millennium.* With Satan bound and banished and the visible glory of the Lord constantly in view, and His iron rule subduing the ambitions and rivalries of the nations, the effect will be a life of unparalleled delight. The nations are to walk in the light of holy Jerusalem, the seat of the king, as it shines with a glory brighter than earth. What a

time it will be for fellowship between the heavenly people, the church, and the earthly people, Jews and Gentiles. A marked feature of prophecy is the large section devoted to the character and conditions of our Lord's millennial reign, two aspects of which will be:

a. The actual absence of Satan from the earth and from his seat of activities, "the air," and his millennial imprisonment.

b. The *actual presence* on earth of Christ, as prince of the kings of the earth. Visibly seen, and having the seat of His universal government at Jerusalem in fulfillment of Psalm 2.

After "the times of the Gentiles," it is now His time, and what a time it will be! The term *millennium,* from two Latin words meaning "thousand" and "years," may not be in the Bible but what it represents is, for six times over John uses the term *thousand years* (Rev. 20:1-7). Throughout this period, Christ will reign and "judge the people righteously" (Ps. 96:10). The saints will share His throne and reign with Him (II Tim. 2:12; Rev. 5:10; 22:5). The Saviour is now sovereign. The sword becomes a sickle, foes are now friends, the people have a paradise.

Of all the plan and program the book of Revelation reveals, no feature is so impressive as the armies of heaven following the Lamb, clothed as He is in a vesture dipped in blood, symbol of His passion and of His victory, and in His wounded humanity seated upon a throne, receiving the prostrate adoration of the glorified saints and the inhabitants of earth. How solemn it is to see Him portrayed as the object of solemn, uninterrupted, and universal worship, and in union with His Father, the almighty, uncreated, and supreme God (Rev. 5:13; 19:1-6). No wonder John, as he gazed in vision upon His glory, fell at His feet as dead (Rev. 1:17).

Forecast: Of all Old Testament predictions of the ultimate reign of Christ, no picture is so delightful and glowing of His millennial age as Psalm 72, which is an inspired poetic prophecy causing our hearts to burn within us in anticipation of such a marvelous consummation of the world's history.

"He shall have dominion also from sea to sea, and from the river unto the ends of the earth" (Ps. 72:8).

"I will establish his kingdom. . . . I will establish his throne for ever" (I Chron. 17:11, 12).

"Yet have I set my king upon my holy hill of Zion. . . . I shall give thee . . . the uttermost parts of the earth for thy possession" (Ps. 2:6, 8; cf. 8:6).

"The sceptre of thy kingdom is a right sceptre" (Ps. 45:6; read entire psalm).

"Of the increase of his government and peace there shall be no end, . . . upon his kingdom" (Isa. 9:7; cf. 11; 40:10).

"A King shall reign and prosper, and shall execute judgment and justice in the earth" (Jer. 23:5).

"And in the days of these kings shall the God of heaven set up a kingdom, which shall never be destroyed" (Dan. 2:44; 7:13, 14).

Fulfillment: "Where is he that is born King of the Jews?" (Matt. 2:2).

"And he shall reign over the house of Jacob for ever; and of his kingdom there shall be no end" (Luke 1:33).

". . . to receive for himself a kingdom" (Luke 19:12).

"But unto the Son he saith, Thy throne, O God, is for ever and ever: a sceptre of righteousness is the sceptre of thy kingdom" (Heb. 1:8).

"The kingdoms of this world are become the kingdoms of our Lord, and of his Christ; and he shall reign for ever and ever . . . thou hast taken to thee thy great power, and hast reigned" (Rev. 11:15, 17).

"They shall be priests of God and of Christ, and shall reign with him a thousand years" (Rev. 20:6).

"For he must reign, till he hath put all enemies under his feet" (I Cor. 15:25).

"Our Lord Jesus Christ... who is the blessed and only Potentate, the King of kings, and Lord of lords" (I Tim. 6:14, 15; cf. Rev. 17:14; 19:16).

How our broken world, plagued by cruel dictators and impotent rulers, awaits the coming of One who will control the world's thrones as He sits on the throne of His glory, and who will enforce peace and justice throughout the whole world! Then the nations shall be glad and sing for joy as Christ judges righteously the people of the earth (Ps. 67:4; 96:13). There will be no duplicity, trickery, intrigues, and lust for power presently characterizing so many who try to govern. God's king will be on the highest throne owned by the myriads of angels and by multitudes of men throughout the universe as their rightful Lord.

The once-persecuted peasant of Galilee, the man of sorrows, the crucified but now exalted Saviour of the world, will then be the sole arbiter and universal king, and the wonder of wonders will be that His redeemed people will share with Him in all the glories of His glorious reign. The question is, Are we preparing ourselves for the coming responsibilities as co-sharers of His beneficient reign on earth? Much as we would like to dwell upon the Eden-like conditions to prevail during the millennium when the cause and curse of sin are to be removed, we must leave the reader to work out more fully these particular aspects of universal blessings –

1. Nature will be delivered from bondage (Rom. 8:19-22).
2. Nature will be perfected (Isa. 35:1, 6, 7).
3. The physical nature of man will be renewed (Isa. 35:5, 6; 65:20).
4. Animal nature will be transformed (Isa. 11:6-9; 65:25).
5. Righteousness will be personal and universal (Ps. 72:1-8; Hab. 2:14).
6. Prosperity and peace will be the possession of all (Isa. 2:1-4; 65:21-25; Mic. 4:3, 4).
7. Satan's evil kingdom and dominion ceases (Rev. 20:2).

A fitting conclusion to our survey of the glorious future is given by Dr. W. T. Davidson in Hastings' *Dictionary of the Bible:*

> In the Person, Life, Sufferings, Death, and Resurrection of Jesus Christ, and in the establishment of His Kingdom on the earth, is to be found the fullest realization of the glowing words of the Prophets who prepared the way for His Coming. For a still more complete fulfillment of their highest hopes and fairest visions the world still waits. But those who believe in the accomplishment of God's faithful Word thus far will not find it difficult to believe that our Lord's words concerning the Law, may be adapted, and that in the highest spiritual sense they will at last be realized—"Till heaven and earth pass, one jot or one tittle shall in no wise pass from the *Prophets*, till all be fulfilled" (Matt. 5:18).

F. *The Great White Throne*

After a millennium of captivity in the bottomless pit, Satan is loosed for "a little season," but what universal revolution he incites in such a brief period of liberty! Although he was away from the earth for so long, his influence in the hearts of men, although prohibited from manifesting itself because of the iron rule of Christ, was nevertheless latent and became patent as soon as the Devil reappeared. Such a widespread revolt among the nations proved that their obedience to the king was only forced and feigned. Those Satan gathered together to battle against Christ in a final effort to overthrow His kingdom were in number as "the sand of the sea" (Rev. 20:7-10).

The first glimpse of the Devil corresponds with the last in Scripture, namely, the deceiver. "And Adam was not deceived, but the woman being *deceived* was in the transgression" (I Tim. 2:14). "Satan . . . shall go out to *deceive* the nations" (Rev. 20:7, 8). This arch deceiver will inspire the "deceiver and antichrist" (II John 7). We are prompted to ask the question, How could the multitudes who have benefited in every way by the magnificent reign of Christ allow themselves to be duped by Satan? Why, in the counsels of God, was he liberated to engage in such a universal revolution resulting in all the deceived being destroyed by divine fire? Was it to manifest for the last time the unalterable innate nature of man apart from the regenerating power of the spirit? As the beautiful environment of the garden did not prevent Eve yielding to satanic deception, so the glorious environment of Christ's millennial peace and righteousness did not eradicate man's old, rebellious nature. Man is without hope of change unless he becomes the recipient of God's transforming grace.

At last the longsuffering of God is exhausted, and with man's malignity fully revealed, the sinning human race is devoured. The long predicted doom of the damned is executed. "The wicked shall be turned into hell, and all the nations that forget God" (Ps. 9:17). Our Lord predicted that eternal fire, had been "prepared for the devil and his angels" (Matt. 25: 41), and now the great deceiver finds himself, along with his two dupes, the Beast, prominent dictator in the political world during the Tribulation, and his lieutenant, the False Prophet, conspicuous ruler in the religious realm, in the fearful Lake of Fire. It was both fitting and necessary that the complete disposal of Satan should take place before the final assize, when all responsible creatures who through past millenniums rejected God are arraigned before the judge for the ratification of a condemnation previously announced. "He that believed not is condemned already. . . . the wrath of God abideth on him" (John 3:18, 36). With divine judgment of Satan and of those who were deceived by him, God's dealing with the earth, whether in grace, mercy, of judgment, is concluded.

Between the doom of Satan and the last judgment, there comes an event of great magnitude and importance, namely, the disappearance of the original heavens and earth. "From whose face the earth and the heaven fled away; and there was found no place for them" (Rev. 20:11). Peter predicted the destruction of earth and heaven by fire:

> The heavens shall pass away with a great noise, and the elements shall melt with fervent heat, the earth also and the works that are therein shall be burned up. . . . Looking for and hasting unto the coming of the day of God, wherein [on account of which] the heavens being on fire shall be dissolved, and the elements shall melt with fervent heat (II Pet. 3:10, 12).

John states the fact only of their disappearance, but Peter foretold that fire was to be God's chosen instrument for the destruction of this present scene. *Fire*, it will be found, is associated with *all* the judgments of the Lord, even with that of believers at the judgment seat of Christ. With the passing away of earth and heaven there takes place the most awesome spectacle in the Bible, predicted millenniums ago by Daniel the prophet. *Forecast:* "I beheld till the thrones were cast down, and the Ancient of day did sit. . . . the judgment was set, and the books were opened" (Dan. 7:9, 10).

Fulfillment: "And I saw the dead, small and great, stand before God; and the books were opened" (Rev. 20:12).

Actually the phrase should be "stand before the throne," not "before God," for Scripture declares that the Lord Jesus is to be the occupant of the august throne. "The Father judgeth no man, but hath committed *all* judgment unto the Son" (John 5:22). Paul also agrees that full authority to execute judgment belongs to Christ (Phil. 2:9-11). The One who was once unjustly judged and crucified is to sit in judgment upon all those who died rejecting Him as the Saviour. Seated upon this last judicial throne, God publicly vindicates His Son in the presence of angels and men, and holds Him forth as the object of universal honor. Refusing to bow the knee before Him in the day of grace, the condemned are compelled to bow before Him in acknowledgement of His Lordship and supremacy.

Although He will sit, however, as the arbiter of the eternal destiny of all His enemies, it must be remembered that this great assize is not a court to determine whether those called to appear before the judge are innocent or guilty, and then pass a sentence accordingly. As we have seen, sinners in the flesh are condemned already and have heard the verdict: "The soul that sinneth, it shall die." Thus, those who will appear at this judgment can enter no plea or earn a benefit of doubt. They are raised from hell to receive the ratification of their condemnation, and banishment to the final and eternal depository of those whose names are not in the Book of Life, namely, the Lake of Fire.

The throne is described as being *great,* as being suited to the dignity of its occupant who is great, and greatly to be praised. It is *white,* as a symbol of the character of the judgment pronounced, which will be according to the holiness of the nature of God. What must be made clear is that no *believers* will be found in the vast, unnumbered throng. Death and hell deliver us. Perhaps you know Martin Luther's expressive poem on *The Judgment Day?*

Great God! what do I see and hear,
The end of things created,
The Judge of all men doth appear,
On clouds of glory seated.
The trumpet sounds, the graves restore
The dead which they contained before:—
Prepare, my soul, to meet HIM!

Great Judge! to THEE our prayers we pour,
In deep abasement bending:
O shield us through that last dread hour,
Thy wondrous love extending!
May we, in this our trial day,
With faithful hearts Thy word obey,
And thus prepare to meet THEE!

Our only criticism of this poem is that Luther, as a child of God, as he truly was, will not appear at "that last dread hour." The only preparation the reformer could make was that of the constant experience of God's saving and sanctifying power, which alone can earn the smile of the Saviour, once translated from earth into His presence above. Only sinners, then, in all their guilt and despair will stand revealed in striking contrast to the dazzling whiteness of the throne that has no rainbow of mercy round about it.

With the end of our Lord's reign, two classes are dealt with, namely, millennial saints who will not die and the millennial sinners or rebels consumed by fire, and since the scene of the throne includes only *the dead* (Rev. 20:12), all who stand before the judge are composed entirely of the wicked dead, two kinds of books being the basis of their judgment, which is upon two grounds – positive and negative.

The Book of Works

Works of the wicked are produced in evidence against them – words being included in their works. Out of their own mouths condemnation is to come.

The Book of Life

The absence of their names from the Lamb's register shows that they have no title to mercy or favor. "And whosoever was not found written in the book of life was cast into the lake of fire" (Rev. 20:15). With no trace of name, works become the ground of verdict (Rom. 3:20).

> The deeds we do, the words we say—
> Into still air they seem to float,
> We count them ever past,
> But they shall last,
> In the dread Judgment they
> And we shall meet!

In the land of the living, it is imperative to warn sinners that "after [death] the judgment" (Heb. 9:27); and that only at the cross is there deliverance from eternal condemnation. It is only in Christ as the Saviour that we can escape from facing Him as Christ the judge. Saved by grace, we shall not come into judgment, but shall pass from death into life. Along with the wicked dead consigned to eternal woe go death and hades. The heaven and the earth are to pass away, but they are to be revived in a new form; but for death and hades there is only divine destruction by Him who has the power over both, and so destroys them judicially. As Christ "must reign, till he hath put all enemies under his feet" (I Cor. 15:25), the *last* enemy, death, is now consumed.

G. *The Surrendered Kingdom*

In a most remarkable passage, in which the immediate subject is that of the Resurrection, Paul seems to cover all dispensations in its scope (I Cor. 5:22-28). Concluding with the millennium, the apostle says that with all antagonistic rule and authority and power having been put down, *then cometh the end!* The judgment throne marks the termination of Christ's mediatorial kingdom. He yields up the kingdom to Him that put all things under Him, and takes a subject place to God that He, henceforward may be "all in all." At long last, Christ sees of the past travail of His soul and is satisfied as He surrenders His earthly kingdom to the Father.

What must be made clear, however, is the fact that Christ's essential deity abides forever. The wondrous revelation is that throughout eternity He will remain not only as God the Son, but He will retain His glorified humanity, moving among the ranks of the redeemed from all ages, all of whom are conformed to His glorious image, as the firstborn among many brethren. Then we shall gaze

> Not at the crown He giveth,
> But on His piercéd hand;
> The Lamb is all the glory
> Of Immanuel's land.

H. *The New Creation*

With the surrender of the earthly kingdom there comes the *eternal state,* wherein God is indeed all in all. John saw in vision the actual fulfillment of the prediction of both prophet and apostle.

Forecast: "For, behold, I create new heavens and a new earth: and the former shall not be remembered, nor come into mind." (Isa. 65:17).

"The new heavens and the new earth, which I will make, shall remain before me" (Isa. 66:22).

"Nevertheless we, according to his promise, look for new heavens and a new earth, wherein dwelleth righteousness" (II Pet. 3:13).

Fulfillment: "And I saw a new heaven and a new earth: for the first heaven and the first earth were passed away" (Rev. 21:1).

"Behold, I make all things new" (Rev. 21:5).

Everything in connection with this new creation will be brought into ordered beauty before God and fashioned according to His own perfect mind. The first creation is like the vessel which Jeremiah saw marred in the hands of the potter. "So he made it again another vessel, as seemed good to the potter to make it" (Jer. 18:4). God will bring forth the new creation as it were out of the sepulcher of the old, but until all His in the old have been accomplished. Is it not wonderful to realize that the Lord Jesus Himself, who rose from the dead, is indeed "the beginning of the creation of God" (Rev. 3:14), and that all who are *in Him* form "a new creation" and are to be part of the new and eternal creation John describes? Inheriting the New Jerusalem, we are to sing a new song, for the former creation with its groans and travail, is past and shall not be remembered.

The new heavens are imperative, as the original ones were polluted by the presence of Satan as prince of the power of the air through succeeding millenniums. A new earth is likewise essential because the old one was marred and broken by man's corruption and violence, and also stained by the ruby blood of God's beloved Son, as well as by the blood of countless numbers of martyrs for His dear sake.

Our finite minds fail in their attempt to compass the thought of eternity. In this we do rest that an eternal inheritance and eternal glory are to be ours. Beyond all ages, we shall find our true and ultimate expectation. "Unto Him be glory in the Church by Christ Jesus *to all generations of eternal ages*" (Eph. 3:21, *Alford*). Everything in this new creation will be perfect, as measured by the holiness of God, and His Church will then be "without spot, or wrinkle, or any such thing." What glories of the New Jerusalem, with the blessedness of its inhabitants John portrays (Rev. 21; 22)! The perpetual sunlight and joy of the eternal presence of God will be ours as He tabernacles among the glorified, as the Alpha and Omega, the beginning and the ending! (Rev. 1:8).

Through all Eternity, to Thee
A joyful song I'll raise!
For oh! Eternity's too short
To utter all Thy praise!

Part Two

SYMBOLIC MESSIANIC PROPHECIES

Prophetic Gleams From Conspicuous Persons
Prophetic Gleams From Historical Events
Prophetic Gleams From Religious Rituals
Prophetic Gleams From Sacred Festivals
Prophetic Gleams From Prescribed Offices

Scripture is rich in symbolism, and the study of same is most profitable. The Eastern mind has ever been pictorial, and as the Bible is an Eastern book, it is but natural that it should abound in figurative language. To read all the Old Testament books without seeing Jesus, not only in direct predictions and promises, but also in veiled pictures and parables, leaves our reading somewhat flat and insipid. When, however, we keep looking for Him, even in most unexpected places, our meditation becomes most satisfying and profitable. Isaac Williams would have us know that

> Truth through the sacred volume
> hidden lies,
> And spreads from end to end her
> secret wing,
> Through ritual, type, and stories
> mysteries . . .
>
> Through every page the universal
> King
> From Eden's loss unto the end of
> years,
> From East to West, the Son of Man
> appears.

As far back as 1657, Francis Roberts wrote that

> In a sword there's hilt, and back, and edge, but only the edge into. In an instrument there's wood, and brass, and belly, and frets, and strings, but only the strings do make the melody. So there are many passages in Parabolic Scriptures subservient to the main scope, which must only be understood with tendency and reference thereunto. The scope of a Parable is the *Key* of a Parable.

While exploration is very necessary in our quest for a fuller revelation of Christ in types, metaphors, or emblems, we must restrain ourselves from exaggeration. We must strive to see things that are there, and not try to discover what is not there. Much care must be exercised in the pursuit of the study of types. A twofold caution should ever be our guide in Bible Typology:

1. Do not seek for types everywhere.

2. Never press the typical teaching to such an extent as to imperil the historical character of the Bible. Professor W. Moorehead says that it "must be remembered that *exposition* is not *imposition,* nor is it interpretation to *draw out* what *we* have first *read in.*" In the time of the Reformation there was a tendency to let imagination run wild in the endeavor to find Christ in unusual Bible characters and events. After His Resurrection, meeting His disciples, He began by *interpreting* the Scriptures to them, and then went on to "unseal the barred doors of their perceptions to make the right inference," or to have the capacity of "adding two and two together" from the Scriptures, whether direct or indirect. It was with glowing hearts that those disciples came to see their Saviour, not only in specific prophecies, but in

symbolic and implied portions of the Word.

The story is told of a famous British artist who painted a sunset so vivid that a lady said, "But I never see a sunset like that!" "Madam," was the reply, "don't you wish you could?" Those who read the Old Testament with cold and critical eyes may not see that "every common bush" is "afire with God." But those who take off their shoes, only these devout and humble hearts can

> Find tongues in trees, books in running brooks, Sermons in stones, and good in everything.

For the reader desiring one of the most complete, thorough, and learned works on Bible symbolism, Dr. Patrick Fairburn's *Typology of Scripture* can be recommended. In the previous pages of our study we have concentrated largely upon the way it pleased God to prepare for the Advent of His Son chiefly by *prophecy*. Yet types and pictures are likewise the media of revelation of Him who came in the flesh. Before we proceed with this fascinating aspect of Scripture meditation, it may be as well to define what a *type* actually is. Nicholls, in his useful handbook on *Helps to the Reading of the Bible,* has this explanation:

> A type has been defined to be an action or occurrence, in which one event, person, or circumstance, is intended to represent another, similar to it in certain respects, but of more importance, and generally future. The Scripture describes a type as "a shadow of good things to come" (Heb. 10:1). Shadows are not exact resemblances, but give only a dark outline; yet with sufficient distinctness to convey some general idea of the body, especially when afterwards we have the body with which to compare them. One distinction between a *Prophecy* and a *Type* is, that a Prophecy is a prediction by something said—a Type, usually by something done, and presented to our sight.

Dr. Moorehead also says that "a type always prefigures something future. In all Scripture types there is Prophecy. Prediction and Type differ in form rather than nature. This fact distinguishes between a *Symbol* and a *Type:* a Symbol may represent a thing of the present or past as well as one of the future . . . A type always looks forward to the future. Another thing in the study of Types should be borne in mind, namely, that a thing is in itself evil, and can never be the type of good."

Our present purpose is to show the prophetical significance of that which is typical. As the whole of Scripture is the *mirror* of the Messiah, we can expect His image to be indirectly, as well as directly, forecast and foreshadowed in its sacred pages. Dr. A. T. Pierson reminds us that if we are "to understand the New Testament records of Christ, then, we must know the whole Old Testament, from Genesis to Malachi, for the two Testaments are as closely related as a medallion and its mould."

The moral use of both specific and symbolic prophecies must be emphasized, for some are not mere anticipations of the future, but are intended, by confirming the faith of the true believer, to inspire and strengthen him for his present obligations.

> Jesus, I love to trace,
> Throughout the sacred page,
> The footsteps of Thy grace,
> The same in every age!
> O grant that I may faithful be
> To clearer light vouched to me!

Chapter One

PROPHETIC GLEAMS FROM CONSPICUOUS PERSONS

Adam	Joseph	Boaz	Elijah and Elisha
Abel	Moses	Samuel	Daniel
Melchizedek	Aaron	Job	Jonah
Abraham	Joshua	David	Hosea
Isaac	Judges	Solomon	Zerubbabel
		Jeremiah	

Prophetic pictures giving indirect forecasts abound in the Old Testament. Such an aspect of study would take a large volume all its own to thoroughly explore. These indirect foregleams all leading to Christ can be distinctly traced through the whole of Scripture. As Dr. Pierson puts it, "We see the convergence of a thousand lines of prophecy (indirect forecasts) . . . as in one burning focal point of dazzling glory." We begin by considering some of the Old Testament characters who, each in his own way, suggest Him who came and lived as *the Man* among men.

A. *Adam*

In the classification of types, we have, first of all, *personal types,* by which are meant those personages of Scripture whose lives or actions illustrate some truth or principle associated with Christ's character and works. The book of Genesis abounds in these personal and historical types. As we shall discover as we proceed, characteristic differences are marked in certain books of the Bible. As *Genesis* is a book of beginnings – of sin and judgment, of failure and forgiveness – we can expect its types to be associated with the person and redemption of Christ the deliverer.

Adam was the first man on earth. Eve and he were the first sinners. The name *Adam* means "man," *homo sapiens,* this Latin phrase signifying "a wise man" or "man as a reasoning being," which was what God created him to be. The first man and the man Christ Jesus bear the same name in Paul's great chapter on *The Resurrection:*

> *"The first man Adam* was made a living soul" (I Cor. 15:45; cf. Gen. 2:7).
>
> *"The last Adam* became a life-giving spirit" (I Cor. 15:45, R.V.).

The phrase, "was made," should be omitted, for Jesus was not *made* a life-giving Spirit; He was this, even before He was born in Bethlehem. He was the fountain of life (John 1:4).

> *"The first man* is of the earth, earthy [natural]. *The second man* is the Lord from heaven [spiritual]' (I Cor. 15:47, 48).

Paul distinctly declared Adam to be a contrasting type of Christ.

> "Nevertheless death reigned from Adam to Moses, even over them that had not sinned after the similitude of Adam's transgression, who is the *figure* [type] of him that was to come" (Rom. 5:14).

Adam was the head of God's original creation; Christ is the head of a new creation, the church. Here, again, the two are in contrast:

> "For as in Adam all die, even so in Christ shall all be made alive" (I Cor. 15:22).

A further contrast can be seen in

that Adam was created *without* any evil bias or propensities — these came upon the human race because of his sin — and Christ was likewise born without any evil bias, but He triumphed over the Devil, where Adam failed.

> "For as by one man's disobedience many were made sinners, so by the obedience of one shall many be made righteous" (Rom. 5:19).

It is in a garden that Adam sinned, and in another garden that the last Adam agonized and died to save man from sins. Sad reminiscences are associated with the Bible history of gardens:

In a garden the first of our race
 was deceived;
In a garden the promise of Grace
 was received;
In a garden was Jesus betrayed to
 His doom;
In a garden His body was laid in
 a tomb.

Along with Christ, Adam shared the title of the Son of God (Luke 3:38; 4:9).

B. *Abel*

The bond bringing Abel and Jesus together was a *blood* one; both men were innocent, yet they became murdered men.

> "And to Jesus the mediator... and to the blood of sprinkling, that speaketh better things than that of Abel" (Heb. 12:24).

The blood of Abel cried out for vengeance; the blood of Jesus ever cries out for forgiveness and mercy. Jesus became the mediator through the shedding of His blood because it spoke of "better things," or more powerfully or excellently. Abel being dead yet speaketh, for his innocent blood calls for revenge (Heb. 9:15-17; 10:29). The precious blood of Jesus, however, speaks with greater power, seeing it asks not for wrath but for atonement. God was the avenger of "righteous Abel," but Jesus Christ the righteous One is our advocate with the Father, and He is the propitiation for our sins (I John 2:1, 2). Jesus spoke of "the blood of righteous Abel" (Matt. 23:35), and we are reminded that "Abel offered unto God a more *excellent* sacrifice than Cain, by which he obtained witness that he was righteous" (Heb. 11:4). As the centurion watched Jesus die, he said, "Certainly this was a righteous man" (Luke 23:47).

Abel's sacrifice of a lamb was surely an inspired prediction of the great purpose of the Messiah's coming, namely the putting away of sin by the sacrifice of Himself as the Lamb of God — the substitution of an innocent for a guilty being. Abel, who was earth's first martyr, and the first human person to pass through the gates of death into heaven, was likewise the first to understand the historic offering of sacrifice. He was the first to experience that by the shedding of the innocent blood of a lamb a sinner became righteous before God (Heb. 11:4), and how, through the shedding of the innocent blood of a human being, a sinner became a murderer and was condemned before God (I John 3:12). Jesus is the One who intervened to avenge the shed blood of Abel and to punish the wrongdoing of Cain.

In Abel's shedding of the blood of the lamb, we have a forecast or foreshadowing of the shedding of the blood of Jesus. Is it not somewhat striking that in the list of Old Testament worthies who were illustrious for their faith and readiness to die for it, *Abel has first place* (Heb. 11:4)? We should have thought that his father's name, Adam, should have headed that roll call, but *Adam's name is not in the list at all.* His commendable son, Abel, "obtained witness" — a characteristic of perfect confidence — born of a faith in God's unfailing word. Abel was alone in what he did, just as Jesus was, and his sacrificial offering is the first suggestive type of Calvary in the Bible. When we read that "the Lord had respect unto Abel and to his offering" (Gen. 4:4), *respect* means to look upon with favorable consideration. Such favor was shown both to Abel and his offering, for God never separates what we do from what we are.

How God bore witness to Abel's righteousness by faith by some manifestation of His favor is not recorded (I John 3:12). Jesus witnessed to Abel's righteousness, and many witnessed to His righteous ways, and the Holy Spirit bears "witness to us" in connection with the sacrifice of the cross (Heb. 10:14, 15). When we read of Abel's sacrifice, "By it he being dead yet speaketh," by the *it* we understand Abel's faith, and such a faith speaks and the message is one of instruction. "Faith cometh by hearing" and goes out to render good service by speaking. Abel's lamb speaks of "the Lamb of God" who was slain before Abel slew his lamb, even "from the foundation of the world" (Rev. 13:8). Murder did not silence Abel, just as Calvary did not silence Jesus. Faith is endowed with immortality and cannot therefore die.

C. *Melchizedek*

During the patriarchal dispensation, God gradually prepared for the coming of the Messiah by saintly souls to whom He was able to reveal His purpose, and thus they became guardians of prophecy, with their history and their worship becoming typical. The somewhat mysterious Melchizedek is one of these divine agents (Heb. 5; 7). From Abraham having paid tithes to Melchizedek, Paul argues that the Mosaic dispensation was intended to be subservient to that of the Gospel (Gen. 14:20; Heb. 7:2ff.). The apostle also made it clear that Jesus, who was "a priest after the order of Melchizedek," united in His person the offices of priest and king, and Melchizedek's mysterious origin typified the divine nature of Christ.

The brief biography of this ancient priest still remains as mystical as the handwriting at Belshazzar's feast, or the phantomed specter that predicted the doom of King Saul. Yet it is because of the veil of mystery surrounding Melchizedek that his record is suggestive. As Henry Thorne expresses it in his studies on *Genesis,* "There are clouds, but they are the dust of the Saviour's feet. No type of the Redeemer could be perfect that was destitute of the element of mystery. Think of the mystery of His Birth, of His Cross, of His vacated Tomb!" The following points of contrast may serve to foster the desire of the reader for a fuller, extensive study of priesthood, further references to which can be found under our section *Prophetic Gleams From Prescribed Offices.* (See PRIEST.)

Melchizedek –

With the Aaronic priesthood, priestly appointments depended upon parentage, but with this shadowy priest it was different. His calling was of divine origin, "priest of the most high God" (Gen. 14:18).

Messiah –

It was so with Jesus who as the priest was not derived from Aaron. Coming from the tribe of Judah and not from the priestly line of Levi, He could not have been a priest according to the ceremonial. Jesus was not only the Son of the Highest, but the priest of God in that He was sent of God (I John 4:4), anointed of God (Luke 4:18), approved of God (Acts 2:22).

Melchizedek –

As both *King* and *Priest* (Gen. 14:18), Melchizedek was a suggestive type of the Messiah who is "to sit and rule...; he shall be a priest upon His Throne" (Zech. 6:13). He bore the title of "King of Righteousness" and his name means "My king is righteous."

Messiah —

Righteous in Himself and made unto us "Righteousness," Jesus will yet reign as a king in righteousness, with righteousness as the girdle of His loins (Isa. 11:5). "Behold, a king shall reign in righteousness" (Isa. 32:1).

Melchizedek —

"King of Salem" was another designation this ancient priest bore. *Salem* means "peace," and true to his name he was for tranquillity and not turmoil in national life. He took no part in the war with the kings and is therefore a fitting type of the peace-loving character of Christ.

Messiah —

"Peace" is not only one of the virtues of our great high priest and supreme king, but a part of His being. He *is* peace! When He takes unto Himself to reign as priest upon His throne of glory, His name shall be called "The Prince of Peace" (Isa. 9:6; cf. 32:17, 18). The kings of Judah were not priests. King Uzziah was struck with leprosy for attempting to burn incense, but Jesus, although from Judah, is a royal priest, after the order of Melchizedek, and will yet rule in Zion, the seat of Melchizedek's kingdom and priesthood.

The king-priest by divine appointment is to carry, or will be *in* Himself, "the rod of thy strength out of Zion" (Ps. 110:2). The word used here is not the scepter, the usual mark of kingly power. It is *matteh*, meaning "ancestral staff," or the mark or badge of the hereditary and lineally descended ruler. It was borne by the head of each village, the *Sheik* of each Bedaween tribe. Because, therefore, in patriarchal times each head of the house appeared in the character of a priest to his own family, the *matteh* marks the priest as well as the prince. Fittingly, then, this was given to Him who is both king and priest, as being the predicted prince of David's direct line. This *matteh* shall be "sent out of Zion," which will be the seat of His governmental control during the millennium.

Melchizedek —

Further, this evidently godly man is said to have been "made like unto the Son of God," but in what respect we are not told, unless it be in the reference either of his typical ministry or to his history, namely, "Without father, without mother, without geneaology, having neither beginning of days, nor end of life." This description has puzzled a good many, seeing that Melchizedek could not have been a human king and priest, without human parents. What is meant, of course, is the fact that we have no official genealogy, no information as to who his parents were, when and where he was born, and died. He suddenly appears in the course of history, plays his part, and abruptly vanishes from the record, except as a foregleam of Christ's dual office as priest and king.

Messiah —

Like Melchizedek, Jesus abideth a priest continually for He ever liveth to make intercession for us (Heb. 7:25), having an unchangeable priesthood (Heb. 7:24). As the eternal Son, He hath neither the beginning of days, nor end of life. "Whose goings forth have been from of old, from everlasting" (Mic. 5:2). By way of contrast, we do know who the mother of Jesus, and likewise His foster-father, were and when He was born and how He died and left the world.

Melchizedek —

Another feature worth noting is that after Abraham's victory over the kings, he was met by Melchizedek, who refreshed the warrior-patriarch with bread and wine and blessed him in the name of the most high God. In response, Abraham gave the king-priest tithes of all the spoil he had taken.

Messiah —

In view of His certain victory over the monarch of hell, Jesus gathered His own around Him for communion with Himself, and the bread and wine were to remind them of all He had suffered and secured. Whenever His saints meet in His name, He lifts up His hands and blesses them, and their gratitude for all He accomplished on their behalf finds expression in the tithes they surrender to Him for the furtherance of His cause.

D. *Abraham*

From the references Paul has to the typical nature of the patriarchal dispensation (see Gal. 4:22-31; Heb. 5:10; 7:1), we are safe in assuming that there are many more types in Old Testament Scriptures than those specially mentioned in the New Testament. But, as we have already mentioned, we must not let our imagination run wild in the matter of typology. The danger of abuse must be guarded against. It is generally safer to dwell only on those types we have Scriptural authority for, ever remembering that in a type every circumstance is far from being typical. For instance, the High Priest, on the Day of Atonement, was eminently a type of Christ. We must not infer, however, that when he offered first for his own sin, therefore Christ partook of our sinful nature. The type breaks down here, for in Him was no sin.

Abraham is one of those persons of foregoing ages who bore some resemblance or representation of Him that was to come, yet who, in yielding to the flesh, contradicted all that Christ was in Himself. This "Columbus of Faith," as Abraham has been called, has been named by God as, "the father of all them that believe" (Rom. 4:11), and is more often referred to than any other patriarch. For instance, nearly one-third of the verses in Hebrews 11 relate to the trials and triumphs of Abraham, "the fountain-head of Hebrew life." He is spoken of as having "received the promises" (Heb. 11:17), and perhaps no person named in the Bible received so many promises from the Lord as did Abraham.

A striking forecast of Christ's influence in the world can be found in the benediction pronounced by God upon Abraham, that by him all the families of the earth would be blessed (Gen. 12:3) — a promise that will receive its perfect fulfillment during the period of millennial happiness during Christ's reign over the earth.

Then the altars Abraham built were fingerposts pointing to Calvary. The Hebrew word for *altar* literally means "the slaughter-place" and foreshadowed the death of the cross. He build his altar "unto the Lord" (Gen. 12:8), suggesting that the way to God is sprinkled with the blood of the Redeemer (Heb. 10:19).

Abraham was indeed a pilgrim, yet he should not have wandered from the path of obedience as he did when he went into Egypt, God having led him to Canaan. In Egypt he yielded to fear of man, and acted a lie that placed his wife Sarah in a position of great moral danger (Gen. 12:10-20). God had said to His servant, "I will make thy name great," but Abraham sacrificed a measure of his greatness by his lapse in Egypt, to which he went because of famine in Canaan. What a contrast is presented by Christ when He was without food in the wilderness! On no occasion did He do anything to dishonor His Father. Bread was only a secondary consideration to Him whose chief concern was obedience to the Father's will (John 4:34).

Above all else, Abraham was conspicuous for his faith, so pleasing to God. His simple trust secured honorable mention both in Romans and Hebrews. Because of his faith he became known as "the Friend of God"

(James 2:23), "the father of all them that believe" (Rom. 4:11), "the heir of the world" (Rom. 4:13), "a father of many nations" (Rom. 4:17). But a greater than Abraham is here, although He came as "the son of Abraham" (Matt. 1:1). As if no honor could be too great for the first man to be called a *Hebrew,* the Lord linked his name with the glory of the Redeemer, where He says, "The God of Abraham . . . hath glorified his Son" (Acts 3:13). But one of the wonders of grace is that this God is *our* Lord, and that we are to be glorified in and through His Son.

While there are many other typical contrasts and comparisons we could adduce, one or two of which we do deal with in our next cameo, we think of Abraham's last days and death. How largely human history is the echo of divine predictions; the patriarch died in a good old age (Gen. 25:8), or "full of years." Alexander Maclaren suggests that "we shall understand the meaning of this expression better if, instead of 'full of years,' we read 'satisfied with years.' He was not *satiated* with life, but *satisfied.*" Having finished his pilgrimage of 175 years, Abraham had no desire that it should reach beyond the appointed end. With almost her last breath the Countess of Huntingdon said, "My work is done, and I have nothing to do but go to my Father."

Did not Jesus say "to the Father"? — "I have finished the work Thou gavest Me to do"; and completing His task, He cried, "It is finished." But unlike Abraham, He did not die in a good old age. He was only thirty-three years and a few months when He ended His earthly course.

> Not one golden hair was gray
> Upon His Crucifixion Day.

"Abraham gave up the ghost, and died" (Gen. 25:8); and Jesus after uttering His last cry "yielded up the ghost" (Matt. 27:50). But as we know, such departure of the soul from the body does not signify cessation of existence. Did not Jesus, in proving to the Sadducees who did not believe in life after death, that Moses called the Lord "The God of Abraham," reveal the continuity of existence and the certainty of resurrection. God "is not a God of the dead, but of the living" (Luke 20:38). As Abraham left the land of the dying, he entered the blissful land of the living above. The patriarch "died in faith" (Heb. 11:13), meaning that the faith sustaining him in life supported him in death. "As he took his last look at the fading vision of the earthly inheritance the eye of faith would behold the undimmed glory of the heavenly." Was this not so with Jesus, who, as He died, committed Himself into the hands of His Father confident that He would rise again?

E. *Isaac*

By his three wives, Abraham had eight sons, but only two of them are referred to, typically, in the New Testament, namely, Ishmael and Isaac, the latter being the only son to be mentioned by name. Incidentally, it is said that after Abraham died "his sons Isaac and Ishmael buried him" (Gen. 25:9). Nothing is said of the other six sons (Gen. 25:1, 2). It was to the credit of Ishmael that he attended the funeral. Dr. Joseph Parker's comment is suggestive, "Abraham gave all he had unto Isaac, yet Ishmael went to the funeral." The large-hearted generosity of Abraham appears again in his firstborn son. Through conflict in the home, Ishmael and Isaac were divided, but death, often a reconciler, brought them together. Sooner or later death will bring us all together.

Paul speaks about Ishmael and Isaac as presenting an "allegory" or a parable. Ishmael was "the son of the bondwoman," meaning that he was born of Hagar, who had been a slave in Abraham's household. Isaac was "the son of the freewoman," or the son of Sarah, Abraham's first wife. The first son represents the law, and the second son, the promise, and Paul argues that the Mosaic dispensation was intended to be subservient to that of the Gospel of divine grace (Gal. 4:22-31). The two sons were typical of the two covenants, one of bondage, the other of freedom – which cannot exist together. Thus, as Cowper wrote,

Israel, in ancient days,
  Not only had a view
Of Sinai in a blaze,
  But learn'd the Gospel too:
The types and figures were a glass,
In which they saw a Saviour's face.

One of the outstanding Old Testament pictures or predictions of Calvary is the offering up of Isaac by his own father. What a memorable foreshadowing of the love of God manifested in the sacrifice and death of His only begotten Son, the obedience of Abraham on Mount Moriah presents (Gen. 22:1-19). In after days both Isaac and Jacob made use of that sacrifice (Gen. 31:54; 46:1). While the offering up of Isaac is not specifically referred to in the New Testament as a *type*, it can be received as such because of its close resemblance to the cross. Nowhere else in Scripture have we a more perfect presentation of the supreme sacrifice at Calvary as in the willingness of Abraham to surrender his son of promise to death on an altar.

If Moriah was the greatest trial in Abraham's life, it was certainly his greatest triumph for the faith that led him to forsake his country at the call of God, enabled him to offer up the only son now left to him as the Lord had commanded him. The promise had been given that he should become "a father of a multitude," as the name *Abraham* means, but could he become such if his son was sacrificed? God had said, "In Isaac shall thy seed be blessed," but how could this promise or prediction be fulfilled if Isaac was knifed to death? But while *reason* is asking HOW?, *Faith* answers IT SHALL BE DONE.

Their's not to reason why,
Their's but to do and die.

Preachers and teachers can find effective material for presentation in the comparisons between Isaac and Christ. For instance, with both:

We have a good and kind father causing his beloved, only, and innocent son to suffer death. Isaac was the only son of promise.

We have Isaac, heir to the promises of the temporal Canaan – through Christ, our heavenly Isaac, we claim the heavenly inheritance.

We have Isaac carrying the wood on which he was bound, in order to be offered up – Christ carrying His own cross on which He was afterwards nailed and put to death.

We have the God-appointed place where Isaac should die – Christ actually dying in the place He said He would die. Both mounts were in the land of Moriah, which means "the manifestation of God." On one mount the Temple stood – on another, the Cross.

We have the term of *three* days, remarkably specified in each history. With Isaac, the three days ended with a substitute dying in his place. With Jesus, the three days ended with His Resurrection.

We have the *Lamb* that Abraham said God would provide – Christ came as the Lamb of God. The ram died for Isaac, and both lambs and rams were associated with temple-sacrifices, and are fitting types of the substitutionary aspect of Christ's death.

We have Abraham's naming of the mountain where his distress was relieved *Jehovah-Jireh*, "The Lord will Provide." But Calvary deserves such a name infinitely better, for there

God provided a perfect salvation for a sinning race.

A. M. Hodgkin, in *Christ in All the Scriptures*, suggests how we should tread softly as we follow step by step, as if on holy ground, the road to the scene of death.

Mount Moriah (Gen. 22)

v. 2 – "Take now thy son."
"Thine only son."
"Whom thou lovest."
"Get thee into the land of Moriah."
"Offer him there for a burnt-offering."
"Upon one of the mountains which I will tell thee of."

v. 4 – Abraham lifted up his eyes, and saw the place afar off."

v 62– "Abraham took the wood... and laid it upon Isaac his son."
"They went both of them together."

v. 7 – "Where is the lamb for a burnt offering?"

v. 8, R.V. – "God will provide himself *the* lamb."
"They went both of them together."

v. 9 – "Abraham built an altar .... and bound Isaac... and laid him upon the wood."

v. 10 – "Abraham... took the knife to slay his son."

v. 11 – "The angel of the Lord called to him out of heaven."

v. 12 – "Thou hast not withheld thy son, thine only son."

v. 13 – "Abraham... took the ram, and offered him up... in the stead of his son." Rams as well as lambs were sacrificial animals.

v. 5 – "I and the lad will... come again to you." Abraham believed he would take Isaac home with him, "accounting that God was able to raise him up, even from the dead." (See Hebrews 11:17-19).

Mount Calvary (Luke 23:33)

Heb. 1:2 – God "hath... spoken unto us by his Son."

John 3:16 – "God... gave his only begotten Son."

John 1:18 – "Which is in the bosom of the Father."

II Chron. 3:1 – "Solomon began to build the house of the Lord... in Mount Moriah."

Luke 23:33 – "The place, which is called Calvary, *there* they crucified him."

Heb. 10:10 – "We are sanctified through the offering of the body of Jesus."

Acts 3:18 – "God before had showed by the mouth of all his prophets, that Christ should suffer."

John 19:17; cf. 18:11 – Jesus "bearing His cross, went forth."

John 10:17, 18 – "Therefore doth my Father love me, because I lay down my life."

John 1:29 – "Behold the Lamb of God, which taketh away the sin of the world."

Rev. 13:8 – "The Lamb slain from the foundation of the world."

Ps. 40:8 – "I delight to do thy will, O my God."

Acts 2:23; cf. Isa. 53:6 – Jesus "being delivered by the determinate counsel and foreknowledge of God."

Isa. 53:10 – "It pleased the Lord to bruise him."

Matt. 27:46 – "My God, my God, why hast thou forsaken me?"

Ps. 22:2 – "I cry in the daytime, but thou hearest not."

Jer. 6:26 – "Mourning, as for an only son." God compares deep grief to the loss of an only son.

Exod. 29:16 – "Thou shalt slay the ram."

Isa. 53:11 – "He shall bear their iniquities."

Matt. 28:6 – "He is not here: for he is risen." Abraham believed God was able to raise up Isaac from the dead, "from whence also he received him in a figure." Isaac was spared at the last moment; but with Jesus, it was different. He died on the cross.

The word used for "figure" is given

as "parable" in the R.V. and indicates that the laying of Isaac upon the altar was a parabolic representation of death – the parable being in action instead of words – and his deliverance from death was therefore a parabolic representation of resurrection. Thus, in Isaac, we have a conspicuous type of Him who was freely "delivered up for us all" and who was received from the dead by His Father (Rom. 8:32; I Tim. 3:16).

Before we leave Abraham and Isaac, there is one further indirect type we can discover in another episode of their history, namely, in the charming story of Rebekah, who was willing to go out from her father's house to go to be the bride of Isaac (Gen. 24). In his old age Abraham was insistent on the accomplishment of the divine revelation as to his seed, and was therefore urgent that Isaac should not take a wife from the daughters of the Canaanites, but find a partner for him among his mother's kith and kin. Abraham's commission to his trusted servant, who was perhaps Eliezer (Gen. 15:2), shows how determined he was to follow closely the divine will. Thus we have a chapter containing a love lyric full of romance and tender beauty.

But, as Henry Thorne reminds us, "Abraham, in his search for Rebekah, was really looking for Jesus. Her marriage with Isaac was to be a link in the chain of events which would lead up to "That far-off Divine event To which the whole creation moves," and which was to result in the fulfillment of the prediction that secured blessing for all the nations of the earth through Abraham. Through the wedding-day Abraham would see that day of Christ in which the church should become the bride of Christ. His long chapter is thus seen to have in it the depth of the great purposes of God "concerning Christ and the church" (Eph. 5:32)." It is in this respect that the servant's search for a bride for Isaac is typical of the ministry of the divine servant, the Holy Spirit, in preparing for God's Son a heavenly bride, even the church. Spiritual commentators have not been slow to find the seeds of profound truths in this memorial chapter with its sixty-seven verses, but its outstanding typical suggestion is that of the security of a bride for the Son of the most high God.

The decision and determination of Rebekah to respond to the servant's offer to take her to Isaac, proves that when faith ventures it finds itself justified. Out she went to Canaan to find a husband, her permanent home, and her true life. The Divine Spirit has been active in the world since Pentecost, gathering out a people for Christ's name, and all who have followed the Spirit's leading to the Saviour have entered into a most blessed union. As soon as Isaac saw Rebekah he loved her, and Christ also loved the church, and will present her to Himself as a glorious bride, not having spot, or wrinkle, or any such thing (Eph. 5:23-33).

F. *Joseph*

The king of glory heaped with all honors, promised to all ages, proclaimed by all inspired prophets, is likewise prefigured by all great examples of whom none is greater than Joseph, who, more than any other Old Testament character, foreshadowed the Saviour of the world. The whole history of Joseph affords an illustration of God's overruling Providence and is calculated to inspire confidence in His unceasing protection of His own. Each of the ancient leaders typifies a particular feature of the Messiah who was to come and fulfill all promises and predictions:

In Melchizedek we see Jesus as the priest of the Most High God;
In Moses, we see Jesus as the mediator between God and man;
In David, we see Jesus as shepherd, ruler, and King;

In Joseph we see Jesus as preserver, provider, and Saviour.

The stirring pages of the story of Joseph — the most lengthy of all the biographies in the book of Genesis — provides us with a history that can be called *par excellence* "The Drama Of Providence." Both in prison and palace Jehovah was with His servant. Even the master saw that "Jehovah was with Joseph." He did not leave his religion behind in his father's home nor conceal it in the house of Pharaoh. He never forgot, nor was he ashamed of the name of Jehovah his God. His light ever shone before men. Joseph was about seventeen years old when he was sold into Egypt and shortly thereafter was thrown into prison till, when thirty years of age, he came before Pharaoh and set out upon his great career as Prime Minister and Governor of all Egypt, second only to Pharaoh.

There are two Biblical summaries of Joseph's life that speak for themselves and act as foregleams of Him who went from prison and from judgment, because He was the Saviour of mankind, and who will yet function as the governor of all nations. The psalmist sketches the destiny of Joseph thus:

> He sent a man before them, even Joseph, who was sold for a servant:
> Whose feet they hurt with fetters: he was laid in iron:
> Until the time that his word came: the word of the Lord tried him.
> The king sent and loosed him; even the ruler of the people, and let him go free.
> He made him lord of his house, and ruler of all his substance:
> To bind his princes at his pleasure; and teach his senators wisdom.
> Israel also came into Egypt; and Jacob sojourned in the land of Ham." (Ps. 105:17-23).

The other brief biography was cited by Stephen in his plea before the council: "And the patriarchs, moved with envy, sold Joseph into Egypt: but God was with him, And delivered him out of all his afflictions, and gave his favour and wisdom in the sight of Pharaoh king of Egypt; and he made him governor over Egypt and all his house . . . And at the second time Joseph was made known to his brethren; and Joseph's kindred was made known unto Pharaoh" (Acts 7:9, 10, 13). A person must be spiritually short-sighted if he cannot see Jesus in many of the experiences overtaking Joseph. With an outline like the following, preachers should be able to present a profitable message on Joseph as an evident type of Jesus:

Joseph was beloved of his father — Jesus was His Father's Beloved Son;
was sold by his brothers at the price of a slave — Jesus was sold for thirty pieces of silver, the price of a slave;
was found taking upon him the form of a servant — Jesus humbled Himself and took upon Him a similar form;
was victorious in resistance of temptation — Jesus was more than conqueror over Satan and his wiles;
was, for his own sake, a blessing to others — God blesses us for Christ's sake (Gen. 39:5);
was condemned and bound — Jesus was unjustly condemned, bound, and made to suffer ignominy;
was exalted to be a prince and a saviour — Jesus was highly exalted because of His finished work and will yet be prince of the kings of earth;
was provider of bread for a famine-stricken nation — Jesus became the bread of life to the world;
was manifested unto his brethren — Jesus will be seen by Israel as the One they pierced;
was second to Pharaoh — Jesus is co-equal with God.

There are two almost parallel passages showing the great salvation in both cases to be the combined result of human wickedness and divine purpose. With true magnanimity, Joseph calmed the fears of his brothers by telling them that he was in the place of God: "But as for you, ye thought *evil* against me; but God meant it unto *good*, to bring to pass, as it is this day, to save much people alive" (Gen. 50:20). Then we have this paragraph from Peter's mighty sermon at Pentecost: "Him, being delivered by the determinate counsel and foreknowledge of God, ye have taken, and by wicked hands have crucified and slain: Whom God hath raised up" (Acts 2:23, 24). How true are the words of F. W. Faber on *The Will Of God:*

> Ill that He blesses is our good,
> And unblest good is ill;
>
> And all is right that seems most wrong
> If it be His sweet will.

G. *Moses*

Behind all Biblical references to Moses stands a man of tremendous worth and achievement, whose mark upon the world is as important as it is incalculable. Of all Old Testament characters, Moses stands out so magnificently as a great man of many parts. He was prophet, legislator, historian, ruler, and champion, all in one. "In the history of the World probably no name ever stirred the heart of a nation as his has done." He was, and still is, the hero of the Jewish nation. The proverb which has sustained the Jews through many a long oppression reads "When the tale of bricks is doubled then comes Moses." The life of this remarkable man, who lived for 120 years, is divided into three periods of forty years each:

Forty years training in the arts of Egypt, and learning to be SOMEBODY.

Forty years training in God's school of the desert, and learning to be NOBODY.

Forty years as Leader and Law-Giver of Israel, and learning that God is EVERYBODY.

As we shall presently see, the great theme of prophecy and performance is the mediatorial character of Christ, which consisted in His being a prophet, priest, and king; and each of these offices was typified by Moses. For the guidance of preachers, these bones could be clothed with a little flesh:

Moses was divinely appointed as the ruler and leader of the Israelites – Jesus is head of His church, and will yet reign as king.

Moses was the outstanding lawgiver, revealing God's mind to a people – Jesus, as a prophet, gave commandments to His own. In the giving of the Law, Moses was a type of Jesus in a twofold way:

1. In delivering the people from their heavy and prolonged bondage – The bondage of sin Jesus delivers from is far more oppressive than Egypt's bondage.
2. In the bringing of a New Law. In His Sermon on the Mount, Jesus shows how much greater He is than the Law, and that His added commandment of Love touches the springs of character and conduct.

Moses, in the first five books of the Bible, laid the foundation of Jewish literature – Jesus is the One dominating the world's literature.

Moses typified Christ as priest, in a twofold way:

1. The Jewish leader was commanded to ratify the Covenant made between God and the Israelites, by the sprinkling of blood, which act reminded them of their unfitness as sinners to

enter into any covenant with God, except through an appointed atonement (Exod. 24:8) — Jesus declared that no one could approach God save through His mediatorial work (John 14:6).

2. In his intercessory ministry, Moses exercised a powerful influence. Through his prayers, countless blessings were obtained, and divine wrath turned away from the people. We think of Taberah, Hazeroth, and Kadesh-barnea (Exod. 15:25; 17:12; 32:11).

While Moses stood with arms spread wide,
Success was found on Israel's side;
But when thro' weariness they failed,
That moment Amalek prevailed.

Jesus was, and ever is, a mightier intercessor than Moses was. He never fails through weariness to plead on our behalf (Matt. 26:36-38; Heb. 5:7; 7:25). Through the shedding of His blood, Jesus completed a covenant between God and man, and now intercedes for His church at the right hand of the Father.

Moses was not able to bear the burden of the people alone, and God gave him others to help carry the load — Jesus bore the terrible burden of our sin alone. Alone, He bore our sins in His own body on the tree.

Moses was not allowed to bring the people into the Promised Land. He represented the Law which may point to Christ but cannot save nor bring one into the fulness of the blessing of the Gospel. Joshua, whose name is the same as Jesus, was given the task of leading the people into the Promised Land, and thereby typifies the Saviour who alone can bring us into the inheritance of the saints.

Moses, after a remarkable career, died, and "God buried him," the only man in history to have God as his undertaker. But he appeared again on earth at the Mount of Transfiguration, and in his glorified form was recognized by Peter — Jesus died and rose again and in His glorified form appeared to His disciples, and to Stephen at his death, and to Saul of Tarsus on his way to Damascus.

Other comparisons proving that Moses was a picture of the Son of man who was to come can be traced in his deliverance from violent death in infancy, in his years of silent training, in his willingness to leave a palace for the wilderness, in his meekness, in his completion of a God-given task and in the authoritative message he proclaimed. See Deuteronomy 4:2 with Revelation 22:18, 19.

H. *Aaron*

The divinely-appointed priesthood under the Old Dispensation is rich in symbolism. The High Priest, priests, and Levites, with their specific ministry and ornate garments, are mirrors of the priesthood of Christ, and of all believers. The book of Leviticus, the name being based on *Levi*, the priestly tribe, offers us many expressive types of the redemption and mediation of Christ. The consecration of Aaron as High Priest, and his priestly office and work, prominent throughout *Leviticus*, is an almost perfect forecast of Him who became our great High Priest; and the consecration of Aaron's sons and of the Levites foreshadow the priesthood of all who are truly born again believers. That access to God can only come through the blood of atonement is seen in the account of Nadab and Abihu, two of the four sons of Aaron, who offered "strange fire" before the Lord and were consumed. The priestly censers had to be lighted from the altar of burnt sacrifice — only with this fire could they approach the Lord.

For ourselves, it is only on the ground of Christ's Atonement that our prayers can arise to God as acceptable incense. Without His blood, we cannot enter the holiest of all. The full typical significance of Aaron and his sons, can only be gathered from an understanding of how and why they came into existence. Moses tells us why God honorably distinguished the tribe of Levi with public worship. It was because the Levites, as the record reads, "observed thy word, and kept thy covenant (Deut. 33:9). Therefore theirs was to be the privilege of teaching the Israelites the things of God and also "They shall put incense before thee, and whole burntsacrifice upon thine altar" (Deut. 33:10). Thus, after the death of Moses, the High Priest became the great medium of communication between God and the people (Num. 27:21-23). After His death and resurrection, Jesus became our perfect High Priest, through whom alone the sinner has access to God. The means of communication were principally kept up by *Urim* and *Thummim,* meaning "Lights and Perfections," suggesting the clarity with which God would impart to the High Priest the knowledge of His Will, when that knowledge was sought by means which He had appointed (Exod. 28:30; Deut. 33:8).

When, in Hebrew, two nouns appear together as in the form here, Urim and Thummim, one is understood to be an adjective, making it especially emphatic. Thus, this combination should be translated "perfect light," for the plural form here is the Hebrew plural of majesty. Some scholars, like Scofield, suggest that we have here a collective name for the stones of the breastplate, so that the total effect of the twelve stones is to manifest the "Lights and Perfections" of Christ, who is the antitype of the Aaronic High Priest. In some way, not revealed, ascertainment of the divine will in particular cases came by way of the Urim and Thummin (Num. 27:21; I Sam. 28:6; Ezra 2:63).

Whatever these were, they had to be placed in the breastplate of the High Priest and borne before the Lord when His will was sought on solemn occasions; and the judgment that came by them was always a true and just one (Num. 27:21). When Paul uses the words "manifestation" and "truth" (II Cor. 4:2), he employs the very terms by which Urim and Thummim are translated in the *Septuagint,* or Greek version of the Old Testament. Typically, the somewhat mystic terms typify the Lord Jesus Christ, our High Priest, "in whom are hid all the treasures of wisdom and knowledge."

Aaron and his sons were consecrated and crowned for the high office of exercising a general oversight in public worship, and to perform the most sacrificial parts of divine service (Lev. 8). The symbolic act of the coronation of the High Priest in Zechariah 6:9-11 united the two great offices of priest and king in one person-type of the person and work of the man whose name is the *Branch* (Zech. 3:8; 6:12), who shall sit on His throne of glory as a priest, the builder of the eternal temple of the Lord, and "bear the glory." The High Priest wore a miter, but on the head of Jesus will rest many crowns.

Further, the High Priest was distinguished by a peculiar and glorious dress, which he wore on particular occasions. Attached to this was the breastplate, upon which, as well as upon the onyx stones on the shoulder, were engraved the names of the children of Israel that the priest might bear them before the Lord continually (Exod. 28:19; 39:14). The miter on his forehead bore the inscription "Holiness to the Lord." Shoulders, forehead, and heart, what do these symbolize but the perfect strength, perfect wisdom, and perfect love which our great High Priest manifests on our behalf? Does He not carry us on His shoulder? Was He not made unto us wisdom? Is not His love personal and eternal? As priests unto God we are clothed in the beautiful robe of His righteousness (Rev. 19:8). The burning of incense, the fragrance of which rose up, represents that acceptable prayer and worship ever pleasing to God (Ps. 141:2; Luke 1:10; Rev. 5:8).

There is the incident of Aaron with his censer of incense running quickly and standing between the living and the dead to make atonement for the people who had maligned him as the High Priest, and who had sinned against God. When the rebellious people had been smitten with a plague, Aaron made intercession for them and the plague ceased (Num. 16:46-50). Is this not a picture of One greater than Aaron, who was blasphemed and rejected and crucified, but who, by His death, made a full atonement for a sin-plagued world; and who ever lives to intercede for those redeemed by His blood? Soon after this dramatic episode, the budding of Aaron's rod was the seal of his spiritual power and authority. God's choice of him was made when He said to Moses, "Take thou unto thee Aaron *thy brother*... that he may minister unto me in the priest's office" (Exod. 28:1). Here, again, we see Jesus of whom it is said that "In all things it behoved him to be made like unto *his brethren,* that he might be a merciful and faithful high priest" (Heb. 2:17).

Although a striking foregleam of Jesus, Aaron falls short of Him in at least two directions. First, he came behind in type because he was a sinful man, and had to present a sacrifice for his own sins, as well as for those of the people (Lev. 4:3, 35). So, although he was Israel's first High Priest, he was not a perfect one, as Jesus is. As the man, He was tempted as men were, yet remained sinless. None could convict Him of error or sin. He was holy, harmless, and undefiled, and therefore *separate* from sinners, but thoroughly identified with their sin. Knowing no sin, He was made sin for them.

In the second place, Aaron, as priest, is not a perfect type of Jesus, because he could only enter into the Holy of Holies *one day* in the year, bearing the blood of atonement. His was not a once-for-all representation. But with Jesus, "the High Priest of good things to come," it is different, for He entered into heaven itself, and is ever in the Holy of Holies of God's presence on our behalf. Aaron went in and out of the most inner court of the tabernacle once a year – Jesus has remained in the divine presence since He entered it at His Ascension, bearing the evidence of His atoning work. Up there, as the glorified man, He *understands our need* to the uttermost; and as the perfect God, He can *meet that need* to the uttermost. On the cross, He bore the world's sin; on the throne, He bears the world's need in intercession (Exod. 30:10; Heb. 9:24-28).

I. *Joshua*

William Caxton (1422-1491) wrote that "it is notoriously known through the universal world, that there be nine worthy men and the best that ever were. That to wit three paynems (pagans), three Jews, and three Christian men." The three Jews Caxton names are:

> The first was Duke Joshua...
> The second David, King of Jerusalem...
> The third Judas Maccabaeus.

While we may not agree with such a selection, Caxton was right in calling Joshua "Duke," which, in its original form, means "leader" or "commander," of which the successor of Moses was a perfect example. The book bearing his name reveals that he is an outstanding prototype of his great successor, the captain of our salvation, who is leading His own on into the Promised Land of full blessing now, and heaven hereafter. It is not hard to trace the Saviour, in his name, character, and history.

His name was originally *Oshea,* meaning "a saviour," or "one saved"; but afterwards Moses called him *Joshua,* meaning 'he shall save," or "the salvation of Jehovah," which was a name indicating the work which God was to accomplish by this warrior. The Greek form of *Joshua* is JESUS, accounting for the use of *Jesus* for *Joshua* in the phrase, "If Jesus had given them rest" (Heb. 4:8). The margin quotes *Joshua.* In name, then, he was a foregleam of the Saviour before His birth, "Thou shalt call his name JESUS: for he shall save his people from their sins" (Matt. 1:21).

As we have already indicated, Moses was not allowed to bring the Children of Israel into the Land of Promise. A new leader with a new commission was necessary to command the people to go in and possess the new land. Moses was the embodiment of the Law, and Christ was the end of it. The Law cannot bring us into all divine grace has provided; only Jesus can do this. Thus the book of Joshua is heavy with types of Jesus.

On the threshold of a great adventure, God gave His people a threefold encouragement to arise and acquire the land, namely:

The Divine Gift. "Every place that the sole of your foot shall tread upon, that have I given unto you" (Josh. 1:3). The land was theirs before their feet trod upon it, but by faith they had to possess their possessions. We have been blessed with all spiritual blessing in the heavenlies in Christ, and our obligation is to appropriate what is *ours* without timidity (Eph. 1:3). It is not without reason that Joshua has been called the Ephesians of the Old Testament. As God gave Canaan to Israel so He gave Christ to the church; and as the gift of Canaan meant the gift of all that Canaan contained, so the gift of Jesus Christ means the gift of all His, and of all He has. What an inheritance we have in "the fulness of the Godhead bodily" and in "all the treasures of wisdom and knowledge"! But the enjoyment of all we have in Him is conditioned by our faith, for He is to us what we trust Him to be. Ours is the privilege to gather all God has given (Ps. 104:28).

The Divine Command. "Arise, go. . . . Have not I commanded thee?" (Josh. 1:2, 9). Without hesitation Joshua obeyed and his book is taken up with his entrance into the Canaan, and of the division of it among the tribes of Israel. In fact, the book is in three general sections:

1. The Conquest of the Land (chs. 1-12).
2. The Distribution of the Land (chs. 13-22).
3. The Death of Joshua in the Land (chs. 23; 24).

Ere Jesus left His own, He commanded them to go out into all the world and bring the nations under His sway, and His last commission has never been withdrawn. There are to be no frontiers to His kingdom (Matt. 28:19).

The Divine Presence. "As I was with Moses, so I will be with thee: I will not fail thee, nor forsake thee" (Josh. 1:5). Fearlessly Joshua went forward, and courageously routed God's enemies and possessed the land for His people. Amid all his testings he was upheld by the promise, "The Lord thy God is with thee whithersoever thou goest" (Josh. 1:9). Did not Jesus have the very same promise for His church? With His "Go ye" there was also His "Lo, I am with you alway, even unto the end of the world" (Matt. 28:20) Then think of the confirmation of His abiding presence His people have in the repeated promise, "He hath said, I will never leave thee, nor forsake thee" (Heb. 13:5).

What a forecast, then, the entrance into Canaan is of our present inheritance in Christ—the good land we are called upon to enter here and now! While hymnists, with poetic license, speak of heaven as our heavenly Canaan, Canaan is *not* a type of heaven. In the Land of Promise, Joshua experienced a good deal of warfare, but there are no enemies nor strife in heaven. We are not yet in heaven but in a hostile world of which the Devil is its god, and as we claim our inheritance in Christ we can expect the highest kind of warfare, a good fight against spiritual wickedness in heavenly places. But for the conflict a full and perfect armor has been provided (Eph. 6:10-18). The divine gift of Canaan did not do away with the necessity of conflict. With the gift there was the guarantee that the conflict would end victoriously.

Among the many lessons we learn from the book of Joshua is that in taking possession of what God has so graciously given us, our strength to appropriate is of God. Is this not the typical significance of the section containing the incident of the appearance of the captain of the Lord's host to His valiant soldier? Knowing that the land was Israel's, Joshua thought that it was to be left to him and his people to take the land the best they could. But on the plains of Jericho, the valiant commander learned that as it was *God's grace* which had given Israel Canaan, so it was by *God's power* they would be able to take possession of the land. It was the captain of the Lord's host who would make actual in experience all He had made possible in promise.

How slow we are to learn that there is always power at our disposal to take possession of what God has given; that when the captain of our salvation is in His right place, enthroned in our hearts, there is nothing promised to the church which may not be experienced by the humblest saint! Can we bear testimony that "not one thing has failed of all the good things which the Lord your God spake concerning you; all are come to pass unto you, and not one thing hath failed thereof" (Josh. 23:14)? There are, at least, three key words in the record of the conquest of the land we should take to heart:

Prepare. Is this not the note sounded at Jordan? Preparation included personal morals as well as sufficient and efficient munitions of war. Thus the opening chapters of the book typify how God's soldiers must be right with God before they can fight God's battles. A good life behind the good fight of faith is a powerful weapon against the enemy.

Pass Over. Are we clean over Jordan? When Joshua's men drew their swords, threw away their scabbards, and crossed the river, they committed themselves to the gigantic odds of victory or death. Out they went in full reliance upon the divine promise of conquest. Does this not teach us that as soldiers of our heavenly Joshua we are only fit to fight His battles if there has been a definite decisive surrender of ourselves to His command?

Possess. Here we have the recurring key word of the book from the fall of Jericho until the whole of the land is subdued and divided. Stories of possession like that of Caleb, who by his faithfulness to God and his courage obtained possession of Hebron, are full of spiritual encouragement for our hearts. Too often we are slack to go and possess the land! In every one of us is an evil heart departing from the living God. Yet our cry is, "How can I take possession of that which is Christ?" and this ancient book supplies the answer. "All things are ours" in Christ, and we must take possession of them experimentally by faith in Him. The destruction of the Canaanites is an emblem of the victory we gain over the world, flesh, and the Devil through Christ, our captain (Heb. 2:10).

Joshua's character, like his campaigns, is highly instructive and typical. The Holy Spirit was in him (Num. 27:18) – Jesus was likewise anointed with the Spirit. In seasons of emergency, Joshua sought by prayer special blessing and help (Josh. 10: 12-14). It would seem as if "efforts and prayer," "zeal and dependence," were clearly his rule. Do not these virtues suggest the dependence of Jesus upon His Father, and His zeal for the Father's business? Further, although Joshua had the divine promise of success, he yet prudently used whatever means were likely to secure victory. He did not rest upon his military prowess, his spies, his well-disciplined forces, but upon the God of battles. He trusted in God, and was careful to keep his powder dry, and came to prove that the discipline of his task had not been unblessed.

The piety and devotion of Joshua are beautifully revealed in his farewell appeals, and the spirit of affectionate submission with which the people received them gives us a favorable impression of his strong influence and of the people's fidelity (Josh. 23). As for the Israelites in Canaan, they looked back on fulfilled predictions, and forward to a glorious future. The last act of Joshua was not only to exhort the people to keep all that Moses had written, and to serve the Lord with all their heart, but to add his personal testimony to the book of the Law of God and set up a great stone as a witness to the renewal of the Covenant, "As for me and my house, we will serve the Lord."

Joshua died at the age of 110 years, and left behind a character without blemish. Such was the continuing influence of his life that after his death we read that, "And Israel served the Lord all the days of Joshua, and all the days of the elders that overlived Joshua, and which had known all the works of the Lord, that he had done for Israel" (Josh. 24:31). Our heavenly Joshua lived for only some thirty-three years, and did not die a natural death. But for well-nigh two millenniums His influence has circled the globe for He is alive forevermore, and will go on conquering till all enemies are under His feet.

J. *Judges*

The sad book of Judges covers one of the darkest periods in Jewish history, stretching from the death of Joshua to the establishment of regal government under Saul, Israel's first king. The book gives us the history of fourteen judges whom God raised up to govern Israel and to deliver them from the oppressions of their enemies. Nehemiah calls these judges "Saviours": "According to thy manifold mercies thou gavest them saviours, who saved them out of the hand of their enemies" (Neh. 9:27). It is in their deliverance of the people from their grievous captivities that these saviours typify Him who came as *the* Saviour from the bondage and thralldom of sin. There were the frequent relapses of the people, and the terrible oppressions that followed, but when they cried unto the Lord, He made possible wonderful deliverances throughout a period of about 300 years from Othniel, the first judge, till Samson the last one.

Under Joshua, and in the fear of God, the people were irresistible, but the tragic story of *Judges* presents the reverse to this. The promises of Joshua had been, "Thou shalt drive out the Canaanites, though they have iron chariots, and though they be strong" (Josh. 17:18). But although *Judges* opens on a note of victory, it was a victory with a reservation, they "could not drive out the inhabitants of the valley, because they had chariots of iron" (Judg. 1:19). Disobedience to divine commands, and lack of faith, brought defeat and bondage, necessitating the raising up of saviours.

It is not our purpose to dwell upon the successive judges raised up to deliver the people from captivity. There were seven distinct departures from God, seven cries of repentance, and seven deliverances by God through the judges. There is very little of a genuine typical nature about any of the fourteen of them. It is *what they did* that is typical of Christ, for these saviours foreshadowed the Great Deliever Isaiah predicted, "He shall send them a saviour, and a great one" (Isa. 19:20). God, in His love, had mercy upon man in his sin and hard bondage, and sent His Son to be the Saviour of the world. The temporary and temporal deliverances recorded in *Judges* shadowed forth the manner in which we are saved by Christ. They were saved in such a way that the glory of their salvation belonged only to God. None could vaunt himself, and say, "Mine own hand hath saved me" (Judg. 7:2). All cause of boasting was taken away, both from the deliverer and from those he delivered. But all praise is His, and His alone for His matchless salvation from the tyranny of sin.

Nor merit of thine own
  Upon His altar place;
All is of Christ alone,
  And of His perfect grace.

K. *Boaz*

Perhaps no Book of the Bible is as rich in its typical teaching as the beautiful idyll of *Ruth*. This brief book is like an oasis after the desert of *Judges*. In such a sweet story we seem to pass from darkness into light. Amid the lawlessness and idolatry of the time there were those, both rich and poor, who feared God and lived simple lives to His praise. It would be profitable to linger over the typical significance of the characters named in "this literary treasure house. Nothing can surpass in beauty this exquisite idyll of early Israelitish life." For instance, Ruth herself, who became an ancestress of Jesus, receiving notice in His genealogical record (Matt. 1:5), symbolizes many precious truths. How her unselfish devotion to God and to duty was bountifully rewarded! Her son, Obed, became the grandfather of King David.

All of us know by heart the calm poetry of those harvest fields of Bethlehem, and of the guiding hand of God in bringing Boaz, the lord of the harvest, and Ruth the reaper, together. Everything about Boaz suggests Christ — the simplicity of his life, the courtesy of his behavior to all who worked for him, his deep regard for the Law, his tracing of every event to God, not only make him stand out in striking contrast against the dark background of his time, but also as a wonderful type of Him who came from the royal line through Boaz and Ruth. Think of how Boaz is presented in the book bearing his wife's name — lord of harvest, dispenser of bread, man of wealth, advocate, kinsman-redeemer, bridegroom, life-giver! Can you not see Jesus in all these facets of the character of Boaz? It is, however, upon him as the kinsman-redeemer we want to dwell, seeing that as such Boaz was a most expressive type of Jesus.

Ruth's virtue and piety, her kindness to Naomi, and her conversion and devotion to Naomi's God, preceded her, and as soon as Boaz learned who she was, he treated her with the utmost respect and kindness. Unmarried, and a new kinsman of Ruth's father-in-law, Elimelech, Boaz was in a position to purchase the inheritance of Elimelech and take Ruth to be his wife. But there was a nearer kinsman than Boaz who had the prior option of redeeming the inheritance, and he was given the opportunity of carrying out such an obligation. Fearing, however, to impair his own inheritance, he refused, and Boaz came forward and fulfilling all obligations the Law demanded bought the inheritance and with all due solemnities made Ruth his wife.

As George H. C. MacGregor states in his chapter on Ruth in *Messages of the Old Testament:*

> Ruth owed her position in no sense to herself. She owed it entirely to Boaz. Her choice of Israel as her nation, her choice of Jehovah as her God, would never have given her position had it not been for Boaz. Her knowledge of her claim, her presentation of her claim, would have availed her nothing had Boaz refused to act.... The nearer kinsman proved himself both unable and unwilling to redeem the inheritance .... Boaz began to act, but Ruth's position was not gained until, by marrying her, Boaz made her one with himself and lifted her into the position of all honour and glory and power that was his. The secret of all that Ruth had was *union with Boaz.*

Is not all this a beautiful forecast of all that Christ made possible when He purchased us by His blood? "With His own Blood He bought her." The word for kinsman is *Goel,* meaning "the redeemer," one whose right and duty it was to redeem the inheritance of a deceased male relative and marry his widow (Deut. 25:5-10; cf. Lev. 25:25-55). Thus the keynote of the book of Ruth is *The Kinsman Redeemer.* Thirty times in this short book of four chapters the word "kinsman" is found and with kindred terms, as "near kinsman," "next of kin," "kindred," suggests a "Redeemer." How clearly the book foreshadows the New Testament doctrine of Redemption (Ruth 4:4-10). In the extreme minuteness of detail we can see the Holy Spirit's guidance in the provision of a typical design.

A *kinsman* means "one of the same race or family," and Jesus became one of our race in order to have the right to redeem. Incarnation was imperative for redemption. God's holy Law can be looked upon as man's nearer kinsman, but the Law could not redeem man from his sin in that it was weak through the flesh (Rom. 8:3). Further, no sinner was able to redeem himself, much less his brother (Ps. 49:7). Jesus, however, became our Boaz (a name meaning "strength" or "ability") and because of kinship and by His power, He purchased us with His own blood. He loved the church, and gave Himself for it. Thus the union of Ruth with Boaz is typical of the union each and all believers have with Christ. He is our glorious kinsman-redeemer. "In all things it behoved him to be made like unto his brethren...to make reconciliation" (Heb. 2:17). As Boaz, the kinsman-redeemer of this charming gem of a book, completed his mission of redemption by uniting Ruth to himself, making her thereby a sharer in all that he had, so is it with Jesus our blessed redeemer.

We can only be saved by union to Him who bestows pardon and power, forgiveness and fulness. How privileged are the redeemed to be made heirs of God and joint heirs with Christ, and partakers not only of His sufferings now, but His glory hereafter! A further type can be found in the fact that Ruth, the Moabitess, and Boaz, the Jew, were becoming one in the Lord. In His true church there is neither Jew or Gentile as such. Regenerated by the power of the Spirit, they become one in Christ Jesus. His mystic Body has no divisions for all its members, sweetly all agree, and "kindly for each other care."

> Love, like death, hath all destroyed,
> Rendered all distinctions void;
> Names, and sects, and parties fall:
> Thou, O Christ, art all in all.

L. *Samuel*

As a Prophet, Samuel was honored as such from Dan to Beersheba. The revelations of God he received, the spirit that distinguished him, his supreme power in the state of Israel, his rule without ambition, his irreproachable integrity in the execution of his office, made him feared and respected by all. Well over 150 years ago, an expositor wrote of Samuel:

> Those who attend to his life may observe that he was modest without meanness, mild without weakness, firm without obstinacy, and severe without harshness. He lived to the noblest purpose—the glory of God, and the good of his country, and died full of years and honour, universally lamented.

We include Samuel in our portrait gallery of prophetic persons because he stands out as a picture of Jesus, the prophet of Galilee.

As to his youth, he manifested early piety, obedience, and respect for Eli, and a strict regard for truth (I Sam. 1:28; 3:5, 18).

As a minister, he was conspicuous in his earnestness and perseverance in leading men to repentance, and in his zeal in teaching them to improve seasons of convictions (I Sam. 7:3).

As a judge, he ruled in the fear of God with unwearied diligence (I Sam. 7:15, 16; 12:3, 4).

As to his example, he gratefully acknowledged God's goodness in his success, and when in trouble was diligent in seeking divine direction (I Sam. 7:12; 8:21). In his reproof and punishment of sin, Samuel was altogether free from the fear of men, even in his rebuke of the king (I Sam. 13:13). When exalted to supreme power, he exercised it for some twenty years, without ambition, oppression, or avarice; resigning without reluctance, when God commanded him. He harbored no envy for his successor, but used his great influence to commend Saul to the people. Rejected by his countrymen, he never ceased to pray for them. When Saul sinned, Samuel tried to turn away the divine anger from him (I Sam. 15:35; cf. 12:23).

Surely it is not hard to trace the Saviour in all these virtues Samuel manifested? Perhaps, it is in his name that he is a fitting type of Jesus. The common interpretation of his name, Samuel, is that it means "asked of God," but a renowned Hebrew scholar, Professor Jastrow, says that in the Assyrian tongue, which is closely allied to the Hebrew, *Samuel* is the word "sumu," meaning *son,* and that Samuel can be translated as "son (or offspring) of God." Hannah, in all sincerity, surrendered her first-born son to God utterly. He became "God's son" from the moment of his birth. "Therefore I have *given* (not "lent" as in the A.V.) him to the Lord. Hannah wanted everyone to know that her son was altogether the Lord's very own.

Thus the Song of Hannah, and the name she gave her first-born, are alike a prediction of Christ. She has the honor of being the first to use the name *Messiah* as we can see by comparing her song with Mary's Magnificat (cf. I Sam. 2:10 with Luke 1:51, 55). Both Hannah and Mary had a vision of earth's full salvation and of the Saviour as the promised Messiah. Hannah sings, "He shall give strength unto his king, and exalt the horn of his anointed [Messiah]." Mary responds, "He hath showed strength with his arm; he hath scattered the proud in the imagination of their hearts.... As he spake to our fathers."

Further, Samuel was a type of Christ in the combination of the three offices of prophet, priest, and ruler; and also in his life of prayer and intercession. Along with Moses, Samuel was chosen as a divine example of intercessor—"Moses and Samuel stood before me" (Jer. 15:1). Of his rebellious nation, Samuel said, "God forbid that I should sin against the Lord in ceasing to pray for you" (I Sam. 12:23). Of Jesus it is said that "he ever liveth to make intercession for them" (Heb. 7:25).

M. *Job*

Last in the form of a dramatic poem, the book of Job, which is probably one of the oldest of the books forming the divine library, is heavy with the atmosphere of sin, sorrow, and silence. It has been referred to as "The Matterhorn of the Old Testament," and is indeed most prominent as a revelation of the philosophic breadth and intellectual culture of the patriarchal age, as Dr. C. I. Scofield suggests. We heartily concur with the estimation Dr. W. Moorehead gives us:

> The Book of Job is one of noblest poems in existence. The splendour of imagery which glows on every page; the personages introduced into it; the mysterious problems which it discusses; the action which sweeps through every emotion of the soul and strikes every chord of the human heart, invest the Book with peculiar interest.

Although we have no account of Job's heritage, no mention of his parentage and early life, we believe that he was an actual being with wife and children and many material possessions, and not a mythical being, as some Bible critics assume. The book records veritable history. If Job is a fictitious character, so also are Noah and Daniel, because Ezekiel identifies all three as servants of God (Ezek. 14:14, 20). Further, the reference of James to "the patience of Job" would be wholly without point if Job were mythical (Jas. 5:11). In a postscript, The Septuagint, or Greek version of the Old Testament, followed an ancient tradition in identifying Job with Jobab, the second king of Edom (Gen. 36:33). Others supposed the patriarch descended from Ug, the elder son of Nahor, Abraham's brother.

Literary giants have praised the quality of the book of Job, the language of which is sublime in its simplicity. Martin Luther regarded it as "more magnificent and sublime than any other book of Scripture." Victor Hugo said of it, "Perhaps the greatest masterpiece of the human mind." Alfred Tennyson, a wonderful poet himself, regarded it as "the greatest poem whether of ancient or modern literature." Thomas Carlyle wrote concerning the book, "I call this Book, apart from all theories about it, one of the grandest things ever written. Our first, oldest statement of the never-ending problem: Man's Destiny and God's Ways with him on earth. There is nothing written, I think, of equal literary merit." Philip Schaff, eminent church historian, says that "The Book of Job rises like a pyramid in the history of literature, without a predecessor and without a rival."

Much as we would like to pause and dwell upon the dramatic features of this ancient poem, very regular and simple in form, with a natural order throughout, and replete with art the most subtle and attractive, we must adhere to the aim of our study, namely, to emphasize the prophetical and typical significance of many Old Testament personages. Although not numbered among the prophets, Job is to be numbered among those who gave witness to the Messiah, predicting Him as the coming redeemer. How Job declared his sublime faith in a living redeemer, and of his own participation in Resurrection glory! Can anything excel the grandeur of the following confession? "For I know that my redeemer liveth, and that he shall stand at the latter day upon the earth" (Job 19:25). Compare this with Christ's own declaration, "I am alive for evermore" — "He should smite the nations" (Rev. 1:18; 19:15).

"And though after my skin worms

destroy this body, yet in my flesh shall I see God: Whom I shall see for myself, and mine eyes shall behold, and not another" (Job 19:26, 27). Compare with, "We shall see him as he is" (I John 3:2). "They shall see his face" (Rev. 22:4). Certainly the root of the matter of Redemption and of Glorification was found in ancient Job, who stresses still further his belief in a blessing immortality through the sacrificial work of the Messiah. Impressive, is it not, that the oldest book in the world teaches the doctrine of a future life? The Septuagint, the ancient version of the seventy, adds to the Hebrew closing of Job the suggestive words, "It is written that he will rise again with those whom the Lord raiseth."

Yearning for death as a way out of all his mysterious suffering, Job asked the question of perennial interest: "If a man die, shall he live again?" (Job 14:14). But he answered his own question when he affirmed that after death he would see his redeemer-God. Then Elihu in his speech to Job gave utterance to a similar hope: "If there be a messenger with him, an interpreter, one among a thousand, to shew unto man his uprightness" (Job 33:23). Compare this with the statement of Jesus concerning the Holy Spirit, the Interpreter, One among a thousand, "He will reprove the world of sin, and of righteousness, and of judgment" (John 16:8). Then we have this unique description of the Messiah's sacrifice: "Then he is gracious unto him, and saith, Deliver him from going down to the pit: I have found a ransom" (33:24; cf. v. 28). Compare with Christ's own declaration as to His mission among men: "The Son of man came . . . to give his life as a ransom for many" (Matt. 20:28). "He brought me up also out of an horrible pit" (Ps. 40:2). When Elihu went on to say, "His flesh shall be fresher than a child's: he shall return to the days of his youth" (Job 33:25). As the risen, glorified Lord it is said, "Thou hast the dew of thy youth" (Ps. 110:3), and His glorified body, as well as the glorified bodies of the redeemed will be fresher than a child's. They will never decay or become wrinkled. Elihu also adds that "he shall see his face with joy" (33:26). In our risen life we "shall see the light," and forever be "enlightened with the light of the living" (Job 33:28, 30; cf. John 1:4).

Thus again and again in the book we have foreshadows of the coming Saviour. We see Him as the offered sacrifice in the accepted sacrifices which Job offered up for his children as his book opens, and then for his friends as it closes. The intention of sacrifice, as a means of turning away God's anger, is evidently implied in the domestic practice of Job himself, and in God's command respecting his friends (Job 1:5; 42:7, 8). The prophecy of the redeemer was sounded forth in earth's earliest ages. Job saw in the One he predicted his Goel, his kinsman-redeemer, not stranger, but One with the right to redeem. He asked the question, "How shall man be just before God?" But we have not to cry, "Oh, that I knew where I might find Him!" We know that He is ever near and that we can only be justified by His blood (Rom. 5:9).

More evident still is the fact that Job's own sufferings as an innocent man dimly foreshadow the cross. The sufferings of both Job and Jesus sprang from the enmity of Satan. All the upright saint endured pointed the way to the suffering, sinless man of sorrows. Further, the trials of Job and Jesus came from a twofold direction. Job was wounded by his so-called friends. Jesus was forsaken by His disciples, and betrayed by Judas. Job was wounded by foes, becoming the song and byword of base men. "They . . . spare not to spit in my face. . . . My soul is poured out upon me. . . . My bones are pierced in me. . . . I am become like dust and ashes" (Job 30:10, 16, 17, 19). The Gospels tell us of coarse men spitting on the face of Jesus, and of the divine sufferer Himself crying, "Now is My soul troubled." Job entered beforehand into "the fellowship of His sufferings." But there is this difference to observe between the two sufferers – Job complained and justified himself; Jesus, the sinless Lamb of God was dumb before His shearers.

The book of Job, however, is conspicuous for other truths, reaching their clearer and fuller development in the New Testament. With apology it touches upon *human depravity* even although the book was written in the cradle of humanity. Think of some of the expressions found in its pages!

"My transgression is sealed up in a bag, and thou sewest up mine iniquity" (Job 4:17; see Hos. 13:12).

". . . abominable and filthy is man, which drinketh iniquity like water" (Job 15:16).

". . . the son of man, which is a worm" (Job 25:6).

". . . those that rebel against the light" (Job 24:13).

". . . the workers of iniquity . . . wicked men" (Job 34:8).

"Behold, I am vile . . . I will lay my hand upon my mouth . . . I abhor myself, and repent in dust and ashes" (Job 10:4; 42:6).

It was in divine light that Job discovered inate wickedness both in himself and in others. "Now mine eye seeth Thee," and such a vision brought Job to his knees in repentance. All his fancied goodness vanished before that majestic presence. It was so with Peter when after witnessing the display of the Master's power, he cried, "Depart from me; for I am a sinful man, O Lord!" (Luke 5:8). Job came before God to debate the problem of his heaped-up suffering, but once before Him there came profoundest humiliation and repentance. Self-justification vanished; self-pride is in the dust, and full blessing ensues. Did not our Lord teach that the depravity of man; that out of his corrupt heart all forms of evil flow? (Matt. 15:18, 19). Then Paul leaves us in no doubt as to the world-wide devastation because of inbred sin (Rom. 1-3).

Behind all evil forces, however, there is an evil figure, even Satan. The original source of depravity is the Devil, and the book of Job is valuable for what it teaches regarding satanic activities. In fact, its threefold design is easily discernable:

1. To refute the slander of Satan as an accuser.
2. To discuss the question of human suffering – particularly the suffering of the righteous.
3. To reveal Job to himself, and remove the self-righteousness hindering the full blessing of God.

In his conflict with Satan, Job foreshadowed Jesus in His fierce temptations in the wilderness, and in his endeavors to prevent Him going to the cross. Both the range and restriction of Satan's power come out in Job's contact with the adversary. The experience of the patriarch also forecasts the truth that James teaches, namely, that while God may *permit* His children to be tempted, He never *provides* temptation (Jas. 1:12-14).

Because of rebellion against God, Satan was cast out from the divine presence, yet in some mysterious way he still has access to God, as Job records, "Satan came . . . to present himself before the Lord" (Job 2:1; see 1:6, 12). But he came, not to worship the Almighty, but to wreck the character of Job. Before God, Satan accused Job of serving God for what he could get out of it. "Doth Job fear God for nought?" In some unknown way, Satan still functions as the accuser of the saints. John, however, foretold of the time when the satanic accuser of the brethren will be cast down who presently accuses them day and night (Rev. 12:10). Our consolation is that whenever the adversary challenges our integrity in the council of heaven, we have, on hand, the advocate to plead on our behalf (I John 2:1, 2), even as God defended His servant Job against the slander of Satan.

A further lesson we learn from this book is that Satan is like a dog on a leash, who cannot go beyond divine permission. As the god of this world, and prince of the power of the air, and the evil spirit working in the children of disobedience, Satan had power to bring up the hordes of hostile Sabeans and Chaldeans to carry off Job's camels, asses, and oxen; and manipulate the lightning to consume the sheep and command the wind to destroy property and persons and to smite Job himself with a terrible disease, but God said, "So far, no further!" Hedged in, by God, as Job was (Job 1:10), Satan knew he could not break through that protecting hedge without divine permission. "All that [Job] hath is in thy power; *only* upon himself *put not forth* thine hand" (Job 1:12).

How comforting it is to know that as His children we have His protection, and that, therefore, no calamity can overtake us except as He permits!

> Not a shaft can hit
> Till the God of Love sees fit.

Later on, we find Jehovah saying to Job, in that marvelous declaration of His Almightiness, "Who shut up the sea with doors?...And said, Hitherto shalt thou come, but no further?" (Job 38:8, 11). Paul assures us that God will not suffer us to be tempted and tried above that we are able to bear, but will even in temptation provide a way of escape (I Cor. 10:13). The furnace of trial will never be hotter than we can endure it. A French proverb has it, "God tempers the wind to the shorn lamb."

Further the book of Job is eloquent with the revelation of the over-ruling Providence of God. Whether He gives, or takes away, He knows what is best for His children and so acts accordingly. In his first monologue (Job 3:1-26), Job's utterances choked with passion and with tears, indicate that somewhat imperfectly he was learning to repeat the Gethsemane prayer, "Thy will be done." Perplexed by God's providential dealings, the reason of which he could not understand, he curses the day he was born, but not his God, as Satan urged him to do through his wife. Through Peter, Satan sought to prevent Jesus going to the cross. Yet somehow amid all his doubts and darkness, there came the magnificent resolution, "Though he slay me, yet will I trust in him" (Job 13:15). At Calvary, God-forsaken, Jesus could yet pray, "Father, into Thy hands I commend My spirit."

Although Job saw through a glass darkly, he was assured that God, as judge of all the earth was doing that which was right, and so was resolved to trust Him where he could not trace Him, even if He should slay him. Thus, while the book sets forth in unrivaled magnificence the glory of the divine attributes, it likewise displays the Providence of God in its inscrutableness and mercy. At the end, Job came to realize that

> Behind a frowning Providence
> He hides a smiling face.

Wrapped up in divine Providence, is the mystery of human suffering, especially the suffering of the innocent. God's own testimony of Job was, "There is none like him in the earth, a perfect and an upright man, one that feareth God, and escheweth evil" (Job 1:8). The professed friends of Job were wrong in affirming that he was suffering because of sin in his life. "Who ever perished, being innocent?" was their contention (Job 4:7). But Job walked with God in integrity of heart and conformity of life, just as Jesus, a greater sufferer still, did, and so knew that the accusation of his friends was false. Perhaps Job was permitted to suffer as he did for "of all men he was the one most fitted to be entrusted with the service of suffering, being chosen as a pattern of the ways of God in the ages to come, for all His children in the service of trial." At present, we may not be able to read the meaning of our tears, but up in heaven we will learn the reason why the dark threads were as needful as the golden ones.

Loved, yet chastened of the Lord, Job learned the all-important lesson of *patience*, the virtue James praises Job for. Because he was patient under trial, the end testified to the pity and tender mercy of the Lord (Jas. 5:11). How happy we are if, like Job, we are able to endure the chastisement of God! The keynote, and key word of the book is *chastisement* (Job 34:31). It was Elihu, a true messenger from God to Job, that revealed God's gracious purpose in the chastisement of His children. Job was sorely tried, but came forth as gold. Touching the Almighty, the patriarch could not find Him out but somehow knew that He never willingly afflicted any child of His. When the mists rolled away and Job could say, "Now mine eye seeth thee" (Job 42:5), all was well, and his end was richly blessed of the Lord. Job trusted the Lord, even though he could not fathom His ways, and the Lord trusted Job and brought him through into a large place.

Can we say that the trying of our faith worketh patience? Jesus has the message for our perplexed moments, "In patience possess ye your souls," and we certainly need patience as we face many of the problems of life. Shakespeare makes one of his characters say, "I am as poor as Job, my lord, but not so patient." May grace be ours to let patience have her perfect work!

> Would'st thou possess this peace?
> be still, be low!
> Peace with the pure abides;
> Yea, all the humble, all the gentle, know
> The shelter where she hides;
> *Rooted in patience*, her fair buds to flowers shall grow.

The last typical feature we gather from Job's character is that of likeness to Jesus in the power of intercessory prayer. Several aspects of prayer are touched upon in the Book of Job:

"Thou . . . restrainest prayer" (15:4).

"Thou shalt make thy prayer unto him" (22:27).

"He shall pray unto God, and he will be favourable unto him" (33:26).

". . . also my prayer is pure" (16:17).

All of these passages are anticipatory of our Lord's teaching on prayer. In his intercessions for others, however, Job foreshadows Jesus who was to plead both for saints and sinners: "My servant Job shall pray for you. . . . And the Lord turned the captivity of Job, when he prayed for his friends" (Job 42:8, 10). What a fitting conclusion to the ancient poem it is to see Job as an intercessor for the three philosophers who had not spoken the right thing as Job himself had done. The patriarch's prayers for his own children were answered (Job 19:17), and when at last, as the chastened, mellowed servant of God, he interceded at the divine command for those who had aggravated his suffering and woe, his own prosperity returns to him, and the friends prayed for were likewise blessed. Job thus foreshadowed Jesus, who was to make intercession for transgressors, and who at His Ascension was to enter upon a perpetual ministry of intercession for His own. How apt are the lines of C. M. Noel which appeared way back in 1891:

Say not, all useful work thou art denied!
Behold! Christ's censer waiteth at thy side.
He in compassion lets it down to thee,
Heap on thy incense! Heap it full and free!
Pray for thy friends! that every deed of love
May be received and registered above.
Pray for the sick who suffer in all lands!
God's prisoners laid in bonds by His own hands . . .
Pray for Crowned Heads, with all their weight of care,
For broken hearts, and all the sorrows there;
For the whole race which He had made His own,
For which He intercedes before the Throne.

N. *David*

In preparation for the coming of the Lord, many outstanding figures are interwoven with the historical part of the Old Testament, in which there are so many predictions of the Messiah. Conspicuous among such is Samuel who played a prominent part in Israel's transference from a theocracy to a monarchy and who was the first of that succession of prophets whose great subject of prophecy was the Coming One (Acts 3:24). Associated with Samuel is David, who in many ways is the greatest personal type of Christ in Old Testament Scriptures. The first time the Messiah, or Anointed One, is spoken of in Scripture is in the prophetic prayer of Hannah (I Sam. 2:10), where also is a grand prophecy of a king before that office was established among the Israelites.

Once the monarchy was established with Saul as its titular head, David, his successor, the man after God's own heart, was to become the ruler more typical of the kingship of Christ than any other Israelite king. Over a thousand times, David's name appears throughout the Bible, some sixty times of which he is mentioned in the New Testament closely associated with Christ. In fact, it opens with Christ as "the son of David" (Matt. 1:1), and ends with Him as "the root and the offspring of David" (Rev. 22:16; see 5:5). In foregleams of the Messiah's coming reign, He is referred to as *David* (Jer. 30:9; Ezek. 34:23; 37:24; Hos. 3:5), and also as the *Son of David* (Matt. 1:1; 9:27; 21:9).

The application of the title of *David* to Christ testifies to Israel's second king as being the ideal of kingly authority (Acts 13:34). That the prophets represent the Messiah in His kingly rule, possessing all the characteristics of the most distinguished princes of the Jewish theocracy and monarchy, is seen in the fact that they speak of His kingdom, either of grace or glory, as the highest perfection of the ancient Jewish economy. It is for this reason that the person and reign of David assumes a prophetic character. Promises to those of old were both temporal and evangelical. To Abraham, the Messiah had been announced, more or less clearly as *The Promised Seed* (Gen. 12:1-3). To Moses, greatest among the Prophets, Messiah was *The Coming Prophet* (Deut. 18:15). To all under the ancient Levitical order, Messiah was to be *The Great High Priest* (I Sam. 2:35). To David, God's choice as successor to Saul, the Messiah was coming as *The King of Zion.* This is why the Psalms depict His authority, the hostility He receives from earthly kings, His scepter of righteousness, His exalted nature, His unchangeable royal priesthood, His victory over sin and death, His universal dominion (Pss. 2; 16; 45; 110, etc). By comparing the most remarkable prophecies respecting the Messiah given in II Samuel 7:12-16 and 23:5, with Acts 2:30 and Hebrews 1:8, we find that "the sure mercies of David" refer to our Lord. David *knew* that God had sworn to him to raise up out of his family the Messiah whose throne should be established forever, and thus had confident expectation of future happiness as one believing in the promised king (Pss. 16:9-11; 17:15).

When Jesus expounded "in the Psalms" the things concerning Himself, doubtless He tarried over those Psalms messianic in character, as well as over the ways in which David himself reflected Him. Let us choose a few foreshadowings of Christ. First of all, there were the *Three Anointings* as king David received.

1. *The divine anointing.* This took place in his father's home when Samuel took the horn of oil and anointed him in the midst of his brothers, and the Holy Spirit came upon him from that day forward (I Sam. 16:13). Saul was the people's choice as king; David was God's choice.

2. *The Judah anointing.* While in exile, although anointed king, Saul still reigned over the people, and sought to slay David. But the day came when the men of Judah gathered to David and anointed him as their king in Hebron, "Thine are we, David, and on thy side" (I Chron. 12:18; see II Sam. 2:4).

3. *The Israel anointing.* David came into his own by degrees. Saul waxed weaker and weaker, but David stronger and stronger, and at last the Elders of Israel, knowing that David alone could deliver the people out of the hand of all their enemies, came to Hebron and "anointed David king over Israel" (II Sam. 3:1-3).

Do not these three anointings portray the successive, expanding manifestation of David's greater Son, the Lord Jesus Christ? For instance, there was:

1. *The divine anointing.* In addition to the Father's choice of His Son in a past eternity to be king (Ps. 2), He experienced the initial anointing by the Father at his baptism. After thirty years' silent preparation for His ministry, there came the Father's benediction and Spirit's enduement, and publicly for over three years, Jesus lived and labored as the One divinely set apart.

2. *Anointed as Head of the Church.* Christ came as king, but was rejected by the world. Presently, He is personally absent from the world, yet spiritually present in His true Church a "head of the body" (Col. 1:18). By multitudes of the redeemed He has been given His coronation as king of their lives. Translated, by grace, into His kingdom, they recognize no other sovereign.

3. *Anointed as King of Kings.* Patiently He awaits His full anointing, when He will take unto Himself His power and reign "where ere the sun doth its journeys run." During His millennial reign, there will be no end to His government (Isa. 9:7). Then upon His once thorn-crowned head, many diadems will rest (Rev. 19:12). At last, He will be crowned Lord of all. Universal sway will be His as prince of the kings of earth (Rev. 1:5).

A second Advent forecast can be found in David's return to Jerusalem after the rebellion and death of his son, Absalom (II Sam. 19:9-43). The people, earnestly desiring the sight of their absent king asked, "Now therefore why speak ye not a word of bringing the king back?" David's sad heart was cheered when he heard of this request and sent an encouraging message to the elders. "And he bowed the heart of all the men of Judah, even as the heart of one man; so that they sent this word unto the king, Return thou, and all thy servants." Out went the elders over Jordan and brought David back to his rejoicing and loyal subjects.

Alas! we do not hear too many words these days about bringing our absent king back. What sinful silence there is regarding the predicted and promised return of Jesus! Did He not declare before His death, "I will come again"? Before long the cry will go forth, "Behold, the Bridegroom cometh; go ye out to meet Him," but many who do not expect and long for His return, will miss the reward to be given those who love and long for the coming of the king.

Why doth He tarry, the absent
Lord?
When shall the kingdom be restored,
And earth and Heaven, with one
accord,
Ring out the cry the King comes?

It was Daivd's passionate desire to build a temple worthy of the Lord he dearly loved, but although he made abundant provision in necessary materials for same, he was not permitted to build it because he had shed much blood on the earth. God promised his servant, however, that a son would be born to him who would realize his father's dream. The promised son was Solomon, who erected one of the most magnificent temples the world has ever seen. But a greater than Solomon is building a more marvelous temple still, that is to endure forever, the temple of the Holy Spirit, the Church.

God also promised David that he would establish his throne forever, and when Jesus was born, the promise was confirmed. "Jesus . . . the Son of the Highest: and the Lord God shall give unto him the throne of His father David: And he shall reign over the house of Jacob for ever; and of his kingdom there shall be no end" (Luke 1:31-33). David's throne is secured permanently, but Solomon's temple crumbled into ruins centuries ago. The sign of the rainbow proclaims that Christ, David's Son, shall sit upon David's throne in Jerusalem. He alone is of David's seed according to the flesh, possessing the right to David's throne (Ps. 89:3, 4, 27-37), and as the root and offspring of David, He will reign from David's royal city when He inaugurates His kingdom. Without doubt, David is a type of the one perfect king.

One of the most impressive and expressive types of Jesus the history of David presents is that of a *shepherd.* The psalmist combined in himself both shepherd and king, and is prominent as the shepherd-king and therefore a striking prediction of Him who came declaring that He was the perfect shepherd of the sheep. Both David and Jesus were born in the small town of Bethlehem, and although Jesus was brought up in his foster-father's carpenter's shop, and David was a shepherd lad, yet Jesus was born while shepherds kept their flocks by night. They were the first to receive the glorious news of His wondrous birth, and this was fitting, as He came as the true shepherd of Israel. Prophecy prepared the hearts of men for His coming to fulfill such an office.

Forecast: "The LORD is my shepherd; I shall not want" (Ps. 23:1).

"He shall feed his flock like a shepherd" (Isa. 40:11).

"I will set up one shepherd over them" (Ezek. 34:23; 37:24).

"Awake, O sword, against my shepherd" (Zech. 13:7).

Fulfillment: "I am the good shepherd, and know my sheep" (John 10:14).

"There shall be one fold, and one shepherd" (John 10:16).

"I will smite the shepherd" (Matt. 26:31).

"Our Lord Jesus, that great shepherd of the sheep" (Heb. 13:20).

"When the Chief Shepherd shall appear" (I Pet. 5:4; 2:25).

Shepherd and king were thus blended in David and in David's greater Son. A true sovereign always has the heart of a true shepherd. When David was king, and judgment fell upon him for his grievous sin, he cried, "I it is that have sinned . . . but as *for these sheep,* what have they done?" (I Chron. 21:17). It will be found profitable to connect three of David's messianic Psalms with the threefold presentation of Jesus as the shepherd. Psalms 22, 23, 24 form a trilogy, a threefold cord that cannot be broken.

Psalm 22 is the Psalm of the *Saviour,* with *grief* as its keynote.

Psalm 23 is the Psalm of the *Shepherd,* with *goodness* as its keynote.

Psalm 24 is the Psalm of the *Sovereign,* with *glory* as its keynote.

What evident prediction of Christ these three Psalms suggest, and how abundantly they are fulfilled in Him who came to save lost sheep (Luke 15)! The New Testament presents Him as *The Good Shepherd* (John 10:11). Jesus took to Himself this symbol, and declared that His shepherd heart would be revealed in death for His sheep, even the cruel death of the cross Psalm 22 so minutely portrays. *The Great Shepherd* (Heb. 13:20) – As the *Good* Shepherd, He died; as the *Great* Shepherd, He conquered death, and is the companion of all His sheep as they walk through the valley of the shadow of death, as Psalm 23 so vividly reminds us. *The Chief Shepherd* (I Pet. 5:4) – The apostle assures us that Christ is coming in His capacity as *Chief* to reward His under-shepherds who were faithful in caring for His flock. But there is the fuller application of Peter's declaration, for when Jesus returns in glory as the Shepherd King, it will be to combat and destroy *The Idol Shepherd* (Zech. 11:17), the Antichrist, whom He will consume with the spirit of His mouth (II Thess. 2:8). Then Psalm 24, with its glorious triumphant note, will be fulfilled. He is the King – the Shepherd King – of glory!

The *King* of Love my *Shepherd* is,
Whose goodness faileth never.

It has been suggested that the opening phrase of Psalm 23 should be repeated over and over again, with a different emphasis each time, thus

The *LORD* is my Shepherd.
The Lord *IS* my Shepherd.
The Lord is *MY* Shepherd.
The Lord is my *SHEPHERD.*

Among David's commendable characteristics was his magnanimity. He was generous and kind towards friend and foe alike. Jealous Saul sought to slay him, and although David had the opportunity of killing him, because Saul was the Lord's anointed he spared him. Jesus never raised a hand in His own defense, and at the cross prayed for His murderers. Absalom tried to steal the kingdom from his father, but although the handsome son was a rebel and ultimately died a tragic death in a wood, David mourned for his wayward son. "The soul of David longed to go forth unto Absalom" as he fled after murdering his brother (II Sam. 13:39, R.V.). "Deal gently for my sake, with the young man, even with Absalom." Is this not a reflection of God's forbearance with sinners, a picture of divine sorrow over the rebellious?

When David heard of the death of Absalom, he wished he could have died for such a rebel, but he could not. So we have his cry, one of the most poignant in literature:

"O my son Absalom! my son, my son Absalom!
Would God I had died for thee, O Absalom, my son, my son!" (II Sam. 18:33).

Does not such a pathetic lament cause us to think of One who was not only willing but able to die in our stead, and did die as the just for the unjust, to bring us nigh unto God?

While we were yet enemies, Christ died for us.

Then there is the charming story of Mephibosheth who was lame in both of his feet, as the result of an accident when his nurse escaped with him after the death of his father and grandfather at Gilboa (II Sam. 4:4). After he came to the throne, David asked if there were any left of the house of Israel he could show kindness to, and Ziba his servant told him of Jonathan's son, who, when David saw his maimed condition, "fell on his face, and did him reverence" and said, "I will surely shew thee kindness for Jonathan thy father's sake" (II Sam. 9; 16:1-4; 19:24-30). Are we not exhorted "to be kind one to another, tenderhearted, forgiving one another, even as God *for Christ's sake* hath forgiven you" (Eph. 4:32)?

Seeing the resemblance of Jonathan in his son, David would recall the love-bond that had existed between Jonathan and himself. "The soul of Jonathan was knit with the soul of David, and he loved him as he loved his own soul." When he heard of the slaughter of Jonathan, David confessed that his friend's love to him was wonderful passing the love of women. In this respect, Jonathan was a picture of Jesus, who "having loved his own which were in the world, he loved them to the uttermost" (John 13:1, R.V.). In the days when David was hounded by Saul, Jonathan and he made an everlasting covenant, and knowing that although he was Saul's son, he himself could never be king, but that David would be, stripped himself of all that was on him, royal robes, sword, bow, and girdle, and gave them to David. Did not Jesus strip Himself of much of His past glory, in order to cover us with the robe of His righteousness? Rich, for our sakes He became poor. Jonathan at the risk of his own life, sought to reconcile his father to David, but failed. Christ had no need to reconcile His Father to us, but as the King's Son, He died to reconcile *us* to His Father, so that we could become sharers of His throne in glory.

David's generosity of spirit towards his foes is seen in his treatment of Shimei, who had cursed him. Some of David's men wanted to slay Shimei for his treatment of the king, but he said to Shimei, "Thou shalt not die" (II Sam. 19:23). Did not Jesus exhort us to forgive those who despitefully use us? Reviled, He never reviled, never paid back people in their own coin.

How admirable was the action of those three mighty men among the thirty chief captains in David's army who, knowing how their king longed for a drink of water from his favorite well at the gate of Bethlehem, risked their lives to bring David a refreshing draught! Because they had jeopardized their lives, David would not drink it. Colored by sacrifice, he poured it out unto the Lord. In later times we read of those who hazarded their lives for the sake and name of the Lord Jesus (Acts 15:26).

Then there was the remembrance of the kindness of those like Ittai, the Gittite who believed that his place, whether in life or death, was by the side of the royal master he loved. How touched David was by such devoted allegiance. Further, there was Barzillai the Gileadite who, when David was a fugitive, provided him with all the sustenance he needed. When David returned to Jerusalem, David wanted Barzillai to come and stay with him, but now an old man, and not having long to live, he declined. Then came the tender scene: "The king kissed Barzillai, and blessed him" (II Sam. 19:39). The devotion of David's true followers, is most touching. When he decided to go to battle, his loyal friends restrained him saying, "Thou shalt not go forth; for if half of us die they will not care for us; *but thou art worth ten thousand of us!*" A millennium later another rejected king is at Jerusalem's gate, but no strong band went with Him, only His eleven friends, and in His hour of trial they forsook Him and fled. He *was* the chiefest among ten thousand, and into the battle He went and laid down His life for friend and foe alike. His price was above rubies, yet He was betrayed for thirty pieces of silver.

> There was no other good enough,
> To pay the price of sin.
> He only could unlock the gate of
> Heaven,
> And let us in.

O. *Solomon*

The covenant God gave to David as to the perpetual dominion of his seed, had a partial fulfillment in Solomon, his son (II Sam. 7; 23:5; I Chron. 28:1-7). David himself understood this covenant to be fully realized in the spiritual blessings to be received through the Messiah, which would come as the sure mercies of David (Isa. 55:3). Peter distinctly declared that David foretold the Resurrection and kingship of Christ (Acts 2:25-36). Paul likewise had no hesitation in identifying the Son that David wrote about as the Son of God whom the angelic host worship (Ps. 2; Heb. 1:5-9).

The reigns of David and Solomon constitute the golden age of the Jewish state. David, as the visible representative of Jehovah, sought the spiritual and material prosperity of the state, and in his determination to "execute all His will," he proved himself to be a man after God's own heart. In his justice and wisdom as king, and, above all, in his adherence to the worship and will of God, he will ever remain as a model of kingly authority and spiritual obedience. Solomon, his son, however, who continued the high purpose and shared the blessing of his father, became a more colorful and illustrious ruler, and stands out as the most erudite and wealthy king in the Bible, with his wisdom more conspicuous than his wealth.

The greatness of Solomon, which in the end betrayed him, was manifest in various ways. As a poet, writer, naturalist, and ruler, he had no equal. His wisdom, sagacity, and virtues were universally recognized. He composed or gathered 3,000 proverbs, many of which remain in the book of Proverbs; and had 1005 songs to his credit, Psalm 127 and The Song of Solomon of which are samples. His productions placed him among the first Hebrew poets, while his perfect knowledge of natural history mark him out as a genius (I Kings 4:29-34). Halley, in his most valuable *Bible Handbook* reminds us that Solomon "as a young man had a consuming passion for knowledge and wisdom (I Kings 3:9-12) and became the literary prodigy of his day. His intellectual attainments were the wonder of the age. Kings came from the ends of the earth to hear him. He lectured on Botany and Zoology. He was a Scientist, a Political Ruler, a Business Man with vast enterprises, a Poet, Moralist, and Preacher (I Kings 4; 9:1)."

Coupled with his wide knowledge of nature, Solomon was endowed with a keen intuition and discernment of character, and insight into the motives of and springs of action. Like Jesus, whom Solomon typifies in many ways, Solomon knew what was in man. Such a gift is remarkably illustrated in the methods he devised to discover the true mother of the living babe. When all Israel heard of his clever handling of this sordid situation, "they feared the king: for they saw that the wisdom of God was in him, to do judgment" (I Kings 3:28). But because his marvelous mind was a gift from the Lord, He is, indeed, greater than

Solomon. As the perfection and personification of wisdom, Jesus had the right and authority to declare, "A greater than Solomon is here," even though a Queen from the uttermost parts of the earth came to hear his wisdom (Matt. 12:42). The divinely imparted wisdom of Solomon was a foreshadowing of Him in "whom are hid *all* the treasures of wisdom and knowledge."

David, in his Psalms, provides us with spiritual devotions, but Solomon, his son, sets before us in *Proverbs* and *Ecclesiastes,* practical ethics. Dr. William Arnot in his work on *Proverbs* speaks of the book as "Laws From Heaven for Life on Earth." That Solomon was qualified in a most unique way to write such a book so eminently practical in its teaching is accounted for by the statement that God gave him "wisdom and understanding *exceeding much,* and largeness of heart, even as the sand that is on the seashore" (I Kings 4:29). The object of *Proverbs* was to impart "wisdom and instruction; . . . justice, and judgment, and equity; to give subtilty [the open mind] to the simple, to the young man knowledge and discretion" (Prov. 1:2-4). What a different state of society would be ours if only the aimless youth of today could be persuaded to read and inwardly digest the laws for daily life and living to be found in *Proverbs!*

One of the impressive features of Solomon's notable literary production is the way he presents wisdom, not merely as a coveted attribute, but as identified in a person, even the Incarnate Word of the New Testament. When the writer says of wisdom, "When he prepared the heavens, *I* was there," he personified wisdom as a co-creator, and as One dwelling with God from all eternity. This wisdom is God's Son, whose name none could tell (Prov. 30:4). It is most profitable to bring forecast and fulfillment together, as A. M. Hodgkin suggests in the following adapted comparisons.

The Wisdom in Proverbs

I was . . . from the beginning or ever the earth was (Prov. 8:23).

When He prepared the heavens, I was there (Prov. 8:27).

When he set a compass upon the face of the depth. When he appointed the foundations of the earth (Prov. 8:27, 29).

Then I was by him, as one brought up with him (Prov. 8:30).

The Lord possessed me in the beginning of his way, before his works of old (Prov. 8:22).

I was daily his delight, rejoicing always before him (Prov. 8:30).

Counsel is mine, and sound wisdom: I am understanding (Prov. 8:14).

If thou searchest for her [wisdom] as for hid treasures (Prov. 2:4).

O ye simple, understand wisdom (Prov. 8:5).

Wisdom crieth . . . Turn you at my reproof (Prov. 1:20, 23).

Whoso hearkeneth unto me . . . shall be quiet from fear of evil (Prov. 1:33).

Doth not wisdom cry? Unto you, O men, I call (Prov. 8:1, 4).

Come, eat of my bread, and drink of the wine which I have mingled (Prov. 9:5).

I love them that love me (Prov. 8:17).

Those that seek me early shall find me (Prov. 8:17).

Whoso findeth me findeth life (Prov. 8:35).

Blessed are they that keep my ways (Prov. 8:32).

Hear; for I will speak of excellent things . . . right things (Prov. 8:6).

I lead in the way of righteousness (Prov. 8:20. See Ps. 23:3).

The Word in the New Testament

In the beginning was the Word, . . . and the Word was God (John 1:1).

The Word was with God . . . the same

was in the beginning with God (John 1:1, 2).

All things were made by him; and without him was not any thing made that was made (John 1:3).

His Son... by whom also he made the worlds (Heb. 1:2).

He is before all things, and by him all things consist (Col. 1:17).

Thou lovedst me before the foundation of the world... In thee I am well pleased (John 17:24; Luke 3:22).

Christ Jesus, who of God is made unto us wisdom (I Cor. 1:30; James 3:17).

In whom are hid all the treasures of wisdom and knowledge (Col. 2:3).

Hid these things from the wise... hast revealed them unto babes (Luke 10:21).

Repent ye, and believe the gospel (Mark 1:15; Luke 13:3).

Come unto me,... and I will give you rest... ye shall find rest (Matt. 11:28, 29).

Jesus stood and cried... come unto me, and drink (John 7:37).

I am the bread of life. Eat this Bread, and drink this cup (John 6:35; I Cor. 11:26).

The Son of God, who loved me (Gal. 2:20).

Seek, and ye shall find (Matt. 7:7).

He that believeth on me hath everlasting life (John 6:47).

If ye keep my commandments... my love (John 15:10).

All... wondered at the gracious words which proceeded out of his mouth (Luke 4:22).

It becometh us to fulfill all righteousness (Matt. 3:15. See 21:32).

These comparisons can act as guideposts if the reader cares to follow through the *Proverbs,* and search out further foregleams of truth brought to fruition in Christ. The comparison of Scripture with Scripture is one of the most profitable methods of exposition. It was in this way that Philip led the Ethiopian to the Saviour (Acts 8).

In other ways Solomon typifies Him who affirmed that the dazzling magnificence of such a wealthy and wise potentate paled into insignificance alongside the beautiful lilies of the field. There is, for instance, his name, for *Solomon* means "peaceable," or "the peaceful one" (I Chron. 22:9). Although this was the name given with divine sanction, and by his mother, the prophet Nathan called him *Jedidiah,* meaning "Beloved of Jehovah," perhaps as an assurance to his father David that his grievous sin had been forgiven (II Sam. 12:24, 25). But *Solomon,* the name by which he was known, with its implications of peace, sprang out of the prediction of his personal nature, and of his reign.

> "Behold, a son shall be born to thee, who shall be a man of rest; ... his name shall be Solomon, and I will give peace and quietness unto Israel in his days" (I Chron. 22:9).

Jesus not only imparts rest, peace, and quietness but is the embodiment of such virtues. "*Thou* art My rest." "*He* is our peace." "In quietness... your strength." All that the name of Solomon implies will be abundantly manifested during Christ's millennial reign as "The King of Peace." Solomon's bloodless reign and peaceable kingdom came as the result of the widespread victories his father David had obtained, which fact provides a further type. Because Christ fought and conquered Satan by His cross, we can enter into the peace of His glorious reign in our hearts. "Peace, and joy in the Holy Spirit" is our portion as we follow Christ in the train of His triumph (Rom. 14:17).

From the prolific pen of Solomon we have Psalm 72, the title of which should read *A Psalm of Solomon.* In this outstanding messianic Psalm, Solomon distinctly predicts the character and extent of the universal sovereignty of the Messiah. It was at the height of his own reign that Solomon pictured a superhuman king ruling an empire which in its character and in its compass altogether transcended his own which extended from the Mediterranean to the Euphrates, and from the Red Sea and Arabia to the utmost Lebanon (I Kings 4:21). But "the extremest boundaries of the kingdom of Israel melt away before the gaze of the Psalmist. The new kingdom reaches from 'sea to sea, and from the flood of the world's end.' It reaches from each frontier of the Promised Land to the remotest regions of the known world in the opposite quarter."

Solomon's reign, the most peaceful, prosperous, and glorious of Jewish history, is without doubt a foreshadowing of the coming universal reign of the Messiah, when "every pot in Jerusalem and in Judah shall be holiness unto the LORD of hosts (Zech. 14:20, 21). The scope of Solomon's kingdom is indicated by the phrase "Solomon reigned over all kingdoms from the river unto the land of the Philistines, and unto the border of Egypt" (I Kings 4:21), but magnificent though his kingdom was, Solomon knew by divine inspiration that a greater sovereign than he would come, whose kingdom would "stretch from shore to shore," and that every creature would rise and bring peculiar honors to their king. When He takes unto Himself His power and reigns, His empire will be "co-extensive with the world: it is also to be co-enduring with time: it will likewise be of a spiritual nature, bestowing peace through righteousness on the world." Earth's last king will not fail as Solomon, with all his glory, did. Perfect in holiness, knowledge, and power, "people and realms of every tongue" will benefit through His reign. "Omniscience alone can hear the cry of every human heart; omnipotence alone can bring deliverance to every human sufferer."

A great event, if not the greatest, during Solomon's reign was the erection of the remarkable temple, the building of which fulfilled a prophecy (II Sam. 7:13), and which when finished became a symbol of God's resting with His people (II Sam. 7:6, 10). It also became both a prophecy and a type – a prophecy of God's continued presence (Jer. 7), and a type of "the habitation of God through the Spirit," the Church. When the temple fell, the Jews were scattered; but when it rose from its ruins, the people regathered in it. Thus Jewish history can be dated with accuracy from the first capture of Jerusalem, and the destruction of its temple (II Chron. 7:20; Isa. 44: 28) by the Babylonians in 586 B.C. The best part of the first book of Kings is taken up with the building and dedication of the temple. We may be inclined to think so many details were not necessary, but, as George H. C. MacGregor so aptly comments:

> God's Word never spends space on what is unimportant. The life and power of Israel as a nation were bound up with the Temple. The whole of Israel's history is a commentary on the word: "Them that honour Me I will honour, and those that despise Me shall be lightly-esteemed. The climax of Israel's glory was reached in that hour when, on the completion of Solomon's prayer at the dedication of the Temple, "The glory of the Lord filled the house, and the priests could not enter into the house of the Lord, because the glory of the Lord had filled the house." When Solomon allowed other gods to share in the worship due to Jehovah alone, the decline of the nation had begun.

The temple was the most unique building of its kind in the world at that time. As God was its architect (I Chron. 28:12, 19), it had therefore in its design and execution all the perfection that infinite wisdom could give it. As the greatest, He is worthy of the best. But as we shall see more fully when we come to examine *Prophetic Ritual,* the temple, like its predecessor, the tabernacle, typifies the person and work of Jesus and of His relations with His people. The foundation of the temple was built into solid rock, foreshadowing Jesus, the Rock of Ages, upon whom the foundation of His temple rests.

Jesus called His body a temple, and in Him God tabernacled among men (John 2:19-21). In His teaching, He said that earthly temples were not necessary to the worship of God, yet He never neglected synagogue worship (John 4:20-24). Paul describes the true church, collectively "the temple of God" through which He reveals Himself to the world (I Cor. 3:16-19). Every believer is likewise a "temple of the Holy Spirit" (I Cor. 6:19), and will have a glory exceeding that of Solomon's temple. But the church is pictured not only as a building but as a bride, which is a fuller type that Solomon gives us in his famous *Song,* the mystic character of which the spiritually-minded alone can understand. Among the numerous expository works on *The Song of Songs,* a small volume by Adelaide A. Newton can be heartily commended. In the preface of same, the authoress says that

> The general character of Solomon's *Song* in contrast to his *Ecclesiastes* is very striking. The latter from beginning to end tells of the vanity of the creature—the former of the sufficiency of the Beloved . . . One verse in John's Gospel gives the contrast perfectly. *Ecclesiastes* in the first half of the verse—"Whosoever drinketh of this water *shall thirst again.*"
>
> *The Song of Solomon* in the latter half of the verse—"Whosoever drinketh of the water that I shall give him *shall never thirst*" (John 4:13, 14).
>
> This latter book is full of Jesus. But it is Jesus in a special character —not "Saviour," nor "King," nor "High Priest," nor "Prophet" . . . No! it is a dearer and closer relation than any of these—it is Jesus as our "Bridegroom," Jesus in marriage union with His Bride, His Church.

Divine ownership pervades Solomon's "Love Idyll." Union and communion are most prominent, and speak of Christ's inheritance in the saints that Paul writes of (Eph. 1:11, 18). "My beloved is mine, and I am his" (Song of Sol. 2:16; 6:3).

That the best of men are only men at the best is evident from the tragic failure of Solomon at the end of his illustrious reign – a failure that resulted in the breaking up of the united kingdom of Israel, and the beginning of civil and national strife and war. We can look upon *Ecclesiastes* as Solomon's testament of the powerlessness of worldly position and possessions to satisfy the soul. All the rivers ran into the sea of his life yet he had to confess that all was vanity. The waters of the earth had failed, and he was thirsty still. Professor W. G. Moorehead, after discussing the polygamy, heathen rites, and idolatrous altars contributing to Solomon's fall, describes how "the great prince sank lower and lower, seduced by the multitude of his wives and mistresses; and he disappears from history under the deepest cloud – though *Ecclesiastes* gives some evidence of his repentance. Failure in David; failure in Solomon; failure everywhere, save in Him who is the faithful and true witness. "Behold a greater than Solomon is here." What a creature man is! How vain, unstable, puerile, fallible, worthless, but "Jesus Christ the same yesterday, and to day, and for ever" (Heb. 13:8).

Before kings became a part of Israel's way of life, God laid down certain prohibitions for the future kings of His people to observe:

> He shall not multiply horses to himself, nor cause the people to return to Egypt, to the end that he should multiply horses . . .

> Neither shall he multiply wives to himself, that his heart turn not away; neither shall he greatly multiply to himself silver and gold (Deut. 17:16, 17).

Solomon failed to give heed to this threefold warning, particularly to the last one concerning women. He only added to his guilt when he took the multitude of his wives from the heathen nations, God had expressly commanded His people not to marry into. So we read that "When Solomon was old ... his wives turned away his heart after other gods: and his heart was not perfect with the LORD his God, as was the heart of David his father (I Kings 11:4). James Ball Naylor (1866-1945) humorously wrote in his *David and Solomon:*

> King David and King Solomon
> Led merry, merry lives,
> With many, many lady friends
> And many, many wives;
> But when old age crept over them,
> With many, many qualms,
> King Solomon wrote the Proverbs
> And King David wrote the Psalms

Because of his disobedience, the reign of Solomon ended in disaster, with the glorious kingdom he had established rent in twain. Vanity and vexation of spirit were his as he came to the end of his days. It is in this connection that the phrase *under the sun* occurs some twenty-eight times in *Ecclesiastes,* giving the book its keynote. Such a phrase occurs nowhere else in the Bible. *Vanity* is used thirty-seven times. Almost forty times in the book, Solomon names the earth and the things belonging to it. Solomon had tried everything *under the sun* to satisfy his heart, but discovered nothing but emptiness. The very best the world can provide cannot satisfy the deepest and truest longings of the human heart. Where and how can such a yearning be met?

The answer to this perennial question is to be found at the end of this mournful book of *Ecclesiastes* where the empty-hearted, disillusioned king climbs *above the sun,* where He who is our sun and shield is found. Listen to Solomon's confession:

> Let us hear the conclusion of the whole matter: Fear God, and keep his commandments: for this is the whole duty of man. For God shall bring every work into judgment, with every secret thing, whether it be good, or whether it be evil (Eccles. 12: 13, 14).

What a different ending Solomon's great life would have had if only he had kept all the divine commandments up to the last! A greater than Solomon could say, "I do *always* the things that please My Father." The king's last word agrees with the New Testament revelation that judgment approaches when both good and evil will receive their just reward, but for our present life untainted joy consists in loving, obeying, trusting the Lord to the limit.

> Live under the sun, rise no higher,
> and doubt and unbelief will ensue.
> Live above the sun, spend the days
> with God and light and peace you
> shall have.

It would appear as if the last chapter of *Ecclesiastes* is Solomon's confession of departure from God, and that from the true shepherd he received restoration (Eccles. 12:11). Even if this is so, he found a new center of life too late to be effective. Attention has been drawn between *Ecclesiastes* 2 and *Romans* 7, both chapters bristling with the personal pronoun *I,* and the result in both being failure and disaster. The big *I* is found thirty-six times in Ecclesiastes 2, and thirty-one times in Romans. Self-centeredly, Solomon takes credit for all he accomplished: "I said," "I sought," "I builded," "I planted," "I got," "I gathered," "I was great." But he came to see that his wretched self had gained mastery over his life and confessed, "Then *I* looked, and behold all was vanity and vexation of spirit."

With Paul, there is the contrast between law and grace, and the conflict between the old nature and the new nature of the believer under the law, and his thirty-one *I's* prove how life is a failure if *self* is its center. But the apostle found a new center – "*I* live yet not *I*." In Christ Jesus he found One who was able to set him free from the law of sin and death, and Christ-centered, he accomplished great and mighty things for his Lord. Everything in his life ceased to revolve around self – Christ had become the center and circumference in all things. It was so with the Saviour Himself, who could pray, "Not My will . . . but Thine be done."

> Not I, but Christ be honoured, loved, and exalted,
> Not I, but Christ, be seen, be heard:
> Not I, but Christ in every look and action,
> Not I, but Christ, in every thought and word.

The last typical suggestion we draw attention to is found in Solomon's association with the Queen of Sheba, to which Jesus referred when He affirmed that He was greater than Solomon. Francis Bacon in his *Essay on Adversity* says that "The pencil of the Holy Ghost hath laboured more in describing the afflictions of Job than the felicities of Solomon." If the king had had more afflictions than felicities, he would have ended his career in triumph instead of tragedy. In His contrast between the Queen of Sheba and Himself, Jesus said that she "came from the uttermost parts of the earth to hear the wisdom of Solomon." Such marvelous mental gifts added to his fame and felicity, and as the queen laid all her hard questions before Solomon and communed with him of all that was in her heart, she was amazed at his deft and clever answers. Then, after admiring all his wealth, the appointments of his kingdom, and the remarkable houses and temple he had built, there was no more spirit in her. The queen, dumfounded, could only say, "The half was not told me: thy wisdom and prosperity exceeded the fame that I have heard . . . Blessed be the Lord thy God, which delighted in thee, to set thee on the throne of Israel."

When we reach the city, with its street of gold, and find ourselves in the king's palace, we shall be lost in wonder, love, and praise as we behold the glory of the king, and listen to the music of His voice. Then we, too, will exclaim, "The half was not told us"; and the perfection of bliss will be ours as we stand continually before Him. As we await the summons to appear before the king, we must rest in the assurance that nothing is hid from Him; that having been made unto us *wisdom*, He is able to answer our hard questions and solve our problems. Wise though he was, Solomon was not wise enough to keep himself from adultery and idolatry. But Jesus is greater than Solomon, in that He never stained His character, and as the Sinless One is able to save us, and keep us safe through His shed blood.

P. *Jeremiah*

The Jews of our Lord's time had a deep reverence for the ancient prophets, so when He asked His disciples, "Whom do men say that I the Son of man am?" They replied, "Some say . . . Elijah: and others, *Jeremiah*, or one of the prophets" (Matt. 16:13, 14). With their peculiar affection for the prophet Jeremiah, we can understand why the Jews identified Jesus with him. In his heart-warming exposition of *Jeremiah*, Dr. F. B. Meyer, in the preface of his valuable book says that

> Jeremiah has always a fascination to Christian hearts, because of the close similarity that exists between his life

> and that of Jesus Christ. Each of them was "a man of sorrows, and acquainted with grief"; each came to his own, and his own received him not; each passed through hours of rejection, desolation, and forsakenness. And in Jeremiah we may see beaten out into detail, experiences which, in our Lord, are but lightly touched on by the Evangelists... Amid names that shine as stars in the hemisphere of Old Testament Scripture, there is not one more brilliant than his. There is an especial message in the ministry of Jeremiah for those who are compelled to stand alone, who fall into the ground to die, who fill up what is behind of the sufferings of Christ, and through death arise to bear fruit in the great world of men, which they passionately love.

Before coming to the comparisons between Jeremiah and Jesus, it is interesting to gather out the forecasts his prophecy contains of the Messiah. Although he may not unfold as much of the Predicted One as Isaiah does, yet he is included in those prophets who gave witness to Christ. Among the heroes of faith named in Hebrews 11, *none* of the prophets, apart from Samuel, are specifically mentioned. Yet all, including Jeremiah, are included, in the phrase "and of the prophets" (Heb. 11:32). The following prophetic glimpses of Christ can be traced through Jeremiah's remarkable book, saturated as it is with the character of his mind. "It is peculiarly marked by pathos. He delights in expressions of tenderness, and gives touching descriptions of the miseries of his people." Christ-like virtues, are they not?

1. Christ as the Fountain of Living Waters (Jer. 2:13).
2. Christ as the Great Physician (Jer. 8:22).
3. Christ as the Good Shepherd (Jer. 23:4; 31:10).
4. Christ as the Righteous Branch (Jer. 23:5).
5. Christ as David the King (Jer. 30:9).
6. Christ as the Redeemer (Jer. 50:34).
7. Christ as the Lord our Righteousness (Jer. 23:6).

In the list of divine titles, *Jehovah Tsidkenu* occupies a prominent place as a prediction of the majestic name of the Godhead of the Lord Jesus, as well as of His humanity, as a descendant of David. Jeremiah, however, not only *revealed* Christ in his prophecies, but *reflected* Christ in his personality. His very name, meaning "He shall exalt Jehovah," was indicative of his whole life, which was spent in the endeavor to promote God's glory. Does not this aim mirror Him who could say, "I have glorified Thee on the earth"? While all that Jeremiah disclosed concerning the Messiah is of deep importance and very instructive, the life he lived spoke with a louder voice of Him that was to come. As Dr. Moorehead expresses it:

> One cannot but see in Jeremiah something of the Spirit of Christ. Indeed, it is not too much to say that on a small scale that Life which is above all other lives is reproduced in this prophet. Jeremiah's love for his people, his anxiety to do them good and naught but good, his tears at the defeat of his efforts to reclaim them, and the hopefulness with which he looks forward to their final recovery and blessing, are but a dim reflection of what was perfect in the heart of the Lord Jesus. Grace and the Spirit of God will make any one like Christ.

Jeremiah's most conspicuous Christ-like characteristic was his sorrow for the sins of those around him. Although he lived centuries before the cross, he was a man with a Calvary-heart, and was prepared to make any sacrifice or endure any pain if only he could see the people reformed and restored. Both of his books – *Jeremiah* and *Lamentations*, are drenched with his tears. He was indeed "The Prophet of the Broken Heart." But his "liquid pain," as tears have been called, was as unavailing as that of Jesus when He wept over Jerusalem.

It added to his profound grief to see that his task was to end in vain; that his was to be a hopeless love; that those he wept over would have none of his counsel. In this, did he not symbolize Jesus, whose sob of a disappointed heart is heard in the cry, "O Jerusalem, Jerusalem, how often would I have gathered thee together... but ye would not"? Thus Jeremiah himself with his tears and trials, "with his sensibilities always bleeding, with his blasted affections weeping out their life in silent injury, is ever before us as we read." Yes, and as we read, ever and anon, there rises before us the figure of another prophet who became a man of sorrows, and was, thereby, mistaken for Jeremiah.

How heart-moving is Jeremiah's lament of the desolation over Jerusalem, the city of the great king, as recorded in his *Lamentations!* With the vividness of an eye-witness, he describes the captivity of Israel, and the city once great among the nations now sitting as "a widow." How his heart was crushed as he saw the city plundered by the Chaldean Army! Later on, the spot where he sat and sobbed was called "The Grotto of Jeremiah." But what happened some 600 years later? Another prophet, greater than Jeremiah, looked out on the same proud city and wept aloud, saying, "If thou hadst known, even thou, at least in this thy day, the things that belong unto thy peace!" Then "sorrow interrupted silence," and when He found voice could continue, Jesus could only add, "but now they are hid from thine eyes ... Thou knewest not the time of thy visitation."

Jeremiah wept over Jerusalem as he foretold the destruction of the city by the Chaldeans, and Jesus wept over it as He predicted its destruction by the Romans. But Jesus went further than Jeremiah in that He not only shed His tears over those who rejected His witness — at Calvary He shed His blood for their sins and salvation. Several foregleams of the cross can be traced in *Lamentations:*

"Is it nothing to you, all ye that pass by? behold, and see if there be any sorrow like unto my sorrow" (Lam. 1:12).

"All that pass by clap their hands at thee; they hiss and wag their head" (Lam. 2:15, 16; Matt. 27:39).

"All thine enemies have opened their mouth against thee" (Lam. 2:16; Matt. 27:13).

"He shutteth out my prayer" (Lam. 3:8; Matt. 27:46).

"I was a derision to all my people; and their song all the day" (Lam. 3:14; Ps. 69:12).

"The wormwood and the gall" (Lam. 3:19; Ps. 69:21).

"He giveth his cheek to him that smiteth him: he is filled full with reproach" (Lam. 3:30; Isa. 50:6; Ps. 69:20).

"Shed the blood of the just." "Ye denied the Holy One and the Just, ... and killed the Prince of Life" (Lam. 4:13; Acts 3:14, 15; I Pet. 3:18).

When Jeremiah received the message of the broken covenant, and learned of the terrible disaster about to overtake Jerusalem, he acquiesced to the divine decree and said, "So be it, O LORD" (Jer. 11:5). For "So be it," the margin gives AMEN! Jesus likewise rested in His Father's will and purpose, saying, "Even so — or *Amen* — Father." But He was also able to pray, "I thank Thee, Father," implying that because of all He is in Himself, God's will is ever best. John predicted the time when the redeemed church, witnessing the overthrow of the great opponent of the Lamb's bride, will add a *Hallelujah* to the *Amen* (Rev. 19:1-6). Often we can say with Jeremiah, "Amen, Lord," but not *Amen, Hallelujah!* At the church's final triumph, however, there will be not only *assent* but *consent* — *acquiescence* and *acclaim*. *Amen* — subjection to the will of God: *Hallelujah* — the triumphant outburst of praise and adoration. Then the hymn of His glorious church will be

> Great and marvellous are thy works, O Lord God, the Almighty; righteous and true are thy ways, thou King of the ages (Rev. 15:3, R.V.).

As we take our farewell of Jeremiah as a type of Jesus it is with the feeling that he will ever remain as one of the truest patriots the world has ever known. Secretly and publicly he wept over surrounding iniquity, and bravely denounced the sins of his nation. He stood forth at the call of God, and proved himself a faithful, fearless champion of the truth, amid reproaches, insults, and threats. It was no easy task to fulfill his divine mission amid deepening apostasy, judgment, and disaster, but like the Master he resembled, he set his face steadfastly toward Jerusalem. Although the sword reached his own soul and he cried, "My heart! my heart! I writhe in pain! the walls of my heart will break! my heart groans within me; I cannot keep it still," (Jer. 4:19 [free translation]), yet struggling against the message of doom, he could no longer hold it in (Jer. 6:11), and so, with tears, delivered his soul. As with Jesus, so Jeremiah had a sob in his voice as he announced predicted judgment.

Raised up by God for the service of others, Jeremiah came to experience what it was to fall as the corn of wheat into the ground and die. The prophet's privations and sorrows crowd his plaintive prophecy. "Death wrought in him, that life might work in Israel, and in all who should read the Book of his Prophecy." As Dr. F. B. Meyer goes on to expound in his book on *Jeremiah*,

> He died to the dear ties of human love;
> He died to the goodwill of his fellows:
> He died to the pride of national patriotism;
> He died to the sweets of personal liberty;
> He died to the meaning he had been wont to place on his own prophecies.

Before George Matheson wrote his famous hymn "O Love, that will not let me go," Jeremiah experienced its sentiment and could sing

> O Cross, that liftest up my head,
> I dare not ask to fly from Thee;
> I lay in dust life's glory dead,
> And from the ground there blossoms red
> Life that shall endless be.

When, like Jeremiah, we are summoned to run God's errands for Him, no matter whether pleasant or painful it is not for us to demur or question why. When Jesus says "Go into all the world," He means just what God had in mind when He told Jeremiah to "Go to Euphrates." The prophet did not plead the distance and hardship of the way. It was enough that God had said *Go*. May we know what it is to rise and follow, and thus imitate Jeremiah, who with charming simplicity records, "So I went to Euphrates"! The Lord grant that you and I may be found girding up our loins and going out to witness as He commands.

The tragedy is that those Jeremiah sought to warn would not heed nor repent nor obey. Through His servant "God exhausted all means, tried every agency, employed every kind of appeal, to move His people and to lead them back to allegiance to Him. Obdurate, hard-hearted, stiff of neck, rebellious, they were insensible to every effort and dumb to every entreaty. And so at length the judgment which could no longer be delayed, broke down upon them in all its appalling fury. Grace despised, mercy rejected, love spurned, and goodness outraged, become at length whips in the hand of offended justice." Would that this godless age of ours could be aroused to a sense of the peril awaiting it!

We take our leave of the weeping prophet with the portrait of him, which Professor Moorehead has sketched for us to gaze at as an incentive to loyal and sacrificial service:

> Jeremiah was to be the solitary fortress, undismayed in any presence; the one, grand immovable figure who pursued the apostacising people and rulers, delivering his message in the temple court, the royal chamber, or the street, whether they would hear or forbear. In consequence he was a prophet of unwelcome truths, hated by all, but feared as well by all. It was a mission requiring courage, faith, strength, will; a mission no weakling could fill, no coward could undertake. Jeremiah is one of the very great men of the world.

And might we add he is one of the most untarnished mirrors of Jesus to be found among Old Testament personalities.

Q. *Elijah and Elisha*

Forerunner and Fulfiller! How wonderfully these two remarkable Old Testament prophets foreshadow the coming of John the Baptist to prepare the way of the Lord, and then the coming of the Lord Himself. As we know from the Gospels, the Baptist is identified as being the counterpart of the rugged prophet of the Old Testament. Then there were those who saw something of Elijah in Jesus, and that when He died it was upon Elijah He called. Both prophets were endowed with power to perform miracles, the number of which illustrates Elisha's request for a double portion of Elijah's spirit to rest upon him (II Kings 2:9, 15). Elijah wrought eight miracles, Elisha sixteen, all of which were parables in action. The majority were mercy-miracles, the rest judgment-miracles.

1. *Elijah*. Amid the darkness of his age, this mantle-clad prophet of the wilderness suddenly burst upon the scene to announce the judgment of God upon the people for their rejection of Him. Having power with God, he therefore had power with men, and when before Ahab, Elijah, knowing that he stood before the Lord, had no fear of the face of man. In his courageous witness he foreshadowed John the Baptist, who, clad similarly to Elijah, stood in the court of Herod and fearlessly denounced him for his sin. When Jesus said of the Baptist that he was Elijah, who was to come (see Mal. 4:5; Matt. 17:12), He did not mean that the prophet had actually come back to earth in the flesh. John himself denied that he was Elijah (Luke 1:17; John 1:21). The prophecy of coming as a messenger was fulfilled in John in that he came "in the *spirit and power* of Elijah." As Elijah was a severe rebuker of sin, in both king and people, so was John the Baptist. Both too were self-denying men (Matt. 3:4).

What impresses us, as we meditate upon the life and work of Elijah, is that he is more prophetic or typical of Jesus than John the Baptist. For instance, his name, *Elijah,* means "My God is God Himself," and Jesus came not only as the Son of Man, but as God Incarnate. He was truly "very God of very God." Then in Elijah's control of the forces of nature, as when he declared no dew or rain would descend, and when he commanded fire to come out of the heavens, he predicted the coming of Jesus, who, upholding all things by the word of His power, would in His miracles reveal His command and control of all forces. The several instances of deliverance by fire coming at the time of the morning and evening sacrifice portray the power of the cross of Jesus, which those sacrifices foreshadowed (I Kings 18:36). Such a miracle presented an unanswerable proof of his divine authority.

When Elijah was commanded to hide himself from the king, he predicted the Saviour, who was compelled to flee from cruel Herod, and who for thirty years was hid in His humble home at Nazareth until He entered His public ministry of mercy and of judgment. Further, when Elijah multiplied the bread, he acted beforehand, the miracle of Jesus in multiplying the loaves and fishes. Elijah raised the dead, after lying on the widow's son *three times* (I Kings 17:21). Jesus raised *three* while here on earth.

Again, Elijah was a man of prayer who knew how to storm heaven with great results (James 5:16-18). Although subject to like passions as we are, he prevailed. Jesus was heard of God in that He feared. Separate altogether from our passions, as the sinless One, He was always heard by the Father (John 11:42). The mighty prayers of both Elijah and Emmanuel teach us that "more things are wrought by prayer than this world dreams of." Then, what about the forty days in the desert without natural food? Does not such an experience foreshadow our Lord's forty days in the wilderness when He was divinely sustained during His temptations?

Yet another type can be seen in that Elijah cast his mantle upon his successor, Elisha, an act implying that he was to continue the ministry of his master. Did not Jesus say that it was expedient for Him to go away so that the Holy Spirit could come to expand His influence among men? At last, Elijah was translated. He was not, for God took him, even as He did Enoch before him. Often the actual, visible translation of Elijah is compared to the Ascension of Jesus, of which of course it was a type. But Elijah did not die, as Jesus died, before His translation. At the Transfiguration, Elijah reappeared on the mount in his glorified body, along with Moses, for the express purpose of having a conversation with Jesus about His death at Calvary.

2. *Elisha*. A gentler character than Elijah, his predecessor in the prophetic office, Elisha, nevertheless, is counted among Israel's great prophets. It has been suggested that Elisha can be used as a type of the Holy Spirit, seeing He took up and continued the work of the One who ascended on high; or as a type of the believer's sanctification because of the blessing that came to Elisha through testing. But we like to think of him as another who was a guidepost to Him who came as the prophet of Galilee. In his prolific miracles of healing and of mercy he was certainly a type of Jesus whose mighty works benefited so many. As Elisha produced the water to banish the barrenness of the land, so Jesus, by His life and work, has enriched the lives of countless multitudes.

As a name, *Elisha* means "God is Saviour." Before His birth, the Messiah was given the name of *Jesus*, which implies the same thought resident in the prophet's name. It was at Jordan that Elisha took up the mantle of Elijah, and at the very same place that Jesus, as He emerged from the water, received His Father's benediction, and the Holy Spirit's enduement for service ahead. Elisha asked for a double portion of the Spirit for the exercise of the prophetic office, and Jesus, ere He ascended promised the Spirit to His own. "Ye shall receive power, the Holy Spirit coming upon you: and ye shall be witnesses unto Me."

The digging of the ditches, in order to receive the water Elisha predicted would come, is likewise full of spiritual significance. We read, "it came to pass in the morning, *when the meat offering was offered*, that, behold there came water by the way of Edom, and the country was filled with water." Is this not a further forecast of universal blessing through the cross? At Calvary, Christ, the meat offering, was offered; and at Pentecost the waters of the Spirit were liberated, and the church of the living God was born. God-given water to assuage soul-thirst is ours through the once-for-all offering of Christ. There is also food for spiritual hunger in Him who came as the Bread of Life. The unselfish command of Elisha, "Give the people . . . to eat," surely forecasts the bidding of One greater than Elisha. The miracle of the loaves was an acted parable reminding men that Jesus was able to meet both their physical and spiritual needs.

Attention must be drawn to the last miracle associated with Elisha, which happened, strange to say, after he was dead. The dead body of another man was cast into Elisha's grave, and as soon as it touched the bones of the departed prophet, the unknown man was restored to life. Thus, "Elisha died and was buried like all other men, but even in death and in the grave he is avouched to be the prophet and servant of God." Is this not a striking illustration of undying influence? Does it not also typify the vivifying power of Christ's death? "Thy dead men shall live, together with my dead body shall they arise" (Isa. 26:19). Hales, a gifted expositor of a bygone century, says of this extraordinary last miracle of Elisha's:

> It was the immediate work of God, and concurred with the translation of Elijah to keep alive and confirm, in a degenerate and infidel age, the grand truth of a *bodily resurrection,* which the translation of Enoch was calculated to produce in the antediluvian age, and which the Resurrection of Christ, in a glorified body fully illustrated.

R. *Daniel*

It was this Hebrew statesman-prophet of Babylon who, under divine inspiration of the Holy Spirit, gave us the most remarkable prophetic book of the Bible. In different parts of our study we have written of the striking prophecies Daniel sets forth, and so, in this section we are not taken up with same, but only with the prophet himself, as being typical of the Messiah whom he wrote about. We are all acquainted with Daniel's outlines of the epochs and events of world history. In a marvelous way he unfolded deep truths concerning Messiah the prince – His Atonement, when He is to appear, His future dignity, and His coming in the clouds of heaven. We see *in act* what David gave us *in words* (Dan. 7:9-14 with Ps. 110). When Jesus applied the words of Daniel to Himself, "Hereafter shall ye see the Son of Man sitting on the right hand of power, coming in the clouds of Heaven," the High Priest accused Him of blasphemy, because he immediately recognized in the declaration Christ's claim to deity.

Because the book of Daniel is so full of Christ, it must have been very precious to Him. That He was very familiar with its prophecies is evident from the way He quoted from them. How impressive was His use of Daniel's forecast of the daily sacrifice being taken away, and the abomination that maketh desolation being set up! Christ spoke expressly of the *prophet Daniel* by name, and of his book added, "Whoso readeth, let him understand." If, then, He commended the study of this book, containing a good deal of unfulfilled prophecy, how can we expect to have an understanding of the times if we neglect it (Matt. 24:15)? As *Daniel* and *Revelation* are companion prophecies, dealing with the same prophetic themes, and using the same symbols, they should be studied together. Daniel and John deal with the stupendous scenes and events of the end of the age we are rapidly approaching.

In God's Portrait Gallery, the picture we have of Daniel seems to bear a close resemblance to a greater prophet still. In many ways, Daniel is typical of the Messiah he predicted should come. Preachers and teachers could find profitable material in the extension of these particular traits and virtues.

1. *He was a man greatly beloved.* Because of Daniel's sterling qualities, God brought him, not only into favor of the prince of the eunuchs, but into his "tender love" (Dan. 1:9). Daniel was among those of the children of Israel who had no blemish, but were well favored, skillful in all wisdom, cunning in knowledge, and understanding science (Dan. 1:4). Further, the prince of the eunuchs was drawn to Daniel because he requested of him permission not to eat the king's meat nor drink his wine. The prophet early learned that low living was the way to high thinking. Then, reading between the lines, it would seem as if the proud and despotic Nebuchadnezzar had a real affection for the prophet he honored throughout his long reign. Darius also had an undisguised regard for Daniel. When the prophet's foes schemed to destroy him, and Darius found what a trap he had fallen into, "he was sore displeased with himself, and *set his heart* on Daniel to deliver him."

But Daniel not only earned the affection of men, he was also greatly beloved by his God he so faithfully served. Three times over we are told that a heavenly voice called him "a man greatly beloved" (Dan. 9:23; 10:11, 19). In the earthly and heavenly love surrounding him, Daniel foreshadows Jesus, who was dearly loved by His Father. Did He not say, "As the Father hath loved me, so have I loved you" (John 15:9)? The disciples He loved, loved Him in return. With vehemence, Peter repeated his feelings toward the Master. "Thou knowest that I love Thee." John, whose deep love for Jesus was but a response to His love for a disciple privileged to lean upon His bosom, reminds us that if we love Him, in turn, we are loved by the Father (John 14:21).

2. *He was a man spirit-filled.* Five times over Daniel received the testimony of others that "the spirit of the holy gods" was in him (Dan. 4:8, 9, 11; 5:11, 14). Nebuchadnezzar was a heathen who recognized many gods, Jehovah among them. Doubtless he had imbibed some notions of the true God, for although he uses the *plural* "gods," he yet applies the epithet "holy," which applies to Jehovah alone, the heathen gods making no pretention to purity (Deut. 32:31; Isa. 63:11). Nebuchadnezzar must have known of Daniel's allegiance to *his* God, and somehow felt that He was the source of Daniel's remarkable ability to interpret the dreams of others. The prophet himself declares that secrets were revealed to him by the God of heaven, and that interpretation came from Him and Him alone.

We have no hesitation in affirming that Daniel was one of those holy men of God who spake as they were moved (borne along) by the Holy Spirit (II Pet. 1:21). Further, as He is "the spirit of wisdom and revelation" (Eph. 1:17), He was the One who, as God the Spirit, revealed deep and secret things to the mind of Daniel (Dan. 2:22). He was the source of "knowledge and skill in all learning and wisdom," which Daniel exhibited. This was why Daniel and his companions were "ten times better than all the magicians and astrologers that were in all his [the king's] realm" (Dan. 1:20). In the vision Daniel received of the glory of God, the assuring voice was heard, "I will shew thee that which is noted in the scripture of truth" (Dan. 10:21). Did not our Lord declare that it would be part of the Holy Spirit's ministry to lead and guide us into all truth?

As with Daniel, so with our Lord, the Spirit of a thrice-holy God was in Him. Filled with the Spirit from His mother's womb, He manifested reliance upon the guide and comforter He bequeathed to His disciples. Such phrases as "I, by the Spirit," "led of the Spirit," "He returned in the power of the Spirit," "Jesus rejoiced in the Spirit," all testify to a life possessed and energized by the Spirit of Life. Even in His risen form, Jesus instructed His disciples in divine truth "through the Holy Spirit" (Acts 1:2). With Daniel, his unique wisdom and understanding in the matter of the interpretation was imparted, but with the Messiah, the prophet foretold, it was different, for he confessed the revelation he received was not from any wisdom he possessed (Dan. 2:30). But the perfect wisdom Jesus exhibited, causing even His foes to ask "Whence hath this man this wisdom?", was not imparted but innate. He *is* Wisdom. With Him, it was not merely an attribute – it was a personification! The privilege of grace is that we, too, are indwelt by the Spirit of God who ever seeks to make us the recipients of spiritual wisdom and understanding.

3. *He was a man of prayer.* To Daniel, prayer was his "native air," his "vital breath." Again and again we read of him looking up to heaven in confidence that his petitions would be answered. Daniel made the promises of God a motive to prayer (Dan. 9:2, 3), just as the disciples prayerfully awaited the fulfillment of their Lord's promise of the Holy Spirit (Acts 1:14). The prophet also revealed the honor God puts upon the prayer of the contrite in heart (Dan. 9:4, 21). The glorious display of the great work of Redemption was made to Daniel when in the act of sin he deeply bewailed personal and national sin. The life of Daniel is a forcible illustration of the truth that "the secret of the LORD is with them that fear him" (Ps. 25:14). Tennyson wrote of those:

> Thrice blest, whose *lives* are faithful Prayers,
> Whose lives in higher love endure!
> What souls possess themself so pure?
> Or is there blessedness like theirs?

Daniel was one of those pure souls whose *life* was a faithful prayer, and whose prayers were accordingly answered. Because of the heavenly bent of his whole being, he could win heaven by prayer.

When Nebuchadnezzar demanded an interpretation of his dream, Daniel and his friends had a united prayer meeting and interceded that the dream itself as well as its secret be revealed unto them. Prayer was answered, and the forgotten dream was recovered and its interpretation given. Daniel publicly acknowledged that it was all of God in answer to believing prayer (Dan. 2:1-36).

When Daniel's three friends refused to bow down and worship the image of Nebuchadnezzar, they were cast into the fiery furnace, but the flames had no fear for them, nor any influence upon them. They knew that the One they worshiped and prayed to would undertake for them, as He did. All the fire did was to burn off their fetters, so that they were able to *walk* in the fire in company with a fourth person, whose form was like unto the Son of God (Dan. 3:25).

When Daniel was made third ruler of the kingdom by Belshazzar because of the interpretation of the writing on the wall, the presidents and princes Daniel was now above became so jealous of the eminent position he had gained as an interpreter of dreams and hard sentences and a dissolver of doubts (Dan. 5:12) that they forced Darius to make a decree that if any man in his kingdom made a petition to God or man, save of the king himself, he should be cast into the den of lions. These envious rulers confessed that Daniel was faultless and faithful, and that they could only trap him in his prayer-life. But Daniel had no dread of the royal decree. He quietly pursued his usual custom, and prayed with his window open toward Jerusalem "as he did aforetime." Against his will, Darius caused Daniel to be thrown to the lions, but set his heart to deliver the prophet he greatly admired. He had no need to be alarmed about the safety of Daniel, who "believed in his God" and who consequently won another royal decree that all in the kingdom should "tremble and fear before the God of Daniel" (Dan. 6:1-28).

When Daniel discovered from the prophecy of Jeremiah the desolation awaiting Jerusalem, and the consequent restoration of the people, he gave himself to prayer and fasting, and made a full confession of his own sin and the sin of his people (Dan. 9:1-5, 20). While praying and confessing, there came to Daniel the prophetic program of "the seventy weeks" (Dan. 9:24). As we have already seen, Jesus prayed and prayed for others, but never had any personal sin to confess, seeing He was sinless.

When during the reign of Cyrus, God designed to grant Daniel a glorious vision of Himself, the prophet spent three weeks in prayer and fasting (Dan. 10:2, 3). What a panorama of the future events he received as the result! This instance of Daniel's prayer-life is notable, however, for the revelation it gives of the unseen forces of darkness arrayed against us when we pray in the Spirit. From the first day he started to pray, God heard him, but for twenty-one days there was a satanic blockage between heaven and his heart (Dan. 10:12), and when at last Daniel had prayed through, he was without strength. What a grim struggle must have been his with the prince of the power of the air!

As a man of earnest, ceaseless, believing, and prevailing prayer, Daniel is a fitting type of the Messiah, whose death he predicted. In the previous section of our study, dealing with *Specific Prophecies,* we gave attention to our Lord's past and present intercessory ministry. In spite of the fierce opposition surrounding Him in the days of His flesh, like Daniel, He kept His window open toward Jerusalem. He not only prayed; He, himself was a prayer. His prayers and supplications, saturated with His warm tears, were heard, in that He feared the God who answers prayer — even although an answer may be delayed as Daniel experienced (Heb. 5:7).

Poor tremblers at His rougher wind,
  Why do we doubt Him so?
Who gives the storm a path, will find
  The way our feet should go.
The Lord yields nothing to our fears,
  And flies from selfish care;
But comes Himself where'er He hears
  The voice of loving prayer.

S. *Jonah*

Although Jonah comes fifth in the order of the minor prophets, he is generally considered to be the most ancient of all the prophets, whose writings we possess. "Elisha's ministry reaches nearly to that of Jonah, and from Jonah we enter the prophetic canon." Appearing as a prophet to the Gentiles, with a special mission to Nineveh, "a city equally distinguished for its magnificence and corruption, its careless merriment and licentious dissipation, Jonah fled from his God-given task, and was punished for his disobedience." The miracle attending divine reproof of his conduct was evidence of his divine mission, and of how God is able to bring good out of evil. There is not much about Jonah's character typical of Jesus. While his prayer expresses deep repentance, yet he appears as a man inconsistent, disobedient, discontented, and petulant.

Yet Jesus used Jonah in a twofold way as being typical of Himself. First, through the preaching of Jonah, Nineveh experienced a marvelous national revival. The prophet had only one sermon – a short one of doom made up of eight words – "Yet forty days and Nineveh shall be overthrown." Because of his peevish nature, there was little of divine mercy in his tone and manner, but the brief message was effective, for, as Jesus said, Nineveh "repented at the preaching of Jonah." Alas! Jesus, so different in temperament from Jonah, also preached to an evil generation as "a greater than Jonah," yet without a mighty revival. Because those to whom He witnessed spurned His entreaty, the repentant of Nineveh will rise up in judgment against the Christ-rejectors (Luke 11:29-44).

Further, referring to the runaway preacher as "The Prophet Jonah," Jesus, answering the Pharisees, who came asking for a sign from heaven, said the only sign they could have had already been given, namely, the sign of Jonah's burial and resurrection. This is the only reference to Jesus in the book of Jonah. The time of the prophet's continuance in the belly of the divinely created great fish was a type of our Lord's period in the grave (Matt. 12:38-41). Thus, as an expositor of a past century remarks, "In the first and oldest of the Prophets, we perceive that the first image, the introductory representation, which meets us in the opening of the prophetic canon when we explore it in a Christian sense, is that of the great fact of Christ's Resurrection." The early Christians, when under severe Roman persecutions, carved on the walls of the Catacombs of Rome their favorite representation of Jonah as a type of the Resurrection.

Urquhart in his *Biblical Guide* says that "On the horizon of the Old Testament there has always blazed this sign of the Death and Resurrection of the Lord Jesus – the sign of the Prophet Jonah." To be a perfect type of Christ, Jonah had to die, be buried for three days, and rise again. As previously mentioned we believe that the watery deep was more than a dungeon for the disobedient prophet – it was a grave. "The earth and her bars was about me for ever." When Jesus spoke of being "three days and three nights in the heart of the earth," He was referring to His *dead body.* By implication, then, if Jonah was miraculously kept alive at "the bottom of the mountains" for "three days and three nights," he was not a true sign of Jesus in His death, burial, and resurrection. This is why we hold that Jonah actually died and that God brought up his life again from corruption.

When Jonah rose again he went forth with all the power and authority of a prophet, just as Jesus was "declared to be the Son of God with power, . . . by the resurrection from the dead" (Rom. 1:4). To quote Urquhart, who is a safe guide to follow in Bible study:

> Age after age the Jew has been confronted with that sign. He helps kill the Messiah, and out of the grave of the Crucified has arisen a power which has changed the lives of myriads all down the ages. Our Lord gave a promise—the rising from the dead —and He has kept it. He has proved His claim to be the Son of God and the world's Saviour.

The Book of Jonah is likewise typical in a broad sense because it is essentially a missionary book. Twice over, Jonah received the commission to go and evangelize Nineveh – a foreshadowing of the great commission to go and preach the Gospel to every creature. Jonah had to learn that salvation was not for the Jews only; that the love and mercy of God were broader than the measure of his prejudiced mind. The Gospel of redeeming grace in the power of God is to *everyone* that believeth. As the sands of time are sinking and world judgment is nigh, we need to obey the clear instruction from God, "*Arise, go, . . . cry!*" (Jon. 1:2).

Millions of transgressors poor,
Thou hast for Jesu's sake forgiven:
Made of them Thy favour sure,
And snatched from Hell to Heaven . . .
Millions more Thou ready art
To save, and to forgive;
Every soul and every heart
Of man Thou would'st receive.

Ours is not an unwilling Jonah sent to make known our sin, but a compassionate and ever-merciful Saviour ready to pardon sinners, and the church's responsibility is to proclaim such a Gospel whether it is accepted or rejected by those who hear it. Such was the Master's application of the preaching of Jonah (Matt. 12:41).

T. *Hosea*

Among the goodly fellowship of the prophets, Hosea is conspicuous as the prophet of love, repentance, and hope. Placed first in the list of the twelve minor prophets, Hosea, in his prophecy gives us a most vivid picture of the times in which he lived, and of the political and moral state of the people. His book gives him an honored position among the literary prophets. It abounds in arrestive figures and metaphors that are sometimes intermingled, and in style that is concise, terse, and abrupt. The way he can jump so suddenly from one topic to another prompted one writer to describe Hosea "as a bee flying from flower to flower, swift and restless, but always gathering and always laden." Dr. G. Campbell Morgan says of the book of Hosea that "it pulsates with power . . . The Book thrills with emotion, and flames with light, from beginning to end . . . The message of this Book is a message to Christendom." While it is not within the province of our present study to expound the teaching of Hosea, but only to point out any typical and prophetical application it may have to Christ, yet preachers desiring to present the topics Hosea deals with can profitably follow the summary Professor Moorehead gives:

1. The relation which God formed between Himself and Israel originally; it was like that of marriage.
2. Israel's unfaithfulness in this relation.
3. Divorcement of the people from the Lord announced.
4. The people's guilt.
5. Punishment certain, captivity predicted.
6. Remonstrances with the guilty people, and entreaties to repent and reform.
7. Promise of a final and genuine repentance and restoration.

It was because Hosea was a man with a broken heart through a family tragedy that he spoke and wrote as he did. "He saw to the heart of the great subjects which he treated, and he did so because in his training for the prophetic ministry his own heart was wrung with anguish. He who has much to teach must suffer much, and he alone can speak of the deepest things in the economy of God who has entered into fellowship with the suffering of God." This is the key to the appealing, powerful plea of Hosea's wonderful prophecy. Entering into God's suffering through his own, it was out of such a fellowship that he witnessed so mightily to his own age, his sentences falling like the throbs of a crushed and disappointed heart.

What was true, *literally*, of Hosea, he applied, *figuratively*, to the nation of which he was part. His domestic sorrow is well-known to all Bible lovers. Gomer, his wife, proved unfaithful and left the prophet to become the paramour of a man who could better satisfy her fondness for luxury (Hos. 3:1-2). But Hosea still loved his wife and bought her back for the equivalent price Judas sold Jesus for. Israel had strayed from God, and became guilty of spiritual whoredom. Yet God still loved His sinning people and endeavored to win them back to Himself, even though they had spent the very gifts of His love in lewdness. Thus what "the sin of Israel meant to God, Hosea learned by the tragedy of his own home and in his own heart; and with fierce, hot anger he denounced kings, priests, and people alike."

While there is much of sin, and of deserved judgment, declared in letters of fire which must have burnt the men who listened, the greatest revelation of the book is that of a ceaseless yearning, and forgiving love. In the last part of Hosea's prophecy, full of the truth of God's unchanging love, three different features are emphasized, namely

The love of Jehovah in the light of past love;
The love of Jehovah in the light of present and continued love.
The love of Jehovah in the light of future love.

Ultimately Hosea's sinning wife was restored to the place of love and privilege at her husband's side. So, as Dr. Campbell Morgan reminds us, a threefold revelation stands out upon the page of this prophecy:

> It reveals sin, as to what it is—
> It reveals judgment as inevitable and necessary—
> It reveals love amazingly . . .
> The only comfort that comes to the heart in the days of the failure of the Church, is that the music of the love of Jehovah is still sounding, and the soul is filled with the assurance that He has not exhausted His methods . . . He will realise the trump of love. Love will triumph through judgment, and over judgment. Love must at last accomplish its purpose.

As to predictions and types of the Messiah in Hosea's amazing book, while these are not numerous, his profound conception of divine love and forgiving grace points more directly than any specific prediction could to Bethlehem and Calvary and the right hand of God, where intercession is made for us. Dr. George Adam Smith says, "There is no truth uttered by later prophets about the Divine grace, which we do not find in germ in Hosea . . . He is the first Prophet of Grace, Israel's first Evangelist." As one of the greatest of ancient prophets, along with Isaiah and Amos, Hosea laid the foundation of *literary prophecy*. What messianic allusions we have are both clear and appealing.

The prediction as to Israel's future restoration of Israel will be fulfilled in Christ, as Paul and Peter confirm. *Forecast:* "Where it was said unto them, Ye are not my people, there it shall be said unto them, Ye are the sons of the living God" (Hos. 1:10). *Fulfillment:* "Which in time past were not a people, but are now the people of God" (I Pet. 2:10; Rom. 11:25, 26).

Then there is the prediction of the present state of Israel – "Without a king, without a prince, without a sacrifice, without an ephod" – the sign of the priest. Such withdrawals came because of their rejection of the heavenly king who was their true priest after the order of Melchizedek, and of their continued rejection of the sacrifice of the Messiah (Hos. 3:4). Yet Hosea goes on to predict Israel's glorious future, when they return to God under a second David. "Afterward shall the children of Israel return, and seek the LORD their God, and David their king" (Hos. 3:5). The David mentioned here is the Messiah, David's greater son (Jer. 30:9). As Messiah is David's son and heir, He is often called by David's name.

Further, twice over, Jesus takes Hosea's words and makes them His own. "I desired mercy, and not sacrifice" (Hos. 6:6; See Matt. 9:13). The phrase "I . . . called my son out of Egypt" (Hos. 11:1), is definitely applied to Christ's flight into Egypt (Matt. 2:15). Israel was the messianic nation, and so its history foreshadowed the Messiah in various ways. For instance, when Hosea said, "O death, I will be thy plagues; O grave, I will be thy destruction" (Hos. 13:14), he uttered words Paul remembered and applied to the Resurrection of Christ, and of His saints. The Resurrection of the new Israel (Ezek. 37), resembled the Resurrection of the Messiah (I Cor. 15:20-55). How explicit is the forecast, "The third day he will raise us up, and we shall live in his sight" (Hos. 6:2). On the third day, "His going forth is prepared as the morning." What a glad and glorious morning that was when Jesus rose from the grave! Other foregleams are clearly apparent such as the magnetism of love.

Forecast: "I drew them with cords of a man, with bands of love" (Hos. 11:4).

Fulfillment: "I, if I be lifted up from the earth, will draw all men unto me" (John 12:32, 33).

When Jesus became the Son of man, He drew us with the cords of a man, and died for us that we might be bound to Him eternally. Further, how specific is the pronouncement, "There is no saviour beside me" (Hos. 13:4). When Jesus was born it was said that "He shall save his people from their sins" (Matt. 1:21); and we are now reminded that "there is none other name under heaven given among men, whereby we must be saved" (Acts 4:12).

There are two words Hosea uses, namely, *ransom* and *redeem* (Hos. 13:14), which foreshadow what Christ accomplished for us when the cross became His bed, and a crown of thorns His pillow.

Ransom signifies being rescued by the payment of a price.

Redeem relates to one who, as the nearest of kin, had the right to acquire anything as his own, by paying the price.

Both words in their most exact sense predict what Jesus accomplished when He shed His ruby blood on our behalf.

As for the predictions of Israel's restoration Hosea gives prominence to (Hos. 1:10, 11; 2:16-20 etc.), we can spiritualize them and apply them to the revival of God's people today. But we must be careful about taking the life-rent of Israel's blessings and leaving the curses. Delitzsch says, "Interpretation is one; application is manifold." The explicit interpretation of Hosea's message is that of God's unchangeable promise to His ancient, chosen people, the Jews. Through the sacrifice of the cross, the redeemed are most precious to the heart of God. May we be preserved from sinning against His love! If we become guilty of grieving Him, such is the tenacity of His love that He will not let us go. How poignant is the divine sob, "How shall I give thee up, Ephraim?" Nothing can exceed the earnestness and love with which God entreated His erring people to return to Him. Grace abounding and love exceeding are revealed in the book of Hosea for the encouragement of all who have wandered away from the heart of love – "O Ephraim, thou hast destroyed thyself, but come home again, come home, and all will be forgiven!"

U. *Zerubbabel*

Concluding this section, as we are, with the renowned prince, Zerubbabel, we are cognizant of the fact that there are a few other Old Testament characters we might have inclured who foreshadow or typify Christ in some way or another. Those whom we have included can act as guideposts if the reader desires to extend such a phase of study. What we have discovered is that both rulers and prophets alike did only deal with the historical forces and temporal conditions of their own time. Many of them were likewise heralds of the coming kingdom of God. "The religious leverage of their message is to be found in their eschatological outlook."

When the Jewish remnant returned to Jerusalem from captivity in Babylon, Haggai, Zechariah, and Malachi became the three prophets to minister to the emancipated exiles. Among the first to return with the prophets were Zerubbabel and Joshua. The former became Governor of Jerusalem, and the latter, the High Priest. This Joshua is not to be confused with the past leader of Israel. Several bear the name in Scripture. Haggai's first address of the four his prophecy contains was addressed to Zerubbabel and Joshua. Haggai sought to arouse them to their responsibility of shaming the people out of their apathy in beautifying their own houses while the House of the Lord lay waste and in ruins. Their ministry had its desired effect for the people gave themselves to the rebuilding of the temple.

Zerubbabel stands out a most commendable ruler, and also as a fitting type of Christ. Here is a brief résumé of his history —

He was the grandson of King Jehoiachin, who was among those taken as captives to Babylon, and as heir to David's throne in Judah.

He spent most of his life in captivity during the Exile (Ezra. 2:2; Neh. 7:7).

He was among those returning to Jerusalem, where he became Governor of Judah (Hag. 1:1), under the Persians until 515 B.C.

He was given the mission to rebuild the temple (Ezra 5:2; Zech. 4:1-14).

He is pointed out as one worthy of reward in the Day of the Lord (Hag. 2:23).

He is mentioned as being an ancestor of Jesus (Matt. 1:12, 13).

Much of what is recorded of Zerubbabel refers partially to himself, and also to David's family, of which he was a member, but more particularly to the one great representative of David's line, namely, the coming Messiah. David who planned and prepared for the temple, which Solomon built, never thought that such a magnificent edifice would be destroyed, but it was when Jerusalem was plundered. Zerubbabel another descendant of David was given the task of rebuilding it and was assured by Zechariah that he would complete his mission (Zech. 4:6-9). He was also given mystic hints of yet another temple to be built by the *branch*, with the help of many from "far off" (Zech. 6:12-15). Zerubbabel was doubtless conscious of his own weakness in urging the people to rebuild the temple, but Zechariah encouraged him by telling him not to despise "the day of small things" for mountains of difficulties would be removed "not by might, nor by power, but by my [God's] spirit" (Zech. 4:6-10).

Haggai, in his last address (Hag. 2:20-23), likewise stimulated Zerubbabel to zealous efforts in the noble work of his hands. Then the prophet spoke again of the supernatural shaking of the universe and of the kingdom, but amid it all Zerubbabel the prince would be as a signet firm and immovable, because chosen of the Lord. In the Day of the Prince Messiah, he would be rewarded. In all this Zerubbabel was a type of Christ. Servant of the Lord, chosen of Him, and set as *signet* or seal upon the hand of the Father — the Express Image of His Person (Heb. 1:3).

The two olive-trees in Zechariah's vision refer to Zerubbabel the Ruler, and Joshua the High Priest, and through them to the Messiah who will combine the offices of prince and priest, who is to sit on His throne of glory as a priest, and builder of the eternal temple of God. (Zech. 3:8; 6:9-17). The *Branch* was to be of Zerubbabel – David's family, the kingly line. But Joshua the priest was crowned as represented as the *Branch* sitting on the throne of David (Zech. 6:12, 13) – a symbolic representation of the merging of the two offices of king and priest in the coming Messiah godly souls of old eagerly looked for (Luke 2:25-38).

As to the homecoming of the Jews from captivity in Babylon, the same is pictured by the prophets as a most glorious display of the Providence of God (Isa. 43:19; 54:17), and with a like deliverance of the Israelites from bondage in Egypt is typical of the liberation of sinners from spiritual bondage, and of their pilgrimage to the heavenly Jerusalem under the care of God their Saviour (Isa. 32:2; 43:16; 61:11).

O God of Bethel, by whose hand
Thy people still are fed;
Who through this weary pilgrimage
Hast all our fathers led: . . .

Chapter Two

PROPHETIC GLEAMS FROM PRESCRIBED OFFICES

A. The Prophet
B. The Priest
C. The King
D. The Daysman
E. The Surety

The Bible is like a vast Hall of Mirrors reflecting Christ in a thousand ways for us to admire and appreciate. The Greeks requested Philip, "Sir, we would see Jesus," and if we would see Him in all His beauty, majesty, power, and grace, then we must look for Him in unlikely, as well as in likely, places. One of the traditional *Sayings of Our Lord* reads, "Raise the stone, and there thou shalt find Me, cleave the wood and there am I." Spiritual eyes can discover Him in the most unexpected areas of the Word. Too often our eyes are holden as we read the Old Testament, and we see only the earthly form of prominent figures like Moses the Prophet, Aaron the Priest, David the King. If, however, we are set on finding the living word in the written Word, then the Lord will reveal Himself to our hearts through the outward type, and turning to Him in glad surprise we will exclaim, "Rabboni, *my dear Master!*"

Throughout our study we are endeavoring to prove that Jesus is prefigured not only in events and in things but also in *persons.* As to the true significance of a *type,* it can be defined as an illustration from a lower sphere of a truth belonging to a higher. What must be remembered is that no single type or symbol is sufficient to anticipate the perfection of the person and performances of Jesus. Further, in no other phase of Bible study is there so much need of "sanctified common sense" as in the handling of types. Fancy, absurd, exaggerated interpretations must be shunned. Typical teaching has suffered much abuse. But "abuse does not take away use," and no study can be so fruitful if it is only pursued prayerfully, soberly, and intelligently.

Among prescribed offices allocated to divinely chosen men in Old Testament days, the three most prominent were those of *prophet, priest,* and *king,* which we can consider together before dealing, particularly, with each separately. As the result of the Fall of Man bringing, as it did, separation from God (Rom. 5:12), his three basic needs as a sinner can only be met by One who combines in Himself the threefold office we are now to examine.

1. Through original doubt and disobedience, man was left guilty, lost, helpless, estranged from God; hence in need of the forgiveness of sin, and the impartation of a righteous character, and restoration to divine fellowship. For this recovery a sinner must have a *priest.*

2. Away from God, the source of light, man found himself in spiritual darkness, and consequently ignorant of the mind and will of God. As a sinner, he is blind to the beauty of divine truth, and in his spiritual unenlightenment requires a *prophet.*

3. The nature of man's first sin was that of rebellion against divine command and control, which quickly expressed itself in antagonism to his fellowmen, hence Cain's murder of Abel. Further, because man is a social creature, a unit in society, he

needs authoritative governmental supervision to prevent him becoming a law unto himself. In this capacity he needs a *king*.

Throughout the Old Testament times, God provided for these three basic needs of man through His chosen prophets, priests, and kings, the majority of whom were godly men. But being only human instruments and thus subject to human infirmities, they sometimes failed in their office work. Foreseeing this, God, in His love and mercy, in a past eternity planned that One should come who would perfectly combine in Himself the ministry of prophet, priest, and king, providing thereby for a needy race perfect Truth, Redemption, and Sovereignty. Fully unfolded in the New Testament is the mediatorial character of the Messiah, anointed with the Oil of the Spirit to exercise His threefold office.

As prophet, He gave commands to His church, and revealed God to man.

As priest, by His sacrifice, He made a covenant between God and man.

As King, He rules over His redeemed subjects, and will yet reign on earth.

Under the old dispensation each office had to be filled by a brother—one of the same flesh and blood, and when the vision of the coming Messiah burst upon Moses, he was given the prediction of—

"A *Prophet* from the midst of thee, of thy brethren, like unto me" (Deut. 18:15).

"Take ... Aaron thy brother, ... that he may minister unto me in the *priest's* office" (Exod. 28:1).

"One from among thy brethren shalt thou set *king* over thee" (Deut. 17:15).

The Scriptures, then, foreshadow Jesus in these three great offices—each incomplete without the others. He was to come as the *prophet,* to instruct and inform; as *priest,* to atone and intercede; as *king,* to subdue and control. Dr. A. T. Pierson tells us that

> These Prophetic, Priestly and Kingly offices cover three periods of history—
> 1. *The Prophetic,* mainly from the Fall to the Cross.
> 2. *The Priestly,* from the Incarnation to Christ's Second Coming.
> 3. *The Kingly,* from His Return to "The End."
>
> During the Prophetic Period, there was a forecast of His priesthood, in the Levitical offices and sacrifices.
>
> During the Priestly Period, a forecast of His kingship, in individual surrender of believers to His sway.
>
> There is no indication in the Word of God that Christ has ever yet assumed the Kingship; yet the whole conception of His mediatorial work rests ultimately upon this idea, as its basis.

Almost half a century ago, while pastoring a sphere in Dundee, Scotland, I had an Office Bearer, a godly man with a gift of poetry, who loved to expound the Scriptures, and set its truths out in poetic form. One of Wm. H. Robertson's productions was on Christ's threefold office—

God's Word declares that Jesus came,
A Prophet of God's Grace,
To cover sin "hath He appeared,"
His Love redeemed the race.

The Word reveals that Christ now lives
A Priest before God's Throne.
He is for us "now to appear,"
By faith, we're not alone.

God's Word foretells our Lord will come,
A King to show God's power,
A second time "shall He appear,"
Our hope in earth's dark hour.

A. *The Prophet*

Although Samuel was the virtual founder of the prophetic line, Moses called himself a prophet, and in some ways functioned as one. Yet, while Aaron was ordained in the office of priest, God said to Moses, "I have made...Aaron thy brother...thy prophet" (Exod. 7:1). While reference has already been made to the function of the prophet, this fuller coverage of same may prove profitable to the reader.

The prophet was consecrated to office by an anointing with oil (I Kings 19:16). Moses, it would seem, was the only man in Jewish history who exercised the office of prophet, priest, and king in his remarkable career. As a prophet, he was God's spokesman and lawgiver; as a priest, he communed with God face to face, and interceded for a sinful people; as a king, or captain, or deliverer, he brought Israel out of bondage. In all his obligations he was faithful (Num. 12:6-8). After his death, Joshua said of him, "There arose not a prophet since in Israel like unto Moses, whom the LORD knew face to face" (Deut. 34:10-12). What a foregleam he was of the Son of man who was to come!

In general, a prophet functioned in a twofold way: he preached and predicted, proclaimed and prophesied.

1. Witnessing for God in his own time, and to his own people, as well as to their enemies, the prophet was a *forth*-teller, heralding forth, without fear or favor, a divine message. As a patriot, he was as an "incarnate conscience" to king and people, with one object, namely, that of keeping both king and people true to God. The primary meaning of the word *prophet* is "one who speaks on behalf of another whose message may or may not include prediction of the future." As interpreters of their own time, the prophets should be read in connection with the history they refer to in order to understand the power of their utterances.

2. Witnessing for God respecting future events, the prophet was a *fore*-teller who predicted what God was to accomplish. Jonah was a *forth*-teller, a witness to his own day only, but Moses, Isaiah, and other prophets were proclaimers and predictors, declaring truths for their present and the future.

That Moses was a type of Jesus in respect to the prophetic office was confirmed by Stephen in his defense before the Council in Jerusalem. After rehearsing the mighty acts of Israel's lawgiver and deliverer, Stephen went on to say

> "This is that Moses, which said unto the children of Israel, A prophet shall the Lord your God raise up unto you of your brethren, *like unto me;* him shall ye hear" (Acts 7:37).

The qualifying phrase here is *"like unto me,"* for Christ was only like Moses in respect to his God-given ability to proclaim and predict truth. As a man, Moses was imperfect, for he slew a Gentile, and was guilty of losing his temper which caused him to speak on one occasion unadvisedly with his lips. In every way, Christ was perfect. There was never any contradiction between His character and His conduct. Let us now see how He perfectly fulfilled the office of prophet.

1. *Foregleams of His prophetic ministry.* While it is true that to Him all the prophets gave witness, it is likewise true that in their particular ministry they typified Jesus, who came as a prophet "like unto Moses." There was never any gap in the prophetic line. Although we have a 400 year silence between the Old and New Testaments, the spirit of prophecy runs on from the Old into the New. Godly souls like Anna, the prophetess, Zacharias, who prophesied, and Simeon, who knew he would not die until he had seen God's prophet from heaven, prove that even in the intertestament era there were those who eagerly anticipated the coming of the Messiah. Then there was John the Baptist, who, recognized nationally as a great prophet, was declared by Jesus to be the greatest prophet of

the former dispensation, had the mission of preparing the way for the appearance of Jesus as the prophet of Galilee (Matt. 11:9; 14:5).

It was, therefore, in this character that the Messiah had been promised and predicted, and looked for by many (Deut. 18:18; Acts 3:22; 7:37). Thus, when He came, seeing His works and hearing His words, the people said, "This is of a truth that *prophet* that should come into the world" (John 6:14). Old Testament prophets represented God to the nation, and delivered a divine message, and, in some cases, wrought miracles. When the Messiah came it would be to represent God perfectly and completely in *person,* in *proclamation,* in *performances.* As we know, because we live on this side of the cross, Jesus proved to Israel and to the world that He was indeed God's ideal prophet (Acts 3:22, 23).

2. *Recognition of His prophetic ministry.* During His public ministry it was as a prophet that He was recognized and revered (Matt. 21:11; Luke 7:16). He was described by His own disciples as "a prophet mighty in deed and word before God and all the people" (Luke 24:19).

Jesus designated Himself as a prophet (Matt. 13:57; Luke 13:33), after His entrance into such an office (John 2:13; 4:54). His quotation from Psalm 69:17 proves that He saw in Himself the fulfillment of such a forecast as a patriot and reformer. From the outset of His ministry, He knew that the nation would reject Him as *prophet,* crucify Him as *king,* and that thereafter His perpetual ministry would be *priestly.*

3. *Manifestation of His prophetic ministry.* Like the ancient prophets, Jesus functioned both as a *forth*-teller and as a *fore*-teller. Preaching to His own time, predicting the future for His own, the Jews, and the nations, constituted His oral ministry. Jesus declared the mind and will of God to the World. "I have declared... thy name, and will declare it" (John 17:26). Here we have a compendium of all that He proclaimed and prophesied. As the great preacher, His constant theme was "the righteousness of God by faith." Truth, faithfulness, salvation, lovingkindness, were some of the things which He made touching the king. Truly, His tongue was the pen of a ready writer.

Jesus, however, not only witnessed to those of His own time, but to the future as we have already seen. As the "Father of Eternity," He emphasized future truth, as well as truth related to the present. The consummation of the Gentile age, the Second Advent, the tribulation and ultimate glory of Israel, the destiny of nations, the blessed future of the church, the millennium, heaven and hell, these were themes He predicted with divine authority, and which must be fulfilled, since the prophet who foretold them is *the Truth* (John 14:6). "I have *foretold* you all things" (Mark 13:23).

B. *The Priest*

The priestly order of the Old Testament, an integral part of Israel's national and religious life, is a most fascinating subject, for it is singularly typical of Christ as priest, and also of the priesthood of all believers. In tabernacle and temple worship, the Jewish hierarchy included high priest, priest, and Levite, distinguished by different functions and different privileges. For the consecration of high priest and priest, the order was more or less the same, namely, the anointing with oil and blood, the wearing of distinctive garments, and the separation unto a solemn office. Priestly service included the offering up of sacrifices; performing the required rites in respect to leprosy, plague, mold in garments and houses; to teach the people and pray for them. It was also the duty of priests to blow trumpets – an alarm of war, at the new moon, and on the Day of Atonement. For their support they depended upon tithes, first-fruits, redemption money, and sacrificial dues of various kinds.

In the New Testament the term *priest* denotes anyone whose function it is to offer a religious sacrifice, and is used of the various ranks in the Jewish priesthood, of a Gentile priesthood (Acts 14:13), which includes Melchizedek, who was a priest before the introduction of the Aaronic priesthood, and evidently a Gentile priest; of the priestly party among the Scribes and Pharisees; of Christ; and of all those saved by His grace and power, who are called by Peter "a royal priesthood." Saved and sanctified they offer up spiritual sacrifices of prayer and praise to God through Jesus Christ (I Pet. 2:5, 9; Rev. 1:6).

Priests were consecrated to office by an anointing with oil. The term *Messiah,* meaning "the anointed One," is applied to the high priest (Lev. 4:3, 5, 16; 6:22; 8:12), and is prophetic of Him who is our high priest. Comparisons and contrasts between forecast and fulfillment are most instructive. When Jesus went up to the temple at Jerusalem, He entered by the *Sheep-Gate,* the priestly entrance, the place where sacrifices were inspected. While He did not assert His priestly office then, nevertheless, it was a highly symbolic act (John 5:1, 2). Tracing certain points of contact between the priesthood of Aaron and of Christ, we note the following.

In the Psalms, the word *priest* in the singular occurs only once, and then as a prediction of Jesus, who would come as a priest after "the order of Melchizedek" (Ps. 110:4). The parents of this ancient priest were not inscribed among the sacerdotal genealogies. Melchizedek was not of priestly descent, as those of Aaron were. Likewise the priesthood of Christ did not come of Aaronic descent. Priests came from the tribe of Levi, but Jesus sprang from Judah, and thus came after the manner of Melchizedek.

The priest of old, chosen by God, was anointed with oil when set apart for his office. *Oil* is symbolic of the Holy Spirit, and, born of the Spirit, filled with the Spirit from His birth, at His baptism Jesus was anointed with the Spirit for His ministry as prophet-priest (Acts 10:38; Ps. 45:7). The priest was distinguished by his many-colored garments, and of Jesus it was predicted, "All thy garments smell of myrrh, and aloes, and cassia, out of the ivory palaces" (Ps. 45:8. See Rev. 1:13).

Further, Aaron's was an "everlasting priesthood," that is, "entailed upon posterity," or secured to him and his seed for many generations (Num. 25:13). Priesthood was short-lived, being frequently interrupted by death. But Christ, as God's appointed high priest, is the only Perfect One, and is alive for evermore (Heb. 7:23, 24).

Priests had to represent God, and offered sacrifices for themselves, as well as for the people. They were, therefore, imperfect, being sinners. Moses of *Hebrews* is devoted to the fact that Christ is God's perfect high priest, who offered up Himself as a sacrifice for sin, but was Himself sinless, and so by His one perfect offering on the cross "perfected for ever" them that are saved through faith in Him (Heb. 9:11-26). Ancient offerings were merely types for "the blood of bulls and of goats," and could not take away sins. They were accepted in lieu of Christ's once-for-all sacrifice (Heb. 10:4, 10-14; 9:25-28; 7:23-28). Constant sacrifices were associated with the Aaronic priesthood, but Christ by His death procured a perfect salvation for a sinning race. His is an "unchangeable priesthood," in that it abides in Him, and can never pass from Him to another.

Ancient priests could only serve in the outer court, and in the holy place, going so far, but no farther. Into the holy of holies only one man, and only one day in the year, might enter, namely, the high priest. But when Christ became an "High Priest of good things to come... by His own blood... entered into Heaven itself, now to appear in the presence of God for us." He opened up for us a way of access by His cross into the holiest for every child of His. He is our mercy-seat, around whom the Shekinah-glory shines – the symbol of God's presence. As the mediating priest was essential to the ancient Jew, our security depends on our interceding priest in heaven.

As a Jew, and set apart from other Jews, the priest was one taken from his own, and shared the infirmities of his own kinsmen. Jesus had a human birth, was taken from among men, was tempted like His fellows, learned obedience through suffering, was separate from sinners in respect to their sin and infirmities, and was so qualified by His own human sympathies and perfection of character to become the great high priest (Heb. 4:15; 5:1). The sacrifices of the Jewish order although imperfect (Heb. 10:1), were yet figures of the true; and the sanctuary in which they were offered was a "worldly" structure (Heb. 9:1), or subject to destruction or decay, but Christ our great high priest is in the indestructible heaven itself interceding on our behalf. In his *Heroes and Hero-Worship,* Thomas Carlyle says that "The Hero can be Poet, Prophet, King, Priest or what you will, according to the kind of world he finds himself born into." Jesus, our Hero, is all four, or whatever you will. In Him, the best in any sphere finds perfection.

Before the Throne of God above
I have a strong, a perfect plea;
A Great High Priest, whose name is Love,
Who ever lives and pleads for me.

My name is graven on His hands,
My name is written on His heart;
I know that while in Heaven He stands
No tongue can bid me thence depart.

One with Himself, I cannot die;
My soul is purchased by His blood;
My life is hid with Christ on high,
With Christ, my Saviour and my God.

C. *The King*

That a monarchical system dominates the Bible is evidenced by the fact that the terms *king* and *kingdom* occur almost 3,000 times throughout its pages. Further, although David, the renowned Jewish king, is the conspicuous type of the kingship of Christ, the first king mentioned in the Bible was a Gentile, Amraphel, King of Shinar (Gen. 14:1. See 10:10). In the New Testament, David is the first one to be spoken of as *king* (Matt. 1:6). As a position, king, implying a sovereign prince, or chief ruler in a kingdom is used in various ways. For instance, it is applied –

To God, the supreme ruler and governor of the world.
"God is the King of all the earth" (Ps. 47:6, 7).

To Christ, who is now King of Love, and will yet be King of Kings.
"Where is he that is born King?" (Matt. 2:2; Ps. 2:6).

To Believers, or born-again Christians, who are heirs of the Kingdom of Glory.
"Made us kings and priests unto God" (Rev. 1:6; 5:10).

To Satan, ruler of all hellish and spiritual foes.
"They had a king over them... Apollyon" (Rev. 9:11).

While predictions of the coming kingship of Christ are scattered throughout the Old Testament, the

Psalms appear to be fuller than any other section of the truth of the glory of His kingdom when He shall take to Himself His right and power to reign in millennial bliss over all the earth. Further, in exact accordance with the revelation and teaching of the New Testament, the Psalms base Christ's kingdom upon His perfect sacrifice. Paul makes it clear that the kingdom, or reign of God, originates in His grace; is founded upon His power, and illustrates His governmental control (Rom. 14:17). All through the psalter we find the constant blending of sovereignty and sacrifice. We see Him as king and priest; prophet and priest, with His offices being interdependent, and inherent in the one person. While in some of the king-passages there may be a reference to Israel's great kings, David and Solomon, the language used is infinitely more glorious and mighty than their respective reigns, and must be thought of as predictions of Christ as king, and His kingdom (Ps. 2:21; 24; 45; 72; 110) are evidence of One who is coming as

A priest greater than Aaron and Melchizedek
A prophet greater than Jonah
A king greater than Solomon.

The two portraits the psalmists sketch of Christ is that of *the suffering Messiah,* as in Psalm 22; and also as the Messiah entering into *His kingdom glory* as in Psalms 2 and 24. These are the two aspects Christ Himself rebuked His disciples for not fully understanding.

> "Ought not Christ to have *suffered* these things, and to enter into His *glory*" (Luke 24:25-27).

Peter reminds us that it was the Holy Spirit who inspired Old Testament prophets to write of "the *sufferings* of Christ, and the *glory* that should follow" (I Pet. 1:11). Thus, as we have previously indicated, the cross gives the crucified Messiah the right to adorn the crown. God will give His strength to reign and prosper to the One whose head was crowned with thorns (I Sam. 2:10). That there are many striking predictions of the Messiah coming as the anointed king to establish His kingdom and reign in righteousness can be gathered from passages like Isaiah 11:1-9; Micah 4:1-5, but, as stated above, the Psalms are permeated with this predictive aspect of Christ.

Psalm 2 forecasts the coronation of Messiah as king on Mount Zion, and His interitance of the nations. When He appears as king, Jerusalem will be the seat of His universal government.

Psalm 45 displays the majesty, beauty, and glory of the king, and of His resplendent, glorious bride.

Psalm 47 emphasizes the deity of the king. Christ, as *God,* will be king of all the earth, and as *God* will sit upon the throne of His holiness.

Psalm 72 is the greatest of the messianic Psalms in that, as a whole, it forms a complete vision of Christ's kingdom so far as Old Testament revelation is concerned. The key word of the Psalm is *righteousness,* which occurs three times, verses 1-3, and describes the character of the Messiah's reign (Isa. 32:18). Here is a serviceable outline on the Psalm which preachers could extend:

1. The king's relationship, the Son of God, verse 1.
2. The king's righteousness, verses 1-3.
3. The king's reign – wholesome, 5-7; universal, 8-11.
4. The king's redemption and compassion, 12-14.
5. The king's riches, 15-17. Reign produces material and spiritual gains.
6. The king's reputation, 18-19. "Who only doeth wondrous things."

Daniel Defoe (1661-1731), in *The True-Born Englishman,* has the expressive lines

When Kings the sword of Justice
first lay down
They are not Kings, though they
possess the crown.
Titles are shadows, crowns are
empty things,
The good of subjects is the end of
Kings.

Christ will prove to be the most perfect king who ever reigned because He will never surrender the sword of justice. His title as King of Kings will not be a shadow, or His crown an empty thing, because of His own blessed and benign character. As no other sovereign has done, Christ will reach the end of kings as He seeks the eternal good of all His loving and obedient subjects. May the day be hastened when as the king, Christ will take over the control of this blighted, broken world of ours!

Hallelujah! hark! the sound,
From the centre to the skies,
Wakes above, beneath, around,
All Creation's harmonies:
See Jehovah's banner furled,
Sheathed His sword: He speaks,
'tis done;
And the kingdoms of this World
Are the Kingdom of His Son.

D. *The Daysman*

Job's intense desire for an arbiter occurs in his third speech, chapters 9 and 10. Bildad, in the previous chapter, containing his first speech had insisted upon divine justice, saying that Job's sufferings were the evidence of sin in his life, and that if he would only turn to God in penitence, relief from trial would be his. But Job answered that he was not wicked (Job 10:7); that God permitted chastisement to overtake the righteous as well as the sinful. He then pleads for one well able to adjudicate the matter.

"Neither is there any *daysman* betwixt us, that might lay his hand upon us both" (Job 9:33).

Later on in the drama, when accused by Eliphaz of stretching out his hand against God (Job 15:35), Job, out of a wounded heart, cries, "O that one might plead for a man with God, as a man pleadeth for his neighbour!" (Job 16:21).

Eli the prophet, in rebuking his sons for their sacrilege, asked, "If a man sin against the LORD, who shall entreat for him?" (I Sam. 2:25). As can be seen, these three passages are related in desire for a go-between, and are all predictive of the One who became the only mediator between God and men.

At the time when the Bible was translated from the Latin into English a common meaning of the word *daysman* was "an umpire," or one able to act as arbitrator at an appointed day – *days-man,* a man who set *days* for the hearing of disputes. The Hebrew is *jakhah,* meaning "to act as umpire, or mediator." As used by Job, the term implies an umpire or referee who hears two parties in a dispute and decides the merits of the case. The custom prevailed in eastern lands for the arbitrator or judge to put his hands upon the heads of the two parties in disagreement to show his authority and ability to render an unbiased verdict. Bildad had sought to act on God's behalf, but Job affirmed that no human being was worthy of acting as judge of God.

Some old translations give us, "Oh, that there were a daysman," instead of "Neither is there any daysman," which corresponds more with Job's later sob (Job 16:21), "Oh, that one might plead." The patriarch came to find a partial mediator in Elihu, but the perfect mediator is in Emmanuel. Job's dilemma was that although he knew that the imposition of the hand of an umpire expressed power to adjudicate between persons, and thought that there might be one on his own level, the one party; he knew of none on a level with the Almighty, the other party. Job felt that there was no possibility of justification with God unless there should be an impartial mediator who could make the cause both his own and reconcile and unite the two in himself. Paul speaks of Moses as a mediator, and says, "A mediator is not a mediator of one," that is, of one party. As W. E. Vine explains, "Here is the contrast between the Promise given to Abraham and the giving of the Law. The Law was a covenant enacted between God and the Jewish people, requiring fulfillment by both parties. But with the Promise to Abraham, all the obligations were assumed by God, which is implied in the statement 'but one is God' (Gal. 3:20)."

As to the qualifications of an umpire, or arbitrator, he had not only to be just, but have a clear understanding of the claims, complaints, and character of each of both parties, and not come to the day of judgment with any bias. The LXX version of Job's request reads, "O that there were a mediator between us!" The Gospel leaves no room for such a complaint, for in the Lord Jesus we have a blessed daysman, who has mediated between heaven and earth. "One God, and one mediator between God and men, the man Christ Jesus" (I Tim. 2:5). The deep need of the human heart can only be met in "God and Saviour" through "one Mediator between God and man – Himself, Man – Christ Jesus, Who gave Himself a ransom for all" (I Tim. 2:4-6, R.V.). That He is the perfect mediator is seen in the glorious fact that He is both God and man. Being with the Father from the dateless past, the Son knew all about the nature and demands of divine holiness and righteousness. Then by becoming man, He identified Himself with the sin of humanity, and heard the cry of hearts for emancipation from satanic thralldom. At Calvary, He had one hand on a thrice holy God demanding death for sin, and the other hand on a sin-cursed world, and through His death procured the sinner's reconciliation with God.

As W. E. Vine comments on Christ as the mediator between two parties, producing peace:

> The salvation of men necessitated that the Mediator should Himself have the nature and attributes of Him towards whom He acts, and should likewise participate in the nature of those for whom He acts—sin apart; only by being possessed both of Deity and Humanity could He comprehend the claims of the one and the needs of the other.

Because Jesus became the God-Man, we know that He laid His hand upon God and man, and as the divine daysman brought them together in peace. The same technical sense of appointing a day for dispensing justice is found in the Greek, "man's judgment," or more literally, "man's day" (I Cor. 4:3). The word *daysman* or *judge* is also immediately connected with the Scripture phrases "the *day* of the Lord" – "the *day* shall declare it" (I Cor. 3:13). If ours has been a personal experience of reconciliation to God through the blood of the cross, then saved and eternally safe we can walk the pilgrim way home singing,

> It is a human hand I hold,
> It is a hand Divine.

E. *The Surety*

Such is the magnificence of our great and glorious Lord that it takes all the direct and indirect types, symbols, and metaphors of the Bible to display the excellencies of His transcendant attributes and virtues. Even the most expressive figure of speech fails to reveal the absolute perfection of His nature and works. Here, again, is another predictive portrait of Him who came as the complete revelation of God, namely, *the surety*. Who and what is a "surety"? In modern, legal terminology he is one who is bound by the same terms as another, known as the principal, for the payment of a debt, or the performance of a duty but who, if he satisfies the obligation, is entitled to reimbursement from the principal. The latest edition of *Encyclopaedia Britannica* goes on to say that in England the term is often used broadly to describe a person who is liable for the performance of another's obligation and this includes what is usually meant by guarantor, that is, one whose liability is contingent on the default of the principal.

Surprisingly, the Biblical significance of a *surety* tallies with the legal description, or perhaps, we should put it the other way round, as many Bible laws are at the basis of many of the laws governing society today. The word has some interesting examples of suretyship, both true and false. The term carries the general idea of a pledge, or a bail, with a person becoming a surety by a solemn oath to fulfill an undertaking for another —a guarantee to be liable for the default of another, or for his appearance in court, payment of debt, etc. The New Testament usage of the term implies a bail who personally answers for anyone, whether with his life or property.

Forecast: "I will be surety for him [the lad]" (Gen. 43:9; 44:32-34).

"Put me in a surety with thee" (Job 17:3).

"Be surety for thy servant for good" (Ps. 119:122).

"My son, if thou be surety for thy friend" (Prov. 6:1; 17:18).

Fulfillment: "By so much was Jesus made a Surety of a better covenant" (Heb. 7:22).

Solomon is emphatic in warnings against the evils of a misplaced suretyship. Modern proverbs re-echo the ancient king's teaching, such as, "Be surety, and ruin or danger is at hand." We wonder whether Solomon had had bitter experiences of those who had failed in the pledge he had made on their behalf?

"He that is surety for a stranger shall smart for it: and he that hateth suretyship is sure" (Prov. 11:15).

"Take his garment that is surety for a stranger" (Prov. 20:16; 27:13).

"Be not thou one of them that strike hands, or of them that are sureties for debts" (Prov. 22:26).

It is the application of the term to Jesus that brings us to a facet of the truth of His substitutionary work so prominent in *Hebrews,* where *surety,* primarily signifying "bail," refers to "the abiding and unchanging character of Christ's Melchizedek priesthood, by reason of which His suretyship is established by God's oath. As the *Surety,* He is the Personal guarantee of the terms of the new and better covenant, secured on the ground of His perfect sacrifice" (Heb. 7:22-27).

Shakespeare has the lines

> The wound of peace is surety,
> Surety secure.

He who came as our peace was wounded in order that we might have a "surety secure." Wounded for our transgressions, but now alive forevermore, the Saviour guarantees the terms of "the better covenant" for His people. He acted as a guarantee so as to secure the redemption from sin which otherwise would not have been obtained. Judah, the son of Jacob, provides us with a striking prediction of all Jesus accomplished when He became the surety for His friends. Dr. William Clow calls the appearance of Judah before his brother Joseph to offer himself as bail on Benjamin's behalf, one of the tenderest scenes of the Old Testament Scripture:

> Read the heart-shaking address of Judah, in which he makes his appeal to spare Benjamin. The cup had been found in Benjamin's sack. The youth seemed to be a wilful, ungrateful, and pitifully foolish thief. There seemed to be no reason why he, and he only, should not suffer the

> full penalty of the crime. But Judah had given *surety* to his father for him. He steps forward, and after declaring Jacob's love and longing for Benjamin, he offers himself as a bondman in his room. Who cries out on the injustice of that sacrifice? Who does not feel that had Joseph been unwilling to accept Judah's bond-service for Benjamin's he would have read his *bond* with the merciless eyes of a Shylock?
>
> So Jesus our Brother stands to bear our sin and to do homage to God's broken law. So He stands in the judgment hall of God for us. As the chief may die for his clan, as the king may die for his people, as the true priest, whether he bear an outward consecration or not, is always dying for men, so Jesus met the shafts of judgment for, and quenched them in His death. Those who accept His death as their sacrifice receive the Atonement.

Through Jesus, as our bail, we were liberated from the bondage of sin, and He is before the Father as our security, for He paid sin's debt. He is our surety because of God's oath, and because of all He is in Himself. He cannot go back on His promise or break His oath. He has given His pledge and cannot go back on it.

> His oath, His covenant, His blood,
> Support me in the 'whelming flood;
> When all around my soul gives way,
> He then is all my hope and stay.

Chapter Three

PROPHETIC GLEAMS FROM HISTORICAL EVENTS

The Ark	The Healing Tree	The Rod of Aaron
The Ladder	The Manna	The Brazen Serpent
The Blood-Sprinkled Door	The Smitten Rock	The Six Cities of Refuge
The Miraculous Bush	The Two Stone Tables	The Mount of Pisgah
The Two Pillars	The Nazarite Vow	The Twelve Stones
The Red Sea	The Magnificent Benediction	

It is to be regretted that Bible typology and symbolism have been carried to excess, with efforts to trace in every detail of some portion of Scripture some fanciful notion or forecast. Such abuse of figurative teaching has brought the study of types into disrepute. As we are discovering in this meditation of ours, a probability of typical intent and meaning, which sometimes approaches certainty, can be gathered from so much of the Bible. There is, therefore, no need to let imagination run wild. Professor Moses Stuart expressed the view that "Just so much of the Old Testament is to be accounted typical as the New Testament affirms to be so, and no more." But such a position is somewhat arbitrary, for New Testament writers did not, by any means, exhaust the types of the Old.

Having dealt with the prophetic and typical significance of persons, we now come to many historical events that under the guidance of Providence became striking predictions of good things to come, as found principally in *Exodus* with its wilderness journey from Egypt to Canaan, and the future picture of the pilgrimage of the people of God in *Numbers*. We readily concede that there are lesser incidents and circumstances in Old Testament Scripture suggestive of symbolic and spiritual truth we could have included in this section, but we have only cited those most prominent episodes as guideposts for the reader's more extensive study of such a fascinating aspect of Bible study and exposition. Our Lord's application of the serpent uplifted on a pole to Himself hanging on a tree proves the validity of typical teaching.

A. *The Ark*

The deluge in Noah's day stands out as the greatest catastrophic event the earth has experienced – a universal catastrophe necessitated by universal corruption. Noah, "a preacher of righteousness" (II Pet. 2:5), bore testimony to a generation that had abandoned righteousness, but without avail, for, apart from his own family, the rest of mankind perished in the waters of the flood. This man of faith (Heb. 11:7), who walked with God (Gen. 6:9), had a character like "a towering mountain that rises from a plain in which there is no other elevation," witnessed among men who had no faith and who walked only after the flesh. God's Spirit, striving with the multitudes to revolt against evil, was persistently resisted, and at last the warning came that the day of grace would end. "God's patience and forbearance," says Matthew Henry "towards provoking sinners is sometimes long, but always limited."

When the die was cast, and the destruction by water of all the corrupt and violent was decreed, we read that such a decision "grieved him [God] at his heart" (Gen. 6:6). Was not such a quality in the divine nature a forecast of the sorrow of the breaking heart of Jesus when, abandoning Jerusalem to its doom, He looked over the city and wept for its inhabitants who had wilfully rejected Him? With our finite minds we cannot enter fully into these sorrows of the divine heart that are the result of human guilt. But there was not a complete annihilation of the whole race. Because of God's promise of a Saviour (Gen. 3:15), Noah, with his family, was spared from the destroying waters of judgment, to give the world a new beginning. Thus we come to consider the Ark of Mercy.

In the *ark* we have a foregleam and figure of the salvation God was to provide for a sinning race, in the person of His Son, who, as the man Christ Jesus, was to become "a covert from the tempest" (Isa. 32:2). For Noah, God provided a *vessel,* but for our deliverance from sin and judgment — *a victim!* Noah had an *ark* — we have an *advocate*. For those who have use of sermonic material we herewith group together a few similarities between fact and figure, subject and symbol, even and extension.

1. Because God saw that the sin of man was great in the earth, He said, "I will destroy man whom I have created from the face of the earth" (Gen. 6:5, 7).

Peter, confirming the fact that the world that then was, overflowed with water, and that a sinful race perished shows that such a dreadful event was a forecast of a still more devastating destruction, when both the "heavens and the earth, which are now, by the same word are kept in store, reserved unto fire against the day of judgment . . . of ungodly men" (II Pet. 3:6-11).

2. The ark was God's plan, and had to be made according to His specifications. "God said unto Noah . . . make thee an ark of gopher wood" (Gen. 6:13, 14). Divinely conceived, the ark proves that God is the Provider of salvation. All symbols of salvation, such as the ark, the Paschal Lamb, the brazen serpent, indicate that they are thoughts of God.

When Jesus came as a Saviour, He came as a revelation of the mind of God. Because He was slain before the foundation of the word, God provided a remedy *before* the disease. The plan of Redemption was God's, "Whom *God* hath set forth to be a propitiation through faith in his blood" (Rom. 3:24, 25). In a past eternity, love drew salvation's plan.

> God's thoughts are love, and Jesus is
> The loving form they find;
> His love lights up the vast abyss
> Of the Eternal Mind.

3. The explicit purpose of the ark was the preservation of life (Gen. 6:19). Noah prepared the ark according to the divine plan "to the saving of his house," consisting of "eight souls"; and also for the elected animals and birds for the continuation of wildlife. The salvation of man and beast consisted in deliverance from the flood, not a spiritual salvation. Noah was an heir of righteousness, which is by faith (Heb. 11:7). While nothing is said about Noah's wife and family being fellow-heirs of righteousness, it may be that they were brought to a spiritual deliverance as the result of the physical one they experienced.

As the ark was a place of safety, so we have fled for refuge, and lay hold of the hope set before us (Heb. 6:18). The Gospel, like the ark, speaks of deliverance from sin, deliverance from the judgment of God upon the ungodly (John 5:24). The only deliverance a sinner can find comes through the operation of divine grace (Eph. 2:5). Thus the ark is a type of Christ, the only refuge of His people from present sin and coming judgment.

4. The ark represented not only *deliverance* for Noah and his family, but *destruction* for the rest of the earth. For the ante-diluvians the flood was one of judgment, with the waves and billows of wrath going over them (Ps. 42:7). Eight souls were saved *from* death; all the rest were swallowed up *in* death.

Is this not so with the Gospel, which either converts or condemns? The same sun melting the wax hardens the clay. This is the dual effect of the truth, and of Christian witness Paul declares when he speaks of believers as being a "sweet savour of Christ, in them that are saved, and *in them that perish*" (II Cor. 2:15, 16).

5. The *conception* of the ark was divine – its *construction* human. So it is said of Noah that "he prepared an ark." God commanded the ark to be made (Gen. 6:14) and Noah made it (Heb. 11:7). Such a co-operation of the human with the divine is found in other directions, such as "The sword of the Lord, and of Gideon."

When it came to Christ, the Ark of our Salvation, conception and execution were combined, for in the Deliverer, a divine nature was united to a human nature, with the Son of God becoming the Son of Mary. For ourselves, we are privileged to be "workers together with . . . God" (II Cor. 6:1). Paul says, "I have planted, Apollos watered; but God gave the increase" (I Cor. 3:6).

6. The ark had to be fashioned of *gopher wood* (Gen. 6:14), believed to be the wood of the cypress which grew in abundance in Babylon. It was from here that Alexander obtained the wood to build his fleet. Renowned for its strength and durability, it was the most suitable material for ship building. "The essence of art is that what you do should be appropriate." The Bible clearly teaches that God chooses that which is fittest for His purpose, even when He uses the things men despise.

For our spiritual deliverance, God chose the very best for the worst of earth, namely His own beloved Son. "There was no other good enough, To pay the price of sin." We are secure in Him, for He is the strongest and mightiest of all. Further, God always provides for us that which He requires us to use in His service, whether it be strength (II Cor. 12:9), money (Ezra 1:6), words (Mark 13:11), wisdom (I Cor. 12:8), or opportunity (Gal. 6:10). In building for eternity we are told of the material to use that will stand the test, not of water, but of fire (I Cor. 3:13).

7. Among the directions Noah received from God for building the ark was the division of its space into various compartments. "Rooms shalt thou make in the ark" (Gen. 6:14). These included living quarters for Noah and his family, and separate stalls for the different kinds of animals. God instructed His servant to distinguish between things that differed. Beasts were not to be treated as if they were human beings, nor human beings as if they were beasts. As Noah's age was a most violent one, we can imagine how the animal creation became contaminated by the same spirit and multitudes of beasts suffered in the judgment of the flood. For those in the ark, there would be separate stalls, for the time for the lion to lie down with the lamb had not yet come.

The principle of arrangement Noah

was compelled to act upon was evidence of the fact that each thing in God's creation has its own proper place. Perhaps the ark was a foreshadowing of those distinctions between the clean and the unclean that became a distinctive feature of the Mosaic economy and also of our life in Christ (Gen. 7:2; Lev. 11:42; II Cor. 6:17). What havoc is wrought when we try to mix the flesh with the Spirit!

8. The ark had to be "pitched within and without," thereby providing it with double resistance against the flood waters seeping in. The Hebrew word for *pitch* suggests a "covering," and as far as the rain was concerned such a covering was invulnerable. Not a drop of water from the stormclouds could penetrate the divinely ordered shelter. With the bitumen surrounding and covering the ark within and without, Noah passed safely through the judgment which the guilty of the earth suffered. The waves and billows of the flood waters beat against the pitch-protected ark in vain.

How rich in symbolism is this specific instruction of covering the ark with *pitch*, especially when we remember that this very word is the same as given in *Atonement* in the Old Testament. "It is the blood that maketh an atonement for the soul" (Lev. 17:11; Num. 5:8, etc.). Is not a continuing cover from sin the prime blessing of Christ's atoning work? As Adam and Eve were covered with the skins of animals offered in sacrifice, so born-again believers are covered by Christ's righteousness. Thus the covering of the Garden, and of the ark foreshadowed the shelter of the cross. "Oh, safe and happy shelter!" It is the redeeming blood that provides us with salvation and safety. In Christ, we will remain unscathed by "the judgment of the great day" (John 5:24). Who or what can touch those who have, by faith, retreated into the shadow of the cross?

9. The ark, like the ancient city of Troy, had only one way by which it could be entered. "The door of the ark shalt thou set in the side thereof" (Gen. 6:16). God not only provided a refuge for Noah, but the exclusive way into it. Further, once Noah and his family and all the selected beasts and birds were in the ark, God Himself shut them in. "The Lord shut him in" (Gen. 7:16) — and the same divine hand shutting them in shut out the multitudes of sinners for whom the day of grace was over. It was impossible for those shut in to get out. How apt are the anonymous lines:

Shut in? Ah, yes, that's so,
As far as getting out may go.
Shut in away from earthly cares,
But not shut out from Him who
 cares.

Shut in from many a futile quest,
But Christ can be your daily Guest.
He's not shut out by your four walls,
But hears and answers all your calls.

Shut in with God. Oh, that should be
Such a wonderful opportunity.
Then after you have done your best,
In God's hands safely leave the rest.

The fulfillment of such a forecast is not hard to seek. Did not Jesus say, "I am the Way," and "I am the Door, by Me, if any man enter in he shall be saved"? Jesus never said, "I am *a* Door," as if there were other ways into fellowship with God. The door into the ark was wide enough for all entering such a ship of safety. The weighty elephant as well as the small lamb could enter. Such is the door set before sinners in the Gospel of divine grace. Greater sinners than Paul (I Tim. 1:15) have found the door wide enough for them to enter. Further, the door was in the *side* of the ark, and it is through Christ's riven side we enter into peace. Jesus used the illustration of Noah and the ark when He warned those around Him about being engrossed with the things of this world *"until*... the flood came and destroyed them all" (Luke 17:26, 27). Once the door of grace is closed, those outside will be irrecoverably lost, while those on the inside will be eternally saved (See Matt. 25:10, 11).

> One Door, and only one,
> And its sides are two—
> Inside—Outside
> Which side are you?

10. Last of all, the ark had a curious *window,* as well as a solitary door. Situated on the top of the ark, this window was something like a skylight – "In a cubit shalt thou finish it above" (Gen. 6:16). About eighteen inches square, through this roof-window the light passed into the whole of the ark, by means of the openings in the floors of each of its stories. It would seem as if the position of this window was God's way of directing Noah's gaze to the blue expanse above. He was not to look *out* on the angry waters of the deluge, but *up* to the everlasting throne, for succor and hope. Daniel, you will recall, opened his window toward Jerusalem (Dan. 6:10). Although Noah's window was small, the uplook was vast. Through a very small piece of dark glass you can look into the face of the sun.

C.H.M., in his famous *Notes,* reminds us that

> The Lord secured with His own omnipotent hand, the Door, and left Noah the window from which he might look upward to the place from whence all judgment emanated, and see no judgment remained for him. The saved family could look *upward,* because the window was "above" (Gen. 6:16). They could not see the waters of judgment, nor the death and desolation which those waters had caused. God's Salvation—*the gopher wood,* stood between them and all these things. They had only to gaze upward into a cloudless Heaven, the eternal dwelling-place of the One Who had condemned the World and saved them.

The question is, Are we enjoying our window, or are we walking in happy communion with Him who has saved us from coming wrath, and made us heirs and expectants of coming glory? Too many are blind and cannot see afar off (II Pet. 1:9); but we are thrice blessed if we are cultivating a diligent, prayerful fellowship with Him who has eternally shut us in in Christ our ark.

B. *The Ladder*

The life of Jacob is crowded with vicissitudes highly symbolic of Christ and of Christian truth. It would seem as if our Lord had Jacob's remarkable vision of a ladder going up from earth to heaven when He said to Nathanael, "Verily, verily, I say unto you, Hereafter ye shall see heaven open, and the angels of God ascending and descending upon the Son of man" (John 1:51). Jacob's flight from home because of parental favoritism, and his experiences during the journey to Padan-Aram, are covered in Genesis 28 – a chapter containing a leave-taking, a wedding, a dream, a soliloquy, a memorial, and a vow. We cannot study the character and conduct of Jacob without seeing how God graciously overrules human folly and weakness. While he reaped what he had sown, God took the occasion to teach the patriarch the deeper lessons of His tender grace and perfect wisdom.

Presently, we are concerned with the wonderful, unforgettable vision Jacob had as he drew near to the ancient city of Luz (Gen. 28:11-15). Compelled to be an exile from his father's home in consequence of parental deceit, and his part in such deceitful acting, yet Jacob would never have learned the meaning of *Bethel* had he remained at home. So, although driven from Isaac's house, he came to taste, in some measure, the blessedness and solemnity of *God's house.* Overtaken by the swift-coming Eastern night, some twelve miles north of Jerusalem, wearied with his journey, Jacob laid his head upon a stone and slept. Being in the helplessness of sleep, God had the weary wanderer in the very position in which He could meet him and unfold His purposes of grace and glory. The physical condition at this time was so typical of Jacob's helplessness and nothingness in himself – a condition necessary for the reception of the unfolding of the divine purpose respecting Jacob and his seed.

> "He dreamed, and behold a ladder set up on the earth, and the top of it reached to heaven: and behold the angels of God ascending and descending on it" (Gen. 28:12).

Four times over we have the exclamation, *Behold!* (Gen. 28:12, 13, 15). Andrew Fuller says: "Almost every particular is introduced by the sacred writer with the interjection *Behold.*" The vision Jacob received was regarded with wonder, for he was made to see things "the angels desire to look into" (I Pet. 1:12). Jacob's dream was full of Jacob's God. May it be so with our dreams! Dreams can be God's voice to our hearts. "The stuff that dreams are made of" may be woven by the hands of the angels, and there may be worked into them the delicate tracery of divine grace, tenderness, and purpose. When Jacob awoke out of his dreams, the polluted suburb of a heathen city seemed to him as "the gate of heaven." All of us love to sing the poetic setting of Poetess Adams, in her memorable hymn *Nearer, My God, to Thee.*

> Tho' like a wanderer,
> The sun gone down,
> Darkness comes over me,
> My rest a stone;
> Yet in my dreams I'd be
> Nearer, my God, to Thee,
> Nearer to Thee.
>
> Then with my waking thoughts
> Bright with Thy praise,
> Out of my stony griefs
> Bethel I'll raise;
> So by my woes to be
> Nearer, my God, to Thee,
> Nearer to Thee.

What actually concerns us about Jacob's dream is the symbolic and spiritual significance of the *ladder* he saw going up from earth to heaven. The bridging of the gulf from earth to heaven the patriarch saw was a prophetic picture of the cross of Christ which has forever bridged the gulf from our lost and helpless condition as sinners into eternal fellowship with Him who dwells above.

1. *The bottom of the ladder touched earth.* The record says it was "set on the earth," meaning in the heathen, Canaanitish city of Luz Jacob found himself. First of all, that ladder symbolized that the way to heaven was an ascent. A ladder, when in use, is placed at the perpendicular for the user to climb *up.* The way to the earthly temple in Jerusalem was uphill, forecast in the *Songs of Degree,* or *Ascent,* Psalms 120-134, where the thought of a gradual ascent is prevalent. The degrees may be regarded as representing the rounds or rungs of the ladder by which pilgrims *went up* to worship (Gen. 124:4).

Often a ladder is not long enough to reach the part of a building needing attention, but the ladder Jacob saw went all the way from earth into heaven. It is blessed to know that there is a way to heaven from anywhere on earth, all because it was on earth that the wondrous works of acceptance with God was accomplished. Jacob was afraid as he realized that the world of everyday was not cut off from the spiritual world and exclaimed, "How dreadful is this place!" But at all times and in all places heaven is open to earth. An English poet of the late nineteenth century wrote of

> The traffic of Jacob's ladder
> Pitched betwixt Heaven and Charing Cross.

It was on this earth that the ladder commenced – when Jesus lived, labored, died, and from which He rose again and also ascended. Through the finished work of Calvary, every obstacle to the fulfillment of the divine blessing for men was removed, and now men can ascend heavenward on the ladder of faith.

2. *The top of the ladder reached heaven.* The ladder formed the medium of communication between two points, far removed from earth by man's iniquity. Dives saw no ladder from hell to heaven. All he saw was a "great gulf fixed" (Luke 16:26). Poets may refer to earth as "The Vestibule of Heaven," but with all its corruption and rejection of heavenly values, it is not much of a lovely vestibule. Yet Jacob could say of the foul spot where he had his vision, "This is the gate of heaven" (Gen. 28:17). Through that gate, and down the ladder, the glory from above shone; and so

> The men of Grace have found
> Glory begun below.

If our feet are on the Ladder of Grace, then, positionally we are already seated with Christ in the heavenlies.

3. *The ladder had heavenly climbers.* Angels ascending and descending the ladder can indicate that the way up to God is a guarded way. The Earl of Leicester said to Queen Elizabeth I, as he saw her once at a high window,

> I would climb to thee,
> But I fear to fall.

This may be one reason why so many do not start for heaven. The ascent seems to be too steep, and they are afraid of falling. They forget all the forces of heaven are engaged to bear them up; that the angels are sent to minister to the heirs of salvation (Heb. 1:14). It is most interesting to observe the movement of the angels. Jacob saw them not *descending* then *ascending*, as we might have thought, as their abode is in heaven, but the reverse, *ascending* and *descending*. The angelic climbers were around Jacob on the earth, and so went up and down. Jesus taught His disciples about guardian angels of little children here on earth with all its perils.

The true interpretation of the ladder is given by Jesus Himself, who saw in it a prediction of Himself as the only way up to God (John 14:6; Acts 4:12). "Jesus is not three-fourths of the way, but the whole way." He is the fulfillment of all Jacob saw in his dream. Now the angels ascend and descend not upon a ladder, but upon the man Christ Jesus. When He was born of Mary, communication between earth and heaven, which Jacob's ladder prefigured commenced, and His presence on earth made it a heaven. The constant activity of angels is evident in His life while here below. These heavenly messengers ministered unto Him in His temptation, agony, death, and resurrection. Yet it was a prophecy Jesus uttered when He said, "Hereafter ye shall see heaven open, and the angels of God ascending and descending upon the Son of man" (John 1:51) – a prediction to be literally fulfilled when He comes again and "all the holy angels with him" (Matt. 25:31).

As for the rungs of the heavenly ladder, what are they but conviction of sin, salvation by faith, blessed assurance, sanctification by the Spirit, meditation of Scripture, unceasing communion with heaven. As for the heavenly climbers, they are ever on the wing, *ascending* with our prayers, worship, devotion, and longings to reach the end of the ladder; and *descending* with the never-ending store of grace, power, and blessing. Jacob's ladder, then, is a striking and suggestive picture of Him by whom God came down into the depth of human need, and by whom also He brings the repentant sinner up nigh to Himself, to be in His presence forever.

> There let my way appear
> Steps unto Heaven,
> All that Thou sendest me,
> In mercy given;
> Angels to beckon me
> Nearer, my God to Thee,
> Nearer to Thee.

C. *The Blood-Sprinkled Door*

If in *Genesis* "persons" are more or less prominent as prophetic portraits of the Christ who was to come, in *Exodus* conspicuous "events" seem to stand as predictions of the life and work of Him to whom Moses gave witness in *The Pentateuch,* or the first five books of the Bible. Among the events Israel encountered, none was so terrible as the last plague — the death plague — so disastrous to the family life and national economy of Egypt as she became a nation with drawn blinds. "There was not a house where there was not one dead" (Exod. 12:30). The full story of the last contest with Pharaoh, and the judgment upon the firstborn in every home, and among the cattle is graphically recorded in Exodus 11-12. As there was light in every Jewish home when the ninth plague of darkness plunged every Egyptian home into a thick darkness that could be felt, so every family circle in Israel remained intact, but death plunged all Egyptians into family bereavement. Thus there was a difference between the Egyptians and Israel.

Moses foretold his people of God's drastic purpose and warned them of the necessity of being ready to leave Egypt as soon as the blow struck, emancipating them from the cruel bondage of centuries. This is why the second book of the Bible is named *Exodus,* meaning "a going out," and is, as we further see, symbolic of the sinner's deliverance from the slavery and thralldom of iniquity. An event of deep significance in Israel's future history, and also in the realm of Christian truth was that of *the Passover,* which was to mark the beginning of a new year for the nation. Israel was to learn that from now on she was to live and act as a redeemed nation. This is why *Exodus* is peculiarly the book of Redemption. C.H.M. *Notes* comments,

> There is here a very interesting change in the order of things. The common or civil year was rolling on in its ordinary course, when Jehovah interrupted it in reference to His people, and thus, in principle, taught them that they were to begin a new era in company with Him; their previous history was henceforth to be regarded as a blank. Redemption was to constitute the first step in *real life.*

Henceforth, Israel was to have relationship with God in worship, fellowship, and service hitherto unknown — all of which is illustrative of those redeemed by the more precious blood of Jesus. Our life is of no account from the divine standpoint until we begin to walk with God, conscious that ours is a complete salvation and settled peace through the blood of the everlasting covenant. When the Redeemer enters a man's heart, life is then spelt with a capital *L,* for he becomes a new creation in Christ Jesus. The worldly speaks of "seeing life," but Jesus said, "He that believeth not the Son shall not *see* life" (John 3:36). The only way to "see life" is to be sheltered by God's slain Lamb. "He that hath the Son *hath life*" (I John 5:12).

In all the particulars, each home had to offer and slay in the evening a male lamb without blemish and then sprinkle the blood on the two sideposts and lintel of the door of every house, we have a remarkable type of the Lamb of God who became "our passover sacrificed for us" (I Cor. 5:7, 8). This settled beyond all question the predictive aspect of the termination of Israel's bondage by blood. Those paschal lambs offered on Jewish altars became both the center of unity and the ground of peace. The blood-sprinkled doors assured all behind them that when death was doing its deadly work in Egypt, it would have no dominion over them.

"When I see the blood, I will pass over you" (Exod. 12:13). It is from this assurance that the term *the Passover* arose. The application of the blood of sprinkling secured protection and peace for every house so marked. The sentence of death was executed upon Egypt, but Israel experienced mercy in an unblemished substitute, a divinely appointed ground of deliverance from death and of inner peace, namely, the blood of Atonement. Egypt suffered death for its sin, but Israel was preserved from death through the death of a lamb – a figure of the True.

Details regarding participation in the paschal feast are most explicit. The lamb had to be eaten at night. Roasted with fire, unleavened bread and bitter herbs were added. Such a process of eating is pregnant with spiritual meaning. We not only shelter under the blood of the Lamb but feed by faith, upon His person. As *leaven* is consistently the type of evil, eating with unleavened bread suggests separation from all that is alien to the holy nature of the unblemished Lamb as Paul makes clear in the exhortation about eating our Passover "with the unleavened bread of sincerity and truth" (I Cor. 5:7, 8). As for "the bitter herbs," the same remind us that we must remember all that the Lamb "suffered *for us*." Our hearts are subdued as we think of the dark night the Lord passed through.

Then there is a further spiritual lesson to be gleaned from this most instructive ordinance. It had to be eaten by those who were prepared to leave behind the land of bondage, darkness, and death, and journey on to the land of promise. So with loins girded, feet shod, staff in hand, the people ate in haste (Exod. 12:11). Having been made a redeemed people, they were now to become a pilgrim, expectant and dependent people. So "the shod feet declared their preparedness to leave Egypt; the staff was the expressive emblem of pilgrimage, leaning on something outside themselves. Precious characteristics of ourselves as members of God's redeemed family."

Further, God ordained the feast to be a *memorial,* and kept as much to the Lord throughout the generations, which the Jews have never failed to do. After thousands of years, *the Passover,* without sacrifice – Israel is now "without a sacrifice" (Hos. 3:4) – is observed the world over by orthodox Jews. For the church, the Lord's Supper He Himself instituted is the memorial feast she observes. It was while, as a Jew, He was keeping the Passover that Jesus gave the feast its fulfillment in Himself as the slain Lamb providing salvation, safety, and sustenance. "Take eat . . . Drink ye all of it" (Matt. 26:17-29; I Cor. 11:12-34). In loving remembrance we sit around His table and meditate upon all He accomplished when as the Lamb He delivered us from the bondage of sin and the fear of death.

By Christ, redeemed, in Christ
 restored,
We keep the memory adored,
And show the death of our dear
 Lord
Until He come.

My favorite illustration is that of a monument to a lamb: A man, fond of travel, always kept his eyes open for anything unique or unusual in the cities he visited. During a tour of a certain town he was attracted by a somewhat remarkable spire over a public building. About two-thirds of the way up he noticed that the stone figure of a lamb had been inserted. Then, from its back, the spire continued its course.

Stopping a passer-by, the traveler said, "Excuse me, friend, but I am a stranger here, and wonder whether you could tell me if there is a story behind that unusual spire?"

"Yes," the man replied, "the spire has a story. I live around here, and saw this building go up. When the masons reached the part indicated by the stone lamb, one of them lost his balance and fell. As you see, it was a good way up."

"Was he killed?" the interested traveler asked.

"No," said the local man, "that's the miracle. When his friends hurried down, expecting to find his mangled body on the pavement, there he was, shaken and badly bruised, but with hardly a bone broken. And the reason for his miraculous escape from death was a lamb. Several lambs were on their way to slaughter, and as the mason fell, he landed on the back of one of them. The lamb was killed, of course, but saved the mason's life. The builder was so impressed with the miracle that he had that stone lamb placed there as a lasting tribute to a lamb dying to save a stoneman from a terrible death."

One can imagine the traveler's reaction to such a story. But what must have been the feelings of the mason whose life had been spared? How he must have been impressed by the fact that he owed his life to an innocent lamb!

Our sins should have crushed us. We deserved eternal death, but the load fell on God's Lamb; He was crushed, and we are free!

But the lamb that was the instrument of sparing the mason's life was an unconscious victim. Having no forethought, it did not know what a terrible death awaited it, and having no will power, it could not have refused to die for a man.

How different was the sacrifice of Christ, God's Lamb, on our behalf! He *knew* He was to die as the sinless substitute for sinners. He was born to die for our sins. His death was a voluntary one, for His life was not taken – it was given. Had He wished, He could have made His blood-stained cross His throne, and meted out judgment upon His enemies. But He remained on the cross. He knew that it was only as "the Lamb, the bleeding Lamb" that He could give eternal life to all who are dying in their sins.

Within many a blood-sprinkled home there may have been those who wondered whether the sight of the blood would guard them from death, or whether they were worthy of being preserved from such. But doubtless a personal unworthiness had nothing to do with their deliverance from death. The divine Word upon which assurance rests was, "When *I* see the *blood,* I will pass over you." Thus all Israelites were not only saved but *safe* within their blood-covered homes. "If a hair of an Israelite's head could be touched, it would have proved Jehovah's word void and the blood of the lamb valueless." But we know the blood of the victim became the means of preservation from the wrath of God; and how by partaking of its flesh, the people were strengthened for their journey as they left doomed Egypt (Exod. 12:27, 46; John 19:36).

Most of the events recorded in Exodus are presented as types of Christ and of Christian experience, and of the symbolic teaching of the Passover Lamb there can be no doubt, for God has told us that it was a prediction of His Lamb who would be led to slaughter. "*Christ our Passover* is sacrificed for us: therefore let us keep the feast." The following list of "Forecast" and "Fulfillment" could form the basis of a message on *Redemption From Death* –

1. *It was a slain lamb.* "Kill it in the evening" (Exod. 12:6). A sacrificial lamb; not a living one, availed for the Israelites in the hour of judgment on Egypt. Paul was determined to know nothing among men, "save Jesus, and *him crucified*" (I Cor. 2:2). True, He is alive forevermore, but we are saved in virtue of the death He died for us.

2. *It was an unblemished lamb.* "Your lamb shall be without blemish" (Exod. 12:5). Had it been deformed, diseased, or old and decrepit, it would not have been a worthy offering to a holy God. We have been "redeemed . . . with the precious blood of Christ, as of a lamb without blemish and without spot" (I Pet. 1:18, 19). The absolute holiness of the life He lived added to the efficacy of the death He died.

3. *It was a lamb whose blood was applied to door-posts* (Exod. 12:7). The sprinkled lintels were the token of safety and preservation. If the Saviour's blood is on us and on our children because of our acceptance of Him, then we are safe forevermore.

4. *It was a lamb with unbroken bones.* "Neither shall ye break a bone thereof" (Exod. 12:46). What a foregleam of Calvary this was! While it was the custom to break the bones of those who were crucified, the Scripture was fulfilled for Jesus: "A bone of Him shall not be broken" (John 19:36).

5. *It had to be a lamb for every home.* "A lamb for an house" (Exod. 12:3). In every Egyptian home, there was a dead child, and a dead lamb – the sign of divine judgment. But over every Jewish home was the blood – symbol of death, yet of deliverance from death. The Jews feasted on the lamb, which was what the Egyptians could not do on the perished carcasses of lambs.

6. *It was a lamb to be memorialized.* "An ordinance for ever" (Exod. 12:14). The people were to reckon their life as a nation from the day of the Passover. God's Lamb came to redeem us from the bondage of sin, and that we might receive new birth (John 3:7; Gal. 4:3-6).

7. *It was by a lamb the people were sanctified* (Exod. 13:1-19). All the firstborn in Israel, redeemed by the blood of a lamb, were to be sanctified, or set apart for the Lord. Does not the New Testament remind us that having been bought with the price of the shed blood, we are likewise sanctified by the blood of Jesus? (Heb. 10:14, 29).

Not all the blood of beasts,
On Jewish altars slain,
Could give the guilty conscience peace,
Or wash away the stain.

But Christ, the heavenly Lamb,
Takes all our sins away;
A sacrifice of nobler name,
And richer blood than they.

D. *The Miraculous Bush*

Before we step out with the Israelites and follow them in their pilgrimage through the wilderness, let us go back a little and think of a most unusual event that happened to Moses. God called him to be the leader and commander of the people until they reached the border of the Promised Land. Already we have considered the prophetic and typical aspects of this great figure of whom Jesus could say "Moses wrote of me." All we desire to stress at this point is the significance of the *burning bush* which he encountered as he received the divine commission to bear the oversight of God's people for forty years. At eighty years of age, Moses saw a common little thorn bush of the desert, ablaze with God, and what he saw and heard became his source of strength for the dangerous and difficult tasks ahead.

After eighty years of brooding over the sufferings and slavery of his people, and over the glorious prophecies and promises of God, the clear, direct call came to deliver His people, and lead them out of Egypt and through the wilderness. Moses might have succeeded Pharaoh, for being the adopted son of Pharaoh's daughter made him a possible heir to the throne. But Moses clung to the religion of his own home, and in spite of all that Egypt offered him, he esteemed the reproach of Christ of greater wealth than all the treasures of Egypt. Thus, at forty years of age he chose rather to suffer affliction with the people of God than delight himself with the passing pleasures of Pharaoh's court and land (Heb. 11:24-26). Out he went into the desert, to spend another forty years, enduring trials, being upheld by the sight of Him who is invisible. How those years of loneliness and hard labor developed the sturdy qualities regarded for the coming leadership of Israel.

While in Egypt, Moses received the highest form of education and became a well-learned man in all the wisdom of Egypt's schools. But he had something more to learn – lessons he could only give heed to in "the backslide of the desert," which was where God and Moses met. To learn of God, he had to be alone *with* God. "In the desert God will teach thee." Paul learnt more in Arabia than ever he had learnt at the feet of Gamaliel. We may shrink from the tuition of the desert, but that is often where nature is laid in the dust, and God alone exalted. There are no distractions in the desert. All is still, and conducive to the sound of the divine voice.

Suddenly the area around Moses was ablaze and there appeared unto him an angel in a flame of fire, out of the midst of a bush. But the miracle was that although the bush burned with fire, it was not burnt. To Moses this was a great sight! (Exod. 3:2, 3). Moses was to become the leader and legislator of Israel, and God, the consuming fire, appears as the great Redeemer of Israel from Egyptian bondage. In our previous treatment of the pre-existence of Jesus, we dealt with the awesome statement *I Am That I Am* and how Moses was brought to learn that the Jehovah who had chosen Israel would be with her in all her tribulations. As Moses received this vision, Israel was in the furnace of Egypt, and it was fitting therefore that God should reveal Himself as a burning bush. The bush was not consumed, neither were the Israelites in their furnace of affliction, for God was with them, enabling them to survive the cruel bondage. Knowing all about their sorrows by reason of their taskmasters, God sustained His own, and would have them know that He would bring them out of their captivity to a land flowing with milk and honey.

That *burning bush* was to be prophetic of the future history of the Jews, who stand out as the most amazing people of history. No other people have been so scattered, blasphemed, tormented, and destroyed, yet the world cannot get rid of them. Adolph Hitler tried it when he brutally massacred millions of them, but there are still some fourteen millions of them scattered throughout the world. Mark Twain once wrote about the indestructibility of the Jews in a most commendable way:

> The Egyptian, the Babylonian, and the Persian arose, filled the planet with sound and splendour, then faded to dream-stuff, and passed away; the Greek and Roman followed, and made a vast noise, and

> they are gone; other peoples have sprung up, and held the torch high for a time: but it burned out, and they sit in twilight, or have vanished.
>
> The Jew saw them all, beat them all, and is now what he always was, exhibiting no decadence, no infirmities of age, no weakening of his parts, no slowing of his energies, no dulling of his alert, aggressive mind. All things are mortal but the Jew; all other forces pass, but he remains. What is the secret of his immortality?

The answer to Mark Twain's question is that the God of that burning yet unconsumed bush is Israel's protector and preserver. President Nasser has a passion to wipe out the Jews, but to do this he must first of all destroy the God who brought them into being as His chosen people. No matter what fiery trials may yet overtake the Jews, they will ever remain an amazing evidence of God's dictum, "I will destroy them that destroy you." Israel has never ceased to experience "the good will of him that dwelt in the bush" (Deut. 33:16).

The burning bush can also be seen as a type of the church of the living God, which in all ages since Pentecost has been as a bush burning with fire yet not consumed. She has been compassed about with corruption from within, and trials and persecutions from without. At times, it seemed as if the fire of affliction threatened the Lord's people with instant and complete destruction, but the church still exists. The reason why she has not been consumed is because of her inner sustaining power. The Lord who bought her is in the midst of her, and she cannot be moved. (Zeph. 3:17).

The miracle of the true church's preservation is graphically pictured for us in the allegory John Bunyan gives us of such a truth he learnt in *The House of Interpreter:* "Pilgrim" came into one of the rooms "where there was a fire burning against a wall, and one standing by it, always casting much water on it, to quench it: yet did the fire burn higher and hotter." The reason for this was that, from the other side of the wall, unseen, one fed the flames continually with oil. In answer to the question, "What means this?" *Interpreter* explained that the fire is the work of grace that is wrought in the heart: he that casts water upon it, to extinguish it, and put it out, is the Devil; and He that pours oil upon it, to renew the fire continually, is Christ. In his own "Auto-biography," Bunyan says that this was his own personal experience:

> Then hath the tempter come upon me with such discouragements as these: You are very hot for mercy but I will cool you: this flame shall not last always: many have been as hot as you, but I have quenched their zeal. Though you be burning hot at the present I can pull you out of the fire. I shall have you cold before it be long.

But Bunyan had a fire burning on the altar of his heart that even the Devil could not extinguish, for his life was hid with Christ in God, and His grace was more powerful than satanic temptation. Archbishop Leighton would have us remember that

> Divine grace even in the heart of a weak and sinful man, is an invincible thing. It must overcome at last. Drown it in the waters of adversity it rises more beautiful, as not being drowned indeed, but only washed; throw it into the furnace of fiery trials, it comes out purer, and loses nothing but the dross which our corrupt nature mixes with it.

Last of all, the burning bush is a striking presentation of the Incarnation of Christ, when God manifested Himself in tangible form (I John 1:1). Such an application of the emblem is intensified when we remember that it was a common *bush* that Moses saw transformed, and not a tree like a *cedar* of Lebanon manifesting His glory (Isa. 2:13). When

Christ came to earth He tabernacled in substance of our flesh – a Babe in a manger. He did not come in pomp and glory but in the likeness of sinful flesh, to condemn sin in the flesh (Rom. 8:2). While He tarried among them, He was the Bush ablaze but never consumed. Religious foes tried to destroy Him but He was preserved until His task was completed. Down the ages deliberate efforts have been made to extinguish Him from the minds of men. Today, Communism, Atheism, Humanism, modernism, and materialism are combined to put out His fire, but on He burns and is still a living, bright reality in the lives of millions around the earth. Our blessed Lord is the fire on the divine altar that can never be quenched.

E. *The Two Pillars*

We read that Solomon cast two massive pillars of brass for the temple (I Kings 7:15), yet in spite of their strength and beauty they perished long ago. Moses, however, tells us of two other *pillars*, more glorious and powerful than Solomon's, which are indestructible, and which were related to Israel's departure from Egypt.

> They took their journey . . . And the LORD went before them by day in *a pillar of a cloud*, to lead them the way; and by night in *a pillar of fire*, to give them light; to go by day and night: He took not away the pillar of the cloud by day, nor the pillar of fire by night, from before the people" (Exod. 13:20-22).

As soon as Pharaoh let the people go, God took over their control and led them forth, not by the shortest way to the desert, which was through the land of the Philistines, but by a circuitous route by the way of the Red Sea. The reason for this long way round was because the strong and warlike Philistines might have frightened the Israelites. "Lest peradventure the people repent when they see war, and they return to Egypt" (Exod. 13:17, 18). When they reached the edge of the wilderness they were to wander in for almost forty years, the people received a most spectacular manifestation of God's presence and protection as the above verses show.

The first appearance of the pillar of cloud and of fire came "at Etham in the edge of the wilderness," which fact holds an instructive lesson for our hearts. "As all roads and canals, cities and villages are left behind, and an untried and trackless wilderness lies before the people, then God provides for them the mysterious cloud which never leaves them till the journey is over, and guidance is no longer required." When Christ said unto His disciples, "Go ye into all the world," He also added, "Lo, I am with you always." God never sends us forth on our own charges. Such was His grace that He not only brought His redeemed safely out of Egypt, so that not a hoof was left behind, and then selected the journey for them, but came down, as it were, "in His travelling chariot, to be their Companion through all the vicissitudes of their wilderness journey." Note these aspects –

1. *The cloud went before them.* What a precious phrase that is, "The Lord went before them." He could not suffer them to go alone. Not only was He to be "a guide, a glory, a defence, to save from every fear," but their abiding companion until the end of their pilgrimage. "God led the people" (Exod. 13:18). Said Jesus, "My sheep . . . follow Me." If only that redeemed company had lovingly and obediently walked with God, what a triumphant journey from first to last theirs would have been! "With Jehovah in their forefront, no power could have interrupted their onward prog-

ress from Egypt to Canaan." Alas! however, tragic delays were experienced, and the journey they could have finished in almost two weeks took them forty years. The cloud, then, symbolized God's presence with His people. "The pillar of the cloud went from before their face, and stood behind them" (Exod. 14:19, 24, 25; 33:9, 10).

2. *The cloud served as a guide for the people.* Because God alone knew all the perils of "the great and terrible wilderness," and how incompetent the people were to be their own guides, He went before them, "to lead them in the way." Later on we read that Moses felt he had need of Hobab's "eyes" to direct the host, but his knowledge of the wilderness was not sufficient – only Jehovah was the sufficient guide (Num. 10:31. See Jer. 17:5-7).

3. *The cloud was adapted for their necessity.* The Israelites marched some part of each day and some part of each night, and thus evaded the full blaze of the sun. In this way a full day's march was completed. So the pillar or cloud having the appearance of light smoke led them by day, and a column of fire gave them light by night (Neh. 9:19). Night journeys are later mentioned (Num. 9:21). Thus the people had at once a signal and a guide. When the cloud moved, the people moved; when it stopped they encamped (Exod. 40:36-38), where it went they followed. As Ellicott comments,

> It bore some resemblance to the fire and smoke signals which Generals used when at the head of their armies, and indicates that God had constituted Himself the General-issimo of the host; but it was altogether of a miraculous and abnormal character.

4. *The cloud was a shelter for the people.* As the people journeyed from Sinai to Kadesh-Barnea, we read that "the cloud of the LORD was upon them by day, when they went out of the camp" (Num. 10:33-36). David says, "[God] spread a cloud for a covering" (Ps. 105:39). This is the precious truth Philip Doddridge has captured in song:

> O spread Thy covering wings
> around,
> Till all our wanderings cease,
> And at our Father's loved abode
> Our souls arrive in peace.

5. *The cloud was a defense for the people.* When Pharaoh and his armies pursued the Israelites to the sea, and it seemed as if any hope of flight from their enemies was cut off, their murmurings and fears were silenced by Moses, and they came to experience the protection of the cloud, which "removed and went behind them," meaning, between the Israelites and their foes. President Nasser of Egypt vowed some time ago to drive Israel into the sea. This is what Pharaoh would have done had it not been for the cloud which plunged Pharaoh and his men into darkness, yet provided Israel with light by night (Exod. 14:19-20). Before an Egyptian could touch a hair of an Israelite's head, he would have had to have made his way through the Almighty Himself, who is ever between His people and every enemy.

6. *The cloud remained until the journey's end.* How suggestive is the phrase "He took not away the pillar of the cloud by day, nor the pillar of fire by night, from before the people" (Exod. 13:22). Does He not promise to guide us continually (Isa. 58:11)? So the cloud remained "throughout all their journeys" (Exod. 40:38. See Num. 9:16; 10:34) and probably disappeared at Abel-shittim (Num. 33: 49). For the child of God today the companionable cloud is Christ, who promised that He would never leave nor forsake His own (Heb. 13:5). Throughout the rugged pilgrimage, by day and night, He is the abiding

companion, and when at last the valley of the shadow of death is reached, He will still be near, whispering, "Fear no evil, – I am with thee" (Ps. 23).

Concluding our meditation on the cloud of His presence and guidance, we re-echo the sentiment expressed by Professor W. Moorehead that

> in all the various offices and movements of the Cloud, that which most impresses the reader is the minuteness of God's care for His people, His personal interest in them. Nothing is too small for Him to do for them, nothing too great. He studies their comfort, attends to every detail of their lives and their happiness. He is just as mindful of His children now. "The very hairs of your head are all numbered" (Matt. 10:30); "He careth for you" (I Pet. 5:7). Over us also He throws the great aegis of His protecting care, and beneath His wings we are safe.

> Forward! be our watchword,
> Steps and voices joined;
> Seek the things before us?
> Not a look behind;
> Burns the fiery pillar
> At our army's head;
> Who shall dream of shrinking,
> By our Captain led.

F. *The Red Sea*

The continuing, entrancing story of this second book of the Bible is the story of divine deliverance, its first chapter being taken up with Israel's national deliverance from Egypt, which was a deliverance through blood-shedding. All the power and destruction of the plagues did not avail. "It required the knife that shed the blood of the Paschal Lamb to sever the cords that kept Israel slaves." While the miracles associated with the plagues prepared the way for Israel's emancipation from bondage, it took another mighty miracle to deliver the nation forever from Pharaoh and his host. At the Red Sea their tyranny ceased, and Israel's new life of freedom actually began, and with it the second chapter of the story of deliverance which *Exodus* tells.

The guiding cloud had led Israel by a most peculiar route until the people found themselves hemmed in on the one side by massive rocks and on the other the sea. But God, who never makes a mistake in His guidance, had a twofold aim in bringing them into what appeared to be an impossible position as far as any escape was concerned. *First,* He was setting a trap for defiant Pharaoh; and *Second,* He wanted an opportunity of performing a great miracle, which through the centuries should be a memorial to Israel of His power to deliver them from any possible, or impossible, situation. He desired to prove that "Man's extremity was God's opportunity."

Hard-hearted Pharaoh, learning of the plight of the Israelites, imagined he had an excellent chance of destroying the people whose God had severely impoverished Egypt, and rousing himself from the stunning blow of the night of death, and, mad with rage and violence, gathered his captains and chariots and pursued hard after Israel, concluding that Moses had made a tactical blunder. Perhaps the Egyptian monarch felt that, after all, the God of Moses was only a local god of circumstances and not one universally wise and omnipotent – a kind of god of the hills but not of the valleys (I Kings 20:28), a god of Goshen but not of the wilderness. Thus, in his mad rage he is typical of the last desperate effort of Satan to destroy the saints (Rev. 17:13, 14).

When the people of Israel saw the armies of Pharaoh coming, their hearts failed them for fear, as they realized that there was no human avenue of escape. Crying out in their unbelieving distress, they upbraided Moses for bringing them out of Egypt. How quickly they forgot the plagues, and how easily their faith was obscured by sight! They became panic-stricken as they saw the war chariots. But Moses, ever magnificent as a leader, calmed the excited host, and assured them that God would fight for them and that they would *hold their peace* – a loving rebuke about their grumbling. Their rescue could only be brought about by a miracle, for with Pharaoh behind them and the sea before them, God alone could preserve them, as He did. "Stand still, and see the salvation of the Lord." Jehovah's glorious work annihilated on the one hand the groundless fears of Israel and, on the other, the proud boastings of Pharaoh. By the aid of the Spirit, let us look closely at this superb miracle, which is the only miracle in the Bible giving birth to a remarkable Psalm of Praise. (See the author's volume on *All the Miracles of the Bible.*)

1. *A divine miracle.* When Moses stretched out his rod toward the Red Sea, the waters parted to make a passage for Israel, but it was not his rod, symbol of divine authority and power, that performed the miracle, only the God who gave Moses the right to act as His chosen representative. Moses had quieted his frightened people with the assurance, "The Lord shall fight for you." It would appear as if Moses was a little anxious himself and betook himself to pray, but God told His servant that it was not the time to pray but act, and so instructed him what to do in view of the coming miracle. When all was quiet and restful in the camp again, Moses held out his rod over the sea, and God performed a miracle not by "suspending the forces of nature, but by wielding them in a fashion impossible with man." That was all He did as the God of the universe, and it was enough.

We totally reject the modernistic trend in some liberal theological circles to treat historical persons and events in the Bible as myths or fables designed to express truth in mythical form, as in *Aesop's Fables.* Further we deem it to be apostate to explain away the miraculous on natural grounds. For instance, those who displace Revelation by reason affirm that actually there was nothing miraculous about Israel walking through the Red Sea. At the point where the people were camped was a very narrow part of the sea, and at that time of the year the water was very low, and so, fortunately, the people were able to walk almost dry-shod through it. But Moses, who wrote the history of Israel, gives us a truthful account of a wonder that the people witnessed and which they celebrated for generations. If we accept the fact of God's omnipotence, then what man may deem impossible is gloriously possible to Him.

As the Creator, He controls the forces of nature and can command them to do His bidding. "The sea is His – He made it," and that it obeys Deity is seen in the miracle when Jesus rebuked the storm-tossed sea and the winds and the waves subsided. He revealed Himself as the master of ocean and earth and sky in that they sweetly obeyed His will. The display of omnipotence at the Red Sea was a foregleam of what happened when Jesus was asleep in the wave-beaten ship (Mark 4:35-41). As Moses held out his rod, God used a "strong east wind" to dry up the sea, causing the waters to stand up "as an heap" thus making a perpendicular "wall on either side" (Exod. 14:21, 22; 15:8). The wind was but the servant of the power of Him who "causeth his wind to blow, and the waters flow" (Ps. 147:18). Are we not reminded of "stormy wind fulfilling his word" (Ps. 148:8)? With the relaxed pressure of the wind, the water returned and there was no defense and the Egyptians were destroyed.

Such precise timing of the separation and then the return of the waters bringing deliverance to Israel but disaster to Pharaoh could only have taken place by a direct miraculous act of God. No wonder neighbor nations were alarmed at this manifestation of divine power (Exod. 15:14-16). See how these phrases stand out in the narrative as evidence of God's Almightiness:

"The salvation of the LORD" (Exod. 14:13).

"The LORD shall fight for you" (Exod. 14:14).

"I will . . . I will . . . I am the LORD" (Exod. 14:17, 18).

"The LORD caused the sea to go back" (Exod. 14:21).

"The LORD fighteth for them [Israel] against the Egyptians" (Exod. 14:25).

"The LORD overthrew the Egyptians in the midst of the sea" (Exod. 14:27).

"The LORD saved Israel that day" (Exod. 14:30).

"That great work which the LORD did" (Exod. 14:31).

In the song Moses and all Israel sang unto the Lord, in which they magnified Him for all He had accomplished, there is not a single note about *self*, its doings, its sayings, its feelings, or its fruits. From beginning to end this remarkable song is all about Jehovah. The keynote of His attributes and actings throughout the song is given at the beginning:

> "I will sing unto the LORD, for *he* hath triumphed gloriously: The horse and his rider hath *he* thrown into the sea" (Exod. 15:1).

The song of Moses is most comprehensive in its range for it begins with redemption by power and ends with glory. "The LORD shall reign for ever and ever" (Exod. 15:18). As soon as the delivered people set foot on the other side of the sea, on the margin of the desert, prophetically, they could sing, "Thou *hast guided* them in thy strength unto thy holy habitation." This was not a vague utterance but a prediction of the actual accomplishment of the divine purpose for His people (see Psalm 78:53, 54).

2. A *double miracle*. Actually, there was only one over-all miracle accomplished at the Red Sea, but it had an opposite double effect, summarized for us in a verse from the song:

> "The horse of Pharaoh went in with his chariots and with his horsemen into the sea, and the LORD brought again the waters of the sea upon them; but the children of Israel went on dry land in the midst of the sea" (Exod 15:19. See Exod. 14:22, 28).

The divine opening in the sea was the pathway of salvation for Israel, but doom for the hosts of Pharaoh. The same waters forming a wall for a redeemed people became a grave for the Egyptians, who were not among the redeemed and therefore under judgment. How wide the dry way was we do not know! It must have been considerable to allow some two millions to cross in one night without being wet by flying spray torn from the waters by the strong wind. Over they went dry-shod as if on dry land because of the water congealed on either side of them, protecting them like massive walls. What a triumphant host of believers they must have been as all night long the Angel of God kept the enormous procession safe by the darkness enveloping the Egyptians and by which Israel was hid from their enemies.

Pharaoh ordered his host to pursue, and "the Egyptians assaying to do, were drowned." The enemies of God should never attempt to do what only the people of God can do by faith. The hard dry sand which Israel had walked over became sodden with the returning waters, and the floor of the sea, like a pavement for God's people, became a bed of quicksand to Egypt. Overcome with fear, Pharaoh and his host gave up the chase. "Let us flee from the face of Israel; for the Lord fighteth for them against the Egyptians," but Israel safely across, Moses, standing on the far shore stretched out his authoritative rod, and the glassy walls broke, as Jehovah released from His grip the vast mass of water which came "tumbling and thundering down like a thousand Niagaras upon the miserable Egyptians, and drowned the entire host in the sea." What terrible judgment overtook proud, defiant Pharaoh as "the sea returned to his strength" – a prediction of a still greater judgment to overtake a godless world (See Acts 13:41).

Such a dual miracle was predictive of the double effect of Christ as His Gospel, both of which are either the savor of life or the savor of death. At Calvary, as Christ died for the sin of the world, one thief accepted Him as Saviour and followed Him into *Paradise*. But the other thief died in rejection and went out into perdition. Nations despising Christ as the foundation and Cornerstone of the church will experience His judicial power as He crushes them as the stone out of the mountain (See Prov. 29:1).

Without doubt, the passage provided for Israel through the Red Sea was a decisive and distinguished miracle, which both Moses and the psalmist have celebrated in poetic form. G. H. C. MacGregor says, "Scarce any story of the Bible rivets the attention of the reader like the first Passover and the midnight departure from Egypt. The whole section is a magnificent song in praise of the power and the Mercy of God." The writer takes the greatest care to impress upon us two aspects of the story of the deliverance. First, from beginning to end, it was the work of God. It was not the hand of Israel but the hand of God that smote Egypt and brought Pharaoh to his knees. It was not the might of Moses but the might of God that sank Pharaoh and his chariots as lead in the mighty waters. At the great crisis of deliverance Israel did nothing; God did all. On the Passover night Israel stood still behind the blood-sprinkled door, while God alone snapped the chains that bound them to Egypt. At the Red Sea Israel stood still and saw the salvation of the Lord, as He swept their enemies into the torrent before their eyes.

Second, Moses takes the greatest care to show that the deliverance was one through blood-shedding. The blood shed and sprinkled saved Israel from death and made them the people of Jehovah. Being redeemed by blood, they became the objects of His concern and preservation, and at the Red Sea He redeemed them by His power (Rom. 8:2). Up to this momentous day there had been little praise, only the cry of deep sorrow as the people toiled in their bondage, but once through the sea, a saved people became a singing people, and so we have the triumphant hymn of praise (Exod. 15. See also Ps. 77:13, 19; 78:13, 14, 53). How prophetic this song is of a similar one called "The song of Moses . . . and . . . the Lamb" (Rev. 15:3), which the saints will sing to God through the endless ages of eternity!

In a passage full of deep spiritual truth, Paul tells us that the experience of the Red Sea was a type that the saints of the Christian age should heed (I Cor. 10:1-3):

> Brethren, I would not that ye should be ignorant, how that all our fathers were *under the cloud*, and all passed through the sea;

> And were all baptized unto Moses in *the cloud and in the sea.*

Here, then, is our divine warrant for interpreting Israel's baptism in the cloud and in the sea, as being prophetic or typical of spiritual truth. It was as a people baptized that Israel entered upon their wilderness journey with "spiritual meat" and "spiritual drink" provided for their needs. Typically, Israel was a people completely dead to Egypt, their watery baptism bringing them the last sight of their foes. The miracle, then, was descriptive of what transpires when being "baptized into Jesus Christ [we] were baptized into his death" (Rom. 6:3, 4). As C.H.M. observes in his *Notes* on Exodus:

> The cloud and the sea were to the Israelites what the Cross and Grave of Christ are to us. The cloud secured them from their enemies; the sea separated them from Egypt; the Cross, in like manner, shields us from all that could be against us, and we stand at Heaven's side of the empty tomb of Jesus. Here we commence our wilderness journey—here we begin to taste the heavenly Manna, and to drink of the streams which emanate from "that spiritual rock," while, as a pilgrim people, we make our way onward to that land of rest of which God has spoken to us.

How assuring and applicable is the beautiful poem of Annie Johnson Flint on *The Red Sea Place in Your Life,* the first verse of which reads

> Have you come to the Red Sea place in your life,
> Where, in spite of all you can do,
> There is no way out, there is no way back,
> There is no other way but—through?
> Then wait on the Lord with a trust serene,
> Till the night of your fear is gone,
> He will send the wind, He will heap the floods,
> He says to your soul, *Go on!*

G. *The Healing Tree*

The happy result of the miracle of the Red Sea was that "Israel saw that great work which the LORD did upon the Egyptians: and the people feared the LORD, and believed the LORD, and His servant Moses" (Exod. 14:31). Alas! however, three days later their music turned into murmuring, and disappointment overtook delight. After such a display of divine power on their behalf, the people found no water in the wilderness and failed to remember that the God who had controlled volumes of water for their deliverance was able to supply streams in the desert. Their fear of and faith in God quickly evaporated, as did their reverence for Moses, for when the people came to Marah, the water there was bitter, and they murmured against Moses, as if he were responsible for the undrinkable water (Exod. 15:22-24).

Both the absence of water, and then the bitter water were in the very path of divine guidance, and represent the trials of the people of God, which are educatory and not punitive. Wilderness experiences are designed to test the reality of our acquaintance with God, and the depth of our faith and confidence in His Word. Setting out after their watery baptism, Israel bounded forward with glad heart, but their joy as a saved people soon received a check from the dry and dusty desert. Often this is so with those who commence their Christian pilgrimage with an exuberance of joy, but who, at the first keen blast of the world, break down, and in their hearts feel like turning back to Egypt.

John the Baptist remained in "the deserts till the day of his shewing unto Israel" (Luke 1:80). Our Lord lived in the desert of obscurity for thirty years before He entered His brief ministry of some three years. Let us not shun the College of the Wilderness, from which we can graduate with the Degree of Reliance upon God. "The disciple of the wilderness is needful," one has said, "not to furnish us with a title to Canaan, but to make us acquainted with God and with our own hearts; to enable us to enter into the power of our relationship, and to enlarge our capacity for the enjoyment of Canaan when we actually get there" (See Deut. 8:2-5). As the events and experiences in Egypt and in Canaan are typical and prophetic of Christ and Christian truth, so are the vicissitudes Israel encountered in the wilderness between Egypt and Canaan.

What must be borne in mind as we now follow the steps of Israel is that while God designed the wilderness for the spiritual preparation of His people for Canaan, He did not plan their wanderings, backslidings, murmurings. The sin of the people delayed their progress, turning a journey of some twelve to fourteen days into one of almost forty years, and likewise robbed them of peace and blessing, even in the wilderness, and also a longer sojourn in the land of promise. The pilgrimage to Canaan makes sad reading, for the people were forever sinning and repenting. After such a miraculous deliverance from Egypt by blood-shedding, and then from Pharaoh at the Red Sea, what a bitter disappointment to God a redeemed Israel was.

Recounting some of the crises in the wilderness trail, Paul says that these are "for types" (I Cor. 10:11), or a divine picture of our passage from bondage to victory. It is thus we pause to think of Israel at Marah, then at Elim. Two phrases lead us to combine what transpired at these two places.

They came to Marah – They came to Elim (Exod. 15:23, 27). As we are to discover both stops on the way are typical of the evangel and efficacy of the cross. In one of Sankey's hymns the saints are depicted as travelers to the better land, o'er the desert's scorching sands. Then come the verses

When at Marah, parched with heat,
I the sparkling fountain greet
Make the bitter waters sweet,
And lead me, lead me on.

When the wilderness is drear,
Show me Elim's palm-groves near,
With its walls, as crystal clear,
And lead me, lead me on.

Taken together, Marah and Elim are predictive of both Christ and the Christian, as the following four key phrases clearly prove. How the Master must have illuminated many of these Old Testament episodes as He expounded from them the things concerning Himself!

1. *The trial.* "They could not drink of the waters . . . they were bitter" (Exod. 15:23). These unpalatable waters gave the place its name, for *Marah* means "bitter," a fact Naomi applied to herself when, returning to her homeland a widow and without her two sons, her old friends cried, "Is this Naomi?" and she replied, "Call me not Naomi [meaning 'pleasant, agreeable'], call me Mara: for the Almighty hath dealt very *bitterly* with me" (Ruth 1:20).

In the experience of Israel, Marah came after the great moments of high triumph as found in the song of Moses. Was it not so in the life of Jesus, for whom, after the exalted events of His baptism in Jordan, there came the bitterness of temptation in the wilderness? Soon after the dove came the Devil. During His ministry many Marahs were His as the man of sorrows. A bitter stream followed Him till the more bitter cross was reached. But unlike Israel He never murmured or complained. He was a silent sufferer. Before His shearers, He was dumb; and in His unruffled demeanor amid the cruel, harsh treatment He received at the hands of merciless men, He left us an example that we should follow His steps.

As with Israel and with Jesus, so with ourselves, the distance is short between the Red Sea and Marah. With a people blessed with a mighty deliverance, notes of praise were soon exchanged for accents of discontent, for they cried to Moses, "What shall we drink?" "Those bitter waters tested the heart of Israel, and developed their murmuring spirit, but the Lord shewed them that there was no bitterness that He could not sweeten with the provision of His own grace." For each of us there is a *Marah*. In the world, said Jesus, ye shall have tribulation. Not until we reach heaven will the waters be clear as crystal.

What is your *Marah?* – a wayward child, an unsympathetic companion, an ungodly home, crushed hopes, physical infirmity, an empty life and heart? Each heart knows its own bitterness. There are right and wrong ways of facing life's Marahs. At Marah, Moses needed water as much as Israel, but as the people murmured, he prayed. True speech is prayer not complaint. The danger is that bitter waters make us bitter. It is only as we believe that such waters are in the plan of God and are permitted for spiritual enrichment of our life, that, like Jesus, we, too, can become noble in suffering. We greatly err if we regard all chastening as being deserved. Some of the saintliest of souls are the deepest sufferers.

There is a vast difference between chastisement and correction by punishment. *Chasten* is associated with "chaste," meaning "pure," and divine chastening results in beauty and purity of character. God only chastens those He loves. "For thou, O God, hast proved us: thou hast tried us, as silver is tried" (Ps. 66:10).

Every joy or *trial*
Falleth from above,
Traced upon our dial
By the Sun of Love.

2. *The tree.* "The LORD shewed him a tree" (Exod. 15:25). While there are some trees which have the power of sweetening bitter water, Ellicott remarks that there were no trees around Marah that were able to render putrid streams palatable. Doubtless the tree the Lord pointed out to Moses had some kind of healing virtue. "God seems to have made use of Nature, as far as Nature could go, and then to have superadded His own omnipotent energy in order to produce the required effect." A study of some of our Lord's miracles reveal the same action.

As the cross is called a *tree* (Acts 5:30; Gal. 3:13), the tree at Marah is a striking prophecy of all the Saviour accomplished at Calvary, which was the culmination of His earthly Marahs. As He died, He refused the offered narcotic to deaden pain. He wanted to be conscious as He drained even the dregs of such a bitter cup. This was why the cross was sweet to Jesus – it was the expression of the Father's eternal will (John 18:11; I Pet. 1:20). He knew that the tree was the only cure for the polluted waters of sin, and, as the carpenter, He fashioned the ark of salvation out of that tree. We often say after some hard test, "If I had known beforehand I could not have endured it." But Jesus knew before He was born that He was to be the tree cast into the waters, and when He appeared among men He walked with a firm step to that tree upon which He was crucified.

The Cross: it takes our guilt away;
It holds the fainting spirit up;
It cheers with hope the gloomy day,
And sweetens ev'ry bitter cup.

When we reach our Marah do we look for the tree? Is grace ours to lay our anguish, all that is sore and sour in life, alongside of Calvary, and experience how all the Saviour endured can rob us of all our bitter feelings and thoughts (Rom. 5:3, 4)? That rugged tree on the hill at Calvary seems to say to us, "How dare you complain about your trials after such undeserved agony and shame?" It is only a sweet resignation to the divine will, whether pleasant or painful, that can enable us to say,

> How bitter that cup no heart can conceive,
> Which Jesus drank up, that sinners might live!
> His way was much rougher, and darker than mine:
> Did Jesus thus suffer, and shall I repine?

3. *The transformation.* "The waters were made sweet" (Exod. 15:25). What a pregnant phrase this verse ends with: "There He proved them"! But although the people failed in the test, God not only sweetened the waters for them, but brought them into a sweeter relationship with Himself, promising to be their Healer (Exod. 15:26). Those purified and agreeable waters at Marah foreshadow the Resurrection of Jesus from the dead. The tree was cast into the deepest, darkest waters – His grave: and for us the sting of death has gone. What a difference to a harsh, sinful world the cross and Resurrection have made! Alive forevermore, Jesus is able to transform the most unwelcome experiences of life. Did He not say, "The cup which my Father hath given me, shall I not drink it?" (John 18:11). Death and the curse were in that cup, but such a Marah is now His Elim, for in every life healed of its iniquity He sees of the travail of His soul and is satisfied.

What do we know about the transforming, transfiguring influence of the untoward and painful experiences of life? Do we find it hard to drink of the waters of Marah because they are bitter, or have we learned how God can made the bitter sweet? The secret of such a change is the loving acceptance of what God permits as being His sweet will for us. If we live 'neath the shadow of the tree, so blood-red, our trials will be transformed into triumphs. Although we may not be able to change adverse circumstances, we must be on our guard lest they change us for the worst. Moses cast the tree into the waters. The divinely appointed remedy had to contact the source of Israel's murmuring.

By ourselves we cannot change the Marahs we meet on our pilgrimage, or right wrongs, or make the bitter beautiful; but Christ by His cross can. The leaves of the tree on which He died are for the healing of national strife, religious schisms, the root of bitterness in our own heart, and those whose lives have become so sour and unwelcome because of sin. Seneca once said, "The good things that belong to Adversity are to be admired." Have we found it so? E. Young has given us the lines

> May Heaven ne'er trust my friend with happiness,
> Till it has taught him how to bear it well
> By previous pain!

4. *The tranquility.* "They came to Elim" (Exod. 15:27). Although only an easy march of some six miles from Marah, Elim must have seemed as an oasis in the wilderness to the grumbling Israelites. They had nothing to murmur about as they took advantage of the twelve wells of water and the shade and fruit of seventy palm trees. The name *Elim* means "strong" and is found in the name *Elimelech,* Naomi's husband, with the extension, "My mighty or strong God is King." The people failed to glory in their tribulation at Marah, but came to experience that the wilderness has its Elims as well as its Marahs – its refreshing springs as well as its bitter waters. Thus, at the green spot of Elim, the hearts of the people were soothed. their murmurings hushed,

and strength gathered for trying days ahead. How delighted they must have been to encamp at such a place!

For the Saviour, a wonderful Elim followed His sorrowful Marah. After His trials accepted as the Father's will, there came peace, tranquility, and a glorious reward. With His exaltation in His heavenly Elim, there were His seventy palm trees of eternal rest and shade. "When he had by himself purged our sins, [he] sat down on the right hand of the Majesty on high" (Heb. 1:3). Then there were His twelve wells of refreshing and life-giving water, for after Calvary there came Pentecost with its sweet waters of the Holy Spirit – the only antidote for all life's Marahs. For Jesus, the Elim of His exaltation and of Pentecost was but a foretaste of all the mighty triumphs He will achieve until He surrenders the kingdom to the Father.

The all-important question is, Have we reached our Elim yet in the wilderness journey of life, or are we still living at Marah? Is ours the risen, Spirit-filled life? If *Elim* means "strong trees," as trees planted by the Lord, are we girded with His strength? Is ours the twofold provision Israel found at Elim?

Refreshment. "Twelve wells of water."

Unlike the bitter wells at Marah, these contained nothing but fresh, pure, sweet and quickening water, and can typify the varied ministry of the Spirit, whose rivers of living water Jesus promised His own. Then the number is significant – twelve. As there were twelve tribes of Israel, a well was at Elim for each tribe. The never-failing springs of life in the Spirit are for each one of us. Each believer can claim all there is in the Well of Water. "All our springs are in Thee."

Rest. "Threescore and ten palm trees."

The psalmist declares that the days of our years are "threescore and ten," so God's provision is sufficient for the span of life. Those beautiful, fruit-bearing, shady palm trees at Elim can represent the flourishing state of the believer, of whom it is said that he should "flourish like the palm tree" (Ps. 92:12). Palms are likewise symbolic of victory (John 12:13; Rev. 7:9). Of the prince's daughter, her lover could say, "Thy stature is like to a palm tree" (Song of Sol. 7:7). Is such a description true of you and me? If our tent has been pitched at some Marah, let us seek the healing tree of the cross, and then strike tent and encamp at Elim where life is more pleasant and profitable. Well over seventy years ago, William Canton left us these most appropriate thoughts on *Elim:*

> Elim, Elim! Through the sand and heat
> I toil with heart uplifted, I toil with bleeding feet,
> For Elim, Elim! at the last, I know
> That I shall see the palm-trees and hear the waters flow.
>
> Elim, Elim! Grows not here a tree,
> And all the springs are Marah, and bitter thirst to me;
> But Elim, Elim! in thy shady glen
> Are twelve sweet wells of water, and palms three score and ten.
>
> Elim, Elim! Though the way be long,
> Unmurmuring I shall journey, and lift my heart in song;
> And Elim, Elim! all my song shall tell
> Of rest beneath the palm-tree, and joy beside the well.

H. *The Manna*

We can imagine how loathe Israel must have been to leave such a pleasurable spot as Elim, the bountiful provision of which should have intensified the faith of the people in God's ability to care for those delivered out of bondage by His power. But it was otherwise. The whole assembly moved on and came to the wilderness of Sin between Elim and

Sinai. The name of the region, *Sin*, may have been derived from the moon-god "Sin" or may have been identical with the desert of *Zin*, which Moses often mentions (Num. 13:21, etc.). Then the position given is somewhat significant and instructive, "Between Elim and Sinai." As we have just seen, *Elim* was the place of the refreshing springs of divine ministry, but at *Sinai* the people left the ground of free and sovereign grace and came under the Law, or a covenant of works.

The wilderness of Sin, therefore, represents a singularly interesting pause and portion of Israel's journey. The people are still the subjects of the same grace which had brought them out of Egypt to Sin, hence, their further murmurings are instantly met by divine supplies, with God acting in the display of His grace. "But when man puts himself under law he forfeits: for then God must allow him to prove how much he can claim on the ground of his works." Israel was in the desert, hungry and disappointed, and so complained to Moses, "Ye have brought us forth into this wilderness, to kill this whole assembly with hunger" (Exod. 16:1-3). What a heartbreak the people were to Moses! They should have believed that when God redeemed them out of their terrible bondage in Egypt, it was not that they should die of hunger and thirst in the wilderness. Theirs should have been the confidence that they were infinitely better to be with God in the desert than at their brickkilns under Pharaoh. And as Moses had been God's agent in their escape from the horrors of Egypt, they should have trusted him, and should not have tormented him as they did.

While the people "murmured against Moses and Aaron" their grouse was against the God they served. "He heareth your murmurings against the Lord." Yet with the rebuke there was grace and mercy, "Behold, I will rain bread from heaven for you" (Exod. 16:4-8). With this promise there also came the first mention in the Bible of the appearance of the glory of the Lord. "Ye shall see the glory of the LORD . . . they looked toward the wilderness, and, behold, the glory of the LORD appeared in the cloud" (Exod. 16:7, 10). Glory in a wilderness? Yes, "Jehovah's chariot was in the wilderness, and all who desired companionship with Him should be there also; and if there, the heavenly manna should be their food, and that alone."

Before we come to our Lord's use of the *manna* as a type of the sustenance to be found in Him, let us observe some of the features of the manna that fell in the wilderness, noting the Messianic foregleams of same.

1. *It was miraculously provided.* While natural substances similar to manna, "concreted into small granular masses" and known as "air-honey," were found in the area and were eaten by the Arabs with their unleavened cakes as a condiment, the *manna* the Bible mentions must be regarded as a miraculous substance and not a natural one. "It pleased the Creator, however, to proceed *on the lines* of Nature, so to speak, and to assimilate His new creation to certain of His old creations." The Lord provided the manna *from* heaven!

Jesus, while made in the likeness of our sinful flesh, was not fashioned after the order of natural generation. Although born of the Virgin Mary, He was conceived of the Holy Spirit, and came as the Lord from heaven. "The bread of God is he which cometh down from heaven" (John 6:33).

2. *It had a secret name.* The words of the original, *man hu*, can either be translated "What is this?" or "This is a gift." *Manan* is the Hebrew for "to give." The Israelites did not know

what the substance was until Moses answered their question, "What is this?" with the reply, "This is the bread which the Lord hath given you to eat" (Exod. 16:15). In contrast to the fleshpots of Egypt, this mysterious bread was what David called *Angels' Food,* or "the bread of the mighty." Unaware of its real nature, the people spoke of manna as "the what-is-it." Almost at the end of the wilderness journey, Moses, rehearsing the guidance and goodness of God, said, "The LORD thy God . . . fed thee with manna, *which thou knewest not, neither did thy fathers know*" (Deut. 8:2, 3). Such language implies that its ingredients were God's secret just as the combination of our Lord's two natures were. His name was called *wonderful,* which is equivalent to *secret* in the Hebrew (Judg. 13:18). After the Red Sea, Moses sang of God as "doing wonders," or "doeth secretly" (Exod. 15:11). By our own reason we shall never be able to find God out.

3. *It came from heaven.* As already hinted, Israel's food was heaven-sent. The divine fiat was, "Behold, I will rain bread from heaven for you," which suggests that such food was not simply "out of the air, but a supernatural, celestial provision for Israel's daily needs." The difficulty with the people was that it demands a heavenly taste to feed on heavenly food, but theirs was an unceasing appetite for Egypt's fleshpots.

Jesus referred to Himself as "the bread of God" and "the bread from heaven." Seven times over He told the Jews of His day that He came down from heaven (John 6:33-58). Paul gives us seven steps in our Lord's descent on His way from the throne of glory to the tomb (Phil. 2:7, 8). We will never know how deep were the depths into which He descended that He might become the Bread of Life to those who were dead in sin, and provide a way for sinners to go to heaven. Like the manna, Jesus came from heaven for the benefit of earth.

4. *It was small.* The original for "small" means "lean," or "thin," hence the reference to manna as a *wafer,* or cake, round in shape. Being very light in weight, it could be easily gathered by children, as well as in a quantity by adults (Exod. 16:14). The town in which Jesus was born is described as being "little among the thousands of Judah, yet out of thee shall he come forth unto me that is to be ruler in Israel" (Mic. 5:2). Christ, in His humiliation, was the One who came down from heaven and was found as a small, helpless babe in a manger. Let us never underrate the possibilities arising out of a small beginning.

5. *It was round.* Its shape and size made the manna convenient to handle. A round ring has no edges, no beginning or ending. Can this not typify Jesus in the circle of His eternal being? He is from everlasting to everlasting, being without a break in His continuity.

6. *It was white, like coriander seed.* We are given a twofold description of the manna. It was "small as the hoar frost on the ground" (Exod. 16:14), which was its appearance as it lay on the ground; and "like coriander seed, white" (Exod. 16:31), which was what it looked like when collected and brought in. This particular seed is "a small round grain, of a whitish or yellowish grey." Because of its color it was quickly discovered. How wonderful it is of our great God to think of such minute details in the display of His miraculous power. In Solomon's Song, the lover is made to say, "My Beloved is white," and John depicts God's beloved Son as having white hair. As our heavenly manna, He was whiter than the whitest. The Gospels pre-

sent Him as the One without sin—the One who wore "the white flower of a blameless life."

7. *It was like wafers, made with honey.* How thoughtful of God it was to make the heavenly manna palatable to human taste! In fact, there is a Jewish tradition embodied in *The Apocrypha* that the taste of the manna varied according to the wish of the eater and "tempered itself to every man's liking" *(Wisdom* 16:20, 21). We know from the experience of Jonathan that honey is a pleasant and delightful food. "His eyes were enlightened" (I Sam. 14:27). "What is sweeter than honey?" (Judg. 14:18). Is not Jesus a delight to the heart? Is not our meditation of Him sweet, or pleasurable and profitable? If the manna of old "tempered itself to every man's liking," does not Jesus, knowing all about my peculiarities and personal taste adapt Himself to my individuality? *"My"*—it may be different from yours—"meditation is sweet." To each believer, with his or her own personality, He is precious.

8. *It was the color of bdellium.* Bdellium is a precious stone, transparent and semi-crystal. A gum also has the same name, and resembles myrrh—fragrant, with a bitter yet pungent taste. When the Israelites came to complain about the sameness of the manna and lusted for the fish and food, they cried, "There is nothing at all, beside this manna before our *eyes.*" Then the following Hebrew description of the manna should read, "the eye of it as the eye of bdellium." But its white brilliance no longer fascinated them. The people lost the sense of wonder in such a divine provision. The poet depicts Jesus as "the Crystal Christ," and like "the pure river of water of life, clear as crystal" (Rev. 22:1). He is conspicuous for His perfect transparency, clarity, and illuminating influence.

9. *It had the taste of fresh oil.* We have just mentioned that it had the "taste of honey"—now it had "the taste of fresh oil," and there is no contradiction between the two ingredients, for the ancients made a mixture of oil and honey in their flour cakes. The manna was ground and beaten, baked like cakes with oil and honey in pans (Num. 11:8). *Oil* is given as a type of the Holy Spirit, and Jesus was ever anointed with fresh oil. Coming as the Bread of God, He was born of and constantly empowered by the Spirit. "I, by the Spirit of God," was the way He described the performance of His miracles.

Dew is likewise a symbol of the Spirit, and we read that "when the dew fell upon the camp in the night, the manna fell upon it" (Num. 11:9). Unless a heart is prepared by the Spirit, Jesus cannot be fully known. When the dew falls, He, the Bread of Life, also falls.

10. *It melted when the sun waxed hot.* While God was most prodigal in His provision, nothing had to be wasted. Exposed to the fierce heat of the desert sun, manna quickly became useless and decomposed, hence the necessity of gathering it every morning, thereby preserving it. It had to be secured and eaten at the right time. As every man had to take a lamb for his family (Exod. 12:4), so with the manna "every man according to his eating," meaning that each fresh morning each man gathered according to his immediate need and that of his family. And just as there had to be no waste, so no one was to accumulate a store of the food. No one was to leave any of one day's supply till the next morning.

The only exception to this rule was on the *sixth day,* when they gathered twice as much, thereby avoiding laboring on the Sabbath. The people secured a certain rate every day, but on the sixth day a double rate, when there was a miraculous doubling of the quantity required, and likewise a miraculous preservation of the extra supply, as at any other time if kept overnight it bred worms. The spiritual application of all these features is clearly evident. As the manna had to be gathered early in the day and eaten at the right time, so it is necessary to seek the Lord while he may be found. How profitable it is not only to seek Him *early* and seek Him *only* as each new day dawns, but also to do so in "life's fair morning." All who seek Him early find Him.

Further, as an Israelite might gather up more manna than he required for one day's food, exhibiting thereby a far more diligent accumulation of the heavenly food than others, yet every crumb beyond the day's supply was worse than useless – it *bred worms* and *stank*. Is this not so with those of us who profess to be Christ's? A mere knowledge of Christ in the head only leads to pride that stinks in the nostrils of God. John Newton reminds us that

> The Bread by which our souls are fed
> Is each day sought afresh,
> For notions resting in the head
> Will only feed the flesh.

The divine instruction about having none of the gathered manna left over was meant to remind Israel of their complete dependence upon God for food from *day to day*, and thus become habituated to absolute trust and confidence in Him. Natural manna, similar in looks to that sent from heaven, was not subject to any rapid decomposition, but if any of the heavenly bread was kept overnight it bred worms and stank. Such a divinely accelerated action is spoken of as a punishment for disobedience. God never gives us grace in advance.

A Christian must *use* what he gathers; he must feed upon Christ as a matter of actual need, and the need is brought out in actual service. As His, our path is to be a practical one, but it is here that so many of us come short. What we gather we hoard, and fail to give. Our knowledge and experience of the Lord becomes doubly precious when shared with others. How appropriate are the lines of Margaret E. Sangster on "Manna":

> 'Twas in the night the manna fell
> That fed the hosts of Israel.
>
> Enough for each day's fullest store
> And largest need; enough, no more.
>
> For willful waste, for prideful show,
> God sent no angels' food below.
>
> Still in our nights of deep distress
> The manna falls our hearts to bless.
>
> And, famished, as we cry for bread
> With heavenly food our lives are fed,
>
> And each day's need finds each day's store
> Enough. Dear Lord, what want we more!

11. *It was enough for all.* The tremendous marvel of the food God provided were the multitudes of mouths that had to be fed in the wilderness. While we are concentrating on the bread God rained from heaven, we should note that He also gave them meat. In the morning, manna was given and gathered – and at evening the quails covered the camp. Abundant in the East, quails were regarded as a delicacy. It was no miracle that quails were found where Israel sojourned from time to time, seeing they are migratory birds. The miracle was in their daily appearance in such vast quantities for almost forty years, being adapted, along with the manna, to Israel's principal nourishment for such a long period.

As for the manna, we read that every man gathered according to his own eating, and for all persons in his tent. The tally for the day was an *omer,* about three English pints. If the families in the whole camp averaged four members, each man would have to gather, on an average, six quarts. If 500,000 men gathered this amount, the daily supply must have been *93,500 bushels.* What a table for God to furnish in a *wilderness!* Think of it! On the basis of this computation, during the forty years the Israelites consumed *one thousand three hundred and seventy millions, two hundred and three thousand, six hundred bushels.* "He fed them according to the integrity of his heart; and guided them by the skillfulness of his hands" (Ps. 78:72).

All food is from God, so what He did directly and miraculously for Israel, He did indirectly and naturally for other living souls. The manna fed a nation, but Jesus as the Bread of Heaven gave His life for the world. In Him, there is grace enough for all. He has bread enough and to spare. Since Jesus became the Living Bread, millions upon millions have been fed and satisfied, and today there are countless numbers all over the world feasting on Him as the heavenly manna. As future generations come and go there will be sufficient spiritual sustenance for them. As the manna never failed for forty years, so Jesus will never fail to feed the hungry who turn to Him for bread that never perishes. If the wilderness provision for a nation was a most extraordinary miracle, worthy of God, and most beneficial to man, is not His provision in Christ for a lost world, a still greater miracle? Our own personal experience of all Christ is in Himself is none the less because untold numbers have shared His infinite love and provision.

> I am sure what I feel, others have felt;
> And all that I know, others have known;
> And yet the joy of what I feel,
> And what I know, is all my own . . .
>
> I think it was God's boundless love
> Made Him create a world like this;
> That so a million million lives
> Might share, and multiply, His bliss.

12. *It was loathed when at Hormah.* Because of the hard road the people had to travel, they became disappointed and disgruntled and spoke against both God and Moses, and complained yet once again about the monotony of their diet. "Our soul loatheth this light bread" (Num. 11:6; 21:5). The word for *light* means something "vile" or "worthless." What an ungrateful way to describe the manna from heaven! The lack of what they deemed more palatable bread caused them to cry to Moses, "Wherefore have ye brought us up out of Egypt to die in the wilderness?" They forgot how the bread from heaven had been their life for so long. They should have loathed themselves for their carnality and rejection of divine bounty.

When Jesus came as manna from above, He found Himself despised, reviled, and rejected of men. Destitute of a spiritual nature, they failed to appreciate spiritual meat. They could not understand, appreciate, or live upon it. Many worldly people today regard Christ, and His church and ordinances as *light bread* – as irrelevant for our times. When professing Christians seek after the things of the world, their carnal desires, like those of the Corinthians, prove that they "loathe" the heavenly manna, esteeming it as "light food." Instead of mortifying the flesh, they minister unto it, and therefore have little appetite for the bread from heaven, which "strengthens man's heart." Can we say that Christ is the exclusive food of our souls, the One we habitually feed on by faith?

> Thou bruised and broken Bread,
> My lifelong wants supply;
> As living souls are fed,
> O feed me, or I die.

13. *It was kept in a pot for a memorial.* Although the people of Israel often murmured about the wilderness food, they were divinely commissioned never to forget – even when they came to the milk and honey of Canaan – the heavenly bread sustained them during their forty years of wandering. "This is the thing which the LORD commandeth, Fill an omer of it to be kept for your generations; that they may see the bread wherewith I have fed you in the wilderness, when I brought you forth from the land of Egypt. . . . As the LORD commanded Moses, so Aaron laid it up before the Testimony, to be kept" (Exod. 16:32-34).

This golden pot (Heb. 9:4), which came to occupy a place in the tabernacle, and which contained one omer, was not only to be a perpetual memorial, but the command concerning it was likewise a prophecy that the manna would continue until Israel reached Canaan. Does not that precious pot of manna, containing as it did one man's daily portion and laid up before the Lord, furnish us with a volume of truth? What a testimony to the unfailing faithfulness of God it was! When the people tried to store up what they could not eat, the manna bred worms and stank. But God preserved the manna in that pot, for it had neither worm nor taint.

How prophetic and typical all this is of Christ, who promises to give of *the hidden manna* to all overcomers when they reach heaven (Rev. 2:17). Manna is termed not only "angels' food," but "the bread of God" (Ps. 78:25; John 6:33). For some 12,500 mornings Israel saw the manna on the ground around the camp. Neither the quails nor the manna were "hidden." But the day's portion in the memorial pot was hidden, screened from the gaze of the people. In heaven, away from the eyes of the world is Christ, our heavenly pot of manna, and we are to feast on Him forever. There we shall learn from Christ Himself the secrets of His life here below when He could not be hid. He will unfold the depths of His humiliation for our sakes, and reveal the moral beauties and perfections of His life hid from the eyes of them to whom He was without form or comeliness.

14. *It was a type of Christ.* In the several features of the manna we have just considered, recognition has been given of their messianic import. We now come to examine more particularly the Master's own use of the wilderness food for Israel as predictive of Himself as the true bread from heaven. Rich, as it is, in its suggestiveness, the old manna was only a type, and, like all other types and symbols, inadequate to fully manifest the person and work of Christ. As we have already seen, Noah's ark was not large enough to represent His great heart of love. Jacob's ladder was not wide enough to reveal the breadth of His compassion. No paschal lamb was ever pure enough to portray His sinless nature; and, in like manner, no angels' food was sweet enough to express the perfect sweetness of the grace of Him whom angels worship and obey. Adapting the lines of Isaac Watts,

> All types are too mean to show His worth,
> Too mean to set my Saviour forth.

15. *He is the true bread.* The principal thought in our Lord's application of the bread from heaven for Israel to Himself is that such a miraculous provision for their need was typical of the supply of all our spiritual need in Him. He is more than sufficient for all the necessities of our pilgrimage through life. In His miracles of feeding the hungry, He acted the truth that He is the source of supply. Now, He first distinctly declares the marvelous message that He

is, in Himself, the living and life-giving bread (John 6:26-60).

Christ claimed faith in Himself as the one great work of God, but the Jewish rulers, offended at this claim, demanded a sign sufficient to substantiate it. They rejected the recent miracle of the feeding of the five thousand as being insignificant in comparison with the miraculous feeding of a nation for forty years in a wilderness. Therefore, they argued, Moses was far greater than Jesus (John 6:28-31). In His reply He presented a contrast between *Moses* and *God*, the force lying upon the words "Moses" and "my Father."

Further, there is the contrast between the manna, *that bread from heaven*, and Himself as *the true* bread from *heaven*. Here the giver rather than the gift is emphasized. Christ reminded His Jewish questioners that even the bread their fathers ate in the desert, which was not the *true bread*, was not given by Moses, but by God Himself. Then, following His frequent custom, Jesus did not directly answer the question asking for a sign, but led His questioners to higher thoughts concerning Himself. All past miracles and signs drew attention to Himself, as the one great miracle and sign. Manna in the desert was but a poor type of Him who became God manifest in *the flesh*.

"Moses gave you not *that* bread," said Jesus. What bread? He had been speaking of "meat which endureth unto everlasting life" (John 6:27, 32). But Moses was not a *life-giver*, and life could not be obtained through him. True, he was a *law-giver* (John 1:17), but no man ever secured life through the Law (Gal. 3:21). The manna, then, was not Jesus, and anything that is not Jesus must be infinitely less than Jesus. Thus the type came short of reality, as everything else of a symbolic character falls short of Him. "The Ordinances; The Ministry; The Church; The Scriptures; The Angels, Principalities and Powers, what are they but fragmentary threads in the carpet of His footstool as compared with Him?"

16. *He is the divine bread.* In the narrative which speaks of that which the manna symbolized, we have the great *I AM*, the Jehovah term, Christ frequently used of Himself in John's Gospel that emphasizes the glorious truth of His divine nature. Thus, as "the bread of life," He is not something but *someone* – a person upon whom men must feed if they would not perish eternally. Christ is "the bread of God, which cometh down from heaven" (John 6:33). What a pregnant description this is of Himself – *bread of God!* If Christ is of God, He must be God, for He claimed to be God. No mere imperfect man could satisfy the craving of human souls for salvation and satisfaction as Christ declared He was able to do. Jesus would never have used words containing the awesome name *Jehovah*, if He had not been conscious that He was the eternal God, and, therefore, as the living God, the living bread.

The manna supplied to the Israelites came from under the heavens, but Jesus is the bread that came down *from* heaven – an evidence of His pre-existence as a member of the Godhead. Rich in glory, for our sake He became poor, that as poor, lost, hell-deserving sinners we might be saved from our spiritual destitution, and fed and satisfied with all that His grace provides.

> Bread of Heaven! Bread of Heaven!
> Feed me till I want no more.

17. *He is life-giving bread.* The manna gathered in the wilderness was not able to give life to the body, but only to sustain the body. Food is necessary for the repair of physical

waste. Sin wastes spiritual strength, and for this reason we need life and Jesus offers Himself as the life of the soul. "I am . . . the life" (John 14:6), and as such He repairs the waste and gives new power (John 6:51, 53). As our "daily bread," He is the support of our life, and because of His inexhaustible resources, He is the satisfaction of our life. By His claim, "I am that bread of life" (John 6:48), we have the assurance that all who receive His as Saviour have everlasting life.

Those who questioned Jesus held that the manna was more wonderful than the miraculous bread He had provided for the hungry thousands. But He replied that all who ate the manna ultimately died, while all who eat of the living bread never die, eternally. Although feeding on Christ as the bread of life does not save us from bodily death, it does assure us of a bodily resurrection. The manna the Israelites ate gave no pledge of resurrection, being only concerned with physical existence on earth. Christ, however, as the living, and life-giving bread is profitable not only for this life, but for that which is to come. "I will raise him up" (John 6:54).

The bread of life, then, is Christ *Himself*, in the fulness of His dual nature, as perfect God and perfect man, and unless He is appropriated by faith, then "ye have no life in you" (John 6:53). Bread is a substance that has been formed by life. As Henry Thorne expresses it,

> There is life in the seed from which we get the harvest, and there is life in the ears of the corn that clothe the autumn fields, and hence there is that in them by which human beings may be fed and nourished. Life can only be sustained by that which has been produced by life. This is true in relation to the physical life, and it is equally true in relation to the spiritual life. Spiritual life can only be derived from one possessed of spiritual life, and who has power to impart it to others. Christ has "life in himself" (John 5:26), and has power to impart that life to others, for He is able to quicken "whom he will" (John 5:21). Bishop Westcott defines "The Bread of Life" as food *of which life is an endowment which it is capable of communicating.*

18. *He is sacrificial bread.* The manna may have been "the bread of the mighty" (Ps. 78:25, R.V.), but it was only something God created for His people, and not God Himself. The soul cannot be fed upon manna which was only *matter.* Jesus, knowing this, gave himself that souls might be fed. Twice over He reminded the Jews that the manna their forebears ate was not able to preserve their bodies from corruption (John 6:49, 58), and that, therefore, it was an imperfect symbol of eternal preservation the sacrifice of Himself would provide. God gave manna *to* Israel, but God the Son declared that He was to die *for* the world, and that because of His death for sinners, He would become their Bread of Life (I Pet. 2:21; 3:18).

> "The bread that I will give is my flesh, which I will give for the life of the world" (John 6:51; Heb. 10:5, 10).

This prediction was fulfilled upon the cross, where He gave His flesh. Christ crucified is the food of His people, as He Himself proclaimed when instituting "The Lord's Supper." He said that the bread broken would be a reminder of His sacrifice, "This is My body, which is given, or broken, for you." He speaks of *His flesh* and *His blood* (John 6:53), for His sacrifice involved both. His flesh was broken and His blood shed that we might have life forevermore.

19. *He must become the appropriated bread.* The Israelites, in order to benefit by the bread from heaven, had to eat it: "Your fathers did *eat* manna in the wilderness," and Jesus

advances the mystic truth that in order to profit by His death, we must *eat* His flesh and *drink* His blood (John 6:54), if we would not die, but live forever (John 6:50, 51). We utterly reject the Roman Catholic notion of affirming that in the Sacrament of the supper, participants in some mysterious way eat His actual flesh and drink His actual blood. Participation in Christ always means spiritual food and sustenance. The Greek word our Lord used for eating is one that means more than the mere sensation of consuming food. It was a strong word implying eagerness of desire for the food eaten, and represents spiritual hunger, a devout craving or yearning of a famished soul for heavenly food. Coming to Christ, hunger ceases, and believing in Him, thirst is ended (John 6:35).

Augustine's instructive comment is,

> This then it is, to eat that meat and drink that blood: namely to dwell in Christ and to have Christ dwelling in us. And therefore he who dwelleth not in Christ, and in whom Christ dwelleth not, without doubt doth neither eat His flesh nor drink His blood: but rather doth unto judgment to himself eat and drink the Sacrament of so great a thing.

The *eating* and *drinking,* then, are actions illustrating our faith in coming to Christ and believing on Him (John 6:29, 35). It would seem as if there is a twofold aspect to the eating of the heavenly manna –

a. *To obtain* eternal life (John 6:54). There must be access to Christ by faith in order to receive this life forevermore. First of all, He must be appropriated as the living bread.

b. *To maintain* the life received (John 6:58). Thus, we pray, "Lord, evermore give us this bread." To have a healthy spiritual life, we must daily feed upon all that He is in Himself. The manna of old ceased when Israel reached Canaan, but Christ, the ever living bread, is our eternal sustenance. Even when we reach heaven, we shall feast upon Him, and He will feed us and lead us "unto living fountains of waters" (Rev. 7:17).

> Jesus, Bread and Wine art Thou,
> Wine and Bread for ever,
> Never canst Thou cease to feed
> Or refresh us, never.
> Feed us still on Bread Divine,
> Drink we still of heavenly wine.

I. *The Smitten Rock*

What short memories the Israelites seemed to have had! The miraculous provision of their daily food failed to beget unquestioning faith in and obedience to their divine companion and provider. Their insensibility to the Lord's mercy, faithfulness, and mighty acts characterized their whole sojourn in the wilderness. The people were forever sinning and coming back again. How they reflect the humiliating evil and backsliding of our own hearts! Shortly before they had witnessed bread coming to them from heaven; now they are "ready to stone" their noble leader for bringing them to another place to kill them with thirst. But what happened at Rephidim reveals that "nothing can exceed the desperate unbelief and wickedness of the human heart save the super-abounding grace of God. In that grace alone can anyone find relief unto the growing sense of his evil nature which circumstances tend to make manifest."

In a portion of our Lord's Sermon on the Mount in which He spoke of trust in divine care as a cure for unbelieving anxiety, He asked two questions: What shall we eat? What shall we drink? (Matt. 6:25). The manna and the smitten rock provide the answers. Our wilderness food is Christ as the bread from heaven, ministered to us by the Holy Spirit, through the Scriptures; and our wilderness drink is the Spirit Himself, who was poured forth after Christ was smitten for our sins. Water out of the smitten rock is a beauteous type, as we shall presently see, of the Spirit as the fruit of Christ's supreme and all-sufficient sacrifice. Living bread (John 6), living water (John 7), these met Israel's needs, and are ample for ours. Fanny J. Crosby has taught the saints to sing

> All the way my Saviour leads me;
> Cheers each winding path I tread;
> Gives me grace for every trial,
> Feeds me with the Living Bread.
> Though my weary steps may falter,
> And my soul a-thirst may be,
> Gushing from the rock before me,
> Lo! a Spring of joy I see.

Continuing their pilgrimage, the children of Israel came to Rephidim, and after pitching their tents found that the experience at Shur (Exod. 15:22) was repeated here – "There was no water for the people to drink" (Exod. 17:1). Only desert travelers know what a privation and agony the scarcity of water is. Because of the severity of thirst under a blazing sun, many perish in the way. The Israelites had plenty to eat in the continuing miracle of the quails and the manna, but the people and their flocks could not exist long without refreshing water in such a barren and extremely dry area of the wilderness.

1. *Rebellion* (Exod. 17:2-4; Num. 20:10). "Ye rebels." Jeremiah had to confess of Israel, "This people hath a revolting and a rebellious heart" (Jer. 5:23), and somehow they found it hard to "unthread the rude eye of rebellion," as Shakespeare puts it. Divine authority expressed through human representations was rejected, even down to the appearance of God's King of Israel, of whom the Jewish rulers said, "We will not have this man to reign over us." The conduct of the people at Rephidim was nothing short of outrageous, for they not only tempted God but felt like killing Moses. They were guilty of opposition to God's minister, a distrust of His care, and indifference to His kindness, an unbelief in His providence, and a trying of His patience and fatherly forbearance.

If only God had transported His redeemed people directly from the Red Sea to Canaan there would not have been the sad and tragic exhibitions of what the human heart is capable of, and consequently they would not have proved such outstanding examples or types for us, as Paul reminds us (I Cor. 10). Israel remains a picture of many of us today who, redeemed out of the bondage of Satan, yet fail to enter into the fulness of the blessing of the Gospel of Christ. A wilderness of rebellion and defeat is ours. May we be kept from "an evil heart of unbelief" which ever reveals itself in departing from the living God.

2. *Request* (Exod. 17:4). As a leader of the hosts of pilgrims, Moses stands out in the magnificent grandeur Michaelangelo presented in his most remarkable sculpture of Moses. A man of lesser caliber would have crumbled under such a load. In reading Sir Walter Scott's *Marmion,* one instinctively thinks of Moses, who was privileged to see God face to face.

> His square-turn'd joints, and strength of limb,
> Show'd him no carpet knight so trim,
> But in close fight a champion grim,
> In camps a leader sage.

When the people chided with Moses, and angrily contended with him to do something about the disastrous water situation, he did not act on his own initiative, but pursued the only wise course of seeking the counsel of the Lord about the matter, "Lord, what shall I do?" His resource was God. Although Moses was chided and threatened with death by stoning, his plea betrayed no signs of resentment or vindictive imprecation on a people who had given him cruel and unmerited judgment. His cry to God was an anxious desire to know what was best to be done in the desperate situation he faced. In his attitude, Moses illustrated the teaching of Jesus, whose day the leader saw: "Love your enemies, bless them that curse you" (Matt. 5:44; Rom. 12:21). Moses prayed for those who despitefully used him.

3. *Remedy* (Exod. 17:5, 6). Moses did not seek the Lord's advice in vain. There came a quick reply to his question. He was to go before the rebellious people and, with his authoritative rod, smite the conspicuous rock in Horeb. Is there not a beautiful touch here concerning the delegated power and prestige of Moses as God's representative, and of His willingness to accomplish a further miracle for His people? "Take . . . thy rod, wherewith thou smotest the river, take in thy hand, and go." So Moses went and smote the *rock,* even as he had the *river.* He was not instructed to smite the people as they truly deserved for their treatment of God and himself, but to smite the rock. Was this not an evidence of divine compassion, and of God's desire for His chosen people to have His provision, as well as His protection and guidance day by day? He did not reward them according to their iniquity. His love suffereth long and is kind.

> The Lord told Moses not to smite the rebels, but the rock; not to bring a stream of blood from the breast of offenders, but a stream of water from the granite cliffs. The Cloud rested on a particular rock, just as the star rested on the house where the infant Saviour was lodged. And from the rod-smitten rock there forthwith gushed a torrent of fierce and refreshing water.

Perhaps this Horeb miracle was the greatest one performed by Moses, and in some respects resembled the greatest of Christ's miracles, namely, His Resurrection; being done without ostentation, and in the presence of a few chosen witnesses. Moses smote the rock in the sight of the elders, and Jesus, after His Resurrection appeared to His disciples. The Israelites doubtless saw the massive rock as soon as they reached Rephidim, and perhaps were impressed by its rugged grandeur, but they could have gazed and gazed upon it and died while gazing. It could yield no refreshment or relief for their dry throats until it was smitten by the rod of God.

Here we have a plain prophecy and picture of Christ, the rock of ages, smitten of God for our iniquities. Water was promised from the smitten rock: "There shall come water out of it that the people may drink"; and from the riven side of Jesus there flowed the double cure from sin's guilt and power. Jesus is the center and foundation of all God's counsels of love and mercy, and thus from Him all spiritual blessings flow to man. It was predetermined that from the smitten Lamb of God streams of grace would gush forth to refresh and quicken a lost world. Cleft by the hand of Jehovah at Calvary, the stricken Lamb opened the floodgates of love.

4. *Refreshment* (Ps. 105:40, 41). The psalmist, in his masterly survey of the history of Israel up until his own time, has this excellent summary of the experiences of the people after leaving Egypt:

> He spread a cloud for a covering;
> and fire to give light in the night.
> The people asked, and he brought
> quails, and satisfied them with
> the bread of heaven.
> He opened the rock, and the waters gushed out; they ran in the
> dry places like a river."

It is this addition to the account that Moses gives us of the miracle at Horeb that we are to dwell upon: "They ran in the dry places like a river." In fact, the whole verse is strikingly typical and prophetic of Israel, Christ, and the church.

a. *Israel*

The Commencement of the Jewish Nation. "He opened the rock."

Isaiah urged the people to look unto the rock from which they were hewn (Isa. 51:1-4). The great starting point in the divine purpose – the time the rock was opened – was with Abraham (Gen. 11; 12).

The Enlargement of the Jewish Nation. "The waters gushed out."

The psalmist says, "[God] increased his people greatly" (Ps. 105:24). In Egypt they waxed mighty, increased abundantly, and the land was filled with them (Exod. 1:7; Isa. 51:2). From the twelve sons of Jacob came the twelve tribes forming the nation (Gen. 35:11).

The Fertility of the Jewish Nation. "They ran in dry places like a river."

God made Israel the channel of revelation and blessing to the world. She functioned as streams in the desert, bringing the idea of God to surrounding nations. In the days of millennial ingathering Israel will be as a missionary nation reaching out to all dry places of the earth. She is predicted as filling the world with fruit (Isa. 27:6).

b. *The Church*

The Basis of the Divine Structure. "He opened the rock."

Referring to His deity and messiahship, Jesus said "Upon this *rock,*" or Himself and upon all He was to accomplish, "I will build My church." He is the impregnable rock of the Christian faith.

The Birth of the Church. "The waters gushed out."

Pentecost witnessed the historical birth of the church which Jesus purchased with His blood, and as the result of the effusion or plentitude of the Holy Spirit, His church became a dynamic force in the world.

The Building up of the Church. "Ran in the dry places like a river."

Is this phrase not descriptive of the rapid growth of the church as recorded in *The Acts?* Converts by the thousands were added to the church. Dry places were evangelized, and His true church is still as a river irrigating the waste and barren places of the earth.

c. *The Lord Jesus*

Calvary. "He opened the rock."

In the concluding section of this meditation on "the Smitten Rock," we deal more fully with Christ as the rock opened at Calvary. The question is, What do we know of the inner meaning of the smitten life of the Cross? A rock suggests something that is hard, stubborn, irresistible, adamant, and needs to be broken. The rock Moses opened was absolutely submissive to the touch of God. Are we opened or as yet unopened, that is, hard, selfish, vain, and carnal? A life can only yield its treasures when it is smitten. Think of the imprisoned forces hanging upon the breaking of a rock-like heart (Acts 16:30)!

Pentecost. "The waters gushed out."

Jesus promised the life-giving waters of the Holy Spirit as the result of His Death, Resurrection, and Ascension. But there would never have been a Pentecost had there not been a Calvary. Job says, "The rock poured me out rivers of oil" (Job 29:6), and *oil* as well as *water* typifies the ministry of the Spirit. Is ours the Pentecostal life, or are we living somewhere between Calvary and Pentecost? We have been saved by the blood of the cross, but as yet we have not experienced the flood tides of the Spirit's power.

The World. "Ran in the dry places like a river."

God so loved the world, and Christ died for its salvation and ever since

He has refreshed dry places all over the world. The reader is referred to the author's two volumes on *The Man Who Changed the World,* in which he has endeavored to trace the remarkable influence of Christ, the smitten rock, for well-nigh 2,000 years. Coming to our personal responsibility as those professing to be disciples of the universal Christ, can we honestly confess that by the aid of His Spirit we are like a river in the dry place in which we find ourselves? Let us not forget the significance of two little words of the psalmist's statement regarding the waters gushing out of the rock—*They ran,* meaning, on their own accord. We are not to force spiritual results, but just let them flow. If nothing blocks the movement of the Spirit in a believer, then He quickly makes a way for Himself through his life, and witness, making him, thereby, a channel of blessing to those around.

5. *Rebuke* (Exod. 17:7). That the Israelites might ever remember their folly at Horeb, Moses gave the place two names, Massah and Meribah: In his final instructions to the people ere they entered Canaan, he said, "Ye shall not tempt the LORD your God, as ye tempted Him in *Massah*" (Deut. 6:16). *Horeb* comes from a word meaning "to dry," and implies waste, or desert, or dried up place. Most typical of the world. *Massah* means "temptation" and is linked to the reminder of Moses, "Because they tempted the LORD, saying, 'Is the Lord among us, or not?'" *Meribah* means "chiding" or "strife" and is the same word translated "provocation" (Heb. 3:8), and serves as a memorial of their disrespect of Moses when the children of Israel chided him. "Why chide ye with me?" To doubt Jehovah's presence as the people did, and to sorely provoke His servant and desire his death, proved the deep-seated unbelief a redeemed people could be guilty of.

6. *Representation.* We now come to deal more particularly and fully with the smitten rock as a type, symbol, or prophecy of the Saviour. Like many other events, what happened at Horeb is rich in predictive and spiritual truth.

First of all, let us think of the figure of the rock itself, which is used so often in Scripture of our Lord. "Thou art my rock," "Lead me to the rock that is higher than I," "The shadow of a great rock in a weary land," "Upon this rock will I build my church." A rock is described as being *unsightly* (Isa. 53:2), *immovable* (II Sam. 22:32), *protective* (Isa. 32:2), all of which applies to Him who had no beauty that man should desire Him. Then there are the numerous provisions associated with a rock, all of which are applicable to Christ.

Living Water (Deut. 8:15).
Strength and Salvation (Ps. 62:3-7).
Refuge and Hiding Place (Num. 24:21; Pss. 32:7; 94:22).
Honey (Deut. 32:13).
Oil (Deut. 32:13).
Shadow and Rest (Isa. 32:2).
Fire of Judgment (Judg. 6:21).

> I hunger and I thirst;
> Jesu, my Manna be;
> Ye living waters burst
> Out of the Rock for me.

Paul, in a most definite way, identifies the rock at Horeb with Christ. The two warnings regarding types, given by Dr. C. I. Scofield are

1. Nothing may be dogmatically asserted to be a type without explicit New Testament authority.
2. All types not so authenticated must be recognized as having the authority of *analogy,* or spiritual *congruity,* merely.

That we have explicit apostolic authority for treating some of the events and experiences of Israel as types can be found in Paul's reference to Israel in the wilderness, in which he deals with the nation's vicissitudes not only as *emblems* but as *examples* of warning (I Cor. 10:6, 11). In his summary of the manna and the smitten rock, the apostle says,

> And [they] did all eat the same spiritual meat; And did all drink the same spiritual drink: for they drank of that spiritual Rock that followed them: and *that Rock was Christ*" (I Cor. 10:3, 4).

By *spiritual* we are to understand that which is divine or supernatural. The *bread* Israel fed on was not prepared by the women from gathered corn. It came from heaven, and being divinely created was spiritual. The *water* the people drank was not already in the rock, for we are distinctly told that "there was *no* water for the people to drink." It was imparted to the rock by the power of God to meet the thirst of man and beast alike, and being divinely produced was spiritual. Although it was literal water, it was not natural to the area; and because it was miraculously provided, it followed Israel through the wilderness.

But Paul did not mean that the *actual* rock or its water followed the people. There is a Jewish tradition to the effect that a fragment was broken off the rock that Moses smote and that this accompanied the Israelites through their wanderings, a tradition Paul used by way of illustration. But that the stream from the rock did not journey is proven by another smitten rock at Kadesh (Num. 20:1, 7-13). The qualifying phrase in Paul's rehearsal of the wilderness experiences is *that Rock was Christ*. He was the spiritual rock who followed a redeemed people. The term "followed" implies attendance on the people to minister to their needs. In most cases, He went before them, and when occasion required it, He followed *behind* (Exod. 14:19). If the Angel God sent to accompany the people and whose voice they were commanded to obey represents a theophanic appearance of Christ, then He was the rock who acted as a fellow-traveler with Israel (Exod. 23:20-23). Ellicott's comment on the Pauline passage reads,

> As Christ was "God manifest in the flesh" in the New Dispensation, so God manifest in the Rock—the source of sustaining life—was the Christ of the Old Dispensation. The Jews had become familiar with the thought of God as a rock (I Sam. 2:2; Ps. 91:12; Isa. 32:2). Though the Jews may have recognised the Rock poetically as God, they knew not that it was, as a manifestation of God's presence, typical of *the* manifestation which was yet to be given in the Incarnation. Paul's *But* is emphatic. *But* though they thought it only a Rock, or applied the word poetically to Jehovah, that Rock *was* Christ.

Christ spoke of the well of water springing up that He would give to all who were athirst (John 4:13, 14), and in ancient times He satisfied all alike as to their bodily thirst whenever water was needed; as on three occasions (Exod. 15:24, 25; 17:6; Num. 20:8), and this water for the body symbolized the spiritual drink from the spiritual rock. It is necessary to distinguish the difference between the latter two occasions, the first occurring at Horeb, the second at Kadesh. At the first Moses was told to *smite* the rock, and at Kadesh to *speak* to the rock, but angrily he smote it with vigor, and sinning with his lips was denied the privilege of taking Israel into Canaan after bearing with the people for forty years (Ps. 106:33). The conduct of the great leader, accentuated by the strife and murmuring of the people, was hasty and passionate. Directed to *speak* to the rock, he *smote* it *twice* in his impetuosity. Instead of speaking to the rock, he *spoke* to the people in a fury. Yet, in spite of the sudden lapse on Moses' part, God did not withhold the demand of the multitude for water. It may be that Moses wondered at the will of God to gratify such a rebellious people. Certainly they were utterly unworthy of such divine bounty, but God deals with sinners by grace (Eph. 2:1-6).

The brief poem of Cardinal H. Newman on "The Meekness of Moses" comes to mind as we think of Moses, the personification of meekness, losing his temper momentarily at the rock –

Moses, the patriot fierce, became
The meekest man on earth,
To show us how love's quickening flame
Can give our souls new birth.

Moses, the man of meekest heart,
Lost Canaan by self-will,
To show, where grace has done its part,
How sin defiles us still.

The smitten rock was a type of the smitten Saviour who was smitten of God and afflicted (Isa. 53:4, 10), and smitten to the heart (Isa. 2:10), and smitten once for all (Heb. 9:28). The Hebrew word for rock in Exodus 17:6 signifies a low-lying bed-rock typical of Christ's humiliation and death; but the word for rock in Numbers 20:8 means "a high and exalted rock" and can be predictive of Christ in His ascended glory. When Moses smote the rock at Kadesh instead of speaking to it, he sinned in that he tried to use what belongs only to God – power! "Ye rebels, must *we* fetch you water out of the rock?" To smite the smitten rock again is tantamount to crucifying the Son of God afresh.

Water, flowing out of the rock, then, is eloquent of the truth of the fulness of the Holy Spirit, and of life by Him. Smitten, the rock is a foregleam of Calvary, and of the outpoured Spirit as the seal of an accomplished redemption (John 7:37; Acts 2). The gift of the Spirit, who came as "the Promise of the Father," was imparted as soon as the smitten one, alive forevermore, entered heaven to take His seat at the right hand of the Majesty on high (Eph. 4:8-10). All the people of Israel had to do was to stoop and drink of the bountiful supply of water miraculously provided (Isa. 55:1). *Drinking* is a picture of faith appropriating all that God has graciously made possible through Christ the rock.

Thou art my Rock, O blessed Redeemer,
Thou art my Refuge where I may hide;
Thou art my Rock to shelter and bless me;
Ever in Thee I safely abide.

Thou art My Rock; when kingdom and nation,
Ruler and Crown have crumbled to dust;
Thou shalt remain my Rock of Salvation,
Rock everlasting, Thee will I trust.

J. *The Two Stone Tablets*

A people redeemed from bondage and brought into a new life in which they are to be dependent upon God for guidance, protection, and provision, and counted as God's people must be taught of Him. Heavenly instruction is the necessary sequence of deliverance, and in her journeys Israel was brought to Sinai to receive it. It was necessary for her not only to be led and fed by God, but taught of Him, and at Sinai she received the Law, obedience to which was designed to furnish the fullest expression for a godly life (Exod. 19-40).

No one can study the Law given at Sinai without having a deep reverence for it. All of its commandments are holy, just, and good, and reveal God's love to man and His desire to have many enjoy Him forever. In the forefront of it is the first and great commandment –

Thou shalt love the Lord thy God with all thy heart, with all thy soul, with all thy strength, and with all thy mind.

Thou shalt love thy neighbour as thyself.

There are laws for the regulation of the details of life, including justice, purity, truthfulness, kindness between man and man. Disobedience merits a just curse; obedience brings the promise of blessing. Laws follow for the regulation of worship with acts, place, and day of worship fully set forth. Explicit instructions are given for the making of the tabernacle, a theme we shall deal with when we come to the prophetic aspect of ritual.

In the midst of all these explicit instructions as to life in the world, and the worship of God, we are reminded that even in the life of the redeemed, there is always the possibility of backsliding, which Israel knew a great deal about. "*Exodus* would be distinctly less valuable, and its picture of the spiritual life distinctly less complete, had it not contained the record of The Golden Calf. It is written for our warning and consideration, to remind us that sin is ever near to us, ready to break out in the most appalling forms; but at the same time to show us that God does not cast away His people, even when they break His Covenants."

Most impressively, we are taught that the secret of victory and all blessing in the spiritual life lies in implicit obedience to the Word and will of God. Man's heart, however, is deceitful and desperately wicked, and the Law can only condemn and never change the heart and make a sinner perfect. The Law could never be a way of salvation. Its function was to reveal the need of a Saviour.

"The Law was our schoolmaster to bring us to Christ." God's Law was originally written on the heart of man, before being written on stone, but sin entered the universe and ruined God's purpose; and divine grace alone can bring the sinner nigh unto God. "The Law was given by Moses, *but* – a most blessed *but* – grace and truth came by Jesus Christ," who came as the end of the Law. It is here that Moses comes before us in a threefold way as a forecast of the coming Messiah.

1. Moses delivered Israel from the terrible bondage of Pharaoh and Egypt; Christ delivers us from the worse slavery to Satan, and from the tyranny of sin.

2. Moses is prominent as the law-giver, who brought from the Mount the revelation of God's will and word for His people – Christ is a far greater law in Himself, as the Sermon on the Mount reveals, for His spiritual law touches every phase of life. While we are not under the Mosaic Law, as those redeemed by blood we are *in-lawed* to Christ.

3. Moses is described as a law-giver, for by him God gave His system of laws to Israel (Num. 21:8; Deut. 33:21) – God or Christ is a perfect law-giver, whose sovereign will is the infallible rule of our conduct, and who is the only Lord of our conscience and the One we must obey (Isa. 33:22; James 4:12).

The term *law* is used in different ways:

To denote the Mosaic economy as contained in *The Pentateuch,* or the first five books of the Bible (John 1:17; Acts 13:39; 18:13).

To denote the Ceremonial Law, or the Covenant God made with the Jews concerning ceremonial observances (Luke 2:27; Acts 15:5, 24; Heb. 9:22).

To denote the moral law, or the Ten Commandments, often described as "The Decalogue" (Exod. 20:3-17; Matt. 5:19; Rom. 7:7), etc.

To denote judicial or civil law (John 7:51; Acts 19:38; I Cor. 6:1, 6).

To denote the Scriptures generally—the whole of *the revealed will of God* the Word contains (Pss. 1:2; 19:7).

To denote Scriptural doctrine and instruction (Prov. 13:14).

As to the object of the Law Moses received while on Mount Sinai, the same was for the direct instruction and guidance of Israel in respect to their duties which the people owed to God, and to each other. Obeying the Law, they were blessed; disobeying it, they were cursed. In such a Law there was the reflection of divine attributes, and comparing themselves with these, the people were able to judge their own character (Rom. 7:7). But the ultimate object of the Law was to prepare man for the coming of our Lord Jesus Christ as a Saviour, or as Paul expresses it, to function as our schoolmaster to bring us to Christ (Gal. 3:24; Rom. 8:7; 10:4). Bishop Hall voiced the prayer

> If the Law was thus given, how shall it be required. O God, how powerful art Thou to inflict vengeance upon sinners, Who didst thus forbid sin; and if Thou wert so terrible a lawgiver, what a judge shalt Thou appear!

Paul says the Law was *weak*, in that it condemned but was not able to save (Rom. 8:3). In a remarkable way the miracles Moses performed illustrated the ineffectiveness of the Law to redeem the one disobeying it. His miracles so frequently inflicted death as the punishment of sin. What a striking contrast we have with the miracles of Jesus, mostly all of which were miracles of mercy (John 1:17)! The Law condemned us to death because of our sinful disobedience, and Christ took that death and made it His own. Thus, through acceptance by faith of all He accomplished as our substitute, we are forever free from the condemnation and curse of the Law (Rom. 7:1-6).

> Free from the Law, O happy condition!
> Jesus hath bled, and there is remission.

The Law discovers to us our sin, revealing it in all its malignity, and pronounces the dread sentence. It lays hold of the sinner, like the creditor upon the debtor, demanding, *Pay me that thou owest!* But Jesus came as a Saviour, for the sinner was unable to pay the debt, so He paid it all, even to the uttermost farthing, and His Resurrection was God's receipt that the debt had been fully paid. Christ died under the curse of the Law, that we might be redeemed and rescued from it (Gal. 3:13, 24). Now in Christ, the believer is dead to the Law, and in a refuge where it cannot reach him to condemn. The Law required *works*—do and thou shalt live! The Gospel requires *faith*—believe and then behave. It is far easier to live and do as the Gospel says, than to do and live as the Law demanded.

Although the saints are no longer under the Law, but under grace (Rom. 6:14, 15), greater obligations are theirs because of the infinite cost of their deliverance from the curse of the Law. Strict adhesion to the ancient laws, and to traditions that gathered around it, produced the Scribes and Pharisees, rigid law-keepers, but heartless, merciless, and cruel. Their hearts were destitute of the peace, obedience should bring and so they plotted the death of Him who came that men might have perfect peace. It was Shakespeare who gave us the lines

> I feel within me
> A peace above all earthly dignities
> A still and quiet conscience.

How true it is that Christ alone, by His redeeming Gospel, can impart to man "a still and quiet conscience," a priceless treasure above "all earthly dignities!"

K. *The Nazarite Vow*

As we have now come to the book of Numbers to gather foregleams of Christ in some of the incidents recorded therein, it is interesting to observe how *Exodus* and *Numbers* are connected by references to the two pillars. *Exodus* ends with the tribute to God's faithfulness, in spite of unbelief, carnality and disobedience of His people:

> The cloud of the Lord was upon the tabernacle by day, and fire was on it by night, in the sight of all the house of Israel, throughout all their journeys (Exod. 40:38).
>
> "So it was alway: the cloud covered it by day, and the appearance of fire by night" (Num. 9:16).

No step was taken without these indications of the divine will, and their movement was instantly obeyed by day or night (Num. 9:21). Two silver trumpets were sounded to call attention to the moving of the cloud. As previously indicated, the covering and guiding cloud is full of spiritual import. Christ at His death bequeathed unto us a guide, and, as many as are led by the Spirit are the sons of God. *Exodus* and *Numbers* are connected by the truth that God's people must wait until the cloud moves, never acting till sure of God's will.

While the name of the fourth book of the Bible is *Numbers,* and is taken from the opening verses in which Moses was commanded by God to number all who formed the people of Israel, historically, *Numbers* is a continuation of *Exodus,* taking up the story of the wanderings of the people where Exodus left it. Typically, *Numbers* describes the service and walk of a redeemed people, which brings us to a consideration of the vow of the Nazarite, briefly referred to under Christ's title, *The Nazarene* (Num. 6:1-8).

The ordinance of Nazariteship, embracing both men and women, is full of practical and spiritual instruction. It involved the setting apart of one's self, in a particular way, from certain things which, though not sinful in themselves, might yet interfere with the intense consecration of heart and life true Nazariteship represented. *First,* there had to be abstentions from wine, the apt symbol of earthly pleasure (Ps. 104:15). During the wilderness pilgrimage, the Nazarite had to sedulously abstain from the fruit of the vine in any shape and form, and thereby be kept from the effects of strong drink. *Secondly,* there had not to be the application of the razor to the hair of the head. The locks of the separated were to be allowed to grow. *Thirdly,* the Nazarite was not to touch a dead body and become polluted.

The reasons for these self-restrictions are obvious. Wine, tending to inflame the passions, intoxicate the brain, and create a taste for luxurious indulgence would be detrimental to whole-hearted service for God. Abstention from wine was "the expression of a devotedness which found all its joy in the Lord" (Pss. 87:7; 97:12; Phil. 3:1-3; 4:4, 10). *The cutting of the hair* was a recognized sign of uncleanness (Lev. 14:8, 9), and its luxuriance was a symbol of professed purity. Long hair was naturally a reproach to man (I Cor. 11:14), but for a Nazarite it was a visible sign of separation and a willingness to bear reproach for Jehovah's sake. The extraordinary length of hair was a constant reminder of the vow taken, and a stimulation for others to imitate a pious example. *Contact with a dead body* disqualified a Nazarite for the work of God, and was carefully avoided as a cause of unfitness. Like the high priest, a Nazarite did not assist at the funeral rites of nearest relatives, preferring duty to God to the indulgence of strong natural affections. There had to be separation from the defiling influence of death because of "the consecration of God upon the head." The Nazarite, then, was one who set out on the path of entire devotedness or consecration to God.

Some Nazarites were set apart to serve the Lord more strictly than others. There were those who devoted themselves perpetually; others, for only a limited time (Num. 6:1, 2; Judg. 13:5, 7; 16:17; Amos 2:11). Some were given the Nazarite consecration by godly parents. Samson and John the Baptist were perpetual Nazarites, being separated unto God at their birth by their parents.

The Lord Jesus is the perfect fulfillment of all that is typified by the religious aspect of the Nazarite vow, in that He was sinless, separate from sinners, utterly separated unto His Father, allowing no natural claim to hinder or divert Him from a God-given course (Matt. 12:46-50; John 6:38). Not for one moment did He allow anyone or anything to come between His heart and the mission He was sent to accomplish. Throughout His life, His eye was single and His heart undivided. He stands out as the world's one true and perfect Nazarite.

For ourselves, we may think that monks are the only ones in our day who approximate to the Nazarite vow, but it is God's purpose that every child of His through faith in Christ should understand the true secret of spiritual Nazariteship, which is entire separation of heart and life to Him who claims all from those redeemed by the blood. Thorough separation from the world's ways and pleasures may not be a popular Gospel to preach. The ancient Nazarite was no ordinary man, like a neighbor who cut his hair, drank wine, and had contact with the dead. His was a peculiar path, and those who are the Lord's are to be a "peculiar people," or a people for His own possession – a people kept in true consecration unto Himself.

L. *The Magnificent Benediction*

The remarkable threefold blessing Aaron was given to pronounce over the people fittingly concludes the first section of *Numbers,* which, as C.H.M. Notes states, is made up of three divisions:

Chapters 1, 2 – The camp is duly arranged; every warrior is set in his proper place.
Chapters 3, 4 – Every workman is set in his proper place.
Chapter 5 – The congregation is purified from defilement.
Chapter 6 – Provision is made for the highest character and separation to God.

> The order is very marked and strikingly beautiful with, not only a cleansed and well-ordered camp, but also a character of consecration to God beyond which it is impossible to go, inasmuch as it is that which is only seen in its integrity in the life of our blessed Lord Himself. Having then reached this lofty point, nothing remains but for Jehovah to pronounce His blessing upon the whole congregation.

A brief consideration of this right royal blessing concluding Chapter 6 is in order, as it is prophetic of the apostolic benediction under grace (II Cor. 13:14), and of the attributes of the three Persons of the Trinity. For centuries it has been commonly recognized that Aaron's blessing is an allusion to the Godhead, just as the threefold *Holy* of Isaiah has been (Isa. 6:1-3). While the occasions on which the blessing was used are not stated, it would seem as if the solemn benediction was pronounced as the people were dismissed at the close of daily service. Mention is made of Aaron blessing the people, but no form of words is given (Lev. 9:22).

The impressive feature of the blessing is the repetition of the sacred name "Lord," or JEHOVAH, three times, expressing the great mystery of the Godhead – three Persons, yet one God. The separate clauses correspond to the respective offices of Father, Son, and Holy Spirit. "There is a rising gradation in the Blessing invoked," comments Ellicott, "until it culminates in that peace which is the highest of those gifts that God can bestow and that men can possess."

Jehovah the Father –

"The LORD bless thee, and keep thee" (Num. 6:24).

"The love of God . . . be with you all" (II Cor. 13:14).

Jehovah the Son –

"The LORD make His face shine upon thee, and be gracious unto thee" (Num. 6:25).

"The grace of the Lord Jesus Christ . . . be with you all" (II Cor. 13:14).

Jehovah the Spirit –

"The LORD lift up his countenance upon thee, and give thee peace" (Num. 6:26).

"The communion of the Holy Spirit be with you all" (II Cor. 13:14).

Then there is an addition to the triad of blessings –

"And they shall put my name upon the children of Israel; and I will bless them" (Num. 6:27).

Jesus said, "These things . . . do . . . for my name's sake" (John 15:21). While Aaron and his sons were commissioned to pronounce this wonderful benediction, it derived its virtue not because it was uttered by the lips of a priest, but because it was of God. Thus the encouraging assurance was added, "*I the Lord* will bless them."

If only Israel had basked in the sunlight of Jehovah's countenance, and lived in the power of all that is implied in the clauses of the benediction what a different story we would have had. But alas! the people soon turned aside from Jehovah, preferring defilement and idolatry to the manifold blessing of separation to God. At *Taberah,* meaning "a burning," so named because of the fire that consumed many of the people, because the righteous anger of Jehovah was kindled against them for their complaint about their divinely provided food and their lusting for the fleshpots of Egypt (Num. 11:1-9).

The disobedience and ingratitude of Israel became an almost intolerable burden for Moses to carry, so much so that he urged God to kill him, and thus deliver him from seeing any more of the wretchedness of the people (Num. 11:15). Such a request reveals Moses' state of mind – agonized and almost overwhelmed by a sense of the undivided responsibilities of his office. Relief from his heavy load was made possible by God in the appointment of the seventy elders to share the leader's tasks. How far removed from the spirit of the divine benediction was Kibroth-hattaavah, meaning "graves of lust," so named because of the way Israel gorged herself with food. God smote the camp with a fatal plague. The many who were buried there, dug their graves with their teeth.

The murmuring of Miriam against Moses, in which Aaron, the priest commissioned to pronounce the benediction, joined, testifies to their departure from the blessing it promised (Num. 12:1-16). Miriam, the ringleader in the revolt against Moses, was smitten with leprosy, which held up the journeying of the camp for a week. Then Israel took up the sour note and murmured against Moses, and also against Aaron and Miriam, and God was set to smite the rebels and kill them as one man, but Moses the intercessor prevailed, and God pardoned the transgressors (Num. 14:1-23) – a forecast of Him who prayed for His transgressors.

M. *Aaron's Rod*

One cannot read the wilderness story of the Israelites without being impressed with these opposite facts. On the one hand we learn what man is – proud, unbelieving, disobedient, self-willed, and lustful, even though redeemed by God. On the other hand, we learn of the exhaustless patience and boundless grace of the God sinned against. These two aspects run together like parallel lines. Korah, a Levite, became the ringleader in a rebellion against Moses and Aaron, which Jude describes as "the gainsaying of Core," or Korah. A man of considerable influence, he gathered many around his banner of revolt, among them being "princes, famous men, and men of renown." Feeling that their liberty was being curtailed, and that too many restrictions were being imposed upon them, these restless spirits confronted Moses and Aaron with the assertion, "Ye take too much upon you . . . wherefore then lift ye up yourselves above the congregation of the LORD?" (Num. 16:1-3). Korah, spokesman for the crowd, bent on equality, inferred that Moses and Aaron were lording it over their fellow Israelites and were interfering with their dues and privileges as fellow members of the camp. Their protest was that they were all on a dead level, and that one had as much right to be used in service as another.

What Korah and his deluded company failed to remember was that their jealous action was not against Moses and Aaron but against God, who had called His servants to their respective tasks. "A man can receive nothing except it be given him from heaven." It is God, therefore, Who calls and qualifies men for ends He has in mind. Moses and Aaron did not assume position on their own initiative. They were ordained of God. Stern justice overtook the restless, rebellious company. The earth swallowed them up with all their possessions, and their names perished from the congregation of Israel (Num. 16:23-35). Moses used the two phrases *The Lord will show* and *The Lord will choose* when speaking of the sovereign rights of Jehovah. Korah and his company accused Moses and Aaron, "Ye take too much upon you." Moses flung the accusation back into their faces, "Ye take too much upon you, ye sons of Levi" (Num. 16:4-7), and their presumption earned for them a terrible death.

All of this is the background to Aaron's rod flourishing. Korah was a Levite, but sought the priesthood, and his sin, or "gainsaying," was rebellious against Aaron, who was God's anointed High Priest. Added to this is "on the morrow," think of it, the very next day after the appalling destruction of Korah and his fellow rebels, "on the morrow, *all* the congregation murmured against Moses saying, 'Ye have killed the people of the Lord.'" With this, the divine sword of judgment was about to fall upon the whole assembly. Divine wrath was manifested in a fearful plague, but the two leaders charged with killing the Lord's people became His instruments in saving the rebellious host. Aaron went out among the plague-stricken, made an atonement for them, stood between the dead and the living and the plague stayed (Num. 16:46-48).

It was because of this controversy with Moses and Aaron regarding the priesthood that a decision and authoritative settlement was necessary. Doubts have to be removed, all murmurings silenced as to who was God's High Priest, so a miracle of a remarkable character decided the issue. All the heads of the tribes who might stake future claims to priesthood were gathered together and from them twelve were selected, and Moses was ordered by God to see that the name of each man was inscribed upon his rod, or wand of office – a practice borrowed from the Egyptians. Aaron, as the head of the tribe of Levi, had his name upon the rod. All of the rods were laid in the tabernacle close to the ark (Num. 17:10; Heb. 9:4), where a token was promised by God that would end the dispute once for all.

These rods, or dry sticks, transmitted from one head of a family to a succeeding head, were there before the Lord, and when Moses went into the tabernacle by the special command of God, he beheld the remarkable spectacle of Aaron's rod bearing fruit in three different stages at once, buds, blossoms, fruit; while all the other rods remained dry, dead sticks. The fruit-bearing rod was kept as a token against those who had rebelled, and if others of the camp should rebel, they would have to pay the penalty of death. After such a striking confirmation of Aaron's divine ordination as High Priest, the attitude of the people should have been, Let us fear and sin not! But they had short memories, even of tragedy and miracle, and sinned yet again.

In the budding of Aaron's rod we have a forceful type of our great High Priest, who was "declared to be the Son of God with power by resurrection from the dead." When brought into the tabernacle *all* twelve rods were alike lifeless; but God, the living God, by that almighty power peculiar to Himself, gave Aaron's rod a resurrection. As the Creator, He can do as He pleases, and so make the rod to bear the fragrant fruits in a moment. Aaron's priesthood was questioned by rebellious Korah, so God Himself confirmed His choice of Aaron (Num. 17:5), by putting life in his rod only. Religious leaders opposed the claims of Jesus as prophet, priest, and king, but in His Resurrection He was owned of God as the great High Priest forevermore. All the authors of various religions have died, Jesus among them, but only He rose from the dead and ascended on high to exercise His priestly intercession (Heb. 4:15; 5:4-10; 7:24, 25). Aaron died on the top of Mount Hor, and the people mourned for him thirty days – our blessed High Priest died but rose again after three days, and is alive forevermore.

N. *The Brazen Serpent*

As we are discovering, many episodes in the wilderness history of Israel, particularly the terrible judgments inflicted upon them, reveal both the innate resistance to divine claims and the constant need of divine deliverance. We have repeated proofs of man's tendency to sin, revealing his need of spiritual assistance to enable him to overcome it. But the prophetic nature of many of the historical events reminds us that it was reserved to the Gospel dispensation fully to manifest, in the work of the Saviour and of the Holy Spirit, the exact nature of the deliverance and assistance a sinner requires. There is no more impressive picture of this fact than in our Lord's use of "the brazen serpent," in which He declared that complete salvation from Satan's power can be found only in Himself. The following features of type and anti-type are clearly apparent to all Bible lovers.

1. *The cause.* While compassing the land of Edom the people of Israel came to the sandy stretch of the wilderness at the head of the Gulf of Akabah, where they yielded to a twofold sin. The first was that of *discouragement.* The journey had been

a rugged one, and in addition to all the hardships and dangers encountered, heartlessness was theirs because of the consciousness that they were turning their backs upon the land of Canaan, instead of marching by a direct course into it. Their intermittent disobedience meant a delayed, zig-zag journey, and the soul of the people was grieved because of such a wait. As Jamieson, Fausset, and Brown state in their *Commentary:*

> Disappointment on finding themselves so near the confines of the Promised Land without entering it —vexation at the refusal of a passage through Edom, and the absence of any Divine interposition in their favour—above all, the necessity of a retrograde journey, by a long and circuitous route through the worst part of a sandy desert, and the dread of being plunged into new and unknown difficulties—all this produced a deep depression of spirits.

Another contributing factor to the severe judgment Israel experienced at this time was the way they despised their unvarying divine provision. Low-spirited, they gave way to a gross outburst of murmuring at the scarcity of water, and at the sameness of the food they had to daily eat. It was the same story over again, an addition to "the murmurs of the wilderness." What offensive language the people used against God, and against Moses:

> Wherefore have you brought us up out of Egypt to die in the wilderness? for there is no bread, neither is there any water; and our soul loatheth this light bread (Num. 21:5).

The word for *light* denotes something vile or worthless, and used here implies bread without substance or nutritious quality. What an ungrateful way to describe the manna given them from heaven! Today there are those who treat "the spiritual meat" which Christ gave to His church in His Word and ordinances in the same contemptuous fashion. Is it not blasphemy to despise Christ, the Bread of God from heaven?

But loathing the manna as being worthless or without nutrition was alien to the experience of the people because on the strength of their heavenly food they performed for almost forty years many hard and toilsome journeys. "They had been indulging a hope of the better and more varied fare enjoyed by a settled people; and disappointment, always the more bitter as the hope of enjoyment seems near, drove them to speak against God and against Moses." By their unbelief, blasphemy, and the attributing of heartlessness to God, the people tempted Him. Because Paul says that the rock that followed them was Christ, he warned the carnal Corinthians:

> Neither let us tempt Christ, as some of them also tempted, and were destroyed of serpents (I Cor. 10:9).

2. *The catastrophe*. The cry of Israel was "Would to God we had died in the land of Egypt!" Before they were hardly aware of it, many of them perished suddenly in the wilderness, for speedily crowds of those complaining, unbelieving people tasted the bitter fruits of their sin. "The LORD sent fiery serpents among the people, and they bit the people; and much people of Israel died" – how many we are not told (Num. 21:6). This divine visitation must have resulted in a terrible catastrophe in the life of the camp.

The species of serpent mentioned is of the fiery kind. Isaiah speaks of it as "the flying fiery serpent" (Isa. 14: 29; 30:6). *Flying*, because of their swift-darting motion; *fiery* because of the color and renown. Some writers suggest that they were so called because of the bright fiery red upon their heads, or because of the blazing color on their scales, or because of their inflammatory and poisonous bite. The Hebrew reads "the serpents, the seraphim," or "the burning ones" (Deut. 8:15; Isa. 14:29). While the particular part of the desert where the Israelites found themselves was the habitat of various venomous reptiles, the multitude of them overtaking the people at once was a miraculous act of the Creator. "The Lord sent fiery serpents among the people," and they proved that the wages of sin is death.

Is there not a suggestive truth associated with serpents as the media of judgment? Was it not "the Old Serpent, the Devil" who beguiled Eve, and was the *source* of Israel's discontent and disobedience during the wilderness journey? Is not this enemy of the Jews at the back of their hostility toward God? Thus, when they were bitten by the serpents, the people would understand the true *character* and *instigator* of their murmurings. As the people of Jehovah, they refused to walk happily and contented with Him, and so suffered the fatal power of the serpent.

3. *The contribution.* The tragic loss and suffering produced by the destructive, poisonous serpents brought Israel to a sense of sin, and after having spoken *against* Moses, they plead with him to pray for them. Repentant, they confessed, "We have sinned, we have spoken against the LORD . . . Pray unto the LORD." Moses, so prominent in his leadership of Israel as an *intercessor,* "prayed for the people" (Num. 21:7). The severity of the scourge, and the appalling numbers of those who died, revealed to the people left the enormity of their transgression and made them contrite of heart. C. B. Shelley wrote that

> Those who inflict must suffer, for they see
> The work of their own hearts, and that must be
> Our chastisement or recompense.

The people of Israel had brought much pain to the heart of God, and in their own suffering they saw the evil of their own hearts, and with their repentance came recompense, for once again they were to prove the grace and mercy of Him they had sinned against. God is never silent to the confession, "We have sinned." Such is the opportunity for Him to display His willingness to pardon.

> Though we have sinned,
> There is mercy and pardon—
> Pardon for you, and for me.

4. *The cure.* How swift God is in answering man's repentant cry! Before the plea is uttered, He answers. No time elapsed between the prayer of Moses for the people and the reply of Heaven, for

> The LORD said unto Moses, Make thee a fiery serpent, and set it upon a pole (Num. 21:8). And Moses made a serpent of brass and put it upon a pole (Num. 21:9).

The unique method for the miraculous healing of the serpent-bitten Israelites was of God's selection. Such a peculiar cure was designed to show that the remedy was not in the lifeless brazen serpent itself but in the efficacy of the power and grace of Him who conceived such an avenue of relief. Why was the divinely ordained remedy "a serpent of brass"? That metal serpent was the very likeness of that which had brought so much death into the camp and was set up for all to see as the channel through which the abundant, forgiving grace might flow down to those who had so grievously sinned against God. The poisonous serpents were the evidence and agents of God's judgment—now a serpent of brass having no venom witnesses to His pardoning mercy.

The *fiery* serpent Moses fashioned was of brass or bronze and resembled the bright, red color of the destructive serpents. *Brass* is deemed to be symbolic of judgment. A people obstinate in sin are likened unto those with a neck like an iron sinew and a brow of brass (Isa. 48:4). Infinite power as well as judicial authority are suggested by the Redeemer's feet of brass (Rev. 1:15). The brazen serpent had to be raised upon a pole, or standard, for all to see. The word used here is the same occurring in Exodus 17:15, *Jehovah-nissi* -- "Jehovah is my standard or banner." The Old Serpent was the cause of sin and death, and that serpent lifted testified to God's dominion over all the wiles of the Devil.

5. *The condition.* Although God provided a cure, those requiring it had to appropriate it. "Every one that is bitten, when *he looketh upon it,* shall live . . . If a serpent had bitten any man, when *he beheld* the serpent of brass, he lived" (Num. 21:8, 9). Those smitten by the serpents had *to look* not at their wounds or the dying around them or at Moses but at the upraised serpent. If the afflicted failed to look, thinking the condition was far too simple, then they died. The verb employed here means more than simply seeing. It implies a believing faith behind the look. Beholding they believed. When we read of those who *looked* for Redemption (Luke 2:38), we know that behind such a gaze there was an expectant faith. The psalmist speaks of those who *looked* to God and were "lightened," or "their faces were made radiant" (Ps. 34:5), which emphasizes the transforming power of beholding believingly.

6. *The consequence.* How immediate and radical the cure! At the moment the eyes of those bitten by the serpents were focused upon the brazen serpent they *lived!* They were not merely healed but *lived.* They became as new creatures and life from God flowed through their poisoned bodies. Looking they lived! They not only "got better" of the serpent's bite; all at once the gift of life became theirs, not through a serpent of brass but from Him who alone is the source of life. The wounded Israelite, if he wanted to live, had to fix his earnest gaze upon God's remedy. The command was explicit, "*Every one* that is bitten, *when* he looketh upon *it,* shall live." He was shut up to God's exclusive remedy for his need. If he looked elsewhere, he remained wounded and ready to die. But if he turned his languid eyes upon the pole, God's provision of life became his.

Traditionally, the serpent is associated with the art of healing. Two serpents twined around a rod are symbolic of the power of medicine. The badge worn by the Royal Army Medical Corps in the British Army is fashioned like two serpents. The ancient Greeks and Romans had a figure of a serpent upon the altars as symbolic of a guardian spirit.

7. *The connection.* The episode of the brazen serpent has a very definite and vital connection with the Gospels in that it is the one type of the death of Christ *He Himself selected* from the many Old Testament ones, and used to illustrate His being lifted up on a cross (John 3:14, 15).

> As Moses lifted up the serpent in the wilderness, even so must the Son of man be lifted up:
> That whosoever believeth in him should not perish, but have eternal life.

As and *so,* these two little words reveal how the serpent on the pole is a great evangelical type. The cure was made in the likeness of the cause of suffering and death – Christ was made in "the likeness of sinful flesh," and was made sin for us (Rom. 8:3; II Cor. 5:21). Through the brazen serpent, the bitten Israelite was healed from the dread effects of poisoning – Christ at Calvary redeemed us from the sting of death and the power of that Old Serpent, the Devil. The brazen serpent had to be set upon a pole – Christ was lifted up on a cross. "Lifted up" was His usual expression of His crucifixion (John 3: 14; 8:28; 12:32, 33). The *tree* on which He died actually means a *stake*.

> Lifted up was He to die,
> *It is finished* was His cry.

The brazen serpent, by itself, was not able to give life to the dying. Such life came from the God who devised the means – Christ, however, had, and has, life in Himself. "I am the Life," and through His death He made possible a perfect deliverance for a Satan-controlled world. The book of Wisdom in *The Apocrypha* has the verse "He that turned himself toward the serpent was not saved of the thing that he saw, but by Thee, that art Saviour of all" (Wisd. of Sol. 16:7). The serpent on the pole was made of brass, symbol of judgment – Christ on the cross bore out judgment, the load of which He felt when He cried, "My God, My God, why hast Thou forsaken Me?" All that the dying Israelite had to do was to look at the brazen serpent – Christ pleads with sinners to *look* unto Him and be saved. Thus the serpent on a pole was a most striking type of the power of faith in Christ to heal all who look to Him of their sins. When Christ said, "Whosoever believeth in him should not perish," the same answered to the *looking* of the bitten Israelite. As a commentator of last century wrote,

> When He bids us look to Him, it is not surely of any single act, still less is it of any more passing feeling of the mind that He speaks. What He means is that our whole lives should be one continual looking unto Him, one continued act of faith in that undeserved and complete deliverance which He wrought for us upon the Cross, should draw our whole hearts to him.

As we know, *looking* is a type of faith common in Scripture. When you look, you *turn your attention* to the object, then sight *rests and dwells on it*. Looking is *expecting*. Looking is *relying*, as when you say to a friend, "I look to you to do it."

> Turn your eyes upon Jesus,
> Look full in His wonderful Face:
> And things of earth will grow
> strangely dim,
> In the light of His Glory and Grace.

The Israelite who looked up at the brazen serpent *lived*, but his life was only lengthened for a little – Christ offers all who look to Him not only a present deliverance from the serpent who deceived the world's first family, but "eternal life," a phrase signifying quality as well as duration. As Christ is the Eternal One, the life He gives is Himself. What must not be forgotten is the fact that each bitten Israelite had to look at the raised serpent for himself or herself in order to receive life. There was intense individuality – "*Every one* that is bitten, when *he* looketh, shall live." It is so with the salvation –no one can be saved by proxy. "What must *I* do to be saved?" Deliverance from sin's thralldom comes to us individually, through an individual faith.

> There is life for a look, at the
> Crucified One;
> There is life at this moment,
> for *thee*.

Whosoever is the word the Saviour used, and it means "each and every one." "When *he* beheld the serpent of brass, *he* lived." And each of us lives as God would have us live if we have beheld the Lamb who took away the sin of the world. When speaking of his conversion as a youth, C. H. Spurgeon used to say,

> I looked at Him,
> He looked at me,
> And we were one forever.

The amazing grace of God is seen in what followed the miracle healing of the serpent-bitten Israelites as they went on their journey. Again, water was a necessity, and reaching Beer they found a dry well, but under the direction of Moses the lawgiver, the princes and nobles of the people re-dug the well, and Israel sang the song "Spring up, O well; sing ye unto it." Drinking of its waters, they went on to defeat their enemies. The spiritual application of these events is easy to make –

a. Healing and Life through the Uplifted Remedy (Num. 21:8, 9; John 3:14, 15).
b. The Provision of Upspringing Water (Num. 21:16; John 7:37-39).
c. The Experience of Ensuing Joy (Num. 21:17, 18; Rom. 14:17).
d. The Manifestation of Power (Num. 21:21-24; Acts 1:8).

Unfortunately, Isreal came to make the serpent of brass a graven image, worshipping it with incense. Under the great spiritual revival in Hezekiah's reign, the king destroyed all graven images, groves for idol worship, and broke in pieces "the brazen serpent that Moses had made: for unto those days the children of Israel did burn incense to it: and he called it Nehushtan" (II Kings 18:4). There is a tradition to the effect that David had used this serpent as a *totem* over his house. *Nehushtan* means "a piece of brass." Such was the contemptuous way Hezekiah described this object of idolatrous worship.

Have we not become guilty of the same folly? Today, the cross is a charm to be worn around the neck as a kind of talisman. In Roman Catholicism, a crucifix is venerated, sometimes with incense. The difference between a cross, often seen in Protestant churches, and a crucifix, so prominent in Catholic churches, is that the cross is *empty*, whereas the crucifix bears the battered image of the supposed Christ and merits the worship of Catholics. Is this not the same kind of idolatry Israel was guilty of in making the brazen serpent a graven image? It is not Biblical to present the image of the blood-stained Christ on a cross, for by dying, death He slew. He is no longer on a cross, which ever remains as a symbol of what He accomplished thereon, but alive forevermore.

O. *Six Cities of Refuge*

The more we follow the wanderings and wickedness of Israel in the wilderness, the more we are amazed at the grace and mercy of God, and of the way He provided for them. As the Eternal One, knowing the end from the beginning, He was cognizant of all that would befall His redeemed people, and so prepared for their future needs and emergencies. This is evident in the commandment concerning the six cities of refuge. In the giving of the Law, among the judgments God told Moses to set before the people was one concerning manslaughter:

> If a man lie not in wait, but God deliver him into his hand; then *I will appoint thee a place whither he shall flee* (Exod. 21:13).

Later on, we are given the exact location and object of these six safe hiding places (Num. 35:6-34; Deut. 19:1-13; Josh. 20:1-9; 21), references the reader should study together for a full understanding of those entitled to security in the appointed refuge, which owed its origin to God. Three cities of refuge were situated on the eastern side and the other three on the western side of Jordan. Meticulous even down to details, God made all arrangements as plain, simple, and easy as possible.

The cities were easy of access and situated through the land at proper distances from each other, therefore convenient to every part of the land, so that wherever there was need of shelter one was at hand. There was always a city within reach of any Israelite exposed to the sword of the avenger. If situated on an eminence, the city would be easily seen from a distance. High roads, kept in good condition, led to each city, the gates of which were always open. Jewish tradition has it that there were signposts at crossroads on which was written "Refuge! Refuge" thus pointing the way, and that runners, knowing the law of God, were stationed to guide fugitives to the city of safety.

Only a person who had unawares and unintentionally slain anyone could use the city. If not overtaken by a pursuer or an avenger of blood, the refugee was safe within the shelter, provided he did not remove more than a thousand yards from its circuit, nor quit the refuge till the death of the high priest in office. God made it clear that these cities of refuge were only for those who had killed any person *unawares* and *unwittingly*, and who had not *hated him aforetime* (Josh. 20:1-6). Such a person was not guilty of any pre-meditated murder. For a murderer, the Law was rigid, unbending, and explicit. "The murderer shall surely be put to death. The revenger of blood himself shall slay the murderer: when he meeteth him, he shall slay him" (Num. 35:18, 19).

Among the conditions imposed upon those fleeing to a refuge were a compulsory trial for man-slaying (Num. 35:24-28), for cases of involuntary murder contemplated by the Law are detailed (Num. 35:22, 23). Then, while in a city the refugee had to support himself by some kind of work, as idleness was not permitted. Although a fugitive, he could breathe freely once he was in the allotted boundary. The moment he crossed the threshold of the gate of the designated city, he was safe. An exile from home and dear ones, he yet knew that not a hair of his head could be touched while he remained within the bounds of the city to which he had fled. He lived as a prisoner of hope, waiting for the death of the high priest, when by Law he would be perfectly free to return to his inheritance.

Bible lovers know how all this is wonderfully predictive and illustrative of Christ our refuge and salvation. Even the names of the cities of refuge are startlingly suggestive, carrying a deep spiritual significance, as we are to see. But before we approach the application of the cities to Christ and His Gospel, let us not forget the picture of Israel herself they suggest. The refuge was for the man who had unwittingly or innocently killed another. Was this not Israel's sin in respect to their Messiah when she became the slayer of innocent blood on Calvary? Did not Peter have this in mind when he condemned the Jews with having killed the Prince of Life? "Brethren, I wot that *through ignorance* ye did it, as did also your rulers" (Acts 3:17). But as A. M. Hodgkin reminds us,

> Israel has been a fugitive ever since, his possession is forfeited, and to all appearances lost. But the High Priest dwells within the veil in the heavenly sanctuary, and one day He will come forth, the Heavenly Priest, and Israel shall receive forgiveness and be restored to his heritage.

One of the most conspicuous types of the Lord is that of the refuge. Three times over in the eleven verses of Psalm 46 we have the phrase "God is our refuge." Fleeing from King Saul after hiding in a cave, David prayed, "In the shadow of thy wings will I make my refuge, until these calamities be overpast" (Ps. 57:1. See also Ps. 142:5). In blessing the tribes before he died, Moses could say "The eternal God is thy refuge" (Deut. 33:27). Then there is the great passage from Isaiah in his description of Christ's future kingdom, "The LORD . . . a place of refuge, and for a covert from storm and from rain" (Isa. 4:5, 6). Scores of our hymns likewise extend the theme as Jesus, the safe and blessed shelter, the most popular of which is Charles Wesley's great hymn:

> Other Refuge have I none,
> Hangs my helpless soul on Thee.

Turning back to the Psalms, where we have the phrase, "God is known in her palaces for a refuge" (Ps. 48:3). The R.V. puts it, "God hath made *Himself known* in her palaces for a refuge," and both translations are true. The refuge is God's revelation of Himself as the sinner's hiding place from sin; and man has discovered God to be the rock in which he can hide. All saved by grace "have a strong consolation, who have fled for refuge to lay hold upon the hope set before us" (Heb. 6:18-20). We thus come to the six named cities of refuge, showing how their names are typical and prophetic of all we have in Christ as the shelter from judgment. Concerning these cities, Joshua has the phrase "They appointed" (Josh. 20:7), which means, as the R.V. states it, "set apart" or "sanctified." How applicable this is of Christ, who, for our sakes, sanctified or set apart Himself as our Refuge!

Once in the land, forty-eight cities with their suburbs, were given over to the Levites; and out of these, the Levites had the privilege of providing six cities as centers of shelter for manslayers. These were

Kedesh in Galilee
Shechem in Mount Ephraim
Hebron in Judah
Bezer in the Wilderness
Ramoth in Gilead
Golan in Bashan – (Josh. 20).

It would be interesting to know why the cities of refuge were limited to six. Doubtless, being strategically placed, they would be sufficient for the needs of the people. In spiritual arithmetic, *six* is *seven* minus *one*, and therefore represents man, even at his best, coming short of spiritual perfection. The *six* cities of refuge offer a most expressive metaphor of Christ, but as with all symbols and types, they are not able to perfectly present Him who exceeds all material portrayals of His majesty and glory. He outshines the most brilliant sun of prophecy.

1. *Kedesh in Galilee.* This Canaanite town, where Barak lived (Judg. 4:6), had an interesting name, for it means "holy place." *Kedesh* is from a root implying "to sanctify." Possibly there was a sanctuary in the area, making it a profitable place for those fleeing to it for shelter. Jesus is the true *Kedesh* for all who are pursued by their sin, unholiness and uncleanness. Testimonies to His holiness came from every quarter:

From God – "Thou wilt not . . . suffer thine Holy One to see corruption" (Ps. 16:10).

From Satan – "I know thee who thou art, the Holy One of God" (Mark 1:24).

From Gabriel – "That which is to be born of thee shall be called Holy" (Luke 1:35, R.V.).

From Peter – "Thy holy child Jesus." "He which hath called you is Holy" (Acts 4:27).

From Paul – "Who knew no sin." "Holy . . . separate from sinners" (II Cor. 5:21; Heb. 7:26).

From John – "These things saith He that is holy" (Rev. 3:7).

Our refuge is not in our own holiness but in the Holy One. When we are urged by Peter, "Be you holy," he does not infer that we are to strive to manufacture the holiness pleasing to our heavenly *Kedesh*. What He commands He supplies. "Faithful is he that calleth you, *who also will do it*" (I Thess. 5:24). His exhortations are enablings. Holiness of life is to be obtained as a gift, attained by effort.

2. *Shechem in Mount Ephraim.* After the conquest of Canaan, the tribes of Israel met at Shechem to hear and to subscribe to the Law. Then it became a Levitical city and one of the cities of refuge Josh. 8:30; 20:7; 21:21). It was also at Shechem that the ten tribes of the north rejected Rehoboam, Solomon's son, as their king (I Kings 12). Because of its situation *on the back* of Gerizim, the name *Shechem* means "back" or "shoulder," coming from a word signifying "strength" or "to burden." What better name could there be for Him whose back is strong enough to bear any burden we cast upon it (Ps. 55: 22)? He is our *Shechem*, in whom we can place absolute reliance, our refuge from all self-effort, self-trust, and anxiety.

a. His Shoulder is the Place of Remembrance and Intercession –

"Aaron shall bear their names before the LORD upon his two shoulders for a memorial" (Exod. 28:12).

"I pray for them." "He ever liveth to make intercession" (John 17:9; Heb. 7:25).

b. His Shoulder is the Place of Abiding Security and Rest –

"He shall dwell between his shoulders" (Deut. 33:12).

"He layeth it on his shoulders, rejoicing" (Luke 15:5; Ps. 91:1).

c. His Shoulder is the Place of Authority and Power –

"The government shall be upon his shoulder" (Isa. 9:4, 6).

"Out of thee shall come a Governor" (Matt. 2:6).

d. His Shoulder is the Place of Messianic Rule –

"The key of the house of David will I lay upon his shoulder" (Isa. 22:22).

"The Root of David, hath prevailed to open the book" (Rev. 5:5; 1:18).

The question is, Have we learned to lean our whole weight upon Him who offers us His shoulder? "Cast *all* your care upon me" is His invitation, and His *all* means ALL. How carefree life would be if only we could rest in His promise! – "Even to hoar hairs will I carry you" (Isa. 46:4).

Yes, for me, for me He careth,
With a brother's tender care;
Yes, with me, with me He shareth
Every burden, every fear.

3. *Hebron in Judah.* Hebron was a town with memorable associations. It was the place to which Abraham came and where Sarah his wife died and was buried (Gen. 13:18; 23:2, 19). For a while David used it as his capital (I Chron. 11:1-3), and it became the center of his son Absalom's revolt (II Sam. 15:7). Doubtless because it was the earliest seat of civilized life and the first home of the Patriarchs (Gen. 35:27), it came by its name *Hebron*, meaning "confederation" or "communion," from an origin suggesting "association" or "fellowship." Here, again, is a name prophetic and typical of Jesus, who is our refuge from all unholy, broken fellowships of sin and death, and the only One in whom we have perfect communion. As our heavenly *fellow*, He offers us holy fellowship – a fellowship both mutual and reciprocal.

What a fellowship, what a joy
Divine,
Leaning on the everlasting arms,
What a blessedness, what a peace
is mine,
Leaning on the everlasting arms.

The Bible presents many facets of this most privileged Fellowship.

There is Fellowship with the Father (I John 1:3).

There is Fellowship with the Son (I John 1:3).

There is Fellowship with the Spirit (2 Cor. 13:14; Phil. 2:1).

There is Fellowship with the Saints (I John 1:3).

> The Fellowship of Kindred minds,
> Is like to that above.

There is Fellowship with Christ's Sufferings (Phil. 3:10).

Abiding in our heavenly *Hebron,* a refuge tried and sweet, abundant blessings are ours. For instance, we have continual light and liberty. "If we walk in the light, . . . we have fellowship one with another, and the blood of Jesus Christ his Son cleanseth us from all sin" (I John 1:7). Such unbroken, undisturbed fellowship involves entire separation from all forbidden fellowship with the unfruitful works of darkness, and an unequal yoke with unbelievers (II Cor. 6:14; Eph. 5:11). Fellowship with Christ means complete harmony with His mind and will, for "can two walk together, except they be agreed?" (Amos 3:3).

4. *Bezer in the wilderness.* This home of the Merarites of the tribe of Levi was a city in the wilderness plateau east of the Dead Sea. Apart from the fact that it was in the territory allocated to Reuben and made a city of refuge, we know little about it (Josh. 21:36; Deut. 4:43). *Bezer* means "a fortification," "a stronghold," and springs from a word meaning "to hew as from a quarry." Perhaps it offered an impregnable position and was adapted as a fortress. If so, then it would make an ideal refuge for those in that area who fled to it from avengers. Is this not another picture of Him who is prophesied and promised as our fortress? "The LORD is my fortress" (Ps. 18:2; II Sam. 22:2). That He is our unassailable *Bezer,* in which we can hide from all our fears and foes, is evident from several Scriptures. All prisoners of hope can turn to Him as the *stronghold* (Mic. 4:8; Zech. 9:12) from –

Trouble – "The Lord . . . is a strong hold in the day of trouble" (Nah. 1:7).

Pride – "Thou shalt hide them . . . from the pride (plottings, R.V.) of man" (Ps. 31:20).

Strife – "Thou shalt keep them secretly in a pavilion from the strife of tongues" (Ps. 31:20).

Satan – "Mighty through God to the pulling down of strong holds" (II Cor. 10:4).

If we have to take refuge in our heavenly *Bezer,* then let us leave all our foes and needs to Him to take care of. Is not His name "a strong tower: the righteous runneth into it, and is safe" (R.V.) "set on high" (Prov. 18:10)? This is the aspect of the divine sufficiency Martin Luther has so forcibly expressed in his Battle Hymn of the Reformation:

> A Mighty Fortress is our God,
> A Bulwark never failing:
> Our Helper He, amid the flood
> Of mortal ills prevailing.
> For still our ancient foe
> Doth seek to work his woe;
> His craft and power are great,
> And armed with cruel hate—
> On earth is not his equal.

5. *Ramoth in Gilead.* This further Levitical city selected as another of the centers for refugees was the place where Ahab was slain in his war against the Syrians (I Kings 22). Jehoram was also wounded here (II Kings 8:28, 29). Some writers think it identical with Mizpah. As a name, *Ramoth* means "height" or "eminence," and comes from a word implying "to be lofty," "exaltation." Perhaps it was so named because of its high, lofty, conspicuous position – a city set on a hill that could not be hid. *Ramoth* is predictive of our Re-

deemer, whom God so highly exalted (Phil. 2:9), and as our refuge affords us freedom from all low, debasing, humbling things and thoughts. He is indeed "high above all the people" (Ps. 99:2).

Higher than the Heavens and the Planets (Job 22:12; Isa. 57:15).
Higher than the Saintliest (Ps. 61:2).
Higher than all Worldly Dominions (Isa. 6:1).
Higher than all the Ways and Works of Men (Isa. 55:9).

As those who have been raised in Him to the heavenlies, can we say that ours is a practical experience of His exaltation as our *Ramoth?* Do we dwell on high, walk upon the high places, praise Him in the heights (Isa. 33:16; Heb. 3:19; Ps. 148:1)? Are we found joyfully responding to His invitation "Come up hither" (Rev. 4:1; Luke 14:10)? What need there is for a higher plane of spiritual experience of holiness, prayer, and communion! "Our conversation is in heaven" (Phil. 3:20). As those who claim to be risen with Him, it is imperative for our victory and His glory to seek those things which are above (Col. 3:1, 2). How slow we are to learn that the only way up is down!

> The highest place that Heaven affords
> Is His by sovereign right:
> The King of kings, and Lord of lords,
> He reigns in perfect light.

6. *Golan in Bashan.* This sixth city of refuge in the half tribe of Manasseh which was given to the Levites (Deut. 4:43) was evidently an important city in its time, although its site cannot definitely be identified. As to the significance of its name, there is a division of opinion. Some say that *Golan* means "happy" or "joy"; others that it implies "circle" or "revolution." Both ideas can be applied to Him who is the refuge of our soul.

a. *Take Happiness*

What is happiness? Emerson would answer, "To fill the hour – that is happiness." But it all depends upon what we fill the hour with. Many crowd useless pleasures and pursuits into the hour, and are the most unhappy people in the world. In his original draft for the Declaration of Independence, Thomas Jefferson laid down certain basic principles in "the pursuit of happiness." John Keats asked,

> Wherein lies happiness? In that which becks
> Our ready minds to fellowship Divine,
> A fellowship with essence.

His "fellowship with essence" can only be found in communion with Him who is the perfection of all true happiness. Paul speaks about "the Gospel of the Blessed – or Happy – God" (I Tim. 1:11), whose beloved Son was anointed with the oil of gladness above His fellows (Heb. 1:9). Minds turned to "fellowship Divine" share divine happiness, for "happy are the people whose God is the Lord." Does not Solomon remind us that "Whoso trusteth in the LORD, happy is he" (Prov. 16:20)?

b. *Take the Circle*

What application to Christ is there in this further suggested meaning of *Golan?* A most ancient statement of unknown origin reads, "The nature of God is a circle of which the center is everywhere and the circumference is nowhere" – which is but another way of describing His unending infinity. Robert Herrick wrote in the 16th century that

> Love is a circle that doth restless move
> In the same sweet Eternity of Love.

This is certainly true of Him whose eternal love encircles a lost world. It is within the circle of His loving will that we live, move, and have our being. "Certainly there is no happiness with this circle of flesh," says Sir Thomas Browne. Rather is our contentment found in the sentiment expressed by John Donne:

> Thy firmness makes my circle just,
> And makes me end where I began.

With a *circle* we have the idea of something without a beginning or ending, or completeness, or that of being compassed about. With Christ, our heavenly *Golan*, there are no broken ends. Everything about Himself and His works are circled about with completeness.

He is Perfect in Himself (Matt. 5:48; Heb. 2:10).
He provided a Perfect Redemption (Col. 2:10; 4:12).
He is the Author of a Perfect Word (Ps. 19:7).
He is renowned for His Perfect Providence (Ps. 18:30; Rev. 4:3).
He is Perfect in Knowledge (Job 36:4).
He bids us rest in His Perfect Will (Rom. 12:2).

With all our human imperfections and failures we are assured that we are complete in Him. Then there is the further thought of encompassment in a circle as in the passage "the angel of the LORD encampeth round about them that fear him" (Ps. 34:7). He ever encircles us as the mountains are round about Jerusalem (Ps. 125:2). How secure the redeemed are, then, in the orbit of His love! And if in the circle of His providential care, then

> Not a shaft can hit
> Till the God of Love sees fit.

Once the cities of refuge were established in the six prescribed centers, fugitives from home and kindred were safe from vengeance all the time the high priest lived. On his death, they were free to return home (Josh. 20:6). How predictive this is of our protection under grace! As a refuge, the Redeemer placed Himself within reach of all, even of such as are in the utmost peril of eternal judgment. Once a refugee entered a city of refuge, he was tried by judges and if found innocent he was allowed to dwell in the city until the high priest died, and with the appointment of a successor, the manslayer could return to his own city and recover his own possessions. But when we fled to Christ we were not innocent but guilty before God, yet He received us, blotted out our crimes, and dwelling in Him as our Royal High Priest, we know that we are secure from man's ancient enemy, The Devil, all the time the priest lives. The glory of the Gospel is that because He is alive forevermore, we have an everlasting security in Him.

That Christ is a more perfect refuge is seen in the fact that while an innocent manslayer could find safety in the city or refuge nearest him, the murderer intentionally killing another was excluded. Under the Law, his life was forfeited for the one he took. But under grace none are excluded from refuge in Christ. "Him that cometh to Me — even murderers — I will not cast out." His blood is able to make the vilest clean. While this does not mean that the *effect* of a man's sin is counteracted, it does imply a salvation from the guilt and thralldom of sin. Of old, the man shedding innocent blood and desiring protection had to flee to a city of refuge; and sinners must come to the Saviour in penitence and faith if they desire salvation. His heartcry, however, was, "Ye will not come unto Me, that ye might have life," and failing to seek the refuge He offered, they perished in their sin. How blessed and eternally safe we are if out of grateful hearts we can sing

> Oh, safe and happy Shelter!

Oh, Refuge tried and sweet!
Oh, trysting place where Heaven's love
And Heaven's justice meet . . .
I take, O Cross, Thy Shadow
For my abiding place.

P. *Mount Pisgah*

While there is only one sad event in the book of Deuteronomy we are to dwell upon, it can be briefly stated that the last book to come from Moses, is taken up with the preparation of Israel for the Land of Promise. The nation is about to enter Canaan *under the Law,* and their sojourn in the land was dependent upon the people *keeping* that Law. If they became guilty of gross disobedience, then they would be cast out of the land. Hence, the condition of continued occupancy was summed up in one word – Obedience. At last God's people, chosen through His electing grace in *Genesis,* redeemed and delivered from Egypt in *Exodus,* worshipping and walking before God in *Leviticus,* tested and disciplined for forty years in *Numbers,* stand on the border of their great inheritance in *Deuteronomy.*

After his final charges to Joshua and Israel in Deuteronomy 31, we have the great song of Moses in the next chapter in which he reminded the people of all awaiting them in blessing or in judgment according to their obedience to God. Chapter 33 is taken up with tribal blessings, and then in the following chapter we have the vision and death of Moses – the lonely, tender scene on Mount Nebo. God says little of the end of His servant, who was denied the privilege of crowning his long and remarkable leadership of the people with the joy of leading the columns into Canaan. Certainly God gave him a vision of *all* the land. "I have causted thee to see it with thine eyes, *but thou shall not go over thither.*" Graciously, God did not remind Moses of the reason why he could not enter Canaan.

That he was able, physically, to finish the divine plan in settling Israel in the land He had destined for the nation is seen in the record that although he was 120 years old, "his eye was not dim, nor his natural force abated." Rashi, the Jewish historian commenting on this scene, says that the Lord showed Moses not only the land, but what should happen therein, in every part. He saw the Promised Land, in all its magnificence, not merely as Israel afterward possessed it, but as God had originally given it. With his remarkable eyesight, he saw more of the Promised Land than those who entered it did. What a commentary this is on the promise. "They that wait upon the Lord shall renew their strength" (Isa. 40:31). Moses is prominent as a man of the Mount. At Mount Horeb he performed the miracle of bringing water out of the rock. At Mount Sinai Moses received the Law for the people. At Mount Nebo he found a grave. At the Mount of Transfiguration, God was so kind to Moses in sending him down to the Land of Promise, so he entered it after all (Matt. 17:3), and his heart-longing was granted. What a glorious visit that was along with Elijah he companied with the Lord of Glory, about whom he had written so much. So

With glory wrapped around,
On the hills he never trod;
And spoke of the strife that won our life
With the Incarnate Son of God.

Why was Moses not allowed to enter Canaan? Although we have briefly touched upon this disappointment, we feel it warrants a fuller treatment. In his inspiring volume published well over sixty years ago, J. G. Greenhough, in *God's Older Picture Gallery,* has a chapter on Moses at Mount Nebo that he calls

A Great Life Un-Finished. Here are a few excerpts from its moving introduction:

> There are some half-dozen pictures in the Bible which stand out with peculiar prominence. They arrest the mind and fix themselves in the memory so fast that they can never be forgotten. People who know least of the Bible scenes and events generally know these. They are either exceptionally grand, or wildly tragical, or tearfully pathetic, and to look on them once is, in a sense, to see them for ever. No one can ever forget Job sitting in sackcloth in his ruined house, or Judas kissing his Master in the garden, or the scene in which the Saviour of the World laid down His life. These pictures are so powerful, either in beauty, pathos or awefulness, that they laid hold of the dullest imagination and retain its place for ever.
>
> Here is one of those great pictures, as striking as any except those in which our Lord figured. Moses, at the end of his earthly pilgrimage, standing on the Mount of Visions, looking down on the land far away, which his feet were not to tread, the land which he had toiled to reach, which he had panted and prayed for for forty years; and dying there, with the one great hope of his life broken off. If that scene does not stir you, your heart must be like stone, and your imagination wood.... He saw there before him the goodly land. The promise was on the verge of fulllment. His people were about to grasp the prize. He had carried forward God's plan a long way. The building only needed the crowning stone. He had done a noble and magnificent work, but the last words he heard were sad, "I have caused thee to see it with thine eyes, but thou shalt not go over thither."

The long life of Moses had been crowned with glorious triumphs. Through him marvelous things had been accomplished. He is conspicuous as one privileged to speak to Jehovah face to face. When called to receive the Two Tables of Testimony, Moses spent forty days and forty nights on the Mount, being miraculously sustained during such a period, for he did neither eat bread nor drink water. When he did return to the people, he came reflecting the glory of the Lord, although he was unconscious that his countenance shone. Was this not a forecast of Him in whose face could be found the glory of God (II Cor. 4:6)? Moses had to cover his face with a veil, such was the blinding effect upon those who saw. But when we see His face, He will not require any covering to hide His effulgent glory, for we shall be like Him. The shining skin of Moses gradually disappeared, but the glory on another face, once marred more than any man's, forever abides. Such was the hallowed intimacy between Jehovah and Moses that Jehovah called His friend by name (Exod. 33:11, 12). Yet his wonderful leadership ends on a minor and somewhat tragic key. Was the penalty he paid for a single fault too drastic?

The incident costing Moses the forfeiture of entering Canaan happened at Kadesh, when he was told by God to *speak* to the rock but he "struck it twice in petulance." Wrought up by the chiding of the people, Moses gave way to temper, and so "spake unadvisedly with his lips" (Num. 20:10; Ps. 106:33). But his momentary loss of self-control sprang from unbelief, for God said, "Because ye believed me not, to sanctify me in the eyes of the children of Israel, therefore ye shall not bring this congregation into the land which I have given them" (Num. 20:12). Unbelief led to disobedience and disobedience to a captious spirit. As his public action as a leader involved God's glory, the punishment of Moses had to be stringent. Sadly disappointed that he could not enter Canaan, he prayed three times for a reversal of the divine decree, just as Jesus prayed three times for the removal of His cup of agony. God's reply to Moses' repeated request was "Speak no more unto me of this matter" (Deut. 3:25, 26). The sin occasioning exclusion from the land was forgiven, but its judicial consequences remained. Thus he remained as a warning to all saints of the tragedy of disobedience.

Moses, the patriot fierce, became
The meekest man on earth,
To show us how love's quick'ning flame
Can give our souls new birth.

Moses, the man of meekest heart,
Lost Canaan by self-will,
To show where grace has done its part,
How sin defiles us still.

Thou, who hast taught me in Thy fear
Yet seest me frail at best,
O grant me loss with Moses here,
To gain his future rest.

The magnanimity of Moses shines forth in his cooperation with God to choose his successor. The blessed man of God exhibited a lovely unselfishness in the need of someone to take up his burden. His was ever a most exquisite spirit of self-surrender – a rare and admirable grace. "We never find Moses seeking his own things; on the contrary, again and again, when opportunity was afforded him of building up his own fame and fortune, he proved very distinctly that the glory of God and the good of His people so occupied and filled his heart that there was no room for a single, selfish consideration." Provided Israel's needs were met, Moses was content. Jealous care for God's glory was his chief concern. Forbidden to cross Jordan himself, he prayed, "Let the LORD, the God of the spirits of all flesh, set a man over the congregation . . . that the congregation of the LORD be not as sheep which have no shepherd" (Num. 27: 15-17). God answered Moses by telling him to ordain the Spirit-possessed Joshua to follow him as leader of the people. When a man has been the controlling head of a nation for forty years and dies in full vigor of his powers, it is not easy to fill his place, but God always knows where to find a man to fill the gap (Deut. 34:7-12).

The death and burial of Moses must have been a poignant scene. When he climbed Mount Sinai, it was to receive the revelation of the will and mind of God for the people. As he climbed Mount Nebo, it was to receive the touch of God in death and hear Him say, "Enter thou into the joy of thy Lord." History has no episode comparable to God's burial of His dear servant. C. H. Mackintosh says that Moses forbidden to enter Canaan was God in government, but taken up to Pisgah in company with Jehovah to have a full view of the inheritance and then dig a grave for His servant and bury him, was *God in grace* – marvelous, matchless grace!

The question arises, Did Moses climb the Mountain of Nebo alone, or did Joshua, who was to succeed him, accompany the one about to die? If Moses went up alone, then to whom were the particulars of the farewell scene given in order to record them for posterity? Ellicott's *Commentary* offers the suggestion that as Elijah and Elisha "still went on and talked" until that chariot of fire appeared which "parted them both asunder," so it was with Moses and Joshua – that Moses' minister attended him until Jehovah withdrew him from his sight. But it speaks well for Joshua's character — in fact, it is altogether characteristic of the man — that in the record of the death of the great law-giver he should have concealed himself and every other figure from sight except Jehovah and His servant Moses.

It was not the fear of death that caused Moses to ascend the Mount. Twice over in his leadership, weighed down by the cares of office and the persistent sin of his people, he asked God to kill him (Exod. 32:32; Num. 11:15). No, it was the thought of dying without the thrill of leading Israel into Canaan, after having brought them out of Egypt and through the wilderness to the border of the Land of Promise. When he did die, it was "according to the word of the LORD," or "upon the mouth of the Lord" (Deut. 34:5). The Jewish tradition is that Moses died by the kiss of God. F. W. H. Myers in his "Saint Paul" has the couplet

> Moses on the mountain
> Died of the kisses of the lips of God.

The most remarkable feature of the death of this grand old man is that he was not only kissed to sleep by God, but that God was actually His gravedigger and undertaker, for "[God] buried him in a valley in the land of Moab" (Deut. 34:5). That grave remained unknown and unmarked, for no man knew where it was. What a signal honor it was to have God perform the last rites for His friend! The calm silence in which Moses died is sublime. His farewell to earth was taken in the company of Jehovah, and so as he passed through the valley of the shadow of death, he had no fear. Just before he died, he wrote about the everlasting arms undergirding the saints. Now he feels their tender embrace in his last hour.

Moses was alone in privileged burial. When the Messiah came and died upon another hill, it was with the feeling of God-forsakenness, and He was buried not by Jehovah but by Joseph of Arimathea, one of His devoted disciples. Moses had a silent, calm, peaceful death. Christ died in agony and thirst and shame. Moses was 120 years of age when he died, but Christ was a few months over 33 years of age when He died upon a cross. Christ rose again in a glorified form after three days in the grave. Moses appeared in a glorified body recognizable by Peter centuries after his death. No epitaph was necessary for the soon-discarded grave of Christ; but Joshua wrote a moving epitaph for the man he loved and faithfully followed —

> And there arose not a prophet since in Israel like unto Moses, whom the LORD knew face to face,
> In all the signs and wonders, which the LORD sent him to do in the land of Egypt to Pharaoh, and to all his servants, and to all his land,
> And in all that mighty land, and in all the great terror which Moses shewed in the sight of all Israel (Deut. 34:10-12).

That the body of Moses, reposing in its unknown tomb, was precious can be gathered from what Jude says about the Devil disputing his right to that body (Jude 9). Why did he contend with Michael, the archangel, for the body? Was it because he knew that Moses was to be raised from the dead, and so resisted his resurrection? When such a resurrection took place we do not know, but that Moses was raised in a glorified body is evident because, along with Elijah, he appeared on the Mount of Transfiguration "in glory." Those two Old Testament warriors were no disembodied spirits, for they were seen by Peter, James, and John, who heard them speaking with Jesus about His coming death at Jerusalem.

How fitting it was for this trio to

meet as they did! Moses represented the Law; Elijah, prophecy; and Jesus came as the end of the Law and the fulfiller of all past predictive utterances. In Him, law and prophecy were happily combined (Matt. 22:40). Moses, the embodiment of the Law, could only bring Israel to the border of the Promised Land, but not *into* it. That required a *Joshua,* or Jesus. As Bishop Wordsworth expressed it, "The Law led men to 'see the promises afar off, and to embrace them' – rather, *to see and greet the promises from afar* (Heb. 11:13), and it brought them to the borders of Canaan, but could not bring them into it: that was reserved for Joshua, the type of Jesus." Through grace, we are brought into the fulness of the blessing of the Gospel of Christ, which is typified by Canaan, and carry with us the assurance of life forevermore with Him who saved us.

> Could we but climb where Moses stood,
> And view the landscape o'er;
> Not Jordan's stream, nor death's cold flood,
> Should fright us from the shore.

Q. *The Twelve Stones*

The whole of Jewish history is suggestive of spiritual truth, and of analogous expressions. *Egypt* is a type of the world: men are *slaves* of sin, their road is through the *desert,* they cross the *Jordan* of death, they enter the *rest* that remains for the people of God, they have their *forerunner,* their *prophet, priest,* and *king.* It is with the historical and prophetic and spiritual significance of Israel's entrance into the Land of Promise that we are now concerned. At the outset, Joshua, who had been Moses' minister or personal attendant and who was now his successor, received the divine assurance, "Every place that the sole of your foot shall tread upon, that have I given unto you" (Josh. 1:3). But what God gave had to be taken. We have the poignant statement, "Moses My servant is dead." For a new dispensation there was a new leader, and so Joshua received the divine commission. "Arise, go over this Jordan, thou, and all this people."

With the commission there was the promise of companionship. "As I was with Moses, so will I be with thee" "I will not fail thee, nor forsake thee" (Josh. 1:5), the promise Jesus gave His own (Heb. 13:5). Once out of Egypt, the great task of Moses was to take the people through the Red Sea. Now, out of the long wilderness journey, the responsibility of Joshua was to lead Israel through the River Jordan. The two water crossings are coupled by the psalmist –

> What ailed thee, O thou sea, that thou fleddest? thou Jordan that thou was driven back? (Ps. 114:5).

While there may be a close connection between the Red Sea and Jordan, in that going down into the bed of the water signified death, yet there is a difference between the two. For Israel, the Red Sea meant death to Egypt and Pharaoh; for the Christian, it typifies death to the world, the flesh, and the Devil. For Israel, Jordan signified death to the failures of the wilderness and the entrance into Canaan with all its provision and possessions; for the Christian, Jordan means the Lord's delightsome land of peace and rest and victory, the exalted spiritual life which *Ephesians,* the New Testament counterpart of *Joshua,* reveals. The Red Sea is our death to the old life; Jordan, our death with Christ and a new life in Him (Rom. 6:6-11; Eph. 2:5, 6). The believer is merely separated from this present evil world by his identification with the cross of Christ; he has also been quickened out of the grave of Christ, raised up, and made to sit with Him in the heavenlies (Eph. 2:5, 6).

We must also pause to say that Jordan is not a type of physical death, and Canaan is *not* a perfect type of heaven. Many of our hymns have popularized the idea that our passing from this life is the Jordan we have to cross.

> When I tread the verge of Jordan
> Bid my anxious fears subside;
> Death of death, and Hell's
> destruction,
> Land me safe on Canaan's side:
> Songs of praises
> I will ever give to Thee.

Then there is the well-known Sankey hymn:

> On Jordan's stormy banks I stand,
> And cast a wistful eye
> To Canaan's fair and happy land,
> Where my possessions lie.

We readily concede that many a powerful and fruitful Gospel sermon has been preached on the verse, "How wilt thou do in the swelling of Jordan?" Dwelling upon Jordan as being typical of death, the evangelist urged sinners to get right with God before being cut down by man's last enemy, and, dying in sin, being cast into a lost eternity. But such an application is not the true spiritual interpretation of Jordan. But Canaan, which Israel entered through Jordan, does not foreshadow heaven, for in the land the people encountered strife and war and spies and sin and death, none of which are to be found in heaven. Because of their unbelief and disobedience, Israel was ultimately driven from Canaan and became scattered among the nations. Once in heaven, no saint can be expelled from it. Even in Canaan, Israel failed to enter into her true rest in God. The saints, with their heavenly Joshua, are at perfect rest forever. Canaan, then, is a foregleam of the present establishment of the believer in Christ in a position where he may fight and conquer, expelling the enemies of Christ from his own heart, or subduing them in it.

1. *Before Jordan.* We have considered a good deal of the history of the people since their deliverance out of the bondage of Egypt, and the miraculous passage through the Red Sea and the miraculous provision for forty years during the wilderness pilgrimage, all of which is symbolic of our spiritual journey. Now, Canaan is ahead, but Jordan must first be crossed, so Joshua receives the divine injunction, "Sanctify yourselves: for tomorrow the LORD will do wonders among you" (Josh. 3:5).

a. *The Human Responsibility — Sanctify yourselves.*

The solemn seasons of life demand special consecration to God. Great tasks necessitate deep preparation of heart. Israel was to witness another miracle of a passage made through water, and of the manifestations of divine power in Canaan, and so they had to put away all that was alien to the holy will and mind of God, not merely by outward ceremonial cleansing but by the cleansing of all filthiness of flesh and spirit. It is a law of the spiritual kingdom that if God is to be glorified through His people, He must first be sanctified in them. A Holy God must have holy instruments to accomplish His wonders among men. Thus Israel must have a serious deportment befitting the solemn ceremony of the coming day. The night before Jesus chose His twelve disciples, He spent its lonely hours in communion with God. Do we fully understand that the security of tomorrow's wonders depends upon today's sanctification?

b. *The Divine Response — The Lord will do wonders.*

Sanctification fitted Israel to behold the manifested presence and power of God. The people came to know that He was in the midst of the camp.

Such preparation of heart also enabled them to appreciate God's mighty work at Jordan and in Canaan. Are we preparing ourselves for God's tomorrow, whether it be in the revelation of His mighty power in a wonderful revival, or in the glorious morrow of the Saviour's return for His saints? Are we clean vessels, prepared to every good work? It is the pure in heart who see God revealing Himself in might and majesty.

2. *In Jordan.* The name means "descender" or "flowing down." The phrase "the waters which came down" (Josh. 3:16) is the same as *Jordan* in the Hebrew. Several specific instructions were given as to the passage of Israel through the waters of Jordan, which, as at the Red Sea, were miraculously parted to allow the people to pass over dry-shod. The miracle has added glory because it was the period of the year when Jordan overflowed its banks, greatly swelling the volume, thereby making the crossing of a great multitude of men, women, children, and cattle an absolute impossibility at such a time. Divine intervention was a necessity.

But there is a difference between the two crossings, however, in that the Red Sea was in God's elective purpose and therefore necessary for Israel. With Jordan it was otherwise, as it was Israel's wickedness and wandering that made such a crossing necessary. Had it not been for their rebellion, the people could have marched straight up from Kadesh-Barnea to Canaan without having to cross the river. What useless trial disobedience causes. Jordan was a crisis that could have been avoided – even though it remains as a forecast of the believer's death and a life of self-trust and self-effort, and entrance into the rest of faith.

3. *The priests* and the ark went first (Josh. 3:6). The usual position of the sacred ark, when at rest, was in the center of the camp and, during a march, in the middle of the procession. But on this occasion it was in the front, being borne, not by the Kohathite Levites, its official bearers, but by the priests, as on all solemn and extraordinary occasions (Num. 4:15; 6:6; I Kings 8:3-6). That ark was the symbol of divine presence, and is a fitting symbol of Christ our ark who ever accompanies His own. He was the first and only One to go to a grave as the substitute for sinners. Now, we have no need to shrink from the formidable waters of trial, for He has said "When thou passeth through the waters, I will be with thee; and through the rivers, they shall not overflow thee" (Isa. 43:2). As soon as the feet of the priests, bearing the ark of the covenant, touched the overflowing river, the water divided, and the priests stood on dry ground in the midst of Jordan until all the people and their cattle were clean passed over (Josh. 3:16, 17). It was the Lord God of Israel who dried up the waters both at the Red Sea and at Jordan, and kept the passage through both until all the people were clean across the divide.

The spiritual counterpart is not hard to seek. Jesus, our great High Priest, stands firm; and His finished work on our behalf ever prevails, and ever will, "till all the ransomed Church of God be saved to sin no more." He will be our companion and protector until we have all gone over to the other side. A further instruction was that of the observance of a space between the ark and the people. As the way ahead was unknown to them, the ark functioned as a guide (Josh. 3:3, 4). Thus the Israelites followed in reverence, knowing that the ark of divine presence would lead the way until the deep waters were crossed. See Hebrews 10:19-22 for the spiritual significance of this edict.

4. The people hasted and passed over (Josh. 4:10). Why the haste? Would not the God who parted the waters not keep them walled up on either side until the last person had crossed? One commentator suggests,

> The unfaltering confidence of the Priests contrasts strikingly with the conduct of the people, who "hasted and passed over." Their faith, like that of many of God's people, was, through the weakness of human nature, blended with fears. But perhaps their *haste* may be viewed in a more favourable light, as indicating the alacrity of their obedience, or it might have been enjoined, in order that the whole multitude might pass in one day.

Perhaps the people hurried across so as not to overtire the standing priests. Sinners need to be warned of the folly of wearying the patience of Jesus. As for the saints, they are urged to labor to enter into the perfect rest of Redemption, lest by their delay they become guilty of unbelief (Heb. 4:9-11). The recurring phrase *clean over* (Josh. 3:17) is impressive. Not a hoof was left behind. "*All* the Israelites passed over." Thus will it be when our heavenly Joshua returns for those redeemed by His blood. *All* who are His will be caught up to meet Him in the air. He will not leave one child of His behind in the Egypt of this world, or in the grave (I Thess. 4:13-18).

5. *Beyond Jordan.* At last Israel is in Canaan, facing an untried life in a new land. The purpose of God is completed – He had brought His redeemed people *out* of Egypt, *through* the wilderness, *into* the Land of Promise, even as He had declared He would do (Deut. 6:23). What marvelous experiences awaited a people so marvelously overshadowed by God in the land which has ever been theirs by divine gift and right! The first action of Joshua was the establishment of a twofold memorial. *Twelve stones* were buried in the waters of Jordan, and another *Twelve stones* were set up on the Canaan side of the river.

Divinely commanded to take twelve men, each representing a tribe, these men, previously chosen for the service of placing these commemorative stones (Josh. 3:12), were not told of their precise task till the time of passage over Jordan. Ordered by Joshua, these picked men selected each a heavy stone from around the spot "where the priests stood" and deposited the twelve stones in the first stopping place, namely, Gilgal (Josh. 4:19, 20-24). Doubtless they were arranged in the form of a memorial cairn as a standing record to posterity of the miraculous deliverance at Jordan.

Then, taking another twelve stones, Joshua placed them in order where the feet of the priests had stood in the bed of the river as a further momento of the miraculous event. In the low, ordinary state of the river these stones would be quite visible. These large remembrance stones can be seen as a foregleam of Him who came as the chief cornerstone. In fact, all that transpired that great day presents us with a striking picture of our salvation through Christ and our present standing in Him. Represented by the ark of the covenant, we see Him going on before His people into the Jordan, or sin-judgment, or death. The waters of judgment are rolled back so that His people pass over unharmed.

The twelve stones in Jordan show us the cross where Jesus died for us. In those stones we see our position as being crucified with Him, or buried with Him "by baptism into death" (Rom. 6:3, 4).

The twelve stones in Gilgal bring us to the Resurrection side, and set forth all the redeemed now in Him in the heavenlies (Eph. 2:5, 6). We are not only dead indeed unto sin but alive unto God through Jesus Christ our Lord (Rom. 6:11; Gal. 2:20). As the Canaanites were afraid of God's redeemed people brought through Jordan, so our position in Christ terrifies our enemies. See Joshua 5:1 with Colossians 2:15; Hebrews 2:14, 15; James 4:7.

We could linger long over the experiences of Israel in Canaan. On the Resurrection side of Jordan there came the renewal of circumcision, or the separated, mortified life. Now in the Promised Land the people must bear the mark of God's separate people (Josh. 5:1-9 with Col. 3:1, 5).

The miraculous manna having ceased, the people now eat of the old corn of the land, which can pre-figure the ascended Christ as "the produce of the heavenly realm" ministered directly to us by the Holy Spirit. Saints now feast upon the risen Christ Himself (John 6:56-58; II Cor. 3:18). There are other events and incidents we would like to deal with, such as what happened at Jericho, the fall of which before Israel marked the first step in the conquest of Canaan. God's plan appeared to be somewhat foolish and unworkable, but obedient faith learns to stand still and see His salvation. There is a somewhat remarkable evidence of divine grace in the use Paul makes of the history of Israel from Egypt to Canaan (Heb. 11:29, 30): "By faith they passed through the Red Sea as by dry land: which the Egyptians assaying to do were drowned." Then there should have followed a reference to the forty years in the wilderness, but there is not a word about it for the next verse reads, "By faith the walls of Jericho fell down, after they were compassed about seven days." Previously the writer said, "Their sins and iniquities will I remember no more" (Heb. 10:17), and he now gives an illustration of this, for the full stop between Hebrews 11:29 and 11:30 represents an omission of forty years of wandering, rebellion, and disobedience which, by grace, is blotted out from divine remembrance.

Before the conquest of Jericho, however, there came to Joshua the vision of the unseen captain, and with it a necessary lesson the new leader had to learn before he could conquer the land. Already, under "The Theophanies," we drew attention to the significance of this appearance, and only return to it to emphasize that the mysterious guest who appeared to Joshua was an ally not an enemy; and that facing his solemn charge, the over-all responsibility of Israel's protection and settlement in the land was the Lord's, not Joshua's. The Lord was the captain of the host of the Lord, and Joshua was but His servant, as he humbly acknowledged himself to be (Josh. 5:13-15). How Israel came to prove "God Himself is with us for our Captain" (II Chron. 13:12)! Then, are we not assured of the fact that Jesus, our heavenly Joshua is the Captain of our salvation (Heb. 2:10), and that as His soldiers we must live to obey His commands?

> Thou wast their Rock, their Fortress, and their Might:
> Thou, Lord, their Captain in the well-fought fight;
> Thou in the darkness drear their one true Light—Alleluia!

As we conclude this section of our study on *Prophetic Gleams From Historical Events,* confining ourselves, as we have, to the more conspicuous experiences overtaking the Israelites during their pilgrimage from Egypt to Canaan, we are conscious that there are many other events in the further history of the nation in Old Testament history, prophetic or typical of Christ and His life and mission, that we might have dwelt with. We trust, however, that sufficient coverage of this particular aspect of our study has been given to act as an incentive for a more exhaustive search on the part of the reader as he endeavors to follow the signposts pointing to Christ in Old Testament Scriptures.

Chapter Four

PROPHETIC FOREGLEAMS FROM RELIGIOUS RITUALS

A. The Construction of the Tabernacle
   1. Its Architect and Structure
   2. Its Appellations and Synonyms
   3. Its Applications and Symbols

B. The Ceremonies at the Tabernacle
   1. The Brazen Altar
   2. The Brazen Laver
   Outer Court
   3. The Golden Candlestick
   4. The Tables of Shewbread
   5. The Altar of Incense
   Holy Place
   6. The Golden Censer
   7. The Ark and Mercy Seat
   Most Holy Place

C. The Commanded Offerings of the Tabernacle
   1. The Burnt Offering
   2. The Meal Offering
   3. The Peace Offering
   4. The Sin Offering
   5. The Trespass Offering
      a. The Two Sparrows
      b. The Red Heifer

To an ordinary reader of the Bible all of the minute data given of the tabernacle and its offerings may seem uninteresting and unprofitable, and the reading of same a weariness to the flesh. In fact, those of us who profess to be Bible lovers, if we were frank, would have to confess that when we come to those chapters in *Exodus* and *Numbers* detailing the precise measurements and construction of the tabernacle, and to *Leviticus,* with its recital of all the intricate instructions as to the offerings and feasts, we tend to skip such portions as those we cannot derive much spiritual profit from. But as we are to see, no other sections of the Bible more amply repays meditation. As we prayerfully and patiently study them, we find them full of the deepest teaching concerning Christ and spiritual things, and of the wisest counsels for the right ordering of our daily life.

As the thrice Holy One, God desired a people to live on a high spiritual level with Himself, and so chose Israel to fashion her into an "holy nation." Thus the people were redeemed by blood, and became God's own, and in the wilderness He planned the tabernacle, and thereafter the temple, as His dwelling place, which likewise became central in the religious life of Israel. Broadly, the Scriptures to study for a full understanding of the history, as well as the typical and prophetic aspects of the tabernacle with all its offerings and services, are *Exodus* 24–40, *Numbers* 1–10, and, of course, *Leviticus* and *Hebrews* together to discover how Christ is the substance of all Old Testament shadows. As we are finding out, He is the magic key to all Old Testament types.

It was with the truth in his mind that Jesus came as the fulfiller of the past religious symbols that John Bunyan, in *The Holy War,* described as taking place in the House of Interpreter:

> Now after the feast was over, Emmanuel was for entertaining the town of Mansoul with some curious riddles drawn up by His Father's Secretary, by the skill and wisdom of

> Shaddai, the like of these there is not in any kingdom. These riddles were made upon King Shaddai Himself and upon Emmanuel His Son, and upon His wars and doing with Mansoul.
>
> Emmanuel also expounded unto them, some of these riddles Himself; but oh how they were enlightened! They saw what they never saw before; they could not have thought that such rarities could have been couched in so few and such ordinary words . . . but when they read in the scheme where the riddles were writ, and looked into the face of the Prince, things looked so alike the one to the other, that Mansoul could not forbear but say, this is the Lamb, this is the Rock, this is the Red Heifer, this is the Door, this is the Way.

That the Redeemer is the only key to the "riddles [that] were writ" is clearly taught in *Hebrews*, as we shall discover as we proceed in our meditation. As Dr. A. T. Pierson expresses it,

> The 300 predictions store up enigmas whose only adequate solution is Jesus Himself.
>
> *The Symbolical Chamber,* with its Tabernacle symbolism, its priestly robes and rites, its fasts and feasts, sacrifices and offerings are meaningless until He is seen as the Tabernacle of God with man, at once High Priest and Victim, Offering and Offered.
>
> *The Historical Chamber* is a picture gallery, with scenic paintings and personal portraits, and He, the living Guide to explain the events and characters of all ages.
>
> *The Sacramental Chamber,* with its ceremonies and ordinances of separation in purification: its anointings and washing, its symbols of fleshly mortification, of burial and resurrection, and perpetual feeding on heavenly food; all these are without meaning until they serve to typify identification with Him in suffering and service, victory and glory.
>
> The Inspired Word and the Eternal Word are forever inseparable. The Bible is Christ portrayed; Christ is the Bible fulfilled. One is the Picture, the other is the Person, but the features are the same and proclaim their identity.

We may be helped to a fuller understanding of the purpose and prophecy of the teaching and types of the tabernacle, if we keep in mind where it was to be erected.

1. *It was not built in Egypt.* During bondage in Egypt, Israel, surrounded by the gods of the country, fell into idolatry, and a sanctuary for God, in which He might dwell among His people, was not possible in such circumstances. They were Pharaoh's slaves, and were not free to serve God as He required. By reason of their affliction, sighs and groans prevented them serving God with gladness of heart. They had to be free and redeemed ere they could have a place where they could worship Him.

2. *It was not built in Canaan.* Because the tabernacle was moveable, it went with the pilgrims from the time of its first erection until they came to Shiloh, where it rested for a time, the vicissitudes overtaking it being recorded for us in the books of Samuel and Kings. But as Israel was permanently settled in Canaan, a permanent sanctuary for God was necessary, for which King David abundantly prepared, and his son, Solomon built in a magnificent way.

3. *It was built in the wilderness.* The tabernacle was for a people on the move, as pilgrims in the desert. They had been delivered from the idolatry and bondage of Egypt, but had not yet entered Canaan with all its bountiful provision. Israel was in the wilderness totally dependent upon God for protection, guidance, food and drink; and so the temporary, moveable sanctuary was designed that the people might know that God was indeed in their midst.

In this age of grace, the redeemed have been delivered from darkness and bondage and translated into the light and liberty of the kingdom of God's dear Son, but they have not yet apprehended that for which they were apprehended in Christ Jesus. They await entrance into His everlasting kingdom, and meantime in the wilderness of this world live for and worship Him whom, seeing not, they yet love.

As we endeavor to classify the rich and abundant typical and prophetic truth associated with the worship of Him who is "glorious in holiness," the following threefold outline may assist us in the assembly of the relevant material.

A. Prophetic Gleams From the Constructed Tabernacle.

B. Prophetic Gleams From the Tabernacle Ceremonies.

C. Prophetic Gleams From the Tabernacle Calendar of Feasts and Festivals.

Under the first point we have the one house God planned and built. As both the Tabernacle and the Temple were essentially on the same model, what applies to the one applies to the other. Under the second point, there is the one order of worship and service in connection with the sanctuary that God decreed and directed for His people to observe. Under the third point, we come to the calendar of fasts, feasts, and festivals God likewise arranged and ordained and which Israel had to faithfully keep.

In each case, as we shall find, there would seem to be a sevenfold completeness. The conspicuous features of the tabernacle were the brazen and golden altars, the lampstand and shewbread, the laver, the ark and mercy seat. The ceremonial requirements included the five offerings, the red heifer, first fruits and tithes.

The calendar called for a sacred seventh-day, week, month, year, a seven times seventh year, and a seventy times seventh, or four hundred and ninetieth, with a dimly forecast final millennium or sabbatical thousand years.

A. *Prophetic Gleams From the Constructed Tabernacle*

To assert our faith in the historical veracity of the record of the tabernacle with all its ritual may seem to be superfluous, yet because of the way the school of higher criticism has attacked and opposed the erection of an actual tabernacle in the wilderness, it is necessary to affirm our belief in its reality, without which its spiritual significance as found in the Epistle to the Hebrews is meaningless. Briefly stated the critical views are that

The Tabernacle never existed except on paper.

The Tabernacle was a pure creation of priestly imagination sketched after or during the Exile.

The Tabernacle was represented as having been built in the wilderness for the purpose of making legitimate the newly priestly code or levitical ritual still preserved in the Pentateuch.

The Tabernacle was only a paper sketch or model of the temple to be built by Solomon.

But the Orthodox view, to which we hold, affirms that

The Tabernacle was built as God directed Moses in the wilderness of Sinai.

It was fashioned according to the pattern God gave to Moses in the Mount.

It was divinely designed to be and was the center of sacrificial worship for the tribes of Israel in the desert.

Centuries later the temple was built by Solomon to the same specifications.

God so decreed that all associated with the tabernacle should be a picture book of Christ's redemptive work.

Further, the Bible evidence of the tabernacle's actuality is overwhelming. Within the Pentateuch itself there are over eighty references to the tabernacle. In the historical books of Joshua, Judges, Samuel, and Kings, it is mentioned some eighteen times. As for Hebrews, this great Epistle is taken up, from a Christian point of view, with the typology and religious significance of the tabernacle. For ourselves, the question of its authenticity is settled by the terse statement of the psalmist, "God . . . forsook the tabernacle of Shiloh, the tent which he placed among men" (Ps. 78:59, 60). The fine summary of that renowned Christian Hebrew, Adolph Saphir, is worthy of repetition:

> There are only two chapters of Scripture to narrate the Creation of the World; but no fewer than sixteen chapters of the Inspired Record are devoted to the description of the Tabernacle. It has been remarked that God only took six days in the work of Creation, but spent forty days with Moses in directing him to make the Tabernacle. The work of Grace is more glorious than the work of Creation. Three times the Book of Exodus gives a full account of all the parts of the Tabernacle—
>
> 1. When the command is given to build it:
> 2. When its full preparation is narrated:
> 3. When it was actually erected.
>
> For the Tabernacle shows for the Redemption in Christ: and the whole world was created that the glory of God should be manifested in Christ and the Church.

In his *Antiquities*, Josephus, the Jewish historian of the first century, has given us a full description of the tabernacle, and something of its history.

1. *The architect and structure of the tabernacle*. The whole concept of this sanctuary, down to the minutest detail, was conceived by the mind of God and conveyed to Moses, who carried out the divine plan to the very letter. One cannot read all of the precise particulars regarding its construction and function without bowing in awe before Him who is the God of Order, leaving nothing to chance.

Every aspect of the tabernacle was a revelation that Moses received, even down to the very pins that were used. Nothing was left for Moses to arrange for. The tabernacle was built according to the pattern he received on the Mount of God. Reading the specification laid down by God, one is impressed with the attention given to insignificant details such as loops, taches, and pins by the divine planner. God did not give Moses a general plan and then leave him to fill in the minor requirements. The plan was all of God, just as the building of the spiritual tabernacle is so that no man can boast. Even the choice of craftsmen to make all the necessary parts and utensils was not left to Moses. God chose Bezaleel and Aholiab, who were naturally and supernaturally fitted to carry out the task, along with the wise-hearted and willing-hearted workers, of completing the building of the tabernacle. Knowing what was in man, God chose the two right men at the right time for the right work.

Divine superintendence is seen in the number of "I have's" where the workmen are mentioned in Exodus 31.

"I have called by name Bezaleel" (v. 2).
"I have filled him with the spirit of God" (v. 3).
"I have given . . . Aholiab" (v. 6).
"I have put wisdom in the hearts" (v. 6).
"I have commanded thee" (vs. 6, 11).

When God sought to redeem men from sin and build for Himself a spiritual house to fill with His own presence and glory, He knew where to find His two workers, namely, the other two of the Blessed Trinity. His beloved Son, our divine Bezeleel, and the Holy Spirit, our divine Aholiab, labor together to complete the temple not made with hands, the church, God's own habitation by Christ and through the Spirit.

Can it be that Moses saw a sketch or model of the tabernacle while receiving full instructions about its erection from the divine architect? See Revelation 11:19. With the completion of it, the verdict was, "According to all that the Lord commanded Moses, so the children of Israel made all the work" (Exod. 39:42).

The plan of salvation, like that of the tabernacle, was all of God and was perfectly completed at Calvary when Jesus cried, "It is finished." Nothing was left to man's merit, effort, or ingenuity. Human reasonings and opinions have no part in the divine scheme of Redemption. If a sinner desires deliverance from the bondage of his iniquity, he must approach the Saviour just as he is without one plea. As to the plan of the tabernacle, it was an oblong creation, being twice as long as it was broad, and made use of three distinct sections yet bound together as one, even as the three Persons of the Trinity are.

a. *The Outer Court*

Encircling the inner shrines on four sides, this enclosure had six outstanding features:

(1). *The north and south sides were 100 cubits (159 feet) long, respectively.*

(2). *The east and west ends, 50 cubits (75 feet) broad, respectively.*

(3). *It was surrounded by a hanging of fine linen, 5 cubits (7½ feet) high.*

(4). *It was supported by 20 pillars on each side, and 10 pillars at each end.*

(5). *It contained the brazen altar and brazen laver.*

(6). *It was entered by only one gate, 20 cubits (30 feet) wide.*

b. *The Inner Shrines*

Within the enclosure at the western end stood the tabernacle proper, which was divided into two sections:

(1). *The Holy Place.* This section was 20 cubits (30 feet) long: 10 cubits (15 feet) broad.

It contained the altar of incense, the table of shewbread, the golden candlestick.

It was entered by a door of fine twined linen.

Its boards were of shittim wood.

(2). *The Holy of Holiest.* This inner sanctuary was square — 10 cubits (15 feet) by 10 cubits (15 feet).

It was divided from the Holy Place by a veil of fine twined linen.

Within it stood the ark, containing the two tables of stone, a pot of manna, and Aaron's rod that budded.

Within the Holy Place, the Holiest of All was covered with colored curtains, goats' hair, rams' skins dyed red, badgers' skins. The Outer Court was uncovered and open.

Into the Outer Court priests and people freely entered. Into the Holy Place the priests alone were allowed to enter. Into the Holiest of All, the High Priest only was permitted to enter, and he only once a year.

Further, as an exponent of tabernacle types has expressed it:

> Between the Jew, in his common and everyday association, and the essential presence of the ever-present God there were *three veils.*
>
> Between the penitent worshiper, who brought his offering with his consciousness of sin, and the

immediate presence of the ever present God there were *two veils.*

Between the minister of God, in his ordinary ministrations, and the presence of the ever-present God there was *one veil.*

Between the High Priest when he entered once a year into the Holiest of All and the presence of the ever-present God there was *no veil* – All of which is richly predictive of the Lord, and ourselves as we shall presently see.

2. *The appellations and synonyms of the tabernacle.* Many names or designations, all having association with the tabernacle, are used in order to give us a comprehensive revelation of its purpose and nature in the life of Israel. Herewith we collate the various titles found in Scripture:

a. *The Tabernacle of the Congregation* (Exod. 27:31; 33:7; 40:34, etc.)

Such an appellation indicates that it was for the exclusive use of the children of Israel, as the center of divinely-appointed sacrifice and worship, and is therefore rightly translated "The Tent of Meeting" (R.V.). It was the one place of reconciliation where the Holy One welcomed those who came in penitence (Exod. 25: 22).

b. *The Tabernacle of Testimony* (Exod. 38:21; Num. 1:50; 17:10, etc.)

This name signifies that God had placed His testimony, or His Word or Law within it, which testified against the sins of His people.

The two tables of stone are described as the *testimony* (Exod. 31:18; 34:29).

The ark is called the ark of testimony (Exod. 25:22; 26:33).

The veil which separated the Holy Place from the Most Holy is termed *the veil of testimony* (Lev. 24:3).

c. *The Tabernacle of Witness* (Num. 17:7; II Chron. 24:6; Acts 7:44)

There may be two reasons for this title. First, because God witnessed against the rebellion of Korah and his fellow rebels. Then, because Aaron's rod stored up in the ark was a witness that God would fulfill His Word regarding His redeemed people.

d. *The House of the Lord* (Josh. 6:24; I Sam. 1:7, 24)

Having been planned by Him, it was indeed His very own, and was His way of having an earthly habitation to dwell among His people.

e. *The tabernacle of the Lord* (Josh. 22:19; I Kings 2:28, etc.)

Akin to the previous name, this one conveys the primary idea of a dwelling place among men. "Let them make me a sanctuary; that I may dwell among them" (Exod. 25: 8). How true it is that the ancient tabernacle was God's first habitation on earth.

He *walked* with Adam in Eden, He *visited* Abraham at Mamre, He *dwells* with His redeemed people in the wilderness, and from then has had a dwelling place here below. After the tabernacle, there came the temple in the land (II Chron. 6:3-6), and when its day was past, the Son from the Father's bosom appeared as God manifest in flesh – He *tabernacled* among us (John 1:14, R.V.), and the glory of God was manifest in the temple of His body. When Jesus went back to heaven, there came the church, bought with His blood, as a spiritual house, an holy temple built of living stones. In His own members of His body, He dwells by His Spirit on earth. In the true church He dwells, for He has desired it (Ps. 132:14). Under the old economy God had a tabernacle for His people; but under grace He has a people as His temple. In the glory to come, "The tabernacle of God is with men, and he will dwell with them, and they shall be his people" (Rev. 21:3).

f. *The Temple of the Lord* (I Sam. 1:9; 3:3)

This description of the wilderness structure actually implies "the Palace of the Lord," in which He is the undisputed sovereign. It is so named not from any eternal magnificence it possessed but because it was the earthly sanctuary from which, at times, the visible glory of the eternal king of Israel, the Shekinah, shone forth.

g. *The Tabernacle of Shiloh* (Ps. 78:60)

Here the structure is identified with the place where it was first established, and where Israel prostituted so many of her privileges as the redeemed of the Lord (Judg. 18:31). Several times Shiloh is mentioned in connection with the tabernacle.

h. *The Tabernacle of Joseph* (Ps. 78:67)

In this somewhat unusual designation we are reminded of the transference of the promised inheritance from the line of Ephraim to that of Judah, the tribe from which Jesus sprang. Ephraim had been honored of God, the tribe to which Joshua the great conqueror, and Gideon, the renowned judge, belonged. But because of sin and disobedience, Joseph's offspring was superceded.

i. *The Worldly Sanctuary* (Heb. 7:1)

The term *worldly* here implies "earthly." The large tent construction in the desert was a visible, tangible object, built with material common to earth. "Thy servants take pleasure in her stones." Under the old covenant God had a local, discernable habitation, but since the coming of Him who is our heavenly sanctuary, every or any place is sacred to those who are holy (John 4:21). Because experiences can sanctify places, there are some spots on earth very dear to men of grace.

3. *The application and symbols of the tabernacle.* We have reached the most fascinating part of our study, namely, the predictive and symbolic significance of so much, if not all, associated with the tabernacle itself, and its offerings and offices, its service and sanctity. Competent, spiritually-minded expositors of Scripture have long recognized the rich typical teaching the tabernacle affords.

> Victims were offered by the Law of God,
> That is a type celestial mysteries told.

A lover of Scripture of a past century wrote of tabernacle typology,

> These similitudes open Christ, and the secrets of God hid in Christ, and have more virtue and power with them than bare words, and lead a man's understanding further into the pith and marrow and spiritual understanding of the thing than all the words that can be imagined.

In his most valuable *Commentary*, Dr. James M. Gray quotes Professor W. G. Moorehead as saying that the tabernacle was—

> A Divine object lesson;
> An Embodied prophecy of good things to come;
> A Witness to the grace and saving power of God;
> It taught salvation through Propitiation, Forgiveness, and and Blood-shedding;
> It taught Access to God and Worship;
> It disclosed the Holiness of God, the sinfulness of man, the reconciliation which in due time should be effected. All these are clearly set forth by the Tabernacle and its Rites.

No one can read the New Testament diligently without seeing how the furniture and ritual of the desert structure was in the minds of some of its writers, particularly the writer of the Epistle of Hebrews, which is the messianic commentary on the divinely conceived tabernacle. There are two aspects of approaching the symbolic teaching of tabernacle types:

a. *There Are the Phrases Used to Contrast the Two Dispensations*

We have at least six terms used in *Hebrews* which are of deep import in an understanding of type and antitype.

(1). *Example.* "There are priests . . . who serve unto the example . . . of heavenly things" (Heb. 8:4, 5). For *example,* the R.V. gives us "copy," or a token, designed to suggest the original. Moffatt translated it "A mere outline." The priesthood of the tabernacle was a specimen, copy, or representation of the great High Priest God was going to send.

(2). *Shadow.* "The shadow of heavenly things" (Heb. 8:5). "A shadow of good things to come" (Heb. 10:1).

A shadow implies a substance. If you were about to turn a corner and saw in front of you the shadow of a man, you would know that in immediate contact with the shadow was the man. One meaning of the word *shadow* (see James 1:17) implies the thought of "a shadow arising from the turning of any body." We have the phrase, "Coming events cast their shadow before." The inference is that the tabernacle and all related to it was a shadow case beforehand by God of Christ. "Which are a shadow of things to come; but the body is of Christ" (Col. 2:17). The tabernacle was the Old Testament *shadow* of Him who came as the eternal substance.

(3). *Signifying.* "The Holy Spirit this signifying [sign-i-fying, or working or teaching by signs], that the way into the holiest of all was not yet made manifest" (Heb. 9:8). It was the divine Spirit, then, who was present with the Israelites of old, instructing them in the symbolism of their religious exercises, and teaching them that the highest mysteries of eternal Redemption were implied by the rites and ritual of the tabernacle which were but *signs* saying, "Know the Lord in His Person, Sacrifice, as High Priesthood." Without doubt, He is prefigured more profoundly and completely by types than in prophecies, properly so called.

(4). *Figure.* "A figure for the time then present" (Heb. 9:9). "Which are figures of the true" (Heb. 9:24). "[Abraham] received him in a figure" (Heb. 11:19).

The word *figure* is given as *parable* in the R.V., and is a word meaning "a placing side by side for the purpose of comparison," which is what *Hebrews* does with the tabernacle and Christ. The former is compared with the latter as an Old Testament parable. (See the author's volume *All the Parables of the Bible.*

(5). *Pattern.* "It was therefore necessary that the *patterns* of things in the heavens should be purified with these" (Heb. 9:23). The inner significance of the term "pattern" is something shown secretly or privately, and bears out a thought previously expressed that while in the Mount, Moses saw not only a sketch or model of the tabernacle, but was given a secret, private preview of the Lord Jesus Christ it portrayed. Moses was able to endure because he saw Him who was invisible at that time (Heb. 11:27).

(6). *Very Image.* "The law . . . a shadow of good things to come, and not the very image of the things" (Heb. 10:1). Moffat translates the passage, "The Law was a mere shadow of the bliss that is to be instead of representing the reality of that bliss." The photograph of a person, although a good likeness, is not the person himself. The tabernacle was a photograph, so to speak, of which Christ is the original. Comparing the picture with the person, we marvel at the resemblance between the two.

b. *The Language Describing the Tabernacle and Christ's Work Are* the *Same*

While we could spend time tracing *all* the references to the ritual of the tabernacle in the writings of the apostles, we herewith offer a sample as an incentive to a fuller search by the reader.

(1). *The Mercy Seat.* "God be merciful to me a sinner" (Luke 18:13). The word for *merciful* means "propitiation," and is the same word Moses used in Exodus 25:17, 18, 21, and which is given for "mercy seat" (Heb. 9:5). Scofield comments, "As an instructed Jew the publican is thinking, not of mere mercy, but of the blood-sprinkled mercy" (Lev. 16:5; Rom. 3:25). Divine forgiveness is ours in virtue of the sacrifice of the Cross.

(2). *The Offering.* "Christ . . . hath given himself for us an *offering* and a sacrifice to God for a sweet-smelling savour" (Eph. 5:2). Later on, we shall see how all the Levitical offerings foreshadowed Him who became an offering for sin — the fragrant offering and sacrifice.

(3). *The Laver.* "Through the washing of regeneration" (Titus 3:5, R.V.). As the margin states *washing* is the word for "laver," which stood before the Holy Place and at which the priests washed their hands and feet before entering the Holy Place to minister.

(4). *The Candlestick.* "The seven golden candlesticks" (Rev. 1:20). Within the Holy Place there stood the candlestick with its seven lights — the symbol of light and of the witness of the people of God.

It is, however, in *Hebrews* that we find the keys to the prophetic and typical interpretation of the ancient structure in the desert. Here Christ is seen as the High Priest of our profession (Heb. 3:1).

As at the Mercy Seat, or throne of grace (Heb. 4:16).

As having entered as our forerunner within the veil (Heb. 6:19).

As the minister of the true tabernacle (Heb. 8:2).

As the Holiest One providing access into God's immediate presence (Heb. 9:8).

As the veil rent by His death (Heb. 10:19, 20).

As the altar and offering by His cross (Heb. 13:10).

As the sacrifice slain without the camp (Heb. 13:12).

As the altar of fragrant incense (Heb. 13:15, 16).

c. *The Sixfold Application of the Historic Tabernacle the New Testament Makes*

(1). *The Person and Work of Christ.* The psalmist declared that "in His temple doth every one speak of his glory" (Ps. 29:9), and every part of the tabernacle, even to its smallest detail, speaks of Christ's glory and magnifies His grace. Take, first of all, His Divine *Person.*

As a tabernacle He was predicted (Isa. 4:6).

As a tabernacle He came (John 1:14, R.V. margin).

As a tabernacle He spoke of Himself (John 2:19, 21).

Then, think of His gracious and glorious *work,* so marvelously pictured in every part of the wilderness erection. At this stage we give a general summary of the typical meaning of the tabernacle articles.

Later on, we hope to deal with them more particularly.

The Brazen Altar – Christ our sacrifice. Atonement through the blood.

The Laver – Christ by His Word and Spirit apply the blood that cleanses.

The Shewbread – Christ, the source and sustenance of our spiritual life.

The Candlestick – Christ, the Incarnate One as the light of the world.

The Golden Altar of Incense – Christ, the perfect and prevailing intercessor.

The Veil – Christ's death witnessed the rending of the veil.

The Ark – All of its contents suggest different aspects of Christ.

The Mercy Seat – Christ, our propitiation, revealing the fulness of divine love.

The Two Tables of Stone – Christ, who glorified the Law, manifesting it in His own Person, and fulfilling its curse and precepts.

The Pot of Manna – Christ as the hidden manna sustaining our inner life on earth, and our eternal source of strength.

The Rod of Aaron – Christ, cut off and given over to death, budding forth in Resurrection power.

The Shekinah Light and Fire – Christ is His effulgent glory and the gift of His Spirit.

It is not without reason that John's Gospel has been called *The Commentary of the Tabernacle* because the order of truth unfolded therein with regard to the Person and work of Jesus exactly corresponds with the order of those objects in the tabernacle, without one particular being violated. No wonder the fourth Gospel has also been named *The Holy of Holies*. If Paul, in *Hebrews*, gives us the *typical* meaning of the tabernacle ritual and furniture, John in his Christ-honoring Gospel supplies the *spiritual* significance.

Christ is the brazen altar (John 1:29).

Christ's Spirit is the laver (John 3:5).

Christ is the drink for thirst – Bread, for hunger (John 4, 6).

Christ is the candlestick (John 8-9).

Christ is the golden altar of incense (John 14-18).

Christ is the veil rent in twain (John 19).

Christ is the two tables of stone (John 19:30). "It is finished."

Christ is the rod that budded (John 20).

Christ is the pot of manna (John 21:9-12). "Come and dine."

Christ is the mercy seat as He ascends on high (Acts 1).

Christ sends His Shekinah fire down (Acts 2).

(2). *The True Church of Jesus Christ*. This further application of the tabernacle can be seen in the language Paul uses of the church, which is the Lord's body –

"Ye are the temple of the living God . . . I will dwell in them" (II Cor. 6:16).

"The building fitly framed together groweth unto an holy Temple in the Lord . . . an habitation of God through the Spirit" (Eph. 2:20-22).

Take the Position of the Tabernacle.

To multitudes of Gentiles outside the camp of Israel, the tabernacle was a token of the God the nation was called to serve. The church, planted in the desert of this world, is a reminder to it of

Him who is her head and Lord. Like the tabernacle, the church is separated from the world, indwelt by God, a medium of revelation. Further, the tabernacle was in the center of Israel, God's redeemed people. What must not be forgotten is that the encampment was arranged by divine command, with a most superb setting.

It was in the form of a hollow square, each side of the square being composed of the camps of three tribes. Within this hollow square there was another hollow square, three sides of which were formed by the tents of the three families of the Levites, while the fourth side consisted of the tents of Moses, Aaron, and the priests. Within this inner square, and thus "in the midst" of the whole vast assembly, stood God's tent, the tabernacle, surrounded by the uncovered rectangular enclosure, the Outer Court. The Lord is ever the center of His church. Whenever and wherever the saints gather in His name, He is ever in their midst. The redeemed gathered around Him are to gather unto Him. He is ever in the midst of them (Ps. 46).

Take the Threefold Part of the Tabernacle.

The Outer Court – *The Gospels* give us the Outer Court of the church which Christ promised to build and died to bring to birth. He is its chief cornerstone.

The Holy Place – *The Acts* and *The Epistles* give us the church inaugurated and established as a dynamic force in the world (Isa. 54:2).

The Holiest of All – *The Revelation* brings us to the church translated, glorified, and reigning with Christ.

To express this application in another way we have

The Outer Court – The visible form of the church, the external exercise of religion.

The Holy Place – The spiritual state sanctified members enter into.

The Holiest of All – The church, saved to sin no more, safe in heaven.

(3). *The Human Body of the Believer.* Paul speaks of the human structure as "the earthly house of this tabernacle, and of groaning in such, yet awaiting another building, eternal in heaven (II Cor. 5:1-4). Peter had been warned by Christ of the putting off of the tabernacle of his worn-out body (II Pet. 1:13, 14). The body of the believer is the temple of the Spirit (I Cor. 6:19). The word Paul used for *temple* refers, specially, to the inner shrine. It was in the Holiest of All that God communicated with Aaron. But the whole life of the believer is a trinity:

The Outer Court, *the body*, connecting him with the world in which he lives.

The Holy Place, *the soul*, where all its powers are priests serving Him.

The Holiest of All, *the spirit*, where the Holy Spirit has His abode.

An Israelite, pointing to the tabernacle, could say, God is there. A Christian, with his hand on his heart, can say, God is in here!

(4). *The Progress of True Christian Experience.* Associated with a deep desire in the heart of a born-again person for a richer experience of God's most perfect salvation is a growing spiritual apprehension of the glorious inheritance he has in Christ.

There are those who give Him a *preferred place* – they are "Outer

Court Christians." They entered through the gate and came to the brazen altar, signifying their salvation by the blood, and to the Laver, typifying their experience of the Spirit's regenerating work, but, alas! they remain all their days in the Outer Court, as if deliverance from past guilt and regeneration were all God has for them.

There are others who give Jesus a *prominent place* — they are "Holy Place Priests," who manifest delight in Him. They look upon the altar and the laver as the starting places of their journey heavenwards, but not as the end. They pass to and fro like the priests of old, serving the Lord in various ways. Knowing that there is more to follow, they enter the veil and learn the secret of His illuminating power as the candlestick, of His sustaining, strengthening life as the shewbread, and of His mighty, prevailing intercession as the golden altar of incense.

There are still others who give Jesus the *pre-eminent place* — they are "dwellers in the Holiest of All." Ever fewer in number, these aspiring saints ever strive to be filled with all the fulness of God. Life they have, but they desire its abundance. As the Most Holy place was the inner shrine filled with the presence of God, so all who hunger and thirst after Him reflect all unconsciously, as Moses did, the glory of His presence within their hearts. May you and I be found in this company!

(5). *The Entire Abode of God.* Through Jeremiah the question comes, "Do not I fill heaven and earth? saith the Lord" (Jer. 23:24). As God is omnipresent, He fills every sphere. We cannot flee from His Spirit (Ps. 139:7-10). Thus, another application of the threefold section of the material tabernacle is evident:

The Earth is His Outer Court. "The whole earth is full of his glory" (Isa. 6:3; Ps. 29).

The Heavens above are His Holy Place. "The heavens declare the glory of God" (Ps. 19:1). The entire universe is His dwelling place.

The Heaven itself, His own immediate presence, is the *Holiest of All.* "I dwell in the high and holy place" (Isa. 57:15). "The holy places made with hands" (Heb. 9:24).

(6). *The Eternal Glory.* This final application of the erection in the desert can be found in the revelation granted to John. "Behold, the tabernacle of God is with men, and he will dwell with them, and they shall be his people, and God himself shall be with them, and be their God" (Rev. 21:3). In a previous passage we read of God spreading His tabernacle *over* His people (7:15, R.V.); but here the preposition is changed from *over* to *with,* which is the way the R.V. puts it — "He shall tabernacle *with* them." Why is the word *tabernacle* and not *temple* used here? Surely the latter term would have been more fitting, as the former was associated with journeyings and was of a temporary nature, while the temple was expressive of a more glorious permanent structure. Might the answer be that even in the new heaven and on the new earth we shall not be permanently settled but ever moving to and fro on divine errands? What glorious service awaits the redeemed of the Lord!

4. *The materials used in the construction of the tabernacle.* We now come to a full and particular coverage of the plan of the tabernacle, the different materials used in its construction, as well as the various arti-

cles it contained. All the offerings associated with its service are reserved for separate treatment after our treatment of the construction and ceremonies of the tabernacle. As we approach the historical data and prophetic aspect of the tabernacle, there are two most profitable matters to discuss.

a. *The People and Their Gifts* (Exod. 25:1-7; 35:4-10; 36:1-7).

Where did the Israelites get all the rich and costly materials that they presented to Moses for the building of the tabernacle? How could they produce such when they were in the wilderness away from all sources of supply? Doubtless questions such as these have troubled the minds of many, but Scripture is its own interpreter. "The Lord knew that they would need these things so He gave them all they required before they left Egypt." If you turn to Exodus 12:35-39, you will see the above difficulties answered:

> And the children of Israel did according to the word of Moses; and they borrowed (i.e. asked, God cannot do much with borrowed things) of the Egyptians jewels of silver, and jewels of gold, and raiment: And the Lord gave the people favour in the sight of the Egyptians, so that they lent [i.e., gave] unto them such things as they required. And they spoiled the Egyptians . . . And flocks, and herds, even very much cattle.

While it is true that God placed no value upon the stranger's or alien's gold to build the tabernacle, which for our age means that the money of unconverted people should not be used in God's work, we must not forget that the best part of what Israel offered to God was first of all gathered from the Egyptians, who represent for us the unsaved. The late General Booth once said, when criticized for receiving money from a well known brewer, "I have redeemed it," so the Israelites gave back to God what the Egyptians gave to them.

After all, is not all money God's — "The silver is mine, and the gold is mine, saith the LORD of hosts" (Hag. 2:8), whether it be in the hand of the saved or unsaved? Therefore He has every right to it. Let us note the method of the givers and their gifts:

(1). *Their Gifts Had To Be Willingly Offered* (Exod. 25:2; 35:5, 21). The word "willing" here employed is translated in various ways, e.g.:

"Free" (II Chron. 29:31). As many as were of a free heart (Ps. 51:12). Uphold me with thy free Spirit.

"Liberal" (Isa. 32:5, 8) "The liberal deviseth liberal things."

"Nobles" (Num. 21:18) "The nobles of the people." (Ps. 83:11). "Make their nobles like Oreb."

"Princes" (I Sam. 2:8). "Set them among princes."

By taking all these meanings with us to the willing offerings of the Israelites, we learn that wonderful beneficence and princely liberality was exhibited by the people. *God loves cheerful givers!* Do not these ungrudging gifts of God's ancient people lead us into two avenues of spiritual truth which, if we but consider them, will reveal unto us the grace of our Lord, as well as our own responsibility?

The first message of the "willing hearted" is that God gave His Son willingly and ungrudgingly for us — "He that spared not his own Son, but delivered him up for us all, how shall he not with him also freely give us all things?" (Rom. 8:32). What an unrestrained, unbounded love is manifested in the gift of Christ!

May we never forget the noble, princely giving of Christ! His offering of Himself was as willing as God's giving. As He left heaven He emptied the storehouse of His treasures at His Father's feet, for "though he was rich, ... he became poor" (II Cor. 8:9), and when He reached the cross He freely offered His blood without stint or reserve for you and me.

The second message that the offerings of the willing-hearted suggests is that our giving to God should be more hearty, willing, and liberal. The house that was filled with fragrance was the one wherein the woman had broken the alabaster box of precious ointment, and the person who made glad the heart of Christ was the one who cast into the treasury her two mites, which represented her all (Mark 14:8; Luke 21:1-6).

If God's people were only more willing and responsive in their gifts, the church would not be obliged to seek assistance from such questionable things as bazaars, whist drives, etc., to carry on its own work. "Freely ye have received, freely give."

We have great need to return to the apostolic days when the possessions of all were laid willingly at the Master's feet, and when the church lacked nothing (Acts 2:44, 45; 4:34-35).

(2). *The Gifts Had To Be Given by All* (Exod. 35:29). If one were to ransack the Scriptures, it is doubtful whether he could find such a wonderful, unanimous response to God's wish and command as was here displayed. From every quarter of the camp, the rich and poor united and came with their respective gifts to Moses. A parallel passage might be found in Judges 5, when Deborah's forceful appeal gathered fighters together from almost every tribe. Some, however, were faint-hearted, and did not come to the help of the Lord. But here, at the building of the tabernacle, Israel as one man gave of its substance to God.

What a great difference it would mean in the church of God, at home and abroad, especially abroad in these days when so many are being forced to retrench, if "every man and woman" realized his or her individual responsibility in the matter of giving to God (II Cor. 8:1-5).

The Men and Women (Exod. 35:22). Such brought bracelets and earrings, and rings, and tablets, and jewels of gold.

The Men (Exod. 35:22-24). Such brought gold, blue and purple, and scarlet, and fine linen, and goats' hair and red skins of rams, and badgers' skins, silver and brass, and shittim wood.

The Women (Exod. 35:25-26). Such are found spinning the fine linen, and goats' hair, giving their lookingglasses (Exod. 38:8).

The Rulers (35:27, 28). Such brought precious stones, spices, oil.

What lessons can we gather from such united efforts?

First all the men headed the list of their gifts with gold. Thus was it with the wise men who came to Christ (Matt. 2:11). Gold symbolizes the best. Let us therefore offer to Him the best, no matter what the gift may be.

Next we see that the women had an equal place with the men in their giving and working. The weak as well as the strong participated. There are those who would seek to discourage women from taking any part in the work of the Lord, and yet the tabernacle was built by women as well as by men. Moreover, even as the women spun the beautiful linen and the lovely white goats' hair which represent the glorious excellencies of our Redeemer, so let us be mindful of this fact when some would discredit the ministry of women. The Lord's body, that most precious, wonderful tabernacle, was fashioned by the Holy Spirit in the womb of a woman, and at Pentecost, when God created the first 120 pillars of the spiritual tabernacle which is His church, the Holy Ghost fell upon and baptized the women as equally as the men.

Further, the princely giving of the rulers at this point is very interesting when compared with the way in which their descendants treated the Saviour whom the tabernacle prefigured. Willingly they gave their precious stones, spices, and oil, but when in after days the Lord of glory came as their king, they sold Him for thirty pieces of silver and heaped upon Him spittle and shame (Zech. 11:12, 13).

Gold, Silver, Precious Stones. Do not these remind us of our "Bema" (I Cor. 3:11; II Cor. 5:10)?

(3). *Their Gifts Had To Be Brought Daily* (36:3). What a procession would be seen outside Moses' quarters every morning! Men and women, rich and poor, all standing together with their hands laden with fresh gifts.

Is our giving to God as fresh as it might or ought to be? Are we not sometimes stale in our giving to God? Why, descendants of these very same people were condemned by God in the days of Malachi (Mal. 1:8), for their lack of honor and zeal in their giving – "Ye offer polluted bread upon mine altar; ... ye offer the blind for sacrifice, ... ye offer the lame and sick" (Mal. 1:7, 8).

Let us not fall behind the Israelites in the wilderness, and like their successors offer to God what is not fresh or unclean. Alas! there are some who seem to think that anything is good enough for God. Every morning, yes, and moment by moment, let there be that fresh dedication of all that we have and are to Him; and that continual, fresh appropriation of Him for all our needs.

(4). *Their Gifts Had To Be Restrained* (Exod. 36:5-7). These people were fired with a burning devotion for God, otherwise there would not have been such a marvelous display of liberality. Love is always liberal, and if we profess to love our Lord, we shall not stop at the bare requirements of His word. Like Himself, we will go a little further, even to the second mile, and become more extravagant in our giving. Jesus not only fed the 5,000; we read they gathered up twelve baskets of fragments (John 6:13). Surely the disciple is not above his Master. Yet in these days people are in no fear of being restrained, rather have they to be constrained by appeals, honorable and otherwise, to give of their means to God.

b. *The Gifts and Their Significance* (Exod. 25:3-7)

It will be found helpful if at this point we bring together all the materials that were given and used by the Israelites of old, noting at the same time their typical and predictive significance.

(1). *Their Number.* By comparing the lists of things mentioned in Exodus 25:1-7; 35:5-29, we discover that there were fourteen outstanding materials given by the "willing-hearted" and "wise-hearted." Is there any special significance in the number? Students of Scripture numerals tell us that seven is the figure denoting spiritual perfection; and that twice seven, which is fourteen, are the figures that represent the double measure of spiritual perfection.

As all these fourteen various articles went to form the tabernacle of the Lord, and as the tabernacle was a shadow of Him who is the substance, can we not see in these particular fourteen materials types of Him who is the acme of perfection?

Who ever possessed such a double measure of spiritual perfection as Jesus? Said Peter to Christ, "How oft shall I forgive my brother, seven times seven?" [and that would have been a good measure of perfection]. No, said our Lord, until *seventy* times seven. *Seventy times seven,* that was ever His way of calculating and giving, for right across His ways, life, and sacrifice we can inscribe those figures of sublime and abounding perfection!

(2). *Their meaning.* Before we proceed further, it may be necessary to give a brief summary of the generally accepted typical meaning of the various materials that are mentioned, in order that we may carry such in our minds, and thus make our further meditation of Christ's person and work more intelligible and edifying.

Gold — The divine glory of the Lord Jesus as the Son of God.

Silver — As such was derived from the atonement money of Israel, it presents the preciousness of Christ as the ransom for sinners.

Brass — The divine character of Christ is able to sustain the fire of God — holiness and justice.

Blue — As this is a heavenly color, it typifies Christ as the manifestation of God as grace and love.

Purple — The kingly glory of Him who was the God-man — God manifest in flesh.

Scarlet — The true dignity and glory as seen in Christ as the Suffering One.

Fine Linen — Christ as the spotless, righteous Son of man.

Goats' Hair — The memorial of the death of Christ as the sin-offering.

Rams' Skin — The outward aspect of Christ as the man of God, whose blood makes atonement.

Badgers' Skin — The outward aspect of Christ toward the world, as having no beauty, no form or comeliness.

Shittim Wood — LXX "incorruptible wood." The incorrupt humanity of Christ.

Oil — The Holy Spirit's fulness shining forth in Christ.

Spices — The perfect graces of the Spirit as seen in Christ's life, death and intercession.

Onxy Stones — The effulgent glories and brightness of Christ.

More particular attention will be paid to the meanings of each article as we reach such in the various aspects of our study.

c. *The Outer Court — Its Name* (Exod. 27:9-18; 38:9-19)

When God gave the pattern of the tabernacle to Moses He commenced with the part of it that we hope to consider toward the end of our meditation, viz., the ark (Exod. 25:40). But although God began with the ark and finished at the Outer Court, i.e., came from within to the without, the Israelite in his approach to God started at the Outer Court and traveled within to the ark.

Such a procedure is true in almost every revelation of God. "He begins from Himself working outward toward man." e.g., in the Levitical offerings, as given in Leviticus 1-4, God commences with the burnt offering and concludes with the trespass offering. But the Israelite in his approach to God begins where God ends, namely, at the trespass or sin offering, and then gradually ascends until he is able to apprehend and offer the burnt offering.

The truth implied by this method of revelation and approach is very apparent. As sinners, we first of all meet Christ in the Outer Court as the brazen altar, and once there, we follow on to know Him as the laver. Then, according to our spiritual desires and apprehension, we enter the Holy Place and discover in Him our sustenance as the shewbread, our light as the candlestick, our mighty intercessor as the altar of incense; and then by the Holy Spirit we are led on within the veil until the beauties and glories of our adored and adorable Lord break upon our ravished souls. May God help us to seek a fuller, deeper spiritual apprehension and enable us not only to begin where God ends, but end where God begins.

There is a further thought that comes to one's mind as he thinks of the Outer Court, and it is this – to the eyes of one who was at a distance, the tabernacle would present nothing that was pleasing or attractive. In this case, distance would not lend enchantment to the scene. Imagine a Gentile standing away on some far-off mound or hill and gazing down upon the tabernacle. How would it appear to Him? Why, with the badger skin turned the reverse way upon the oblong shape of the Holy and Most Holy Places, it would look like a coffin resting upon desert ground and surrounded by a curtain. To behold its beauty he must come down to the plain and enter the gate of the Outer Court.

In like manner, no soul can ever discern the attractiveness of the radiance by standing afar off. To the sinner in his unbelief and ignorance, the Lord Jesus is as "a root out of a dry ground," and "there is no beauty that we should desire him" (Isa. 53:1-3), but when faith draws near and enters the gate and reaches the altar, then what loveliness and magnificence meets the gaze – gold, silver, precious stones, fine linen, etc.

If men and women would only enter the Outer Court and discover, as some of us are trying to do, that He is the altogether lovely One. As it made all the difference to one of old where he stood, so no one can appreciate Christ until they enter in through the gate. So many are trying to understand Him from "without," when the Word makes it plain that we must come "within" (John 3:1-16; Ps. 25:14).

The hangings or curtains that were suspended upon sixty pillars and which covered a space of 150 ft. by 75 ft., bore the name of "Outer Court." Such was the line separating the Israelites from the outside, and at the same time separating him unto the presence and worship of God within.

The Outer Court, then, stands for separation – "Almost every ancient temple stood within a sacred enclosure, which isolated it from the common working world, and rendered its religious character more distinctly apparent." Once the Israelite entered the gate of the Outer Court, he stood upon holy ground.

To the Spirit-anointed eye the lesson is very clear. Christ yes, and in Him, His people, are cut off, separated from the world and made holy unto God. With Him we have been separated unto every good work. If the Outer Court, as some have suggested, is typical of the outer or earthly life of our Lord, then we can see how, in every way, the truth of separation is applicable to Him. Although in the world He was not of it. Said He, regarding His own people, "They are not of the world, even as I am not of the world" (John 17: 14). In these days of compromise and apostacy, when it is so hard to distinguish many professing Christians from the ordinary men and women of the world, may the Lord make the Outer Court of our separation more distinct and apparent.

d. *The Outer Court – Its Dimensions*

As we have already observed, its length was 100 cubits and its width 50 cubits. The recognized English measure for a cubit is 18 inches and we therefore reach the sizes already quoted, viz., 150 feet by 75 feet. Its length was twice its width.

What typical truth is there for us here? Why, Christ's Person is greater and more glorious than His Gospel. His message is indeed wide, very wide, for "whosoever will may come," and those outstretched arms upon the cross reveal in symbol the great width of His invitation. But, beloved, what a length He came! Think of it, He traveled down from the realms of pure delight to this earth of ours with its sin and cruel shame and mockery! He, who was the very God of very God, condescended to become a babe, and was found wrapped in swaddling clothes. He came "from the Throne to the Manger – from there to the Cross." Truly His work and message are great, but He Himself is infinitely greater. His length, like the pattern of Him we are considering, exceeds His width.

e. *The Outer Court – Its Pillars* (Exod. 27:10-19).

The curtain wall that formed the sacred enclosure was suspended upon sixty pillars, including the four that were utilized for the gate, and as all that was connected with these pillars is most suggestive we must consider them more particularly:

(1). *Their Nature.* What these sixty pillars were made of and what design they had we are not told. Scripture is silent upon the point, and although it may be inferred that they were made of the shittim wood that was hewn down by men, it is always wise to observe the silences of God! The best course to pursue is to make the silence regarding their nature productive of an edifying truth. There are many things that we can understand about God and His Christ. To the spiritual mind, vast avenues of truth are unfolded, especially as the tabernacle is meditated upon as a type of Christ, but the puny mind of man cannot apprehend or comprehend everything. There are heights that we shall never scale and depths we shall never fathom in the wonderfulness of His nature and Person. No man, by searching, can find out God is the testimony of Old Testament writers (Job 11:7; Isa. 40:28). Truly Solomon was right when he declared in Proverbs 25:2, "It is the glory of God to conceal a thing."

(2). *Their Number.* Altogether there were sixty of these pillars. Why were there sixty and not seventy-five, or more or less? Is there anything to be gained from the exact number that were erected? Some think there is! The number sixty is made up of twelve fives. Twelve is a perfect number and signifies the perfection of *government.* Five is the number that denotes *grace. Twelve* is the number of the tribes of Israel. Therefore twelve fives, which makes sixty, is grace in governmental display before the world. That Christ has perfection of government is evident from Isaiah 9:6, 7, and that He is grace is proven by various passages. The glory of His reign is that He mixes grace with government – the day is fast coming when the grace of Christ will be displayed in governmental perfection on the behalf of His people and the world.

(3). *Their Sockets.* From Exodus 27:9, 10, we discover that these particular pillars rested in a foundation of brazen sockets. Such is expressive of a twofold thought.

Brass was an enduring substance and would therefore give firmness and stability to the pillars as they stood erect in the sandy desert. Is there not a firmness and stability in the work of Christ that defies all the storms of criticism and blasts of apostacy? Why His position, yes, and ours in Him, is impregnable! "Fastened to the Rock which cannot move, founded firm and deep in the Saviour's love."

Brass in Scripture Is a Type of Judgment. This is seen by the nature of the altar within the court, and also in the serpent that Moses raised upon the pole – both were of brass (Num. 21:6, 9). Was Christ not the One who endured the wrath and Judgment of God?

> The tempter's awful voice was heard,
> O Christ, it broke on Thee!

Yes, and as the brass is the metal that can endure and sustain the flames of the fire, so our blessed Lord bore willingly until He had exhausted the fiery heat of God's righteous judgment for our sake.

(4). *Their Silver Hooks and Fillets and Chapiters.* Passing from pillar to pillar was a rod, or fillet, and upon such were silver hooks from which hung the curtains of fine linen. At the top of each pillar there was a chapiter or headpiece of silver (Exod. 27:9-19). *Exodus* itself provides us with the meaning of silver. In Exodus 30:11-16, we discover the every Israelite, rich and poor alike, had to give a ransom of ½ a shekel (1/4½d) for the atonement of the soul. And in Exodus 38:28 we are told that this particular ransom, or atonement money, was used for the hooks, fillets, and chapiters of the tabernacle.

What a beautiful lesson there is here of the work of our Saviour. There is no redemption or atonement for mankind apart from the blood of Christ. The giving of His life upon the Cross was the one-half shekel Christ gave. Possibly Peter had that Old Testament requirement in mind when he wrote those words that set forth the preciousness of Christ's work (I Pet. 1:18, 19).

f. *The Outer Court – Its Hangings*

Suspended from the silver hooks that were upon the silver fillets or bar that went from pillar to pillar was a massive curtain of fine twined linen (Exod. 25:9-15) – 150 feet on the north and south sides respectively – 75 feet wide at the west end – 45 feet wide at the east end, 30 feet being allowed at this end for the gate – 7½ feet deep all round.

(1). *Their Meaning.* Here again we are helped as we compare Scripture with Scripture. From Revelation 19:8 we learn that "fine linen is the righteousness [the righteous acts, R.V.] of the saints." As the saints have no righteousness of their own (Rom. 3:10), the righteousness referred to must be His. "THE LORD OUR RIGHTEOUSNESS" (Jer. 23:6. See Rev. 19:8).

The fine twined linen reflects the righteousness of Christ, which was known to all. His garments of life and speech were without spot. He was that holy, harmless, undefiled, separated one of whom Pilate said, "I find no fault in Him." Such moral purity as Christ possessed was necessary for Saviourhood, and equal to all the demands of God.

> His life was pure without a spot,
> And all His nature clean.

(2). *Their Message.* What must be remembered is that there was no way through the hanging into the Outer Court, just as there is no salvation or redemption for the sons of men in the human righteousness of Christ. Such, of course, was imperative, for had there been one flaw in His character, He would have forfeited the right to become our Saviour. We are saved, not by the pure, holy life that He lived, but by the sacrifice of that thrice holy, spotless life on Calvary's tree. That cross is the gate by which we enter in; and he that climbeth up some other way the same is a thief and a robber (John 10:1).

g. *The Outer Court – Its Pins* (Exod. 27:19; 38:20)

How minute God's instructions were to Moses! Even the pins, or tent pegs, which were among the smallest of the materials, were not overlooked by God. What praise should be ours for One who counts even the hairs of our head and marks the grave of every common sparrow. "Little is much if God is in it," so let us try and see God in the little things of life.

(1). *They Speak of Stability.* These pins or pegs were driven into the ground and thus held the pillars and the hangings secure and firm against all adverse weathers. Does this not remind us of Him who was so steadfast unmovable? What power on earth or in hell could swerve Him from His purpose? "He set His face steadfastly towards Jerusalem." Those pins were made of brass, speaking of that which can endure, and consequently suggest Him who was ever strong in His God.

(2). *They Speak of Death.* Yet again those tabernacle pins were driven into the earth and the earth symbolizes death (John 12:24). Here we have another vision of the cross. The pin or peg was driven into the place of death, and the deeper in it went, the more secure was the erection.

What a message for our hearts! It is because the divine pin went down into the dust of death, down, down, until He destroyed him who had the power of death, that He came forth offering eternal life to all. The spiritual erection of His church is secure, for, builded as it is upon His death and resurrection, the very gates of hell cannot prevail against it.

This precious lesson cannot only be applied to Christ; the same is equally applicable to ourselves, as we are all one in Him. If we want to manifest that steadfastness, immovability, and power to resist the storms of passion, doubt, and unbelief when they beat against us, we must learn how to be buried in the desert of death. The further out of sight we get or the more we enter into the death of the cross, the more do we display the rock-like nature of Christ. The stability of the tabernacle of the Holy Spirit, which is your life and mine, depends upon its pins. Doubtless it is unpleasant to be buried out of sight but when we are willing to "lay in dust, life's glory dead," then, and only then, do we make it possible for the ground to blossom red, and with "life that shall endless be."

(3). *They Prophesy of Christ.* One other thought deserves attention ere we leave the pins. The word *pin* that is used here is elsewhere translated *nail,* as in Judges 4:21, 22; 5:26, where we find that the tent pin or iron nail was the implement used for Sisera's destruction.

The word is also used in Isaiah 33:20; 54:2, for "stakes," i.e., pegs or pins of a tent. With these meanings in mind, it is helpful to realize that the prophets spoke of Christ as a "nail." Look at such passages as Isaiah 22:20-25 and Zech. 10:4. He is the "nail" firmly securing all God's counsels of love, mercy, and blessing, and connecting them with this earth. Isaiah 22:5 refers to another "nail" who is the antichrist. He will be the nail securely fastened by Satan's power, but displaced and removed when the Son of man shall appear.

h. *The Outer Court – Its Cords*

Henry Soltan observes that

> Some of the Cords were the charge and burden of the Merarites (Num. 3:37; 4:32). The rest of the Cords were the charge and burden of the Gershonites (Num. 3:26; 4:26). This is rather a remarkable exception to the arrangement made for the charge and burden of the Tabernacle, its curtains and hangings. In no other instance did the Merarites and Gershonites carry any similar portions of the Tabernacle, but the distribution of the burden was in every other case kept quite distinct. It may be the object of God in thus altering the rule, was to give us a little intimation of a truth important to be remembered, viz., that however varied and different the gifts and occupations of His servants, yet they are members of the one body of Christ. There are mutual interests which link them together. There are common ties which unite them firmly as one assembly of God's people. There are bands of brotherhood which inseparably bind them in one bundle of life.

Scripture does not state of what material these cords were made. Possibly they were fashioned of the same material as the curtain (Exod. 35:5-19; 39:60). They were fastened to the pins, and thereby kept the pillars erect, and were also thrown over the external coverings of the tabernacle proper to keep them from being lifted by any blast of wind, and possibly were taken somehow underneath the coverings to keep them from sagging. Such can be made illustrative of

Christ's Grace. "I drew them with the cords of a man" (Hos. 11:4).

Israel's Past Desolation and Future Prosperity (Isa. 54:2; Jer. 10:20).

The Trinity. "A threefold cord is not quickly broken" (Eccles. 4:12).

Sacrifice. "Bind the sacrifice with cords" (Ps. 118:27).

Judgment. "When he had made a scourge of small cords" (John 2:15).

Shall we now try to gather up the various truths we have sought to outline and understand in some measure the progress of doctrine that is unfolded regarding Christ and His doctrine? The sockets of brass were possibly taken first of all and sunk in the ground: and as such represent judgment. There is the foundation of God's righteous judgment upon sin which must be endured and satisfied.

Then into the sockets of brass were placed the pillars, and as the nature of such is unknown, we have Christ stepping forth as the One whose name is *secret* (Judg. 13:18), and whom men knew not when He came among them (John 1:10, 26, 31). He was placed into the socket of brass ere He left heaven, for He was the Lamb slain before the foundation of the world (Rev. 13:8). Then in the fulness of time, He was stricken, smitten of God, and afflicted.

Then there followed the preparation of the curtain, and as such typifies the righteousness of Christ, we here see the next step in the divine pattern, viz., the Incarnation of Christ and the consequent holy life that He lived among men.

Then there came the hanging of the fine twined curtain upon the silver hooks and fillets; and as silver represents atonement, we see Christ finishing the work He came to do. As the linen curtain was hung upon silver bars, so Christ, whose character was more perfect and purer than the purest texture, is found hanging upon the tree.

The pillars were crowned with silver and the crown of our Saviour's mission was the Redemption that He affected by His precious sacrifice upon the cross.

The whole was made secure by the brazen pins and cords, which symbolize His faithfulness bringing all His work together. Beloved! what soul absorbing mysteries are unfolded here:

The wilderness of man's sin and iniquity.
The brazen sockets of God's judgment upon sin.
The fine twined linen of Christ's perfect type, who alone could bear such.
The silver death on the cross, whereby God's judgment is removed; God's broken law is satisfied, God's creatures delivered.

Well might we sing with grateful hearts, "Hallelujah! What a Saviour."

i. *The Outer Court – Its Gate* (Exod. 27:16; 38:18, 19)

As the provision of this gate forcibly illustrates man's need of salvation, and the grace of God in meeting such a need by the gift of His beloved Son, it will be found helpful to dwell fully upon this entrance into the Outer Court.

If you draw a straight line from the center of the gate to the mercy seat, you go through the brazen altar, through the laver, through the door, passing the table of shewbread on your right hand, and the golden lampstand on your left. Then you go through the altar of incense, through the veil, to the ark covered by the mercy seat, in the Holy of Holies. Is this not a mirror of the true Pilgrim's Progress from the camp outside to the immediate presence of God?

(1). *The Three Entrances.* It will be remembered that there were three different words used to describe the entrance into the three respective parts of the tabernacle.

There was the entrance to the Court, which was called the *gate* (Exod. 27:16).
There was the entrance to the Holy Place, which was called the *door* (Exod. 26:36).
There was the entrance to the Most Holy Place, which was called the *Veil* (Exod. 26:31).

Turning to the New Testament we discover that the same three terms are employed to unfold the Person and work of our Redeemer.

In Matthew 7:13, 14, He is the *gate* by which we enter.
In John 10:7, 9, He is the *door* by which we enter.
In Hebrews 10:20, He is the *veil* by which we enter.

(2). *The Messages They Proclaim.* These three avenues of approach declare two very important truths: *Separation From God.*

Each of the three hangings that formed the entrance speak of the same thing, viz., something which hid or covered the interior from the exterior. They were used not so much as to shut God in, but to shut man out.

The Israelite was separated from the Outer Court by the gate.
The priest was separated from the Holy Place by the door.
The High Priest was separated from the Holiest of All by the veil.

Taken together, then, they teach us that separation from God has come about through the sin of man. In the far off days of Eden there was no veil, or door, or gate between God and man, for the creature walked in the cool of eventide with his Creator, and held sweet converse with Him. But through disobedience, this communion was broken, and the flaming cherubim formed the first barrier between man and God, and the word of Isaiah became true for the whole human race thereafter—"Your iniquities have separated between you and your God, and your sins have hid his face from you" (Isa. 59:2).

Yet in those early days of human history although the heart of God was grieved over the separation that man's sin occasioned, we can see when we read the short biography of Enoch that He still hungered after man's fellowship, for this seventh one from Adam "walked with God." And the companionship was so sweet to God that He took him away altogether—"He was not for God took him." The well-known hymn suggests the experience of this Old Testament saint:

Nothing between, Lord, nothing
between;
Let me Thy glory see,
Draw my soul close to Thee,
Then speak in love to me—
Nothing between.

Nothing between, Lord, nothing
between;
Shine with unclouded ray,
Chasing each mist away,
O'er my whole heart bear sway—
Nothing between.

Salvation Alone Through Christ. All the three curtains were made of the same materials and were arranged in precisely the same order, viz., blue, and purple, and scarlet, and fine-twined linen. The three were also of the same dimensions, as regards their area, for the gate was 20 cubits (30 feet) wide by 5 cubits (7½ feet) high, making a 100 square cubits (20 multiplied by 5), while the door and the veil each occupied a space of 10 cubits (15 feet) wide and 10 cubits high, or a 100 square cubits each. This similarity in material and measurement in these typical curtains or coverings set forth the same truth, namely, that it is only through our Lord Jesus Christ, who is God manifest in the flesh, that we have any salvation at all. With one united voice the gate, the door, and veil proclaim that there is no access to God of any kind, whether it be of the initial distant worship of the Outer Court, or the closest intimacy of the Most Holy, except through Him who Himself declared that "no man cometh unto the Father, but by me" (John 14:6).

j. *There Was a Gate*

What a blessed thing it was that God condescended to provide a way by which the sinning Israelite could enter the tabernacle and be cleansed, and thereafter enjoy His presence and worship before Him. Although man was the one who caused the barrier to be raised between his own heart and God, God was the One who made the first effort to restore the broken fellowship, hence His command to Moses, "Let them make me a sanctuary; that I may dwell among them" (Exod. 25:8). Think of what the absence of that tabernacle would have meant for Israel, taken out as they were from the other nations, and then left to wander in the wilderness alone! Think of them groaning under the broken Law, with consciences smitten with guilt and with no promise or provision of atonement! What darkness and despair would have been theirs!

What a world of misery and woe ours would have been had the Lord Jesus not have come! Think of the world with no church, no Bible, no Gospel, no holy men and women! Why such a world would be but a reflection of hell! But let us ever be grateful to God that there is a gate divinely provided whereby mankind can enter in and be reconciled to God.

There is a gate that stands ajar,
And through its portals gleaming
A radiance from the Cross afar
The Saviour's love revealing.

> Oh, depth of mercy; can it be
> That gate was left ajar for me?
> For me—for me,
> Was left ajar for me.

k. *It Was the Only Gate*

Any Israelite approaching the tabernacle leading his sacrifice and with a deep desire to atone for his sin knew that there was no way to reach the brazen altar but through the gate that God had appointed to be set toward the east.

He could not enter through the hanging around the court for that was all closely woven together, and as we have already seen, no sinner can be saved from sin by the holy, righteous life that Christ lived upon earth, but only through the offering up of such a spotless life.

And then the height of the court made it impossible for an Israelite to enter apart from its only entrance, for being 7½ feet high it debarred him from looking and walking over or jumping. Yet, how many there are who are trying, like Cain of old, to please God, not in God's way but in their own. They are seeking to climb over the high curtain by self-righteousness and self-effort, or by religion, but says our Lord of such, "He that . . . climbeth up some other way, the same is a thief and a robber" (John 10:1).

Bunyan has illustrated this truth for us in his *Pilgrim's Progress:*

> He espied two men come tumbling over the wall on the left hand of the narrow way; and they made up apace to Him. The name of the one was Formalist, and the name of the other Hypocrisy. So, as I said, they drew up unto him, who thus entered with them into discourse.
>
> *Christian*—Gentlemen, whence came you, and whither go you?
>
> *Formalist & Hypocrisy*—We were born in the land of Vainglory, and are going for praise to Mount Zion.
>
> *Christian*—Why come you not in at the gate which standeth at the beginning of the way? Know you not that it is written, that he that cometh not in by the door, but climbeth up some other way, the same is a thief and a robber?
>
> *Formalist & Hypocrisy*—They said, that to go to the gate for entrance was by all their countrymen counted too far about; and that therefore their usual way was to make a short cut and to climb over the wall as they done.

But there are no "short cuts," for as there was only one gate for the rich and poor, prince and beggar, in Israel by which they could enter in, so for us "there is none other name under heaven" (Acts 4:12).

Yet in these days we are counted narrow-minded or bigoted if we contend for the only way by which souls can be saved. To insist upon the absolute necessity of regeneration, which is the divinely appointed gate into the true church of God, is to be counted old-fashioned. What the world wants is a popular Gospel, an Outer Court with gates all the way round – "Oh, it does not matter what a man believes if only he is sincere" is its repeated cry. The contention of the people who talk thus is not against us, but with God, for the narrow gate is of His own making and is just as narrow as He Himself made it. Thus, no matter whether it be a Nicodemus and a Saul, or a Mary Magdalene and a dying thief, all must enter through the same, and only, gate.

l. *It Was a Wide Gate*

It is interesting to observe that the gate was 20 cubits, i.e., 30 ft. wide. This means that the width of the three openings would be somewhere about 10 feet wide each – wide enough to admit any Israelite. It was also 7½ feet (5 cubits) high which means that it was high enough to admit any Israelite who cared to enter.

How wide is the gate of salvation? Why, can we not write across its portal, "Whosoever will may come"?

Think of the Width of God's love – John 3:16. "For God so loved the world."

Think of the Width of Man's need – Romans 3:23. "For all have sinned and come short of the glory of God."

Think of the Width of Christ's Redemption – I John 2:2. "He is the propitiation for our sins; and not for ours only, but also for the sins of the whole world."

Think for a moment of the size of the gate of the Outer Court and then compare it with that of the door, or the veil.

The height of the gate was 7½ feet, while that of the door and the veil was 15 feet.

The width of the gate was 30 feet, while that of the door and the veil was 15 feet.

In the gate, we are taught of that great liberty of access a sinner finds as he draws nigh to God. There is sounding in his ears the sweet music of the Saviour's message – "Him that cometh unto me." No matter what his depth or breadth is as a sinner, the gate is both wide and long enough to admit him.

The door, however, symbolizes by its increased height and narrowed width that enlarged spiritual experience and clearer vision can only come by further renunciation. The nearer we travel inward to God, the more do we learn the meaning of the word about "denying ourselves and taking up the cross."

m. *It Was a Strong Gate*

From Exodus 27:16, we learn that this way into the Outer Court was composed of four pillars, and, like the other fifty-six that formed the enclosure, they were strong and immovable, being kept secure by their sockets, pins, and cords. Turning to the New Testament, we discover that the work of our Lord was supported by four infallible pillars, i.e., the four Gospels, and such are able to bear all the stress and strain of the storms of modern criticism. As it took four pillars to uphold the gate, so it takes the whole of Matthew, Mark, Luke, and John to depict in various aspects the glories of Him who is "The Way."

Matthew says – *"Behold your King" (John 19:14).*

Mark says – *"Behold the man" (John 19:5).*

Luke says – *"Behold my servant" (Isa. 42:1).*

John says – *"Behold your God" (Isa. 40:9).*

But although there were four pillars, there were only three avenues of approach through such into the Court as one can see by the following sketch,

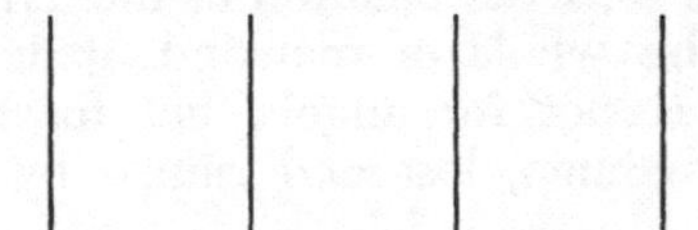

which clearly illustrates the Saviour who Himself declared that He was the *Way, Truth, Life* (John 14:6). Across these three openings we can also write His threefold title, so fragrant to sinners saved by His grace – LORD JESUS CHRIST.

Lord – eloquent of His pre-existence, deity, sovereignty.

Jesus – related to His humanity and Saviourhood.

Christ – declaring Him to be God's anointed One.

But the number of the pillars has another message for our hearts. Four is the number of material completeness. It is made up of three and one – 3 + 1. Three is the number of divine perfection and has a special reference to the Trinity –

The Father is One in sovereignty.

The Son is the second Person in incarnation, salvation, deliverance from the enemy.

The Holy Spirit, the third Person,

realizing in us and to us the divine things.

Four, then, is the revelation of God in the Trinity through His creative works. After the revelation of the Trinity, Creation is always the next thing; and therefore the gate is the gracious work or creation of the Trinity. *Four* is the number that connects the Father, Son, and Holy Spirit to the earth and man. It is the great number of the world as we see from the following:

Four great elements of the earth – earth, air, fire, water.

Four regions of the earth – north, south, east, west.

Four division of the day – morning, noon, evening, midnight.

Four seasons of the year – summer, autumn, winter, spring.

The gate of salvation is strong because it is the creation of the Trinity for the whole of mankind. Redemption is not for angels, but for men and women, lost and ruined by the Fall.

Turning to the Four Gospels again, we see how they are divided into 3 and 1. Matthew, Mark, and Luke are always connected and called the "Synoptic Gospels," as they present one truth that is common to each, viz., the perfect ministry of our Lord. John is the one who sets forth the deity of our Lord. In the Gospel that bears his name, we enter into a more intimate knowledge of the Saviour as very God of very God.

n. *It Was an Illuminated Gate*

The tabernacle, and also the tents of Israel, were pitched toward the east (Num. 2:3). This meant that the gate of the Outer Court always faced the east, i.e., toward the rising of the sun.

In Scripture the east is connected with that which illumines –

In Isaiah 41:2, you have righteous light – "The righteous man from the east."

In Matthew 2:1, you have intellectual light – "There came wise men from the east."

In Matthew 24:27, you have destructive light – "For the lightning cometh out of the east."

In Numbers 2:3, you have beneficial light – "The east side toward the rising of the sun."

The gate, therefore, was pitched before the light, and as soon as the sun rose in all its grandeur and glory, it shed its penetrating beams upon this beautifully colored portal of the tabernacle, and any Israelite entering had to do so in the full blaze of the sun's light.

As no entrance could be secured apart from the light-strewn way, let us turn to the New Testament and listen to what our Lord has to say about this gate of light – "And this is the condemnation, that light is come into the world, and men loved darkness rather than light, because their deeds were evil. For every one that doeth evil hateth the light, neither cometh to the light, lest his deeds should be reproved. But he that doeth truth cometh to the light, that his deeds may be made manifest, that they are wrought in God" (John 3:19-21).

Any sinner desirous of entering God's appointed gate must be willing for the light to reveal all his sin. Doubtless there will come a thorough searching and consequently deep humbling of soul before God as the sun of righteousness arises upon the wakened soul but what the light of the Holy Spirit reveals, the precious blood of Christ can cleanse.

o. *It Was a Gate of Life*

The Israelite entering the gate of the Outer Court had to do so leading his sacrifice, which was offered at the first thing his eyes gazed upon, namely, the brazen altar. Once within the gate, and at the altar, he knew that God had accepted him and that he could go out into the camp again conscious that there was nothing between his heart and God. Through the death of the victim he had brought, life was imputed unto him. The manner of entering in was simple, the man had but to take one step across the dusty threshold, and yet that one step meant everything, for once it had been taken, the man was on thrice holy ground.

How quickly does it take for the sinner to pass from death into life? The truth of the Gospel is most expressive –

Only a step to Jesus!
A step from sin to grace.

Of course, in reality, there were two steps for the Israelite to take from the gate to the altar, but in Christ there is only one, for He is both the *gate* and the *altar;* yes, and the sacrifice too. Experimentally, we decide at the gate, we are justified at the altar – The one is our act, the other is God's. One represents conversion, the other regeneration.

But we must bear in mind the solemn truth that as the Israelite walked under the gate, he did so with brass under his feet and silver over his head, for the four pillars that formed the gate, like the other fifty-six pillars of the Outer Court, were placed in sockets of brass and had their hooks, fillets, and chapiters of silver. And so what means life to us meant death to another. As the Israelite went between the brass and the silver, so we are shielded by the One who endured the righteous judgment of God upon sin by dying upon the cross as the ransom for all sinners.

p. *It Was a Beautiful Gate*

When Peter and John went up to the temple to pray, they found a man who was born lame sitting at the gate which is called *beautiful* begging for alms (Acts 3:2). And over this gate of the Outer Court that we are considering, we could suitably inscribe the words given to that sanctuary gate of old – "the Beautiful gate" (Acts 3:10).

Think of the beauty that would meet the eye of the Israelite as he approached the gate of the tabernacle. The bright rays of the sun would be shining upon the four colors that must have made the entrance pleasing and attractive to all – blue, purple, scarlet, and fine twined linen. The order of these beautiful colors, blue, purple, and scarlet, is repeated some twenty-four times in the book of Exodus. They are found mentioned in the –

Gate of the Outer Court (Exod. 27:16).
Door of the Holy Place (Exod. 26:36).
Veil of the Most Holy (Exod. 26:31).
Girdle of the High Priest (Exod. 28:8).
Ephod of the High Priest (Exod. 28:6).
Breastplate of Judgment (Exod. 28:15).
Hem of the Robe (Exod. 28:33).

Seeing, then, that these particular colors are found so often in the same rotation, let us seek to trace their meaning in order that we may fully apprehend the beauty of Christ as the way of salvation.

Blue, purple, and scarlet, we take it, were simply colors, displayed upon the groundwork of the fine twined linen.

(1). *The Colors.* Attractive loveliness, as well as utility, appears in God's design for the tabernacle, in which His presence was to be manifested. And that He is a lover of beauty is seen in the world He created in which "every prospect pleases." The distinct and pleasing colors referred to not only symbolize spiritual truths but remind us of the necessity of worshiping the Lord "in the *beauty* of holiness."

(a). *Blue*

The Hebrew word rendered "blue" is primarily the name of a shellfish, and derivatively of the brilliant dye yielded by it. This bright color ranks as the pre-eminent one, being always mentioned *first* in the frequent lists of colors.

We are told that the equivalent word used by the LXX translators is one that is applied by the ancients to the clear heavens and to the deep blue sea. Therefore, we are to understand it as indicating a heavenly color. "Heaven above is softer blue."

Man needed something to suggest the idea of heaven as a place from which God reveals Himself more fully than on earth, as the color of heaven was taken to suggest something which in its nature and origin was heavenly. Is not the loveliness of the blue seen in the life of our Lord Jesus Christ? Was He not the One who was not only heavenly in His origin but in His very nature and ways? Turn to John 3:12, 13, and what do you find Him saying? – "If I have told you earthly things, and ye believe not, how shall ye believe, if I tell you of heavenly things? And no man hath ascended up to heaven, but he that came down from heaven" – and here comes the word that is paradoxical – "even the Son of man which is in heaven." How could our Lord "come down from heaven" and yet be in heaven at the same time? Why, the simple meaning of the passage is that His whole life was lived in the atmosphere of heaven, for as Dr. Weymouth translates it, "There is no one who has gone up to Heaven, but there is One who has come down from Heaven, namely the Son of Man *whose home is in Heaven.*"

This seeming contrast is also true of all believers, for we are not only in the world but seated with Him in the heavenlies. May this heavenly blue be more manifest in our lives! The blue, then, represents Christ as the heavenly One, who manifested the grace, love, and power of Him who is the God of heaven.

As with the Israelites, so with us, we first of all meet the blue, for as we approach Him we exclaim, "He that cometh from heaven is above all" (John 3:31).

(b). *Purple*

Syrian purple dye was furnished by two particular Mediterranean sea-snails. Small shells were pounded, but from the larger ones the snails were pulled out and crushed. These particular creatures were found in great heaps on the Syrian shore.

The cloth of purple was much prized by the Greeks and Romans. It was looked upon as the imperial purple, the purple of kings. That it was a kingly color is seen from Judges 8:26, where the kings of Midian were clothed in purple raiment when slain by the Hebrews under Gideon.

Then the Chaldean king, Belshazzar, offered to anyone who could interpret for him the fearful writing on the wall that he should be the third ruler in the kingdom and wear purple and gold as appropriate insignia of his high position (Dan. 5:7, margin).

It was also looked upon as the fitting color for the heathen deities to wear, for in Jeremiah 10:9 we read that "blue and purple is their clothing." Such usages suggest the idea of royal majesty and authority, and so when we come to the Crucifixion of our Lord we find that it was the color He wore when as the King of the Jews He was clad with a purple jacket which doubtless had been discarded by Pilate or one of his soldiers.

Now purple is formed by mixing the other two colors mentioned here, viz., the blue and scarlet, and it is to this mingling that purple owes its peculiar beauty. Does this not intimate a most important truth? Blue suggests someone who is heavenly-minded. Scarlet, as we shall presently see, denotes something which is earthly – manhood.

Purple is a combination of both, which translated means that Christ is both God and man. He is "God manifest in the flesh" – the God-man. Henry Soltan has a thought that emphasizes this truth:

> If we were to place the blue and the scarlet side by side, without the intervention of some other colour the eye would be offended with the violent contrast, for, though each is beautiful in itself, and suitable to its own sphere, yet there is such a distinction, we might say opposition, in their hues, as to render them inharmonious if seen in immediate contact. The purple interposed, remedies this unpleasing effect: the eye passes with ease from the blue to the scarlet, and vice versa, by the aid of this blended colour, the purple. The blue gradually shades off into its opposite, the scarlet, and the gorgeousness of the latter is softened by imperceptible degrees into the blue. The purple is a new colour, formed by mingling the two: it owes its peculiar beauty alike to both: and were the due proportion of either absent, its especial character would be lost.

So we do not deal with a holy God who only resides in heavenly beauty and grandeur, or on the other hand with a pure man who was only of the earth, earthy, but with Him who was both the Son of God and the Son of man. In some mysterious way He combined both natures in His own when he took upon Himself the likeness of sinful flesh. And this blending of deity and humanity is seen in everything connected with the words and works of Him who was "the Word made flesh."

(c). *Scarlet*

This is the well known color or emblem of blood and of death. It is the color that belongs to the earth, just as the blue belongs to heaven. Let us trace the suggestive meanings of the scarlet. One of its connections or derivations is that of "Adam." *Adam* means "red" or "of the red ground," or better still, "taken out of the red earth." The *scarlet,* therefore, speaks of the sin of the first Adam, who was taken from the earth and through whom a curse passed upon the earth. His color, found as it was, upon the gate, door, and veil, speaks of Him who, as the last Adam (I Cor. 15:45-47), took upon Himself the curse of the whole earth and bore it away.

Another of its derivations is that of the "worm." The word *scarlet* that is used here is the same almost as that which is found in Job 25:6. "The son of man, which is a worm," and in Psalm 2:6, "I am a worm, and no man," and in Isaiah 41:14, "Fear not, thou worm Jacob." The scarlet dye is derived from a particular insect or worm called by naturalists *coccus ilicis,* which is found in large quantities on certain species of oak. The Arabic name of this insect is "Kermes," the root of our word "crimson." How blessed is the truth taught here! In that great messianic Psalm, Christ declares that He is "a worm and no man," which implies that He was not only self-abased, insignificant, weak, and despised when He came to earth, but that He was the "coccus ilicis" of God from which the precious crimson or scarlet blood was extracted, and which is efficacious to change the scarlet color of our sins into the pure whiteness of the wool and snow (Isa. 1:18).

(2). *Fine Twined Linen.* As we have already seen, this represents the earthly life of our Lord, which was "holy, harmless, undefiled" – "white and clean." The thought he emphasizes in this connection is that as the aforesaid colors of blue, purple, and scarlet were worked somehow upon the texture of linen, so in and through the offering up of Christ's spotless life upon the cross, heaven's love was revealed: God and man were made one, the curse of sin upon the earth atoned for. (One would fain linger upon the fuller significance of each word that is used here – *1* Fine; *2* Twined; *3* Linen.)

What a beautiful gate we have in Jesus! How miserable would have been our lot had He not come and combined all that the colors of the gate suggest in that wondrous life of His? Yes,

> How helpless and hopeless we
> sinners had been
> If He never had loved us till
> cleansed from our sin.

Hallelujah, what a Saviour! He is my blue! my purple! my scarlet! and my fine twined linen!

What exclusions were ours! Driven out and kept out from the presence of Him, whose delight is with the sons of men! But,

> Love found a way to redeem my
> soul,
> Love found a way to make me
> whole,
> Love sent my Lord to the Cross
> of Shame,
> Love found a way, O praise
> His holy Name!

The Saviour was the way and the place! He became the gate to life!

One other thought as we leave our "beautiful gate." The fourfold nature of that gate prefigures the fourfold nature of God that excluded man from His presence on account of his sin.

Blue

The color of heaven's love! God by His love excluded man from entering. Ah, but you say, "it is impossible that the love of God could come as a barrier between Himself and the object of His love." Let us remember that "our God is a consuming fire," and if we were to go into that Holy of Holies uncleansed, unpurified, we should be utterly and hopelessly destroyed.

Purple

Being the color that denotes royal authority and majesty, it speaks of the truth that God is ruler of the encampment. As a king, God has been rebelled against by man. "We will not have this man to reign over us," was what man said when this heavenly monarch exerted His authority. Thus rebellion shut man out from His presence.

Scarlet

This color, speaking as it does of blood and death, proclaims the message of the Old Testament that "the soul that sinneth, it shall die"; and the message of the New Testament, that "without shedding of blood there is no remission" (Heb. 9:22). Both of these are written large across the portals of the gate. We would be blind indeed if we did not see that the only way into the presence of God is by the execution of the demanded death penalty.

Fine Twined Linen

As this fabric typifies righteousness, it reveals the sad fact that man has broken God's law and by human righteousness is unable to meet its claims. God's perfect righteousness and holiness excludes the sinner, but, if accepted by faith as a garment, includes him in the divine family.

B. *Prophetic Gleams From the Tabernacle Ceremonies*

The Old Testament is conspicuous as a book of religious ceremonies which only receive their full explanation and interpretation in the New Testament. The Bible presents a progressive revelation, and further light reveals that ancient ceremonies were meant to portray the true methods of approach to God, the basis of which was the Passover sacrifice of Redemption. The sacrifices of *Leviticus*, with their ritual, are predictive of One who would offer up a "better sacrifice." As to the laws of purification, they teach us the necessity of holiness in drawing near to God. Laws as to the priesthood remind us of the agents by which we can draw near.

Among the Jews, as among all ancient nations, sacrifices formed the most essential part of religious worship. This is why the laws governing the same, scattered over the books of the Pentateuch, must have our closest study. Very early in the history of the human race, Abel learnt the truth of divine approach and acceptance, even though his sacrifice of a lamb meant the cost of his own life. Abel was the first one on earth to rear a sacrificial altar, and from Eden to Calvary the altar unfolds three infallible facts:

1. Every time a sacrifice was made, it testified to the depravity of man.
2. Every time a sacrifice was made, it testified to the inefficiency, and to the weakness and failure of the Law to save.
3. Every time a sacrifice was made, it pointed to the *sacrifice to be made on Calvary*. This was why Christ's blood spoke of better things than that of Abel's.

The tabernacle, with its construction, ceremonies of sacrifices, and calendar of feasts and festivals, were designed by God to embody vital truths – "parables for the time then present" (Heb. 9:9), an object lesson to the faith of God's ancient people. What did it teach? Professor Moorehead gives us this summary of what Israel learned and we can learn from "the Church in the Wilderness."

1. It symbolized God's presence with His people. (Exod. 25:8; 29:44-46; II Cor. 6:16).
2. It taught the necessity of holiness. God's dwelling with His people in the Tabernacle demanded holiness on their part (Lev. 20:26; 21:8; Num. 5:3). The object of all the moral, dietary and sanitary laws were to impress the people that the God among them was thrice holy. His holy presence with them made them what they were. He identifies Himself with His children now more intimately than then (John 14:23; Eph. 2:20-22; I John 4:16). Once He dwelt *among* His people, now He dwells *in* them. By and by there will be a more glorious and ineffable tabernacling with the redeemed (Rev. 4:3, 4).
3. It was a figure of God's plan of bringing sinners to Himself (Heb. 9:23). By means of the blood of beasts the people were made ceremonially clean, and relationship with God was maintained. By the blood of Christ we are brought into eternal fellowship with Him. The Altar of Sacrifice set forth the truth about Pardon, Justification—The Laver, Cleansing and Sanctification. In short, the Rites of the Tabernacle were a type of God's method of Salvation.
4. It was a symbol of the Incarnation of the Son of God (John 1:14). The Lord God dwelt with His people according to His promise in the Sanctuary (Lev. 26:11, 12). But now He has come to take up His permanent abode with them by "wedding Himself forever to His flesh."

We note a sort of progress in the manifestation of God to men.

First—His presence in the Tabernacle
Second—His Incarnation
Third—The Indwelling of the Spirit
Fourth—The Descent of the New Jerusalem, the Heavenly Tabernacle, into a glorified earth

The Outer Court – Its Contents. Although at the west end of the Outer Court the Israelite would observe as he entered the gate the covered section known as the Holy Place and the Holiest of All, his immediate attention would be taken up with two outstanding vessels, viz., the brazen altar and the brazen laver, which stood in a straight line between the gate of the Outer Court and the door of the Holy Place. These two vessels were visible to all, and the services at both of them were more or less of a public nature, while those vessels within the Holy Place were seen only by the priests whose right it was to enter and officiate there. The character of the vessels differed – those within were composed of gold and wood, while those without were made of brass and wood. This difference emphasizes two important lessons:

Inside, God is seen in His divine glory by His saints with whom He graciously condescends to fellowship with.

Outside, we have God dealing in righteousness with sin and uncleanness. There are some who see in the Outer Court and the tabernacle proper, the twofold aspects of the Saviour's work.

> *The contents of the Outer Court typify the work of Christ* down here. Sacrifice and Cleansing, the Altar and the Laver, are the result of His Death.
>
> *The vessels within the Holy Place speak of Christ* as risen and glorified, and of His continuous work on behalf of His people as Intercessor.

All who entered the Outer Court by way of the Gate would behold two large objects, the altar and the laver.

1. *The Brazen Altar.*

a. *Its Names*

Scripture designates this place in many ways, all of which denote its real meaning and purpose.

The Terms Used

There are at least some seven names by which this altar is called.

(1). *The Altar of Shittim Wood* (Exod. 27:1). As we shall presently see, this represents the humanity of our Lord and illustrates the truth of Hebrews 4:15-17: "Touched with the feeling of our infirmities."

(2). *The Brazen Altar* (Exod. 38:30; I Kings 8:64). Brass being an enduring substance, it encased wood; otherwise it would have been quickly charred and destroyed, and is thus illustrative of the divine strength that supported Christ until He bowed His head and died.

It also represents the righteous justice of God, and thus reveals the truths of Christ bearing the stroke that was due to sinners.

(3). *The Altar of Burnt Offering* (Exod. 35:16). The burnt offering is the first one that God commences with in the order of His revelation in Leviticus 1:3, and as every part of this offering was consumed upon the altar, it typifies the entire devotion of the Lord Jesus Christ to the accomplishment of the Father's will, no matter what that will involved. "I delight to do thy will, O my God" (Ps. 40:8; Heb. 10:7).

(4). *The Altar* (Exod. 29:12; 40:30). This short title with strong emphasis upon the article *the* speaks of its pre-eminence. There had to be no other altar in Israel. The one and only meeting between any sinning Israelites and God was at God's divinely appointed meeting place, the altar of sacrifice. Specific commands are given regarding the erection of other altars in such passages as Leviticus 17:8, 9 and Deuteronomy 12:13, 14. How true it is that a sinner under grace has no other meeting place than the cross of Christ! In these modern days many try to rear private altars of their own, but Acts 4:12 is still true – "Neither is there salvation in any other: for there is none other name under heaven given among men, whereby we must be saved." The only altar that we can repair to is the one Paul refers to in Hebrews 13:10, where he remarks, "We have an altar." As Bishop Westcott puts it: "The only earthly altar is the Cross on which Christ offered Himself: Christ is the Offering: He Himself is the feast of the believer."

(5). *The Altar at the Door of the Tabernacle* (Lev. 1:5). Israel learnt the precious lesson that there could be no worship without sacrifice, and so the altar was at the door of the gate of the Outer Court, where none could pass it. The sinner's first glimpse of Christ is as the brazen altar – the sacrifice for sin. But alas! what multitudes try to worship God without knowing the meaning of the altar and the laver. What disaster would have overtaken the priest who passed the altar and the laver by without performing all that was necessary at both and then attempted to walk straight into the Holy Place!

Of course he would never have been allowed to commit such sacrilege, and yet there are many who trample "under foot the Son of God" (Heb. 10:29) when they seek to worship God without meeting Him first of all at the altar where Israel had to meet Him of old. Hard though it may seem, yet it is taught here by this old-time construction in the wilderness, that no worship, however beautiful, refined, and pleasing to the flesh, is acceptable to God, unless the worshipers have experienced all the salvation and cleansing which the altar and the laver imply.

(6). *The Table of the Lord* (Mal. 1:7; Lev. 21:6, 22). Possibly this name has some reference to one of the particular offerings that was made upon it, and which satisfied both God and the offerer, viz., the meal offering. Such was composed of fine flour and is sometimes referred to as the food of the altar. How true it is that Christ, crucified and risen again is the Table that God has furnished for us in this wilderness. His complete sacrifice both satisfied the heart of God, and the souls of men.

(7). *The Altar of the Lord* (Mal. 2:13). It was an altar of His own provision. He did not leave its plan to man. Every detail regarding it was given to Moses by God when they met upon the Mount: and such details are followed up with the special injunction – "Make it: as it was shewed thee in the mount" (Exod. 27:8). In like manner, the cross was God's own provision. The reply of Abraham to Isaac was, "God will provide himself a [as a] lamb for a burnt offering" (Gen. 22:8). Redemption, let us never forget, originated in the heart of God, for Christ is the Lamb slain from the foundation of the world (Rev. 13:8). Away back in the past eternity, the plan of our salvation was conceived and virtually completed, and then in the fulness of time, when His Son was born of a woman, God, who had ever loved the world, actually gave His only begotten Son (John 3:16). And so redemption is precious because it was the Lord that found a ransom for our souls.

The Meaning of the Terms Used

There is a twofold significance about the name itself that is worthy of our consideration.

(1). Altar *means "a high place" or that "which ascends" or "lifts up."* The sacrifice brought by the Israelites was lifted up after it had been slain and placed upon the brass grating of the altar by the priest, where it remained lifted up from the earth; and it was thus that through this action the offerer was lifted up again into fellowship with God. How descriptive this is of that word of our Lord's regarding the altar of His cross (John 3:14; 12:32). Because He was lifted up between earth and heaven, the sinner can now come and experience the raising power of the cross, for Christ lifts us up again into contact with the Father.

But there is another deep truth

taught by this particular meaning of the word. This altar of burnt offering lifted up all that was laid upon it. The sacrifice was lifted up in the form of smoke by the consuming fire that burned continually thereon. Heart-searching truth! Are we willing that our bodies should be turned into smoke for the glory of God? Have I been lifted up, crucified with Christ? Is the fire of the Holy Ghost feeding upon my life? Am I wholly yielded up to Him? and is He causing my whole being to ascend as a sweet savor unto God? The sacrifice, being dead, was unconscious of its own virtue. Moses wist not that his face shone. Oh, for such a blessed state of such unconsciousness!

(2). *The Name* Altar *also implies "to kill," or "the place of sacrifice or slaughter."* The animal offerings were all slain at such and consequently it was always red with blood. It was the place of death. And if it be true that Calvary, which means "the place of a skull," was so named, not only because of its skull-like shape, but because it was a place of skulls, the conscious ground of death, then we can more readily understand this particular significance of the word. The truth, however, to enforce is that Christ was killed. He came to the place of slaughter – "And when they were come to the place which is called Calvary, there they crucified Jesus." Said Peter, when he faced the murderers of Christ: "Him . . . ye have taken, and by wicked hands have crucified and slain" (Acts 2:23).

But we all had a part in that cruel slaughter. The offerer in those far-off days had to slay his own beast while the priest dealt with the blood that was shed. My hand helped to slay Him, for it was my sin that laid Him upon His brazen altar. Therefore, let me bow in daily, deep humiliation at the foot of the cross and remind my cold, ungrateful heart of the part I played in His agony and shame; and then let me never add another sharp thorn to His brow or a nail to His hands or feet. Since it was my sin that crucified Christ, God help me to hate it with all the abhorrence that can fill a human soul.

b. *Its Position* (Lev. 4:7)

We have already seen from one of the names that the altar was known by that it was the first object that met the eye of a person as he entered the Outer Court, thus reminding him that atonement was the first necessity in approaching God. What is the first blessing that the Lord desires to meet us with as we return to Him? Is it not the forgiveness of our sin? Such is not possible apart from the altar of sacrifice, for "without shedding of blood is no remission." You remember how in the miracle of the healing of the palsied man Christ gave the sufferer the very thing he least expected to receive, viz., the forgiveness of his sins. The man desired physical healing first of all, but Christ deals in the first place with the root of the man's disease, and then with its result.

To approach God disregarding the altar meant death. Cain tried it; he ignored the blood, the sacrificial altar that made his brother Abel's altar so acceptable to God, and consequently he brought the curse of God upon his head. Yet even to Cain, God revealed the message of the cross, for said He, "If thou doest not well, sin lieth at the door." This phrase "sin lieth at the door" is most expressive (Gen. 4:7). The word for "sin" is the same as the one that is used for "sin-offering." So in effect the words of God mean, "If you have sinned against Me there is a sin-offering at the door; identify yourself with that and thus become reconciled to Me."

c. *Its Size*

Some very profitable truths are

suggested by the measurements or dimensions of this first Outer Court vessel.

(1). *It was Four-square* (Exod. 27:1). That phrase "the altar shall be four-square," that is, the same size on all sides, indicates equality. There is an equality of need for the word of Paul in Romans 3:22, 23 about there being "no difference," applicable to sinners of all ranks and conditions.

But praise God, Christ is the same for all. Men talk glibly in these days about equality, but where do we find one like Him whose ways are equal (Ezek. 18:25, 29; 35:19, 20)? He has not one Gospel for the rich and another for the poor. "The same Lord over all is rich unto all that call upon him" (Rom. 10:12).

(2). *It was 5 cubits long, and 5 cubits broad.* As five is the number that denotes "grace," we can see in such that the altar is the perfect answer of Christ to God's righteous requirements and to what was required of men. The Redeemer's work is equal and perfect, no matter whether you view it from the Godward or manward side. In the altar, then, grace is seen in God's giving, and in Christ's sacrifice, and in the acceptance of man through such. "By grace are ye saved" (Eph. 2:8).

(3). *It was 3 cubits high. Three* being the number that speaks of divine perfection, with a reference to the Trinity, we at once realize the provision of the altar was divine in its origin. Atonement emanates from God. Further, *three,* standing as it does for completeness, suggests that the work of the cross, in which the three Persons of the Godhead had a share, is solid, real, and complete. Being only this high it was easily reached.

(4). *It was twice the height of the mercy-seat.* In Exodus 25:10 we discover that the mercy seat was 1½ cubits high, while the altar of burnt offerings was 3 cubits. Thus, as Dr. C. I. Scofield reminds us, "the Atonement more than saves *us* – it glorifies God" (John 17:10).

(5). *It was the largest Vessel.* By comparing the measurements given of the other vessels with that of the altar it would seem that the latter had sufficient capacity to contain all the rest. The profound message here is that the One great sacrifice of the cross comprehends every other spiritual blessing. Is this not the meaning of such passages as Ephesians 1:1-15 and Romans 8:22?

Again, what spiritual blessing can we have apart from the atoning death of Christ? All that God does for us now is founded upon that cross. In fact, the outstanding lesson of the tabernacle appears to be that death is the only foundation of all approach to God and revelation of as well as blessing from God. To summarize, all the materials used in the construction of the tabernacle can be stated thus:

There was the fine linen which was produced from the seed that first of all had to fall into the ground and die.

The colors, blue, purple, and scarlet were extracted from certain insects who had to surrender their little lives.

The gold, silver, brass, precious stones had to be dug out of the earth, where they had been long buried.

The wood for the boards had to be cut down and sawn into their right shape.

The coverings of the tabernacle represented animals that had been slain or sacrificed.

The shewbread had to be made out of corn that was bruised and broken.

Death, then, was written everywhere. Therefore, let us never weary of extolling the death of Christ! Let us, like the apostle, "glory . . . in the cross" (Gal. 6:14), for it is the only foundation of all our vast, spiritual inheritances.

I take, O Cross, Thy shadow
For my abiding place;
I ask no other sunshine than
The sunshine of His Face;
Content to let the world go by,
To know no gain or loss,
My sinful self my only shame,
My glory all the Cross.

d. *Its Nature*

The materials that composed this altar at the gate all speak of many many truths concerning the Lord Jesus.

(1). *Shittim Wood* (Exod. 27:1). Doubtless it was called "an altar of shittim wood" because its greatest bulk would be composed of such timber. The Greek word that the LXX translators have used for *shittim* is "incorruptible," and so it is called "incorruptible wood." This suggests the incorruptible humanity of Christ, for are we not told that He was not suffered to see corruption (Ps. 16: 10)? He was the truly human One, "the Man Christ Jesus." The Scripture does not err when it calls Him "the son of Mary" (Mark 6:3) or the Son of man (John 5:27). A body was prepared for Him (Heb. 10:5), and that body He still possesses in a glorified form. "This same Jesus" is up there for us, and is to return for His redeemed people (Acts 1:10, 11).

(2). *Brass* (Exod. 27:1). The altar made of wood was covered, or overlaid with *brass* (Exod. 27:2). This takes us to the other side of our Lord's nature. He was not only the virgin's seed but "the mighty God" (Isa. 9:6). *Brass* reveals the strong, encuring character of Him who was "God manifest in the flesh." The altar was a brazen one, and the Lord, for your sake and mine, "laid help upon one that is mighty" (Ps. 89:19). Human perfection and divine strength are united in Christ and both are necessary for our needs while in the flesh.

(3). *Earth* (Exod. 20:24). Sometimes an altar was made of earth, and this is very fitting, for the mother dust, or "earth, was made for man's nourishment: bears the witness of his sins, and is the drinker in or receiver at death, his forfeited life." Christ, as our altar, was taken out of a dry ground and was given for man's nourishment, bears the witness of our sin in the marks of the nails, and at death receives us unto Himself. Earth ready on the spot was to be used for building up a sacrificial place. Are we not here taught to lay no stress upon the imposing ceremonials with which men seek to please the eye and gratify the imagination in religious observances? "Worship in spirit and in truth" is what God requires; and the very absence of pomp and fleshly dignity will conduce to lowliness of heart and self-abasement, and will at least help towards reality as drawing nigh to God. The altar of earth was a lowly thing and stood out in contrast with the high places, erected by the heathen nations of Canaan for their places of worship. Calvary was a place of no esteem. The cross had no attractiveness for the eye and He who hung on it had "no beauty that we should desire him" (Isa. 53:1, 2).

(4). *Unhewn Stones* (Exod. 20: 25). The plain, unfinished rough stones were to be used, for Moses received definite instructions from God regarding dressing or facing or ornamenting such material (Deut. 27:5, 6). The stones in their native state as they came from the hand of God were the only acceptable material. "To lift up a tool" upon it would pollue it. Here, again, the same truth is recorded with additions. "The Cross of shame and woe, and curse, has in modern days been turned into an ornamental device. It is stamped in gold, emblazoned in colours; and worn as an ornament of female dress, or as a charm. Truly it is polluted by being thus handled by human fancy!" In Isaiah 65:3, we find how hateful man's art and devices were to God. The Israelites made their altars of brick, which of course represented human effort, agency, and skill. The lesson is not far to seek. God will have us add nothing to Christ's death. The cross has been called "The Old Rugged Cross," and rugged and repugnant as it may appear to many, it must remain so, for the art and skillful efforts of sinful men would only mar, and not aid, that glorious work. Some would have us take Christ down from the cross as many desired Him to descend on the Crucifixion day. What they want is a Christ of example, One whose garments are not dyed with blood, but who is only robed in beautiful, pleasing garments. But, says Paul, "We preach Christ crucified" (I Cor. 1:23).

Yet again, are we not reminded of Ephesians 2:9, 10 – "Not of works, lest any man should boast. For we are his workmanship," as we keep in mind the unhewn stones?

(5). *No Steps* (Exod. 20:26). This implies that it stood upon the ground and was therefore equally accessible to all. Being only 3 cubits, that is 4½ feet high, it could be seen and reached by young as well as old. So it is with Christ's cross. It is near to all and within the reach of the youngest who has the power to understand.

The prohibition of "steps" also acts as a type of the immediate access that we have into God's presence. Steps of self-effort, self-righteousness, self-cleansing, and self-improvement are not necessary. In fact, God will not allow them, for the only fitness He requires is the consciousness of our utter, appalling need. The priests were not allowed to ascend "steps" because, owing to their particular dress, they would display the naked parts of their body. "Every attempt of man to reach God, every step higher, is only a further discovery of the nakedness of the flesh. Every outward amendment as a plea for the mercy of God, is a fresh exposure of the uncleanness and evil of the heart."

e. *Its Horns*

Upon each corner of the altar was a horn made of the same material as the altar itself (Exod. 27:2). Facts to note are:

(1). *Their Connection.* The reading of the A.V. of the above verse says "his horns shall be of the same," but in the R.V. there is this important alteration: "his horns therefore shall be of one piece with it," or, as we have it more forceful still in the LXX rendering, "the horns shall be of the same [margin, *out of*] piece." Thus these horns were not ornaments nailed or soldered on to the corners of the altar, but one piece with it, or a vital part of it. They grew out of it, so to speak. And as the horns speak of power and might, we see in them that there is no power apart from Christ's Person. Often we ask or seek for power as if such is something apart from Christ Himself, but the power "is one piece with" the Person. His Person and His power are one.

At this point it is well to remember that some of the blood of the victim that was slain had to be sprinkled upon the horns of the altar (Exod. 29:12; Lev. 8:15; 9:9; 4:24, 30, 34). The blood was upon the power! If only men would realize when they talk about the power and influence of Jesus as an example or teacher that His most effective power is the power or strength that has His blood-drops upon it! The might He wields is His because of Calvary! It was after the cross and as the result of it that He said to His disciples, ere He sent them forth, "All power is given unto me." The horns of the altar were sprinkled with blood!

From this same thought of the connection of the horns with that of the altar, we can gather the precious message of our union with Christ. Mysterious and wonderful though it may seem, yet it is blessedly true that through faith in Christ's finished work we have been made one with Him.

To use His own figure, we are the branches and He is the vine. Now branches are not tacked or fastened on to the vine; if they were, of what use would they be to the vine, or the vine to them? No, they grow out of the vine: they are one with the vine (John 15). We are one with Christ (John 17:21). What a gracious love on His part it is to make us a part of His very self! The body and the members are one (I Cor. 12:12-27), even as the horns and the altar were of old, because there is a blood union between them.

(2). *Their Uses.* By gathering together some of the outstanding references to the horns in Scripture we are enabled to understand what such are symbolic of.

Place of Mercy (I Kings 1:50; 2:28). "Joab fled unto the tabernacle of the LORD and caught hold on the horns of the altar." Is this not typical of the poor sinner who flies for refuge to lay hold on the hope set before him in the cross of our Lord?

Place of Sacrifice (Ps. 118:27). "Bind the sacrifice with cords, even unto the horns of the altar." The sacrifices of old were bound, unwillingly, upon the altar and the cords were their bonds that held them captives. But Christ required no cords or even nails to keep Him fast bound to His altar, for did He not say "No man taketh it [my life] from me, but I lay it down of myself. I have power to lay it down, and I have power to take it again" (John 10:18)?

Place of Power (Deut. 8:3-20; Rev. 17:12). In these references power other than Christ's is referred to, but still the dominating thought is that of might or strength, and thus the horns of the animals are taken as a figure to represent such. Mercy and might then are what the horns suggest! They are predictive of that prevailing power and protection the blood of Christ affords to every sinner that lays hold upon such. To grasp the altar's horns in faith meant to the Israelite that he was laying hold of Jehovah's strength. As He is "the horn of my salvation" (Ps. 18:2), let us daily appropriate Him as our strength. "Let him take hold of my strength" (Isa. 27:5) is His message for our hearts. Our spirits should rejoice in that He has "laid help upon one that is mighty" (Ps. 89:19).

Place of Eminence (Isa. 5:1). Turning to the above passage, we observe that the "horn" is equivalent to a "high hill." Here is the LXX version of the text – "My beloved had a vineyard on a high hill [Gr. and Heb. "horn"] in a fertile place." As the horn is the highest part of the animal, it is carred aloft as a badge of power and the honor consequent of power, and is therefore used as a sign of elevation. So "to lift up the horn" is to exalt either in the physical or in a figurative sense. The horns of an altar may be intended, therefore, to symbolize still more emphatically the elevation of the earth on which the sacrifice is offered toward heaven, the residence of the Being to whom it is presented (See Ezek. 43:15).

(3). *Their Direction.* Being upon the four corners they doubtless pointed not only upward but outward in every direction, thereby predicting the glorious truth of Christ's power in and through His cross to gather men and women from the four corners of the earth (Matt. 8:11; Rev. 21:13. See Mark 1:4). As the horns of the altar looked every way – north, east, west, south, so the power of His cross looks over this poor sin-stricken earth of ours, and as in the days of His flesh, so now, the weary, the sin-sick come to Him, the Saviour of the world.

Upon those of us who know Him there rests the solemn responsibility to obey His command and preach the Gospel to every creature throughout every quarter of the world (Mark 16:15).

Shout while ye journey home,
  Songs be in every mouth;
Lo! from the North we come,
  From the East, and West, and
    South,
City of God, the bond are free;
We come to live and reign in Thee.

f. *Its Vessels* (Exod. 27:3-5)

The various necessary utensils that were used in connection with the service of the altar each possess their own significance and symbolism.

(1). *The Pans to receive the Ashes* (Exod. 27:3). Great care was bestowed upon these ashes. They were not taken outside the camp and thrown anywhere. To the Israelite, they were precious because they spoke of a sacrifice that had been made on their behalf and accepted by God. They were the evidence that the victim or offering had been received in the Israelite's place. In the ashes lay the merit of the sacrifice. What does the dead body of Christ or the ashes declare but that God's claims have been fully met and that He has accepted Christ in the place of sinful men. As He bowed His head and died, the Saviour cried, "It is finished"; and as we gaze at Him who suffered on the cross, we know that in Him we have been accepted.

What happened to those ashes? Why, they were carried out in the pans and laid in a clean place. And this command to carry forth the ashes without the camp unto a clean place may have some reference to the burial of our Lord, for the place where He lay had all the requirements of a clean place. No corrupt body of fallen man had ever lain there. After His sacrifice, He was carried forth and placed in a sepulcher, hewn in stone, "wherein never man before was laid" (Luke 23:53; John 19:41). The phrase "poured out" is used in connection with the ashes as well as the blood (Lev. 4:12), and thus continues the thought of the entire pouring out of His life as our atoning sacrifice.

It is interesting to notice that ashes were used for cleansing any defilement (Num. 19:2, 9, 17, 19; Heb. 9:13). Such could be applied to the unclean, because in them there lay the merit of the sacrifice that had been made. But look for a moment at one verse in that nineteenth chapter of Numbers – "For an unclean person they shall take of the ashes of the burnt heifer of purification for sin, and running water shall be put thereto in a vessel" (v. 17). So there were two ingredients, ashes and water. Now from John 7:37-39 and Ephesians 5:26, we understand that water is a type of both the Holy Spirit and the Word of God. Therefore we see in the ashes His blood, and in the running water the life-giving Spirit operating through the Word.

When Christ died upon the cross He made our redemption *possible;* and now as the Holy Spirit works through the message of the Gospel, He makes that same redemption *actual* in our lives. On Calvary, we see the ashes; at Pentecost we see the running water, and both are gloriously combined for the cleansing of our sinful lives.

(2). *The Shovels.* These were possibly used to clear away the ashes from the altar and place them into the pan.

(3). *The Basons.* Such received the blood from the victims that were offered upon the altar (Exod. 24:6), and retained it for the purpose of sprinkling and for the pouring of the blood at the bottom of the altar. And being poured out at its very base meant that the altar was thus established upon blood (Isa. 53:12; Ps. 22:14).

The blood was counted as a precious thing because it represented life — "the life thereof, which is the blood" (Gen. 9:4). Thus, when the blood was poured out at the foot of the altar, it symbolized the pouring out of an accepted sacrifice before God. How typical this is of Calvary.

(4). *The Flesh-hooks.* The flesh-hook was an instrument with three prongs and used for placing the pieces of the offering upon the altar (See I Sam. 2:13). Such can be made to represent the dark hour of our Lord's death, when by the coarse, cruel soldiers, *His flesh-hooks,* He was placed upon His altar.

(5). *Fire-pans.* Possibly these are the censers mentioned in Leviticus 16:12 that were used to carry the fire from off the altar into the Holy Place for service at the altar of incense. There is a vital connection between these two altars. It is the brazen altar that helps to sustain the altar of incense. Christ's intercessory work is powerful and prevails because of His work upon Calvary. His wounds are effectual prayers.

(6). *The Brazen Grating* (Exod. 27:4, 5). In the middle of the altar, i.e., half way down, there was placed a grating of brass, upon which the sacrifice was laid and bound to rings and then consumed. This network of brass was in the heart of the altar and it was there that the fire burned so fiercely. As it was of brass, does it not speak of the strong, unswerving passion and zeal that burnt in the heart of Christ to fulfill His Father's will? Could He not say, "the zeal of thine house hath eaten me up" (John 2:17)?

Another thought is this. The network was 1½ cubits from the ground, the altar being 3 cubits in all, i.e., the grating was exactly the same height as the mercy seat (Exod. 25:10). The altar speaks of severity of justice, and the mercy seat of goodness, of mercy and love; and both the network of the altar and the mercy seat are the same height; they were in a level line with each other. Never let us speak of the mercy of God at the expense of His justice, or of His justice at the expense of His mercy. Says Paul, "Behold therefore the goodness and severity of God" (Rom. 11:22); they are parallel, equal, the same height. And the psalmist could write, "I will sing of mercy and judgment" (Ps. 101:1). As all the vessels were made of brass, the symbol of judgment, God's judgment upon sin at Calvary is ever before us.

g. *Its Fire*

The fire that consumed the sacrifice is emblematic of several deep spiritual truths regarding the nature of God, and of Christ's work.

(1). *Fire is symbolic of God's holiness.* As such it expresses God in three ways, as Scofield suggests:

In judgment upon that which His holiness utterly condemns (e.g., Gen. 19:24; Mark 9:43-48; Rev. 20:15). The fire upon the Altar speaks of the holiness of God condemning sin in the body and death of Christ.

In the manifestation of Himself, and of that which He approves (e.g., Exod. 3:2; I Pet. 1:7; Exod. 13:21). Christ was the manifestation of God and the One of whom He approved.

In purification (I Cor. 3:12-14; Mal. 3:2, 3). Christ whose eyes are as a flame of fire, tries, searches and cleanses the hearts of men.

(2). *The Fire of the Altar Was Divinely Provided.* The Israelite provided the sacrifice, the priest offered it, but God supplied the fire (Lev. 9:24). The fire coming out from

God's presence represented His holiness and justice; and when it rested upon the sacrifice, it became the visible token of His presence with His people. Because our God is a consuming fire, the flames of holiness and justice leaped out upon His beloved Son at Calvary. Some of the Rabbis say, "the fire crouched upon the altar like a lion, bright as the Sun, the flame solid and pure, consuming things wet and dry alike, without smoke." May we never lose sight of the fact that the fire should have consumed us, for we were worthy, but it spent its fiery heart upon Christ.

The Brazen Altar smokes no more,
On which the Victim lay,
Where sin's unmeasured doom He bore,
When I had nought to pray.

(3). *The Fire Was Continuous.* "The fire shall ever be burning upon the altar; it shall never go out" (Lev. 6:12, 13), was the divine Word. The bright flame never died down. Night and day, the column of smoke ascended heavenward, which spoke to God and to men of a justice that had been satisfied. The continual fire holds a twofold lesson for our hearts.

(a). The claims of God's holiness and justice are ever the same; they never die down. The Lord will never lower or alter His divine standards. As the fire never went out, so the holiness of God continues. The unquenchable flame of that "eternal fire" in which Christless ones must forever dwell is an awful witness of the abiding holiness of God. His holiness and hell are two fires that are never quenched.

(b). The other lesson is that the continual fire taught the Israelites that God was always ready to receive them through sacrifice, for His willingness to cleanse and save is as perpetual as the fire that burned (Heb. 7:25). In those far off days the continual descent of fire required the continual sacrifice, and the sacrifice, the fire; but in the one great offering of Christ upon the cross, God's holiness and justice were fully and finally met (Heb. 7:27; 9:28; 10:10; I Pet. 3:18).

No blood, no altar now,
The sacrifice is o'er:
No flame, no smoke ascends on high,
The Lamb is slain no more.

(4). *The Divine Fire was sufficient.* No other fire but that which was divinely provided was allowed to burn upon that old-time altar. Severe judgment fell upon Nadab and Abihu because they offered strange fire upon the altar (Lev. 10:1; Num. 3:4); God requires no carnal means to satisfy or meet His claims. Since it is His holiness which is at stake, we can add nothing to the fire.

h. *Its Staves* (Exod. 27:6, 7)

The provision of these staves adapted it for the wilderness journey. As the camp moved, it was covered with a covering of badgers' skin and a cloth of purple (Num. 4:13), and carried by the Kohathites. The altar, therefore, was always with them, and this implied that the time for their final rest had not yet come. They were strangers and pilgrims in the desert. Until our last breath there will be need of the blood.

In Ezekiel's temple, which is a picture of Israel's kingdom-age, the altar has no staves or rings (Ezek. 43:13-17). What is it that helps to bear the message of a crucified Lord to all mankind? Is it not the staves of shittim wood overlaid with brass, or men and women, human channels, made strong to resist all the onslaughts of the Devil? Think of some of our lonely missionaries in the regions beyond, who are helping to bear the message of Christ's altar to those who are in darkness – how human, how frail they are! And how could they stand the climate, the loneliness, the sacrifice, the persecution, if they were not overlaid with brass? Underneath them, and around them are the everlasting arms. But as in Ezekiel's vision, so with us, the day is fast dawning when our altar will require no staves, for when all the ransomed church of God is saved to sin no more, when all her wilderness journeying is over and she enters her final rest, Christian witness will be no longer necessary.

All heralds of the cross will then feed upon the Lamb, and turn all their energies into new and eternal channels of devotion and service.

i. *Its Holy Character*

It was sanctified (Exod. 29:44; 40:10).

So was Christ as our altar sanctified, i.e., set apart for a purpose (John 17:17).

It was anointed with oil (Exod. 40:10; Lev. 8:10, 11).

As an oil is a type of the Holy Spirit, we see here the truth of Acts 10:38.

It was Most Holy (Exod. 29:37; 40:10).

During His earthly life many testified to Christ's holiness.

It imparted Holiness (Lev. 20:7. See Num. 4:15).

We have a fitting illustration of this in Mark 5:30.

It was only served by Holy Men (Num. 18:2, 3).

"Be ye holy," "Be ye clean" (I Pet. 1:16; Isa. 52:11).

It was profaned and removed (II Kings 16:9-16).

"If another Gospel be preached—accursed" (Gal. 1:8, 9).

It provided material support (I Cor. 6:9).

"They which preach the gospel . . . live of [it]" (I Cor. 9:14).

It was the place of presented gifts (Matt. 5:22, 24).

Wise men of Matthew 2. What gifts have we brought? Are we right with others?

It sanctified all the gifts (Matt. 23:18, 19).

It accepted nothing unholy or unblemished (Lev. 22:22; Mal. 1:7, 8). Is there any blemish in our giving to God?

It is thus a fitting type of Christ (Heb. 13:10).

j. *Its Message*

Under this section let us seek to summarize the truths that have been set forth. Standing as it did at the gate of entrance, the altar of burnt offerings represented the claims of God. He is a holy and righteous God and His claims as such must be fully satisfied before He can meet man, in mercy and grace. He has decreed that "the soul that sinneth it shall die"; and failure to exact the death penalty from every Israelite in the shape of his individual offering would have meant the violation of His own truthfulness and honor. "God is not a man that he should lie" (Num. 23:19; I Sam. 15:29; Titus 1:2). The altar must be filled with a sacrifice ere man can approach God in peace.

How all this pre-figures our Saviour! When God purposed in His heart to redeem mankind, Christ offered Himself as the One upon whom all the death that was due to sinners on account of their sin, and when upon His cross He uttered the dying cry "It is finished," He implied that all the claims of a Holy God had been fully met. In Him "mercy and truth are met together; righteousness and peace have kissed each other" (Ps. 85:10). Calvary, which is our altar, became "Heaven's trysting place where love and justice met."

God is still the same as He was to Israel; but through the cross, He, while maintaining His justice, becomes the justifier of those who believe in Jesus (Rom. 3:23). Therefore let us praise Him, who is our altar, our sacrifice, our priest, yes, and the offerer too!

2. *The Brazen Laver* (Exod. 30:17-21; 38:8; 40:7, 30). Leaving the brazen altar and reaching the brazen laver, we realize that God would have us make progress in our Christian life and experience for the use and the message of the laver signifies a closer walk with God, resulting in holiness of life and a deepening spiritual apprehension.

The laver marks advancement in our thought and conception of the profound truths illustrated for us in the services and furnishings of the tabernacle. How true is the word of Hosea just here – "Then shall we know, if we follow on to know the LORD" (Hos. 6:3) – which, in effect, is what Paul says when he declares that we must leave the altar and pass on to the laver. "Therefore leaving the principles of the doctrine of Christ, let us go on unto perfection" (Heb. 6:1).

a. *Its Name*

The term "laver" is a very simple one meaning a bath or similar utensil containing water for the purpose of washing. Besides being quoted often in the Old Testament in connection with the tabernacle and Solomon's temple, the word finds a place in New Testament Scriptures, and its place in this latter part of the Bible gives us our authority for using the "laver" as a type or symbol.

(1). Ephesians 5:25, 26, R.V. "Christ also loved the church, and gave himself for it; that He might sanctify it, having cleansed it by the washing [margin – Gr. *laver*] of water with the word."

(2). Titus 3:5, R.V. "According to his mercy he saved us, by the washing (margin – *laver)* of regeneration and renewing of the Holy Ghost."

(3). Hebrews 10:22, R.V. "Let us draw near with a true heart in the fulness of faith, having our hearts sprinkled from an evil conscience, and our bodies washed with pure water." Here the laver is implied.

These passages, as one can see, all refer to the constant physical purity demanded of the Jewish priests when in attendance upon the tabernacle, and the application is made by Paul that believers in the church age must be likewise pure and clean. The features of the laver form an impressive type.

"Thou shalt also make a laver of brass . . . and thou shalt put water therein" (Exod. 30:18). Here are two things – the laver and the water, and the water was in the laver.

From Ephesians 5:26 we learn that the laver itself is the Word of God, i.e., the Bible – "the washing of water with [or through, or in] the word."

From Titus 3:5 and John 7:37-39, we realize that the Holy Spirit is the water. Water is the Saviour's great symbol of the divine Spirit.

In Hebrews 10:22 you see the water in the laver, or, in other words, you have the power and presence of the Holy Spirit working through the Word of God upon the heart of the believer, cleansing and washing him from the daily defilement of his sin.

Psalm 119:9. "Wherewithal shall a young man cleanse his way? by taking heed thereto according to thy word."

John 15:3. "Now ye are clean through the word which I have spoken unto you."

John 17:17. "Sanctify them through thy truth: thy word is truth."

May this meditation of the laver, with its wonderful spiritual meaning, be constantly before us. If it is, our minds will be enlightened, our hearts blessed, and our lives purified. There are other passages that can be cited to prove the cleansing efficacy of the Word as it is used by the Spirit.

b. *Its Position*

If there is one part of the Old Testament more than another in which our Lord must have spent much time over the exposition of those truths concerning Himself as reflected in type and prophecy, it must surely have been all that is associated with the tabernacle. How those saints He met on the Emmaus Road must have been amazed as He unfolded the Gospel significance of all that Moses was commanded to prepare for the religious life of Israel in the desert!

(1). *Its Position in the Bible.* Doubtless you have noticed that in the previous intimations given by God to Moses regarding the tabernacle and its furniture, the laver is not mentioned. The first reference to it is in Exodus 30:18, where we find it connected with the priests. The law that governs the first occurrence of a word is one that calls for the closest study because it usually heralds its consequent meaning or significance.

The laver is added and mentioned here in Exodus 30 for the first time because hitherto God has been dealing with sin and sinners. Therefore prominence is given to the altar and to its sacrifices. But with the reaching of the laver, there is an advance of thought, as priests only are found at it, where their particular cleansing equipped them for worship and service.

Does this not explain the word of John, "The Holy Spirit was not yet given; because that Jesus was not yet glorified" (John 7:39)? The laver prefigured the ministry of the Holy Spirit in connection with believers; the altar, the work of Christ on behalf of sinners.

Therefore, the position of the laver in the Word of God exactly corresponds to our Christian experience. The Holy Spirit always comes as Jesus is glorified. The laver follows the altar, it never precedes it.

Then, possibly, the reader has observed that the laver is the last vessel to be appointed for construction. See the references in Exodus 30:17-21; 38:8; 40:30-72. Is there not a divine intention in this, as well as in the thought just expressed? The laver is illustrative of the power of the Word of God and inspired and used by the Holy Spirit. The laver signifies the Spirit-inspired Scriptures.

Thus, being the last appointed vessel for construction, the laver suggests the finality of the Bible. God's last, final revelation to men is in the covers of the Sacred Book, which He caused to be written by men who were divinely led and inspired by the Holy Spirit. God has nothing more to say to man, for within His Word He has given us the last word from heaven regarding the revelation of His own purposes for the world and mankind. Did not our Lord teach the finality of the Scriptures in these solemn words? – "They have Moses and the prophets; let them hear them" (Luke 16:29-31).

Yet in these apostate days men are craving for new revelations of the eternal, while some are professing to have discovered truth unknown to the Bible. We are warned to beware of false teachers. God's Word is final and complete. He has nothing to add to it or take from it. What He has done, and is doing, and will yet do for believers and unbelievers, is clearly set forth, and the Word of Revelation rejected is the Word by which the rejector will be judged and condemned.

(2). *Its Position in the Tabernacle.* It was placed between the door of the Holy Place, which is called "the tabernacle of the congregation" in Exodus 30:18, 19 and "the tent of the congregation" in Exodus 40:7, 30, and the altar.

(a). *It came after the altar*

The appointed priest, as he entered

the gate of the Outer Court, faced the altar, where he had to receive atonement or remission of sins through blood-shedding. Like any Israelite, he had to offer up sacrifices for his own personal sins. Once beyond the altar he was ready to act as a serving priest and so at the laver he prepared himself for the further service of God. He had the right to enter the Holy Place, for he had passed the altar; but the condition necessary for using his title, or right, was cleanness of body, and so at the laver he washed himself.

The priest did not stay at the altar, but moved on to the laver. And in the order of Christian experience, as well as of the tabernacle construction, the altar precedes the laver. Yet how many there are who try to reach the laver without tarrying at the altar? The altar spells redemption through sacrifice, the laver, fitness for service, but often people try to serve God in multitudinous ways without a definite experience of regeneration or salvation. What God desires first of all is the life, the heart, and that He always receives when souls in lowly penitence bow at the cross and acknowledge His Son to be their Saviour. Then He willingly meets them at the laver, and by His Holy Spirit equips them for service, and uses all they seek to do for Him. Salvation and then service. The altar and then the laver!

(b). *It was connected with the altar*

Possibly the best way to show the vital contact between the altar and the laver is in the following tabulated manner. We must be careful, however, to remember that although we are treating the altar and the laver as separate vessels, and passing from one to the other, yet in their spiritual significance, the one is incorporated within the other. We carry the altar to the laver or, to put it in another way, we never leave one initial blessing of salvation or regeneration. It always abides although we travel in to experience more of God.

At The Altar

Christ's work on the cross
Christ's work for us

Calvary

Justification through the grace and power of God. Makes us clean.

Deliverance from the guilt and penalty of sin through the shed blood.

Sin as a principle dealt with.

The cause of estrangement removed.

The root of sin

Our position and standing (Isa. 1: 12).

Definite crisis once for all.

At The Laver

Christ's work by the Spirit
Christ's work in us

Pentecost

Sanctification through the Spirit-inspired truth. Keeps us clean.

Deliverance from the power and defilement of sin through the indwelling Spirit.

Sins as a practice dealt with.

The effect of estrangement removed.

The fruits of sin

Our experience and state (I John 1:7).

Daily process according to need.

Both aspects are combined in that verse that John records in his Gospel – "One of the soldiers with a spear pierced his side, and forthwith came there out *blood* and *water*" (John 19:34). First the blood, because it speaks of the need of justification; then the water because the justified soul needs a daily sanctification. Uniting the altar and the laver, we sing

Let the Water and the Blood
From Thy riven side which flowed
Be of sin the double cure
Cleanse me from its guilt and power.

(c). *It came before the Door*

How heart-searching this truth is! Within that door were vessels that symbolized the presence of One before whose holiness no priest dare stand with any trace of uncleanness upon him. "Be ye holy even as I am holy" was the message that faced the priest and so at the laver, he waited, and washed, until all defilement was removed.

Although he was a priest and had served at the altar, yet because of uncleanness upon him, he was unfitted to exercise his priestly office within the Holy Place until he had received cleansing at the laver.

The tabernacle, as we have seen, offers a type of the church, as the habitation of God. As it was impossible to pass through the door into the Holy Place without washing at the laver, so it is just as impossible to enter, and become a member of the true church except by and through Regeneration. It is only too evident that there are many in the visible, organized church who have never been born anew by the Holy Spirit.

Has the truth gripped our hearts? The laver was before the door! "LORD," says David, "who shall abide in thy tabernacle? who shall dwell in thy holy hill? He that walketh uprightly, and worketh righteousness, and speaketh the truth in his heart" (Ps. 15:1, 2). Beloved, if our works and ways are not right in His sight, if our lives are not clean and thoroughly adjusted to His mind and will, how can we enter the door of fuller service and blessing? It seems as if we can write that word "without" over both the altar and the laver. Upon the altar we can place the inscription "Without shedding of blood," while around the laver we can inscribe the solemn words, "Without holiness no man."

(d). *It came between the door and the altar*

This is not useless repetition of thought. The binding link between the altar and the door was the laver. So there were these three, the altar, the laver, the door, and says Solomon, "A threefold cord is not quickly broken." God has bound these three things inseparably together and what He has joined together let no man dare to put asunder. Together they set forth the successive steps in a soul's true progress in drawing nearer to God.

The altar, which speaks of justification and acceptance. The Work of the Son.

The laver, which speaks of sanctification and holiness. Deeper experience of Psalm 139. Searching of v. 1 and v. 23. The sanctification of the Spirit.

The door of the Holy Place, which speaks of entry into worship and service. The surrender to the Father (Rom. 12:1, 5).

Where does this meditation find us? What spiritual progress are we making? Are we still at the altar? Can it be true that we are content to live with only the forgiveness of past sin? Knowing that we are definitely saved by grace, are we no further than the cross?

Are we at the laver? It is sadly possible to reach the laver and discover our own disobedience and sin, and yet be unwilling to pay the price of a clean and a sanctified life!

Or have we reached the door of the Holy Place? If so, let us enter with all boldness. To whatsoever He calls, let there be willing, quick obedience. Let us be among the number "which follow the Lamb whithersoever he goeth" (Rev. 14:4).

c. *Its Size*

One outstanding feature of the laver, which is also shared by the golden candlestick within the Holy Place, is that no measurements or particulars are given as to shape and size. The fact is simply stated that the laver and its foot had to be made by Bezaleel (Exod. 31:1-9). Was this an oversight on the part of Moses as he communicated to Bezaleel the divine instructions regarding the tabernacle? No, it was no oversight nor omission, for when men are working as the wise-hearted of old did to the exact word and dictatorship of God it is impossible to be guilty of omissions or oversights. Therefore the absence of size and shape is significant.

Further, we are not told how it was conveyed through the desert. The altar had its staves and rings as we have already seen; but the laver is not mentioned as having such additions for transport, all of which purposed silence is suggestive and typical.

The laver speaks of the need of personal cleansing.

The laver speaks of the Word of God.

The laver speaks of the Holy Spirit operating through the Word.

The laver speaks of holiness made possible.

Combining all these thoughts, what have we? Why, the laver is left unmeasured to us because God would have us realize something of the need of our own human heart, a need which we cannot measure; and of His own immeasurable, inexhaustible grace and power to meet that need.

(1). *There is the unmeasured need of personal cleansing.* Who can tell the size and shape of sin in the human heart? The more the laver of the Word discovers to us our uncleanness, the more conscious do we become of unknown territories of greater and more heinous sins. We become companions of Isaiah in his "Woe is me" (Isa. 6:5).

They who fain would serve Thee best,
Are conscious most of sin within.

(2). *There is the unmeasured influence of the Word of God.* The Bible, symbolized as it is by the laver, is also without measurement. It has no shape nor size in respect to its influence and power. Every day beholds fresh triumphs and conquests. As quickly as possible it is taking on the strange, unknown languages of those who sit in heathen darkness, and by its gracious message of the Redeemer's love is conquering the benighted nations of the earth.

Who can measure its size when it comes to exert a personal influence over our own lives? Every time we read it, there flashes out new truth! Fresh revelations of God and of Christ break upon our vision as we prayerfully and reverently handle it. The Sacred Word is forever urging new claims upon our wayward hearts, calling us upward and onward to lives of deeper faith, love, holiness, and intercession. Our unwilling spirits would measure the distance to travel, but the Bible has no measurement for obedience, holiness, and service. It is forever urging us to go the second mile, to go a little further, to give freely – that is without size, shape or measurement.

(3). *There is the un-measured and un-measurable power of the Holy Spirit.* Although the water of the laver is our Lord's type of the work-influence of the Holy Spirit, yet upon another occasion He referred to Him as "wind," and said, "The wind bloweth where it listeth, and thou hearest the sound thereof, but canst not tell whence it cometh, and whither it goeth: so is every one that is born of the Spirit" (John 3:8).

Who can measure the work of the Spirit of God upon a human soul? How wonderful, mysterious, unfathomable, and immeasurable are

His ways! Why, they are past finding out. Yet some would seek to confine Him to creeds, dogmas and organizations. But He is without measure. With our little tape measure of human wisdom we try to measure the ways of God and confine Him with certain prescribed bounds. What folly it is to limit the Holy One of Israel! This is the Scriptural way of looking at His influence, for said our Saviour, "God giveth not the Spirit by measure" (John 3:34, R.V.). How true, then, the prophet's description of His influence (Isa. 40:13, 14).

(4). *There is also the suggestion of unmeasured holiness.* If through the water in the laver the priests were cleansed and thereby made fit for the sacred service of the Holy Place, what can the Holy Spirit not do in your heart and service if only you are kept in a state of continual purity? Let us never limit what God the Holy Spirit is able and willing to do for us. What great possibilities there are within each believer if only the Holy Spirit is allowed to work.

No saint has yet been able to contain all that the Spirit is waiting to bestow, for no matter how full we are, or how holy we think we are, there is always more to follow. This old world of ours has yet to witness how holy the Spirit of God can make a person, and what He can do through such a man or woman who is willing to pay the price of utter abandonment to His influences and power. The laver was without size, therefore, let us hold up our little lives to Him it typifies, for if we can't hold much we can overflow a great deal. What He wants is not merely receptacles that only hold His supply, but channels that convey His inexhaustible fulness to others.

Ere we leave this question of the laver's measurement or shape, there are one or two more observations to note:

(5). *Possibly the laver was round.* Such, of course, is only a conjecture. But a round vessel would be the most convenient shape for washing purposes. Assuming then that it was round, what spiritual application can such produce? The laver typifying as it does the Word of God, we see in its round shape the figure of completeness. If a thing is completely round, with no breaks or joints or corners, it becomes a circle of perfection. Is this not descriptive of the Bible? Is it not round or complete? It has no ugly corners of unreliability or soldered joints of fraudulent composition. It is not made up of fable and truth, of myths and miracle, in the way some modern writers would have us believe.

It is one whole, complete book and cannot be broken. The psalmist declares that "the law of the Lord is perfect," and the evidence of its perfection is the "converting of the soul." He again declares that "the statutes of the LORD are right," and consequently, they "rejoice the heart" (Ps. 19:7, 8).

(6). *It had no staves.* How it was carried we are not told. The altar and other vessels had staves and rings by which they were carried about. Surely the lessons is not far to seek.

Take the altar – it represents a work accomplished. It stands for the death of Christ upon the cross for our sins. The message of such can be transmitted or carried to others by the staves of confession and ministry.

But the laver represents not a work so much as a worker. Rather would we say, at the altar we see the work of a Person; while at the laver we see a Person at work. When the Holy Spirit enters your heart, He comes to abide, and you cannot convey Him to another soul as you can the message of the cross. We cannot give another the oil of the Spirit; they must come to Him and buy for themselves (Matt. 25:8, 9).

(7). *It had a foot.* In the majority of references to the laver, one finds this added phrase "and his foot." What purpose this foot served we are not told. "Perhaps it was a little outlet through which the waters could more easily flow within the reach of one that sought cleansing. The laver itself was too high to be easily reached, at least at its brim, but through this little pipe, which probably could be opened by a simple mechanism, the waters flowed to the ground and were always within the reach of those who had need of same."

How truly this illustrates the blessed nearness of the Holy Spirit. He is our paraclete, the One alongside of us to help us—"A Guide, a Comforter bequeathed, With us to dwell." The Spirit's constant nearness is suggested by the laver's foot.

(8). *It had a maker.* Bezaleel and his assistant, Aholiab, and all the wise-hearted, we are told in Exodus 31:1-11, were responsible for the fashioning of the laver, as well as the other necessary parts of the tabernacle. They were specially equipped for their work. God filled them with "the Spirit of God, in wisdom, and in knowledge, and in understanding, and in all manner of workmanship." Bezaleel was not able to make the water within the laver. That was supplied by God. The Bible, in one sense, is a human production. Its inspiration was supplied by God. As the laver itself is suggestive of the Word of God, do we not discern here a truth regarding its compilation and authorship? By whom was the Bible formed or written? How came we to possess such a wonderful product? Why, says Peter, "Holy men of God spake as they were moved by the Holy Ghost" (II Pet. 1:21).

These men were skilled in all manner of workmanship. Some were kings, prophets, statesmen, herdsmen, fishermen, scholars, yet all their minds were subject to one great mind. As the Holy Spirit made the laver possible by possessing Bezaleel and the rest of the workers, so He has made the Bible possible by His presence within the heart of each of its writers. Behind the human writers there was the divine author, for we must remember that there is only one author of the Bible, namely, the Spirit Himself. But He used many writers to fashion the book that causes everything to live wherever it goes. "All Scripture is given by inspiration of God, and is profitable for doctrine, for reproof, for correction, for instruction in righteousness" (II Tim. 3:16, 17).

d. *Its Composition*

Many interesting and profitable lessons can be gleaned from the material that composed this laver, and its foot.

(1). *It was composed entirely of brass.* In this it differed from the altar, which as we have observed, was made of shittim wood and brass. There was no inter-mixture of wood in the formation of the laver. Is there not a double truth here?

(2). *The wood was typical of humanity.* But there is nothing human about the actual Word of God. Some would have us believe that the Bible, as a whole, is not the Word of God. It may contain the Word of God, that is to say, you have a mixture of God's words, which, of course, are reliable, and of man's words, which are not to be trusted. We affirm, however, that there is no mixture in the Word of God. It not only contains the Word of God, it *is* the Word of God, from beginning to the end.

(3). *The water of the laver is typical of the Spirit.* Therefore the other typical side of the laver represents the Person of the Holy Spirit, and in Him there was no mixture. Our Saviour was the incorruptible wood overlaid with brass, a symbol of His two natures, one human, the other divine. The Holy Spirit has never possessed a human body of His own, He only indwells others. He indwelt the body of Christ, and since our Lord's Ascension, He has tabernacled in the bodies of believers. The Holy Spirit is one Person, possessing all the powers of deity.

(4). *The brass of the laver is also significant.* From the following passages we further learn that brass is

(a). *The symbol of what is strong, firm, lasting*

"He hath broken the gates of brass" (Ps. 107:16).

"I have made thee . . . brasen walls" (Jer. 1:18).

"I will make thee unto this people a fenced brasen wall" (Jer. 15:20).

"His thighs of brass" (Dan. 2:32-35 [Macedonian Empire]).

"I will make thy hoofs brass" (Mic. 4:13).

(b). *The symbol of hardness, obstinacy, insensibility*

"I knew that thou art obstinate, and they neck is an iron sinew, and thy brow brass" (Isa. 48:4).

"They are all grievous revolters, walking with slanders; they are brass and iron" (Jer. 6:28).

"They are brass, and tin, and iron, and lead, in the midst of the furnace" (Ezek. 22:18).

How applicable are the foregoing meanings when applied to the laver of God's divine Word!

(a). *It is strong, firm, lasting*

Peter in two very descriptive phrases testifies to the durability of the Bible. In the first chapter of his first epistle, he speaks of "Being born again, not of corruptible seed, but of incorruptible, by the word of God which liveth and abideth for ever." And again, "The word of the Lord endureth for ever" (I Pet. 23-25). Ages come and go! New systems of truth arise with every passing generation. So called "Gospels" are produced to meet the needs of each succeding epoch; but God's unchangeable and unchanging Word still stands and ever will, because it endureth "forever." To adapt Tennyson's lines

> Men may come, men may go,
> The Word goes on forever.

(b). *It is hard and obstinate*

Centuries of hate and opposition and adverse criticism have not made the least impression upon the Bible. Although it has been burnt, confiscated, torn asunder, denied, wounded in the house of its friends, it still holds up a brazen face to all who seek to destroy its influence and wreck its power.

Like Joseph's sheaves of old, it lifts up its proud head and compels all other books to bow in obeisance before it. It is the anvil that has worn out many hammers! It is the impregnable rock that never moves! Like the three Hebrew youths, it has passed through not one but countless fiery furnaces, and it always emerges without even the smell of fire about it, for the simple reason that it comes from and presents to all the divine Person whose form "is like the Son of God."

(c). *It is the symbol of slavery*

In those far off days, "brass" was an emblem of servitude. This is seen in the history of Samson, who, when taken by the Philistines, was compelled to serve in "fetters of brass." It was the metal used and worn by slaves.

> The Bible is a Book of preparation for the service of God. It is not a book simply for thrilling us with happy feelings and bringing us peace and joy; it is a Book of preparation

> for the service of God. We were saved that we might serve. We were sprinkled with the precious blood of Christ, but we were first bought with it, and we are bond-slaves of our Lord and Saviour Jesus Christ. The great motive of our Christian life should be, not that we may be happy, or peaceful, or joyful, or even saved; the compelling force of our religion should be full consecration to the Lord.

(d). *It was composed of brazen mirrors*

The fact that the laver was made from the brazen mirrors or looking glasses brought by the women of Israel who assembled at the door of the tabernacle is a most enlightening one. Symbolism of this fact is significant.

There is the Thought of Reflection

In a twofold way those women of Israel could see themselves.

First of all by looking into their own Polished Mirrors.

How many there are who seem quite content to gaze into their own looking glasses of self-righteousness, and self-pride. Then they could see themselves by standing at the door of the tabernacle, as they often did, and looking into the mirror of the piercing light of the presence of a holy, sin-hating God. But how few there are who surrender their own mirrors and seek, like Isaiah, to look into the mirror of God's holiness and have reflected the uncleanness of their own hearts. Then think of a suggested contrast!

Those looking glasses could only reveal the beauties or blemishes of a person. They could not make the beholder any better or worse. Neither can our own ways, efforts, righteousness improve us in God's sight.

We must surrender our mirrors, and then gaze into the laver, and, as we see our defilement, allow the water to wash such away. As those priests looked into the polished brass they saw their need and then as they washed in the laver's water their need was met.

The Bible is our looking glass and only such and thus of itself can only reveal our uncleanness and defilement of heart and life. But it does not leave us there. It points us to the water, and so what "the light reveals, the blood can cleanse." Smitten and scorched by the Word of God, we turn to the Holy Spirit, who applies "the cleansing the blood doth impart." But alas, so many see their need and are unwilling to seek the full cleansing. It is here that we understand the figure that James employs. "If any be a hearer of the word" (James 1:22-25).

There is the Thought of Sacrifice

It must have meant a good deal for those women to surrender their glasses to Moses in order that Bezaleel might fashion them into the laver, but they were "willing-hearted" so surrendered them without a grudge. What a surrender there is of our own mirrors of self-effort, self-glory, or our own ideas and fancies, yes, and of our sins and weights, when we realize that the submission of such will enable others, as well as ourselves, to live cleaner, holier lives. Have we caught the truth that the submission of some mirror we love, the letting go of some vanity we are clinging to, may help some priest of God to see his own deep need and thereafter live a cleaner more useful holy life? Our surrender of vanities, yes, and of our supposed virtues, too, always results in the spiritual blessing and quickening of others.

Then there is this further message that we can apply to our hearts. If only we consecrate to God our talents, wealth, beauty, influence, rank, and whatever we possess, then to what high and holy purpose can the Lord not put them? "Except a corn of wheat" (John 12:24).

e. *Its Use or Office*

The laver served one great purpose, namely, the washing and cleansing of the priest from all the defilement that he had contracted at the altar of offerings. Ere he entered the Holy Place "to bear the vessels of the Lord," meaning to attend to the requirements of the golden candlestick, the table of shewbread, and the golden altar of incense, he had to tarry at the laver until every stain was removed from his hands and feet. As the teaching of this part of the tabernacle is deeply spiritual and blessedly profitable, let us seek the definite guidance of the Holy Spirit Himself because no other part of the tabernacle so fully illustrates His sanctifying ministry in our lives as the laver. There is, first of all, then,

(1). *The cleansing of the priests.* Turning back to the first intimation of the laver in Exodus 30:18, 19, we discover that it was not for all Israelites to assemble at as they could at the altar. It was for a particular class.

(2). *It was for priests only.* Do we understand the spiritual significance of this fact? Can anyone worship or serve God aright if they are not washed and anointed as priests, or in other words, regenerated by the Spirit of God? Is the ministry of any preacher, or the so-called worship of any church member, or the service of any Sunday School teacher, or worker in some other branch of church work, acceptable to God, if the person — whether he be minister, member, or worker — does not possess the salvation of the cross the altar typifies?

The laver spells sanctification and the consequent door of the Holy Place with its service and worship, but such were not for any common Israelites.

And sinners, no matter how educated, refined, reverent, and religious they may be, can ever enter into the Holy Place if God has not been met and dealt with at the altar of burnt offerings.

(3). *Their cleansing was initial and complete.* One cannot get away from the thought that in the tabernacle God has given us a most perfect representation of Christ's relationship to ourselves, and of our relationship to Him. The progress of the pilgrim is clearly set forth from the wicket gate to the celestial city. In a series of fascinating types, He has shown us His way down to man, and man's way up to God. And if we truly experience the meaning of the laver, the rest of our Study will be a spiritual feast.

Turning back to Exodus 29:4, we learn that Aaron and his sons received a very definite washing ere they were consecrated as priests unto God. Here is the command — "Thou shalt wash them with water."

Now the word *wash* here means, as it is translated by the LXX, to "wash all over." And this washing, as you will observe, was performed not by the priests themselves, but by Moses — "Thou," said God to Moses, "shalt wash them"; and once washed they "were washed for ever." The act by Moses was never repeated. Therefore this particular washing was initial and complete. Once for all these priests were taken and their bodies washed all over and then followed their clothing, anointing, and order of service.

This cleansing, or thorough washing, answers to our Regeneration, or our cleansing or washing in or through the precious blood of Christ. At the moment of our conversion we were taken out of the guilt and penalty of sin and planted in Christ forever. Now we stand complete in Him. "What God doeth is forever." Regeneration can never be repeated either by God, or man. Like the priests, we were washed all over once and for all by another, even by the

Lord Himself, and are able to join in John's doxology and sing, "Unto him that loved us, and washed us from our sins in his own blood" (Rev. 1:5, 6). Regenerated once for all. Thus our position is unalterable, no matter what our experience may be like. A regenerated person may become degenerated through disobedience and defilement but never unregenerated again. Once born-again, he cannot be *born again.*

(4). *Their cleansing was continuous and partial.* At the laver we encounter another washing that was necessary for the priests, for in the first account of the laver that is found in Exodus 30:18, 19, its use is proclaimed. By comparing this verse with the one already discussed we see these three contrasts:

(a). *Here the Cleansing is Partial*

The word that the Spirit of God used for *wash* here is a different one altogether from the one found in Exodus 29:4. It signifies the partial wash, or washing of particular parts and not the whole body. God says, in v. 19, "Aaron and his sons shall wash their hands and their feet."

This cleansing, then, differs from the other because the two washings represent two blessed truths in our Christian experience which are vitally connected.

Our Salvation — that is our deliverance forever from the awful guilt of sin. With grateful hearts we look back and sing, "Tis done, the great transaction's done."

Our sanctification — that is our deliverance from the power, dominion, and defilement of sin. The washing of the laver is really the Old Testament illustration of Romans 8:1, 2.

The two specific parts of the body that were detailed for cleansing at the laver were the hands and feet.

The Hands.

At the altar the hands of the priests became defiled through handling the slain sacrifices and their ashes, and thus, before they handled the holy vessels in the Holy Place, they had to cleanse them at the laver.

The Feet.

Standing continually upon the blood-sodden earth at the altar, their feet presented a very unsightly appearance and so, ere they walked into the sanctuary and trod upon the holy ground, they had to seek the washing away of all their stains.

Taken together these two parts typify our need of partial cleansing.

The Hands — Our Work.

Our hands represent what we do, or our service, our works, and express our relationship toward God. And how great is our need of cleansing just here. Why, there is not a part of our labor that is not marred in some way or another by selfishness, pride, disobedience!

How defiled our hands must appear in the presence of a Holy God, in whose sight the very heavens are not clean.

> Let no man talk of sinless perfection this side of the grave. I can hardly speak a word that is not sinful. I can hardly think a thought that is not in some way unclean. I can hardly do a thing that is not imperfect. I can hardly have a motive that is not stained with selfishness.

The Feet — Our Walk

Our feet represent where we go, or our life, our ways. They signify our relationship toward the world. How solemn the thought is — would that it exercised a greater influence over our lives! We cannot stand in the Holy Place with unclean feet. The feet that stray away into disloyalty to God's Word, or that are found standing in places where He is not honored, such as centers of worldly amusement and pleasure, can never tread the sacred precincts of His Holy sanctuary.

How wonderful it is that our Lord has combined these two washings in one verse, giving to each its distinctive meaning. "He that is washed [i.e., washed all over, for the word here is the LXX one of Exodus 29:4] needeth not save to wash [i.e., the word of 30:8] his feet, but is clean every whit [washed all over, once for all]: and ye are clean, but not all" (John 13:10).

(b). *Here the Cleansing Is Continuous*

The first cleansing of the priests was complete. They were washed all over, once for all. But here at the laver the cleansing was a daily one. Whether the priests were conscious of their need or not, they had to wash themselves before they entered the Holy Place. It is what God sees and not what we are only conscious of that makes cleansing necessary.

Have we all realized the need of perpetual cleansing from the defilement of sin? Do we all believe in, and have we all experienced the power of Him who saves us to the uttermost or entirely? That wonderful verse in Hebrews 7:25 is not first of all for sinners but saints. It describes the salvation that God has for saints, his full salvation which is typified by the laver.

Some of you possibly have stumbled over what is known as "Keswick" teaching. Somehow you have never understood its message aright. You have thought it to be too ideal for your life of constant struggle and defeat.

Now what does it mean? Simply this – when you came to Christ as a poor lost sinner, He received you in virtue of His death and transferred to you immediately the full merits of His cross so that had you died the next moment, as the dying thief did, you would have gone straight to heaven. What was it that happened at your conversion? Why Christ dealt with sin in you as a *principle*. When you were born into this world you were born a child of Adam, meaning you inherited all the propensities to evil that are to be found in everyone born since Adam's day. As you grew up, that inherited sin of Adam's grew with you until it became the ruling principle in your own life. Not only were you born in sin, but by your own desire you lived in sin. Original sin became acquired sin.

Upon the cross the Last Adam who was born sinless, because He was born of the Holy Spirit and not by human generation died, and by dying He destroyed the sin of the First Adam. When you received Christ as your Saviour, He imparted to you deliverance from Adam's sin and transgression which you had made your own. Thus you became a new creature in Christ Jesus, or no longer a child of Adam, but being born again, you became a child of God. Grace entering your heart brought a new principle with it.

But here is the trouble. You ran well for a while, and then as the glow of your early joy began to fade you realized when you came up against the hard facts of life that somehow you were not fully delivered, and possibly today you are troubled with sins of failure, sins of wrongdoing, sins of temper, sins of selfishness, sins of willful and negligent ignorance, sins of self-pride and glory, sins of unclean desires. The constant reappearance of these sins is being used by the Devil to make you doubt the fact of your initial salvation.

This brings us to the truth and the message of the laver. Christ not only died upon the cross and dealt with sin, but He rose again and went back to heaven, and after reaching there He sent forth the Holy Spirit. But what is the office of the Holy Spirit? Why, although Christ washed us once for all by His royal blood, and gave us a new nature, He did not take away the old nature, or our old body with its remaining corruption, neither did He deliver us from a world that is full of evil and defilement. But in the Person of His Holy Spirit, He provided One who would enter our regenerated lives and thus keep back all the powers of the old nature and make us dead to its claims, and cause the new nature to gradually assert itself until our whole life grows into the likeness of the Lord.

Why is it that, although you are a Christian, you are not enjoying that life of constant victory over sin that you so much desire? How is it that you find yourself continually baffled and beaten by forces within and around you? How is it that your testimony is crippled because of your temper, or your confession so fruitless because of your crookedness, or your labor so futile because of your living? Simply because you are ignorant of the Holy Spirit whom God has placed within you, or, if you are conscious of His indwelling, you are unwilling to follow Him on to the higher planes of spiritual experience. The washing and the teaching of the laver represent a life of continual holiness made possible by "the Holy Spirit who stands ministering within the heart and ready every moment to wash away the faintest touch of evil, and keep us undefiled and perfectly accepted in His sight." Because of our constant liability to contract the stains of earth, the atmosphere of which, as we breathe it, seems to be so laden with the breath of evil, this cleansing that the laver typifies will remain necessary and continuous until our old body is changed and we are delivered from the sinful environment that surrounds us and receive the redeemed, glorified body that will correspond to the redeemed spirit we now possess.

In Ezekiel's temple, no laver is mentioned. The truth is surely apparent. When we stand in the light of His Glory there will be no further need of cleansing, for when we see Him we shall be like Him – for He will present us to Himself a glorious church, not having spot, or wrinkle, or any such thing but holy and without blemish (Eph. 5:27).

Till then, however, the laver stands, and as "we walk in the light, as he is in the light, we have fellowship one with another, and the blood of Jesus Christ his Son cleanseth [mark the present tense] us from all sin" (I John 1:7).

The Laver stands. If earth-defiled,
Go, wash thy hands, thy feet;
And simply as a pardoned child,
Approach the mercy-seat;
Within the veil thy censer bring,
And burn sweet incense to the King.

(c). *Here the Washing Is Personal*

Let us seek to make our study practical. When the priests were selected they were washed all over by another, even by Moses, who was God's representative. But here, at the laver, they are left to cleanse themselves. Each priest applied the water to his own hands and feet as need required.

While it is true that we are made holy by another and that sanctification is not an effort but a gift, not an attainment but an obtainment, not a life of struggle but submission, yet there must be a deliberate turning from sin on our part, hence the meaning of injunctions such as Philippians 2:12 (Work out), Titus 2:11, 12 (Teaching us), II Corinthians 7:1 (Let us cleanse ourselves), Ephesians 4:20-22 (Put off), Hebrews 12:1 (Let us lay aside).

When we plead with sinners to accept Christ, we make it very clear that God cannot save them against their will, but often we forget that He cannot sanctify saints against their will. It is His will that they should be sanctified but if they have no great desire for holiness of life and service, then God's will is thwarted. "Ye will not come to me" (John 5:40). We must seek to cultivate those desires for likeness to Him. In other words we must come to a point of decision as we did at conversion and trust the Holy Spirit to undertake for us, or as Evan Hopkins, theologian of *Keswick* delighted to put it, there must be the "Crisis before the Process." Are you willing for the "crisis" at this very moment? Will you turn deliberately from all known sin and then go out to constantly obey the voice of the Holy Spirit as He speaks to you through the Word of God and thus make the process of sanctification effectual in your whole life?

(5). *The Claims of Divine Holiness.* The other thought that the brazen laver represents and which is so closely connected with the cleansing of the priests is that of the claims of God's holiness. In fact, it was God's holiness that made the laver a great necessity in the experience of the priests. The demands of divine holiness are seen in the fact that any priest refusing to comply with the divine command, and attempting to enter the Holy Place without engaging in his ablutions at the laver, had to forfeit his life (Exod. 30:20, 21).

Possibly it may seem hard that a man should die for such a trivial thing as the failure to wash his hands and feet, but the principle involved made such punishment imperative. Because God was of purer eyes than to behold iniquity, He had to deal drastically with the one who was bearing what He hated. Does this solemn fact of immediate death not overwhelm us with the sense of God's holiness? Do you never tremble as you think of Him who is "glorious in holiness, fearful in praises, doing wonders" (Exod. 15:11)? What hatred for sin the laver represented! Not only the laver, but the whole tabernacle witnessed to the truth that God hated sin. There was no fellowship at the altar unless there was the sin offering. There was no service within the Holy Place unless there was cleansing at the laver. There was no yearly entrance into the Most Holy Place unless the blood that satisfied the claims of God's holiness was sprinkled upon the mercy seat. Well might the seraphim cry, Holy! Holy! Holy!

Would that we had the same divine hatred for sin! The difficulty is we entertain some secret desire for it—we regard iniquity within our hearts and so the Lord does not hear the request of our life for holiness. Yet the Holy Spirit can shed abroad in our hearts love for God's holiness and at the same time scatter through every part of us that divine hatred and abhorrence for sin. If only we hated sin as God does, we should understand the meaning of the laver and experience more fully the privilege of the Holy Place.

Then there is that solemn question of death that overtook the priest who disobeyed the divine injunction to cleanse himself from defilement, the application of which is not hard to seek. Unless we desire that daily equipment for service that can only come through the daily renunciation of these works and ways which are absolutely hostile to God's holy nature, then what can follow but death? Refuse the voice of the Holy Spirit as He calls you to a life of deeper holiness, resist the claims of God for fuller consecration as He urges them upon you through His Word, and you will die in many ways: your testimony dies, your power for Him dies, your fruitfulness dies, your holy desires die, your love for souls and for the things of God die.

Despising the laver, with its washing, which for believers signifies dying to sin and living entirely unto

God, we become as withered branches that are fit for destruction by fire and at the judgment seat of Christ we shall face a lost life, through the burning of the wood, hay, and stubble – retaining only our regenerated spirits because such are wholly of God. So as we leave the Laver in our study and pass on to the door of the Holy Place let us ever keep in mind the precious truths that with unceasing voice it proclaims. May the Holy Spirit Himself help us to remember that –

We are priests of the Most High God.

Aaron and his sons are typical of Christ and His Church.

As such we are called to consecrated service.

(Phil. 3:14; II Thess. 1:11; II Tim. 1:9).

This service can only be rendered by those who are clean.

"The pure in heart... shall see God" (Matt. 5:8).

We can never be clean while our defilement remains.

(I John 1:8, 9).

This is but one means of cleansing.

(I John 1:7).

(a). *For Aaron and His Sons*

This specific injunction included the priests, and excluded any other class. The laver was for priests and priests only! Who were the priests? and what was their ministry? and why was the laver for them alone? are questions that naturally arise. There are three outstanding things that seem to characterize their work:

Offer Sacrifices. At the altar the priest offered up on his own behalf the sacrifice that God demanded.

Worship the Lord. This they did when after they had washed themselves they entered into the Holy Place and waved the incense before the Lord.

Serve the Lord. Their constant attendance was required at the golden candlestick, table of shewbread, golden altar, and at such as well as in other matters outside, they served the Lord.

The application of these facts is clearly evident.

(b). *Believers Are Priests.*

There is no longer a separate priesthood as in Israel's day; no favored class who hold the monopoly of the service and work of the Lord. Whether we are ministers, evangelists, missionaries, laymen, counts or clerks, male or female, if we have met Christ at the altar of His cross and have the assurance that we have been purchased by His blood, and that we belong to Him, then He is our great High Priest, and we are priests unto Him.

The priesthood of believers is a precious truth that sadly needs emphasizing in these days when certain people would lord it over God's heritage; and also, when even the heritage appear to be unwilling to recognize the nobility of their calling. The priesthood of all believers is fully taught in the Word of God.

We are called priests.

Take the references in I Peter 2:4 and Revelation 1:6; 5:10; 20:6. Notice the order of our respective offices. First *kings,* then *priests.* We must learn, first of all, how to rule the passions of the flesh and desires of the mind and have all our powers under the control of our heavenly monarch ere we can act as a kingdom of priests in the capacity of service, worship, and intercession (Exod. 19:6).

We exercise Priestly Offices (I Pet. 2:5). "An holy priesthood."

As priests of the most high God, think of the sacrifices we offer unto Him!

Joy (Ps. 27:6).

Broken Spirit (Ps. 51:17).

Thanksgiving (Ps. 107:22; 116:17; Heb. 13:15).

Prayer (Ps. 141:2).
Bodies (Rom. 12:1; Phil 2:17).
Benevolence (Phil. 4:18; Heb. 13:16).
Martyrdom (Phil. 2:17; II Tim. 4:6).
Spiritual Sacrifices (I Pet. 2:5).

(6). *The Worship of Priests.* Leaving the laver and entering the Holy Place, the priests learned how to "worship the Lord in the beauty of holiness." How often do we worship the Lord?

Too often we come as beggars to One who is rich. We are such a bundle of needs and wants that we are forever asking, asking. And, blessed be His name, He delights to give for He has enjoined us to ask, seek, and knock. Do not let us forget, however, that we are priests as well as paupers! Worshipers as well as suppliants! God looks for true spiritual worship and although such is not easy, it can be cultivated. Closing our door and bowing down before Him, let us try to forget our material needs for the time being, for your heavenly Father knoweth that ye have need of these things "before you ask Him," and endeavor to meditate upon the thought of His love, His holiness, His majesty. Realizing that we are in the presence of the thrice holy One, let us simply adore and praise Him for what He is. Like the seraphim, may we cover our faces and our feet and allow the thought of His holiness and glory to fill our worshipful hearts.

(7). *The Service of Priests.* As the priests entered the Holy Place to attend to the respective vessels therein, are we not called to minister unto Him in some way or another? Is not our whole life – even our so-called secular life which comprises our home life, our business life, our social life, as well as our religious life – to be looked upon as the Holy Place wherein we can witness for Him? May the golden candlestick of testimony burn brightly everywhere and never flicker. Let our consistent witness be a means of sustenance and strength, as the shewbread to others. Let the holiness of our lives be as fragrant as the golden altar of incense. Then, no matter who, or what we are, we shall be acting as priests, serving priests unto God.

f. *The Inner Sanctuary* (Exod. 26:15, 21, 29; Eph. 2:14-22).

We have now reached various aspects of Levitical service and worship, reflecting in a magnificent way the glory of Him who is the Lord of all glory.

We realize the danger of pausing to give a detailed exposition of every part of the tabernacle, particularly its seemingly insignificant portions. It may not be necessary to examine every blade of grass in order to gain a satisfying view of the landscape. Still, as *all* the sections and services of the tabernacle were "figures of the true," we deem it imperative to discover "figures" even in details.

Although it is true that the tabernacle in its entirety was sacred to the Jews, yet the section we are about to consider moved the people to stand in awe, for such represented in a very real way God's dwelling place among men – and man's meeting place with God. It may give us a clear and profitable understanding of the tabernacle proper if we summarize relevant material thus:

The Outer Structure, comprising the *Boards* and the *Curtains.*
The Inner Shrines. *The Holy Place* and *The Holiest of All,* with their respective sacred contents.

(1). *The Outer Structure.* Both of the compartments, which were really one oblong structure, 45 feet long and 15 feet broad, divided into two separate places by a veil, was formed of *48 boards* and *5 pillars.*

There were 20 boards on the north

side, 20 on the south side, and 8, counting the two corner boards, along the western end. Over such were arranged various sets of curtains or coverings, while upon the 5 pillars at the east end, there was another covering called "the door."

(a). *The Boards*

As the particular boards that were used are very typical both of Christ and His church, it will greatly enlighten our minds and deepen our admiration respecting God's marvelous provision, if we dwell somewhat fully upon them.

i. *Their Nature.*

They were composed of "shittim" or "acacia" wood, a tree which grew in the desert. The LXX, as we have already seen, translates the word *shittim* as "incorruptible." After they had been fully prepared, these boards were overlaid with gold.

Here we have the blessed truth of our Lord's twofold nature, typified. He is "The Son of God" and "The Son of man" – He is "the God-Man." The foundation of Christianity is the message symbolically foreshadowed by the combination of the shittim wood and the gold, "God manifest in the flesh." Placed in silver sockets we have the threefold truth of deity and humanity combined in Christ for the accomplishment of Atonement.

Man, as a sinner, has a twofold need, which is fully met by Christ who is represented here as these gold-covered boards.

He needs a sympathizer

That is one who understands his case, one who will not unduly condemn him without knowing what sin or temptation really are. Man is human and meets with trials, difficulties, and sorrows and must have another person whose heart beats like his own. And has man not this One in Jesus? Jesus is His human name connecting Him with our humanity (see Heb. 4:15). We have not.

He must have a deliverer

That is someone who, although upon his level in respect to the experiences of life, is yet greater, more powerful than himself. One who can say, "I know your needs. I have felt them myself, but they need not overwhelm you as my life shows." And here, again, we turn to the Saviour for He is the One and the only One who can deliver. As the man, the *shittim tree,* He sympathizes. As God, *the gold,* He delivers. Both combined – Job 9:33. Neither is there any daysman betwixt us, that might lay his hand upon us both.

ii. *Their Preparation.*

These boards, standing as they did together, within the enclosure, thus forming the meeting place between God and Israel, symbolize in a marked fashion the Church of God, which He has purchased with His own blood. The very preparation of those boards is suggestive of spiritual truth that we cannot lightly ignore.

They were of the earth

Striking their roots away down into the earth, they formed part of it, and thrived and were sustained by what they received from the ground. In such, these acacia trees lived, and moved, and had their being. Are they not representative of Him who came as a root of the dry ground (Isa. 53:2)?

Further, our previous nature as sinners has been fully and faithfully described by the apostle, "of the earth, earthy" (I Cor. 15:47-49). Before we formed part of that spiritual tabernacle called "the church," we were children of this world and of wrath even as others. We lived upon its ways and pursuits! It alone supplied our sustenance! What ultimate connection there was between the world and our lives!

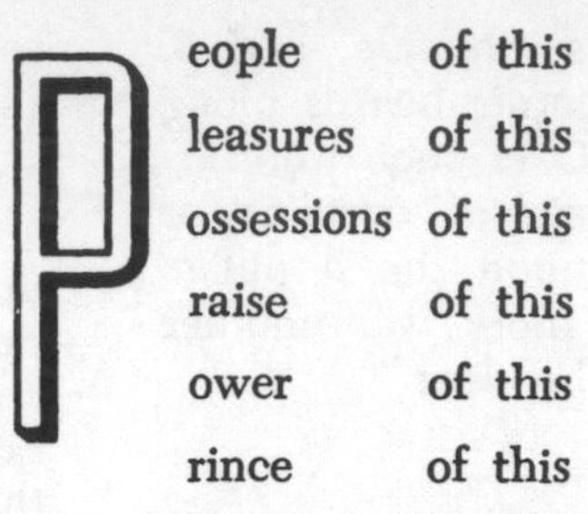

We companied with the	P	eople	of this	W	
We lived upon the		leasures	of this		
We sought for the		ossessions	of this		
We fed upon the		raise	of this		orld
We were controlled by the		ower	of this		
We served the		rince	of this		

They were cut down

There came the day when the people felled the trees with their axes, thus severing forever the connection they had long held with their natural surroundings. Suddenly and swiftly these acacia trees were made to fall at the feet of the axe-men. What was your conversion and mine, but as the Baptist puts it in Matthew 3:10, 11, "The axe laid unto the root of the tree." Like Saul on his way to Damascus, or the jailer in the prison at Philippi, the Spirit of the Lord dealt with us and in a moment we were smitten down, and by one strike of the divine axe of regeneration, severed forever from the world with all its evil ways. Applied to Christ, we think of His severance from heaven at His Incarnation, and of the way He was cut down at the cross.

They were stripped

All the stately boughs, with their fine foliage must go! Those trees of the desert must be made as nothing! They must be shorn of everything and left as bare, plain boards ere they can be cut to their prescribed size and shape and take their place in the sacred sanctuary. How humiliating!

Yet, is it not just here that a good many seem to turn back and walk no more with the Lord? After conversion, the stripping process begins. His divine woodman begins to deal with all the stately boughs of pride, with their foliage of self-centeredness, that hitherto marked the old life, and because they are not willing to become as nothing, nothing, nothing, they deny themselves the joy and privilege of adorning the temple of the Lord. To "put off the old man with his deeds" is too drastic a stripping, but profitable when allowed. Job cried, "He hath stripped me of my glory" (Job 19:9). Christ led the way to self-renunciation when He humbled, emptied, stripped Himself of all His past insignia of glory in order to become man and die for our salvation.

They were dried

The sap that had satisfied the life of the trees in the past had to be thoroughly dried up and all greenness removed before the shaping process could begin. It was necessary for the wood to be dried before use, otherwise it would be warped. "His roots shall be dried up beneath, and above shall his branch be cut off" (Job 18:16).

Does such not teach us that all the old sap of iniquity must be dried up in our lives, and all of the green, old nature dealt with if God is to fulfill His plan in and through our lives? We can never become "trees of the Lord, full of sap" unless the old sap ceases, and the new is poured into us.

Our Saviour knew all about this process. In that messianic twenty-second Psalm, He is represented as saying, as He died upon His cross – "My strength is dried up like a potsherd" (Ps. 22:15). Think of it! The omnipotent God crying, "My strength is dried up!" For you and me this drying up process means death-union with our Lord. Moffat's translation of our Lord's command reads, "If any man will come after me, *let him cross himself out*" (Matt. 16:24). If the stripping of the trees was the outward process, the drying of them was the inward process.

They were overlaid with gold

What a change had been wrought upon these trees by the wise-hearted men who had been endowed by the Holy Spirit to prepare them for the sanctuary! How beautiful they looked as they stood there adorned not with their natural beauty, but with that precious, magnificent gold! This was something different and outside of themselves.

Do we not praise God for the change that has been wrought in and upon our lives? Beloved, the gold is ours, for have we not been made partakers of the divine-nature? We present no longer the old carnal beauty. The beauty of the Lord our God is upon us. We are complete in Christ, accepted in Him, the beloved and beautiful, and thus beautiful in the eyes of God, although, perchance, without comeliness in the eyes of men, even as He was (Isa. 53:2). "Thy renown went forth among the heathen for thy beauty: for it was perfect through my comeliness, which I had put upon thee, saith the Lord God" (Ezek. 16:14).

They were placed in sockets

Later on we shall deal more fully with the foundation of these boards, therefore let one word suffice at this point. No longer do these prepared trees rest within the desert ground. They have been taken from such and their roots destroyed. Now, two tenons, or hands, securely fasten each board within a massive silver socket. What a picture of our new position in Christ! No longer are we sending our roots away down into the earth of sin or worldliness for life and nutrition. Our roots, or old desires, have been removed, and with our two hands we are laying hold upon and resting in Him because His redemption is our great silver socket. It was the great and glorious task of Atonement that brought Him down from the ivory palaces.

> My faith has found a resting place,
> Not in device nor creed:
> I trust the ever-living One,
> His wounds for me shall plead.

Howbeit, this sacred edifice was built in the wilderness. It had no floor save the dusty, desert earth. Thus, the sockets with their boards were still connected with the earth in one sense. Both the silver and the wood had been taken from the earth, and then sent back into it.

This suggests, does it not, the fact that we are still in the world though not of it. The boards were in the earth but not of it. The sockets separated the boards from the earth, just as Christ separates His own from the world. And so we remind our hearts that we are still passing through the wilderness, but that the day is fast dawning when the church will be complete and then she will no longer be in the earth witnessing for her absent Lord, but reigning with Him over the earth in millennial glory.

They stood up

We are distinctly told that the tabernacle boards were made of shittim wood, "standing up" (Exod. 26:15). Hitherto they stood up in the desert supported by their own strength. Now they stand erect because they are all securely bound together with five strong bars, and rest in a firm foundation of silver sockets.

Surely there is a type here of ourselves. The time was when we tried to stand before God in our own strength and righteousness. Erect and firm we stood, but we were "trees whose fruit withereth, without fruit, twice dead, plucked up by the roots" (Jude 12). But by the Holy Spirit we were made to realize our deep need of the entire support of Christ's cross and then by faith we embraced His righteousness and became justified (see Zech. 3:1). Thus we are now able to stand up with all boldness before God because of our absolute dependence upon the merits of His Son, who ever pleased His Father.

They were fitly bound together

Further on in our study we hope to view this truth more particularly. Just now look at those forty-eight boards standing close together, and kept together by their bars, rings, and sockets. They were "set in order" (Exod. 26:17). Says the apostle, "Set all things in order." If they could have spoken, unitedly they would have said, "We are not divided. All one body we." Yet each board was distinct from the other. Although one in faith, we retain our individuality. Does this not prefigure the unity that exists among the members of His body? The *Keswick* motto, "All one in Christ Jesus" — which, after all, is the New Testament designation of the church — is here, in type, in the boards standing close together. Yes, right together with nothing between. Jesus could say, "I and My Father are One." And what better commentary of this truth can we have than the words so finely put by Paul in Ephesians 2:20-22?

> Elect from every Nation,
> Yet one o'er all the earth.

They were covered

Four specific curtains or coverings, were laid in an orderly manner over these acacia boards after they had been erected and placed together. Such closed them in, thus forming the sanctuary. Such coverings would also protect them from the elements outside. Is it possible to have a more perfect representation of the wonderful protection that we enjoy when sheltered by all that these four coverings suggest of Christ? Was He not covered by all that these curtains suggest? Every believer has the assurance, or should have, that between himself and the Father, there is nothing and no one except the Saviour, who is our covering.

Think of the shelter that Christ affords to His Church! Once our life is hid with Him, we are protected and that continually, from

- God, and His just and righteous claims,
- The Devil and his evil accusations of the brethren,
- From the past with all its guilt and penalty,
- From the present with all its fear and anxiety,
- From the future with all its gloom and despair,
- From the world and all its seducive allurements.

Like those boards, we, too, are covered with

- Gold — His deity is my protection. For He is my Mighty God (Isa. 9:6).
- White linen curtains — His sinlessness is my protection. If not such, then He has forfeited the right to save.
- Goat's hair curtains — His impartial righteousness is my protection. This shelters the claims of justice.
- Rams' skins dyed red — His consecration is my protection (Heb. 10:10).
- Badgers' skins — His active holiness is my protection, and covers me from all outward elements of evil.

They were numbered (Exod. 26: 17-19, 26-28; See Acts 2:41-45)

As we have already observed, there were 20 boards on each side of the tabernacle and 8 at the west end, making a sum total of 48. Why there were exactly 48 we are not told. It is sufficient to know that this was the precise number revealed to Moses by God, for the tabernacle as a whole was fashioned in every particular according to the pattern shown in the

Mount. But as there is a spiritual significance regarding the numbers of Scripture, it is quite possible that the number of boards referred to, being a multiple of 12, 12 x 4 = 48, represents a very high, perfect form of heavenly government; as 12 according to some expositors speaks of "*governmental perfection.*"

In the Old Dispensation there were the twelve tribes of Israel.

In the New Order of Things, there were the twelve apostles.

In the New Jerusalem of Revelation 21, there are several twelves – 12 foundations, 12 gates, 12 pearls, 12 angels. Therefore we can take the number of 48 as signifying the church of God in its completeness, governed perfectly by Him who is its head. What the ultimate numbers of those who form the church invisible will be is beyond all human calculation. The magnitude of such was overwhelming when John saw them, for he declared that they were as "a great multitude, which no man could number, of all nations, and kindreds, and people, and tongues" (Rev. 7:9).

Associated with the brilliant-looking boards were one or two accessories, necessary to their security in the sand of the desert. For instance,

There were tenons

At the foot of each board there were fixed two tenons. What they were precisely like we are not told. The Hebrew word given in the A.V.M. is "*hands,*" while the LXX translates the word as "joints." Possibly they were two fixtures spreading themselves out like two hands, one on either side at the bottom of each board, thus enabling the boards to rest firmly in their sockets. Each board had two tenons, or "hands"! Can these not symbolize our appropriation of the finished work of Christ? As believers "we . . . have fled for refuge to lay hold upon the hope set before us" (Heb. 6:18). As those two tenons were fastened within the silver sockets, so our faith and hope rest in the twofold aspect of the work of Christ, namely, His Death and Resurrection.

Or again, we can liken these two tenons or hands unto the twofold result of our committal to the Saviour. For, says the apostle in Romans 15:13, "Now the God of hope fill you with all joy and peace in believing, that ye may abound in hope through the power of the Holy Ghost" (See also II Tim. 1:12, 14).

There is yet another application. As each board had two hands, or tenons, which were necssary to secure an upright position, so each believer has two hands without which his life can never be upright and pleasing to God. His two hands are *faith* and *obedience.* We often sing,

> Trust and obey; for there's no other way
> To be happy in Jesus, but to
> Trust and Obey.

There were sockets

As we have already observed, the silver provided for the sockets, as well as the other silver parts of the tabernacle, was the Atonement money of the people. Every one numbered among Israel's host, rich or poor, had to bring an half shekel of silver as a ransom for his soul (Num. 3:44-51; Exod. 30:11-16). The Atonement silver is therefore a type of the redemptive work of Christ. There are five recorded facts in connection with these sockets:

COMMANDED

Everything, except the silver that was required for the erection of the tabernacle, was willingly given as a free gift by the Israelites, but the silver was given in response to God's command. "This they shall give" (Exod. 30:13). In such there was no option of refusal. How solemn the thought! The cross of Christ, our silver socket, was an imperative necessity. God's command was, "The soul that sinneth it shall die," and such a command was obeyed by the One who gave it, for in the person of His Son He died for all sinning souls. On Calvary, the Lord "was stricken, smitten of God and afflicted."

FOUNDATION

The silver sockets formed the foundation of the tabernacle. There they were hidden in the sandy desert firmly supporting and holding up the gold covered boards with their curtains. And so the church of God is secure at all times for she has the redemptive works of her Lord as her only foundation. "Other foundation can no man lay than that is laid, which is Jesus Christ" (I Cor. 3:11). Once she attempts to lay another she ceases to be His church.

On Christ the solid rock I stand,
All other ground is sinking sand.
All other ground is sinking sand.

FIRST

It is also interesting to note that in the conditions set forth by God for the rearing up of the tabernacle, the silver sockets are foremost. Ere the Merarites handled the boards, the massive silver sockets were first placed in the sandy soil. Now does this not correspond to the place that we ought to give to the cross in our preaching? "Make much of the precious blood," urged a Welsh preacher. The blood of Christ was ever upon the apostle Paul's lips. To the Corinthians, yes, and to the world at large, "Christ, and him crucified" (I Cor. 2:2), was his dominant theme.

COSTLY

How costly was that silver foundation? As each socket weighed a talent of silver, the total value of the hundreds of sockets that were used represents a figure somewhere around $11,650 worth of silver. But what is silver and gold in comparison with the value of the precious blood of Christ? The value of such can never be estimated, for "the Church of God . . . he hath purchased with his own blood" (Acts 20:28). Surely Peter must have had this figure in mind when he wrote his first epistle, "Ye were not redeemed with corruptible things, as silver and gold . . . but with the precious blood of Christ" (I Pet. 1:18, 19). Beloved, let us constantly bow before the cross and meditate upon the infinite cost of our salvation.

Oh, make me understand it,
Help me to take it in,
What it meant to Thee, Thou
holy One
To bear away my Sin.

NUMBER

Each board, we are told, possessed two sockets, thus giving a double security to them as they stood erect in the desert. Although the silver speaks of Redemption, we must never forget that such has a double aspect which has been prefigured for us in the two sockets of each board. By turning to Romans 4:25, we discover this to be so – "Who was delivered for our offenses." That was Calvary, and such satisfies the claims of God regarding sin.

"Was raised again for our justification." That was His Resurrection, and such was God's receipt for Calvary. The Resurrection is the evidence of divine approbation of Christ's redemptive work, and the token that we have been received by the Father, on Christ's behalf. How secure, then, is every believer! A crucified Saviour! A risen Lord!

There is, however, another lesson that we draw from these two sockets. Each board had two of them. Typifying as they do the redemption of Christ, these two sockets under each board speak of a two-aspect of that Redemption which every believer can lay claim to.

There is the Redemption of the Soul. And such is appropriated by faith the moment a person seeks the Saviour. Immediately there comes the consciousness that "the blood maketh atonement for the soul" (Lev. 17:11). The Holy Spirit is the *earnest*, or pledge, of the Redemption Christ provided for us. The Spirit is the assurance of our inheritance until the redemption of the purchased possession (Eph. 1:14).

There is the Redemption of the body. Paul in Romans 8:23 speaks of this. Such is necessary to complete the first installment. This will be blessedly realized as the result of the cross when our eyes behold the returning Saviour, "who will change our vile body" (Phil. 3:21). Our present duty in Eph. 4:30, "Grieve not the Spirit of God, whereby ye are sealed unto the day of redemption."

There were bars

To fasten the 48 boards together, thus forming them into one whole structure, *five bars,* made of the same material, namely, shittim wood overlaid with gold, were supplied. Four of these bars were fastened around the boards, while the other one was passed through the boards in a kind of groove. Such would bind all the boards firmly together, giving to them that wonderful unity which was necessary for the purpose they served. Surely this is a fitting type of the way in which we are encircled as believers by the arms of Almighty God? As these bars were around the tabernacle, so is He ever embracing and holding His own together. These bars can

REPRESENT GIFTS TO THE CHURCH

These five gold covered bars that clamped the boards together into one compact structure can fitly represent the five gifts of the ascended Lord, to His church. Turning to Ephesians 4:7-11, we have them set forth in their true order –

Apostles,
Prophets,
Evangelists,
Pastors,
Teachers.

REPRESENT MEANS OF GRACE

By comparing the passages where the nature and purpose of the bars are set forth, it is very evident that the five were divided into two sections.

Four, which were placed around the outside, and which consequently were visible to man.

One, which was passed right through the middle of the boards and were thus invisible to the eye of man.

The Outer Four

These suggest the binding influences that characterized the early church and which should also mark the life of the present church. Let us turn to that record of the rearing of the spiritual tabernacle, the church of God. The testimony she bore was that "all that believed were together" (Acts 2:44). Yes, but what kept them together? Why, four bars Luke tells you in Acts 2:42.

The Apostles' Doctrine

What this "doctrine" was is not difficult to determine. Read carefully Peter's sermon in 2:14-41, and you will find how comprehensive the doctrine was. It covered all the essentials of the faith once delivered to the saints. The church enjoyed unity because of her purity of doctrine. Now, however, division has rent the church's unity. And the numberless sects or denominations are a pitiful contrast to that united front that she presented to the world at her inception. Did not our Lord declare that the unity of His church would become the great factor in bringing the world to His feet? When the church loses her doctrine, she also loses her dynamic. "That they also may be one in us: that the world may believe that thou hast sent me" (John 17:21).

Fellowship

This is what is known as "the Communion of Saints." That is, the coming and binding together of those who have believed and received, and whose lives illustrate the Apostles' Doctrine.

> The fellowship of kindred minds
> Is like to that above.

But alas! alas! the present day system of church government makes such sweet fellowship impossible because saved and unsaved alike are allowed to form one so-called visible church. And, says Paul, "What fellowship hath righteousness with unrighteousness? and what communion hath light with darkness?" (II Cor. 6:14). But our responsibility is perfectly clear. "Be ye not unequally yoked together with unbelievers."

Breaking of Bread

To the early church this holy feast was a potent force in keeping her unity intact. Its commemoration had a wonderful cementing influence. But when in later days she fell away from the simplicity and necessity of this sacred Sabbath institution, or "means of grace," she found herself torn into shreds.

The sacrament of the Lord's Supper is a bar that binds us, first of all to the crucified, for as we remember *Him* by the bread and the wine, our hearts and lives are drawn out to Him. It is also a strong bar binding us to each other bidding us so to act one toward another as we ought to, as members of the same heavenly family.

Prayers

Such a word seems to indicate the public aspect of prayer which the church has learned in her very infancy. For on the day of Pentecost, her spiritual birthday, she was found in the upper room, praying. Not reciting prayers, but breathing out in simple language the deep needs that faced her. Dr. Moffat translates this word "praying together." It therefore suggests those frequent gatherings for definite intercession as is illustrated in Acts 3:1, when "Peter and John went up together into the temple at the hour of prayer."

But somehow the church has lost this gold-covered bar. She has her gifted ministry, her beautiful music, her palatial buildings, yet, that mighty spiritual influence that comes another way is missing. The cold, formal, mechanical prayers so often recited are not those great, dynamic forces that bring multitudes, as on the day of Pentecost, to their knees, or that compel proud empires like that of Rome to yield to the Christ of God.

The one thing so conspicuously absent from church life is this "praying together," as Dr. Moffat puts it. Members, in general are ever ready to do many things together, but ascertain how many are present when the minister conducts a prayer meeting and you will usually find the same few faithful souls who alone have caught the passion. May the Lord cast around His church again that mighty bar of prayer!

The Inner One

Doubtless you will have noticed a specific reference to the third bar, which is called in Exodus 26:28 "The Middle Bar." Now this middle bar is found "in the midst of the boards," or, as it is put in Exodus 36:33, "he made the middle bar to shoot through the boards." Such implies that right in the center of each board a groove or opening had been cut that allowed this third and central bar to pass through. It was thus a hidden, invisible binding influence. For when once the tabernacle was erected, the eye of man only discerned the four outer bars, binding the sacred structure together. Is it not that that apart from the four outward unifying influences that we have already mentioned, there is a hidden, invisible, gold-covered bar that binds all God's people together? Is not the visible power of the invisible Lord so evident in the early church? It was the unseen Lord who added to the church.

How is it that God's people gather with one desire in their hearts to learn more of their precious Lord? What brings and binds Christian hearts together? We sing

> Blest be the tie that binds
> Our hearts in Christian love

but what is the tie that holds us all together? Is it not the blessed invisible presence of our Lord by His Spirit? Did He not say "Where two or three are gathered together in My name there am I *in the midst* [the same phrase] in the middle, of them"? His presence, then, is not only a promise but an actual fact to be realized. And such keeps the boards of the Spiritual tabernacle together. "Whom having not seen" — no, He is the invisible bar — "we love."

Ere we leave these five bars, let us look at them again and seek to see reflected in them a direct application to the Lord Himself. In that wonderful tabernacle every part spoke of His glory. There were five bars made of shittim wood overlaid with gold. The wood and the gold signify, as we have already seen, the humanity and deity of our Lord.

Now turn to Hebrews 1:3, and see in Him the five bars:

1. Who being the brightness of His glory,
2. The express image of His Person,
3. Upholding all things by the Word of His power,
4. He had by Himself purged our sins,
5. Sat down on the right hand of the Majesty on high.

What security is ours when we are embraced with such bars as these! Then notice that the middle bar is one of great importance. "Upholding all things by the Word of His power." All else rests upon this invisible omnipotent power of His.

There were rings

It is computed that upon each board there were three rings through which the bars passed and these were composed of pure gold. Cannot these three typify the Most Holy Person or Things necessary to complete our security as spiritual boards in the spiritual tabernacle?

1. There are Three Persons in the Trinity — God the Father, God the Son, God the Holy Spirit.

As there were three rings to each board, so the power of the Trinity is at the disposal of the humblest believer.

2. Yes, and the church's benediction is a threefold one.
   The Grace of the Lord Jesus Christ,
   The Love of God,
   The Communion of the Holy Spirit (II Cor. 13:16).

Hence the gates of Hell cannot prevail against her.

3. All such are made actual by the three golden rings of our testimony.
   Faith — We look back to Calvary and think of our appropriation of Christ that brought us peace.
   Hope — We look forward to His Return when our redemption will be completed as we are transformed into His likeness.
   Love — We look upward to Him with gratitude, seeking to please and obey Him as we await His Coming.

(b) *The Curtains*

Having considered the boards and their accessories we now approach an examination of the curtains. As we do so the same voice that spoke to Moses as he received his commission to act as the leader of Israel's host, ringing in their ears — "Put off thy shoes from off thy feet, for the place whereon thou standest is holy ground" (Exod. 3:5) is heard again. Truly the ground is holy! most holy! for what we are to consider brings before us in such a beautiful way the adorable person of our blessed Saviour. May the Holy Spirit therefore enable us to handle the sacred truth with the deepest reverence of heart and mind. Once the gold-covered boards had been placed in their silver sockets and bound securely together with the five bars, reposing in their golden rings, there were stretched over the tops of the 48 boards four different coverings thus forming a kind of a roof for the sacred enclosure.

The References.

The references regarding these coverings can be easily traced in the following chapters of Exodus.

a. The Divine Instructions regarding them (Exod. 26:1-14).
b. The making of them by the Wisehearted (Exod. 36:8-19).
c. The Conveyance of such to Moses (Exod. 39:33, 34).
d. The Placing and Anointing of Them (Exod. 40:2, 9, 17-19).

Their Number.

Covering the boards were four distinct coverings divided into two different sets.

i. *The Two Curtains*

These were the ten fine-twined linen curtains, the eleven goats' hair curtains. Such were the inner set of curtains and are called the tabernacle (Exod. 26:1-3). The Hebrew word for tabernacle conveys the idea of a dwelling place and is indicative of the fact that such covered the place where God dwelt and manifested Himself to the worshipers within.

ii. *The Two Coverings*

These were the rams' skins dyed red, the badgers' skins. Such were the outer set and therefore have the specific name of "coverings" in contrast to "curtains." These outer coverings are called "the tent." Being seen by the people from the outside, they represented the fact that such was a place where they, as sinners, could meet God, provided they came in the appointed way. All of which reminds us that we must never lose sight of the twofold aspect of the cross. The cross is trysting place between God and the sinner. In infinite love and mercy, and yet with all holiness and justice, God comes down to the cross to meet the Sinner. With nothing but sin and utter failure, the sinner travels up to the cross and through what Christ accomplished upon such, he is reconciled to God. Speaking broadly then, the curtains present Christ as He really is, while the coverings present the qualities that marked Him down here.

Their Order.

Before we consider these four coverings in detail it is interesting to observe how the Spirit of God has guided the setting forth of this particular part of the tabernacle. The instructions for the coverings are given before the boards. It is as if a builder arranged for the roof before setting about the walls. But such is a mark of spiritual accuracy, for the boards, as we have seen, represent the believer, while the coverings foreshadow the fullness of Christ.

Then in respect to the coverings themselves, it will be noticed that the list commences with the fine-twined linen curtains, and then travels down through the goats' hair, the rams' skins dyed red, and then reaches the badgers' skins. To the Israelite, however, as he entered the Court, or to the outsider, the badgers' skins were first observed, being as they were the topmost covering. It was only as the priest gradually proceeded and, leaving the altar and the laver behind, entered the door of the Holy Place, who had the joy and privilege of gazing upon the beautiful curtains that could only be seen from the inside.

The message is very apparent. The order given in the Sacred Record is the divine estimation of the Person and work of Christ. God ever thinks of His beloved Son as the fine-twined curtains. But in order to reach man, He willingly suffers Him to pass from the fine-twined curtains to the goats' hair, and then to the rams' skins dyed red, and then to the badgers' skins, the full meaning of which we are to see.

From the manward side Christ is badgers' skins. Then, as the love of the heart deepens and faith is aided by the Holy Spirit, there comes a growing comprehension of the truth of Christ, which is suggested by the inward progress from the badgers' skins to the fine-twined linen curtains.

We may find it spiritually profitable to start from the outward covering and thus unfold the four successive aspects of our Saviour's work, and thereby discover where we are in spiritual apprehension.

i. *The Badgers' Skins*

It is somewhat uncertain to classify the particular skins that are here mentioned. The R.V. has "sealskins." The R.V.M. puts it as "porpoise skins." The LXX renders it "skins of a blue color." Whatever the nature of the skins is, this truth is surely evident that they were meant to act as a covering or protection for the rest. They convey the idea of protection. This can be seen by the way that these skins were used as external coverings to protect the vessels when the camp was on the march (Num. 4:5-15). The same idea with possibly the addition of the thought of separation can be gathered from the fact that the only other reference to badgers' skins outside of their use in the tabernacle is found in Ezekiel 16:10 – "I . . . shod thee with badgers' skins."

What is the import of this? Why, they speak of what Christ was to man! Any Israelite viewing the tabernacle proper from some outward angle would see nothing very beautiful or attractive about it. To him, the oblong structure called the *Holy Place,* and the *Holiest of All,* when covered with the badgers' skins would look like a long, dark coffin.

Do we not see here the estimation of men concerning Christ? What was He to them? Nothing but a coarse, hard badger skin. The prophetic word in Isaiah 53:1, 2, was literally fulfilled. For when He came among men they saw nothing attractive about Him. Is this not the carpenter? they said, and consequently they received Him not. He

> Came to a world, polluted and
> defiled,
> Came to be scorned, neglected
> and reviled.
> Came to be hated, scourged and
> crucified,
> Astounding theme! Immanuel
> groaned and died.

Is this not the present day estimation of our Lord Jesus Christ? What do the vast majority of people see in Christ but the badgers' skin, a simple peasant of Galilee? But to those of us who have opened our hearts to Him He is more than the unadorned or unattractive badgers' skin. He is the altogether lovely One and "the chiefest of 10,000 to our souls." Lovingly, we look up into His face and exclaim, "Whom have I in heaven but Thee? There is none upon earth that I desire beside thee!" (Ps. 73:25). One other thought ere we leave this first covering. It was the badgers' skins exposed to the burning heat of the sun, and the fury of the storm and tempest that entirely hid the glories of the curtains beneath and also the beautiful contents of the tabernacle. So Christ in His earthly humiliation exposed to the fires of man's hatred, and to the fury of Satan's antagonism, hid the glories of His own glorious nature from the irreverent and unholy gaze of men. He did not give that which was holy unto the dogs, nor yet cast His pearls before swine. To such, He appeared as the man of Galilee, sometimes weary, sometimes hungry, sometimes thirsty, sometimes weeping.

Once, however, the badgers' skins were removed, and three pairs of adoring eyes upon the Mount of Transfiguration saw something of His inner glory. But so dazzling was such that they were smitten with partial blindness. When they opened their eyes they saw Jesus only – the human One. Can any good thing come out of Nazareth? Adoring faith answers – Come and see!

ii. *The Rams' Skins Dyed Red*

The ram was the animal of consecration. This can be traced in the consecration of Aaron and his sons in Exodus 29:15, Leviticus 8:18-29. At this solemn service one ram was sacrificed as a burnt offering. The other was slain and its fat and inwards offered as a burnt offering while the breast and shoulder became food for the priests. At the consecration of Aaron, he was anointed first with oil and then with blood. And the three parts touched by blood signified that the whole man had been set apart for God. The tip of the right ear, signifying hearing. The thumb of the right hand, signifying service. The great toe of the right foot, signifying ways. The ram, therefore represents absolute devotion to the service of God.

What is the second truth that we learn regarding the Saviour? Is it not the precious truth of His entire submission to the will of God? Being born and anointed of the Holy Spirit, He steps forth to accomplish the divine plan and purpose. He entered the world with one definite purpose and concentrated all His energies and powers upon the fulfillment of such. One has only to look at the successive stages of His life to see this:

At the early age of twelve He is found in God's house saying, "Wist ye not that I must be about my Father's business?" (Luke 2:49).

At Jordan as He enters out into His ministry He commands the Baptist to baptize Him saying, "Suffer it to be so now: for thus it becometh us to fulfill all righteousness" (Matt. 3:15).

At the half-way stage of His work, when many diverting influences surrounded Him, He declared, "My meat is to do the will of him that sent me, and to finish his work" (John 4:34).

At Gethsemane when the shadow of the cross lay across His path, He did not falter. "Not my will but Thine be done." "The cup which my Father hath given me, shall I not drink it?" (John 18:11).

At the end He could say, and triumphantly assert, "I have finished the work which thou gavest me to do," or "It is finished" (John 17:4).

The keynote of His whole life, in the past glory, during His earthly life, and now in the Father's presence, yes, and forever is: "I come to do thy will, O God" (Heb. 10:7).

Notice that the rams' skins were dyed *red!* Here we have the absolute devotedness of Christ to the will of God proclaimed in a double way:

Being skins suggests that the rams were slain for consecration.

Being dyed red, that is with their own blood, suggests that they bore the mark of sacrifice.

How stupendous the thought! Christ was entirely yielded up to the will of God even to the point of death. He allowed God to do what He thought best!

But as we leave these two outer coverings there is this peculiarity to observe. There are no measurements or dimensions given of such. This is a marked contrast to the careful and repeated measurements of the next two curtains we are to consider. Is there not a message in this silence for our blood-washed hearts?

No measurement for the badgers' skins!

No, none, because they represent the humiliation and rejection of Christ by man. And who can measure the profound depths of such?

> None of the ransomed ever knew
> How deep were the waters crossed,
> Nor how dark was the night that the Lord passed through.
> Ere He found His sheep that was lost.

No measurement for the rams' skins dyed red!

No, none, because they speak of the Saviour as the One absolutely yielded to the Father's will, whatever that will involved. What son of man can measure the devotedness of that sacred heart that broke upon the cross in accomplishing the will of God? One can only pause at Paul's word – "He became obedient unto death, even the death of the cross." We can, however, measure our own submission alongside His – only to find that, alas! it pales into insignificance.

iii. *The Goats' Hair Curtains.*

In Lev. 16:5-10 we are reminded that on the annual day of Atonement the goat was selected as the preeminent sin-offering – which brings us to the inner view of Christ, for in this set and the following set of curtains we behold Christ from the Godward side.

The badgers' skins represent what Christ was to man. "Can any good thing come out of Nazareth?" The rams' skins dyed red, the outward sufferings and sorrow that His devotion to God's will occasioned. Men saw "His visage marred." The goats' hair curtains, however, reveal to us what God has made Christ to be for man, namely, his sin offering, His Atonement.

In the old Jewish economy two goats were brought to the gate of the tabernacle and lots were cast upon them. The Lord's lot fell upon one, and the people's lot upon the other.

The goat chosen by God was then killed, and its blood carried by the High Priest into the Holiest of All, where he sprinkled it upon and before the mercy seat.

The other goat, chosen by the people, and called *the scapegoat* was taken by the priest who, laying his hands upon its head, confessed over such the sins of Israel, and then sent it away into a far-off land uninhabited.

What a perfect type all this presents of our blessed Lord!

> The goat slain to meet Jehovah's holy and righteous claim.
> The goat banished met and satisfied the people's need.
> The goat slain told of substitution.
> The goat banished spoke of impartation.

Both of these aspects of Atonement are associated with Christ, for He was the goat slain! The lot of Jehovah fell upon Him and He was "stricken, smitten of God, and afflicted." But as the High Priest He went right into the Holiest of All, with the memorials of His work as the sin-offering. "Five bleeding wounds He bore."

He has taken our sins away, as the live goat did the transgressions of Israel. They have been banished to a land not inhabited, for "as far as the East is from the West, so far have I removed your transgressions from you." Where they have gone does not, or should not, concern me! "God has blotted them out, I'm happy and glad and free." If, in mercy, He has banished them beyond recall and remembrance, why should I trouble to bring them back again? "Dead men," they say, "tell no tales." If, therefore, I am dead with Christ, the tale of my past life should be silent history. There are two simple thoughts emerging from the context that we cannot afford to miss.

The Material

It is seen that "hair" is in italics, which means that the word is not in the original. One writer suggests that the material was of a very fine texture, more like the modern cashmere shawl. Doubtless it was pure white, and therefore suggests the spotless holiness of Him who became our sin offering. Although He was made sin for us, the apostle is clear about the point of the Saviour's sinlessness. "He knew no sin." Had He sinned in the least degree He would have forfeited the right to die and thereby save.

The Position

One section of this goats' hair covering, which was made in eleven pieces, was folded in a particular manner and placed over the door of the tabernacle so that the priest approaching the Holy Place might see it hanging there and then pass through beneath it. The same would speak to him of the abounding grace of God, and testify to the fact that entrance into the Holy Place was only possible on the ground of sin punished, atoned for, and put away. The section that hung over the door was the eleventh curtain, the extra one, for the next set as well as here, were two sets of five. Then there was one extra to hang over! Our God is the God of the *extra!* Yes, we have a God who is plenteous in mercy and redemption.

> Plenteous grace with Thee is found
> Grace to cover all my need.

iv. *The Embroidered Curtains*

This last set of curtains, so beautiful and gorgeous, were the first to be placed over the boards and then covered with the other three we have considered, and were therefore seen only from the inside by the priest as he ministered at the holy vessels. As we have already detailed at the gate of the tabernacle the meaning of the fine-twined linen with its various colors, a brief word will suffice here.

Linen

This is the texture that when worn, symbolizes righteousness "Let thy priests be clothed with righteousness" (Ps. 132:9). "Fine linen is the righteousness of saints" (Rev. 19:8).

Linen, then, representing holiness of life and walk is suggestive of our Lord Jesus Christ as the One who was perfectly righteous and holy in life.

Fine

This particular word defines the nature of righteousness. There was nothing coarse, hard, or vulgar about our Lord's nature. No ugly knots or twisted ends are to be found about Him. His linen was fine!

Twined

That is, His righteousness was woven into every part of His life. Such was one complete whole, in which every act and word had each its fitting place. What He was and what He did were inseparably and harmoniously bound together. Then the colors wrought upon the linen are descriptive of those beautiful unveilings of Christ.

Blue

This, as we have seen, is a heavenly color. The Hindu has no word for "heaven." The nearest approach to it in his language is "blue." It therefore speaks of Christ's heavenly origin and nature (John 3:12).

Purple

As already indicated, this is a royal color, being worn by kings and rulers. Such then reveals Christ before the gaze of adoring eyes as the King of Kings and Lord of Lords. Purple is a mixture of two colors, blue and scarlet. Here, again, we have a symbol of the twofold nature of our Lord. The blue stands for His heavenly nature, the scarlet, as His earthly nature. Therefore, the purple, being a combination of blue and scarlet, speaks of Him who combines both God and man. He is the God-man.

Scarlet

This is an earthly color being connected with the name "Adam," and also with blood and death. Scarlet dye is extracted from a particular worm. In fact scarlet and worm are the same in passages like Job 25:6: "The son of man, which is a worm," and Ps. 22:6: "I am a worm, and no man." Christ was the worm whose precious body was crushed and which has produced the scarlet blood that cleanses away the sin and guilt of men.

Cherubim of Cunning Work

The figures of the cherubim that were skillfully and exquisitely wrought upon the curtains in the three colors already mentioned proclaimed a wondrous truth to the priest who beheld them from within.

Believing as we do in the law of first mention, it is interesting to turn to the first reference to cherubim found in Genesis 3:24. After his expulsion from the garden because of his sin, Adam was prevented from reentering by the cherubim, who had been placed with flaming swords at the entrance. The cherubim, therefore, represent the righteous government of God, the cherubim themselves being the executors of God's righteous judgment. But the cherubim woven into these fine twined linen curtains, which so beautifully speak of Christ, declare a precious truth that ought to quicken our hearts into deep love. In the book of *Ezekiel* the cherubim illustrate the abundant *life* of the Lord's redeemed people (Ezek. 1:1-28). A. T. Pierson points out that in Solomon's temple

> the wings of the Cherubim touched one another in the midst of the Holiest of All, and being stretched forth reached with their lips the side walls, thus spanning the entire breadth of the Sanctuary. Who can think of them without at least being reminded of the two great Dispensations, which, touching each other in the midst of History at the Cross of Calvary, where God was manifested in the flesh, reached backward to the limits of past history in Creation and forward to the limits of future history in the new Creation, at the end of the ages!

The Cherubim Had No Sword.

No, for it had been plunged into the Saviour's breast. He endured the judgment due to man for sin: the transgression of God's commands. No sword bars the way to the garden now. The entrance into bliss is open wide and all that Adam lost is restored and more beside.

The Cherubim Speak of Judgment.

Because such were worked upon the curtains, they typify Him into whose hands the Father hath committed all judgment. The day is coming when the glorious Lord, although far lovelier than blue, purple, and scarlet can make Him, will exercise His judicial authority and administer the judgment of God (John 5:22-27).

So much, then, for the curtains and coverings themselves. One would fain dwell upon the significant measurements of the curtains, and upon the profitable study of the loops and taches binding such together, but we close this section of our meditation by drawing one or two lessons and conclusions. First of all, these four coverings that formed the roof of the tabernacle can be likened unto

THE FOUR GOSPELS

1. *Matthew is the badgers' skins.* Christ is the king in disguise. Although born king of the Jews, His own people rejected Him.

2. *Mark is the rams' skin dyed red.*

Christ within such is the suffering servant of God, the One who in all things sought to please and obey the Father.

3. *Luke is the goats' hair.* Christ is here seen as the Son of man, with absolute purity of life, offering up Himself on man's behalf.

4. *John is the fine twined linen curtains* with their blue, purple, scarlet, and cherubim. In this fourth Gospel, we have the innermost view of Christ as the Son of God, the image of the invisible One, God manifest in the flesh.

THE FOURFOLD DIVISION OF THE TABERNACLE

These four coverings can represent the four different divisions of the Old Testament sanctuary.

The badgers' skins, which correspond to the coarse, bare wilderness around the tabernacle.

The rams' skins dyed red, which are met with in the outer court, at the altar where the sacrifices were offered.

The goats' hair, which, being pure white material, can fitly represent the Holy Place.

The fine twined linen curtains, which because of their intrinsic worth and beauty can describe the Holy of Holies.

THE FOURFOLD EXPERIENCE

These four coverings can also teach us the successive steps of those who, after receiving Christ, follow on to know Him more fully.

The badgers' skins, which answer to our natural state when having little sense of our guilt and need we saw nothing very attractive in Him who claimed to be our deliverer.

The rams' skins dyed red, which speak of the change that came into our lives through the appropriation of Him who, because of the offering of His body, as the whole burnt offering, has sanctified all who believe once for all.

The goats' hair, which because of its whiteness or purity of color proclaims the progress of the saint. Being delivered from the guilt of sin, he desires to be kept daily clean, hid in God, and overshadowed by His power. The goat was a daily sin-offering. Therefore Christ is appropriated day by day.

The embroidered curtains, which because of their bright and beautiful colors, and of their innermost setting, reveal the ideal of God for every life, namely, a life of constant unbroken fellowship in the Holiest with our Glorified Lord. A life of continual walking in the light, as He is in the light, and appropriation of His fulness that is implied by the lovely curtains.

A friend, after hearing Dr. Andrew Bonar speak upon the Four Coverings of the Tabernacle, wrote him to this effect.

> That's my spiritual history—
> I first learned Christ as a Covert from the Storm—
> The Badgers' Skins.
> Then His Blood as a Substitute—
> The Ram's Skins Dyed Red.
> Then His Righteousness on Me—
> The Goats' Hair.
> Then the Royal Dress on Me—The Embroidered Curtains, on being made kings to God.

Where are we in spiritual experience? What do we know of His abundance? What is He to us? After all, it is only as we come to know Him in all His wonderful fulness that we can understand the truth regarding Him.

Do we only see and know Him as the badgers' skins? Is there nothing attractive about Him? Is our view of Him simply an outside one? While others seem to find great delight in sitting under His shadow, and feasting upon His vast provision, are we looking on like starved, hungry souls? Then may the Holy Spirit anoint our eyes with eyesalve that we may see hidden beneath the badgers' skins One who is surpassingly lovely, One who is fairer than the sons of men.

Do we see and know Christ as the rams' skins dyed red? Have we got the length of conversion and are we content with being saved, merely from past sin? Do we say, once saved always saved, therefore it matters little if our life is spiritual or otherwise? Have we been attracted to Christ merely by the force of His wonderful example of submission to God? Then, may we quickly discover that example will not suffice!

Do we see and know Christ as the goats' hair? Could we have been led a little further in than others? We have longings to be holy. We want a life which, like the goats' hair, representing Christ's holiness, is so pure and white. But His holiness and holy requirements mock us, "For watch and struggle as we may, Pure we are not."

Do we see and know Christ as the embroidered curtains? Beloved, this is where God wants us to live! As spiritual priests dwelling in the Holiest, He desires us to meditate upon His transcendent beauty, His inexpressible loveliness, His unmeasured devotion, His infinite excellencies and then cease struggling and simply rest in the joy of what He is.

g. *The Inner Shrines* (Read Hebrews 9:1-10).

We have now reached a consideration of the two compartments, the Holy Place, and the Most Holy, with their respective sacred contents. Already we have observed that this particular section of that ancient structure was one oblong erection divided into two by means of a veil. The first compartment being called *the Holy Place*, and covering a space of 30 feet in length and 15 feet in breadth. Then there came the next small enclosure, 15 feet square, known as *the Holiest of All*, or the Most Holy Place, where the High Priest alone entered and he only once a year.

(1). *The Holy Place.* In connection with this, we look first of all at the entrance into such, namely,

(a). *The Door*

By turning to Exodus 26:36, 37; 36:37, 38, one gathers all that there is to know regarding the entrance that admitted the priests into the Holy Place. It was a beautiful hanging that stretched across the east side of the tabernacle.

The teaching regarding the door is most instructive in that it brings us to our privileges and responsibilities as believers; and bids us question our hearts as to whether we are entering into the fulness of blessing that the Holy Place so fully represents. Therefore, let us seek the definite guidance of the Holy Spirit, that we may fully apprehend the truth the door portrays.

The message of the epistle of *Hebrews* should be read along with the tabernacle, "Let us go on." It is one of the writer's characteristic phrases, and therefore makes his epistle "the Epistle of Christian Progress." And it does seem as if the door of the Holy Place proclaims the same message "Let us go on" in, it echoes forth. Cognisant of and grateful for all that we have experienced and seen in the past, we reach the door only to realize that there is still more to follow. For we must remember that "the path of the just is as the shining light, that shineth more and more unto the perfect day" (Prov. 4:18).

The Presence of the Door

Possibly one may say, but why was it necessary to have a door excluding the priests from entering the Holy Place in an open fashion? If they had passed the altar and laver, surely they were ready to serve God? Yes, certainly, they were ready to engage in the holy service of the sanctuary, for the laver proclaimed to the priests that "the cause of God is holy and useth holy things." But leaving the laver they faced a barred entrance, a hanging, stretched across the whole of the Holy Place.

First of all, the door, signified to the host of Israel that within such a specific enclosure, God's presence could be realized and localized. Within such the Holy One could be met, served and worshiped. And through Him who is the door, we know that human though we be, we can realize the presence of God and serve Him acceptably with reverence and godly fear (Heb. 12:28). "Draw nigh to God, and he will draw nigh to you" (James 4:8).

Then the door excluded the light, fragrance, and sustenance of the Holy Place from the exterior. No matter how near the priest might have been to the door he could not behold anything within until he raised or drew aside the hanging. Then, and not till then could he gaze with wonder upon the beauty of the curtains and delight in the fragrance of such an inner place. Beloved, the deeper things of God are not lightly gained. We never behold the glories of Christ unless we are prepared to pay the price of entering the door which means for you and me absolute and entire surrender to Him – "The secret of the Lord is with them that fear Him."

Then the door meant that only certain people were allowed to enter the Holy Place. Any Israelite could pass through the gate of the Outer Court, but only priests, washed at the laver, were permitted to enter the Holy Place and engage in the service of God (Heb. 9:6). Surely it is unnecessary to press the point! Priests we are, for Peter calls us "A royal priesthood" (I Pet. 2:9), but alas! so few believers realize their priestly standing before God (I Pet. 2:5). "An holy priesthood, to offer up spiritual sacrifices, acceptable to God by Jesus Christ."

Every believer, saved by infinite grace, has the right and privilege, yes, and the joy, of passing through the door and realizing all that God has provided, but how few feast upon the vast inheritance they have in Christ, or ever allow the Lord to get all the pleasure that He ought to have out of their worship and service.

The message of the door, then, is that of possessing our possessions!

The Measurement of the Door

There is one feature of the three veils:

The gate of the Outer Court,
The door of the Holy Place,
The veil of the Most Holy Place,

which is somewhat remarkable, and that is, although the dimensions were different, yet the area was the same.

The gate was 20 cubits wide by 5 cubits high, making an area of 100 cubits.

The door was 10 cubits wide by 10 cubits high, making an area of 100 cubits.

The veil was 10 cubits square, making an area of 100 cubits.

Such signifies that it is the same Lord with whom we have to deal, whether we come as sinners or as saints. It is through Him and Him alone that all men have access by one Spirit unto the Father (Eph. 2:18).

But there is another message in these measurements that will greatly help us if we but comprehend it.

The gate was wider and lower than the door – 20 cubits by 5 cubits.

The door was higher and narrower than the gate – 10 cubits by 10 cubits.

The gate represents the entrance into salvation. It is the gate for sinners and is very wide and low. Wide – for whosoever will may come. Low – because we can suffer the little ones to come.

The door, however, is different from the gate in that it admitted priests only into worship and service. It is the door for saints! But alas! not all who experience the blessing of salvation appreciate the true nature of spiritual worship. Therefore the door is made narrower and higher than the gate. Remember that John 10:9 is for believers, or those who know the Shepherd – "I am the door: by me if any man enter in, he shall be saved, and shall go in and out, and find pasture."

The door is narrower and higher than the gate, then. This speaks of true spiritual apprehension: deeper desires for fuller knowledge of the Lord: aspirations for a life of close intimacy with our High Priest. But so many stop before the narrow, high door and hesitate to enter in. How many there are who seem content to remain mere Outer Court Christians – content with the blessings and provision of the altar, content with being merely saved, but who never travel beyond such to live and act as God's spiritual priests.

The message of the door, then, is this: It is narrow, therefore every weight and sin must be laid aside. It is high, and therefore implies higher heights to scale. In effect the door says to you and me, "Do not stay outside in the Court, content with believing the Gospel but go on to know the graces and glories of Christ and ever seek to behold fresh beauty and loveliness in Him through whom we travel as the door."

> Have you on the Lord believed?
> Still there's more to follow:
> Of His grace have you received?
> Still there's more to follow,
> Oh, the grace of the Father shows!
> Still there's more to follow!
> Freely He His grace bestows,
> Still there's more to follow!

"Let us go on unto perfection" (Heb. 6:1).

The Composition of the Door

There are a few significant facts about the materials used in the formation of the door that set forth in a fascinating way the glorious excellencies of Him who called Himself "the Door."

The Pillars

The hanging called *the Door* was hung upon five gold-covered wooden pillars.

Their Number.

In the specific number of pillars used there is a precious truth for our hearts to feed upon. There were five! And five is the number of grace! "Grace" means "favor." But what kind of favor? for favor is of many kinds.

Favor shown to the miserable we call mercy.

Favor shown to the poor we call pity.

Favor shown to the suffering we call compassion.

Favor shown to the obstinate we call patience.

Favor shown to the unworthy we call grace.

And it is the last aspect that we receive, for we are so unworthy and can never merit God's favor, yet He bountifully and freely blesses us. There is a very helpful interpretation of what "grace" really is in Romans 3:24, "Being justified freely by his grace through the redemption that is in Christ Jesus." The word "freely" here occurs in John 15:25 and is there translated "without a cause" ("They hated me without a cause"). Was there any real cause why the Lord Jesus was so hated? No! none whatever. Is there any cause in us why God should ever justify us? No. He does it freely, or without any cause, except the reason of His own peerless love.

The pillars of the Door, then, being five in number suggests that all that it is possible to enjoy of worship or service is all of grace. None of us can ever get nearer to the Lord by human merit. Both sinners and saints are debtors to grace. In the tabernacle *five* is the all pervading number, for nearly every measurement was a multiple of *five* setting forth in type that everything connected with salvation or with communion is all of grace lest any man should boast.

But then the figure "five" has another message to proclaim. It coincides, does it not, with the prophetic titles given to Him in Isaiah 9:6? In this connection let us combine the nature of the pillars, as well as their number. They were made of shittim wood overlaid with gold, which typifies the humanity and deity of our Lord. Now let us turn to the prophet Isaiah's wonderful word.

"Unto us a Child is Born" – Here we have the shittim wood – the humanity of our Lord.

"Unto us a Son is Given" – Here we have the gold – the deity of our Lord.

"Government shall be upon His Shoulder" – Here we have the pillar crowned – the royalty of our Lord.

His Name	1. Wonderful
What five	2. Counselor
Massive	3. Mighty God
	4. Everlasting Father
Pillars!	5. Prince of Peace

Or again they can	1. King
express the wonderful	2. Eternal
conception that the	3. Immortal
Apostle Paul had of	4. Invisible
Him.	5. The only Wise God.

I Tim. 1:7.

Or again they can stand for the letters that compose the name which was the name given to Him before His wondrous birth and which is the sweetest name in a believer's ear (Matt. 1:21). Thou shalt call His name

Jesus
Eternally
Saves
Us
Sinners

The Sockets

Beneath the five gold covered pillars there were five brass sockets which enabled the pillars to stand firm and erect. These sockets were different from the sockets of the board which, as we have seen, were made of silver, thus speaking of Atonement. Brass on the other hand is the metal which indicates judgment and therefore proclaims the solemn truth that Christ has become the door by reason of the judgment which He took upon His sacred head for you and me. As the priests crossed the threshold of that door, they were reminded of the fact that all the privileges and pleasures of the Holy Place were only possible because of the righteousness and justice that had been fully satisfied.

It may be fitting to point out that "copper" or "bronze" and not "brass" is the metal that is meant, although in our studies we are keeping rigidly to the word used in the A.V. Brass is not a perfect type of our Lord.

Brass will crack and not stand the heat and therefore fails to represent the endurance of Christ. He stood the awful heat of divine judgment even to the length of having "endured the cross" and "despising the shame" (Heb. 12:2). Copper on the other hand, will stand any heat and is therefore more descriptive of Christ's endurance.

Brass is a mixed metal, an alloy, being composed of copper and zinc, and was not discovered until the thirteenth century A.D. But copper has no mixture and therefore symbolizes Him who had no alloy in His nature. And that this was the testimony of those who knew Him is evident, for says Hebrews 7:26, where you find Him as the five sockets. For such an high priest became us – Who is

Holy
Harmless
Undefiled

Separate from sinners
Higher than the heaven

A further thought can be gleaned from the brazen foundation of the pillars. Righteousness and justice are ever the foundation of His dealings with us. "Righteousness and judgment are the habitation of his throne" (Ps. 97:2). Therefore, when John saw Him, he discovered that "his feet [were] like unto fine brass, as if they burned in a furnace" (Rev. 1:15).

The Crowns

The chapiters, or crowns, that covered the top of these pillars were of pure gold. What a contrast! Brass beneath the feet of the priest as he entered the door and gold above his head! But those pillars speak of Him who, although He suffered as the just for the unjust to meet God's righteous demands regarding sin, is now crowned with glory and honor.

The Head that once was crowned
with thorns
Is crowned with glory now.
A Royal diadem adorns
The Mighty Victor's Brow.

"When he had by himself purged our sins," said the apostle in Hebrews 1:3, He became the brazen sockets, and then "sat down on the right hand of the Majesty on High" and was crowned with the golden chapiter. The day is coming, when upon His head will be placed many crowns.

The Highest place that Heaven
affords
Is His by Sovereign right
The King of Kings and Lord of
Lords,
He reigns in perfect Right.

The Hanging

Upon these five pillars there was suspended by means of hooks a hanging or curtain, composed of "blue, and purple, and scarlet, and fine twined linen, wrought with needlework" (Exod. 26:36). Having already dwelt with the significance of the various colors it is sufficient to say that being found here again, they suggest the heavenly glories of Him who became the door. There is one noticeable feature, however, about the hanging. Unlike the curtains over the boards, it has no *cherubim* worked upon it. Why this omission? Because the cherubim speaks of justice or righteous judgment, but as priests we enter into fuller blessing by the way of purest grace. No timid priest need be afraid to pass through the door, for God can be met and communed with on the ground of absolute grace.

No curse of law, in Thee was
Sovereign Grace,
And now what glory in Thine
unveiled Face!
Thou didst attract the wretched
and the weak,
Thy joy the wand'rers and the
Lost to save.

There is one other feature to observe ere we leave the hanging. It is distinctly declared that it was wrought with "needlework." The word "needlework" used here is translated in Psalm 139:15 as "curiously wrought." Take the whole verse "My substance was not hid from thee, when I was made in secret, and curiously wrought [embroidered] in the lowest parts of the earth." This passage suggests the wonderful way in which the body is formed in pregnancy. Is it not possible that such can suggest the Immaculate Conception of our Lord when within the womb of the virgin? Humanity and deity were curiously wrought or embroidered together into one blessed piece.

The Significance of the Door

We have already touched upon the fact that the door was for priests alone. None but Aaron and his sons had the right or privilege to pass through such into the Holy Place. And as it led into fuller service, we are taught something of what the deeper life, or priestly service and communion, really means for ourselves.

It was the Door to the Altar of Incense

As soon as the priest passed through the door his eyes would meet the golden altar that stood right before him in front of the veil. As such speaks of intercession, the truth emphasized is that the more precious the Lord Jesus becomes to us, the more precious will the habit and place of prayer become. Prayer to one within the door is always a delight and never a drudgery. Tell me how much time you spend at the throne of grace, and I will tell you how near the Lord you are.

It was the Door to the Candlestick

To the south side of the Holy Place the priest would see the beautiful golden candlestick, with its light that never went out. Now the candlestick represents our testimony or witness for the Lord – "Shining for Jesus" as the hymn puts it. The message here proclaimed is that only those who approach the Lord in holy nearness are those whose light is never dim. Often our shining is very erratic, sometimes bright, at other times obscured, but the light of the Holy Place never went out, and when we realize the fulness of Christ, there is that constant steady witness that magnifies the Lord.

It was the Door to the Table of Shewbread

Right opposite the golden candlestick the priest would discover on his north side the table containing its shewbread. This symbolizes fellowship or communion. We can never experience what sustenance we have in Christ until as priests we have been fully cleansed at the laver and thus made ready to enjoy His provision. When fully surrendered we know what it is to walk in the light as He is in the light, and have fellowship one with the other. Once within the door we learn what it is to "Abide in Him."

It was the Door to Safety

Once within the Holy Place no matter how wet or stormy the weather was outside, all was quiet and calm within. The priest had the assurance that he was being protected by the presence of God. Although general protection was promised to all who abode under the cloudy pillar, yet this protection of the Holy Place was a special one – one to be enjoyed by the priests only. Once within the door they became God's hidden ones. But it may be that we are living as Christians under the Pillar of Promise, and yet not experiencing the calm and peace of divine safety that comes as the result of holiness and which marks God's hidden ones. "Not a surge of worry, touch the spirit there."

Think of what we have if we really know what it is to be hid with God. (See Psalm 83:2; Prov. 28:12; II Cor. 4:2; I Pet. 3:4).

It was the Door to the Holiest of All

How imperative it was to have this door. Why such was the way, not only for the priests whereby they could enter the Holy Place but also the only way by which the High Priest could enter within the veil and there in the Holiest of All commune with God. How conscious both the priest and the High Priest must have been of nearness to God as they passed through the five-pillared door! How solemn! How awful, or full of awe, must have been the atmosphere of those places (I Kings 8:10, 11)!

Beloved, are we there? What do we know of nearness to God? It is true – "Near so near, nearer I cannot be," but such describes our position by grace that can never be altered. The question is "What of our experience? Does it correspond with our position?" God's description of Israel was that of "a people near unto Him" (Ps. 148:14).

Do I live as if I dwelt in the unseen Holy? If I do, then something of the fragrance of the Holy Places will be found wherever I go. When Moses came down from the Mount, after dwelling there for some time with his Lord, "the skin of his face shone," but, "Moses wist not that the skin of his face shone" (Exod. 34:29-37). If we but enter the door and seek by the Holy Spirit to live in the Holiest with our Lord, there will be the going forth of that unconscious holiness that will commend Christ to others around us. As the Lord blessed even the shadow of Peter as he passed along, so our very presence will act as a sanctifying influence and benediction.

We have one last thought to express as we close this portion of our meditation. The was no *floor* within the Holy Place, or Holiest of All! What a contrast such afforded! Beautiful curtains above, gold covered boards around, soft pleasing light, sustaining food, lovely fragrance, exquisite golden vessels, and yet a bare, sandy desert floor. Is not the application obvious? The great spiritual blessings and privileges are for our present earthy state. Deeper holiness, fuller dedication does not mean detachment from the common round, or the trivial task. It means, or it should mean, the ennobling or transforming of them until the glory of God is seen in the most commonplace things.

Said Peter to our Lord as he beheld Him glorified upon the Mount, "Lord it is good to be here. Let us build three tabernacles and stay here." But Peter had to realize that the glory of the Mount was to prepare him for the work of the multitude below, and so down he came into the valley of need but with the glory of the Mount to inspire him. Paul commences his Ephesian epistle in the heavenlies and ends it in the kitchen, and the two, although extreme, should never be divorced from each other. The pivot of the epistle is 5:18, "Be filled with the Spirit," and it is the fullness of the Holy Spirit, or entering the door of the Holy Place that can bring the heavenlies down to the kitchen or lift the kitchen up to the heavenlies, whichever way you like to put it.

(b). *The Candlestick* (Exod. 25:31-40; 27:20, 21; 37:17-20; 39:37; 40:4, 24, 25; Lev. 24:1-4; Num. 8:1-4)

Now that we have considered the significance of the door of the Holy Pace, let us pass through and seek to understand, by the inspiration of the Holy Spirit, the spiritual meaning of all the beautiful contents within. In doing so we turn our attention first of all to the *golden candlestick*, the full information of which is given in the above references, and which should be read together. Ere we come to the candlestick proper, there are one or two introductory thoughts to bear in mind, namely,

The Necessity of Light in the Holy Place

Light was very necessary in the Holy Place because there were no windows or apertures of any description through which the natural light could come. With the coverings over the boards and the hanging over the door, the sanctuary was in total darkness. Hence the need of light! That tabernacle of old had three forms of illumination:

The Outer Court was lighted naturally, that is by the sun and such was the only light that could be seen by those outside. And, moreover, the rays of the natural light never penetrated into the Holy Places. There is a natural light, called by Paul "the wisdom of this world" (I Cor. 1:20), and this natural light of human reason can never illuminate the darkness of the world. In fact, this natural light receiveth not the things of the Spirit of God (I Cor. 2:14).

The Holy Place was lighted artificially, by the golden candlestick and such light was confined to the Holy Place, being seen only by those within. This is the light which the outside world cannot behold or realize simply because they are outside. The light of the Holy Place answers to the spiritual illumination of the Holy Spirit that every true believer is conscious of.

The Holiest of All was lighted supernaturally, or by the Shekinah glory of God's presence, and such a light, so brilliant and penetrating, was witnessed by one and only one man, the High Priest, as he entered within the veil once every year. So there is a light surpassing even the present light of Revelation that we possess and that is the Shekinah glory of God's presence, in which we shall eternally dwell. The brightness of this wonderful light must be overpowering, for the Seraphim we are told cover their faces (Isa. 6:2)!

It is quite possible that these modes of illumination can be traced in John's vision of Revelation 22:5:

> And there shall be no night there.

No darkness, no need of illumination as the outside and inside of the tabernacle required.

> they need no candle;

That is no Candlestick, artificial light, as in the Holy Place.

> neither light of the sun;

As the Israelites did in the Outer Court.

> for the Lord God giveth them light;

As the Shekinah Glory of His presence did in the Holiest of All.

Examining the golden candlestick, it may help us to group our thoughts around three sections. i). Its Formation, ii). Its Ornamentation, iii). Its Illumination.

i. *Its Formation.*

The Golden Candlestick standing as it did on the south side of the Holy Place, as the priest entered by the door, must have presented a wonderful appearance. It was a most magnificent and valuable piece of workmanship, and outstanding for its beauty and loveliness.

The Name

Although the name "candlestick" is employed, we are not to think of it as such, although we shall keep to this word that is used. Rather must we get into our minds the thought of a seven-branched lampstand, bearing seven lighted lamps. Candles were unknown then. In the margin of the R.V., the word given for "candlestick" as Revelation 1:13 is "lampstands."

The Composition

That the composition of the candlestick was a piece of superb work is easy to trace.

Made of Pure Gold

It was fashioned of pure gold and is therefore called "the pure candlestick" (Lev. 24:4). There was no alloy or mixture, neither was there any combination of shittim wood like the boards or pillars, which as we have seen were composed of shittim wood overlaid with gold.

In the golden candlestick there is no such combination. It is made of pure gold and thereby typifies that which is entirely divine in its origin. Perhaps it may be well to state briefly what the teaching of the candlestick is. Its central shaft and six branches represent the blessed inseparable union that exists between Christ and His church. The pure olive oil that made the light possible speaks of the Holy Spirit, and so by taking all things together the candlestick is a fitting symbol of the church of Christ indwelt by the Holy Spirit who causes her to shine and bear a bright testimony for her Lord in a dark world of sin. We have already emphasized that the candlestick was made of pure gold! And such signifies the absolute divine character both of Christ and His church. Christ Himself is of the purest gold, being the Very God of Very God. And His church, which is His mystical body has been made a partaker of the same divine nature.

Beaten Work

This is a very arrestive phrase! It implies that a massive piece of gold was taken and by the hard, constant blows of the hammer was flattened out and then worked into its respective shape and beauty. The beating is suggestive of suffering! May we never forget that Christ and His church are made of beaten work. Think of the beating, the scoffing, the shame that Jesus, that piece of pure gold, endured! But the beating out of such has meant the presence of His church, for the death pangs of Calvary were but the birth pangs of the Saviour which produced the church. Beloved, we are where we are in grace today because of His agony, because the pure gold was beaten!

Where was the pure gold that ultimately formed the candlestick hammered out? Not in the Holy Place, that is certain. It stood there finished! It was outside, somewhere in the camp, that the Spirit-anointed workman, with wondrous skill and after much hard, incessant labor, fashioned the gold into a vessel of surpassing beauty and worth.

In like manner Christ, to form His church, had to go outside the camp. He was within the Most Holy Place enjoying His Father's presence but out He came into a cold, bare world and there without the camp, God's precious gold was beaten out!

There is a green hill far away,
Without a city wall,
Where our dear Lord was crucified,
And died to save us all.

Of One Piece

It is distinctly recorded that all that appertained to the golden candlestick should be without sections or joints. That means that the central shaft and the branches, with all the bowls, knots, and flowers were of one piece. The branches were drawn or beaten out of the center piece, while upon both the shaft and the branches the bowls, knots, and flowers were fashioned. Two thoughts are suggested by this requirement.

That the golden candlestick, before it was ever touched by the skillful workman and made visible, was of one piece. The metal was hid somewhere in the bowels of the earth as one solid piece. Nothing was added to it but its outward form and beauty. This brings us to a very deep New Testament truth in reference to Christ and His church. Such were all of one piece to begin with. In the divine purpose, the Lamb was slain and we were chosen in Him before the foundation of the world (Eph. 1:4). All of one piece before the world began! Let us bow before such a mystery and yet manifestation of divine grace.

The second thought is that of the inseparable union that exists between Christ and His church. All of one piece! The New Testament explanation of this is given in Hebrews 2:11 — "For both He that sanctifieth and they who are sanctified are all of one," or, as Moffat puts it, "have all one origin." The divine commentary regarding this holy indissoluble union is given by Paul in I Corinthians 12:12: "Many members yet one body."

A Talent of Pure Gold

The weight of this golden candlestick was that of one talent of pure gold, which is equal to a sum of $15,000 to $18,000. Such a mass of gold made the candlestick not only the most beautiful, but the most costly vessel of the sanctuary. Five to six thousand pounds! But what is that in comparison to the worth of Christ to us, or the worth of the church to Christ? He is indeed precious to us — for "unto you therefore which believe he is precious" — or *"the preciousness"* (I Pet. 2:7). We are precious to Him, because we represent the result of His bloody sweat, His pierced hands and feet, His smitten side. Precious to Christ! May it be so in every respect! May this sublime truth be our objective!

The Measurement

Like the laver, the golden candlestick is given without measurement. It is not to be wondered at that these two vessels are given without definite dimensions. They speak of the two great mysteries that no human mind can fully comprehend and will never fathom this side of eternity, if ever on the other side.

The laver stands for the work of the Holy Spirit. Who can measure what He is prepared to do for any life that is fully yielded or surrendered to Him?

The candlestick prefigures the Lord and His church, and who can measure the bounds of such? Why their influence is infinite! Each day fresh members will be added to His body, until there are un-numbered multitudes even "ten thousand times ten thousand, and thousands of thousands" (Rev. 5:11).

Another interesting feature regarding this unmeasured beautiful vessel is that there is no description of the foot or pedestal upon which it stood or rested. Such an omission turns our thoughts to the unearthly standing of the church; it has no home, no resting place here below; it has no foot, no dependence on or connection with the earth. Here she has no abiding place, or continuing city. We come now to examine the composite parts of the candlestick, and as we do so, may there be the application of the truth to our hearts, as well as the apprehension of it by our minds.

THE SHAFT

The central column or upright part was called the shaft and was probably higher than the branches. And standing out so distinctly and prominently, it afforded a true figure of Him who in all things must have the pre-eminence. If the shaft was taller and more conspicuous than the branches, such is as it should be, for Christ has been anointed with the oil of gladness *above* His fellows (Heb. 1:9).

It is helpful to notice that the word "shaft" is rendered "thigh" in Genesis 24:2 and "loins" in Genesis 46:26. As children came from the *shaft* or *loins* of Jacob, so the branches came forth from the shaft. In like manner, the church came from the riven side of Christ as Eve came from Adam's.

Again, in Exodus 37:18, this center stem is termed the "branch," and thus bears the same name as its offshoots. The word, you notice, is in the singular. *His branch*, thus distinguishing it from the plural word "branches" which occurs in the next verse. He calls us the branches under the figure of the vine in John 15, and yet here He is Himself pre-figured as a "branch." This reminds of His condescension, for He was made like unto His brethren and is not ashamed to call them brethren. It also suggests the prophetic name that was His. The prophet Isaiah says, "In that day shall the branch of the LORD be beautiful and glorious" (Isa. 4:2).

THE BRANCHES

Spreading out from the shaft or middle branch were six branches, three on either side, which were probably curved upward, until each pair formed a half-circle. They were made of the same nature as the shaft, namely pure gold, because they were a vital part of it. The church, like her Lord is divine in her origin and nature.

The branches sprang out from the shaft. Let us note this! They were not soldered on or artificially connected with the central stem but an inseparable part of it. This fact opens up a question which has perplexed the minds of many, namely,

If a believer has been made a vital part of the Lord, can he fall away and be lost? If he is a branch of the candlestick, can he drop off? If he is a member of Christ's body, can such a body be complete if he cuts himself off? These thoughts constitute what is known as the falling away doctrine and such a doctrine is contrary to Revelation. Texts that are used to propagate it are often wrested from their context. For instance,

Warfare. "Lest that by any means, when I have preached to others, I myself should be a castaway" (I Cor. 9:27).

Fruitfulness. "If a man abide not in me, he is cast forth as a branch" (John 15:6).

But passages like "Married to another, even to him who is raised from the dead" (Rom. 7:4).

"But he that is joined unto the Lord is one spirit" (I Cor. 6:17).

"For we are members of his body, of his flesh, and of his bones" (Eph. 5:30).

serve to show how the believer is everlastingly united to the risen Christ and is made forever one, even as the branches and stem were one in that candlestick. And what God hath joined together, no man, or devil, can put asunder.

Further, the strength of the branches lay in the shaft. It was thus that they were supported and enabled to spread themselves out and hold their respective lamps. And, says our Lord, "Without Me, the central Shaft, ye, the branches can do nothing."

Then again, the beauty of the shaft was upon each branch. Yes, the knops, bowls, and flowers adorning the center, were exquisitely wrought upon each individual branch. Is this not beautiful? It is the will of God that the church should be like her Lord. "As he is so are we in this age." May the prayer of the psalmist be answered for Christ's blood-washed ones, "Let the beauty of the Lord our God be upon us."

THE ACCESSORIES

No one can read the minute particulars that are given in connection with all the different sections of the tabernacle without adoring the God who planned it. Although so mighty that He can create and control vast worlds, yet we here find Him as careful regarding the smallest matters such as tongs, snuffers, and snuff-dishes. Nothing was omitted that was absolutely necessary, thereby showing how perfect the wisdom of God was, and is!

The Tongs, or Snuffers

These accessories, which like the candlestick itself were made of pure gold, were used for trimming the wick of the lamp. It was the daily duty of the priest to remove all the dead material that hindered the light from shining as brightly as it ought to. Before the days when electricity was so general, some of us can remember how the oil lamps, before they could burn properly, had to have wicks trimmed with a pair of scissors. This, then, was the reason for the snuffers!

Is it not true that there is something to remove even from the best of us? Lights we are, if we belong to Christ, but often the snuffers have to be applied to the dead material that hinders the light from shining. What is the tribulation of Romans 5:3-5, and the chastening of Hebrews 12:11, and the trial of your faith of I Peter 1:7 but the snuffers the Lord uses to remove all the ill-smelling wick which is both an offense and an hindrance? Remember it was the High Priest who trimmed the lamp; and as Aaron typifies our Lord Jesus Christ, what better hands could we commit the sanctification of our lives to? Therefore, in the hour of trial and affliction let us think of the golden snuffer and allow the Lord to remove all that would extinguish the light.

These tongs were also used to raise up the wick in order that the light might be more bright. The priest would gently place his tongs upon the wick and lifting it up increase the light of the lamp. Does this not explain a rather difficult passage in John 15:2, "He taketh away" or as it can be translated, "He lifted up."

The Golden Snuff-dishes

These little golden cup-like vessels were used for receiving the waste or snuffings from the lamp and for removing such out of the Holy Place. The gracious, divine Lord removes from your lips and mine, as His Temple, all that is displeasing to Himself.

ii. *Its Ornamentation*

Not only was this vessel costly, being made of gold, and indispensible, being the only light within the Holy Place, it was also beautiful as well, for worked upon the shaft and branches were three sets of ornaments known as bowls, knops, and flowers.

The Bowls

These bowls or cups, which likely contained a sufficient quantity of oil to feed the lights were made like unto *almonds.* The almond tree, we are told, is the first tree to awake from the sleep of winter, thus acting as a herald of Resurrection. The almond bowls, therefore, speak of Resurrection. This can be proved by referring to Aaron's rod, that comprised all the three ornaments worked upon the candlestick. In Numbers 17:8 we are told that Aaron's rod, although dead, budded, blossomed blossoms, and yielded almonds. We here see Jesus, pre-eminent in Resurrection, for, says Paul in Romans 8:29, Christ is "the firstborn among many brethren." But as the candlestick also typifies the church as well as her Lord, so the same title is applied to her — the "church of the firstborn" (Heb. 12:23). Thus the almond bowls, symbolizing Resurrection, are found upon the shaft and branches.

The Knops

As it is somewhat difficult to define what kind of ornaments are meant by the knop, we cannot be certain about their purpose or significance. Josephus renders the word "pomegranates." One writer, however, suggests that the knops were like opening buds, out of which the branches apparently sprouted. Such would answer to the buds upon Aaron's stick. Buds speak of promise of flower and fruit.

The Flowers

These flowers, so beautifully worked upon the candlestick, must have proved how great was the skill that the Holy Spirit had given to the workman who had fashioned them. Both the LXX and Vulgate versions call them "lilies." This was the special flower that our Lord called attention to in Matthew 6:30, because of its graceful beauty and fragrance. Here again, we turn to Aaron's rod and upon such we find flowers, for it bloomed blossoms.

So there were three exquisite ornaments.

Knops, answering to the buds of Aaron's stick.
Flowers, answering to the blooming blossoms.
Bowls, answering to the yielded almonds.

And all three speak of the Lord Jesus and of His redeemed church.

The knops, the buds, answer to our Lord, who in His boyhood was like a bud so full of promise. Think of Him at the age of twelve saying, "Wist ye not that I must be about My Father's business?" What promise He gave!

The flowers, blossoms, answer to His earthly manhood, which like a lily so pure and white was so beautiful and fragrant, and yet, withal, so delicate and sensitive as lilies are.

The bowls, like almonds, which is the fruit that came as the result of the buds and then the blossoms, speak of Christ in His risen manhood. For although like Aaron's rod, which was dead, behold He is alive forevermore, yielding almonds.

But we must remember that the same beautiful ornaments were worked upon the branches as well as the central shaft that sets Christ forth as the chiefest among ten thousand. Beloved, what about these graceful, lovely figures? Are they to be found adorning our lives as the branches?

The Knops

These can represent those whose lives have recently opened to the Saviour. Grace has entered their hearts and they have been made part of His blessed body. And now, being His, they are like buds, so full of the promise of flowers and fruit. Let those who are newly saved take heed lest some withering frost of sin or worldliness blasts the bud and thus destroys its promise.

The Flowers

These can typify those who are growing into the full stature of Christ. Through daily contact with the pure and holy one, whose life is as fragrant as a lily, their lives through implicit obedience are catching the fragrance of the divine lily and manifesting the same purity of character. Should we not all seek to adorn the flowers of holiness and likeness to our Lord?

The Bowls

Although risen and seated with Christ, yet for you and me the almond bowls signify the glorious Resurrection that will soon be ours when the Blessed Lord appears. Then, and not till then, will our lives perfectly satisfy His loving heart, for in glory we shall serve Him day and night in His temple and thus yield almonds for His enjoyment continually.

iii. *Its Illumination*

As we have remarked, the light of the golden candlestick was the only illumination the Holy Place had, because the created light of the sun and the borrowed light of the moon were denied it (Exod. 27:20, 21).

Light is a characteristic symbol of witness and testimony!

It is used of God. "God is light" (I John 1:5). "God is a Spirit" (John 4:24). "God is love" (I John 4:16).

Threefold description of God.

It is used of Christ. "I am the light of the world" (John 8:12). Seven words – seven lamps. "In him was life; and the life was the light of men. And the light shineth in darkness; and the darkness comprehended it not" (John 1:4, 5).

It is used of the church. "Ye are the light of the world" (Matt. 5:14-16). Seven words, seven Lamps. "Ye shine as lights in the world" (Phil. 2:15). Seven again. "The seven candlesticks . . . are the seven churches" (Rev. 1:20). "He was a burning and a shining light: and ye were willing for a season to rejoice in his light" (John 5:35).

It is used of the Gospel revelation. "Men loved darkness rather than light" John 3:19, 20).

There are many precious truths for our hearts to meditate upon in the brilliant light of the candlestick.

The Seven Lamps

The divine command was: "Thou shalt make seven lamps," which means that a separate lamp rested upon the end of each branch, three upon either side, and one upon the center shaft, thus making seven.

Seven is the number denoting "perfection" and suggests in this connection the perfect witness to Christ that the Holy Spirit makes possible through the church of God. This figure is found again, you remember, in John's vision of Revelation 1:4; 3:1; 6:5, where the seven spirits of God speak of the Spirit in all the plenitude of His light and power, who works through the seven churches or the perfect body of our Lord.

One Light

The remarkable feature about the references to the light from the candlestick is that although there were seven lamps yet there was only one light spoken of. Seven lamps, seven lights, yet their light was one! The lamps sent forth *the* light, the oil ministered was for *the* light to cause it to burn continually (Exod. 27:20; Lev. 24:2 [Hebrew].

What a beautiful thought there is here. Seven lamps yet one light! As believers we may differ one from the other in multitudinous ways but being His there is no conflict between His testimony and ours, between His message and ours. *Many lamps — yet one light!* That is the Lord's ideal for us! Alas, today there are many lamps and many lights in the visible church of our Lord. She has departed from the Word of truth and consequently lacks that unity of witness that should characterize her. Let us beware lest we stray outside the borders of divine revelation, which can be found only in Scriptures, in order to secure light! Whatever light men have apart from the Word is darkness. Many false lights are shining around us, professing to have the power to enlighten men. But Christ, the Living Word, is the perfect light of God, and the Bible, the written Word, is the only perfect revelation of God and apart from such there is no united testimony or illumination.

Again, as the candlestick was the only light within the Holy Place scattering its darkness, so there is no other source of illumination for the darkened minds of men and women in this benighted world apart from the blessed evangel of the risen Lord which the Holy Spirit empowers the church to give witness to.

Our responsibility is very clear — "Go ye into all the world and preach the Gospel." Therefore, let us realize that as there was complete darkness without the light of the candlestick, so the darkness of this world would be more dense if it were not for the presence of Spirit-filled men and women. The Lord Jesus came as a light to lighten the Gentiles and is still seeking through His people to shed His radiant beams abroad.

The Oil

The substance that produced the light was called "pure oil olive, beaten for the light" (Exod. 27:20). Here we reach the precious truth regarding the ministry of the Holy Spirit in connection with the witness of Christ and His church.

OIL

Oil, as we know, was the liquid used when the prophet, priest, and king were anointed in Old Testament times. And as "anointing" and "unction" are the same word in the original, so in passages like

"The wise took oil in their vessels" (Matt. 25:4),

"Ye have an unction from the Holy One" (I John 2:20),

"He . . . hath anointed us" (II Cor. 1:21),

we have Scriptural authority for using the oil as a type of the Holy Spirit. Oil in the candlestick was the illuminative medium! The light was not in the lamp, or branches, not in the gold, but was derived entirely from the oil. Who but the Holy Spirit can enlighten our minds? We have no light of ourselves, although some would disparage such a statement. The spiritual divine light comes solely from the Spirit of God.

Was it not this particular function of the Spirit's ministry that our Lord referred to in

John 16: v. 7 "It is expedient for you that I go away."
v. 14 "He shall receive of mine, and shall shew it unto you."
v. 15 "He shall take of mine, and shall shew it unto you"?

OLIVE

In Scripture the olive tree is symbolic of many things:

Richness "The olive tree said... Should I leave my fatness?" (Judg. 9:9).
Fertility "I am like a green olive tree" (Ps. 52:8).
" A green olive tree, fair, and of goodly fruit" (Jer. 11:16).
Beauty "His beauty shall be as the olive tree (Hos. 14:6).

The Holy Spirit, then, as olive oil, is the One who possesses a vast fulness – richness, fertility, and beauty are all His in an abundant measure.

PURE

One is greatly struck with the repetition of this epithet!

The central shaft of the candlestick had to be made of pure gold.
The six branches springing out of such had to be fashioned of pure gold.
The knop, flowers, and bowls ornamenting the candlestick had to be wrought out of pure gold.
The tongs, or snuffers, and snuff-dishes had to be composed of pure gold.
The priests who ministered within the Holy Place had likewise to be pure.

Hence the need of the laver outside the door! Over their clothing – "Holiness unto the Lord."

The oil for the light had to be compounded of pure olives. Representing the Spirit, such is an appropriate epithet, for is He not called the *Holy* Spirit? About one hundred times referred to as "Holy," He is indeed the *pure* olive oil!

So everything within that Holy Place had to be pure, or like the place they were in, holy. How solemn the truth! Are we prepared for it? Without holiness no man shall see the Lord! Belonging to Christ, as we do, let His message sink deep into our hearts that "the pure in heart see God." Purity of heart means clarity of vision!

BEATEN

The olive berry had not to be squeezed or pressed only, but beaten. We have already seen that the gold that formed the candlestick was once a piece of shapeless gold but that the workman's hammer had beaten it out until it formed the seven-branched light, and such as we observed speaks of the intense sufferings of Christ. He was the smitten and beaten One.

Here we have the same word and process in connection with the olives. The olive oil represents the Holy Spirit. But was He ever beaten? Did He suffer? Yes, He did! He is called the Spirit of Christ, which means that entering our Lord's body at His Incarnation, He remained within Him until His death, and residing in Him, He suffered with the Saviour. There was perfect sympathy between the Spirit and the Son and so our New Testament shows that during our Lord's earthly life, their lives were mingled one with the other. May we always remember that the olive oil was beaten! The sufferings of the Holy Spirit were as real to Him as the Third Person of the Trinity as the sufferings of the Saviour were to Him as the Second Person of the Trinity.

Olives! Why are they associated with Gethsemane? Here is a thought that staggers one's heart, namely, that a believer can continue the sufferings of the Holy Spirit, yes, even to the length of giving Him a Gethsemane!

In Ephesians 4:30 we read, "Grieve not the Holy Spirit" and the word *grieve* there means "to afflict with sorrow," and is akin to that pathetic Gethsemane passage of Matthew 26: 37 – "He began to be sorrowful." May we be delivered from causing the Holy Spirit the sorrow of Gethsemane!

APPLIED BY THE HIGH PRIEST

It is very evident from the reference to the candlestick that it was the duty of Aaron, the High Priest, to attend to the requirements of the light and supply the beaten oil when such was needed and also to dress the wicks – "He shall order the lamps" is the inspired command. How sweet is the message hidden here! The Lord Jesus, who is our High Priest, is the only One who can supply the pure olive oil. Was not the Holy Spirit the distinct gift that He poured out upon His church at her inauguration upon the day of Pentecost? And did not this divine unction cause her to shine so brightly that Jerusalem, Judea, Samaria, and ultimately the uttermost parts of the earth were penetrated by the brilliant beams of the golden candlestick of His early church?

The High Priest supplied and applied the olive oil! And He is still doing so! The Saviour Himself is God's gift to a lost, ruined world, while the Spirit is the Gift of the risen, ascended Lord to His people. But what do we know of this gift? Certainly we have the Holy Spirit if we are believers, but has He the possession of us? Do we realize and enjoy the gift bestowed? Or, realizing how dim our light is, shall we ask the great High Priest to fill our lamps with oil? He alone can trim and dress them, supply the oil and thus keep them brightly shining! John declares that He is the One who baptized with the Holy Spirit and with fire. So let us

Take the Gift of Pentecost
Take the Promised Holy Ghost.

COMMANDED (Exod. 27:20)

The word *command* is seldom found in the making of any particular vessel. The tabernacle as a whole was fashioned according to the command of the Lord. The *command* in connection with the beaten oil can be linked on to the New Testament command to be filled with the Spirit (Eph. 5:18).

The Purpose

There are just one or two brief points to mention in respect to the light ere we end our meditation on the golden candlestick.

It was for the Holy Place

The purpose of it was to illumine the Holy Place. Without it the priest could not see to serve the Lord, or behold the wonderful glories and beauties above and around him. So apart from the illumination of the Holy Spirit, we cannot realize the fulness of Christ.

It was for the Lord

We are told that it had to shine "before the Lord." It was there not merely for the benefit of the priest but also for the Lord. "God first," it seemed to say. In fact, the three vessels in this Holy Place had as their primary aspect something for the Lord.

The golden candlestick was lighted "before the Lord" (Exod. 40:25).
The bread was on the table "before the Lord" (Exod. 40:23).
The incense on the golden altar was "before the Lord" (Exod. 30:8).

Although the priests saw the light, smelled the incense, tasted the bread, yet in each case God was first. Says the apostle, "Whatsoever ye do, do it heartily, as to the Lord, and not unto men" (Col. 3:23). Before the Lord! Beloved, shall we not make these three solemn words the dominating desire of our hearts, as we think of our own individual lives, in our homes, our business, or our service? Let our whole life be lived before the Lord!

It was to Shine Continually

"The light was ever burning," it never went out while the tabernacle stood. Extinguishers, you will notice, were not supplied, the Holy Spirit thus signifying that God expects us to maintain a steady, continuous witness for Him. We must confess, however, that our light is sometimes extinguished! Often we are like flashlamps; our light is erratic, it goes in and out. Our Lord warns us against two extinguishers – "the bushel" and "the bed" (Mark 4:21). "Is a candle brought to be put under a bushel, or under a bed? and not to be set on a candlestick?" The former represents the world's merchandise, an illustration of which you have in Genesis 13: 10, 11, when Lot hid his light in Sodom. The latter speaks of ease, slothfulness, and finds an echo in David's history when in II Samuel 11:1, 2, he rose "from off his bed."

But how precious it is to realize that it was the High Priest alone who trimmed and dressed the lamp (Lev. 24:3; Num. 8:1-33) every morning. So if the wick of our testimony is dry, if some dead, unnecessary matter has gathered over it, if the light is being extinguished, then it is the hands of the Lord Jesus who can put things right. No other hands dare meddle with our sanctification.

Then are we told that to do away with the obnoxious smell that was caused when the lamps were being trimmed, Aaron burnt fragrant incense upon the altar (Exod. 30:7, 8)? "Snuffs do not give forth a very dainty perfume," says Spurgeon, "therefore Aaron before he trimmed the lamp kindled the incense."

How like the Lord Jesus this is! How graciously He tries to counteract the influence of your mistakes and mine! Why, if only we could see it, we should discover that our great High Priest is forever burning the incense as He trims our black, dirty, dry wick! (See Gen. 50:29).

It is only as the Holy Spirit has unhindered flow into and through us that our light can burn continually. "By all the grace of God I continue." Then let us be warned by the history of the candlestick.

At a future date it was carried away into captivity (Jer. 52:19), and bondage dimmed its brilliance. It was desecrated by Belshazzar, and so the writing was over against the candlestick. It was being used for man's pleasure not God's glory and so judgment fell (Dan. 5:2, 3). Our Lord, in Revelation 2:1, speaks about removing the candlestick and, therefore, let us give heed to such solemn consequences of extinguished light.

It was to Shine upon Itself

The words "Give light over against it" (Exod. 25:37) imply that the lamps were all turned towards the center, thus focusing all their light upon the beautiful shaft, causing its perfect, exquisite workmanship to be seen. So the one great purpose of the Holy Spirit is to exalt Jesus. He does not shine away from the golden candlestick but "over against it." He takes of the things of Christ and reveals them unto us. In like manner, all Spirit-filled believers who have been made as branches of the candlestick should allow the Holy Spirit to fulfill the same through them, namely, exalt Jesus. Often your light and mine is turned upon ourselves, and people see not the beautiful golden candlestick but your little lamp and mine. We cannot make much of Christ and of ourselves at the same time.

It Shone upon the Table

From Exodus 26:35 we gather that the candlestick was over against the table or directly opposite to it, so that its light could be cast upon it, and thereby display the purity of the bread, with its covering of frankincense arranged upon it. Christ is the Bread of Life, the only true sustenance of our souls, and it is the Holy Spirit who reveals Him as such. Moreover, when we are shining for Jesus, as we ought to, we always shine upon the table of shewbread, that is causing the perishing ones around us to behold Christ as the food they need to satisfy them. The light illuminated the table. We read, "The two disciples heard John speak, and they followed (not him) but Jesus." As a burning and a shining light, for that is what John is called, he sent all his light toward the center, even toward Him who is the table of shewbread, thus causing many to say, "We have found the Christ."

We are living in an empty world where multitudes are "feeding upon ashes." Like the prodigal of old, they are filling themselves with husks, while in the Father's house there is bread enough and to spare. Who can lead them to the source of plentiful supply? Why, we can. The only way by which we can do it is to shine upon the table! That is, let the world see how wonderfully Christ satisfies our hearts, until with hungry hearts they seek your Saviour and mine with the cry,

> Thou bruised and broken Bread,
> My life long wants supply.

(c). *The Table of Shewbread* (Exod. 25:23-30; 37:10-16; 39:36; 40:4, 22, 23; Lev. 24:5-9)

Leaving the meditation of the golden candlestick and turning to the spiritual teaching of the table of shewbread, one is forcibly reminded of the opening verse of Psalm 27, where we have the thought of the candlestick and shewbread combined:

The Lord is my light – The Golden Candlestick.

The Lord is the strength of my life – The Table of Shewbread.

The golden candlestick speaks of the light or testimony of the church of God as she is indwelt and controlled by her Lord.

The table of shewbread, on the other hand, indicates the life of the church, which is continually sustained as every individual believer feeds upon Him who is "the Bread of Life."

Coming, then, to the table of shewbread, it may help us if we summarize its teaching thus:

The Table Itself
The Contents of the Table

i. *The Table Itself*

This sacred article within the Holy Place should have our closest attention because its typical significance reveals to us the only way by which our spiritual lives can be strengthened and thereby delivered from their weak, anaemic, powerless condition.

Designation

Think, first of all, of the name given to the table of shewbread. It is in connection with this piece of holy furniture that we find the first reference in Scripture to the name "table." Bearing in mind the truth that we can never over-emphasize, namely, that the first mention of anything affords a certain clue as to its meaning, we discover that the word *table,* occurring in Exodus 25:23 as it does for the first time, is associated with mutual fellowship and communion, inasmuch as the bread upon the table was there both for God's pleasure and the priests' sustenance.

At once, then, we arrive at the spiritual significance of the table of shewbread. It represents the blessed fellowship that the church of God enjoys with the Father and with His Son, Jesus Christ, and of the inward life of the believer that is sustained and strengthened thereby.

The calling of the church is to have communion and fellowship with her Lord. In his unfallen state, Adam had around him in the garden many things in which he could take delight with God. But through disobedience, this happy intercourse was broken, and he was driven from the presence of the Lord. And while man remains in sin, that fellowship with God is forfeited, for "What communion hath light with darkness?... What concord hath Christ with Belial?" (II Cor. 6:14, 15).

But the privilege of the redeemed, who constitute the church of God, is that they have been restored into the presence and favor of the Lord. By faith they have unhindered access to Him and find, daily, that sweet communion with the Father and the Son is open to them.

Our Lord gives us a picture of this in Luke 15. After the prodigal had been restored and welcomed back by his father, and reinstated into the family circle, and clothed with the robe, ring, and shoes, there came the fulness of blessing, when the father commanded his servant to kill the fatted calf and said, "Let us eat, and be merry. For this is my son who was dead, and is alive again; he was lost, and is found. And they began to be merry" (Luke 15:23, 24).

So the teaching of the table is that of the believer's joy and privilege of feeding upon Him who, in infinite mercy, became the fatted calf. Upon the table was the bread that the Father beheld for one whole week, and which thereafter was eaten by the priests. Our blessed, adorable Lord is the food both for the satisfaction of God and for the sustenance of His people. As at the table in your household there is friendly intercourse and communion, so here at the table of shewbread, blessings are enjoyed and partaken of in common between the head and all the members of the family. The same food is spread alike before all, and consequently the same sources of refreshment and joy are alike presented to all who are drawn together.

The word *table,* therefore, occurring here for the first time, signifies fellowship and communion, and thus interprets for us the typical importance of the shewbread.

The last reference in the Old Testament to the table is also interesting to observe. It is found in Malachi 1:12, where the prophet says, "The table of the LORD is polluted." May the gracious Lord Himself deliver us from prostituting our privileges or despising our rights!

Dimensions

In the specifications as to the dimensions of the table itself, it is stated to have been 2 cubits in length, 1 cubit in breadth, and 1½ cubits in height, or to adopt English measurements, 36 inches in length, 18 inches in breadth, 27 inches in height.

There is not much one can say about these measurements except it be that the height of the table and the ark within the veil were the same, possibly implying that Christ is the same to God as He is to us, namely one of human and divine perfection. The ark was a little longer and broader than the table, suggesting that there is a wider and greater presentation of God's grace as seen in Christ that we have yet to witness. Let us not forget the extensive aspect of our Lord's Person. What He really is will always exceed our comprehension.

A further suggestion given is that

> the lesser lengths and breadth would indicate that whilst the Mercy Seat has in view typically the whole world, for Christ "as the propitiation for our sins, and not for ours

only, but also for *the sins* of the whole world" (I John 2:2), the Table of Shewbread stands typically in relation to the Lord's people only. The Mercy Seat stood in relation to all, the Table was only for the Priests. Its height, equal to that of the Mercy Seat, sets forth that the believers' communion is commensurate with the fulness of the place won through the atoning death of Christ.

Descriptions

Regarding the composition of the table itself, there are one or two very enlightening features to notice.

It was Made of Shittim Wood

The command was to make the table of shittim, or acacia wood, the only timber used in the construction of the tabernacle and its vessels, and which being a desert wood suggests the humanity of Him upon whom we feed. Our human souls are truly fed as we meditate upon Him as the man Christ Jesus.

It was Overlaid with Gold

The absolute quality and purity of the gold are imperatively insisted upon in that the wooden table had to be overlaid with *pure* gold. The table sets forth, as other parts of the tabernacle do, the twofold nature of the Lord, for the gold speaks of the other side of His nature, namely, His deity. Pure gold He certainly is, seeing He is without any alloy or mixture of sin.

The gold, of course, is of a different substance or material from the wood, nevertheless it adds preciousness, firmness, and eternal stability and glory to the wood.

The Crown of Gold Round About

Round about the upper part of the table there was a crown, or an ornamental rim or "moulding," as the R.V. puts it in the margin of Exodus 25:11, 24. Such a rim or border would serve to retain the bread securely in its position on the table so that it might not be displaced by the Kohathites who carried it on their shoulders when Israel was journeying.

In this, one sees the twofold thought of Christ and the believers' security. God, as the crown of gold, purest deity, continually guards the precious truth regarding His Son. In spite of all apostacy there is the same fragrance of Christ ever under the eye of God on our behalf. Christ, Himself, is unchanged by any feebleness, failings, or wonderings of His people below. He is both sure and steadfast.

Being in Christ we are also kept secure by the Father's power. The New Testament is eloquent with the truth of the security of the believer! The crown of gold is round about us while we are being carried through this wilderness upon His living shoulders. Therefore, let us rest in the fact that the government of our lives is with Him — "Now unto Him that is able to keep you from falling" (Jude 24).

The Border of an Hand-breadth

In Exodus 25:25 and 27:12, we read of a border of an hand-breadth round about which also had a crown or rim of gold adorning it. Says Henry Soltau,

> The use of this border or shelf added to the Table was, it seems, to form a place of support for the golden vessels attached to the Shewbread Table, whereon they probably were placed during the journeys. The object of the crown or ledge attached to the border would then be to render the vessels secure in their position when carried on the Table. We are here reminded of a careful and diligent foresight on the part of our God, to secure and maintain unshaken all our blessings in Christ.

The border was an hand-breadth, or the breadth of a hand, signifying that it is a divine hand that safely guards all that the table holds. On God's part there was no failure to keep everything upon the table intact. Would that the church in these days of doubt and unbelief manifested the same diligence and desire to preserve intact all that our blessed Lord is represented to be by the table of shewbread!

The Four Rings and Their Staves

Fastened securely to the feet of the table were four rings, one at each corner, over against the border (Exod. 25:27), through which the staves were passed, thus enabling the table to be carried in its journeys. There are several truths we can combine under this section.

They were *rings* that were fastened to the table. A ring, being an unbroken circle, suggests the eternity of our Lord, who has an unbroken existence being "the Father of eternity" (Isa. 9:6, R.V.). These rings were made of pure gold, thus indicating His absolute deity. The staves were made of shittim wood overlaid with gold foreshadowing the oft-repeated figure of His twofold nature.

The staves and rings enabled the Kohathites to carry the table about and so the Israelites had constantly with them in their wilderness condition the table of shewbread. The conclusion of the matter is that our experience here below is one of change and journey, for at the best we are a pilgrim host, having no abiding place but seeking one to come. The glory of the Gospel is that it presents to us a Christ who is adapted to all the vicissitudes of a wilderness life. Although in a world of turmoil and unrest, our fellowship and communion with the Lord need not be interfered with, for He is well able to make us the recipients of the pleasant bread spread upon a table in the presence of mine enemies.

ii. *The Contents Upon the Table*

Having viewed the gold-covered table itself, let us now turn our attention to the articles that were placed upon it by the priests.

The Golden Vessels

From Exodus 25:29 we learn that there were four distinct sets of golden vessels placed upon the table, all of which were kept in their place and position by the hand-breadth golden border.

The Dishes

This word *dishes* in Exodus 25:29 is translated "charges" in Numbers 7:84, and seems to represent a large, hollow vessel like a deep dish for conveying the loaves to and from the table. Is it not blessed to realize that our Lord is not only the object of our fellowship, not only the bread sustaining our hearts, but the provider of the means whereby He Himself is communicated unto us? The "dish" may be the Word or the ministry of it by some teacher, still the means of grace, that is, the medium by which He is brought to us to feed upon is of His own providing.

The Spoons

The Hebrew word for *spoons* seems to denote a small hollow vessel holding about a handful. Probably such were used for conveying the frankincense and spreading it over the tops of the loaves.

Soltau, however, thinks that these spoons were used for conveying the incense to the golden altar, thus combining the table of shewbread with such.

> In the enumeration of the various vessels of the Sanctuary we shall find none specified for holding incense except these: when, therefore, the High Priest had to put incense on the Golden Altar, he would have to go to the Table of Shewbread to fetch the spoonful from thence. In this act he would link, as it were, these two vessels, the Altar and the Table together; he would remember, whilst he sent up a cloud of fragrance from the burning coals on the Altar, to cover any ill-savóur that might have been exhibited by Israel, that at the same moment the perpetual bread presented, on the Golden Table, an unchanged aspect of perfectness on their behalf; and thus, whilst defect had by the one vessel to be met and covered over, perfect-

ness was on the other still preserved unaltered under the gaze of the Lord. And does this not afford a true type of the ministration of our High Priest? Because He ever liveth to make intercession for us (like the Incense Altar with its fragrant cloud), does He cease at the same time to present the full aspect of perfectness on our behalf, as typified by the Shewbread? In a word, is not His the power to combine the presentation of all perfection with the covering over of all imperfection, one great blessing of His Priesthood? The Priest who lights the Incense Altar has his thoughts full of the remembrance of the pure Table and its twelve presence loaves, from whence he has taken the golden spoon full of the perfume.

The Covers and Bowls

The R.V. gives the word *flagons* for *covers.* These two remaining sets of vessels, namely flagons and bowls, were used as it is stated in Exodus 25:29, "to pour out withal." Often these libation vessels are overlooked in the study of the table of shewbread, partly because it is forgotten that the flagons and bowls represent liquid food, even as the loaves represent solid food.

By turning to Numbers 28:7, we see that there is a command to pour out strong wine unto the Lord as a drink offering. The presence of the flagons and bowls were therefore necessary in that they were directly employed for the drink offering unto Jehovah, ministered in the Holy Place.

We need both food and drink for the sustenance of our spiritual life, and we have both in Christ, for He is not only "the bruised and broken bread," but also "the true life-giving Vine."

Turning to John's Gospel we find that our Lord is the drink who satisfies all thirst in Chapter 4, and the bread who sustains all life in Chapter 6. In fact, in those mystical words of His in John 6:53-56, our Lord presents Himself as our meat and drink.

In connection with all the vessels mentioned, it will be noted that they were made of gold. As such vessels were used for the purposes of conveyance, they proclaim the solemn truth that Christ can only be ministered to by means that are pure. What a lesson there is in this for our hearts as believer-priests! Then there was no wood in the composition of those vessels, signifying the fuller truth that it is the Holy Spirit alone who has no humanity but entire deity in His nature, that can convey to our hungry spirits the revelation of Christ that sustains and satisfies. "He shall take of Mine," said our Lord, "and shew it unto you."

(d). *The Shewbread*

We have now reached the particular section of our theme that reflects in a most blessed way the adorable Person of our Lord. And if we but humbly look to the Holy Spirit for guidance, our souls will delight themselves in fatness.

i. *The Description of the Loaves*

As it may not be generally known why the bread placed upon the table was termed "shewbread," let us seek to examine the various descriptions or designations that are used.

The Shewbread

In the text of the A.V., it is the ordinary word *shewbread* that is used, indicating that the loaves were exhibited or shown upon the table for seven consecutive days. There they were for the eyes of the Lord and of the priests to gaze upon.

Presence-Bread

Turning to the R.V., however, we discover in the margin the phrase "presence-loaves," which means to give the original thought of the word, "bread of the Presence" or "bread of the faces."

How precious is this thought! The

"shewbread" was the "bread of the faces," that means the twelve loaves were not only placed with their faces, as it were, turned toward the eye of God; but so placed and left upon the table that the face of God – or better still, seeing the word is plural – the faces of the Trinity, of Father, Son, and Holy Spirit, yes, and of believers too, for the faces of the priests were directed toward the loaves, might constantly behold them. With delight Jehovah gazed upon the bread that was continually before His face, for it foreshadowed Him upon whom He ever feasts with satisfaction. Christ is our "presence-bread," for He is now in the presence of God appearing for us and as "The Bread of Life," our unfailing Sustenance.

Bread of Ordering

There is another meaning of the term "shewbread" that the reader will observe by turning to passages like I Chronicles 9:22; 23:29, etc., where in the margin will be found the rendering "bread of ordering" or "arrangement." The word *row* in Leviticus 22:6, 7 is an identical term. This translation indicates the orderly arrangement of the bread upon the table in two rows. The bread of ordering or arrangement. How suggestive! Why our Lord is such, for did He not come as the bread from heaven according to the divine plan or ordering? In the fulness of time, at the precise moment, God sent forth His Son. Not only so, but in all His ways, our Lord was most orderly and careful. Nothing slipshod can be found in His earthly life. On rising from the tomb there was that evidence of His orderliness in the napkin folded neatly by itself. Truly He hath done all things well, or "beautiful," as the word sometimes signifies.

Hallowed Bread

During his flight from Saul, David came to Ahimelech the priest. Tired and hungry, he sought food and found that the priest had just changed the bread on the table. Fresh, hot bread was placed there by Ahimelech, while the previous loaves were about to be eaten. These David consumed, for the priest gave him "hallowed" or "holy" bread, as it is put in the R.V., I Sam. 21:4-6.

Holy bread it was, for it had been made by *holy men*, with *holy material*, that is without leaven, and had stood in the *holy place* before the thrice *holy God*, and was not removed until the *holy day*. Can we not call our Lord Jesus Christ the hallowed or holy bread? Why, as the Bread of man, and of God, He must be Holy, and Holy He is, as men, angels, demons, and the Father affirmed.

The Typical Teaching

Shall we not linger to ascertain the spiritual significance of the shewbread? What is the teaching? Is it not that Christ is the sustenance of our life, even as He has so fully illustrated under the same figure of bread in John 6:1-7?

Whenever bread is referred to typically in the Scriptures, it is used to represent not what man is to God, but what God is for man. Therefore, in Christ as the bread, we see what God has become for man. Bread, we are told, is the staff of life, and in the Bible, bread is emblematic not only of life itself, but of all the necessities and blessings accompanying life.

So in Christ we have life and not only life itself, but all that accompanies it, for, says the apostle, "Shall he not with him also freely give us all things?" (Rom. 8:32). Alas! how few there are who see and find in Christ all the sustenance they need. He is their only daily bread, but somehow they fail to come to Him every morning with the prayer that He Himself gave us, "Give us each day our daily bread." Says one writer,

> There are thousands of Christians, men and women, today whom one would not, for the world, un-Christianise—but whose Christianity is puny, weak, infirm, hopeless, complaining, fretful, miserable; of whom you cannot think as "good soldiers of Jesus Christ." Soldiers! They are more fit for a hospital than a battlefield. They have no joy, no peace, no testimony; they are victims of the world, the flesh, and the Devil, almost without resistance; and the whole secret of it is this, they starve their "souls," as they call them, every day. They have neither time nor inclination—or if they have inclination they have not the time, and if they have the time they have not the inclination—to seek for, and feed upon, the Bread of Life through those channels which God has provided for its reception.

Shall we ask God for a healthy appetite, and also for a growing one, in order that as the days go by we may appropriate and assimilate more and more of Christ, and thus enter into the life more abundant? Do not let us live upon the husks that the swine do eat, when for every one of us there is bread enough and to spare in Him who is our meat and drink.

ii. *The Composition of the Loaves*

In the preparation of the bread used in the Holy Place, one can discern several features of our Lord's Person and work. In the directions regarding the bread as we have them in Leviticus 24:5, 6, we gather the following facts.

Fine Flour

Such material indicates the same truth that is set forth in the *fine linen,* namely, the spotless perfection of the character of Jesus. Flour is a product of the earth and becomes flour after the wheat has been bruised and crushed. So our Lord in one sense was a product of the earth, a root out of a dry ground, and as "the corn of wheat," He was bruised and crushed and thus made fine flour.

Look at the earthly life of Christ! Why, Pilate had to confess that he found no fault in Him! As one remarks,

> He was without spot. As fine flour He was tested and tried—tempted at every point by God, and man, and demons, but always and everywhere He was the same. No unevenness, no irregularity, everything was methodic, uniform, straightforward, pure. You turn "fine flour" anyway you may, it is still fine flour. No sifting, pressing, or bruising can alter its character. How does our character correspond with the fine flour? Are we the same joyful trusting Christians in adversity as in prosperity? Are we always and everywhere alike? Does change of circumstances never bring out any pride, coarseness, impatience or self-seeking? Alas! Alas!

Baked

This fine flour was thereafter baked into twelve cakes before being presented before the Lord. This baking process typifies the final agonies and sufferings of Christ. During His earthly life He had to be bruised and crushed, and such bids us remember His trials, sorrows, and temptation that beset His pathway. But at last the fine flour was baked, for upon the cross, when all around was dark and fearful and full of wrath and terror, our Saviour bows His head and dies. What a fiery furnace He passed through! But through it He went, and now our souls feed upon Him who is the bruised wheat and the baked cakes. He could not become the food of His people apart from sorrow and death, and die He did that we might live forevermore.

No Leaven

In the composition of those loaves, no other ingredient was used apart from the fine flour mixed with water. No leaven or artificial baking powder were used. No leaven was used because throughout the Bible it is the type of evil. And as the bread is a figure of Christ, the absence of leaven is in order, for in Him was no guile. He alone could say, "The prince of this world cometh, and hath nothing in me" (John 14:30).

Two Tenth Deals

The tenth speaks of responsibility. Jacob gave a tenth of what he had to God. *Ten* represents responsibility, Godward and manward, as can be shown by the Ten Commandments, five of which have a Godward aspect, and the other five a manward aspect. In the formation of the loaves, there were two tenth deals, and the ten being doubled speaks of full and adequate testimony regarding Christ. He fulfilled all obligations, Godward and manward, and such is testified to in a sufficient manner by the fulness of testimony, Jewish and Gentile.

Sprinkled with Frankincense

After the loaves were placed upon the table in two rows they were sprinkled with frankincense (Lev. 24:7). The word *frankincense,* we are told by Henry Soltau, springs from a word signifying "to be white." The word *Lebanon* is derived from the same root, so called because of its snow-clad summits, and the Hebrew word for "the moon" is also from the same root, so called because of its silvery whiteness.

Having such a white appearance has suggested the thought that possibly the modern practice of "frosting" cakes, used on certain special occasions, such as marriage, etc., may have arisen from some tradition respecting the white aspect of the holy loaves of shewbread thus covered with frankincense.

Frankincense, being a growth of the earth (See Song of Sol. 4:16), as well as the flour, and then added to the cakes upon the table, seems to express another aspect and truth respecting the Lord Jesus as a Man, namely, the purity and fragrance manifested by Him towards God in all His ways, actions, and thoughts. The purity of the ways and words of Jesus was not an affected sanctity, neither was it attained by separation from the haunts of men; it was not the mere result of habit, because observed by others, nor was its object the applause of men; but it was the natural result of the spotlessness of His own nature. This can be more clearly seen when one considers the epithet "pure" that is attached to the word in Exodus 30:34.

The word "pure" here is a different one from that which is used in connection with the gold employed in the formation of some of the Sanctuary vessels. The word "pure" when used in reference to the gold is "Zachar," and signifies the "intrinsic purity of nature, as contracted with uncleanness of nature; it is therefore used to designate beasts that are clean."

The other word used in connection with the frankincense is "Tahore" indicating "a purity practically developed and manifested." He, therefore, that was "Tahore," pure like the gold by nature, was also "Zachar," pure like frankincense in His ways.

Further, the Bread had no fragrance of itself pure though it was, and the death of the Cross that Christ passed through, and which is seen in type in the Baked Bread had no fragrance in itself for two others died the same death at the same time. Christ's death is efficacious in that the One Who died was not a malefactor, but the Mighty God. It is because of what He was that His death is able to accomplish what it does.

The frankincense upon the Bread speaks then, of the Divine worthiness of the offering of Christ, a worthiness imputed unto us as believers.

If we are continually partaking of Him who is so fragrant, then we shall become like Him. Says another exponent of the tabernacle types,

> We shrink rather sometimes, do we not, from the consideration of this truth, that our lives should be fragrant? Fragrant, sweet, and holy in-

> cense in the presence of our God, they ought to be. Not only our spiritual life or our Church life, but our daily life also, ought to be sweet and holy and fragrant; a life that should come up "as the evening sacrifice" before our God, and diffuse its perfume among our fellow men, that they might be charmed with the beauty of our Christianity.

But alas! it is not. Our spiritual life should be fragrant and beautiful, free from bitterness and uncharitableness; gentle and loving towards the fallen and the lost; pitiful and kind and gracious; deep and fervent in its love for God; but too often it is not. Yet this fragrance is one of the first and highest objects of our Christianity, which should purify and sweeten and enrich our lives.

> Like a watered garden,
> Full of Fragrance rare,
> Lingering in His Presence,
> Let my type appear.

iii. *The Order of the Loaves*

Under the orderly arrangement of these loaves, with their white covered tops there are one or two spiritual thoughts for our faith to lay hold upon, and for our hearts to feed upon.

Their Number

Seeing that the number of loaves placed upon the table was twelve, we naturally infer that such a number represents the twelve tribes of Israel, one loaf for each tribe. Although there was a vast difference between the tribes, both in respect to their numbers and character, yet there was one loaf for Reuben, "unstable as water," one for Dan, "a serpent in the way," one for the royal tribe of Judah, and one for the favored tribe of Benjamin.

There was no difference regarding these loaves, they were of the same material, of the same weight, and of the same size. "What a picture of our high calling as Christians! There may be differences and distinctions among us, but we are all alike before God. Our gifts, talents, and experiences may differ one from the other, but being 'accepted in the Beloved' we are 'all one in Christ Jesus.' The same Christ in all His wholeness is at the disposal of the most humble believer."

Their Arrangement

Although it is very apparent that the loaves were set in two rows, six in each row, yet there has been diversity of opinion regarding their exact arrangement. Our God, is One of Order, not of confusion. "Order is Heaven's first law." When Dr. A. Bonar was showing his model of the tabernacle in a cottage, he put the question to a company of shrewd old women as to whether the loaves should be piled up in two columns of six each, or set forth in two rows of six each. At once one of them said, "Not piled up one on another." "Why?" "They would mold before the end of the week." Under this thought, there are some deeply spiritual thoughts in an homily by Dr. Alexander Smellie in his *Secret Place*. The heading of his daily portion for August 20 reads, "Who sweeps a room as for Thy laws." Dr. Smellie then develops many sweet truths upon the following points:

> The Cakes were baked by busy and skilful hands.
>
> Are they not a symbol of the daily task in which I must occupy myself?
>
> The Cakes are laid on the pure Table before the Lord.
>
> So my common duties are performed in His sight and under His scrutiny.
>
> The Cakes are Sprinkled with Frankincense.
>
> Invest my craftsmanship . . . with greater loveliness and costlier worth.
>
> The Cakes are a delight to God.
>
> In my homeliest labour I would be ambitious to bring happiness to God.

Their Removal

The cakes remained in all their freshness on the table for a week, seven days, that is, a complete cycle or period of time. Every Sabbath freshly baked cakes, fragrant with frankincense, were placed by the priests upon the gold covered table. Christ was before God during the whole of His life even as the bread was before God in the Holy Place seven days. *Seven* is the symbol of perfection, and, seven days being a complete or perfect period, suggests that God discovered no trace of evil in His well beloved Son during the complete cycle of His life.

But there is another thought that we can take out of this Sabbath changing. "Every Sabbath he shall set it in order," and says Dr. Bonar, "Sabbath days are well-days in the desert journey – days when we fill the waterskins to journey on to another well." Truly this is the meaning of our Sabbaths! God intends these holy days when we turn aside from the world with hungry hearts to be days when we can feed afresh upon Him who is the only true sustenance of our souls. The bread was changed every Sabbath! Let us strive to eat fresh bread! We cannot keep fresh if we live upon the stale bread of old experience. We ought to have a renewal at least once a week.

iv. *The Partakers of the Loaves*

The table, as we have suggested, speaks of fellowship, and the instructions regarding these twelve loaves in respect to their consumption sets forth in a most expressive way the glorious mutual fellowship that God and man have in our Lord and Saviour, Jesus Christ.

Before the Lord

We are told that the bread had to be set in order and then left "before the Lord" for seven whole days, suggesting thereby God's side of the feast. For that complete period of a week Jehovah gazed upon the loaves and had them so to speak "all to Himself." Christ is the Father's delight, is He not? Looking down upon those twelve loaves – pure, white, fragrant loaves – He would think and feast upon Him who was the object of His love. Listen to the way in which God speaks of Him:

"Behold my servant, . . . mine elect, in whom my soul delighteth" (Isa. 42:1).

"Before the hills was I brought forth . . . I was daily His delight" (Prov. 8:25, 30).

"This is my beloved Son, in whom I am well pleased" (Matt. 3:17).

"Christ also hath loved us, and hath given himself for us an offering and a sacrifice to God for a sweet-smelling savour" (Eph. 5:2).

Yes, Christ was, and is, and will ever be, "the Bread of God."

For the Priests

The presence-bread after the seventh day became the food of the priests. "And it shall be Aaron's and his sons'; and they shall eat it in the holy place" (Lev. 24:9; 22:2). After these twelve loaves had been before the Lord for a week, gladdening and satisfying His heart, they became the food of Aaron and his house. And are not we priests unto Him?

Is the true church of God a holy priesthood? And is it not our privilege, our portion, to feast upon the same object of delight as God's? We cannot fully comprehend this truth, yet here it is. Feasting upon Christ! Men feast with God upon the Saviour, for "truly our fellowship is with the Father and with (yes, and over) His Son, Jesus Christ."

Beloved, we are called upon to participate with God in that which is so exceedingly precious to Himself. Are we feeding thus? The Priest was called to be a partaker with His God, and this is communion. What do we know of such holy communion? Is Christ the same source of joy and delight and fragrance to us as He is to the Father? We must feed upon Him not just every Sabbath, but every moment of every day. Then it must be remembered that the priests had to eat the hallowed bread not outside the tabernacle but in the Holy Place. No believer can find enjoyment in Christ unless he is holy. Sanctification and sustenance go hand in hand. The more I desire to be holy, the more shall I be strengthened and sustained as I think of Christ. Holy bread must be eaten in the Holy Place by Holy men!

For the Priests Only

In the instructions given regarding the eating of this bread, it is specifically stated that priests only had the right to eat of such. Two extreme cases where such a law was waived aside can be found in I Samuel 21:4-6 and Matthew 12:4.

In turning again to Leviticus 22, we gather that several restrictions were imposed upon them by God. Let us look at them for our spiritual profit, and observe at the same time that the Lord does not give that which is holy unto the dogs, neither does He cast His pearls before swine. As none but a holy priest could feed upon the bread, so none but God-like men and women can appreciate the worth of Christ.

Restriction regarding Defilement

In the fourth verse of Leviticus 22, we read "What man soever of the seed of Aaron is a leper, or hath a running issue, he shall not eat of the holy things, until he be clean." Such a person was prohibited from eating the holy bread not because he was outside the priestly house; that point was settled for it is, "what man soever of the seed of Aaron," but because as a priest he was defiled, by reason of his defilement he was for the present disqualified from enjoying the privilege of feasting upon the bread. Fellow priests, shall we not examine our own hearts and see if there is any taint of the leprosy of indulged or cherished sin unfitting us to hold communion with such a holy God? Christ can only be enjoyed as the holy bread, as we seek to obey the injunctions regarding uncleanness laid down for the priests of Aaron's house in Leviticus 22:5-9, and for believers of the Church of God in II Corinthians 6:14-18.

Restrictions regarding Strangers

"There shall no stranger eat of the holy thing" (Lev. 22:10). That means one who was not an Israelite, a chosen one. But we were all strangers once, for in our unconverted days we "were without Christ, being aliens from the commonwealth of Israel, and strangers from the covenants of promise, having no hope, and without God in the world" (Eph. 2:12), and as such we had no part or lot in Christ, for we hid as it were our faces from Him. But we have been made nigh by the blood of Christ, and are now "fellowcitizens with the saints, and of the household of God." This restriction still holds good, for what stranger, or unregenerated person, can comprehend the truth of Christ or derive any spiritual sustenance from the sacred emblems he partakes of upon the Communion Sabbath? The stranger cannot eat the holy bread.

Restrictions regarding Sojourners

"No sojourner of the priest," adds the Word. A sojourner was one who, although an intimate friend of the priest, only tarried for a short time under his roof, but did not belong to the priestly family. How many sojourners there are in the professed church! John refers to such in his first epistle. "They went out from us, but they were not of us" (I John 2:19).

They appeared to be believer-priests but they were only sojourners after all.

To treat it in another light. Are you a sojourner of some priest? Or, to put it thus, have you some connection with godly friends? Are you a child of many prayers and entreaties? Then do not be deceived, your attachment or connection with such will never bring to you the true worth of Christ. There must be the priestly character and the personal contact or appropriation of Christ, ere the treasures of His grace are opened. Yet again, as a sojourner is one who passed from place to place, let us never imagine that we can enjoy the fulness of Christ if we fail to abide with and in Him!

Restrictions regarding Hired Servants

"Nor an hired servant shall not eat of the holy thing," says the Lord. One who serves for wages, and who is seeking to work in the service of the Lord merely because it is his profession or calling, as the ministry is often termed, then he is an "hireling," to use the designation of our Saviour, the true shepherd of the sheep. A hired servant is one who acts upon compulsion and only works when there is no other alternative. Such a one can never enter into the real spiritual truth regarding the Lord. Talk, preach, and write about Him he may, but like the two men upon the Emmaus Road, the eyes are "holden." It was only when their eyes were opened that they knew Him (Luke 24:16, 31).

Bought Ones

"If the priest buy any soul with his money, he shall eat of it" (Lev. 22:11). Have we not every right, as believers, to feed upon Christ in holy fellowship? We are His bought ones, paid for with the purchase price of His own precious blood (I Cor. 6:19, 20; I Pet. 1:18, 19; Rom. 8:14-17). We likewise appreciate and appropriate Christ as we labor for Him. How many souls have we bought with our prayers, tears, and entreaties?

Born Ones

"He that is born in his house, they shall eat of his meat." Here again we see our right to enjoy Christ, for have we not been born in His house (Rom. 8:15; I John 3:1-3)? Hence, we have regeneration as born ones, as well as redemption as bought ones, our birth and His blood, as our right and privilege to feast upon the holy bread of heaven.

Priest's Daughter Unequally Yoked

In verse twelve of Leviticus 22, there is a passage that should cause many to think—"If the priest's daughter also be married unto a stranger, she may not eat of an offering of the holy things." Here we have a solemn warning for those believers who take the fatal step of becoming unequally yoked together with unbelievers. Notice in the restriction before us that the relationship was unaltered, the woman remained a priest's daughter, "but through an unholy alliance, having united herself to a stranger, she had acted in direct disobedience to God; her communion was broken, her high privileges were forfeited." Never tell me that a believer can be the same spiritually if there comes any willing alliance with any person or thing that is not of God. Why, there are tragic stories that many breaking hearts could tell, of lost peace, joy, fellowship, and of spiritual blessing just because there has been some marriage with a stranger, or an alliance with some worldly thing. The next verse shows the pathway back to restored fellowship—"If the priest's daughter be a widow, and have no child, and is returned to her father's house, as in her youth, she shall eat of her father's meat." The message is very plain—let there come separation, repentance, and return to God, and then His generous hand will bestow its richest blessings and once again the restored one can gather with joy at His feet; and feast upon His love and presence.

Partial Appropriation

Turning back to Leviticus 21:16-24, we discover a few particulars regarding priests who had some physical defect. What is to be done with these priests who are not as whole as they ought to be, not through any apparent fault of their own, but because they are found so? Why, although not privileged to "come nigh to offer the bread of his God," yet he could "eat the bread of his God, both of the most holy, and of the holy" (Lev. 21:21, 22). So there are many of us with defects of some nature or another. We may be feeble, lame, or dwarfed, as the case may be, but we are not thereby excluded from the fellowship of the saints. The Lord is very gracious with us, and if we are walking up to the light we have received, then all is well. With our growing spiritual apprehension, we experience as we daily feed upon Christ and find our desires for Him intensified, greater spiritual health and strength. Many there are who are lame from their spiritual infancy, thus resembling Mephibosheth, who was lame on both feet from childhood as the result of carelessness. Yet he came to feast regularly at the king's table.

Do not let us be too severe upon those who cannot enjoy Christ as we can. Possibly, like Mephibosheth, they are lame because of some carelessness, the careless living of some saint, or careless teaching received at or soon after the time of spiritual birth. Let us pray for them unceasingly, that Christ may be formed in them. For as they continue feasting upon the holy bread, it will not be long before they pass from their apparent defects into likeness to the Lord. What more can we say? Simply this, in closing. The ordinance of the loaves is spoken of as a "memorial," an "everlasting covenant." Christ will be our food for ever. Sweet to our taste now! But how much more will He be when we see His face, and feast upon Him through all eternity! We would fain linger upon this blessed theme of fellowship, but enough has been written to whet our appetite for more of Him, who is our soul's heavenly meat and drink.

> Saviour, of Thee we ne'er would tire;
> The New and living Food
> Can satisfy our heart's desire,
> And life is in Thy Blood.

(e). *The Golden Altar of Incense*

For full information respecting the directions given, as to the function of this altar, one is referred to Exodus 30:1-10; 37:25-29; 39:38; 30:5, 9, 16, 26, 27; Leviticus 4:7, 18; 16:12; Numbers 4:16; 16:17, 40, 46.

Having now reached the third and remaining vessel within the Holy Place, we enter into a fuller knowledge of our Lord's gracious Person and work. Such, of course, is the purpose of God, for traveling inward as we are to the Holiest of All, there is unveiled to us, step by step, a deeper insight into the august truths that surround the glorious Saviour we love.

Looking for a moment at the two vessels we have already considered and at the one we are now to meditate upon, we discover that these three vessels within the Holy Place beautifully sum up not only our Lord's character and work, but also our privileges and blessings as part of His body. "And," says Solomon, "a threefold cord is not quickly broken" (Eccles. 4:12). Shall we think of them thus?

The golden Candlestick speaks of Light.

The Table of Shewbread speaks of Life.

The Golden Altar of Incense speaks of Liberty.

Light, life, and liberty, these three, and the greatest of these, as we shall see, is liberty. We can also express it in this way. As priests unto God, we have a threefold need of light, food, and communion, and all three are symbolized in the three articles within the Holy Place.

As believers, the correct order of these three vessels in respect to their spiritual application can be set out as follows:

The inward life, represented by the table of shewbread, and sustained by Him who is the Bread of Life.

The upward liberty, represented by the golden altar of incense, and which signifies the liberty of access that we have into His presence, to pray.

The outward light, represented by the golden candlestick, and which is made possible by Him who is our light.

Then, again, a believer is one viewing his life in this threefold way:

Christ begets and sustains the inward life.

Christ makes it pleasing to God and to Himself.

Christ causes it to be beneficial to those around.

There are other very interesting ways in which we can treat the threefold truth unfolded here in these three golden pieces of furniture:

A believer has a threefold nature.

The mind is illuminated by Him who is the light.

The heart feeds upon Him who is the meat and drink.

The will is made submissive by contemplating Him who is the golden altar of incense.

Or spirit, soul, and body can be fittingly applied.

A believer has a threefold charge. He must — witness, and so confession is meant by the golden candlestick.

wait, and so meditation is typified by the table of shewbread.

worship, and so intercession is represented by the golden altar of incense.

A believer has a threefold need of Christ.

He has — darkness, caused by ignorance and disobedience, and this is scattered by the illumination of the Lord.

weakness, caused by lack of spiritual food, and such is banished by feeding upon Him who is our heavenly sustenance.

defectiveness, caused by the failure of prayer, but such is remedied as we contemplate Him who is our intercessor.

A believer has need of the Trinity. Surely it is not straining the symbolical aspect of these three vessels when we seek to find in them sublime truths that suggest the three blessed Persons who form the Trinity.

The golden altar of incense brings us to the Father, inasmuch as our intercessor is before Him appearing on our behalf.

The table of shewbread leads us to the Son, who is the food, and the only food for His redeemed ones.

The golden candlestick connects us with the Holy Spirit, who is the only divine source of illumination.

Let us now turn our concentrated attention to the golden altar of incense and endeavor by the guidance of the Holy Spirit to fully apprehend its all-important teaching. For the sake of clarity it may be best to group our material around these two aspects:

The Golden Altar
The Fragrant Incense

i. *The Golden Altar*

Regarding the golden altar itself,

there are several very arrestive features that demand our earnest thought and study.

Designation

In Exodus 39:38, this "altar to burn incense upon" is termed "the golden altar." And such it was, not only because it was overlaid with pure gold, but because it is in definite contrast to the other altar in the Outer Court, which was a brazen altar. We must not forget that there were two altars distinct in their respective office and offerings –

There was the brazen altar in the Outer Court, upon which the sacrifices were offered.

There was the golden altar in the Holy Place, upon which nothing but incense was offered.

At the brazen altar there was continual bloodshed, occasioned by sin.

At the golden altar there was perpetual fragrance, occasioned by incense.

The one is a necessary complement of the other, and taken together they both reflect the glories of Jesus Christ, our Lord.

At the brazen altar we see our Saviour upon the cross dying for us.

At the golden altar we see our Saviour, risen and glorified, living for us.

Out at the brazen altar He stood for us in the place of death, and met our deep need as guilty sinners.

Within at the golden altar we learn that He lives for us in the presence of God, and that all our need as saints and worshipers is met by Him.

Moreover, the divine order must never be reversed. It is still the altar of sacrifice first, then the altar of worship. Man would reverse the order by seeking to appease God, and merit His favor by prayers and religious acts, but there is only one way by which man has access to God and is acceptable in His sight, and that is upon the ground of the finished work of Calvary, as typified by the altar with its sacrifices.

Commenting on the verse of the much-loved Evangelical hymn,

> Just as I am without one plea,
> But that Thy Blood was shed for me,
> And that Thou biddest me come to Thee,
> O, Lamb of God, I come—

a preacher of a past century said, "We have His Blood and His Bidding as our only ground of approach, and what more do we need?"

There is one other interesting feature that it is as well to draw attention to ere we leave the point under consideration. It is this – that the mention of the golden altar is omitted in the enumeration of the vessels of the tabernacle, when the command was being given to Moses. Such an omission is very apparent, as can be gathered from a careful reading of this verse: "Thou shalt set the table without the veil, and the candlestick over against the table on the side of the tabernacle toward the south: and thou shalt put the table on the north side" (Exod. 26:35).

There is no reference to the golden altar until we come to Exodus 30. Why is this? Well, the reason is not hard to find! The golden altar was connected with High-priestly ministration; it represents a ministry in heaven, so to speak, therefore it is not mentioned or described until after Exodus 28 and 29, which have to do with the choosing, clothing, and consecration of the High Priest and the priestly family.

Such is as it should be, for as priests, we must first of all be sure of our calling and consecration ere we can effectually serve God at the altar of incense. As W. Lincoln puts it, "Now the priesthood has been instituted there can be priestly worship." Personal fitness before personal fragrance!

Another significant omission is found in Hebrews 9:2 – "There was a tabernacle made; the first, wherein was the candlestick, and the table, and the shewbread; which is called the sanctuary." Here, again, we find the other two vessels of the Holy Place referred to, but no word regarding the golden altar, the reason being that *Hebrews* speaks of the veil being rent that divided the Holy from the Most Holy Place, and spiritual incense being offered at "the blest Mercy Seat." The golden altar is now in Heaven – "Let us therefore come boldly unto the throne of grace, that we may obtain mercy, and find grace to help in time of need" (Heb. 4:16).

Blessed be His name. "Through him we both (Jew and Gentile) have access by one Spirit unto the Father" (Eph. 2:18). Here we see the Trinity connected with the fragrant intercession of our Lord. Well might we sing,

> Arise, my soul, arise
> Shake off thy guilty fears;
> The bleeding Sacrifice
> In my behalf appears;
> Before the throne my Surety stands;
> My name is written on His hands.

Dimensions

In common with all the altars described in Scripture, the golden altar was "foursquare" (Exod. 30:2), its length and breadth being equal. According to English measurements, this altar was 18 inches long, 18 inches broad, 36 inches high.

First of all, it was foursquare. Now "a square is a compact, even-sided figure, and seems to have been especially selected for the form of the altars, in order to represent the completeness and fulness of the work effected thereon, whether of sacrifice or incense. The same perfect measure and estimate was thus presented every way, whether towards God, or towards man. Firmness also, and stability, are betokened by the same figure." Thus, being foursquare, the golden altar represents the perfection and fulness of our Saviour's gracious intercessory work.

Then it was 36 inches high, which means, if we compare it with the other measured vessels of the Holy and Most Holy Places, that it was 9 inches higher than either the mercy seat or the table of shewbread. Thus, the golden altar took the lead in the sanctuary, teaching us the lofty standing of our great High Priest in the presence of God. For truly He is "higher than the heavens" (Heb. 7:26).

Having gone into heaven itself, there to continually intercede for His people, His intercessions are ever effectual because they are answered according to the value of the sweet fragrance and merit of His own peerless name. How blessed it is to know that although we cannot fully appreciate the full value of the Saviour's work and worth, God can – and that He does bless us according to His own high estimation of the work and worth of His well-beloved Son!

Description

Although there is the repetition of many things under this point that we have mentioned several times, yet it is well to refresh our memories regarding all the excellencies and glories of Him who is our great and gracious intercessor.

It was fashioned out of shittim wood

Here, again we are brought face to face with His humanity. Is it not consoling to know that as a man, Christ proved the value of prayer? Who can fathom the depths of a verse like this? – "Who in the days of his flesh, when he had offered up prayers and supplications with strong crying and tears unto him that was able to save him from death, and was heard in that he feared" (Heb. 5:7).

It was overlaid with gold

These two materials, wood and

gold, combine the glory of His Person as we have often seen. In the epistle to the Hebrews, an epistle which forms a wonderful commentary upon the tabernacle, there is set forth in a very wonderful way this twofold aspect of our Lord's nature.

In Hebrews 1, the writer proves the deity of Christ from Old Testament Scriptures, showing Him to be the Son of God – "Unto the Son, he [God] saith, Thy throne, O God, is for ever and ever" (Heb. 1:8).

In Hebrews 2 from the same inspired Word the apostle proves the humanity of Christ – "He took on him the seed of Abraham. Wherefore in all things it behooved him to be made like unto his brethren" (Heb. 2:16, 17).

Bearing in mind that the golden altar signifies the truth of Hebrews 7:25 – "He ever liveth to make intercession for them," let us see how this twofold view of Christ's Person helps us to understand the efficacy of Christ's priestly intercession.

The altar of incense was made of shittim wood and Christ became flesh, was made like unto us, and therefore because He was made like unto us, and resorted to the ministry of prayer when tempted in all points like as we are, so now He fully understands all our cares, needs, and daily perplexities.

But the altar was overlaid with gold, and as such speaks of His deity. As the man, He understands our infirmities, but as God He helps and succors us and meets our needs. So both truths are combined in Hebrews 4:14-16 – "Seeing then that we have a great high priest, that is passed into the heavens, Jesus the Son of God [humanity and deity combined], let us hold fast our profession. For we have not an high priest which cannot be touched with the feeling of our infirmities; but was in all points tempted like as we are, yet without sin." With this blessed result – "Let us therefore come boldly unto the throne of grace, that we may obtain mercy, and find grace to help in time of need."

It had a crown of gold around the edge

"Thou shalt make unto it a crown of gold round about" (Exod. 30:3). In this command we see how the coals of fire were kept upon the table. The crown was simply a ridge or rim encircling the table, thus preventing either the burning coals or the holy perfume from being scattered or displaced. The altar of incense thus crowned with gold indicates that the priestly power of Christ is preserved and assured because He Himself is now crowned with honor and glory.

Says the apostle, "We see Jesus, who was made a little lower than the angels for the suffering of death, crowned with glory and honour" (Heb. 2:9). Here we can see the two altars. But there was no crown around the altar outside, the holy place where the victims were slain, where goats, lambs, and bullocks tasted death for every man. No, nothing but blood and ashes there!

This reminds us of Calvary. There was no diadem of glory on the brow of the Holy Sufferer there; only the tangled thorn-crown with the ruby blood-drops – jewels of priceless value to the believer's heart. But on that very brow, where wicked hands entwined a crown of thorns, the hand of God has put a crown of glory and honor. His "sufferings" are past, His "glories" must follow.

The crown of gold is round about Him now! Can we not add to its luster by living holy, fragrant lives of submission and intercession? "We see Jesus crowned"! But by altering one word can we say "We have Jesus crowned"? God has crowned Him with "glory and honor." Shall we not likewise

> Bring forth the Royal Diadem
> And crown Him Lord of All?

It had four horns

At each corner of the golden altar there was a horn fashioned out of shittim wood and overlaid with gold. Remarks Henry Soltau,

> Horns are peculiarly a characteristic of all the altars of which a description is given in the Word of God (Exod. 27:2; 30:2; Ezek. 43:15).
>
> The readers of Scripture are familiar with the constant use of these emblems, as types of power and dignity. The power and strength of the altars seems to have been concentrated in the horns.

Taking the horns, then, as the symbol of power, we have unfolded the blessed truth of the power of our Lord's intercession. A very fitting illustration can be gathered from Peter's experience in Luke 22:32 – "I have prayed for thee, that thy faith fail not."

Then, being four in number suggests that as the four camps of Israel took up their several positions with reference to the tabernacle – Judah, east; Reuben, south; Ephraim, west; and Dan, north – a horn would point toward each of these four camps and the incense from the altar would have equal reference in all its value and power to each of the tribes. The spiritual substance of this shadow is that Christ's intercessions are equally efficacious for all. Scattered as they are to the four quarters of the earth, believers everywhere can rejoice in the fact that He ever liveth to make intercession for them.

It had two golden rings and staves

From Exodus 30:4; 37:27 one gathers that there were only two rings for the staves, instead of four as on the table of shewbread. These two rings were placed at two corners immediately under the crown, or ridge, and meant that the altar was carried cornerwise, instead of what we should familiarly term *square;* and as it was carried so it would be deposited, and would stand in the tabernacle.

The presence of the rings and staves proclaim that the altar was ever ready for the march, and that wherever the Israelites traveled the golden altar was by their side. What is the lesson here? Is it not that in every need, circumstance, or place we can prove the value of our Lord's priestly intercession? Was this not the secret of Paul's midnight prayer in that Philippi prison? He certainly proved that

> Prison bars can not control
> The flight, the freedom of the soul.

"Lo, I am with you alway," or "day by day," as Dr. Weymouth adds. Do we live in the enjoyment of this truth? The altar had two rings: and we have the two golden rings of His faithfulness and love. Therefore let us seek to realize that our golden altar of incense is ever with us, no matter where we are, or may go.

Directions

Seeing that the altar of incense, like all other parts of the tabernacle, prefigures Him whose name is like ointment poured forth, particular and minute instructions are given relative to the position and service of the altar.

Before the Veil

"Thou shalt put it before the veil" (Exod. 30:6). This command Moses fulfilled (Exod. 40:26). The veil was then hanging because it was the type of Him who would break down the middle wall of partition between the Father and sinners, thereby making it possible for all to enjoy direct access to the Holiest of All.

"Now, no veil intervenes to hinder our approach into God's presence: and not only have we access with boldness into the holiest through the blood, but there is also 'an High Priest over the house of God,' Who has living active sympathies, ever presenting on our behalf a sweet fragrance of holiness and purity before the throne of Grace." Now it is our privilege to "Draw near with a true heart in full assurance of faith" (Heb. 10:19, 22). May we be delivered from creating any veil of our own that would in any way interfere with our approach to Him!

> May no earth-born cloud arise,
> To hide the Saviour from our eyes.

Before the Lord

Another name characterizing it and distinguishing it from the altar of sacrifice is the altar "Before the Lord" (Lev. 4:7, 18; 16:18, 20). In Revelation 8:3, it is designated as "the golden altar which was before the throne." Does not our intercessor appear in the presence of God for us? Is it not in His name that we speak to God? Are not our prayers effectual and our lives victorious because He, the living witness of purity and holiness, is ever before the Lord for us; Himself a speaking testimony and proof of the value and efficacy of His name? "Who is he that condemneth? It is Christ that died, yea rather, that is risen again, who is even at the right hand of God, who also maketh intercession for us" (Rom. 8:34).

Covered by Priests

"Upon the golden altar they shall spread a cloth of blue, and cover it with a covering of badgers' skins" (Num. 4:11). The altar in preparation for its journeys was first covered with a cloth of blue, and hence heaven's own color wrapped it up; over that was spread the badgers' skins, thus effectually protecting it from outward defilement or hurt. Is this provision for the wilderness experience of the altar not suggestive? Christ's intercessions are ever guarded, and so are ours. Protection is promised for our prayers and priestly service. Often our intercessions are Spirit-inspired, and doubtless we mean them because at the time they really came from our hearts, but we leave them uncovered, and within a few minutes or seasons of holy intercession, we go out to do or say something that exposes our prayers, thus causing them to lose their fragrance as they ascend to God, and their power as they are offered on behalf of others. The Devil does not fear our prayers so long as we do not cover them over with the cloth of blue, that is, with the covering of a heavenly, holy life.

ii. *The Fragrant Incense*

As we enter into the inner significance of the incense offered upon the golden altar just considered, shall we not silently ask the gracious Holy Spirit to surround our minds and hearts with the fragrance of the Lord's most holy presence in order that the spiritual message underlying such might lay hold of us? We should seek not merely to comprehend the truth, but to have the truth fully apprehend us.

Commands Regarding the Incense

Let us take this holy material and reverently examine it, for it is beautifully descriptive of Him who is more fragrant than all the incense and frankincense compounded together.

Its Ingredients

This holy perfume was composed or compounded of four different ingredients — "Take unto thee sweet spices, stacte, and onycha, and galbanum; these sweet spices with pure frankincense" (Exod. 30:34). We have dwelt upon the frankincense already, but here are three spices mentioned, stacte, onycha, galbanum, that are not mentioned elsewhere in Scripture, and of which no satisfactory description can be given.

These three perfumes are unknown to us. Possibly

> They may have been selected on that very account; in order thereby to designate a sweetness and fragrance not appreciable to human sense, but understood and valued by God alone. Who is able to enumerate the varied graces of Christ? or who can estimate their value? Our souls may and do indeed say—"He is precious," the fragrance of His sweet perfumes is wafted towards us; but our thoughts are poor, our words and expressions weak, when we seek to portray the beauties and excellencies of His Person.

Its Proportions

"Of each shall there be a like weight" (Exod. 30:34). Although each of the four ingredients weighed the same, and had its own peculiar aroma, yet when they were all blended together they formed one most fragrant perfume. And just as these spices which formed the incense were of even weight, no one preponderated over the other; varied as each was, so within such we see a type of Him in whom every grace had its due proportion, and its right place. Grace, mercy, truth, righteousness, all had their place in Him, and gave their fragrance to each thought, word and action. There was no preponderating feature to His character, so as to overpower or eclipse other graces; all was perfect, and all of even weight.

Its Formation

There is a most helpful thought in the words "Thou shalt make it a perfume, a confection after the art of the apothecary, tempered together, pure and holy" (Exod. 30:35). Coming at once to the anti-type, we discover, to use Soltau's words, that

> Together with all the sweetness exhibited in the ways of Christ, and the grace and love displayed by Him, attractive to the poor weary soul, there ever ascended also to God the fragrance of perfect purity and holiness. Here was purity, unmingled with one particle of human taint—motives that may be sifted, and most minutely scrutinized, and which will be found altogether fragrant, and free from the slightest shade of that selfishness and independence of God which so pervade even our best and fairest actions.

Then in respect to the formation of this fragrant perfume, are we not told how its aroma was really produced in a twofold way?

IT WAS BEATEN SMALL

The Divine command was, "Thou shalt beat some of it very small" (Exod. 30:36).

The purpose of finely pounding the incense was in order that its fragrance might be the more developed and to evidence the fact that each minute fragment had all the varied perfumes of the whole.

Coming to Christ's earthly life, can we not find in every word, every movement, however small, the diffusion of a sweet odor, pleasant alike to God and man? In the trivial and unnoticeable things He was as particular about pleasing His Father as in the greater matters of life. He once said, "He that is faithful in that which is least is faithful also in much." And Christ lived or practiced His own precepts. What a lesson there is for us in this truth!

IT WAS BURNT WITH FIRE

"He shall put the incense upon the fire before the LORD" (Lev. 16:13). Here we have another secret regarding the production of the fragrant smell of the incense. It was mixed with fire! After it was beaten small, the incense was thrown upon the burning coals taken off the brazen altar. It was the fire which consumed the sacrifice that brought the delightful aroma of the incense: the Holy Spirit thus signifying that it was Calvary that gives a continual, sweet fragrance to the intercessions of Christ.

Its Uniqueness

How clear, and yet solemn are the instructions given in Exodus 30:9, 37, 38, regarding the imitation of this holy incense! Anyone found making incense like it for his own use suffered a severe punishment. No imitations of the perfume were to be made. But how active we are with the manufacture of incense of our own! Many there are who seek by the savor of self-righteousness, and sweet incense of religiosity to please God; but such are an abomination unto the Lord. It is only the fragrance of Christ's life and work that makes anyone acceptable to God.

What "strange incense" (Exod. 30: 9). For there is strange incense, as well as "strange fire" the people of God try to offer! "How much of what passes for Christian grace and sweetness is really but a spurious fabrication of the human heart, for its own self-exultation, and the feeding of its own vanity! An apparent austerity passes under the name of holiness; a seeming lowliness gets the credit of humility; a smoothness or liberality, which speaks well of all, is called charity; and many an act which is attributed to self-denial nourishes the flesh instead of resisting it." May God deliver us from all imitations and substitutes! "Ye shall offer no strange incense thereon." These words must burn themselves into our minds.

Its Typical Import

It may be found helpful to gather together at this stage all the spiritual teaching of the altar and its incense. From various parts of Scripture we find that such is typical both of Christ and His believer-priests.

OF PRAYER OFFERED IN HIS NAME

How precious is the truth unfolded in passages such as Psalm 141:2 – "My prayer . . . before thee as incense."

Revelation 5:8 – "Golden vials full of odours [incense], which are the prayers of saints."

Revelation 8:3 – "There was given unto him much incense, that he should offer it with the prayers of all saints."

It is from these words that we have Scriptural authority for affirming that the golden altar of incense is a type not only of our prayers but of what makes our prayers acceptable, namely, the merit of our Lord.

> To Him shall endless prayer be made,
> And endless praises crown His head;
> His Name like sweet perfume shall rise
> With every morning sacrifice.

OF CHRIST HIMSELF

Turning to passages like Hebrews 7:25, "He ever liveth to make intercession," II Corinthians 2:14, 15, "A sweet savour of Christ," and many other indirect references, we learn that the golden altar of incense points to Christ. He is our great High Priest, who has passed through into heaven and who, in virtue of His death and Resurrection, is able to plead effectually for His people. At the right hand of the Majesty on high, in the presence of our Father and our God, He pleads our cause. And it is His powerful, prevailing, and priestly intercession that guards our earthly lives, succoring us in our need, and helping in all our priestly failure.

Further, our own prayers are often imperfect, being stained with selfishness and carelessness, our praises are so meager, our service for Him so weak and feeble, yet somehow they become acceptable to God because our gracious intercessor presents them richly perfumed with the sweet fragrance of His own intercession.

Then there are further glimpses of Him as our incense altar in these passages –

His Name. "Thy name is as ointment poured forth" (Song of Sol. 1:3).

Love from and for Him (Song of Sol. 1:12; 4:10; John 12:3).

OUR SERVICE FOR HIM

Coming to ourselves, we discover that our prayers, praises, and service are also likened unto incense ascending up to God as a sweet smelling savor, as these aspects prove:

Kindness to the Saints. "Gift . . . an odour of a sweet smell, a sacrifice acceptable, well-pleasing to God" (Phil. 4:17, 18).

Our continual praise to God. "Let us offer the sacrifice of praise to God" (Heb. 13:15).

Our benevolence to all Men. "Do good . . . communicate . . . for with such sacrifices God is well pleased" (Heb. 13:16).

Our Priestly Service. "An holy priesthood, to offer up spiritual sacrifices" (I Pet. 2:5).

Commands Regarding the Offering of the Incense

Summarizing the particulars given in respect to the offering up of the fragrant incense, one is deeply impressed with the further unfolding of our Lord's Person and work.

It had to be burnt upon the altar

This incense, "a perfume, a confection after the art of the apothecary, tempered together, pure and holy," had to be consumed upon the altar (Exod. 30:1). Is it not significant that the word for "altar" here is the same as that that is used for the brazen altar, namely "a place of slaughter"? The holy incense was burnt upon the altar – the place of slaughter! The truth unfolded is a precious one.

Already we have seen that the intercession of Christ is effectual because of His work upon the cross, but here the truth is developed. In fact, one can combine with this thought another that must not escape our attention, namely, that the blood was brought from the brazen altar and placed upon the horns of the altar of incense. The horns, we have indicated represent power and strength, and the blood being placed upon such suggests that the source of our Lord's priestly power as our intercessor is the death of Calvary. So with truly grateful and adoring hearts we sing,

> Five bleeding wounds He bears,
> Received on Calvary;
> *They* pour effectual prayers,
> They strongly plead for me;
> "Forgive him, oh forgive," they cry,
> "Nor let that ransomed sinner die."

Then again, we have a further expansion of this glorious fact in passages like Leviticus 16:12; Numbers 16:46, where we learn that the incense had to be mixed with the fire from off the altar of sacrifice. Does this not teach us that our Saviour's vocal prayers are powerful as with the silent plea of His wounds, because of the furnace of His agony? Not only so, we cannot come as suppliants into the presence of God at all save as we take our stand upon that mighty sacrifice offered on that great world-altar of Calvary. Our prayers are of no avail in His sight unless they are founded upon, and sanctified by the blood of our Lord and Saviour, Jesus Christ.

Yet again, let us notice that no strange fire, that is, any other fire save the fire from the brazen altar had to be used in the burning of the incense. What a solemn portion of God's word is Leviticus 10:1-10, where we have the awful judgment that overtook Nadab and Abihu because they offered strange fire, that is, other than the divinely commanded fire of Leviticus 16:12, before the Lord.

These two men were true priests and had true incense within their censers, but they used strange fire, fire that did not come down from heaven (Lev. 9:24). May God help us to dread the use of strange fire! Often it is mingled with our incense of service and intercessions, to our spiritual loss. The use of carnal means to carry on God's work, the fleshly, selfish ways that often characterize our lives, the desire for the praise of man, the glory of self – these and many other unworthy things from the strange fire.

It had to be Offered in Censers

This fact can be proved by looking at Leviticus 10:1 and Numbers 10:17, 46. The censers! Let these represent the heart that bears up and offers the petition or intercession to God. Why "nothing can be more glorious than to take the needs, cares, sorrows, hopes, fears, desires, and petitions of others, put them into one's censer, and go into the presence of our God and offer them there in priestly intercession that there might be brought down upon those for whom we pray the blessing of the Highest." Have we ever realized that privilege?

The word for *burn,* here, in connection with the incense burnt in the censer is a very arrestive one. It means, as we saw in connection with the burnt offering, "to consume or burn up." Are we burnt up, consumed with desires for holy intercession?

Twice over, in connection with the golden candlestick, the word *burn* signifies "to cause to go up." Shall we not borrow this thought also, and have continually that fragrant life of intercession, prayers ever going up to the great intercessor for ourselves and others? But let us not forget that worship is a large word covering intercession, prayer, adoration, fellowship, contemplation. May all ascend to Him!

It was Offered by Priests

References like Numbers 16:40; Deuteronomy 33:10 prove this. Have we not the privilege and joy of coming to the Lord in prayer? Are we not priests unto Him? A person unsaved may say prayers, but it takes a priest to pray effectually.

I often say my prayers,
But do I ever pray?

is a couplet that contains a solemn question for both saint and sinner. And, moreover, it is this truth that explains the sorrow and death that overtook those who were not born into the priestly family of Aaron, as for instance, Uzziah (II Chron. 26:18; see II Chron. 13:10, 11; Deut. 33:10; I Chron. 6:49; 9:30). None but those who have been born again can offer incense to God. Korah and others (Num. 16:1-35) – "The gainsaying of Korah" that Jude refers to was intrusion into the priests' office.

It was Offered by the High Priest

The ministry of the priests speaks of our intercession, and of its sweet fragrance that ascends to God, and at the same time of the blessing it brings to man; but the bearing of the incense by the *High Priest* into the Most Holy Place (Lev. 16:11-13), indicates the glorious intercessory of Him who has passed within the veil. "All the year round" says one, "the incense was offered by the common priest until on the Day of Atonement, it was gathered up as it were and consummated by the High Priest who put incense into his own censer and passed into the presence of the Highest. We said we were intercessors; yes, we are, but we are intercessors through Christ Jesus. . . . Without Him we can do nothing." So we have in this a beautiful figure of our Lord's intercession (Heb. 7:25; 9:24; John 17).

It will also be noticed that when the High Priest entered into the Holiest of All, once a year, and stood in the presence of the Shekinah glory, he was shielded by a cloud of incense, "that he not die" (Lev. 16:12, 13). Says the psalmist, "The LORD God is a sun [the Shekinah glory] and shield [the cloud of incense]" (Ps. 84:11).

It was Offered Night and Morning

When the morning and evening sacrifices were placed upon the brazen altar, fresh incense was put on the censer upon the golden altar; and doubtless it is to this that the psalmist refers in Psalm 141:1, 2: "Lord, I cry unto thee: make haste unto me; give ear unto my voice, when I cry unto Thee. Let my prayer be set forth before thee as incense; and the lifting up of my hands as the evening sacrifice."

These set times of worship and sacrifice were often times of special crisis and answered prayer. Read very carefully passages like Elijah, I Kings 18: 29; Ezra 9:5; Daniel 9:21; Peter and Cornelius, Acts 3:1; 10:2, 3, 30.

Is it not blessed to realize that "at the time our Saviour died on the Cross, the priest in the Temple must have been offering incense, and thus was probably standing in front of the veil when it was rent (Luke 23:44, 45; Matt. 27:45, 46, 51)." The *hour* of the Lord's death was foretold in the daily offering of the incense and the evening sacrifice, the *day* was foretold in the Passover; and the *year* in Daniel's prophecy (Dan. 9:25, 26).

Here are two sweet thoughts for us to feed upon — offered night and morning!

The Ceaseless Intercession of our Lord

As the morning opens for us with all its dangers, opportunities, needs, and cares, as we go out upon the unknown journey of each new day, how comforting to know that we leave behind us the morning intercession of our Lord, and that such is a guarantee of security and blessing.

Then when we return at night with the dust of the day upon us, with conscious failure, disappointment with a daily life that has not been altogether pleasing to Him, how blessed to know that He ever liveth to make intercession for us and that His evening incense is being offered for us.

The Continual Intercession of the Believer

As it was for the priest of old, so surely there is for those who are called to worship God in the service of the sanctuary the offering of the incense night and morning. We must have our set times of devotion with our Lord when we wave our golden censers containing saintly prayers before Him or else the fragrance of our life will disappear. May grace and desire be ours to emulate the example of David, who said, "Evening, and morning, and at noon, will I pray" (Ps. 55:17).

Not only so, but shall we not seek to make our whole life fragrant with prayer? Good it is to have our precious seasons of communion, private and public, but is it not better still to cast around every hour of the day whether we be in home, factory, or business, the perfume of prayer? It is the aroma of such a life that fills all the house with a delightful odor (John 12:3).

It was Offered Perpetually

"Aaron . . . shall burn incense upon it, a perpetual incense before the Lord throughout your generations" (Exod. 30:8). Such a thought is an expansion of the previous one: and what a blessed development it is. Christ not only intercedes night and morning, but perpetually!

Your Lord and mine intercedes throughout the generations. His prayers are forever efficacious on behalf of His people; and moreover I can rely upon them throughout this little life of mine, and throughout the earthly sojourn of His church. Perpetually, will He intercede for such until she is caught up to meet Him in the air, and then be forever without the range of having any needs requiring His priestly intercessions. But until that "day break," let us understand the twofold power of intercession that enfolds us. We have —

The Holy Spirit's intercession within us (Rom. 8:26, 27).

The Blessed Saviour's intercession above us in glory (Heb. 7:25; Rom. 8:3). The Holy Spirit intercedes within that we might not sin. The Saviour intercedes, and pleads His blood, above, if we do sin. Shall we not allow such mighty intercessors to create for us a life of priestly intercession, which like the perfume of the incense of old was pure and holy?

(f). *The Veil* (Exod. 26:31-37; 36: 35, 36; 39:34; 40:3, 21). The New Testament Anti-type is found in Hebrews 10:19, 20.

Turning from the holy vessels we now pause at the veil, as the priests must often have done, and behold its wonderful beauty and superb workmanship; and seek to penetrate by the Holy Spirit that which was hidden from the mind of any Israelitish priest as he looked upon the veil, namely, its spiritual application to Christ and to ourselves as believer-priests.

Regarding many parts of the tabernacle, there may be difference of opinion and judgment in respect to their spiritual interpretation, but of this we are certain, that the typical signification of the veil is beyond dispute, because, as we hope to show, we have definite Scriptural authority for treating the veil separating the Holy Place from the Most Holy Place as a God-given symbol of the glorious work that our Saviour has so perfectly accomplished.

It may be as well to refresh our memories by remarking that there were three veils, or coverings, connected with the three courts of the tabernacle in the wilderness.

There was the first veil, called the *gate*, which admitted any Israelite into the Outer Court, as he came to offer his sacrifice to Jehovah.

Then there was the second veil, called the *door*, admitting priests — and priests only — into the inner court, or Holy Place, in order that they might serve and worship Jehovah.

And then there was the third veil, the one we are now considering, which admitted the High Priest, and he only once a year, into the innermost court, or the Holy of Holies.

These three veils predict the Work of Christ:

He is the *gate* through which we enter, and in doing so we come to the altar of sacrifice which also is Himself (Matt. 7:14).

He is the *door*, leading us into all the holy privileges of the Holy Place. He calls Himself "the door" (John 10:1).

He is the *veil*, rent in twain as we shall presently see, thus providing immediate access into the presence of God.

Coming then to this third veil, we have these aspects:

i. *The Significance of the Veil*

Under this section there are one or two helpful thoughts to meditate upon in reference to the name given to the veil, and to the position it occupied in that structure of old.

The Name

According to one scholar the word *veil* is derived from an unused verb signifying "to break," and in a secondary sense "to separate." As one can easily see, such an interpretation of the word discloses part of its use or function. The veil was used for the purpose of separating, or breaking off the Holy Place from the Most Holy. In fact all the three veils spoke of separation.

The gate of the Outer Court separated the Jew from God.

The door of the Holy Place, the priest from God's holy service.

The veil of the Most Holy Place, the High Priest from God's most holy presence.

That veil also taught that God was not only *invisible,* but also *unapproachable,* except under strictly defined conditions. We can only come before Him on His own terms, and when accepted, the veil is only a *veil,* not a brick wall; not some immovable mass, but a light hanging even a child could lift or draw aside.

Moreover, these veils are a witness against sin, for in the beginning God and man lived together in blissful fellowship, but as the prophet Isaiah puts it, "Your iniquities have separated between you and your God, and your sins have hid his face from you, that He will not hear" (Isa. 59:3). But the glory of the Gospel is that the Lord Jesus has broken down the middle wall of partition separating us from God.

Turning to Numbers 4:5, we find this veil spoken of as "the Veil of Covering." Such a term appears to convey the idea of concealment. The veil covered or hid something that could not be seen. The women of the east veiled their faces.

The veil covered the ark, mercy seat, and the symbol of the divine presence from the sight of the priests while the tabernacle was standing (Exod. 40:3).

Then the veil was used to throw over and cover the ark itself when the tabernacle was dismantled and Israel was traveling through the wilderness (Num. 4:5). So it is aptly called "the Covering Veil."

It is in the thought of the veil hiding or covering something that we glean a precious truth regarding our Lord. The veil that covered the face of Moses concealed the glory gleaming within. The veil of unbelief over the heart of the Israelite Paul refers to in II Corinthians 3:13-18 hid the soul from the glory of God, as seen in the face of Jesus Christ.

Coming to our Lord, we find that the veil speaks of His body, and that such, like the veils referred to, had the power of concealment, for His body was the veil hiding the glory of His divine character from the gaze of men. Once, however, the veil was drawn aside upon the Mount of Transfiguration, and three disciples for one brief moment saw the covering removed and with awe-struck vision "beheld His glory, the glory as of the only begotten of the Father, full of grace and truth" (John 1:14).

Then in reading Hebrews 9:3, one finds the veil termed "the second veil," thus distinguishing it from the door that covered the Holy Place. The significance of this "second veil" is that "the presence of God could not be entered, His glory within could not be witnessed so long as the Veil stood unrent and the Mercy Seat unstained by blood – the witness of death."

The Position

The veil was hung between the Holy and Most Holy Places, right in front of the ark and mercy seat. Thus it is called "the veil of the testimony." And, being in such a position it revealed the fact that access to the mercy seat could only be gained as the veil was removed. The order of its removal was as follows:

The High Priest alone could remove it (Heb. 9:6, 7).

And he was not allowed to move it at all times, but only once a year (Lev. 16:2; Heb. 9:7).

Moreover, the High Priest could only remove it as he entered bearing the blood of sacrifice (Lev. 16:3; Heb. 9:7).

Once the veil was behind the High Priest, he stood within the Holiest of All, face to face with Jehovah, having nothing between. What a moment that must have been when the High Priest and God thus met!

How beautifully all this prefigures our Saviour's work upon Calvary. The veil had to be removed. Well, Christ became the veil, yes, and as such He must be removed, if God and man are to meet in holy communion, and removed He was. He was set aside, was He not, when those sin-blinded priests and rulers cried, "Away with Him! Away with Him!"? What was that experience but the tearing aside of the veil?

ii. *The Structure of the Veil*

Coming to the materials that composed the veil, we realize that it must have been an exquisite and lovely example of the highest skill and design. It certainly proved that the Lord had fulfilled His word in giving the makers of it special wisdom and qualifications. And the fact that it was made under the direct orders of God was a guarantee of the perfection and rare beauty of the work (Exod. 35:30-35). As we have already considered the spiritual significance of some of the thoughts suggested by the composition of this veil, let a brief reference suffice at this point.

The Curtain

The curtain or veil itself was made of fine-twined linen. And such is a type of the absolute, moral purity of our Lord in the days of His flesh. With perfect right He could stand and say, as no other, "Which of you convinceth Me of sin?" (John 8:46).

The Colors

The three colors woven or worked into the fine-twined linen have each their own divine message, as we can see by turning back to what we have said of them. The three were these:

The blue, being a heavenly color, depicts His association with heaven (John 3:13).

The purple, being a mixed color formed by mingling blue and scarlet together, speaks of Him as the God-man becoming our mediator.

The scarlet, being an earthy color, suggests the fact of His condescension in taking upon Himself the likeness of sinful flesh; and as a worm (for the scarlet dye is extracted from a particular worm), allowing Himself to be crushed in order that His crimson blood might cleanse our sin away.

Truly we can trace the Gospel in these colors!

The Cherubim

Covering the whole of this beautiful veil could be seen the lovely figure of the cherubim, which doubtless were worked into the linen in the three colors referred to. As the veil represents the earthly life of our Lord, that is, from His incarnation to His death upon the cross, there are four blessed truths connected with His character that can be gleaned from the symbolic reference to the cherubim in the book of *Ezekiel* (See Ezek. 1:5-10). In this passage the cherubim are represented as four living creatures having each one four different faces.

The Face of a Man

This particular face is indicative of mind, reason, sympathy, and of all the powers of a human being. And in this we behold our Lord, for as the man Christ Jesus, He had perfect human intelligence.

The Face of a Lion

In Scripture, the lion possesses a fourfold quality, all of which speaks of Him who came from the tribe of Judah whose ensign was the figure of a lion.

Strength — "A lion which is strongest amongst beasts" (Prov. 30:30).

Terribleness — "The king's wrath is as the roaring of a lion" (Prov. 19:12; 20:2).

Majesty — "The Lion of the tribe of Judah" (Rev. 5:5).

Dignity — "He also that is valiant, whose heart is as the heart of a lion" (II Sam. 17:10).

How descriptive these four qualities are of Him who sprang from the tribe of Judah, and who displayed

His lion-like power in overthrowing the power of him who is termed "the raging lion."

The Face of an Ox

There are at least two features of the ox that are noted for us in the Word of God:

Patient, persevering, enduring labor:

"Much increase is by the strength of the ox" (Prov. 14:4).

"That our oxen may be able to bear burdens" (Ps. 144:14, margin).

Knowledge of its master, or owner.

"The ox knoweth his owner, and the ass his master's crib" (Isa. 1:3).

Do we not find these two characteristics in connection with our Lord's life? They "prefigure the persevering resolution of Him Who unflinchingly set His face to the arduous work committed to Him by His Father, and Who always recognized His Father's will, and delighted to do it."

The Face of an Eagle

Such a symbol expresses "quickness and power of sight, and almost equal rapidity of action."

"She seeketh the prey, and her eyes behold afar off, . . . and where the slain are, there is she" (Job 39:29, 30).

"Too wonderful . . . the way of an eagle in the air" (Prov. 30:18, 19).

How blessed to know that keenness of sight and swiftness of execution fitly describes Him whose eyes search the depths of the heart and who is as rapid in discovering where the lawful prey is as in delivering it from the power of the destroyer. Is it not interesting to observe that the four Gospels that record the life and death of our Lord, that is, the veil whole and rent, each give us a portrait of the Saviour, as indicated above.

Matthew is – the face of a lion. In his Gospel we have the majesty and dignity of Christ. It is the *Gospel of the king,* stating His royal power.

Mark is – the face of an ox. It is the Gospel recording the gracious service and labor of our Lord. It is the *Gospel of the servant.*

Luke is – the face of a man. In this third Gospel we discover the full fragrance of our Lord's earthly life. It is the *Gospel of the man.*

John is – the face of an eagle – Here we see Christ as God. Here He rises higher than man, servant or earthly king. It is the *Gospel of Godhead.*

Thus, spread all over the veil were these figures, depicting Him who in the days of His flesh combined *in His gracious Person* all the glorious truths that they prefigured.

The Cunning Work

The sacred record tells us that the veil was made of "cunning work," or as it might be put, "the work of a deviser." It was skillfully wrought with wisdom and cunning device; a matchless fabric, copies from a heavenly pattern and never again to find its equal on earth."

Here we come to the deep mystical texture of our Lord's life, namely His wondrous birth. Truly the veil of His flesh was made of "cunning work" or "the work of a designer." And the cunning, or skillful, workman was none other than the Holy Spirit – "The Holy Ghost shall come upon thee, and the power of the Highest shall overshadow thee" (Luke 1:35).

Cunning work! Yes, our Lord's birth was such, for who can explain the mystery of His nature, who in the womb of the virgin became the God-man? Woven together into one glorious Person was deity and humanity. Cunning work the veil truly was, for "great is the mystery of godliness, God manifest in flesh."

iii. *The Supports of the Veil*

The divine command regarding the support of the veil was as follows: "Thou shalt hang it upon four pillars of shittim wood overlaid with gold: their hooks shall be of gold, upon the four sockets of silver" (Exod. 26:32). They were, first of all,

The Pillars

Passing by the composition of these, which were made of shittim wood overlaid with gold, the significance of which we are fully acquainted with, we pause to consider the truths suggested by the number of pillars employed. There were four, and not five, as at the door leading into the Holy Place.

A Universal Number

Four is a universal number, speaking of that which concerns the earth at large, e.g., there are four quarters of the earth, four seasons of the year, etc. So, when God was planning the redemption of the soul, He had in mind the salvation not only of an elect few but all mankind. Therefore Christ came as the propitiation for our sins: and not for ours only, but also for "the sins of *the whole world*" (I John 2:2). Now the way into God's presence is open for any and every poor sinner who comes to Him through Christ.

A Fourfold Description of Christ

We also have a fourfold view of Christ given to us by the apostle in I Corinthians 1:30. Christ Jesus, who of God is made unto us –

Wisdom – He imparts to us knowledge of God and of self and *is* the truth.

Righteousness – He gives us a new standing before God, an imputed righteousness.

Sanctification – In Christ we are assured of a holy state as well as a righteous standing.

Redemption – This expresses the final goal, the Resurrection of the body.

The Two Testaments

There is a deeper truth than most people imagine in some of these details we are considering. For example, the two Holy Places can be likened to the two parts of the Bible.

There is the Old Testament, akin to the Holy Place. Light there is, but it is dim in comparison to the Shekinah glory of the Most Holy Place. Now the entrance into the Holy Place was through a door suspended upon five pillars.

Have we not the five pillars at the entrance of the Old Testament? There is the *Pentateuch*, that is the first five books of the Bible which are called *Pentateuch*, a word meaning "five books." And such are full of our Lord, for He Himself said, "Moses wrote of me."

Then you have the New Testament, which is "the Holiest of All." Fuller and more glorious light bursts upon our vision as we pass through it. Entrance into "the Holiest of All" was through a four pillared veil, and this answers exactly to the four gospels that open our New Testament and present Christ to our adoring gaze.

Moreover, it is interesting to observe that these four pillars of the veil, unlike those on which the door hung, had no capitals; they ended abruptly, that is, they lacked the ordinary architectural completeness of a pillar. Does such a fact not suggest various passages of Old Testament prophecy like –

"He was cut off out of the land of the living" (Isa. 53:8),

"He shortened my days" (Ps. 102: 23, 24)?

Turning to the four Gospels, what do we find? Why, they all present at the close of each a Saviour *"cut off," crucified, and slain.*

The Sockets

These four gold-covered pillars safely reposed within, and were held securely by four silver sockets. The silver, connected with Atonement (Exod. 30:15, 16), testifies to the glorious foundation that we rest upon. Yes, and the sockets were unseen by the eye of man; and there was that in the cross of suffering and woe which man could not witness—"His *soul* was made an offering for sin"—and that God alone could fathom.

The Hooks

These were made of gold and were used for fastening the veil to the pillars. And what was it that fastened our Lord as the veil to the pillar of the cross, in order that He might be rent and thus open up a way for us into God's immediate presence? Why not Roman nails merely, but golden hooks, even the golden hooks of divine righteousness. Beloved, the veil was hung up by the hooks until it was rent in twain!

iv. *The Symbolism of the Veil*

Having classified the facts that concern the veil of the Most Holy Place, let us now enter more fully into its true spiritual teaching. From Hebrews 9:8 we learn that the Holy Spirit recognized the spirtual significance of the veil—"The Holy Ghost this signifying, that the way into the holiest of all was not yet made manifest, while as the first tabernacle was yet standing: Which was a figure for the time then present." It is these verses as well as others that form the basis of our symbolism or spiritual interpretation of the veil.

The Incarnation of Christ

Turning to Hebrews 10:20, we read, "Through the veil, that is to say His flesh." Such a verse turns our thoughts back to the Incarnation of our Lord, and proves the truth of the Christmas Carol, "Veiled in flesh the Godhead see."

During our Lord's earthly life, His human body veiled or covered the full manifestation of His deity. But "mere incarnation can do nothing for the sinner," says one.

> We are saved by the death of Christ. The antitype of the unrent veil is seen at Bethlehem, at Nazareth, and all the life long of the Christ of God. The miracles of grace wrought during His ministry were like the swaying of the folds of that veil before men's eyes; and so were His words of grace from day to day (Luke 4:22; John 7:46): while Matthew 16:21 is as if, standing before the veil and pointing to it, He had said, "That veil must be rent."

The Death of Christ

Such a thought brings us to the most sublime message of the veil, and as we ponder it may our gratitude to Christ be intensified as we think anew of His "free grace and dying love." In the Gospels we discover that at the hour of our Lord's Crucifixion, the beautiful veil was rent and removed forever, thus proving to us that such was a God-given type of the life and work of Christ.

It was a Divine Rent

Matthew and Mark both tell us that the veil in the temple was rent in twain from the top to the bottom at the very moment that our Saviour died (Mat. 27:50, 51; Mark 15:37, 38).

Why was it rent from "the top to the bottom" and not from the bottom to the top? Because the rending of the veil typified the Redemption of Christ as a divine work. Had the veil been rent from the bottom, it would have meant that man had done it, but it was divided from the top, that is, from God's end, and by such an act He represented that He was smiting His well-beloved Son for mankind.

We cannot fully understand this mystery, although we do rejoice in all that it means; but there it is in His blessed Word for our adoring hearts to feed upon. Shall we turn to three passages?

"He that is hanged is accursed of God" (Deut. 21:23).

"Thou hast brought me into the dust of death" (Ps. 22:15).

"Stricken, smitten of God," "The LORD hath laid on Him," "Pleased the LORD to bruise him" (Isa. 53:4, 6, 10).

What a mystery! Yet, what great love! Can we take it in – the same hand that slew the Lamb rent the veil! Rent in twain from the top to the bottom! No human hand rent the veil in twain; neither was it torn from the bottom towards the top; but a hand from above rent it from the top to the bottom. Access to the heaven of heavens was to be laid open; no love and no power could either have devised or accomplished this but the love and power of God. Truly, salvation is of the Lord.

It was a Central Rent

Luke gives us a different expression that adds another blessed feature to our Lord's great work upon the cross. In recording the incident of the veil being rent, he uses the phrase "the veil of the temple was rent *in the* midst" (Luke 23:45). Not from the "top to the bottom" only, as in Matthew and Mark, but "in the midst." Why was the veil rent in the midst? Because the death of Christ has opened up a direct way that leads us straight into God's presence. In the Holy Place the veil was hung upon four pillars, and within the Most Holy Place in a line with the center or middle of the veil there stood the mercy seat, where between the cherubim the God of Glory dwelt. The veil, then, was rent in the midst. There was no side access or entrance, but one open way through the rent veil into the Holiest of All. The veil being rent in the middle, the eye of the priest would immediately see the mercy seat. And so faith brings us not by a roundabout way but into immediate fellowship with God.

It was a Complete Rent

Turning again to Matthew and Mark, we pause to notice the specific language used. The veil was rent completely even from the top to the *bottom*. No covering was left. All that hitherto barred the way was gone and gone forever from the God-ward side. Facing the priest on that dark day as the Saviour died was nothing but the two halves of that destroyed covering, and a great opening, wide and complete, into the Holiest of All. Rent in the middle! Rent from top to bottom! How complete! Such speaks of the absolute, complete work of our Lord for Jew and Gentile alike. As the veil was being completely rent, He cried, "It is finished." And so it was. Every barrier and difficulty has been removed and now there was nothing between.

For Israel

The entire rending of that veil signified to the Jews that the Old Dispensation had come to an end. For 500 years or more that beautiful covering had hung in all its splendor, concealing the glory and presence of Jehovah, and confining Him, so to speak, to one small apartment, but now the whole system of sacrifice and worship is set aside. No more high priests: no more altars of blood and sacrifice; no more of the service of the tabernacle or temple, all have at last found their fulfillment in Him who became "the true Tabernacle, which the Lord pitched, and not man" (Heb. 8:2). All the parts of that earthly structure were but "figures of the true" (Heb. 9:24).

For Ourselves

One could fill pages with the

blessed privileges that are ours through the complete work of Christ upon Calvary. The best thing that one can do is to take the epistle to the Hebrews, and carefully reading it through, note at the same time the access that we have into the inner and outer courts of priestly privilege and service. In fact, there is no other part of the sacred Word that illuminates the work of Christ like *Hebrews.*

There is just one phrase, however, to which we must draw attention. Turning to Hebrews 6:19, we read the words "within the veil." To the High Priest of old these words "within the veil" must have sounded somewhat fearfully upon the ear. With what solemn thoughts he would draw near, and entering the Holiest of All, once a year, gaze upon the glory of God.

Such a sentence should not cause us to dread, but raise in our hearts thoughts of blessed nearness, and happy confidence and fellowship with God our Father. "Within the Veil." What a privilege! What holy intimacy and communion are ours! Are we possessing our possessions? Are we taking advantage of our access? In living, daily experience, are we within the veil? Of course, we are there positionally, as believers; but often there is such a difference between our *practice* and *position;* our state and standing, our life up there in the heavenlies, and our life down here on the earth.

Coming to a fuller knowledge regarding the liberty of access that we have into His presence, and living in daily enjoyment of all that that means, let us seek out those who are still afar off and proclaim to them that Christ has broken down the middle wall of partition between their hearts and God, and that by the appropriation of the Saviour's finished work they can be "made nigh."

Dr. Scofield remarks that, "it is deeply significant that the priests must have patched together again the veil that God had rent, for the temple services went on yet for nearly forty years. That patched veil of Galatianism – the attempt to put saint and sinner back under law (Gal. 1:6-9). *Anything* but 'the *grace* of Christ' is 'another gospel' and under anathema."

But having a deep experience of His grace, we have no other desire than to preach to all men that there is nothing between. No human priest, no earthly veil of morality or righteousness, nothing to do and nothing to pay. All that God requires is a sincere, naked faith in His infinite provision, and once He has this, He does all that is necessary in the transforming of the heart and life.

My faith has found a resting-place,
Not in device nor creed:
I trust the ever-living One,
His wounds for me shall plead.

The Holy Privilege of the Believer

In drawing our sacred meditation to a close, shall we come to a practical application of the teaching regarding the beautiful veil?

First of all there is a sense in which our bodies, like the earthly body of our Lord, act as a veil. His body concealed His glory from man, and "our bodies are but veils which hide from us the face of our loving and glorified Lord. Death is but the rending of the veil, the opening of the way for our access into His immediate presence. Absent from the body, present with the Lord. Just now – how sweet the thought – only a *veil* between."

But here is a deeper thought. In reality there is no veil between the Lord and ourselves. We have an open heaven, liberty, glorious liberty, immediate access right into His presence, but we create many veils of our own that unnecessarily shut Him out from our gaze. From our side is there any earth-made veil, no matter how cunningly devised, that hides the Saviour from our eyes?

Our beings are like the tabernacle of old in that they are formed of three distinct parts.

There is the Outer Court of the body, connecting us with the outer world. Through the body we have *world-consciousness.*

There is the Holy Place of the soul, holding a central position like the Holy Place of the tabernacle. The soul is *self-consciousness,* the place where all the powers are, or ought to be, acting as true priests serving God.

There is the Holiest of All of the spirit, linking us up with God; and which being the most spiritual part is called *God-consciousness.*

The question to settle is this, Is there any unnecessary veil between these different parts of our being? To make the matter individual, I profess to be a believer-priest, a child of God, and as such I am possessed by the Holy Spirit, that is, He has entered my being and taken up His abode forever within my spirit, thus fashioning my body into His temple.

But, when I speak of the fulness of the Holy Spirit, what do I really mean? Why, simply this, that between my soul and my spirit, that is between my self or soul life and the inner spiritual part of my nature, there is often a veil drawn, a veil of self-will, self-seeking, self-dependence, self-glory, and that when such is rent in the midst or when I allow God to rend it from the top to the bottom, even as He did the temple veil, then the Holy Spirit rises and passes through the rent veil and fills my self-life with the Christ-life until my position is, Not I but Christ.

Often there is a veil between my soul and my body. Said our Lord in John 7:38, "Out of his belly shall flow rivers of living water." But somehow there is not this outlet or overflow. My body is the medium of revelation, even as God spoke to the High Priest in the Holiest of All, and then the High Priest revealed the divine message to the priest, and then from such it passed out to the Israelite, and through him to the outside world.

Through this body of mine God is wanting to express, reveal, declare Himself, but there is often a veil between, the veil of fear, of timidity, of unwilling confession, of disobedience to His commands. Beloved, shall we not rend forever the veils that cover His blessed face from our hearts, and the hearts of others? The veil was rent in the midst! Open access to God!

Such is our position in grace! May it also be ours in daily experience as believers! To put it in another way, the rent veil in our lives means, as Evan Hopkins expresses it:

Nothing between, Lord, nothing
between;
Let not earth's din and noise
Stifle Thy still small voice;
In it let me rejoice—
Nothing between.

Nothing between, Lord, nothing
between,
Nothing of earthly care,
Nothing of tear or prayer,
No robe that self may wear—
Nothing between.

Nothing between, Lord, nothing
between;
Till Thine eternal light,
Rising on earth's dark night,
Bursts on my open sight—
Nothing between.

(2). *The Holy of Holies.* Now that we are within the veil, we put off the shoes from off our feet, for we are about to visit the most sacred spot on earth to the Israelite of old (Exod. 25:10-22; Heb. 9:1-10).

Within this innermost chamber, the secret place of the Most High, called the Most Holy Place, we have the local dwelling of God, where, for long years, He dwelt in the unutterable darkness of the sacred enclosure and held communion with man. Moreover, this Most Holy Place proclaims the message of silence, a silence that must have filled the heart of the High Priest with holy awe and reverence. For instance, this reserved part of the tabernacle could only be entered once a year, the rest of the year being a time of silence. Further, we have no record that the High Priest ever uttered an audible word when he passed through the veil into the presence of Jehovah.

Neither have we any definite knowledge of what transpired between the Lord and the High Priest when they came together. Emerging from the holy presence of God, the priest apparently felt that silence best befitted him regarding all that he saw and heard as he faced the Shekinah glory.

Is it not incumbent upon us to observe more silence as worshipfully we "Approach the Mercy Seat, Where Jesus answers prayer"? Often the Lord cannot reveal His purpose unto us because of our eagerness to talk to Him, but the nearer we come to God the more we are inclined "to keep silence before Him." Often what we see and hear are far too holy for us to speak about. Like Paul, we hear unspeakable words which it is impossible for a man to utter (II Cor. 12:1-4). What do we know of the power of silence and stillness as we come before the Lord? Shall we not endeavor to make Martin Luther's version of Psalm 37:7 – "Lie still, and let Him mold thee" – our daily desire and attitude?

Therefore, says one,

> The Holy of Holies must be entered with bowed head and unsandalled feet for Jehovah on His throne is there. How awful the presence chamber of the Lord of Hosts. Here no human voice is heard, only the voice of God. Here no seat for man is found, Jehovah sits alone and that on the throne of glory and righteousness. Here no created light, as sun, nor artificial light, as the candle illumines the apartment, the glory of God fills the Holiest with its own Divine radiance. Here, too, all is Divine and we breathe another atmosphere than that of Creation.

(a). *Its Name*

This third division is called, among other titles, which all imply more or less the same thought, "The Holy of Holies." Such a name indicates its purpose. It was the abode of Him who is the holiest of all. The presence of God makes any place holy, therefore our bodies as believers are called "holy temples" because, like the innermost sanctuary of the tabernacle, they are indwelt by the Holy One.

The designations given to this dwelling place of Jehovah are:

Sanctuary (Lev. 4:6; Ps. 20:2).
Holy Sanctuary (Lev. 16:33).
Holy Place (Exod. 28:29; Lev. 16: 2, 3).
Most Holy Place (Exod. 26:31-33).
Holiest of All (Heb. 9:3).
Oracle (I Kings 6:5, 16, 20).

(b) *Its Size*

This Most Holy Place was a small, square apartment, fifteen feet every way. Yet although it was so small, God condescended to manifest Himself and dwell there. He who had omnipresence and cannot be confined by space, limited and localized Himself to the Most Holy Place, a picture, surely, of His greater condescension in taking up His abode within our hearts. Great it was to dwell within that cube-shaped erection long ago, but greater still is His desire to dwell within the narrow confines of our hearts (Isa. 57:15).

(c). *Its Significance*

Coming to the typical implication of the Holiest of All, it would seem as if such represents three very important truths.

Christ

Not only is Christ the veil rent in the midst; but also that which the real veil gave entrance to, namely, the Holiest of All with its contents. In fact, one of the names given to this innermost chamber is applied to our Lord, as one can find by turning to Daniel 9:24, where the prophet speaks of Him as "the most Holy."

The Presence of God

The words "Having therefore, brethren, boldness to enter into the holiest" (Heb. 10:19) undoubtedly refer to the immediate presence of God, and are a figure of speech that the apostle has taken from the tabernacle. Believers are invited to draw near into the holiest – to Him that dwelleth between the cherubim. What a privilege it is to turn aside from the world and, within the veil, pour out our hearts before God. But, alas! we so often fail to take advantage of the liberty of access we have.

> Oh, what peace we often forfeit
> Oh, what needless pain we bear—
> All because we do not carry
> Everything to God in prayer.

Heaven Itself

Passages like Psalm 102:19 and Hebrews 9:12, 24, bid us think of the Holy of Holies as a fitting type of heaven. And so it is! for just as the High Priest entered within the veil once a year and came into direct contact with God, so Christ tore aside the veil and went right back to the bosom of His Father, thereby making it possible for us to go to Himself at the hour when the veil of our earthly body, or tabernacle, is rent by death.

There was no light within this Most Holy Place, nothing to illuminate it but the Shekinah glory of God's presence. God Himself was the light of that place. So is it with heaven! Here we need the light of the candlestick. We need His Spirit to teach us, His word to guide us and make Him real to us; but when the veil of flesh is removed and we enter the Holy of Holies above, even heaven, then we shall prove the significance of John's words,

> And I saw no temple therein: for the Lord God Almighty and the Lamb are the temple of it. And the city had no need of the sun, neither of the moon, to shine in it: for the glory of God did lighten it, and the Lamb is the light thereof (Rev. 21:22, 23).

(d). *Its Contents*

Within the veil there was little to be seen in the way of furniture. Outside in the Holy Place there were three golden vessels but here with the Holiest of All only one, or two if we count the golden censer as well as the ark. If the furniture was scant, it was because there was no need for much else where God Himself is found. Having Him we have all things and abound.

The furniture is good, but the Lord is better. Let us never forget that the presence of the Lord is more important than the vessels of the Lord. There is the danger of knowing all the spiritual truth regarding our life as believers as implied in many parts of the ritual of the tabernacle, and yet not come to know the Lord Himself, and of meeting Him face to face, not once a year as it was the High Priest's privilege to do, but every day, nay every hour of every day.

To those who teach and preach the Word of God there comes the subtle temptation to be taken up with the holy furniture, that is, with the mere letter of the word, and neglect personal fellowship with the Lord Himself. Now, although it is important to know about Him, it is more imperative to know Him, an ambition Paul knew something about – "That I may know him" (Phil. 3:10).

Looking at the contents of the Most Holy Place, we find, first of all –

i. The Censer

It would appear from passages like Leviticus 16:12, and Hebrews 9:4, that this particular vessel remained within the Holy Place all the year round and that on the solemn day of Atonement when the High Priest entered into the Holiest, he first took this golden censer, and filling it with burning coals from the altar of sacrifice, added to it a handful of sweet incense taken from the golden altar and thus stood in the Holiest of All surrounded with a cloud of fragrant perfume as he remained before the mercy seat.

By the golden censer the Holy Spirit would have us think of our Lord Jesus as the intercessor. R. M. McCheyne remarks,

> This is the Angel of Intercession whom John saw (Rev. 8:3), offering up the prayers of all saints with much incense. The prayers of the highest believers are all sinful and polluted. There is so much unbelief, so much selfishness, so much forgetfulness mingling with all, that every prayer is sin. But if you put them into the Golden Censer, Jesus Christ the righteous will cover all the sin and offer them up with much incense. This is the only way of acceptable worship. Is this your way of praying? Have you such a sense of sin that you are ashamed of your prayers? or do you put them into Christ's censer? It is an appealing thought that the censer of Christ is so often empty—so few prayers put into it.

ii. The Ark

In reaching this most sacred of all vessels to Israel, one cannot fail to be greatly impressed by its significance both to Israel and to ourselves, and also of its wonderful history as given to us in Old Testament Scriptures. Ere we deal, however, with the ark itself it may be as well to state that there are three arks to be distinguished even though they have a similar application.

Noah's Ark (Gen. 6:14).

This huge covered-in building resembling a ship with a closed in roof is called an *ark,* and was the means of securing deliverance for Noah and his family.

Moses' Ark (Exod. 2:3).

To escape the cruel edict of Pharaoh, the mother of Moses made a small cradle-like vessel which is called an *ark,* and placing her precious babe within it, hid such away among the bulrushes. Here, again, the ark stood for deliverance, for Moses was delivered, or "drawn out," as his name means, from the water of death, and became as the son of Pharaoh's daughter.

Israel's Ark (Exod. 25).

This is the *Ark of the Covenant* we are now to consider and which proclaims the same sweet message of deliverance and salvation. In connection with this ark, let us seek to view its teaching in the following way:

Its Mention

Doubtless it has been observed that the ark is the first named of the tabernacle vessels, and the first to be made ready to receive the testimony given by Jehovah to the Lawgiver.

God commenced with the ark, but for Israel the ark was the last vessel to be reached in the order of the tabernacle, the reason for which is both beautiful and instructive. God begins with Himself and works outward toward man, reaching him at last at the brazen altar of sacrifice, but man begins where God ends and with growing spiritual apprehension travels inward until with the High Priest of old he stands at the ark within the Holiest of All. The ladder of grace is one that has its first rung in heaven, and then reaches down until its last rung touches the earth.

Then the ark stood as it were in the center of the camp of Israel, and God always begins at the center, and works out to the circumference. Christ is our true ark and mercy seat, and God begins with Him for He is His center, and it is from Him and through Him that every blessing comes.

If we are to rightly understand the truths concerning the tabernacle, we must have right thoughts about Christ, and such right thinking will lead to right living. As John Newton put it,

> What think ye of Christ? is the test
> To try both your state and your scheme,
> You cannot be right in the rest,
> Unless you think rightly of Him.

Its Names

The following are the names given to the ark, all of which have their own significance as one can easily discern by the particular designation used.

The Ark of the Testimony (Exod. 25:22).
The Ark of the Covenant (Josh. 3:6).
The Ark of the Covenant of the Lord (Num. 10:33).
The Ark of the Covenant of God (Judg. 20:27).
The Ark of the Lord of all the Earth (Josh. 3:13).
The Ark of the Lord (Josh. 4:11).
The Ark of the God of Israel (I Sam. 5:7).
The Ark of God (I Sam. 3:3).
The Ark of Thy Strength (II Chron. 6:41; Ps. 132:8).
The Holy Ark (II Chron. 35:3).
Called "His Strength" and "His Glory" (Ps. 78:60, 61).

Its Size

The Hebrew word for ark is *chest*, so in thinking of this ark, let us try and keep in mind an oblong chest something like one that we may use for ourselves in respect to its size:

53 inches long
32 inches broad
32 inches high

Its Composition

As we have frequently referred to the spiritual teaching of the materials used in the formation of the ark, a brief mention should suffice at this stage.

It was made of Shittim Wood

The desert wood called shittim wood, or acacia, and translated "incorruptible wood" in the LXX version, is said not to rot and is therefore a fitting symbol of the humanity of Him who is all that the ark prefigures.

It was covered with Pure Gold

Gold represents the deity of the Son of God. But turning to the divine instructions, there is one particular feature to notice. The divine command was to overlay it with pure gold "within and without" (Exod. 25:11). The table of shewbread, and the altar of incense in the Holy Place were overlaid with gold, but here in the ark no wood was seen at all. To all appearances it was a golden box or chest. Our Lord's deity was both inward and outward. Not only had He those gracious outward acts that betokened deity, such as the raising of the dead, etc., but He had blessed inherent deity. Both His nature and His ways were divine! The ark of our salvation was overlaid with pure gold within and without.

It had a Crown of Gold

"Thou shalt make upon the ark a crown of gold round about" (Exod. 25:11; 37:2). This word translated "crown" occurs only in connection with the ark, shewbread table, and incense altar, and signifies "a border or edge," coming from a root meaning "to bind together."

This crown, then, was not a regal crown, but simply a ledge or binding of gold made of ornamental workmanship, and used for keeping the mercy seat in its proper place and for exactly covering up the ark. God has taken every precaution to preserve the all-glorious Person of His Son, but let us guard ourselves lest we fall into the error of the men of Bethshemesh. "Because they had looked *into* the ark of the LORD, even he smote of the people fifty thousand and threescore and ten men" (I Sam. 6:19). They could not look into the ark without putting aside the mercy seat. They did what many do now who put Christ on one side, and who look at the Law and think they can keep it and get life by it. To do this is death, for without Christ we can do nothing, and without Christ we can have nothing. May we be delivered from the folly of uncovering what God has hid!

It had Rings and Staves

There were four rings of gold, one at each corner of the ark, and two staves made of shittim wood and overlaid with gold which were passed through the rings, thus providing for the transport of the ark from place to place. One feature, however, demands attention. These staves had to be left within the rings even when the ark was resting in the Most Holy Place. "The staves shall not be taken out" (Exod. 25:15). Such a command symbolizes that the church of God is still a pilgrim host traveling through the wilderness.

> This is not our resting place
> Our's a city yet to come.

Wherever believers are found, there the Lord is also, and His grace is adapted to the need.

Following the history of this ark, we discover that when the marching days of Israel were over and the ark was transferred to the temple, its staves were removed and kept by its side as a token of remembrance (I Kings 8:8; II Sam. 6:6, 7; II Chron. 5:9). Ere long, our earthly journey will be over, and we shall enter into our rest, and in heaven the remembrance of Christ with us in the journeys and experiences here below will be one of the richest joys of the paradise of God.

Its History

Although one is tempted to tarry at this point and show from Scripture how instructive and full of import the historical study of the ark is from its first mention to its last, yet it may be best to refer the readers to the articles dealing with this aspect of the ark as given by Soltau, *The Holy Vessels; The Text-Book* by Habershon; Walter Scott on *The Tabernacle.*

Its Contents

From Hebrews 9:4, we learn that there were three things deposited within the ark — "wherein was the golden pot that had manna, and Aaron's rod that budded, and the tables of the covenant."

These three articles represent, as we are to see, what Christ has secured on behalf of His people because the ark, as a whole, speaks of Him as the fulfiller of all righteousness. Taking the contents separately we have —

THE TABLES OF THE COVENANT

Within the bosom of the ark were the two tables of stone on which God wrote with His own finger the Ten Commandments. Such were given to a people who clamored for a written declaration of His will, thus the ark is called the "Ark of Testimony," for there within it was the evidence of their own testimony or confession regarding it. "All that the LORD hath spoken we will do" (Exod. 19:8).

But man could not keep the law, and so in the fulness of time, there came One who had the Law shut up within His heart even as it was laid up in the ark:

"Thy law is within my heart" (Ps. 40:8).

"Thus it becometh us to fulfill all righteousness" (Matt. 3:15).

"By the obedience of one shall many be made righteous" (Rom. 5:19).

Then, the holy Law, broken by others, was shut up in Him. He kept it. He keeps it still. It was magnified in Him. Now He has taken it out of the way as an obstacle to man's salvation, and has nailed it to the cross (Col. 2:14).

THE POT OF MANNA

During their forty years in the wilderness, the people of Israel were fed and nourished by God, who "satisfied them with the bread of heaven" (Ps. 105:40). At the time He fed them with this "angels' food," He commanded them to preserve an omer of it (enough for one person) in a golden pot, "that they may see the bread wherewith I have fed you in the wilderness" (Exod. 16:32-34). In Hebrews 9:4, Paul tells us that it was a golden pot that held this memorial bread. Here again with enraptured hearts we discern the face of our Lord.

This manna was hidden in the ark, that is, it could not be seen because it was covered by the mercy seat. Is not our Lord the hidden manna of His People (Rev. 2:17)? Is He not within the veil as the secret soul-satisfying food, not only in the wilderness, but for eternity?

The meaning of the word *manna* is "What is it?" The host of Israel could not find a suitable name for this heaven-sent food, because its composition was mysterious. It came from heaven and was therefore outside the range of earthly experience. How applicable is this to our blessed Lord! He is our manna – What is He? None can ever find Him out by searching. He "possesseth knowledge."

This much, however, can be said, the Israelites had to gather it fresh every morning, even though they could not explain the constituents of their heavenly food. If our lives are to be spiritually healthy and robust, there must be that daily appropriation of Christ. Depths there are in Him we shall never never fathom, but such transcendant glories need not keep us away from Him. Let us beware of having an experience of Christ that is stale. It is not the Lord I knew some months, or years ago, but the Lord I know and love at this present hour that others want to hear about.

AARON'S ROD

The full story of this remarkable rod can be found in Numbers 16:17. As we have already indicated, it was but a dead stick, yet it was made to bud, blossom, and bear fruit. This rod God commanded Moses to keep in the Holiest of All. Who can doubt that this rod represents Christ? "Originally an almond wand, growing in the wilderness, it represents Jesus the root of a dry ground without form or comeliness, having no beauty that we should desire Him – the Man Whose name is the Branch."

The Rod represented Authority

The budding of Aaron's rod while it was before the Lord was an evidence to Korah, Dathan, and Abiram, who had grumbled about the position of Moses and Aaron as God's chosen ones (Num. 16). As all in connection with Aaron's rod speaks of our Saviour, we see in it, first of all, the fact that God was with Him and behind His work and Word with full authority. Christ is God's chosen, authoritative witness, as is evidenced by the fact that He distinctly stated, "The works that I do in my Father's name, they bear witness of me" (John 10:25). Yet again He speaks of being sent by the Father.

The Rod speaks of Resurrection

Originally Aaron's rod was a dead, dry stick, but when placed before the Lord it "brought forth buds, and bloomed blossoms, and yielded almonds" (Num. 17:8). Such a type brings us to the Resurrection of our Lord. He became the dead stick, but behold He is alive forevermore, and such a victory over the grave is a witness and proof of the efficacy and power of His cross.

This rod was in the ark within the veil, and the priesthood of Christ within the veil is founded upon His death and Resurrection. And let us shrink from underrating the power of His Resurrection. At times, one wonders whether the message of the cross is not a little over emphasized at the expense of the Resurrection. His death, of course, was great, wonderful, sacrificial, marvelous beyond compare, but suppose He had remained dead – What then? Why, our faith would be vain and we should be still in our sin, according to the argument of Paul in I Corinthians 15.

Our message is a twofold one. "Jesus our Lord . . . Who was *delivered* for our offences, and was *raised* again for our justification" (Rom. 4:24, 25). Both sides of such a theme must be equally proclaimed. We need a dead Saviour to meet the claims of a guilty past, and a living Lord to keep us saved. And we have both in Him who died and rose again.

Combining, then, the truth of the three vessels contained in the ark, we have

The hidden law, satisfying the justice of a Holy God.

The hidden manna, satisfying the heart of a believing soul.

The hidden rod, satisfying the needs of all.

Ere we leave these three vessels, mention might be made of the fact that twice over (I Kings 8:9; II Chron. 5:10) no reference is made to the manna, and Aaron's rod as being within the ark. The reason is this – there was nothing in the ark save the table of covenant, because of a deep spiritual truth that the Holy Spirit would direct our attention to. The ark is now in the temple, its wanderings are over, and so the manna and the rod are removed because both were memorials of the murmurings and rebellion of Israel. How like God this is! When we get to glory all will be removed that has marred our pilgrim lives down here.

The two tables of stone remain because they represent God's Law and that is unalterable and eternal (Rev. 11:19). There is a legend that the tables of the Law were of sapphire and therefore, like the Law itself, imperishable. Of course, we must distinguish between the moral Law of God and the ritual Law, which we call the Law of Moses. The *former is eternal* and is of the very essence of God's nature: *the latter* is temporary and passes away, because it merely embodied a code of ordinances.

Seeing that the cherubim are first of all connected with judgment, as one can find by turning to Genesis 3:24, it is quite reasonable to accept the view that the cherubim are emblematic of the judicial power and authority of God, and that as the cherubim were of one piece with that of the mercy seat, so God's grace, seen in the mercy seat, and His justice, seen in the cherubim, are all of one piece, inseparably connected. Thus Soltau remarks, "The Mercy Seat and Cherubim, being all of one piece, represents, it is believed, Christ as the One Who holds all the glorious power of God, associated with mercy, and in and through whom God is able to display His power and righteousness ever inseparably linked on with mercy and grace."

THE POSITION OF THE CHERUBIM UPON THE MERCY SEAT

To the mind of the believer the details in respect to the position and attitude of these cherubim are full of holy instruction and spiritual profit.

They Stood upon the Mercy Seat

Standing there in all their splendor and beauty, those two cherubs must have been the object of admiration to the High Priest as he yearly gazed upon them. If they represent the justice of God, then it is blessed to know that the wondrous work of Christ as our propitiation is overshadowed by the holy righteousness of God. Or if we use the cherubim as emblems of the church, then like the cherubim she also stands upon the mercy seat. Christ is her only foundation (I Cor. 3:11).

I stand upon His merit,
I know no other stand.

Their Wings were Outstretched

No longer had the cherubim swords in their hands; judgment is now past, but their hands were folded and wings were outstretched, suggesting the wonderful protection and daily care of God vouchsafed to all who have escaped judgment through approaching the mercy seat (Pss. 91:4; 61:4; Ruth 2:12).

Or their outspread wings can speak of the spread of the Gospel far and wide, and of the instant readiness, as their wings are outstretched as if in flight, of the eagerness of God to apply His deliverance to all. And surely to those of us who realize our solemn responsibility, there is intimated here the fact that we must

Bear the news to every land,
Climb the steeps and cross the waves,
Onward, 'tis our Lord's command,
Jesus saves, Jesus saves.

They looked toward each other

How suggestive are these words of the sacred text – "Their faces shall look [*notice,* italics] one to another" (Exod. 25:20). Such speaks of that brotherly fellowship and love that John the apostle of love, refers to in I John 1:7. And this should be the attitude of all who are resting upon the mercy seat. Can it be that any of us, although we claim to be the Lord's, have a face that is turned away from the face of some brother or sister? Then let us think again of these two cherubs with their faces turned inward, and then seek to put everything right that has caused us to turn our face away from another.

They looked down upon the Mercy Seat

Although these cherubim were turned toward each other, they did not look, as it were, into each other's eyes, but downward with a fixed gaze at the blood-sprinkled mercy seat – "toward the Mercy Seat shall the faces of the cherubim be" (Exod. 25:20).

As true believers we should look, not at each other, in the spirit of self-adoration, but upon Him who has purchased for us the blessed, holy privilege of entering the Holiest of All.

And when our eyes are truly opened we become like the disciples upon the Mount who saw no man save Jesus only. Possibly there is also a reference in this attitude of the cherubim to the reverent adoration of the angels that Peter mentions – "which things the angels desire to look into" (I Pet. 1:12).

They enjoyed the Presence of God

It was between the cherubim that the Shekinah glory of Jehovah rested – "There I will meet with thee... commune with thee... between the two cherubims" (Exod. 25:22). How grateful we should be that there is a meeting place! God rested on the mercy seat waiting to meet with man. Communion is now possible because of the atoning blood. In the Person of Christ, our sacrifice and mediator, God can be met in pardon and mercy.

Gathering the facts together in respect to this aspect of the truth, we discover that God

Spoke from above the mercy seat (Exod. 25:22; Num. 7:89).

Appeared above it in the cloud (Lev. 16:2).

Dwelt over it (Ps. 80:1).

Such gives the divine side of the blessed fellowship that is realized in the presence of God.

From the manward side it was treated thus –

Covered with a cloud of incense on the Day of Atonement (Lev. 16:13).

Sprinkled upon and before with the blood of sacrifices (Lev. 16: 14, 15).

"On the great day of Atonement," says one, "Israel's annual cleansing from sin – Aaron the priest, robed in Linen garments, entered within the veil with the blood of a sin-offering. This was sprinkled on the Mercy Seat once, and before it seven times. Once was enough for the eye of Jehovah, but seven times – the perfect number – for the eye of the worshipper. We need to be reminded often of the perfectness of the atonement of Christ, but in the estimate of God it is ever the same."

The question for us to answer is, Are we coveting and enjoying that full communion opened up to the redeemed by the greater sacrifice of Christ? Are we entering into the deep significance of our Lord's words? "At that day ye shall know that I am in my Father, and ye in me, and I in you" (John 14:20). Surely such a fellowship is a foretaste of the eternal enjoyment of His presence – "Behold, the tabernacle of God is with men, and he will dwell with them, and they shall be his people, and God himself shall be with them, and be their God" (Rev. 21:3).

WHAT IT SYMBOLIZES

Already we have hinted that the mercy seat is a type of Christ's glorious work, but let us, as we draw our meditation to a close, seek to gather into a brief statement one or two distinctive features of the Saviour's work prefigured by the mercy seat.

CHRIST

First and foremost, the mercy seat is a divinely given symbol of our Lord's atoning death.

The Name

The name given to the covering of the ark, "mercy seat," is somewhat significant, especially when we take the two words separately.

Seat

This golden lid was called a "seat." Now a seat suggests rest. The mercy *seat* was therefore a resting place for God. There was no seat in the tabernacle for the priests, because their work was never done. They *stood* to minister in the Holy Place (Heb. 10:11, 12). The only seat there was the mercy seat, the throne of God. And is it not blessed to know that God does find a place of rest in the finished work of His dear Son? Further, there is no other place where the weary soul of man can find rest from sin but where God has found it, in the Person and work of Jesus Christ.

From every stormy wind that blows,
From every swelling tide of woes,
There is a calm, a safe retreat;
'Tis found beneath the Mercy Seat.

Mercy

Then observe what this seat is called. It is not a judgment seat but a seat of mercy. Grace and mercy were sitting there upon the ark, because the broken law within was covered and because all over the seat itself there was the sprinkled blood. Today, as then, God sits upon the seat of mercy, and He can meet with man and deliver him from his sin in virtue of the shed blood of Christ. Alas! the day is coming when He will be found sitting upon a judgment seat, judging men for their rejection of His mercy.

There is a place where Jesus sheds
The Oil of Gladness on our heads,
A place than all beside more sweet;
It is the blood-stained Mercy Seat.

The Meaning of the Name

The root idea of the name *mercy seat* is "to cover," and is intimately connected with the word Atonement. Coming to our New Testament, what do we find? Why, the Holy Spirit used the very same word – *mercy seat* of Christ Himself and thereby makes this part of the Most Holy Place a heavenly type.

Turning to Romans 3:24, 25, we read, "Christ Jesus: whom God hath set forth to be a propitiation through faith in his blood." The word used here for "propitiation" is the same Greek term for "mercy seat." In Luke 18:13 you have the same thought – "God be merciful to me a sinner." Here the word for "mercy" is really "propitiation" as the R.V.M. shows, or "mercy seat." Commenting upon Romans 3:25, Dr. Scofield observes,

> A propitiation, literally a propitiatory (sacrifice), through faith by His blood, Greek, *hilasterion,* "a place of propitiation." The word occurs I John 2:2; 4:10 as the translation of *hilasmos*—"that which propitiates," "a propitiatory sacrifice." The Mercy Seat was sprinkled with atoning blood on the Day of Atonement (Lev. 16:14), in token that the righteous sentence of the law had been (typically) carried out, so that what must else have been a judgment seat could righteously be a Mercy Seat (Heb. 9:11, 15; 4:14-16), a place of communion (Exod. 25:21, 22).
>
> In fulfilment of the type, Christ is Himself the *hilasmos,* "that which propitiates," and the *hilasterion,* "the place of propitiation"—the Mercy Seat sprinkled with His own blood —the token that in our stead He so honoured the law by enduring its righteous sentence that God, Who ever foresaw the Cross, is vindicated in having "passed over" sins from Adam to Moses (Rom. 5:13), and the sins of believers under the old covenant (Exod. 29:33), and in justifying sinners under the new covenant. There is no thought in propitiation of placating a vengeful God, but of doing right by His holy law and so making it possible for Him righteously to shew Mercy.

THE THRONE OF GRACE

Does it not seem as if the apostle had the appropriation of the privileges of the mercy seat by believers in mind when he penned these words, "Let us therefore come boldly unto the throne of grace, that we may obtain mercy, and find grace to help in time of need" (Heb. 4:16)? Here we have provision made for our twofold need.

As pilgrims on earth we always need mercy, to wash our feet, to restore to us the joy of salvation, to heal our backslidings, and bind up our wounds. There is need for the grace, and grace for the need.

Then we also need help – wisdom, patience, daily bread – all is treasured up for us in Christ our mercy seat. The sanctuary is also the treasury: the High Priest is also king. Therefore let us come boldly. Let the constant attitude of our hearts be

Approach my soul the Mercy Seat,
Where Jesus answers prayer;
There humbly fall before His Feet,
For none can perish there.

Chapter Five

PROPHETIC FOREGLEAMS FROM LEVITICAL OFFERINGS

A. The Burnt Offering
B. The Meal Offering
C. The Peace Offering
D. The Sin Offering
E. The Trespass Offering
The Two Sparrows
The Red Heifer

As we take up the specific study of the Levitical offerings, endeavoring to trace the Gospel of redeeming grace and mercy within them, we shall discover that it takes all of them to convey any idea of the perfection of Christ's supreme sacrifice. As we proceed, it will become evident that there are at least three distinct objects presented in each offering, namely, the priest, the offerer, the offering; and a definite understanding of each of these is necessary if we would understand the offerings aright.

Further, we shall see how the Lord Jesus is the substance of all these Old Testament shadows, and of how, in Himself, He fulfilled all that the Jewish ritual predicted.

1. For the service of the Tabernacle, Aaron and his sons were set apart as priests, together with the tribe of Levi, who were to execute the duties assigned them under the direction of the priests (Exod. 28; Num. 4). Jesus became the priest—"We have a Great High Priest, Jesus the Son of God" (Heb. 4:14). Aaron had to offer sacrifice for his own sins, as well as for those of the people. Jesus was sinless, and required no atoning blood.
2. The offerer of old brought the sacrifice he could afford. If not a lamb, then a couple of pigeons. The intrinsic value was in the willingness of the offerer, and in the blood of the animal or bird slain. Jesus was also the offering, as well as priest—"Who gave himself for us, that he might redeem us from all iniquity" (Titus 2:14). Because of who He was, His sacrifice is eternally efficacious.
3. The offering had to be voluntarily given, and one that was without any blemish. "The offering of the body of Jesus Christ once for all" (Heb. 10:10).

An impressive and inescapable feature of all the offerings, as we shall indicate in our coverage of them, is the insistence upon the very best, seeing they were to be presented to God. The edict was, "It shall be perfect to be accepted; there shall be no blemish therein" (Lev. 22:21). As the God of the best, nothing less than the best must be offered to Him. These unblemished offerings were a foregleam of Him who was perfect in every way, and who, by His perfect sacrifice, secured a perfect salvation for imperfect men.

A. *The Burnt Offering* (Lev. 1–6:8-12)

Leviticus is the great book of sacrifice in the Old Testament and should be studied along with *Hebrews*, which is its counterpart in the New Testament. The offerings and ritual of the tabernacle were provided by

God for the Israelites, whom He had gathered out from among the other nations of the world. In the waste, howling desert, Moses created the mystic tabernacle, and the Lord sought by sacrifices and ceremonies to instruct His people in the things pertaining to true worship and service.

How true it is that many regard these Levitical offerings as antiquated Jewish customs! The very reading of the record of these rites and ceremonies is a weariness to the flesh, because having no spiritual light or understanding they fail to detect within them all divine instruction regarding the various aspects of our Saviour's blessed work for us, and of our worship of and service for Him. *Leviticus* presents the Gospel of the offerings.

At the outset we must realize that these offerings in themselves never satisfied the heart of God. "It is not possible that the blood of bulls and of goats should take away sins" (Heb. 10:4). The importance of these offerings is in the fact that they symbolized the Person and work of our Lord Jesus Christ (Heb. 10:5). Taken together, the five offerings present a full view of Christ. They are like five mirrors, arranged in such a manner as to reflect, in different aspects, the perfect sacrifice of a perfect Redeemer for imperfect people.

It is well to realize as we proceed that the five offerings we are about to consider include all the offerings and sacrifice referred to in Israel's history. Again and again you will find these five offerings mentioned in different ways and aspects. Offerings that bear a different name, such as thank or voluntary offerings, are just aspects of one of these five Levitical offerings.

The number of offerings is five — burnt, meat, peace, sin, trespass — and when viewed separately they present five different portraits of one offering, meeting the various needs of the people in connection with access, communion and worship.

These five are divided into two classes: the sweet offerings — *burnt, meat, peace* — and the non-sweet offerings — *sin, trespass.*

The first three are called *sweet offerings* because they speak of that which God can accept, and accept with pleasure (sweet savor — a savor of rest). They typify Christ in His perfect life of obedience and devotion to the Father's will. His whole life was fragrant to God.

The last two are named *non-sweet offerings* because they are connected with sin and bear the shame and demerits of the sinner. And yet even these typify Christ because by His cross He suffered for our sin and disobedience.

Burnt offering — The entire devotion of Christ to the Father's will even though it meant death.
Meat offering — The personal character of Christ — God's will in His human life.
Peace offering — Fellowship with God through Christ, who is our peace.
Sin offering — Christ became our substitute when made sin for us.
Trespass offering — The Spirit's adaptation of Christ's sacrifice to our needs.

A word as to the order of these offerings. The order revealed in Leviticus is not the order in which Israel presented them. She began at the last of the five, the trespass offering, and worked back to the first one, the burnt offering. The point to keep in mind is that the burnt offering sets forth not the meeting of the sinner's need but the presentation to God of that which is acceptable to Him. Both aspects end at the cross, the burnt offering portraying Christ fully surrendered, doing the Father's perfect will, the trespass offering eloquent with the truth of Christ as the sin-bearer.

When God begins telling out what He has in Christ, He commences with the burnt offering and descends to the trespass offering. But when a guilty sinner comes to realize what he has in Christ, he must begin where God finishes, namely, at the trespass, or sin offering. Here we have God's side – outward toward us; our side – inward and upward to God. By looking at Leviticus 14:12, 13, we see this reversed order illustrated in the cleansing of the leper; and in Leviticus 8:14, 15, the same order from the trespass offering upward is connected with the consecration of the priesthood. So is it for us all. As sinners we come to know Christ as the One who "died for our sins." Order corresponds to our apt apprehension of Christ, and then passes on to know Him in all the fulness of His sacrifice and Person. We ascend until we come to the burnt offering. We can never go beyond that – absolute perfection of Christ's devotion and dedication.

1. *The Character of the Burnt Offering* (Lev. 1:3). It is called the "burnt" offering because the victim was wholly consumed. No part of it remained, either as waste or for consumption, as in some of the other offerings. Moreover, the fire that consumed the sacrifice ever burned. It never ceased to burn night or day.

The word rendered "burn" is really *holah,* or "that which ascends." It is a word of peculiar interest and is used in connection with incense (Lev. 6:15; Deut. 33:10; Exod. 30:1; Jer. 44:21, etc.). The connection of the word is that this particular offering was one that ascended to God, and is so fragrant because of its perfect nature and character. How wonderfully descriptive of Christ's sweet-savor offering this is!

The other word "burn" used in connection with the sin offering signifies to burn anything in general (See Gen. 40:3; Lev. 10:16; II Chron. 16:16). This was burnt without the camp – the burnt offering was burnt upon the altar. Thus the Holy Spirit uses different words to describe the two different burnings.

The distinctive feature in the burnt offering is that it was wholly for Jehovah. It represents the unreserved devotedness of the Lord Jesus – His perfect surrender to God in life and in death. Hence it ascends in sweet fragrance, affording Him great satisfaction and delight. "He gave Himself for us an offering and a sacrifice to God of a sweet-smelling savour" (Eph. 5:2).

2. *The Creatures Acceptable for Sacrifice* (Lev. 1:5, 10, 14). *Had to be male.* Speaks of Christ's strength, also of His humanity. "The glory of a young man is his strength."

Of the first year (Exod. 29:33). This gives the idea of freshness (See Mal. 1:8, 13). Christ died in the bloom of youth.

Without blemish, meaning perfection (I Pet. 1:19). A blemished sacrifice of no avail. Redeemed – precious blood of Christ, as of a lamb without blemish, without spot. Thus God claimed and received from Christ the very best. Is it so with us?

Had to offer either bullock or ox, sheep or lamb, goat, turtle dove, or pigeon. Possibly these are specified in order to show that the offerer could bring the sacrifice that he could afford – the richer the person, the more costly the sacrifice. But the spiritual mind will see in the various creatures mentioned different aspects of Christ's own sacrifice for us on the cross.

a. *The Bullock or Ox* (See I Cor. 9:9, 10; Heb. 12:2, 3; Isa. 52:13-15; Phil. 2:5-8). This represents Christ as the patient and enduring servant – "obedient unto death."

b. *The Sheep or Lamb.* Such speaks to us of Christ's self-surrender to the cross (Isa. 53:7; Acts 8:32-35).

c. *Goat.* Speaks first of all of the sinner (Matt. 25:33). Goats to the left. Used sacrificially, it symbolizes Christ being numbered with transgressors – Our substitute (Isa. 53:12; Luke 23:33; Gal. 3:13; II Cor. 5:21).

d. *Turtle Dove or Pigeon.* A dove symbolizes mourning, innocency (Isa. 38:14; 59:11; Matt. 23:37; Heb. 7:26). It is also associated with poverty (Lev. 5:7). Christ became poor (Luke 9:58). His poverty began at the incarnation and ended at the cross whereby we are made rich (II Cor. 8:9; Phil. 2:6-8). The sacrifice of this poor man becomes the poor man's sacrifice (Luke 2:24).

There are some who think that different degrees of faith are here represented in these creatures – some being more feeble to apprehend the full meaning of Christ's work than others. How true it is that even the best fail to fully understand all that they have in Him.

3. *The Presentation of the Offering* (Lev. 1:2, 3). Had to be offered voluntarily. "His own voluntary will" (Lev. 1:3). The word "voluntary" brings out the grand idea of burnt offering in reference to Christ. Keep in mind two views of the Cross:

The place of sin-bearing.
The place of accomplishing the will of God.

It was the former that Christ shrank from in the garden, but never from the latter. "I delight to do Thy will."

So the burnt offering presents voluntary devotedness of Christ as manifested in the death of the cross. In the sin offering we see His "life taken" (Isa. 53:8). In the burnt offering His life was voluntarily given (John 10:17).

Had to be offered at "the door of the tabernacle" (Lev. 1:3). There is no way of approach to God but by passing the altar. Sin has blocked the door and there could be no access except on the ground of sacrifice.

So this typifies the open door. The burnt offering is the open door from God's side and the sin offering is the door open from our side.

Had to be offered individually (Lev. 1:2) – "If any man." Three things are taught here:

a. Represents his individual confession of need.
b. Represents his individual acceptance of God's way of salvation.
c. Represents his individual recognition of the excellency of his offering.

Had to offer such in order that he may be accepted (See R.V. of Lev. 1:3), "that he may be accepted *before* the Lord." How acceptable Christ is, and how acceptable we are when we present Him! Accepted and acceptable in our beloved (Eph. 1:6). "Accepted in the beloved" – not accepted because of our love or our faithfulness, but because of Him and because we are in Him. "The Lord taketh pleasure in His people" (Ps. 149:4), because all are in Christ.

> The love wherewith He loves the Son,
> Such is His love to me.

4. *The Laying On of the Hand* (Lev. 1:4). By this act the offering and the offerer became one. It speaks of a oneness secured for the offerer through the acceptance of his offering. There are two important truths that one can discern in this action of the offerer. There was a double transfer: the unworthiness of the offerer was transferred to the victim; and the acceptableness of the offering was transferred to the offerer. The word *put* can mean "lean," "place," or "press." This all sinners can do.

The act implied the identification

of the offerer with his offering. When by faith I lay my hand upon that dear Head of His, I identify myself with Christ. I stand in Him complete and I receive complete acceptance from the Father because I am identified with Christ. I stand as Christ does before the Father. "Near so near – nearer I cannot be, For in the Person of His Son I am as near as He." Remember, there are no degrees of acceptance, of justification or salvation. If I am in Christ at all, then I am complete in Him. Of course, there are degrees of the enjoyment of justification, degrees of knowledge, of the fulness and extent of justification, degrees of the power and desire to manifest justification in life. But we must be careful not to confound the degrees of its enjoyment, extent, or power, with the great fact itself.

The next thought suggested by the hand upon the victim is the transfer of the offerer's obligation of guilt to the victim as his substitute (Lev. 16:21). How true this is of us. We have nothing of our own – nothing but sin and even that the Saviour made His. Standing with his hand upon his victim's head he virtually said, "I have no devotedness, no preciousness, but I present this perfect offering for my acceptance before the Lord." The moment he did this, the whole value of the offering became his. From that moment it ceased to be a question of what he was – it became a question of what his Offering was. How blessedly true this is of Christ and ourselves. No longer is it "Just as I am," but "Just as Thou art." We are nothing – He is everything! "It shall be accepted for him." So God accepts Christ for me. "Make an Atonement," not in the sin offering sense. Perfect surrender of Christ to the Father – this is the highest pinnacle of Atonement.

It was Isaac Watts who taught us to sing

> My faith would lay her hand
> On that dear head of Thine
> While like a penitent I stand
> And there confess my sin.

5. *The Slaying of the Victim* (Lev. 1:5). *The sacrifice was killed by the offerer himself* (Lev. 1:5). "He shall kill the Bullock." This surely represents my personal responsibility regarding the sin which crucified Christ. In my unregenerate state I was among the number who cried, "This is the heir – come, let us kill him." I must never lose sight of the part my sin played in slaying the sacrifice on Calvary.

Killed before the Lord (Lev. 1:5). This gives us the other aspect of Christ's death. He died not only by man's hand, but before the Lord. "It pleased the Lord to bruise Him. He hath put Him to grief." Although my finite mind cannot grasp the truth, yet the fact is Scriptural that God not only allowed Christ to die. But in Christ God virtually died Himself. "God was in Christ, reconciling the world unto Hmself."

6. *The Sprinkling of the Blood* (Lev. 1:5). The sprinkling of the blood was performed by the priests. Here I have a change of my relationship. I am no longer a guilty sinner; my substitute has been accepted. I am now a "worshipping saint." Aaron is a Christ, and his sons typify the believers. The action of sprinkling typifies what I do as I approach God. I come in the spirit of true worship and communion, presenting the perfect dedication of a perect saviour. I have entrance continually and through Him.

The sprinkled blood still speaks. "To Jesus the mediator of the new covenant, and to the blood of sprinkling, that speaketh better things than that of Abel" (Heb. 12:24).

7. *The Flaying of the Pieces* (Lev. 1:6). This was also done by the offerer and is beautifully typical of

Christ and ourselves. Possibly the sacrifice was flayed, that is, all the outward covering was removed in order that the inner substance might be revealed, so that the offerer might see the thorough excellency of his offering. To flay means "to strip off." So it was flayed and cut in pieces, not merely to make it more convenient for burning but to reveal the intrinsic value of every part. It was not sufficient for the creature to be outwardly unblemished – its hidden parts must be of the same character – hence the dissection of the whole.

Blessed be God, there are no weak parts without or within connected with our most acceptable burnt offering. Examine Christ where you will and never will you be able to detect the slightest blemish. The life and work of Jesus were not superficial. Why, the more we penetrate the inner character of our sacrifice, the more we realize the wonderfulness of surrender and devotion. His smallest act was prompted by obedience to God and was therefore fragrant to Him.

"Cut in Pieces." This is subject to another interpretation. The Holy Spirit delights to dwell upon the sweetness of Christ's sacrifice not only as a whole but in the most minute details. "Little is much if God is in it" – and so as we "cut in pieces" His person and work, we discover that He was faithful and devoted in that which is least, as well as in that which is much.

8. *The Placing and Washing of the Pieces* (Lev. 1:7-9). The altar was prepared by priests' sons, who then placed the respective parts of the offering in order. Here again, we see ourselves not as lost, guilty sinners, but as we are in Him – a kingdom of priests. We have the high position and privilege as believers of standing before God and beholding and pleading the perfect sacrifice that has been made.

Laid in Order (Lev. 1:8). There was order even in Christ's offering of Himself. His devotion and surrender were not spasmodic or unregulated but guided and ordered aright. The head, the fat, the fire, "Upon the Wood" – this can prefigure nailing on the cross.

The head represents the seat of all that is valuable and precious. The powers of the head are innumerable.

The fat is that which burns most quickly.

The fire is symbolic of holiness in Scripture. And so placed together the three mean this, that holiness and zeal regulated and consumed the voluntary, perfect, conscious, sacrifice of Christ at Calvary.

"His Inwards and His Legs shall He wash in Water" (Lev. 1:9). The *inwards* stand for the inner substance. The legs for the outer. It simply means that the offerer had to see to it that his offering was clean, without and within. Do we not see Jesus in this? Was He not the perfect offering?

The inwards suggest the inner motives, thoughts, feelings, and contents of the heart. These were all clean before God. "In Him dwelt no evil thing."

The legs typify the outward life and conduct of Jesus, which were ever in agreement with His inner life. Our blessed Lord was the same all through. His inner and outer life were of the same holy texture.

9. *The Burning of the Whole* (Lev. 1:9). "Burn all on the Altar." In some of the offerings, as we shall later see, the priests partook of the offering. In others, the people. But in this burnt offering the offering was wholly for Jehovah, the entire sacrifice was His portion. He demanded all because the offering stood for His acceptance of the offerer who had been made acceptable by the offering. The whole

sacrifice within and without was pure, therefore, God had it exclusively for Himself. It became His food. It was a sweet-savor unto Him because of its purity and entirety.

How true all this is of Jesus – our burnt offering! On the cross, He gave all. He kept nothing back. God demanded all and a sin-cursed world required all that a Holy One could give and our Lord Jesus kept nothing back. He broke His alabaster box of precious ointment and the fragrance of it pleased the heart of the Father and has filled heaven and earth with sweetness ever since.

What a sacrifice! All was burnt upon Calvary's altar.
He left all at His Incarnation.
He gave all at His Death.
He got all at His Ascension.

Now for us His word is "I have given you an example, that ye should do as I have done to you" (John 13:15). Dare we pay the price and follow Him? The burnt offering typifies the entire dedication of the Saviour to the Father's will, no matter what that will involved. It is the offering that sets forth not the exceeding hatefulness of sin as the sin offering, but the unshaken and unshakable devotedness of Christ to God. This offering was not for the sinner's conscience but for the heart of God. "My all is on the Altar." We cannot sing this hymn until we are prepared to be absolutely at the Father's disposal. But do not hesitate to present your burnt offering. The Holy Spirit is able to make all grace abound toward you and be assured "that when your Burnt Offering begins the Song of the Lord will also begin."

The Law of this offering is found in Leviticus 6:8-13.

The Linen garments of the Priest set forth in type the personal righteousness of Christ. Having given Himself up to the death of the cross in order to accomplish His Father's will, He enters heaven in His own eternal righteousness bearing with Him the ashes, or memorials of His finished work.

The "ashes" declared the completion of the sacrifice, and God's acceptance of same.

The ashes of the burnt offering declared the acceptance of the sacrifice.

The ashes of the sin offering declared the judgment of the sin.

The fire, we read, "shall never go out." So the heart of God and our own hearts as well, can feed continually upon the Holy One.

B. *The Meal or Meat Offering*

It may be well at the outset of our study of this particular offering to refresh our memories regarding the significance and order of the offerings as a whole. The following table may help to fix their sequence on our minds.

Order			*Leviticus References*
Burnt Offering			
Meal	do	Chp.	1. 6:8-13
Peace	do		2. 6:14-28
Sin	do		3. 7:11-21
Trespass	do		4. 6:25-30
			5. 6:1-7
			7:1-7

Typical Significance

Entire dedication of Christ to Father's Will.

Christ, the perfect man, tested by human sacrifice.

Christ our peacemaker with God.

Christ, the sinless substitute for sinners.

Christ the Redeemer, restorer, repairer of the effects of sin.

We have already seen that the order given in the first five chapters of Leviticus is the divine order. They represent the presentation of the Lord Jesus from the Godward aspect. When the sinners of Israel, and in fact all sinners, return to God, they have to commence where God leaves off, namely, at the trespass offering or sin offering. Once saved, the ladder is ascended according to spiritual apprehension.

This can be illustrated by a ladder to someone in need. The rescuer descends and then the rescued ascends with the rescuer. How full of spiritual significance this is! We have already seen that the burnt offering, which God commences with, represented the life of the Lord Jesus dedicated to the Father's will, no matter what that will involved.

The meat offering represents the same blessed Person with a life dedicated to man.

The burnt offering typifies Christ satisfying God, surrendering to Him what belongs to Him.

The meat offering represents Jesus, as a perfect man satisfying man and bestowing upon him that which meets his spiritual need.

The burnt offering is His life – Godward.

The meat offering, His life – Manward.

1. *The Character of the Offering.*

a. *It was a meal or meat Offering*

In the A.V. it is called the meat offering, but in the R.V. the meal offering. The meal offering is the correct translation because it describes the nature of the offering presented. The inclusion of the word "meat" is accounted for in the following way. Meat was the term generally used when our Bible was translated to describe food in general and as meal constitutes the staple food of man, the presence of the word "meat" is easily understood. It is used in Scotland still in a general way. Meal or flour is one of earth's most precious products and in this we see our Lord Jesus, who, as the Bread of Life, is the most precious product not only of earth, but of heaven and upon whom both God and man feed.

b. *It was a Bloodless Offering*

In the other four offerings there is blood! Blood! Blood! Blood! but in this one no victim is slain – no blood is shed. This feature is in perfect order because it represents the beautiful life that our Saviour lived upon the earth. The meat offering teaches the pure and perfect manhood of the man Christ Jesus.

c. *It was a Free-Will Offering*

The word for "meal" is "*Minahal,*" which signifies a present, a free gift, or something presented not to obtain admittance but to secure favor. It implies the handing over of a gift from an inferior person to that of a superior (See Gen. 4:3). The Lord Jesus is my Minahal, my gift, the One who came "so freely to this earth to live my human life." When we come before God, He is the One we present. We are the inferiors coming with the gift to the superior in order to secure His favor.

d. *It was an Approach Offering*

The word for "offering" used here is *Korban,* which is derived from *Karab,* meaning "to draw near" or "to make to approach." To this very day in the East one has to bring a *Korban* or "admittance offering" in order to secure an audience or to find access to the presence of a person of superiority. Hence it is called a "free offering" (See Judg. 3:18).

The symbolic application is clearly evident. Christ is our *Korban.* With Him "we venture nigh," and "find liberty of access" into God's presence (Eph. 2:18).

e. *It was a Most Holy Offering*

We have two classes of seven holy things referred to in the Levitical order of worship and service – three holy, four most holy.

Holy

Thank-offerings (Lev. 23:20; Num. 6:20).
Firstborn (Num. 18:17).
Firstfruits (Lev. 2:12).

Most Holy
The Incense (Exod. 30:36).
The Shewbread (Lev. 24:9).
The Sin-Trespass Offerings (Lev. 6:23-29; 7:1; 6; 16:13 etc.).
The Meal Offering (Lev. 2:3).

"It is a thing most holy of the Offerings." This reflects does it not the One who was "holy, harmless, undefiled, separate from sinners"? The New Testament presents us with the anti-type of this offering in Jesus. In Luke 1:35 the angel said, "That holy thing which shall be born of thee." Why is the precise language of this Old Testament offering employed here? "A thing most holy" – "That holy thing." Is it not because He was the most holy of men but unlike them, in that He was born of the Holy Spirit?

f. *It was a Voluntary Offering*

No emphasis was brought to bear upon the person. "When any will." The offerer could come when he liked and with as much as he liked, for no quantity of fine flour is prescribed. Its quality alone is greatly emphasized, as it is with Christ. Was His human life not a voluntary offering as was His death? It took Him three hours to die, but thirty-three years so to live among men in order to understand them fully. As the meat offering represents the perfect human life of Christ, let us try to understand more fully the voluntary aspect of His birth, temptations, sorrows, tears, hunger, humiliations, as well as His glorious sacrifice on the cross.

g. *It was a Sweet-savor Offering*

"A sweet savour unto the Lord." In this, it is connected with the burnt offering and peace offering, because all three speak of our Lord Jesus in the perfection of His surrender and devotion to the Father's will for whatever purpose He deemed best. The perfect human Christ, Emmanuel in the flesh, was the One who brought perpetual joy and gladness to the Father's heart. The earthly life of our Saviour ascended with sweet fragrance to God. "This is my beloved Son in whom I am well pleased." This testimony was given by the Father after thirty years of His Son's human life spent amid the common trials and cares of His home life. Of His own life, our Lord could say, "I do always the things that please My Father."

2. *The Elements of the Offering*. The substance, or elements used in the presentation of the meal offering were varied according to the need of the offerer, or to the manner of bestowal. Still, the outstanding composite parts, which are all beautifully typical, are as follows:

a. *Fine Flour*

The first and foremost ingredient used in this particular offering was fine flour. Now flour is only produced as the result of a bruising, grinding process. Into the mill the wheat is cast and made subject to the process that makes it more palatable as the staple food of man. Moreover, it had to be "fine" flour. There had to be no coarse or hard lumps, no roughness within it, but as smooth to the touch, as only fine flour can be.

What a picture of Jesus this is! He called Himself "the Bread of Life," but ere He could be enjoyed as such He had to pass as "a corn of wheat" into the mill. The precious wheat of His earthly life had to be crushed and bruised. "It pleased the Lord to bruise Him." What satisfying food He is! Lord, evermore give us this bread!

Our Lord was not only flour, but "fine" flour. Cast your mind back to His sojourn on the earth. Was there such a thing as roughness or coarseness, or unevenness about His life? Think of Him in all the varied circumstances and experiences and what do you find? Why, the same quiet, patient, unruffled spirit even when things were so adverse and trying. What evenness — what perfection — what smoothness of touch! Why, of Him it was true —

> Not a surge of worry
> Not a shade of care,
> Not a blast of hurry
> Touched His spirit here.

Moses was the meekest of men, but he sinned with his lips. Jesus was the finest of wheat! He never made one mistake.

b. *Oil*

This ingredient was used in a twofold way —

It was poured upon the fine flour.
It was mingled with the fine flour.

Both processes typify the work of the Holy Spirit in connection with our Lord's earthly life. They speak of His anointing and indwelling by the Spirit. Oil, as we know from Scripture, II Cor. 1:21-23; I John 2:27, is a type of the Holy Spirit.

(1). *The oil was poured upon the fine flour.* Does this not answer to Luke 3:22; 4:1, where our Lord was divinely anointed with the Holy Spirit by the Father? This pouring forth is confirmed by Peter in Acts 10:38. "God anointed Jesus of Nazareth with the Holy Spirit and with power (for His service among men as a Meal Offering for men) and He went about doing good, and healing all that were oppressed of the devil, for God was with Him."

(2). *The oil was mingled with the fine flour.* What does this suggest but the inseparable connection between the Lord Jesus and the Holy Spirit? His life and work were saturated through and through with this divine oil. Think of the oil, mingling with His nature at His birth, for was He not born of the Spirit? Take notice of all that transpired from His birth to His death; was not everything made possible "through the Eternal Spirit"?

(3). *The oil was on every piece.* Every section had oil without and within. Take the knife of reverent inquiry and cut in pieces our perfect meal offering and what do you find? Why oil within and without. Our blessed Saviour's life, even to its smallest detail, was permeated with the Holy Spirit's presence and power. "I, by the Spirit of God" was characteristic not only of His work in casting out demons but of His every action.

c. *Frankincense* (Lev. 1:1, 2, 15, 16).

There are one or two things worthy of our notice in connection with the presence of this particular element.

Flour) Body
)
Oil) Spirit
)
Frankincense) Soul

all surrendered to God for men.

(1). *Its Nature.* Frankincense is not to be confounded with *incense,* to which it was sometimes added, but very often used apart from incense. Incense is prayer (Rev. 5:8).

Frankincense is a certain form of resin obtainable from a particular species of tree. "Trees of frankincense" are referred to by Solomon in *Song of Sol.* 4:14. What the constituents of frankincense were Scripture does not say. Incense, on the other hand, is made up of various perfumes, as we know from Exodus 30:34. How typical this is of our gracious Lord! There is the sweet incense of His perfections that we can apprehend — there is the frankincense of that which God saw in Jesus, but which the mind of man cannot understand or express, for "great is the mystery of Godliness."

(2). *The Fire increases its fragrance.* Whenever frankincense is burned it produces a bright flame and sheds forth a most delicious fragrant odor. What a glimpse of Christ this presents! Why, it was the fire of His sorrows and trials that brought out the wonderful fragrance of His life.

The frankincense was all for God. "All the Frankincense thereof." What does this symbolize but the presentation of His life exclusively for the glory of God? "I have glorified Thee on the earth" was His own testimony.

The oil typifies the source of power in Christ's ministry – The frankincense the sole object of His ministry – for the Glory of God.

d. *Salt*

This particular offering had to be seasoned and offered with salt. Salt is that which preserves from corruption. It is used the wide world over to season particular foods and check the action of disease and decay. What is the salt in our Lord's life as our meal offering? What typical teaching does this ingredient reveal? Surely this, that the perfect words and ways were the influences that arrested the corruptions, evil powers around Him. Wherever Christ goes into the human heart or society, he delivers from all the tainted, corrupting influences. It was also a figure of His own incorruption. "He whom God raised saw no corruption." He was the salt of the earth. His speech was always seasoned with salt, and the truths of Matthew 5:13; Mark 9:49, 50; Colossians 4:6 are for us as well.

(1). *The Salt of the Covenant.* In Moses' day, and in the East at this present time, salt stands for the symbol of an enduring covenant. (Numbers 18:19 confirms this – "A covenant of salt for ever before the Lord unto thee and to thy seed with thee." Among the Arabs, when men eat together and enter into an agreement of any kind, salt is used as a symbol of cemented friendship, hence the expression "There is salt between us." "He has eaten of my Salt." Being a preservative it became a fitting type of an enduring covenant (See Ezra 4:14, R.V.; Num. 18:19; II Chron. 13:5). God and I are friends today. We have entered into covenant with each other, He to keep me eternally, I, to serve Him continually: and what is the binding influence of the covenant? why, Jesus. He is God's guarantee, and also mine, that the covenant between us will not be broken. When a covenant is made by two people, salt is partaken of by each as a sign of indissoluble alliance (See Luke 25:14).

e. *No Leaven*

"Ye shall burn no honey in any offering of the Lord made by fire." Now leaven is always the symbol of evil and corruption. True it is included in one or two other offerings (see Lev. 23:17), but here, mankind is symbolized as having corruption within it. But the offerings that typify Christ, such as the meal offering, were baked without leaven; because in Him there was no evil. The meaning of *leaven* is "sour," something that ferments and puffs up – in Christ this was not found. It represents fermenting dough. Its first reference in Exodus 12:15 means something to be "put away."

f. *No Honey*

"Nor any honey." Now honey is good in itself. Canaan was a land flowing with milk and honey. *Leaven* stands for that which is evil, *honey* the symbol of that which is sweet and attractive. Not only so, but because of its very sweetness it may cause harm or injury. "Hast thou found honey – eat so much as is sufficient for thee lest thou be filled therewith and vomit it."

The spiritual application of the honey is that things so sweet and attractive are harmless within themselves may yet cause pain and sorrow. There was no honey in this offering because it prefigures Christ. What do you find as you think of Him? Why, that He turned His back upon the sweet, attractive, harmless, legitimate things and associations of life, in order to serve God absolutely. He never allowed nature's claims to interfere with the presentation to God of Himself for the service of man. Nothing is so difficult as to adjust the claims of natural relationship so that they never interfere with the claims of Christ. It is also said that in ancient times honey was used to produce fermentation in the preparation of vinegar and that when it boiled it frothed up and thus was regarded by the Hebrew expositors as a symbol of pride. Well, in Him there was no honey of pride or desire for flattery or applause. His words are sweet to our taste because they come from One who is the perfection of sweetness.

3. *The Mode of the Offering.* The meal offering had to be baked through the process of fire in an open pan or oven and such a preparatory process offers one or two suggestive glimpses of Christ.

a. *The Baking and the Fire*

These at once convey the ideas of suffering. Our Lord had much suffering, not only on the cross, but in His earthly life. Sometimes we ask ourselves whether we realize sufficiently the sufferings of His life, as well as His death. Paul speaks about "filling up the sufferings of Christ" (Phil. 1:29, 30). This cannot mean the cross aspect of His trials, for He bore it all alone, and for all. The sufferings of this life through which our Saviour passed were the trials, sorrows, disappointments, insults, persecutions, that men heaped upon Him. Truly He was baked by fire.

b. *Baken in an Oven*

Now an oven is closed up – hidden from the gaze of man – when the door is closed no one can see what the interior of the oven held. This represents the hidden, secret inner sufferings that our Lord passed through (Heb. 2:18; Matt. 27:45, 46). What unseen agonies were His! None of the ransomed will ever know how deep were the waters He crossed.

c. *Pan. Frying Pan*

This is an open utensil, upon which all was seen at once. In such we have suggested the more open, evident sufferings of Christ (Matt. 27:27-31). Men saw His tears, His bruised body, His precious blood. They looked upon Him whom they had pierced. What a blessed Saviour He was to pass through such hidden and more open trials and sufferings for you and me!

4. *The Conditions of the Offering.* All of the conditions regulating this offering are blessedly prophetic of our Lord.

a. *Had to Be Offered on the Burnt Offering Altar* (Exod. 40:29)

The burnt offering, as we have seen, is typical of the Saviour's entire dedication to God. It speaks of His absolute surrender to His Father's will. The meal offering stands for Christ as a perfect man meeting all that man is heir to, in order to succor men themselves. What is the connection? Why, this – the burnt offering is the basis or foundation of the meal offering. Christ's work as a man among men was fruitful because it rested upon His devotion to God. Work for others is dependent upon our surrender to God.

b. *Had to Accompany All Burnt Offerings* (Num. 15:3-12)

With the burnt offering, a meal offering. Our Saviour was a twofold servant, a servant of the Lord and a servant of man. His submission to

God's will did not isolate Him from His service among the diseased and sinful. No, it accompanied it! Surrender to God and service for men went hand in hand.

(1). *Had to be Offered by the Priest and his Sons* (Lev. 6:14, 20). We have already seen that Aaron is a type of Christ as our High Priest and that Aaron's sons typify the saints as members of His body. When we come to apply the meal offering to ourselves we realize that we cannot offer it as lost, helpless sinners. Our relationship must be changed. We must become worshiping saints or priests. How can we work for man if our hearts are not right with God and destitute of His grace?

c. *Part Eaten. Priests* (Lev. 1:10; 6:16). *Part Given to Jehovah* (Lev. 1:9; 6:15)

A part burnt upon the altar unto the Lord, the remainder eaten by Aaron and his sons. Does this not mean that there is a mutual enjoyment regarding Christ? God's part came first, the priests' portion after. God delights to feed upon Him; so do we. He is the object of divine and human satisfaction and sustenance. He is the bread of God – the bread of man.

d. *Eaten in Holiness*

(1). *All who touched it had to be holy* (Lev. 6:18). This refers to the ceremonial cleanness necessary in the priests who officiated and partook of it (See Haggai 2:12). Because the offering was most holy it had to be handled with holy hands. Ere we can enter into the blessed enjoyment of our Lord as our meal offering, we must have His healing touch, His cleansing from all the defilement of sin. "Be ye holy, even as I am holy."

(2). *Shall be eaten in a Holy Place* – in the court of the tabernacle of the congregation (Lev. 6:16). It is impossible to appropriate or apprehend Christ anywhere. An unspiritual believer will never enter into the full delight of the Lord through the things and ways of the world. The offering must be eaten in a holy place. The import is this, that our very practices and associations must be holy, if we are to understand, and experience, the fulness of Christ.

(3). *Eaten by holy Males* (Lev. 6:18). This limitation to males spiritually implies Hebrews 5:14, "strong meat belongeth to them that are of full age, even those who by reason of use have their senses exercised to discern both good and evil." The truth taught by the limitation is that spiritual growth and the development of faith come as we feed on Him." All the males" speaks of energy and strength in the priestly nature, and this is developed in all saints as they feed upon the divine nature.

5. *It was Offered Morning and Night* (Lev. 6:20). How perpetual are the blessings and benefits of Christ's work! How adaptable to our every need! In the morning we offer "the half of it" – that is, we appropriate the man at His right hand for all the needs of our human life during the day. He knows our every need, so we go out in Him. At night "offer the other half." If we pass through the day having allowed sin or disobedience to mar our peace, and we come to the night in sincere contrition, Jesus is our substitute, our intercessor, ready to forgive. By grace we can retire conscious that we are accepted in Him. We read that "it came to pass in the morning when the Meal Offering was offered, water came by the way of Edom and the country was filled with water." When Christ is fully recognized and appropriated, there is always revival blessing (II Kings 3:20).

c. *The Peace Offering*

Just as it takes all the colors to complete the rainbow, so one must place all the Levitical offerings together in order to possess a complete portrait of Christ. It will help us to appreciate more fully the significance of each offering if we keep in mind the fact that each is only a part of the whole — that each has some feature peculiar to itself. "God has taken Christ and shewn Him to us in Parts. Each proclaims in its own measure, the worth and beauty of the Lord Jesus."

The peace offering differs from the burnt offering in that the threefold action of "flaying," "cutting in pieces," and "washing the inwards and legs" is entirely omitted. And this is quite in order.

In the *burnt offering* we have the complete surrender of Christ to the Father's will.

In the *peace offering* we have presented the communion of the worshiper. Christ enjoyed by man as well as God.

In the *burnt offering* the offerer only gazed upon this offering, wholly consumed for God.

In the *peace offering* I not only gaze but feed upon the very portions that I read.

In the *burnt offering,* see Jesus commanding the admiration of the heart.

In the *peace offering,* establishing peace of conscience and meeting the deep and manifold necessities of the soul.

Further, comparing this offering with the meal offering, a leading difference is manifest.

In the meal offering, no bloodshedding. In the peace offering there is blood-shedding. As the redeemed we begin where God finishes, namely, at trespass and sin offerings. Passing through our peace offering we come to know the friendship and peace of God's children, because of the redemptive work of Christ. No one can enjoy or feed upon Christ as the meal offering unless, and until, they have a solid foundation for their communion, namely, identification with an accepted substitute.

Notice the place assigned to the peace offering in Leviticus 7. In the order of the offerings as given to Israel it occupies the third position. Here, in the Laws, it is given the last place, because the peace offering has to do with the communion of the offerer and serves to show that communion and fellowship are based upon and flow from a full knowledge and enjoyment of all that the other four offerings foreshadow. Not until we have died with our sins and ourselves can we delight in God (Col. 1:12-14).

In a beautiful way you find these burnt three offerings brought together in John 14:6. As the burnt offering, Jesus is *the life,* as the meal offering, He is *the truth,* as the peace offering, He is *the way*. That the offering before us prefigures Christ is clearly evident. It symbolizes Him as the foundation of that happy, restful communion with God, that feasting at His table sharing his divine and holy life (Zech. 6:13). "The Counsel of Peace shall be between them both."

"His name shall be called — Prince of Peace" (Isa. 9:6).

"He is our peace — So making Peace" (Eph. 2:13, 14, 15).

A type of what He does for all (Luke 23:12).

1. *Its Character*. Peace offering. The word *peace* denotes "being quits" with another. Actually the word for peace is in the plural, and signifies all kinds of peace. There is peace in man, peace among men, peace between God and man, and all these phases of peace are covered by this offering. The term implies not only the negative side, such as peace coming after cessation of hostilities, but

positive joy and prosperity. The word itself has a threefold meaning.

a. *Completion*

Something definitely accomplished. The war between my heart and God is over. The enemy has been defeated. Christ has become the victor, reconciler. Peace is the basis of a completed work. Now all is well. He is my peace. I am complete in Him. The word that is used for sacrifice here is one that is never used in the first seven chapters of Leviticus with the exception of the peace offering, where it refers exclusively to animals slaughtered, reminding us that only death can bring peace.

b. *Compensation*

"Peace" derived from *Shalom,* a peace on the ground of the perfection of compensation. Christ is my peace, and I am at peace with God. Why? Because Christ has compensated God. With Him, the Father is well pleased. God is my friend because Christ has compensated all claims of the broken law of holiness.

c. *Peace*

This is joy or happiness as an outcome or river. There can be no inward peace until there is peace with God. The term is used of a spiritual offering (Ps. 57:18; Rom. 12:1; Heb. 13:15, 16; I Pet. 2:3; Phil. 4:18).

We have

peace with God.	Rom. 5:1.
peace of God.	Phil. 4:7.
peace from God.	I Cor. 1:3.
peace made by God.	Col. 1:20.
peace as a sermon.	Eph. 2:17.
peace in a person.	Eph. 2:14.

(1). *Thanksgiving Offering* (Lev. 7:12, 13, 15. See also II Sam. 24:25; Judg. 8:31). As such it was used for praise on all occasions for thanksgiving. As the redeemed of the Lord we give thanks in everything and offer the sacrifice of praise, continually, for mercies received (Ps. 107; Heb. 13:15). This aspect of the peace offering signifies peace procured. Praise to Him for redemption (Rev. 1:13-15).

(2). *Votive Offering* (Lev. 7:16; 22:11. See Gen. 35:10; I Sam. 1:11-28). Given or presented when vows were made, token of definite desire to fulfill same, and is connected with service (Ps. 66:16). Christ paid His vows unto the Lord.

(3). *Consecration Offering* (Lev. 7:35). Had to be consecrated as priests before work with offering. Also used Exodus 29:22. Consecration of priests (Num. 6:6-14), and of Nazarite vow. All of these features can be applied to Christ.

(4). *Voluntary Offering* (Lev. 19: 5; 22:11). As such not offered on any external occasion. This aspect speaks of peace possessed. The spring of joy and gratitude (Eph. 5:18, 19; John 14:26; 15:11). What can I give Him? How can I best serve God, now I am His?

(5). *Sweet Savour Offering* (Lev. 3:5-16). Common with burnt offering and meal offering. Emphasizes the truth. Christ hath loved us and hath given Himself for us. Offering and a sacrifice to God for a sweet-smelling savour (Eph. 5:2).

The perfect fellowship God enjoys with man because of Christ's finished work makes His Son fragrant (Isa. 42:1).

2. *Its Elements.*

a. *An Animal*

Ox, Lamb, Goat (Lev. 3:1, 7, 12). Can signify different degrees of appreciation of Christ by believing people.

Ox — Christ, strong and patient. His service as peace offering.

Lamb — His gentleness and meekness. He was a man of peace — Now peace for man.

Goat — Despised and rejected as a

sinner. So Christ not only for sin, but as us (I Cor. 12:12).

b. *No turtle-dove or pigeon here*

Because connected with sacrificial meal in which several parts of a small bird were insufficient. We cannot feed on a small Christ. We must have a full One.

c. *Male or Female*

Different from other offerings. He is no restriction, age or sex. In other offerings Christ is seen. Here we have the mutual communion of offerer by the priest. So in Christ there is neither male or female. All are one in Him.

d. *Without Blemish*

Christ was within and without. Demons confessed "Thou art the Holy One of God." What a perfect offering (I Pet. 1:19; Heb. 10:5-10; Isa. 53:11)! Because of His unblemished life and vicarious death peace is possible for all.

e. *Unleavened Cakes* (Lev. 7:12)

This is a form of the meal offering and signifies some cooked varieties offered with peace offering when presented as a thanksgiving. Here we have the common meal, where God, priest, and worshipers sit down, as it were, together in token that there is nothing which separates them and that all causes of displeasure on the part of God are at an end. Here Christ is seen as our peace. God and man enjoy fellowship because of Him. Both feast in sweet fellowship upon Christ. He had no evil, no leaven. He is here presented as One, making a common meal possible. Here we have a true picture of Christ. Any true thanksgiving must present Him as the offering without leaven, mingled with oil, meaning a life permeated with the Holy Spirit.

f. *Leaven Bread* (Lev. 7:13)

Here the figure is changed. Type of church who feeds with God. Must remember whenever we meet around Christ as the peace offering that as believers we still have the evil principle within us. We are not perfect yet (I John 1:8). "If we say we have no sin we deceive ourselves and the truth is not in us." See Amos 4:5, where Israel is leaven before God. But when Christ comes, His will be "glorious church, not having spot or wrinkle or any such thing, holy and without blemish" (Eph. 5:27).

2. *Its Order.*

a. *For the Offerer*

(1). *Had to bring it himself* (Lev. 7:29, 30). Not come by proxy. If we want peace we must come personally. "His hands shall bring it." So we come personally with a personal Christ in the presence of God Most High.

(2). *Had to lay hand upon its head* (Lev. 3:2, 8, 13). Either ox, lamb or goat. This act speaks of identification. This is all the sinner can do. We place the hand of faith upon the head of Christ saying, "Here, O God, is my peace." Here we have personal identification and appropriation. The word *lay* implies "to press the whole weight upon." As we turn to Him for peace, this is all we can do – lean hard on Him! Further, the hand on the head depicted a double transfer – the transfer of guilt to the sacrifice, the transfer of the peace of the sacrifice to the repentant guilty one.

A true peacemaker must be trusted by both parties. The work of Christ does this: identify by faith (Rom. 5:1).

(3). *Kill it himself* (Lev. 3:2, 8, 13). Let us never forget that it was our sin that killed Christ. "Him . . . ye . . . have . . . slain" (Acts 2:23). Here is death. The life of Christ before the cross could not save. A bloodless Christianity cannot save. Sacrifice is the basis of peace. Christ is here, not so much the sin offering bearing sins. Having already borne them, He is the ground of peaceful, happy fellowship with God. Killed at the door of the tabernacle. Ere Christ passed into the Father's presence, He was slain at the door of the cross. The offering was killed at the door of the tabernacle.

(4). *Wave before the Lord* (Lev. 7: 20). Swung towards the altar, offered to God, and swung back, received again from Him, as consecrated gifts for reverent consumption. So "heave" up to God, down from God to man. Fat with breast was waved before the Lord. Offerer waved such backward and forward. Priests heaved it up and down, a token of their dedication to God first, then received back again for their use. This is also an acknowledgment of the goodness of God. Waved before the Lord, Christ is, first of all, God's, then God gives Him back to man. It was called *heave offering,* because it was lifted up on high and presented to Jehovah. All that is lifted up is separated unto His service as a token of devotion to Him.

It is called *wave offering,* because it is taken and shaken, or tossed to and fro, not up and down as the heave offering. Swung to every part of the world it denoted God's universal dominion, and presented to the four quarters of the earth, prefigured the extent of the Redeemer's sacrifice (Lev. 7:1).

b. *For the Priest*

(1). *Sprinkle blood upon altar* (Lev. 3:2). Altar – place of offering toward God, speaks of just claims. Blood on the altar speaks of God's acceptance of offering, whom we present as our substitute as we approach God.

(2). *Had to offer fat, kidneys, caul* (Lev. 3:2, 4, 9, 11, 14-16). These inward parts were the choice and richest parts. *Fat* answers to suet. *Kidneys* to the seat of inward affections, "reins" (Ps. 26:2).

Offered with frankincense, all these parts were burnt in the fire on the altar to God. The typify the hidden and inward excellencies and affections and energies of the Lord Jesus which were not valued or appreciated while He was here below. These best parts were burnt by fire, reminding us that the finest, noblest, and most excellent must be placed upon the altar. *Fat* is applied to everything excellent of its kind. We speak of "living off the fat of the land" (See Gen. 14:18; Deut. 33:14; Num. 18:18; II Sam. 1:22). That which is choicest food for man, when surrendered, yields the utmost satisfaction as an offering to God.

(3). *Burnt upon the Burnt Offering Altar* (Lev. 3:5; 6:12). The fact of Atonement is the basis of acceptance. Some are hoping to enjoy Christ, but not the Christ of the cross. Such can never experience the peace of God. The burnt offering came first, and the peace offering was laid upon it (See also Judg. 21:6; I Sam. 10:8; I Kings 3:15).

(4). *Feed upon Shoulder and Breast* (Lev. 7:31, 32, 134). These parts first consecrated and then waved before the Lord and then given back (Lev. 7:24). Shoulder means *strength* (Isa. 9:7). *Breast* means affection, love. So love and power come by His cross (Song of Sol. 8:6; Ps. 98:1). The breast shall be Aaron's sons. Let us feed on Him for we have a place in His heart – a place on His shoulder. He loves me and carries me.

God, priest, and offerer were fed by this offering (Lev. 7:16; 3:8). By it they had communion one with another. As it was eaten by the priestly family (Lev. 10:14, 15), we, as priests unto God feed on Him who satisfies both God and man.

Often this offering took the form of a family or communal commemoration or of a joyous and festal character (I Sam. 20:29; 11:15). It was a joint repast in which three took part and represents our fellowship with the Father and His Son. Jesus is not only the object of heaven's delight, He is also the Source of joy and fellowship for the Church of God (I John 1:3).

When the Prodigal Son returned home, his father killed the fatted calf and merriment prevailed because of restoration. So the peace offering is an expression of joy as the result of reconciliation between God and man.

> See, without a cloud between,
> The Godhead reconciled.

There is a sense in which the Lord's Supper reflects the feast of old. By faith, we feast upon His shoulder, and drink of His blood. Eating and drinking speaks of a peace received and possessed. The feast of thanksgiving proclaims an accomplished Redemption.

The Israelites had liberty to invite their friends to the feast which was an occasion for joy even for the youngest and feeblest (See Num. 18: 19; Deut. 12:4-18). No matter who came, so long as they were of the priestly family they could eat. If, out of Christ, we eat and drink at His table to our condemnation (I Cor. 11: 27-29).

(5). *Directions About Eating* (Lev. 7:15-17).

(a). *When offered as a Thanksgiving, it had to be eaten the same day* (Lev. 7:15)

This speaks of instant appropriation. Peace with God through Christ is not to be lingered for or looked at, but definitely and promptly accepted. Instant faith brings immediate salutations. The moment Christ as the peace offering is trusted and received, peace and soul satisfaction are at once enjoyed.

Not only so, but it speaks of instant praise for what we receive. Whenever we feed upon Him who is our peace and receive some token of His love and goodness, do not let us forget to offer immediate praise. Don't leave it until the morning.

When offered as a vow, or a voluntary offering, it could be eaten on the same day, and on the second. This shows the enduring character of our praise or service. As the vow, or voluntary offering, was connected with service. Eating the remainder upon the second day may signify the outcome of our immediate praise to the Lord. When we live upon the ever-fresh peace offering we discover that the next day has a delight that we never experienced before in Him. Again, the first day may refer to this day of grace. Eating the remainder on the second day, or on the morrow, can suggest the coming day of glory. On the morrow of His return, ours will be the delight of feasting to the full.

(b). *Remainder of Sacrifice consumed by fire on the third day* (Lev. 7:17-18)

This limitation of time in respect to the remaining portions was very necessary in a hot climate, as the heat brought about a speedy corruption of flesh.

But the restriction is capable of bearing one or two spiritual truths. The first is that nothing is of value to God which is not immediately connected with Christ. There may be a good deal that looks like worship and sacrifice, but which in reality is not acceptable to God (Eph. 2:13). In these days of so-called modern advance and enlightenment when music, art, literature, science are exerting their powerful influence upon religion, let us beware of a religion that is bloodless and Christless.

Then again, this "third day" may warn us against an experience that is stale, or far off from Christ. When the manna was kept, it stank. Why, it is possible to know only the Christ

I met years ago at conversion. Past experiences are relied upon, Jesus is not the living Lord, the ever-fresh ground of access and the Holy Spirit the ever-present power that They ought to be. God save us from beginning the first day so well with praise, beginning in the Spirit, and then come to finish the third in the flesh, or in corruption.

Possibly there is a prospective reference here to the Saviour's Resurrection. The third day points to Resurrection. But our peace offering is never allowed to experience corruption – nothing left over to burn (Ps. 16:10). Blessed be He; we can feed upon His love and rest in His strength until the third day, the blessed Resurrection morn.

May He keep us fresh by living upon Him every moment of each day. May He keep us from lives that grow stale because the outward acts of service and worship stretch beyond our inner experience and enjoyment of His presence and power.

(c). *Eaten in Holiness* (Lev. 7:19-21)

This ceremonial cleanness was absolutely essential because the offering presented was holy and because as we read, it "pertained unto the Lord." Cleanness then was an absolute condition. Of course, an Israelite who contracted any defilement remained an Israelite, but his uncleanness caused him to suffer the loss of communion with God and His people. He was "cut off," as the record says.

All this is full of solemn warning for our own hearts. Where there is uncleanness, unconfessed sin, something contrary to God's will indulged in, there can never be true inward peace with God. Sin suspends the sweetness of communion. Is this not taught in I Peter 1:15, 16? "But as he which hath called you is holy, so be ye holy in all manner of conversation; Because it is written, Be ye holy; for I am holy." How can we enjoy or have any contact with such a Holy One if there be uncleanness upon us? "If we say that we have fellowship with him, and walk in darkness, we lie, and do not the truth: But if we walk in the light, as he is in the light, we have fellowship one with another, and the blood of Jesus Christ his Son cleanseth us from all sin" (I John 1:6, 7).

So let us examine our own hearts. Christ is our peace offering and as such, He stands for the peace, friendship, fellowship, harmony that ought to exist between our hearts and the Lord. As our peace offering He provides a daily feast, for He has made it possible for us to have "fellowship with the Father" and with Himself. Have we been "cut off," am I out of touch, has the friendship and fellowship been broken by uncleanness? Well, let us listen to His voice calling us back again. He is still our peace offering and waits to restore the communion. Let us appropriate Him anew, and trust Him to put away our sin, for "if we confess our sin he is faithful and just to forgive us our sins." Then we enjoy "Peace, perfect Peace," because the blood of Jesus whispers peace within.

D. *The Sin Offering* (Lev. 4; 6:24-30)

"Without shedding of blood there is no remission" (Heb. 9:22). This is the divine truth arresting our mind as we come to meditate upon the sin-offering. In this offering and in the trespass offering which is akin to it, we see our blessed Saviour as the one and only substitute for poor but helpless sinners. All that we have and enjoy now as believers we owe to Him who took our place, bore our curse, died our death. Now we sing,

> My hope is built on nothing less
> Than Jesus' blood and righteousness.
> I dare not trust the sweetest frame,
> But wholly lean on Jesus' name.

As this offering and its neighbor, the trespass offering, are given at the end of the Levitical order, we emphasize the truth that God ends where the sinner begins. The descending ladder reveals the Father's love and gracious provision, as well as the greatness of the Saviour's obedience and sacrifice. He left heaven as the burnt offering to carry out entirely the Father's will, even though that will was the salvation of sinful men and women through His death as the sin offering upon the cross. For our instruction the following table, key words, and verses will prove helpful:

The Burnt Offering	Surrender	Rom. 12:1; Heb. 9:14.
The Meal Offering	Suffering	Heb. 2:10.
The Peace Offering	Satisfaction	Col. 1:20; Eph. 2:16.
The Sin Offering	Substitution	Eph. 5:2; Gal. 2:20; II Cor. 5:21.
The Trespass Offering	Sacrifice	Heb. 10:12; 9:28; I John 1:8, 9.

Our classification of this present study is in the following way: The offering itself. The Respective Offerers. The Order of the Offering.

1. *The Offering.*

a. *Sin Offering* (Lev. 7:3)

It is called in our Bible the sin offering, that is, an offering that God accepted because of its value, and by which it was possible for Him to cover the sins of the respective offerers.

(1). A particular kind of sin is mentioned here as being covered by the blood, namely, the sin of ignorance (Lev. 7:2). But whether a person was ignorant of his sin or no, the need of substitution was just the same, because judgment is upon sins of omission and commission. Take any particular law of the land. Suppose a person, ignorant that such a law exists, contradicts or breaks it, will his ignorance justify his breach and bring him immunity from punishment. No! So is it, then, with us all. We need to be cleansed from secret faults, or faults secret from ourselves, unknown, undiscovered sins which His holy eye can detect. There are many things that a man's conscience may pass over but which God condemns. Thus the sin offering presents Christ atoning for sin according to God's measurement of sin, and not our own.

We need to be taught that sin is sinful whether it is recognized by the sinner or not, and requires remission just the same (Ps. 19:12; I Cor. 4:4, R.V.). "For I know against myself yet am I not hereby justified but he that judgeth me is the Lord."

(2). Again, sins of knowledge were covered as the result of the offering brought as we see from Leviticus 4:28. Both forms of sin required the shed blood of a substitute.

How this offering prefigures our blessed Saviour! When I become conscious of my sin, I look to Him, the One whose blood alone can cleanse me. Then as His eye beholds the hidden depths of need that mine cannot, and a desire to walk in the center of His will, His precious blood cleanses me from what I don't know as well as from what I do know.

(3). The word that is used for sin here is worthy of our attention and study. It means "to miss the mark," or "to err from God's ways." Moreover the word *offering* is not attached to the word *sin* in the Hebrew. The word for "Sin" is *Chattath* and covers both "Sin" and "Offering." This is seen in Genesis 4:7, where the same word *Chattath* or "sin" is only translated. So we can read Leviticus 4:3, "A young bullock without blemish unto the Lord for—the sin."

What a mysterious truth this proclaims! It takes us to II Corinthians 5:20, R.V. "Him who knew no sin he made to be *sin* on our behalf." Our sin, our substitute became identified as one (Rom. 8:3; Gal. 3:13). What grace!

Moreover, this particular word *Chattath,* when traced through the Word is found to mean "to cleanse or purify," as if the Holy Spirit would teach us that a soul can only be cleansed through the One who was made sin.

b. *It was an Offering that Atoned* (Lev. 4:20, 26)

This does not mean that the blood of bulls and of goats satisfied the heart of God and removed the offerer's sin. "It is not possible that the blood of bulls and goats should take away sins." The word here means "to cover," and what the legal sacrifice did was to remove the death penalty that was due for sin committed. God accepted the bullock in place of the offerer and forgave him because his offering covered his sin. But no sin was forever taken away until Christ came as the sin offering. "He bore away the sin of the world." So the Israelite's offering was accepted in virtue of the cross. Until Calvary, God passed over, or covered the sin of a guilty people (Rom. 3:25; 4:7, 8).

c. *It was a Commanded Offering* "Let him bring – He shall bring" (Lev. 4:2, 3)

In the offerings already considered, we noticed how voluntary they were – "of his own voluntary will" – but here in the sin offering that aspect is not found. It is not a free-will offering, but a commanded and demanded one. The reason for this is apparent. Because of His holiness, God must have remission before He can have any contact with sinners. The claims of His character and His broken law demand or command death. Hence the absence of the voluntary aspect in this offering. But what a God we have! What He commanded, He provided. "The soul that sinneth it shall die." "Christ died for the ungodly."

In the burnt offering we see Jesus offering Himself willingly and voluntarily to God for whatever service He desired. In the sin offering we see Jesus being delivered for our offenses. In the burnt offering He is the Father's Son. In the sin offering the sinner's substitute.

The need of a type to present and prefigure Christ shrinking from the consequence of imputed sin is set forth in the sin offering. In the burnt offering Christ reveals divine affections, accomplishes the will of God, and is precious as a complete Sacrifice. In the sin offering Christ meets the depths of human need. Seeing the hatefulness of sin, He became the bearer of it. The burnt offering says, "The cup which My Father hath given Me shall I not drink it?" The sin offering cries, "Father if it be possible let this cup pass from me" and "My God, My God, why hast Thou forsaken me?"

d. *It was a Non-Sweet Offering* (Lev. 4:12)

The first three offerings belong to the sweet savor class because they speak of Christ in all His perfections, and of His entire submission to the Father's will. The sin and trespass offerings are the two non-sweet offerings and represent Christ bearing the whole demerit of the sinner. God has no pleasure in sin nor in that which bears sin. "He is of purer eyes than to behold iniquity."

e. *It was a Most Holy Offering* (Lev. 6:25)

This offering was counted holy because of the fact that it represented the only way by which unholy ones could be counted holy. If there had been the least flaw in Christ's holiness He would have forfeited the right of acting as the substitute for unholy men and women. "He was tested in all points like as we are — yet without sin!" Hallelujah, what a Saviour!

2. *The offerers.* Four are named.

The priest that is anointed (Lev. 4:3).

The Whole Congregation of Israel (Lev. 4:13).

A Ruler (Lev. 4:22).

One of the Common People (Lev. 4:27).

Such shows how all-inclusive sin is and also how all embracing the sin offering was when every section of life found shelter in virtue of their respective sacrifice. There is a worldwide need, "for all have sinned and come short of God's glory," and nothing short of Christ as the all-inclusive Saviour is sufficient for this need.

The offering of each party was different from that of the other. For instance,

The priest brought a young bullock without blemish unto the Lord (Lev. 4:3).

The congregation had to bring a young bullock also (Lev. 4:14).

The ruler had to offer a male kid without blemish (Lev. 4:23).

The private individual, a female kid or lamb, without blemish (Lev. 4:28-32).

According to their position, so was the application of the value of the blood. The sin of a priest or a ruler would exert a wider influence than that of a common person — (an anointed priest could sin — the sins of teachers are teachers of sins) hence the gradations in the offerings presented correspond to the gradations of the consequences of sin. "He that knew his Lord's will and did it not shall be beaten with many stripes, but he that knew not his Lord's will and did it not 'beaten he must be,' but 'with few stripes.'"

Each found adjustment in their sin offering and so the Lord Jesus avails for all, for the Scripture hath concluded all under sin. When He died, He died for all men, and so, irrespective of position, all men must seek Him as the divinely appointed substitute.

3. *The order.* The order of presenting the offering was practically all the same in the case of all the four offerers mentioned. Is this not wonderfully typical of ourselves as sinners and Christ as our substitute?

a. *The Hand and the Head* (Lev. 4:4-15, 24, 29, 33)

This action was common to all four and speaks of the offerer's identification with the particular offering presented. In the burnt offering you remember the hand laid upon the head of the sacrifice, but there you have the worshiper cleansed and made holy, identifying himself with the unblemished offering. Here in the sin offering it is the guilty sinner who approaches God with his offering, and the hand laid on the head signifies in this case the offerer's identification, not so much with the offering, but with the sins of the offerer imputed to the sacrifice. The just treated as unjust — unjust accepted as just.

The laying on of the hand did not imply the laying on of the person's sins and so, as the hymn suggests, "I lay my sins on Jesus, the spotless Lamb of God." This is not Scripturally true, for Isaiah 53:6 says that "the LORD hath laid on him the iniquity of us all."

When I came as a lost sinner and placed my hand of faith on that dear Head of His, I did not lay my sins on Him but I identified myself with the sin that He bore for me. We confess our sins on Him; not lay them on Him.

My faith would lay her hand
On that dear head of Thine
While like a Penitent I stand
And there confess my Sin.

Guilty, vile and helpless we,
Spotless Lamb of God was He.

Such is our humble and continual position. The moment the hand of faith is laid on the head the offerer is accepted in virtue of offering who bore the judgment.

b. *The Offering Killed* (Lev. 4:4, 15)

In each case the offerer had to kill his own offering before the Lord. This brings us to the truth that we have already indicated in connection with our Lord's sacrifice, namely, the twofold cause of His death. It was demanded by God and it pleased Him to bruise Him, yet it was wicked men, yea, ourselves, who slew Him and hanged Him to the tree. There is no Christ but the One sacrificed as the substitute for sinners.

c. *The Blood Applied*

It was applied in a fourfold way in the care of the priest and the congregation, and in all probability with the other two, although no mention is made of the "veil" in the presentation of the blood by the ruler and a common person.

(1). *It Was Sprinkled Seven Times Before the Lord* (Lev. 4:6, 17). As seven is the number of spiritual perfection, we see in this sevenfold action of sprinkling the perfect standing that we have before God in virtue of our sin offering (Heb. 10:19-22). Some, however, see in this the awful death that our Lord Jesus died. To sprinkle means to throw or splash, hence it may prefigure the gushing forth of His precious blood.

(2). *It Was Sprinkled Before the Veil of the Sanctuary* (Lev. 4:6-17). This again can suggest two rich spiritual truths. The first is that of access. Is it not by the blood of Christ that we receive boldness to draw nigh and to enter within the veil, there to enjoy that sweet communion with the Father?

But the veil can also represent our Saviour's human nature, for that was indeed the sanctuary veil we "enter into the holiest, by a new and living way, which he hath consecrated for us, through the veil, that is to say, his flesh" (Heb. 10:19, 20). It is by this we are saved, by His dėath, not His life (Eph. 2:13). The blood was sprinkled as He gave up the ghost.

(3). *Some of the Blood was Placed on the Horns of the Altar of Sweet Incense* (Lev. 4:7, 18, 25, 30, 34). This altar is a type of Christ as the intercessor. What intercessions were and are His. Think of His earthly intercessions. Repeatedly we find Him pleading for men and women! Think of dark Gethsemane. Think of Calvary, where He made intercession for His transgressors! Think of His mighty prevailing intercession in heaven now!

The horns stand for strength, and are we not told that it was with "strong crying and tears" that He supplicated God (Heb. 5:7)? Sacrifice is the only basis of true worship and prayer.

But is this not capable of yielding another truth? Is not our own worship, praise, and intercession marred by sin and selfishness? Is not the altar of our hearts in need sometimes of the sprinkled blood?

(4). *The Rest of the Blood was Poured at the Bottom of the Burnt Offering Altar* (Lev. 4:7, 18, 25, 30, 34). The pouring out of the blood in this way suggests, does it not, the pouring out of our Redeemer's blood? He poured out His soul unto death. In the Levitical offering the blood reached and covered the ground around the bottom of the altar and our earth became stained with His blood.

Again it can signify the way that God comes out to meet us now, since Christ's death. In the burnt offering the blood was burnt upon the altar and went upward to God. In the sin offering it went downward and outward, being poured out on the ground. So the priest is seen sprinkling the blood of his way out, from the veil before the Lord to the bottom of the altar. Salvation is of the Lord. The way out is from God to sinners and now when a sinner approaches God he meets the outpoured blood at Calvary's altar. The blood is at our "door," but when our individual need is met, it passes on within the veil. This differs from heathen practice in which sacrifices are brought to heathen gods. When we approach God, He presents His sacrifice on our behalf, namely, His Son, our Saviour.

d. *The Burning of the Interior* (Lev. 4:8, 19, 26, 31, 35)

The fat, kidneys, and caul had to be removed from the respective offerings and burnt upon the burnt offering altar. This part is called a sweet-savor offering unto the Lord (Lev. 4:31). This brings before us a most blessed view of our Lord as our sin offering. True it is that He was made sin for us, blessed be His name! But there was no sin within Him. We must never confound *what He was* with *what He became*. Even though He became our sin offering, He Himself remained divinely holy. Within Himself He was perfect.

So the burning of these particular parts typify the inherent spotlessness of our divine substitute, His intrinsic excellency, even though He became the bearer of our sin. It was with such that the Father was well pleased.

e. *The Burning of the Exterior* (Lev. 4:12, 21)

Here is another sublime truth — the skin, flesh, head, legs, inwards, and dung were all taken to a clean place without the camp and there burned with fire. Here we have a different place, a different burning.

(1). *The body of the offering was burnt without the Camp.* In the burnt offering, the victim was wholly consumed upon the altar because such symbolized the full surrender to and the acceptance by God of the offerer. In the sin offering, the body was burnt outside the camp, being despised and rejected of men and bearing their sin. Christ, wishing to sanctify sinners with His own blood, suffered without the gate (Heb. 13:11, 12). Let it be remembered that our Lord was not burnt without the camp. As our sin-bearer He could not stand within a holy place. The camp, which signifies Judaism; religion without blood-shedding was unholy. So an unholy camp was an unfit place for a holy sin-offering. The body was burnt in a clean place. As the holy prophet, He did not perish in Jerusalem. Where did our sins go to? (See Jer. 50:20).

(2). *The body was burnt in the place where the ashes were poured out.* As these ashes were the ashes of the burnt offering, is there not a sublime message to be gathered therefrom? The burnt offering is the basis of the sin offering. All through the latter you have a vital connection between the former. The sin offering was slain in the place where the burnt offering was slain (Lev. 6:25). The blood and the sin offering was poured upon, and around, the burnt offering altar. Here the body of the sin offering was mingled and burnt with the remains of the burnt offering. First of all, perfect surrender to God, and then sacrifice for man. Christ's surrender was the basis of His sacrifice.

(3). *Then again, a different word is used for burning here.* In the burnt offering the word is a fragrant one — one that is connected with incense, something that ascends. Here in the sin offering the word for *burn* is connected with wrath and anger and implies destruction. Beloved, what a truth! He was burnt with fire without the camp. How true it is:

> The tempest's awful voice was heard,
> O, Christ it broke on Thee.
> Thy open bosom was my ward,
> It braved the storm for me.
> Thy form was scarred, Thy visage marred,
> Now cloudless peace for me.

The body burnt without the camp – this is where I first meet Christ and then, bringing His blood within the veil, find peace and safety. After such, I learn the inner meaning of going forth to, and with Him, without the camp (Heb. 13:11, 12). If our Master suffered without the gate, we cannot expect to reign within the gate.

> His path uncheered by earthly smiles,
> Led only to the Cross.

f. *The Priests Ritual* (Lev. 6:24-30)

Up till now there has been an absence of the usual phrase met with in the previous offerings, "the priests, Aaron's sons." This is in order, for the sin offering presents us not as worshiping saints or priests, but as guilty, convicted sinners, under the solemn judgment of sin. We become a kingdom of priests through the awful travail of Him who became our sin offering but who is now our great High Priest.

(1). *The one who offered – ate* (Lev. 6:26). What part he consumed is not given, but does this not symbolize the truth that our sin offering is now our meal offering. The dual truth is proclaimed here, namely, that as my sin offering, Christ gave His life *for* me, but now as my High Priest in heaven, He gives His life *to* me.

(2). *It had to be eaten in a holy place by holy people.* How full of heart-searching this truth is for us! He was the offering most holy, and without holiness He can never be seen or appropriated.

(3). *Earthen Vessel had to be broken. Brazen pot scoured and rinsed* (Lev. 6:28). Here, again, we are taught that if we would constantly receive we must be constantly cleansed. There must be the breaking down of the earthen vessel of our self-life and the scouring and rinsing of the brazen pot of our very lives.

(4). *Eaten by the Males* (Lev. 6:29). The male signifies strength. "The Glory of the young man is his strength." Spiritual weaklings cannot apprehend the full significance of Calvary. Strong meat, says Paul, is for us of full age and the more we appropriate Christ, the more spiritually mature we become.

What an Offering! What a Saviour! All blessings flow from the cross.

Atonement – "It is the blood that maketh an atonement" (Lev. 17:11).

Forgiveness – "Redemption through His blood, even the forgiveness of sins" (Col. 1:14).

Sanctification – "The blood of Jesus Christ his Son cleanseth us from all sin" (I John 1:7).

Justification – "Being now justified by his blood" (Rom. 5:9).

Nearness to God – "Made nigh by the blood of Christ" (Eph. 2:13).

Victory in conflict – "Overcame . . . by the blood of the Lamb" (Rev. 12:11).

Entrance in glory – "Made them white in the blood of the Lamb" (Rev. 7:14).

Frances Havergal tells of a poor woman, who on a Good Friday was so filled with a sense of the dying love of Jesus that she could only look at His cross and say, "Enough for Justice, enough for God, enough for me."

And of another, equally filled with the same sense of His wondrous Redemption, who would repeat, "I come over to one verse, then I conquer. 'The blood of Jesus Christ, His Son, cleanseth me from all sin.' Satan can't face the blood: I lose him there."

Jesus, my Great High Priest,
Offered His blood and died;
My guilty conscience seeks
No sacrifice beside:
His powerful blood did once atone,
And now it pleads before the
Throne.

E. *The Trespass Offering* (Lev. 5–6:1-7; 7:1-7)

We have now come to the list of the historical offerings, which, in many respects, is closely connected with the last offering we considered. In fact many expositors connect the first thirteen verses of chapter 5 with the sin offering in chapter 4. We, however, prefer to link the whole of chapter 5 on to the trespass offering and to see in such a continuation and development of the sin offering.

In all previous offerings, sin is viewed as affecting the sinner himself, and the offering presented is connected with the offerer and God. But here sin is dealt with not so much in its nature as in its results and effects. When a man sins, he sins not only against himself and God, but also against his neighbor, and so the trespass offering presents Christ as the repairer of the damage caused by sin, both Godward and manward.

The trespass offering deals with the evil deeds committed, rather than with the evil person. We commence where God finishes, namely at the trespass offering. When a sinner's conscience is quickened by the Holy Spirit, he is immediately troubled about his sins – the fruit, rather than with the sin – the root, of his past evil life. He thinks of the damage caused by his sins – to others, to God, to himself. So his first glimpse of Christ is as the trespass offering, as the repairer of the breach, and the restorer of the path (Isa. 58:12). The prophet bears this out in his prophecy regarding our Saviour. "Thou shalt make his soul an offering for sin" (Isa. 53:10). The Hebrew here for *offering* is "trespass offering."

Being "dead in trespasses and sins," the sinner identifies himself with Christ, the trespass and sin offerings, then after the quickening influences of the Holy Spirit has the blessed assurance that the Lord has forgiven all his trespasses (Col. 2:13). Christ's work upon Calvary fully compensates God, our fellow man, and ourselves for the damage caused by sin.

1. *The Trespass Offering.*

a. *Its Nature*

In some aspects this offering is closely akin to the sin offering, especially in its order as we shall later see.

(1). *It was a Trespass Offering* (Lev. 5:6, 15). In order to understand the spiritual significance of this offering, we must understand the meaning of the word *trespass.* "To trespass" means to impugn upon the rights of others; it is a breach of a given commandment. You come to a field it may be, and see a sign that forbids your entrance into it. "Trespassers will be prosecuted." But you disregard the notice and walk into the field. What have you done? You have impugned upon the rights of another. The field is not yours but another's. You are a trespasser, and your trespass is against your neighbor. The sinner is a trespasser. He breaks God's commandment, he impugns upon His rights, he breaks commercial, social, and spiritual laws, he causes damage all around; but Christ is the divine provision for all trespass and trespassers. He is the repairer, restorer, and redeemer, both Godward and manward.

(2). *It was a Most Holy Offering* (Lev. 7:6; 14:13). This aspect of the trespass offering prefigures the Lord Jesus in a remarkable way. If I am to be forgiven all my trespasses, it can only be upon the basis of an offering that knows no trespass. Think of Jesus; what perfect holiness was His both Godward and manward! He never trespassed against any commandment of His Father. Nor did He once impugn upon the rights of His fellowmen. His life is open to the closest inspection, and, examine it where we will, we find the same holy standard maintained. With the dying thief, we confess, "This Man hath done nothing amiss." He was the elder brother who could say, "Neither transgressed I at any time thy commandment" (Luke 15:29). Hence, His qualification to act as our trespass offering. He was most holy. Born holy, He was holy in word, deed, and thought.

(3). *It was a Non-sweet-savor Offering.* One misses the phrase in this offering which is common to the burnt offering and the meal offering, namely, "a sweet savor unto the Lord." The omission is in keeping with the offering. Christ is here seen bearing the trespasses of the sinner. It is the aspect of the cross that found expression in the cry, "My God, my God, why hast Thou forsaken me?"

b. *Its Order*

For the sin offering and the trespass offering, the order is exactly the same (Lev. 7:7), and the Law when the offering was a kid, sheep, or ram, was as follows:

The hand was laid on the head of the offering.

The offerer killed his offering in the place where the burnt offering was killed.

The blood was applied in a fourfold way—

(1). Sprinkled seven times before the Lord.

(2). Sprinkled before the veil of the sanctuary.

(3). Some placed upon the horns of the altar of sweet incense.

(4). Rest poured around bottom of the burnt offering altar.

The interior of the beast was burned upon the burnt offering altar.

The exterior was burnt without the camp.

The priests ate certain portion.

(1). Eaten in holiness in holy place.

(2). Eaten by males.

2. *The Trespass.* This section of our study opens up a wide field of very important truth regarding the responsibilities of an Israelite both in divine and human relationship. Trespass is outlined as committed against the trespasser himself; against the Lord; against man.

a. *Against Himself* (Lev. 5:1-13)

The Trespasses (Lev. 5:1-4)

(1). *The Trespass of Silence when one ought to Speak* (Lev. 5:1). Sometimes we say that "silence is golden," but here it is seen as criminal. "Silence gives consent." If when I come into contact with sinners I remain silent regarding this particular sin of swearing that is mentioned here, I virtually condone the trespass. Let us never be silent because of the fear of what the swearer may say or do. We must rebuke in a loving, Christlike way, or the witness will not be fruitful.

(2). *The Trespass of Defilement through unclean associations* (Lev. 5:2, 3). Unclean connections or associations forever bar a person from the presence of God. He can never have true fellowship with those who in any way are conscious of trafficking in unholy things.

(3). *The Trespass of Swearing and Pronouncing Oaths* (Lev. 5:4). Here the sin is not so much the swearing mentioned in v. 1., as the oaths that men sometimes make or take upon themselves. Sometimes as Christians we trespass in this respect, and it is a trespass we must seek forgiveness for.

The Confession (Lev. 5:5).

"He shall confess that he hath sinned in *that* thing." Confession here is seen to be particular. The trespasser had to come and confess, not in a general way, but detail his particular trespass as he stood by his offering. Complete restoration for ourselves is only along the line of confession in this respect. Israel committed a trespass in the accursed thing we are told (Josh. 6). But when Joshua came to search out the matter, he had to come to one particular man, Achan, and from him he received a detailed confession of the sin that delayed Israel's victory at Ai. If we are conscious of any trespasses, let us not shrink from confessing them minutely before the Lord. "If we confess our sins" — one by one (I John 1:9).

The Offering (Lev. 5:6, 13)

In this section we have a variety of offerings mentioned. A female lamb or kid, two turtle doves, or two young pigeons. One-tenth of an ephah of fine flour. Such a variety was no doubt allowed to meet the need of the poorest offerer. Some could afford the lamb, others who were not so wealthy, the doves, pigeons, or flour. But we must not forget that whether the lamb or flour are presented, such made no difference in respect to the acceptance of the offerer. The full value of the power of the sacrifice was imputed to the man with his small portion of flour, as well as to the offerer with his lamb or kid.

Is it not possible that their respective offerings typify our apprehension of Christ's work? There is also the thought of the adaptability of the all-sufficiency of the sacrifice to meet the need of all. A weak, poor faith can hold a strong Redeemer. No matter how poor a believer's estimation of Christ as the trespass offering may be, he is perfectly forgiven. There are no degrees of justification. The full value of Christ's sacrifice is imputed to the most unspiritual believer, as well as to the most saintly. Of course, the more spiritual he becomes, the sooner will he pass from the handful of flour to the Lamb.

b. *Against the Lord* (Lev. 5:14-19)

Here we encounter a different phase of the trespass committed. "A trespass in the holy things of the LORD" (Lev. 5:15). "He hath certainly trespassed against the LORD" (Lev. 5:19).

The Trespasses

These are of a twofold nature.

(1). *Ignorant trespass in the holy things of the Lord* (Lev. 5:15). What holy things these were the verse in question gives no light. But applying it to ourselves is it not true that we often trespass in the holy things? Why, our best service, our holiest seasons, our most hallowed exercises, our deepest desires for likeness to Him are often marred by selfishness of insincerity!

(2). *Ignorant, or conscious, Trespass against the Commands of the Lord* (Lev. 5:17). These commandments were no doubt connected with Israel's life as the peculiar people of Jehovah. His will regarding her had been revealed, and disobedience of such made the presentation of a trespass offering a necessity. A feature is introduced here that we cannot pass over without notice. "If a soul sin . . . though he wist it not, yet is he guilty" (Lev. 5:17). This proves that ignorance is not innocence. Because of my limited nature it is not possible to fully understand the absolute claims of God's holiness. Even in my most holy experiences there are imperfections which the eye of God can detect, hidden depths of trespass that are only visible to Him. But ignorance of each does not absolve me from guilt, for even if I wist it not, I am guilty (See I Tim. 1:13; Ps. 19:12).

God in His infinite mercy can forgive all manner of trespasses, but He cannot pass over one jot or tittle, even where the trespasser is ignorant of such. His grace is perfect, and in His trespass offering all can be forgiven, but His holiness is also perfect and such prevents Him from passing anything over. Christ is my trespass offering and He presents me faultless before the Father, because sins of omission and commission are dealt with by Him.

The Sacrifice

In both cases such had to be a ram without blemish (Lev. 5:15, 18). The ram or male sheep is a fitting type of our Lord's work on Calvary. It presents Him as the One who was despised and rejected of men. It speaks of Him as the One who took all our trespasses upon Himself, and bore them as our substitute. This is also typified in the experience of Abraham, Isaac, and the ram caught in the thicket. Christ was the Lamb offered up in the stead of sinners. But although He was made to bear sin, yet He had no sin within Himself. He was the ram "without blemish." The order of its slaughter and presentation, as we have already seen, was the same as that of the sin offering.

The Restitution

In this section of the trespass offering we have a new feature introduced. When the trespass was committed against the Lord even in holy things or in respect to His commandments, the offerer had to add to his offering the value of such in money and another one-fifth of such thereto, and thus make amends for the harm he had done (Lev. 5:16, 18).

This lesson of restitution is one that is sadly neglected in our Christian life and service. But I can never make ample restitution to God or amend Him for all the harm I have done. And, let it be said, He does not ask me to do so in respect to the guilt of my sin. Christ has done this completely, as we shall presently see, but only to the actual damage done in respect to His cause. Paul turns back upon that Damascus road to preach the fulness of Christ to those whom hitherto he had persecuted. If, as believers, we rob Him in any holy thing, then restitution has to be made in tithes and offerings. Alas, however, we forget to add the one-fifth part to our trespass offering. God is seldom amended insofar as we are concerned for the harm we cause both God Himself and His cause.

This question of restitution in connection with trespass against the Lord reveals the wonderful work of Christ as trespass offering, in that it fully compensates the Father for all the trespass of man. With Christ, God has received His estimation and one-fifth added thereto. Christ caused God to gain more than He lost. Through the ruin of sin, God lost the fellowship of innocent man, but now through Christ He has had restored to Him not only the fellowship of innocent but of holy men. God has in glory now not only His divine Son, the One who was equal with Him from all eternity, but a perfect man, One who vanquished death and Satan. Why, the Lord Jesus is a greater wonder to the heavenly hosts and of more value to God, now, than before the cross. Think of it, He has added the one-fifth part of "his glorious church to himself."

So God has, or will soon have, in glory, what He could never have had apart from Calvary, namely a vast multitude bearing the same likeness and image as His Son. God gains more by Redemption than He lost by the Fall. Through the cross He reaps a richer harvest.

We observe that what God required first, when the Trespass was against Him, was *sacrifice* and then *restitution.* As a holy God, He can accept nothing from unholy men and women. An offering must be made. Blood must be shed ere God can receive the amends of men.

The attitude of some is this. It does not matter about the past. No doubt I have trespassed against the Lord, but I will try now to give God His due and watch myself more carefully. I shall strive to witness more, live better, devote more time and money to His cause. But God says, No! Not your restitution first, but your sacrifice. First, clean hearts and consciences adjusted to His divine claims, then the acceptance of as much restitution as we like to offer.

c. *Against Others* (Lev. 6:1-7)

In this particular phase of the offering there are further truths for our hearts to ponder.

The Trespasses

Five trespasses, more or less akin, are found in the first three verses of this chapter. We observe, however, that the trespasses are all outward, that is, they all are committed against others. Trespasses against the man himself give the *inward* aspect of this offering. Trespasses against the Lord, an *upward* aspect. While this last phase presents us with the *outward* influence — the damage sin does, not only to the man himself, and to God, but to his neighbors.

But we must not fail to observe that although these particular trespasses in chapter 6 are committed against a neighbor, yet they are associated with the Lord as well in verse 2. No man can sin against another without sinning against the Lord. This principle is broadly recognized in Scripture. In II Samuel 12:13, we read, "David said unto Nathan, I have sinned against the LORD," and the same incident is in his mind when he penned Psalm 51:4, "Against thee, thee only, have I sinned." Yet in deed, he had sinned against Uriah, and Bath-sheba his wife. This is also made clear in Luke 15. The Prodigal, returning home confused, says, "I have sinned against heaven, and before thee." His trespass was certainly against his father, but before heaven in the first instance. Trespass against others is the outcome of trespass against God, hence the connection of the two here. Our conduct among others is conditioned by our character. The list of trespasses mentioned as against the neighbor and also against the Lord, who, after all, is our closest neighbor, are given in detail.

(1). *If a soul sin and commit a trespass against the Lord and lie unto his neighbor in that which was delivered to him to keep.* This trespass suggests the betrayal of some sacred trust. Possibly it implies the misappropriation or the careless use of anything that one has entrusted to the care and guardianship of another. One is afraid that this applies very forcibly to all of us. How often we trespass against our neighbor in that we fail to keep the confidences they entrust us with. "Confidence in an unfaithful man in time of trouble is like a broken tooth."

(2). *In Fellowship.* This no doubt covers dishonesty in social relationship and business transactions wherein one has proved unscrupulous regarding the interests of those associated with him. It implies the conscientious observance of all social laws that glorify Christ, such as prompt payment and no bad debts. "Be honest in the sight of all men."

(3). *A thing taken away by violence.* A brother need not use arms to take anything from another brother by violence. One can oppress another by using one's influence or position and thus rob him deceitfully, as we see in the tragedy of Naboth's vineyard. "Defraud no man."

(4). *Deceive his neighbor.* We have constantly to be on our guard against the wiles of the Devil in this direction. He is a deceiver and his purpose is to blight believers in this respect. Are there not some who are so nice to your face and you count them among your friends, but who, when occasion arises stab you behind your back? Sometimes we say one thing and mean another.

(5). *Or hath found that which was lost and lieth concerning it and sweareth falsely* (Lev. 6:2). The only way to escape the tempter's snare is to restore lost property at once, or even property that is not lost. How often a book or something also is kept, when lent by a friend yet kept with no compunction of conscience.

There is a notable omission in reference to the trespasses here, namely, the absence of the phrase that we have been familiar with in other aspects of this offering and the sin offering – sin through ignorance. Such an omission is easily understood. When it comes to the claims of God it is possible to sin and trespass against Him ignorantly. In fact, the demands of His holiness will never be known by us. If a man reached great saintliness of character, there would still be undiscovered depths within him. "In me that is in my flesh," says Paul, "dwelleth no good thing." Hence our ignorant sin is never excused or condoned. But when it comes to our neighbor, ignorance is omitted because it is not possible to deceive, destroy, tell a lie, or swear without knowing it.

The Restitution (Lev. 6:4, 5)

Here, again, we notice something new. There is a reversal of order. When the trespass was against the Lord in holy things, it was sacrifice first then restitution. Now it is restitution and reparation first, and then the offering. The reason of this is obvious. Where God is damaged, blood must ever be first and prominent. Where man is damaged by trespass, restitution naturally comes first, and after such is settled, then the trespasser can enjoy communion with God through Christ his trespass offering.

Look for a moment to the New Testament and see how this is emphasized (Matt. 5:23, 24). "If thou bring thy gift to the altar, and there rememberest that thy brother hath aught against thee; leave there thy gift before the altar and go thy way; first be reconciled to thy brother, and then come and offer thy gift." Again, in Matthew 6:15, "If ye forgive not men their trespasses, neither will your Father forgive your trespasses." How is the injured one to receive the injurer? "Lord, how oft shall my brother sin against me and I forgive him? till 7 times? Jesus said unto him, I say not unto thee until 7 times, but until 70 times 7."

This is how God forgives those who trespass against Him. May He help us to follow His example (Col. 3:13).

Again, the teaching regarding restitution from the manward aspect needs to be greatly emphasized in these days when earnest Christians are seeking revival. One of the outstanding evidences of revival is *restitution.* This can be gathered from the experience of Zaacheus. No doubt it is very humbling to pride to confess one to another, but it always paves the way for deeper and fuller blessing. It is easy to talk about resting in the blood of the trespass offering and at the same time keep back the one-fifth part and the restoration of the principal. There is nothing more dishonoring to God than to imagine that because we belong to Christ there is no need to regulate our conduct toward others and manifest practical holiness all around (I John 3:10).

One call to the unsaved is – Get right with God – One call to the Christian is "Get right with man." It may be possible the reader is blocking revival, because he or she is not right with someone else (Eph. 4:28-32).

But let us look at this restitution in another light. We saw how God had been amply and gloriously compensated through Christ's work on the cross. Now let us see how Christ restored the principal and added one-fifth more thereto in respect to the sinner. Man gains, as well as God, through Calvary. Before the Fall man was innocent. Now because of the cross, he is, or can be made, holy. Before conversion we were natural – now we are divine. Although sin abounded – grace much more abounds. Think of the "much mores" of the New Testament. What boundless streams – what privileges and possessions are ours that Adam never had.

Man gains enormously through the cross. Christ is a wonderful repairer of the damage, for He not only deals with sin as a principle but with sins as a practice – "He transforms the sinner from a curse into a blessing: from a moral player into a channel of divine mercy: from an emissary of Satan, into a messenger of God: from a child of darkness, into a son of the light: from a self-indulgent, pleasure-seeker into a self-denying lover of God: from a slave of vile, selfish lusts into a willing-hearted servant of Christ." Bless His name! He adds the one-fifth thereto. May grace be ours to do so in all our dealings with others.

May God help us to put matters right between ourselves, for this is the last lesson that the trespass offering teaches us. When the Philippian jailer got converted, the first thing he did was to wash the stripes that he had inflicted upon the backs of Paul and Silas. Practicing stripe-washing is God-like. For ourselves it is a conspicuous evidence of our confession and also a means of keeping our communication clear with heaven.

The Sacrifice

This, as we observe from Leviticus 6:6, is the same as in the trespass against the Lord – a ram without blemish. Here, as previously indicated, is a type of Christ. He is our trespass offering and His blood covers all our need.

Then observe as we conclude that the sacrifice comes last here. When the trespass was against God it was first and the restitution next. Here the order is reversed, and the truth is surely plain. No child of God can truly enjoy or appropriate Christ or come into God's presence with Him as the needful offering if matters are not as they ought to be between ourselves and others. Fellowship with God is not possible unless there be fellowship with man. We must first be reconciled to our brother. Says John, "He that loveth not his brother whom he hath seen, how can he love God whom he hath not seen?" (I John 4:20). Could anything be more explicit?

Tennyson has the plea,

> O Man, forgive thy mortal foe,
> Nor ever strike him blow for blow;
> For all the souls on earth that live
> To be forgiven must forgive—
> Forgive him seventy times and seven!
> For all the blessed souls in Heaven
> Are both Forgivers and Forgiven.

In connection with the sin offering for the people, attention is drawn to the two goats associated with same. They were chosen by lot – one goat for Jehovah, and the other for "Azazel," as the R.V. translates *scapegoat* (Lev. 16:8. See Lev. 16:6-26). It has been suggested that Azazel is one of the names of Satan. After the sacrificial goat had been offered to Jehovah, the High Priest laid his hands on the other goat, confessing over it the sins of the people, which was then sent away into a solitary land, bearing with it the sins of the people. As we shall see, this is another of God's historical fore-pictures of all His Son accomplished by His death and resurrection. Moorehead expresses his belief that Azazel means "for removal" or "for the complete bearing away."

The two goats formed but one offering, the two being needed to complete the type. Both animals were charged with the sins of the people; and the reason for the use of one, as in other sacrifices, was probably because of the physical impossibility of combining all the features that had to be set forth in the sin offering of one animal. Thus "the cognate truths of Atonement and Remission are vividly taught in this sacrifice." We can express it thus:

The Slain Goat predicted Christ's death as the sin offering, whereby He made a perfect Atonement for sin. As the sinner receives the Saviour, his sin is covered by the blood. The claims of a righteous God upon the sinner must be met by punishment. Christ was delivered for our offenses. He made the sinner's punishment His own (Isa. 53:6, 12; I Pet. 2:24).

The Scapegoat spoke of the removal of sin. Liberated, this goat showed that perfect pardon had been granted the people. The putting away or complete removal of their sin was assured by the ceremonial dismissal of the living goat into a land not inhabited, bearing the load of sin upon him. Typically, the freed goat declares the pardon Christ procured by the sacrifice of the cross (Gal. 3:13; II Cor. 5:21).

So the *punishment* of sin, and the *pardon* of sin are the twin truths taught by the twin goats. We may feel that this double sacrifice was altogether out of proportion to the need – two goats for the sins of the people for a whole year. Did not God purposely design such to prove that the whole Levitical system of offerings was temporary and typical? "It is not possible that the blood of bulls and of *goats* should take away sins" (Heb. 10:4). They were accepted in virtue of a perfect God providing a perfect man to atone for our sins (Heb. 1:2, 3; 2:14; John 1:29).

> The Scape-Goat on his head
> The people's trespass bore,
> And to the desert led,
> Was to be seen no more:
> In Him our Surety seem'd to say,
> "Behold I bear your sins away."

In connection with the cleansing of the leper we have the priest using two sparrows, one slain, the other spared, as in the ceremony of the two goats (Lev. 15:1-7). Leprosy has ever been thought of as a type of sin, and the leper had to stay outside the camp until the instructions regarding his cleansing were carried out. One bird was slain, then the living sparrow was dipped in the blood of the sacrificial sparrow and released. The leper himself was also sprinkled with the blood of the dead sparrow. These two sparrows predict the twin aspects of our salvation. Christ was not only "delivered for our offences" but "raised again for our justification" (Rom. 4:25). The upward flight of the living, blood-stained bird was the token that the leper was clean.

As for the earthen vessel, with its overrunning water, in which the sparrow destined to die was killed, the same can typify the humanity of

Christ, as the running water speaks of the Holy Spirit as the "Spirit of Life." Christ was "put to death in the flesh, but quickened by the Spirit" (Rom. 8:2; I Pet. 3:18). Incidentally, God's merciful provision is seen in that sparrows, like pigeons, were within reach of the poorest.

Action was required by the leper himself after the ritual of the two sparrows. Ere he could return to the camp he had to wash himself with water, and then his head, hand, and foot had to be sprinkled with the blood of the trespass offering, and then anointed with oil. Through the precious blood of Christ we have both justification and sanctification, and for our service, the anointing oil of the Spirit. Ear, thumb, and toe can symbolize all our powers under divine control.

Dipt in his fellow's blood,
  The living bird went free;
The type well understood,
  Express'd the sinner's plea;
Described a guilty soul enlarged,
And by a Saviour's death discharged.

As we conclude our coverage of the offerings, there is still another we would like to mention, namely, that of *the red heifer* (Num. 19). The dictionary explains the heifer as a young cow or a cow that has not had a calf. Held in reverence, even as India deems the cow *sacred,* the heifer is identified with religious ritual (Gen. 15:9; I Sam. 16:2). Israel, Egypt, and Chaldea are compared to an heifer (Jer. 46:20; 50:11; Hos. 4:16). The ashes of this animal, added to running water, formed the most powerful means known to the ancient Hebrews for the removal of defilement produced by contact with a dead body. And the ceremony offers a striking symbol of "the eternal truth that purity and holiness are the essential characteristics of the people of God."

Out of the ashes of the sacrifice of the red heifer, the water of purification and separation was prepared, an aspect the writer of *Hebrews* alludes to – "The ashes of an heifer sprinkling the unclean, sanctifieth to the purifying of the flesh" (Heb. 9:13). In the book of *Numbers* there is no mention of the laver. "The water of purification appears to have taken the place of the laver in some measure during the pilgrim journey of Israel," observes Moorhead. The cleansing efficacy of the water consisted in the hiefer's ashes, offered as a sin offering, with which it was mingled. Thus, as a cleansing based upon Atonement it foreshadowed the continual cleansing of the blood of Jesus from sin in the lives of those who walk in the light (I John 1:7).

An outline on the symbolism of the ceremony of the red heifer, found in the Scofield Reference Bible at Numbers 19, is most profitable for preachers and teachers to follow and expand. "It is a type of the sacrifice of Christ as the *ground* of the cleansing of the believer from the defilement contracted in his pilgrim walk through this world, and illustration of the *method* of his cleansing." The order is –

(1). The *slaying* of the sacrifice.

(2). The sevenfold sprinkling of the blood, typical public testimony before the eyes of all of the complete never-to-be-repeated putting away of all the believer's sins as *before* God (Heb. 9:12-14; 10:10-12).

(3). The reduction of the sacrifice to ashes which are preserved and become a *memorial* of the sacrifice.

(4). The cleansing from defilement (sin has two aspects – *guilt* and *uncleanness)* by sprinkling the ashes mingled with water. *Water* is a type both of the Spirit and the Word (John 7:37-39; Eph. 5:26). The operation typified is this – the Holy Spirit uses the Word to convict the believer of some evil allowed in his life to the hindering of his joy, growth, and service. Thus convicted, he remembers that the *guilt* of his sin has been met by the sacrifice of Christ (I John 1:7). Instead of despairing, the convicted believer judges and confesses the defiling thing as unworthy a saint, and is forgiven and cleansed (John 13:3-10; I John 1:7-10).

Chapter Six

PROPHETIC FOREGLEAMS FROM FEASTS AND FESTIVALS

A. The Seven Feasts of Jehovah – Commanded
   1. Feast of Passover
   2. Feast of Unleavened Bread
   3. Feast of Firstfruits
   4. Feast of Pentecost
   5. Feast of Trumpets
   6. Feast of Atonement
   7. Feast of Tabernacles

B. Minor Feasts – Uncommanded
   1. Feast of Purim
   2. Feast of Dedication
   3. Feast of Jubilee

More is found in the Bible of feasts and festivals than fasts and funerals, because God desires His redeemed people to be joyful, content, and satisfied. This is why the inspired record as to what the Jewish feasts constitute not only affords one of the richest dispensational studies of the Bible, but also a wonderful panorama of Christian truth. The ritual of these feasts is heavy with symbolic significance. Taken together, these festivals give us the particular occasions on which the people could worship God. Daily, weekly, yearly, seventh year, jubilee year, and other festive services were all so many times of preparation for the worship in spirit and in truth of all times and places. Each seventh and fiftieth year was kept with peculiar solemnities. They likewise point forward: "Christ our Passover was sacrificed, therefore *let us keep continual festival,*" as the Greek expresses it.

In the momentous portion outlining the feasts of Jehovah (Lev. 23), the Sabbath seems to be separated from these feasts (Lev. 23:1-3), yet, for Israel, the weekly Sabbath was the fundamental one of all the "set feasts" given by Jehovah to His redeemed people, and to them alone as the seal or token of their national relationship, as His peculiar people. "I gave them My Sabbaths" (Exod. 31:12-17; Ezek. 20:12, 20). The *weekly* festival, then, was the Sabbath, a day devoted to rest and cheerful devotion, when additional sacrifices were presented, children were instructed, house of God visited for worship and exposition (Lev. 24:8; Num. 28:9; Ps. 68:25-27; Acts 13:15).

The Law of one day's cessation from labor in seven is connected with the day of God's rest after Creation, and also with Israel's deliverance from Egypt (Exod. 20:8; Deut. 5:12-15). This observance belongs to a whole class of Jewish feasts regulated by the cycle of the phases of the moon, and is therefore classed among what we know as *lunar feasts.* In the course of time, religious leaders, like the Scribes and Pharisees made the Sabbath a drudgery not a delight, a burden not a blessing – which called forth strong protests from Jesus. The only *Sabbath* revealed in the Bible is the seventh day, but we are not under Israel's seventy-day obligation. The Christian's *Lord's Day,* or *Sunday,* has no original connection with the *Sabbath* of Israel. Christians are not to be judged "in respect of a Sabbath" (Col. 2:14, 16), because for them the eighth day, or the first day of the week, when Christ rose again, and became the head of a new creation, His church, in His day.

The *monthly* festival was celebrated on the day of the new moon, and was announced by the sound of silver trumpets (Num. 10:10). Labor did not cease, but additional sacrifices were offered. The new moon of the seventh month, Tisri, or October, commenced the civil year. Legal codes prescribed numerous burnt offerings on the recurrence of each new moon, with a special sin offering. Such days as they came around were used for consulting the prophets (II Kings 4:22, 23), for special sacrificial meals in family life (I Sam. 20), as days of rest (Amos 8:5). For the new moon of the seventh, or sabbatical, month, special sacrifices were offered. Such a day was called *The Feast of Trumpets.*

As to the annual historical feasts, there were three ordained by Law. Later Judaism reckoned *the Passover* and *the Feast of Unleavened Bread* as one, but originally they were distinct, and we are to deal with them separately. When these annual festivals were held, all the adult males in Israel were required to appear at the sanctuary (Exod. 23:14-17). These yearly occasions were intended to be seasons of joyous thanksgiving, and were commemorative of the kindness and favor of God toward His chosen people.

A. *The Seven Feasts of Jehovah — Commanded*

1. *Feast of the Passover* (Num. 23: 4-5). In our coverage of Israel's deliverance from Pharaoh after the disastrous tenth plague (which consult), we dealt somewhat fully with this yearly festival. The sprinkling of the blood of the paschal lamb was a remembrance of the sign by which the Hebrews were separated from the Egyptians. This feast was kept on the fourteenth day of the first month, Abib, or Nisan — the first month of the Jewish sacred year, equivalent to our April. On this day of remembrance, a common sacrificial meal, in which a lamb was eaten — as in the peace offering; its blood sprinkled — as in the ritual of Atonement; its flesh and bones wholly consumed — as in the burnt offering. Evidently the observance of this feast was eminently calculated to promote family godliness (Exod. 12:3, 12, 26).

It was in connection with this feast, and toward its close that our Lord instituted the Last Supper, which foreshadowed Him as our *Passover* crucified for us (Matt. 26:26-29; I Cor. 11:23-29). When the third cup, called "the cup of blessing" had been drunk, praises were sung (See I Cor. 10:16-21). The Jews would sing or recite Psalms 115-118, and sometimes, in addition, Psalms 120-137. It would be some of these Psalms that Jesus and His disciples sang as He went to die for our deliverance from the bondage of sin. The yearly Feast of the Passover was "a memorial, and brings into view *Redemption,* upon which all blessing rests." Said Jesus as He inaugurated His memorial feast, "This do in remembrance of me."

Thy body, broken for my sake,
  My bread from Heaven shall be;
The cup of blessing I will take,
  And thus remember thee.

2. *Feast of Unleavened Bread* (Num. 23:6-8). There is a close association between the previous feast and the one before us, in that the *Passover* foreshadowing Christ crucified has its call to holiness of life in the *Feast of Unleavened Bread* (II Cor. 5:17; I Pet. 2:24). It would appear that in the *Passover* the historical association was grafted upon an older image of the offering of the firstlings of the flock to God. Similarly the *Feast of Unleavened Bread,*

known as *Maggoth,* had an agricultural origin, and signified the offering unto God of the firstfruits of the field.

This feast of the Lord began on the fifteenth day of Abib, or Nisan (April), and lasted seven days. On the second day a sheaf of new corn was offered, with a lamb of the first year. All *leaven* was excluded from Jewish homes during the days of the feast because of its historical association with Israel's hasty retreat from Egypt (Exod. 12:24). The connection of *leaven,* however, with ceremonial pollution appears to be much older (Exod. 23:18). The root idea of *Maggoth* seems to be that of the separation of the fruit of the new year from the leaven of the old.

As *leaven* is the consistent symbol of moral and doctrinal evil (Matt. 16:6; I Cor. 5:5-8; Gal. 5:9), the prophetic feature of the waving of the unleavened bread before the Lord is obvious. The life and witness of the Christian must be without any leaven or malice, wickedness, insincerity, and error, as Paul emphasizes in his exhortation to holiness of walk and life (I Cor. 5:8). This feast typifies full, unbroken communion with Christ, who is the perfect unleavened wave-loaf, for in Him was no sin – the experience of the fulness of the blessing of our Redemption in Him. The divine order is Redemption, The Passover, then, a life lived for the glory of the Redeemer – Feast of Unleavened Bread (II Cor. 7:1).

3. *Feast of Firstfruits* (23:10-14). John termed the feasts of Jehovah as "the feasts of the *Jews,*" doubtless because of their moral rejection of Him as their Messiah (John 1:10, 11), and of the way they had prostituted the spiritual import of the feasts. When, after years of desert wandering, being fed miraculously, Israel found herself in the land of promise, she lived off the land by her own labor. As harvests were reaped, a sheaf of the firstfruits were brought to the priest, who waved them before the Lord, an action demonstrating that all good things around us come from heaven above. Then, as we can see from the context, a burnt offering, drink offering, meal offering were associated with the ritual of this feast which not only was designed to promote godliness and gratitude on the part of the Israelites, but instituted to prefigure the greater blessings of the Gospel.

Firstfruits represent "Resurrection." Hence, in his Magna Carta of Resurrection, Paul speaks of his risen Lord as "Christ the firstfruits" (I Cor. 15:23), and of the saints to be raised at His coming as His firstfruits. When He rose from the dead, He became "the firstfruits of them that slept," that is, a sheaf-token of a still greater harvest of resurrected souls. Christ's victory over man's last enemy was the earnest or pledge that the whole resurrection harvest will follow. Thus our faith is not in vain, nor our hope limited to this life. Paul probably wrote *First Corinthians* about the time of the Passover Feast (I Cor. 5:7). The day after the Passover Sabbath was that for the offering of *the firstfruits* (Lev. 23:10, 11), and the same was the day of Christ's Resurrection, hence, the appropriateness of Paul's use of the image. As the firstfruits are of the same nature as the rest of the harvest, so Christ, the bringer of life, is of the same nature as the race of men to whom He brings it.

4. *Feast of Pentecost* (25:15-22). This further yearly feast is also known as *the Feast of Weeks,* and was a festival of the completed wheat-harvest, observed fifty days after the offering of the firstling sheaf. On the fiftieth day sacrifices like those of the days of unleavened bread were offered, but the central feature of this feast was the offering of two

loaves of the new wheat (Exod. 23:16; 34:22; Deut. 16:9-12). The Greek term for *Pentecost* means "fifty" and is from *Pente*, meaning "five." On the fiftieth day after the second day of the Passover, came the Feast of Pentecost, and became known by the above title Feast of Weeks, because it was held seven clear weeks from the sixteenth Abib. Actually it was the feast during which Jews residing out of Palestine generally choose to visit Jerusalem.

As a Thanksgiving for the wheat harvest, it was also called The Feast of the Harvest or The Day of Firstfruits (Num. 28:26), and emphasized the necessity of expressing gratitude for the common mercies of life. Prophetically, it typified the Pentecost of Acts 2:1, when there came the first ingathering of the firstfruits of the Christian church – a glorious harvest as the result of Christ, as the corn of wheat, falling into the ground, and dying. Looking at the instructions given as to the observance of this Feast of Weeks, *leavened* loaves had to be used. If these particular loaves represent the church, then the presence of leaven is suggestive, for the visible church in itself is not good. The church was not long in existence before two of its members were smitten with sudden death for lying against God the Spirit (Acts 5:1-10; 15:1). The leavened loaves became acceptable through the sin offering (Lev. 23:19).

Scofield would have us observe that "*Loaves;* not a sheaf of separate growths loosely bound together, but a real union of particles make one homogeneous *body*. The descent of the Holy Spirit at Pentecost united the separate disciples into one organism (I Cor. 10:16, 17; 12:12, 13, 30)." Further, "the wave-loaves were offered fifty days after the wave-sheaf. This is precisely the period between the Resurrection of Christ and the formation of the Church at Pentecost by the coming of the Holy Spirit (Matt. 16:18; Acts 2:1-4; I Cor. 12:12, 13). With the wave-sheaf no leaven was offered, for there was no evil in Christ, but the wave-loaves, typifying the Church, are 'baken with leaven,' for in the Church there is still evil."

5. *Feast of Trumpets* (23:23-25). Trumpets were used to summon people publicly to hear an important announcement, or to rally fighters to war. On the first Sabbath of the seventh month, the trumpets proclaimed a holy convocation, and on the day, no servile work was to be done, and the people had to offer an offering made by fire unto the Lord (Num. 29:1). There was a celebration of this feast after the return of the Jews from the Babylonian Captivity (Neh. 8:2). This feast, held on the new-year's-day of the year, reminded the people not only of their duty of conducting all the worldly employments of the year in the fear of God and to His Glory, but also of the promise of their final gathering to their land and God (Ps. 81).

Prophecies like Isaiah 18:3; 27:13; 58:1; Joel 2–3:21 in connection with the *trumpets,* are connected with the regathering and repentance of Israel after the church, or pentecostal, period is ended. This feast is immediately followed by the Day of Atonement. For the true church, the trumpet to listen for is the one Paul associates with the return of Christ for His own; and what a gathering there will be in response to its silver tones!

6. *The Feast of the Day of Atonement* (23:26-32). The tenth day of the seventh month was appointed as a day of public fasting and humiliation, on which the nation were to afflict their souls on account of their sins, and seek atonement for them (Lev. 16:29; 23:27; Num. 29:7). Here we have the only *fast* appointed by

the Law (Lev. 23:27-29; 25:9; Acts 27:9). The required ceremonial expiation was made by the High Priest, who on this solemn day alone entered into the Holy of Holies, where he sprinkled the blood of the goat which had been sacrificed. We have already indicated the significance of the two goats, the one slain and the other spared. All features of this day were connected with the expiation for the sins of the people (Lev. 16:11-19). Affliction of theirs on account of their rejection of the Messiah, and their forgiveness is referred to by Zechariah in his prophecy (Zech. 12:10; 13:1).

The word *atonement* means "to make propitiation by expiation," implying the satisfacton or appeasement of God's holy wrath against sin by suffering to the utmost its penalty. This is what Jesus accomplished on our behalf at Calvary, and is now able to deal with us in mercy. For us, the Day of Atonement was indeed "a shadow of good things to come." Prophetically, this day looks forward to the repentance of Israel as she looks upon Him she pierced and is regathered in her own land as the Messiah comes to set up His Kingdom (Deut. 30:1-10). Dr. A. T. Pierson says that,

> The High Priest, on the Great Day of Atonement, went from the altar of sacrifice into the Holiest and shortly returned to bless the people. These few moments which elapsed between his disappearance within the veil, and his re-appearance in the court, typify the whole interval between our Lord's Ascension and Second Advent, already protracted over nineteen centuries. "God's "little while" often proves man's long while, and especially when events are seen in *perspective* as in prophetic vision. We must not stumble over the difficulty of delay. "Long" and "short" are relative terms: everything depends upon the scale.

To God a prolonged interval is but as a moment – one day is as a thousand years and a thousand years as one day.

Since the destruction of the temple in 70 A.D., the Jews have not offered sacrifices. Services of prayers replaced them. There is a custom among some Jews, however, known as *Kapparah*, about which the Jewish Encyclopaedia has this to say:

> An animal used as a sort of vicarious sacrifice on the day previous to the Day of Atonement. As a rule, a cock is taken by a male, and a hen by a female person, and after the recitation of Psalm 107:17-20 and Job 33:23, 24, the fowl is swung around the head three times while the right hand is put upon the animal's head. At the same time, the following is thrice said in Hebrew: "This be my substitute, my vicarious offering, my atonement. This cock (or hen) shall meet death, but I shall find a long and pleasant life of peace!" After this, the animal is slaughtered and given to the poor, or, what is deemed better, is eaten by the owners while the value of it is given to the poor. The custom has been strongly opposed by such authorities as Nahmonides, Solomon ben Adreb, and Joseph Caro as a pagan one in conflict with the spirit of Judaism, which knows of no vicarious sacrifice.

Does not such a quotation reveal the deep need of the Jewish people for a spiritual knowledge of the Lamb of God who died for their sin, as well as that of Gentiles? Their "Service of Prayer" cannot replace what God said long ago to the House of Israel. "The life of the flesh is in the blood: and I have given it to you upon the altar to make an atonement for your souls: it is the blood that maketh an atonement for the soul" (Lev. 17:11). What the Jew needs is not *Kapparah* but Calvary.

7. *The Feast of Tabernacles* (23:34-44). This feast, perhaps the most joyful of all the feasts, was kept from the fifteenth to the twenty-second day of the seventh month, or Tisri (October). Its historical associations were

connected with the wanderings of the Israelites in the wilderness, and commemorated by the usage of living in tents or booths during these days. The origin of the feast is indicated by its other name, *the Feast of Ingathering* (Exod. 23:16). It was the festival at the end of the harvest of fruit, oil, and wine. Numerous sacrifices were prescribed for this feast (Num. 29:12-40). In later times many further ceremonies were added, making it the happiest of all feasts. Among these were the carrying of water from Siloam to the altar, the lighting of many lights, a daily procession round the altar, and the singing of many Psalms, particularly the *Hallel* (Psalms 113-118).

The specific purpose of this feast was the keeping in memory of the years Israel had spent dwelling in the booths or tents in the wilderness (Lev. 23:30-44). Both Ezra and Nehemiah refer to the way the feast was kept (Exra 3:4; Neh. 8:14-17). It was on the last day of this feast, with its outpouring of water, that Jesus proclaimed His message about the varied ministry of the Holy Spirit He would send (John 7:37). One of the great lessons we can learn from the ceremony is that of cherishing a grateful remembrance of God's past mercies both to our forefathers and to ourselves. What must not be forgotten is the remarkable promise God gave to those who, in obedience to His command, left their homes to attend the annual festivals of the Passover, Pentecost, and Tabernacles (Exod. 34:24).

For Israel, *the Feast of Tabernacles* held a prophecy of the future, for as they observed it they exulted in the glad kingdom of the glory yet to come to them on earth (Ps. 147; Isa. 2:2-4; Jer. 31–33; Zech. 14:16). This feast, like the Lord's Supper for the church, is both past and prospective, memorial and prophetic. *Past* — as a memorial of Israel's redemption out of Egypt (Lev. 23:43); *prospective* — prophetic of the kingdom-rest of Israel after her regathering, restoration, and entrance into millennial glory (Zech. 14:16-21). What perfect rejoicing there will be when God can say, "Israel My glory!"

There is one interesting feature of the feast, however, that carries a spiritual message for all our hearts. The people had to bring the boughs and branches of certain trees and rejoice before the Lord for seven days. Two parts of the tree world are specifically mentioned, namely, "Palm trees . . . willows of the brook" (Lev. 23:40). What striking contrasts these present! Let us think of the distinctive meaning of each.

a. *Take the palm.* It grows upright in the sun, and is renowned for its manifold uses. Because it has no equal in the benefits it bestows, it has been called "the King Among the Grasses," and "the Prince of Vegetation." The palm is the symbol of triumph, so victors were crowned with palm leaves. It stands, then, for all that is brightest and best in life. God's desire is that we should flourish as the palm tree (Ps. 92:12).

b. *Take the willow.* God said to the willow, "Stand by the water-courses and weep." So we speak of it as the "weeping" willow tree. Israel's tears were associated with willows (Ps. 137:2). The palm reaches upward, but the willow droops as it grows, and is therefore emblematic of sadness, humiliation, captivity, death. It is the reverse to all the palm suggests. Yet each year Israel had to bring the willows as well as the palms before the Lord in the spirit of rejoicing. We may find it easy to rejoice over our palms, or over the good and welcome things of life, but very hard indeed to bless God for the willows, the sorrowful, inexplicable experiences overtaking us. Yet we triumph in life when we are able to thank Him for the things we do not like, as well as those bringing pleasure.

When the late Sir Winston Churchill came to make his farewell speech to the House of Commons, he said,

> The glory of light cannot exist without its shadows. Life is a whole, and *good* and *ill* must be accepted together.

Shakespeare, in "All's Well That Ends Well," echoes a similar sentiment in the phrase "The web of our life is of a mingled yarn, good and ill together." Dr. W. L. Watkinson in one of his volumes tells of an organist who contrived a somewhat unique overture. It was a mixture of "The Hallelujah Chorus" and "The Dead March of Saul." Like Israel, we go through the wilderness with a palm in one hand and a willow in the other. Smiles and sighs, pleasure and pain are intermingled. Thus, when the people rejoiced with palms and willows in their hearts, they were grateful, not only for the benefits provided, but for the way God had over-ruled all the unwelcome and untoward experiences encountered, making them work together for their spiritual good.

B. *Minor Feasts — Uncommanded*

Having considered the seven feasts Jehovah commanded, there are one or two minor ones Israel observed, which were not of divine appointment.

1. *Feast of Purim. Purim* means "lots" and was historically connected with the deliverance of the Jews from Haman, who had extracted an edict from the Persian king Ahasuerus, then monarch of the world, to exterminate all Jews. Through the overruling providence of God they were spared (Esther 3:7; 9:15-32). The feast was observed on the fourteenth or fifteenth of Adar (March), and was also called Mordecai's Day (II Macc. 15:36), because of the part he played in the preservation of the Jews. The book of *Esther* was read on the night of the thirteenth amid loud imprecations against Haman and his house: the whole feast was one of boisterous mirth. This feast is still observed by orthodox Jews when *Esther* is read.

2. *Feast of Dedication.* This particular feast was instituted by Judas Maccabeus in 164 B.C. It celebrated the re-establishment of divine worship in Jerusalem after the temple had been cleansed of its pollution by Antiochus Epiphanes (I Macc. 4:52-59). The festival, which began on the twenty-fifth of the month Chislea (December), lasted for 8 days. Because of the joyful illumination of every house during the feast, it was also called *the Feast of Lights.* Our Lord's attendance at this winter festival justifies the observance of religious seasons of human appointment (John 10:22).

3. *Other Feasts.* Other solemn seasons, more or less festive in character were the *Sabbatic Year* (Lev. 25:2-21), and the *Jubilee,* held in the year after every seventh sabbatical year (Lev. 15:8). There are references to added feasts by Zechariah, but since the observance of them is not particularly noticed in the Bible, they are not here noticed (See Zech. 7:5; 8:19). As to the moral and spiritual applications of all of the Jewish festivals, we cannot do better than quote the summary of Dr. Joseph Angus as we conclude this fascinating section of our study.

> They all tended to unite the people in a holy brotherhood and to separate them from the heathen. They preserved the memory of past mercies. They illustrated the Divine holiness. They lightened the load of poverty, checked oppression and covetousness, and were either types of Gospel blessings, or suggestive, to a spiritual mind, of Gospel truths.

Chapter Seven

PROPHETIC FOREGLEAMS FROM CHRIST'S OWN TEACHING

A. The Double Function of the Prophet
B. Christ's Predictions Fulfilled
C. Christ's Predictions in Process of Fulfillment
D. Christ's Predictions Yet to be Fulfilled
E. Apostolic Prophecies of Christ

Having endeavored to set forth the predictive element concerning Christ associated with Old Testament personalities, events, institutions, and festivals, we now come to the New Testament to gather together some of His own prophecies related to Himself, to His Church, to Jews and Gentiles, to world events, to man's future beyond the grave. Christ's personal predictions cover a very wide area. As the prophet from God, He was well qualified to prophesy. Because He is Alpha and Omega, the beginning and the end, past, present, and future were as an open scroll to Him, and He was therefore able to predict, unerringly, all that was not revealed to men.

A. *The Double Function of the Prophet*

Earlier in our study we noted that the ancient prophets were inspired to *foretell,* as well as *forthtell:* that as *preachers* they proclaimed stirring messages for their own time; but as *predictors,* they uttered truths for ages far beyond their own. That Christ functioned in this twofold way is obvious from the four Gospels and the book of *Revelation,* which contain His declarations. No man spake like this man! As the preacher *par excellence,* His sermons and messages blistered consciences, liberated the sinbound, and won converts. Pearls of truth leaving His holy lips are still treasured by millions, after almost two millenniums.

But Christ was also a mighty prophet, able to draw aside the veil, and reveal coming events, some of which have been fulfilled – others, in process of fulfillment – and still others relating to the course and consummation of the Gentile age, the rapture of the church, the great tribulation, the judgments, the millennium, which, because no prophecy of His can possibly fail, will be realized to the very letter. "I Am . . . The Truth."

When we come to deal with the oral ministry of our Lord, whether His utterances were prophetical or doctrinal, we recognize that His revelations were *gradually* disclosed, and never fully till after He had risen from the grave. What a remarkable coverage of truth concerning Himself He must have given to those Emmaus disciples (Luke 24)! While among His own in the days of His flesh, strong prejudices and the lack of spiritual understanding on their part necessitated a *gradual* unveiling of truth, for they were slow of heart, not only to believe Old Testament propheices of Him, but what He Himself declared. Christ had to tell His disciples that they were not able to bear the full blaze of truth.

His method was to reward *faith* in a little, by imparting more, as He daily taught His followers. At first, He hinted at some prophecy, doctrine, or event, then repeated it more explicitly, often telling His disciples that when the Holy Spirit came He would lead and guide them into all truth, and likewise show them things to come. The whole prophetic plan or doctrine, He did not exhaustively propound. He accomplished the works that were at the foundation of His teachings. As Angus puts it,

> He suffers, and hence the Doctrine of Atonement.
> He pleads, and hence the Doctrine of Spiritual Influence.
> He rises from the grave, hence the Doctrine of Resurrection and Glory.
> Our Lord came down from Heaven, not so much to *teach* the Gospel as to be Himself the *Subject* of it, leaving the Spirit to be the chief Interpreter. We study, therefore the Law in the Gospels; the Gospels in the Epistles; and all *in Christ*.

To give a complete classification and exposition of *all* the prophetic utterances of Christ, as well as of *all* apostolic prophecies concerning the coming mission of Christ, would require a large volume all its own. We are only able, because of the limitation of space, to outline this absorbing aspect of Bible study. In *Appendices* we have supplied the reader with a few guideposts to follow. Our Lord's foretellings can be gathered under the threefold division of

His Predictions Fulfilled

His Predictions in Continuous Fulfillment

His Predictions Yet to be Fulfilled

B. *His Predictions Fulfilled*

Under this heading we have those prophecies concerning Himself, and others, He made before He ascended on high, and which have been fulfilled — many of them before He left the earth. Jesus predicted —

The Nature and Purpose of His Incarnation (John 3:17; 10:10).

The Benediction of His Angel Host (John 1:51; Matt. 4:11; 15:31; Mark 1:13).

The Rejection of His Claims by Religious Leaders (Matt. 21:38, 42; Acts 4:17).

The Defection of His Disciples: Judas (Matt. 26:21); Peter (Luke 22:31, 61); All of the Disciples (John 16:32).

The Martyrdom of Peter (John 21: 18, 19; II Pet. 1:13, 14).

The Preparations for His Supper (Mark 14:13; I Cor. 11:23).

The Brutal Treatment of His Foes (Mark 10:34; Luke 18:32).

The Cruel Death He should Die (Matt. 20:18, 19; 26:2; John 12: 32).

The Burial of His Body (Matt. 12:40; John 12:7).

The Resurrection of His Body From the Grave (Matt. 26:32; John 2:19).

The Ascension and Exaltation to Glory (Luke 24:51; John 6:32; 20:17).

The Coming of His Spirit (John 14:26; 15:26; 16:7, 8; Acts 1:5; 2:1-4).

The Creation of His Church (Matt. 13:45, 46; 16:18; Acts 2:40, 47; I Pet. 2:6, 7).

The Destruction of Jerusalem (Matt. 24:1, 2; Luke 19:44).

The Universal Ingathering of Souls Through His Gospel (Mark 13: 10; 16:17; John 10:16).

The Fulfillment of His Predictions (Matt. 24:34; 26:13; Mark 13:31; 14:8).

Why Jesus adopted the predictive and parabolic form of declaring truths concerning Himself He clearly states in passages like John 13:19; 14:29; 16:4.

C. *His Predictions in Continuous Fulfillment*

In His prophecy of the destruction

of Jerusalem, which was fulfilled in 70 A.D., when Emperor Titus wellnigh obliterated both the city and the temple, Jesus referred to Jerusalem as being "trodden down of the Gentiles, until *the times of the Gentiles be fulfilled*" (Luke 21:24). These times began with the captivity of Judah under Nebuchadnezzar, when God said to him through Daniel, "Thou, O king, art a King of kings" (Dan. 2:37), and through the centuries we have witnessed Gentile monarchies and dominion, and we live in the Gentile Age which will end when Jesus returns as King of Kings, and assumes world-dominion (Rev. 17:14; 19:16). Jesus lived in the times when Gentiles governed the land He was born in, and thus many of His prophecies are related to the *course* of the Gentile age, which His return to earth will *consummate*. What were these predictions He made concerning the characteristics of the period between His Ascension to heaven and His return from it?

For an understanding of our times, it is important to follow the explicit foreshadowings of present-day happening for Jesus said, "When these things *begin to come to pass,* then look up, and lift up your heads; for your redemption draweth nigh" (Luke 21:28). Reviewing the conspicuous features of our age, as predicted by our Lord, may seem like indulgence in a fit of gloomy pessimism but actually such kindles with our hearts a wondrous hope, even the return of Him who predicted things to come. Amid gathering darkness ours is the glowing optimism born of faith in the veracity of our Lord's inspired utterances. Among the manifold characteristics or signs He gave as betokening His own promised and prophesied return, mention can be made of the following features:

Continuing and developing apostacy (Luke 18:8; II Thess. 2:1-3, 10-12; II Pet. 2:1-3).

Continuous appearances of false Christs (Matt. 24:4; 23; Mark 13:5).

Continuous opposition to His Gospel (Matt. 10:34-36; Luke 12:49-53).

Continuous world hatred of His followers (Matt. 18:7; John 15:18-21; 16:33).

Continuous ministry of the Spirit on behalf of His own (John 7:37-39; 14:16, 17; 16:7-15).

Continuous intercession in glory for His church (Heb. 7:25; I John 2:1; Rom. 8:34).

Continuous salvation by grace of Jews and Gentiles (Luke 19:9; John 4:22; 10:16; 11:52; Acts 13:14, 46).

The most remarkable prophetic section of the New Testament is that part of our Lord's *Olivet Discourse,* in which He vividly described the course of this age, and also what is to follow the dispensation of grace (Matt. 24–25). From the time of His Ascension, the characteristic features He spoke of have been common to men. What is implied is the fact that as the time He spoke of nears its end, these portents will appear with greater intensity.

Satanic and messianic deception (Matt. 24:4, 5, 11, 24).

International wars and rumors of war (Matt. 24:6).

Development of world confederacies (Matt. 24:7).

Universal catastrophes (Matt. 24:7).

Universal anti-semitism (Matt. 24:9, 10).

Abounding iniquity and spiritual declension (Matt. 24:12).

Jerusalem compassed about with armies (Luke 21:20-24).

International upheavals, distress, and unrest (Luke 21:25, 26).

Manifestation of Jewish and Gen-

tile nationalism (Luke 21:29-33).
Warnings as to the snare of worldliness (Luke 21:34-36).

These are by no means the only indications our Lord gave of the history of the world between His Ascension and Advent, but they are sufficient for us to see that the events of our time are heavy with prophetic significance, and most pertinent as incentives to holiness of life.

D. *His Predictions Yet to Be Fulfilled*

This last section brings us to the divine prophetic plan for the ages to follow the privileged age of grace Jesus inaugurated by His Incarnation, Death, Resurrection, Exaltation, and His sending of the Holy Spirit to build and complete the divine habitation, the church, which is His body. Prominent among His predictions not yet accomplished is that of His return for His church, known as *the Rapture.* In His High-Priestly prayer, Jesus expressed the wish to have all redeemed by His efficacious blood with Him in heaven.

> Father, I will that they also, whom thou hast given me, be with me where I am; that they may behold my glory, which thou hast given me." (John 17:24).

This prayer will be answered when, according to His own promise and prediction, He will come from heaven to take His church there.

> I will come again, and receive you unto myself; that where I am, there ye may be also (John 14:3, 18, 28; 21:22; Acts 1:10, 11).

Once the church has been raptured, then there will come the rapid fulfillment of what Jesus predicted concerning the Great Tribulation (Matt. 24:15-26); His return in power and glory to assume control of world affairs (Matt. 24:27-31), His righteous and authoritative judgment (John 5: 26, 27, 30); His universal reign and dominion (Luke 1:32, 33; John 18: 33-37).

As the last Book of the Bible is named "The Revelation of Jesus Christ" (Rev. 1:1), its contents are not only *about* Him but *from* Him to John. What He revealed of Himself and of all the events bringing in His covenanted kingdom, John was commissioned to write in a book (Rev. 1:11, 19), which he did. "Write the things which thou hast seen [Past], and the things which are [Present], and the things which shall be hereafter [Prospective]" (Rev. 1:19). The latter section covers all the prophecies Jesus gave to John that await fulfillment. All of the momentous events before, during, and after the millennium form a phase of prophecy many have written about. For a coverage of same, the reader is referred to the author's volume by the publisher of the book in your hand, namely, *Prophetic Studies in the Book of Revelation.*

E. *Apostolic Prophecies of Christ*

Before Christ left the apostles He had called and trained, He assured them that after His Ascension He would send them the Holy Spirit, who, as He Himself expressed it, "shall glorify me: for he shall receive of mine, and shall shew it unto you" (John 16:12-15). This enlightening ministry of the Spirit of wisdom and revelation included the unveiling of the future — "He will shew you things to come." One cannot read *The Acts* and *The Epistles* without realizing how fully the Spirit inspired the apostles to bring to fruitage the germinal prophetic utterances of Jesus. He was the glorious center and circumference of their predictions as to coming events, and they lived and labored under the impact of same. From Pentecost on the apostles were children of the dawn with eyes scanning the horizon for the promised sunrise. "They waited for His Son from heaven."

Apostolic expansion to brief, predictive messages of Jesus can be traced through *The Epistles*. For instance, He stated the bare fact of His return for His saints in the words, "I will come again, and receive you unto myself" (John 14:3). Paul, by the revelation granted him by the divine promiser Himself, extended this prediction, and expounded all that would take place when the Lord descends from heaven, namely, the Resurrection of the dead, the transformation of the living saints, the translation of both the raised and changed to meet Him in the air (I Thess. 4:13-18). Further expansion of the Advent hope, and related aspects, as indicated by Jesus, can be found in other Pauline epistles (Phil. 3:20, 21; Titus 2:12, 13, etc.).

Peter, likewise, who ever remembered the words of his Lord, had stored away in his memory what he had heard Him say about Advent signs in the sun, moon, and stars, and in after years came to assure the saints that the Master would not be slack in fulfilling His predicted return. The apostle then went on to extend the reference to cataclysmatic changes in the heavens, and the inauguration of a new universe altogether at the coming of the Lord (II Pet. 3). What a tremendous chapter this is, especially in its appeal to holy living in the light of future events!

John is another who, under the Spirit's guidance, had the truths Jesus uttered in his hearing, brought to his remembrance, and in turn, developed them for the enlightenment and edification of the saints. John was the apostle who recorded what he had heard Jesus say about coming again to take His saints to be with Himself. As he reflected upon this first indication in the Gospels of the return of his Master for His church, he enlarged upon it, and came to write about being like Him at His appearing, and of the purifying influence of such a blessed hope (I John 3:1-3).

Prophetic truths dealt with in convincing language are

False teachers, and religions (I Tim. 4:1-5; II Tim. 3:5; 4:1-4; II Pet. 2:1-3; II Thess. 2:11-12).

The glorification of the saints of God (Rom. 8:17-25).

The judgment seat of Christ (Rom. 14:10-12; I Cor. 3:12-15; II Cor. 5:10; I John 4:17).

The final triumph of Christ (I Cor. 15:24-28; II Cor. 6:16).

The apostles knew how poor words were to convey what they felt as to the glories awaiting them, yet unfathomable joy, endless delight, a cloudless sky, a sweet, all-enfolding, unhindered love for the Lord, intimate fellowship with Him, and the vision of His transcendent majesty — these were the experiences beyond all telling they had as they lived under the impact of the glory yet to be revealed.

Well, our task has been a long and arduous one, but most inspiring and rewarding, for in multitudinous ways we have discovered how wonderfully true the Master's own word is:

IN THE VOLUME OF THE BOOK IT IS WRITTEN OF ME!

We cannot do better than close our Christological study with the words the late Dr. T. T. Shields used in the conclusion of a lecture he gave in London, England, in 1934, on *Spurgeon's Testimony to the Inspiration of Scripture:*

> We have followed Jesus—through historical wildernesses, and biographical mountain solitudes, and through genealogical deserts, only to find that the wilderness and the solitary place are made glad for Him; and in His presence the desert rejoices and blossoms as the rose. In Psalmist's melodies; in words of transcendent wisdom; in pregnant type, and glowing

symbol; in which that are dreadful; in chariots of fire; in seraphic visions of enraptured spirits of Prophets, Priests, and Kings, we have seen and heard the voice of our Beloved; until, at last, He has come to us out of the grave, being declared to be the Son of God with power, according to the Spirit of Holiness, by the Resurrection from the dead, and with perfect knowledge of both Worlds, He has joined us on the Emmaus Road; where with burning hearts we had heard Him, beginning at Moses and all the Prophets, expound unto us the things concerning Himself.

Therefore by the illuminating of His presence in all its pages, by the seal of His authority upon all its principles, and precepts, and promises, and prophecies; by His own invariable assumption of the Scriptures' infallibility, there is wrought into our deepest spiritual consciousness the unwavering conviction that the Bible is the Word of God that liveth and abideth for ever!

Should all the forms that men devise
Assault my faith with treacherous art,
I'd call them vanity and lies,
And bind the Gospel to my heart.

APPENDICES

A. Prophetic Foregleams From Words and Metaphors	B. Christ's Quotations From the Prophets C. Old Testament	Prophetic Witness to Christ and Christian Truth

A. *Prophetic Foregleams From Words and Metaphors*

When we set out upon our study it was our full intention to have a section devoted to the above profitable aspect, dealing with symbols like *dayspring, day-star, bridegroom,* etc., with their predictive content. Then there are certain words like *Maranatha,* meaning "the Lord Cometh" we had in mind to deal with. But as there have been requests for a volume on *All the Illustrations of the Bible,* as a further addition to the *All Series,* our next work will cover Scripture types, symbols, metaphors, emblems. Thus, as many of these will require consideration of their prophetic import, publishers and author alike felt it advisable to include all that we might have written under the above heading to the book to follow – which should prove to be a valuable asset for preachers and teachers in its provision of illustrative material.

B. *Christ's Quotations From the Prophets*

When our Lord said, "In the volume of the Book it is written of Me," He was referring to Old Testament Scriptures, seeing the New Testament was not written until several years after His Ascension. But a reading of the Gospels reveals how the mind of Christ was saturated with Old Testament truth, and it was therefore easy to expound in Moses and all the prophets those things concerning Himself (Luke 24:27). Here is a partial list of His quotations:

Matt. 13:14-17, from Isa. 6:9, 10.
Matt. 15:8; Mark 7:6 from Isa. 29: 13; Ezek. 33:31.
John 6:45 from Isa. 54:13.
Matt. 21:13; Mark 11:17; Luke 19: 46 from Isa. 56:7.
Matt. 11:28-30 from Jer. 6:16.
Matt. 21:13; Mark 11:17; Luke 19: 46 from Isa. 56:7; Jer. 7:11.
Matt. 24:15; Mark 13:14 from Dan. 12:11; 11:36.
Matt. 9:13; 12:7 from Hos. 6:6.
Matt. 12:39-42 from Jon. 1:17; II Chron. 9:1-12.
Matt. 10:36 from Mic. 7:6.
Mark 14:27 from Zech. 13:7.
Matt. 11:10 from Mal. 3:1.

(See further under last half of next section.)

C. *Prophetic Witness to Christ and to Christian Truth*

Luke the historian reminds us that "To him [Christ] give *all* the prophets witness" (Acts 10:43), and Christ Himself expounded the messianic prophecies in the Law of Moses, the Psalms, the prophets, in fact in "all the scriptures" (Luke 24:27, 44). The following list gives direct references or predictions from the prophets, with corresponding fulfillment in the New Testament:

From *Isaiah*

Chapter	with
1:9	Rom. 9:29.
2:10, 19, 21	II Thess. 1:9.
6:9-10	John 12:40; Acts 28: 26, 27.
7:14	Matt. 1:23.

8:12	I Pet. 3:14.
8:14	Rom. 9:33.
9:1, 2	Matt. 4:15, 16.
10:22, 23	Rom. 9:27.
11:10	Rom. 15:12.
21:9	Rev. 14:8; 18:2.
22:13	I Cor. 15:32.
25:8	I Cor. 15:54.
27:9	Rom. 11:27.
28:16	Rom. 9:33; 10:11; I Pet. 2:6.
29:10	Rom. 11:8.
40:3	Mark 1:3; Luke 3:4, 5; John 1:23.
40:7	James 1:11.
40:6-8	I Pet. 1:24-25.
40:13	Rom. 11:34; I Cor. 2:16.
42:1-3	Matt. 12:18-21.
45:23	Rom. 14:11.
49:6	Acts 13:47.
49:10	Rev. 7:16.
52:5	Rom. 2:24.
52:7	Rom. 10:15.
52:15	Rom. 15:21.
53:1	John 12:38.
53:4	Matt. 8:17.
53:4-6	I Pet. 2:24, 25.
53:7, 8	Acts 8:32-33.
53:9	I Pet. 2:22.
53:12	Mark 15:28; Luke 22:37.
54:1	Gal. 4:27.
55:3	Acts 13:34.
57:19	Eph. 2:17.
59:1, 8	Rom. 3:15-17.
59:20, 21	Rom. 11:26.
60:1	Eph. 5:14.
64:4	I Cor. 5:2, 9.
65:2	Rom. 10:21.
65:17	II Cor. 5:17.

From *Jeremiah*

Chapter	with
9:23	I Cor. 1:31.
9:23, 24	II Cor. 10:15-17.
31:15	Matt. 2:18.
31:31-34	Heb. 8:8-12.
31:33	Heb. 10:16, 17.

From *Hosea*

Chapter	with
10:8	Rev. 6:16.
11:1	Matt. 2:15.
13:14	I Cor. 15:55.

From *Joel*

Chapter	with
2:28-32	Acts 2:17-21.
2:32	Rom. 10:13.

From *Amos*

Chapter	with
5:25-27	Acts 7:42, 43.
9:11, 12	Acts 15:16, 17.

From *Micah*

Chapter	with
5:2	Matt. 2:6.

From *Nahum*

Chapter	with
1:15	Rom. 10:15.

From *Habakkuk*

Chapter	with
1:5	Acts 13:41.
2:3, 4	Heb. 10:37, 38.
2:4	Rom. 1:17; Gal. 3:11.

From *Zepaniah*

Chapter	with
3:13	Rev. 14:3.

From *Haggai*

Chapter	with
2:6	Heb. 12:26.

From *Zechariah*

Chapter	with
9:9	Matt. 21:5; John 12:15.
11:12	Matt. 27:9.
12:10	John 19:37.

From *Malachi*

Chapter	with
1:2, 3	Rom. 9:13; Luke 1:17.

Still keeping to the witness of all the prophets, we herewith cite those quotations in the New Testament from the prophetical books, including those explicit references to them by Jesus Himself, which the reader will find marked with a *. To indicate and classify all references from other Old Testament books in the New Testament is a task beyond our scope. Notice of many of these has already been made in the body of this volume.

From *Matthew*

Chapter	with
1:23	Isa. 7:14.
2:6	Mic. 5:2.
2:15	Hos. 11:1.
2:18	Jer. 31:15.
4:15, 16	Isa. 9:1, 2.
8:17	Isa. 53:4.
9:13	Hos. 6:6*.
10:35	Mic. 7:6*.
11:10	Mal. 3:1*.
11:29	Jer. 6:16*.
12:7	Hos. 6:6*.
12:18, 21	Isa. 42:1-3.
12:39	Jonah*.
13:14, 15	Isa. 6:9, 10*.
15:8, 9	Isa. 29:13*.
21:5	Zech. 9:9.
24:15; 27:9	Dan. 12:11*.

From *Mark*

Chapter	with
1:2	Mal. 3:1.
1:3	Isa. 40:3.
7:6	Isa. 29:13*.
9:44	Isa. 66:24*.
11:17	Isa. 56:7; Jer. 7:11*.
13:14	Dan. 12:11*.
14:27	Zech. 13:7*.
15:28	Isa. 53:12.

From *Luke*

Chapter	with
1:17	Mal. 4:6.
3:4, 5	Isa. 40:3.
4:18, 19	Isa. 61:1, 2*.
7:27	Mal. 3:1*.
12:53	Mic. 7:6*.
19:46	Isa. 56:7; Jer. 7:11*.
22:37	Hos. 10:8.
24:27	All the prophets.

From *John*

Chapter	with
1:23	Isa. 40:3.
6:45	Isa. 54:13*.
12:15	Zech. 9:9.
12:38	Isa. 53:1.
12:46	Isa. 6:9, 10.
19:37	Zech. 12:10.

From *Acts*

Chapter	with
2:17-21	Joel 2:28-32.
7:42, 43	Amos 5:25-27.
8:32, 33	Isa. 53:7, 8.
13:34	Isa. 55:3.
13:41	Hab. 1:5.
13:47	Isa. 49:6.
15:16, 17	Amos 9:11, 12.
28:26, 27	Isa. 6:9, 10.

From *Romans*

Chapter	with
1:17	Hab. 2:4.
2:24	Isa. 52:5.
3:15-17	Isa. 59:7, 8.
9:13	Mal. 1:2, 3.
9:27	Isa. 10:22, 23.
9:29	Isa. 1:9.
9:33	Isa. 28:16; 8:14.
10:11	Isa. 28:16.
10:13	Joel 2:32.
10:15	Isa. 52:7; Nah. 1:15.
10:21	Isa. 65:2.
11:8	Isa. 29:10.
11:26	Isa. 59:20, 21.
11:27	Isa. 27:9.
11:34	Isa. 40:13.
14:11	Isa. 45:23.
15:12	Isa. 11:10.
15:21	Isa. 52:15.

From *First Corinthians*

Chapter	with
1:31	Jer. 9:23.
2:9	Isa. 64:4.
2:16	Isa. 40:13.
14:21	Isa. 28:11.
15:32	Isa. 22:13.
15:54	Isa. 25:8.
15:55	Hos. 13:14.

From *Second Corinthians*

Chapter	with
5:17	Isa. 52:11.
10:17	Jer. 9:23, 24.

From *Galatians*

Chapter	with
3:11	Hab. 2:4.
4:27	Isa. 54:1.

From *Ephesians*

Chapter	with
2:17	Isa. 57:19.
5:14	Isa. 60:1.

From *Second Thessalonians*

Chapter	with
1:9	Isa. 2:10, 19, 21.

From *Hebrews*

Chapter	with
8:8-12	Jer. 31:31-34.
10:16	Jer. 31:33.
10:17	Jer. 31:34.
10:37, 38	Hab. 2:3, 4.
12:26	Hag. 2:6.

From *James*

Chapter	with
1:11	Isa. 40:7.

From *First Peter*

Chapter	with
1:24, 25	Isa. 40:6-8.
2:6	Isa. 28:16; 8:14.
2:22	Isa. 53:9.
2:24, 25	Isa. 53:4-6.
3:14	Isa. 8:12.

From *Revelation*

Chapter	with
6:16	Hos. 10:8.
7:16	Isa. 49:10.
14:5	Zeph. 3:13.
14:8	Isa. 21:9.
18:2	Isa. 21:9.